INTERNATIONAL
PEACE OBSERVATION

INTERNATIONAL
PEACE OBSERVATION

A History and Forecast

DAVID W. WAINHOUSE
in association with
BERNHARD G. BECHHOEFER   JOHN C. DREIER
BENJAMIN GERIG   HARRY R. TURKEL

THE JOHNS HOPKINS PRESS,
Baltimore and London
in co-operation with
THE WASHINGTON CENTER
OF FOREIGN POLICY RESEARCH, SCHOOL OF
ADVANCED INTERNATIONAL STUDIES,
THE JOHNS HOPKINS UNIVERSITY

FOREWORD

It has long been known that conflict, like disease, is more amenable to remedial action when positive steps are taken in the incipient stages of the situation. It is then that commitments are less deeply entrenched, that prestige factors are less emotional, and that consent is more readily secured for some degree of third-party intervention.

While this theory seemed well founded in both reason and experience, it is only in recent times that attempts have been made to codify the concept in international law and practice. Indeed, it was not until 1920 that an international instrument was adopted which provided that it should not be considered unfriendly for a disinterested third country to call attention to any situation the continuance of which might endanger the peace. And it was not until 1945 that this principle was supplemented by empowering the Secretary-General of the United Nations to call the attention of the Security Council to any matter that might threaten international peace and security.

When the attention of an international body is called to a threatening situation, the first and most limited action that can be taken is to ascertain the facts. If hostilities are already in progress the first action is to call for and perhaps supervise a "cease-fire," pending further action. For these immediate and limited purposes the term "peace observation" has come into usage within the last decade. The United States, through the Arms Control and Disarmament Agency, was the first, in April 1962, to present to the 18-Nation Committee on Disarmament a plan that included the establishment of a standing peace observation corps which could *inter alia* promptly investigate any situation threatening the peace.

On the initiative of the Arms Control and Disarmament Agency, the present study of past experience and the future role of peace observation was undertaken by The Washington Center of Foreign Policy Research of The Johns Hopkins University School of Advanced International Studies. It was believed that the experience in the period since 1920 of the principal international bodies in applying peace observation procedures to threatening situations would serve to clarify the uses as well as the limitations of this device. Some seventy cases under the League of Nations, the United Nations, and the Organization of American States—as well as several multinational cases outside of these organizations—were examined. No such exhaustive assembly of case studies has been undertaken before. The study presented to the Agency has been revised and brought up to date (that is, April 1965) for the purpose of this publication.

The Washington Center entrusted the task to a research staff of experienced and competent persons consisting of David W. Wainhouse, former

Deputy Assistant Secretary of State and U.S. Minister to Austria, as director of the study; Bernhard G. Bechhoefer, formerly State Department official and adviser to the U.S. Disarmament delegations; John C. Dreier, formerly U.S. Ambassador to the OAS and presently Professor of Latin American affairs at the School of Advanced International Studies; Benjamin Gerig, formerly Director of the State Department Office of Dependent Area Affairs and Adviser to United States delegations to the United Nations; and Harry Turkel, formerly Ambassador to the Inter-American Economic and Social Council and Director of the Inter-American Regional Office of Economic Affairs, Department of State. Messrs. Wainhouse and Bechhoefer are mainly responsible for the section dealing with the United Nations and multinational cases; Messrs. Turkel and Dreier for that dealing with Latin American cases; and Mr. Gerig for the section on the League of Nations cases. Part II is an integrated product in which all the authors participated.

During the course of the study, the research staff had the benefit of the advice of the following, to whom the authors wish to express their gratitude: Francis O. Wilcox, Dean of the School of Advanced International Studies, formerly Assistant Secretary of State; Andrew W. Cordier, Dean of the School of International Affairs, Columbia University, formerly Executive Assistant to the Secretary-General of the United Nations; Joseph E. Johnson, President of the Carnegie Endowment for International Peace, formerly Chief of the Division of International Security Affairs, Department of State; James Barco, formerly U.S. Deputy Representative to the United Nations, and United States Deputy Representative to the UN Security Council; and General Byron V. Leary (Ret.), formerly Deputy Chief of the UN Truce Supervision Organization in Palestine.

The authors are deeply indebted to many other persons, particularly officials in various Government Departments, in the United Nations and in the various UN missions abroad, who willingly responded to requests for information relating to the study.

Special thanks are due to Evelyn Breck for her editorial assistance in preparing the manuscript for publication, and to Marilou Righini for research assistance throughout the course of this undertaking.

Finally, The Washington Center of Foreign Policy Research wishes to express its appreciation for the expert and cooperative assistance of Dr. Thomas Irvin of the U.S. Arms Control and Disarmament Agency.

The views and judgments expressed in this volume are solely those of the authors and do not necessarily reflect the views of the United States Arms Control and Disarmament Agency or any other department or agency of the United States Government.

ARNOLD WOLFERS, Director
The Washington Center of
Foreign Policy Research, School
of Advanced International Studies

TABLE OF CONTENTS

PART I: CASE STUDIES

A. CASES UNDER THE LEAGUE OF NATIONS

B. CASES UNDER INTER-AMERICAN ORGANIZATIONS AND PROCEDURES

Contents

C. MAJOR CASES UNDER THE UNITED NATIONS

PART II: STRENGTHENING PEACE OBSERVATION

LIST OF ABBREVIATIONS

GOC	Good Offices Committee
IAPC	Inter-American Peace Committee
ICC	International Commission for Supervision and Control
MAC	Mixed Armistice Commission
NNSC	Neutral Nations Supervisory Commission
OAS	Organization of American States
OAU	Organization of African Unity
PCC	Palestine Conciliation Commission
POC	Peace Observation Commission
UNCIP	United Nations Commission for India and Pakistan
UNCOK	United Nations Commission on Korea
UNCURK	United Nations Commission for the Unification and Rehabilitation of Korea
UNEF	United Nations Emergency Force
UNFICYP	United Nations Peace-Keeping Force in Cyprus
UNMOGIP	United Nations Military Observer Group in India and Pakistan
UNOC	United Nations Operation in the Congo
UNOGIL	United Nations Observation Group in Lebanon
UNSCOB	United Nations Special Committee on the Balkans
UNTCOK	United Nations Temporary Commission on Korea
UNSCOP	United Nations Special Committee on Palestine
UNTEA	United Nations Temporary Executive Authority
UNTSO	United Nations Truce Supervision Organization
UNYOM	United Nations Yemen Observation Mission

INTRODUCTION

THIS BOOK IS CONCERNED WITH THE METHODS AND PROCEDURES THAT HAVE been tried since 1920 to prevent threatening situations anywhere in the world from developing into international conflict, or, failing that, to circumscribe the conflict and prevent its spread. It deals in particular with one method, now generally known as peace observation, whereby the organized international community initiates a third party intervention as early as possible in a threatening situation with a view to permitting calmer judgments to allay the potential or actual conflict. This method has evolved as a result of experience gained since 1920 when it first became possible to use it through the establishment of the League of Nations. The League provided for prompt action to be taken in situations that endangered the peace. The scope of its application was further amplified under the United Nations and the Organization of American States. This experience has shown its value in averting or terminating a number of international crises the continuance of which might have endangered international peace.

The purpose of the study is to analyze and evaluate past precedents and to make recommendations for the future based on this experience. Some seventy international situations, to which some form of peace observation under official international auspices has been applied, have been examined by the authors. In many of the recent instances, they have consulted with officials directly involved. These case studies, under the League, the Inter-American System, and the United Nations are analyzed in Part I and furnish the basis for conclusions regarding the future possibilities of peace observation in Part II.

The study assumes that during the immediate future the United Nations will continue to be used as an important instrumentality for peace-observation. The Security Council, with its primary responsibility under the Charter for the maintenance of international peace and security is the organ that will generally, but not exclusively, authorize establishment of most of the peace-observation efforts. The Secretary-General is likely to continue to have an increasing role in the initiation and application of peace-observation functions. Acting under the Charter and supported by precedent, he may himself initiate fact-finding and peace-observation missions. Usually, however, he will not act without the consent of the Security Council unless requested to do so by all the parties concerned.

The study also assumes that the Inter-American System will continue its interest in maintaining peace in the Western Hemisphere and will use the machinery provided under the Inter-American System to accomplish this objective. The Inter-American System cannot compel its members to grant access or cooperate with peace-observation missions, but can impose sanctions if a state fails to cooperate.

The study draws a distinction, now generally recognized in official usage, between "peace observation" and "peace-keeping."[1] Peace-keeping is a form of collective action by which a considerable military force is used to bring about a cessation of hostilities. Peace observation, on the other hand, does not rely primarily on military force. However, activities that are in the nature of peace-keeping may also use peace-observation methods. Likewise peace-observation missions may have to use methods of peace-keeping. Peace observation is an international device that came into use after World War I to denote international action to deter, discourage, prevent, or terminate threatened or actual hostilities. The concept may be closely allied to or may include other responsibilities such as efforts to settle a dispute, for example, mediation or conciliation, or action based on the use of force to maintain law and order, and to suppress or prevent the spread of hostilities, for example, peace-keeping.

In its simplest form, peace observation may go no further than to train the eyes of the organized international community on a situation, which, if ignored, could endanger the peace of a region or the world. It presupposes that the parties immediately and directly involved will be amenable to the informed opinion and judgment of the international community, whose interests could be affected by the conflict.

Peace observation is a flexible instrument. It may function through the presence of one individual, possibly assisted by a small staff, as in the case of Jordan, where the United Nations Presence, on the one hand, is designed to express international concern for the state, and, on the other hand, to act as the eyes and ears of the Secretary-General. The Secretary-General can establish this type of presence on the request of a member state without the formal approval of the General Assembly or the Security Council. In the cases of Palestine and Lebanon, a large mission was sent to the area, in the former case to oversee armistice agreements and supervise the cease-fire, in the latter, to ensure against illegal infiltration of personnel or the supply of arms and other material across the borders.

In the cases examined, one case has rarely been like another. Flexibility in application has been necessary. Many different patterns have emerged, and valuable lessons have been learned.

[1] In April 1962, the United States, through the Arms Control and Disarmament Agency, presented to the 18-Nation Committee on Disarmament an *Outline of Basic Provisions of a Treaty on General and Complete Disarmament in a Peaceful World*. This document included the establishment in Stage I of a United Nations Peace Observation Corps with a standing cadre of observers, who could be dispatched promptly to investigate any situation that might threaten or breach the peace. Arrangements in Stage I would establish in Stage II a United Nations Peace Force. This document is referred to as the *Outline* in this study.

The development of the peace-observation concept has been pragmatic, depending, as the analyses of the cases show, largely on specific conditions and prevailing political circumstances. Historically, under the Inter-American System, peace observation was generally confined to conducting an inquiry by consulting only representatives of the governments involved. In the postwar period, the Peace Committee of the Organization of American States and the Investigating Committees under the Rio Defense Pact have been directed to make on-the-spot fact-finding. An observer group was sent to the troubled area, preferably, but not always, with the consent of the governments concerned to investigate the facts and to report on its findings. The United Nations peace-observation missions, four in particular, have carried on a wide variety of functions that would not ordinarily be associated with peace observation in the usual sense.

This relatively recent development has taken many forms. It has been based on varying degrees of authority, and it has been accompanied by varying degrees of success. Frequently, it has succeeded only in reducing or ending hostilities, which was the main objective, without bringing about a settlement. In some cases where hostilities have ceased, peace observers have remained on the spot to prevent their resumption pending a settlement. Almost always observation has gained some time for cooling-off processes to begin, although at times it has failed altogether.

As a flexible instrument, a peace-observation mission may, and quite often does, have functions that go beyond observing and reporting. In Latin American practice, peace-observation missions have usually engaged in conciliating or mediating whether these functions were specifically mentioned in the terms of reference. Under the United Nations, the resolution setting up a mission, especially a Security Council resolution in the early years, has generally been specific in the terms of reference. The recent tendency in both the Security Council and the General Assembly has been to set forth general terms of reference and to empower the Secretary-General to implement them. In the process of implementation, the Secretary-General must interpret the resolution, the language of which often is purposely vague and conflicting—a vagueness and a conflict that reflect the power rivalries in the Security Council and the General Assembly. These rivalries have resulted in enhancing the responsibility and authority of the Secretary-General and the office has assumed an importance not clearly envisaged by the authors of the Charter.

United Nations peace-observation missions have been dispatched to the troubled spots only by invitation of the country or countries involved. Even where consent has been obtained, there are instances where one or the other of the parties has failed to cooperate or to assist the mission in carrying out its mandate. Chapter VII of the Charter and, in a limited scope, Article 34 of Chapter VI authorize the Security Council to act without the consent of the parties, since consent to abide by decisions under these provisions has already been given by the member states under Article 25.[2] In all situations with which this study is concerned, however, the United Nations has thus far avoided binding decisions in peace-observation situations. Therefore, peace observation has depended on the consent of the party or parties involved in the individual cases.

Peace observation is only a first step in the process of peaceful settlement. In appropriate circumstances, it must be accompanied or followed by other means such as conciliation, mediation, or judicial settlement. The experience of the League of Nations indicates that mediation or conciliation was regarded as an important stage in the pacification process. Under the Organization of American States, conciliation has been exercised by peace observers as an integral part of their function whether spelled out in the terms of reference or not. Under the United Nations, experience is somewhat mixed. In the Indonesian case, conciliation played the primary role with peace observation giving important support. The Kashmir operation at all times has involved both conciliation and peace observation with separate staffs after the first year. In Lebanon, there was no conciliation officially. In Yemen, the terms of reference initially excluded mediation from the duties of the mission. Subsequently, the need for mediation was recognized. In Cyprus, the Security Council resolution provided simultaneously for both a mediator and an international force to maintain law and order.

How best can peace observation and fact-finding now and in a disarming world be institutionalized? Should the Security Council or the General Assembly create a peace-observation group on an *ad hoc* basis, in each instance calling for peace observation and fact-finding, as is presently the case? Should there be an earmarking of peace-observation officers by the various states, officers trained by them in cooperation with the United Nations for this special task to be placed at the disposition of the United Nations on call? Should there be, in addition to the earmarked officers by the various states, a small UN group of twenty-five to fifty officers, some of whom might form the cadre of a peace-observation team? Should there be a standing corps of trained peace observers ready to be sent promptly into any situation where their services could help to safeguard the peace?

These questions are discussed in the final section of this study, which considers the future character and role of peace-observation arrangements under the United Nations.

[2] Leland M. Goodrich and Anne P. Simons, *The United Nations and the Maintenance of International Peace and Security* (Washington, D.C.: Brookings Institution, 1955), pp. 180–81.

PART ONE

---◆---

CASE STUDIES

CASES UNDER THE
LEAGUE OF NATIONS

———————— •◆• ————————

PREFATORY NOTE

Some thirty situations or disputes, twelve of which are analyzed in this study, were dealt with by the League of Nations in the period 1920–1940. In some of these cases, consideration by the Council and adoption of resolutions addressed to the parties proved effective. In others, especially those involving great power aggression, action by the League was ineffective. In a number of instances, the League developed and successfully used peace-observation procedures—commissions of enquiry, plebiscite commissions, administrative commissions, and judicial panels. In two cases, Upper Silesia in 1921 and the Saar in 1935, international forces were organized to assist the international commissions in carrying out their assigned duties under orderly conditions.

The majority of cases handled by the League had one similar feature: they generally involved disputed claims over frontiers and territory resulting from the break-up of the Austro-Hungarian and the Russian Empires.[1] Most of these were in Europe. However, the League was also involved in cases in Asia (Mosul and Manchuria), in South America (Chaco[2] and Leticia), and in Africa (Ethiopia).

CONSTITUTIONAL BASIS FOR
PEACE OBSERVATION UNDER THE LEAGUE

When the League was established in 1920, Article 10 on preserving members against external aggression, and Article 16, authorizing members to apply sanctions against an aggressor, were

[1] Thus Sweden and Finland disputed over possession of the Aaland Islands; Lithuania and Poland disputed over Vilna and Memel; Germany and Poland over partition of Upper Silesia; Albania with Yugoslavia and Greece over undelimited frontiers; and Greece and Bulgaria over the location of the Macedonian border.

[2] The League action on this case is discussed with concurrent efforts in the Inter-American system. See pp. 94 ff.

considered to be the basis of action to maintain peace. In practice, however, Article 11 was invoked in most of the disputes dealt with by the League. Under this article, war or threat of war, whether it immediately affected any member of the League, was declared "to be a matter of concern to the whole League" which "shall take any action deemed wise and effectual to safeguard the peace of nations." In several cases, Article 15 was invoked at the same time or later. This enabled a dispute "likely to lead to a rupture" to be submitted to the Council or the Assembly, which could make an investigation and adopt a report without counting the votes of the disputing parties. If a disputant disregarded this report and resorted to war, the full sanctions of Article 16 could come into effect. Article 16, however, was invoked only once, ineffectively, when Italy attacked Ethiopia.

The numerous cases analyzed in this study show that the experience gained in applying Article 11 proved its worth. A jurisprudence developed whereby in the case of hostilities a "cease-fire" and "separation of the combatants" was the first action to be taken before the Council would consider the settlement of the dispute. The party that refused the Council's order to cease hostilities was likely to be declared the aggressor even if that party was initially attacked. The plea of "legitimate defence" was also rejected by the Council if a nation took action before appealing to the Council.

The League Covenant gave identical powers to the Assembly and the Council. Each could deal "with any matter within the sphere of action of the League or affecting the peace of the world."[3] In practice, the Council was always appealed to first. But under Article 15 (9), the Council itself could refer the dispute to the Assembly, or either party to a dispute could do so if the request were made within fourteen days after it was submitted to the Council. The Manchurian case was so referred in 1932.

The Council or the Assembly, acting under Article 11, was competent to intervene or mediate in any circumstances affecting the peaceful relations of members of the League. Between 1920 and 1936, hostilities or a resort to arms occurred in ten cases. The Council developed the following procedures: (1) immediate intervention by the President of the Council who issued a warning to the disputants and called for a cease-fire; (2) immediate convening of the Council, to which representatives of the disputants were summoned, for the

---

[3] Articles 3 and 4.

purpose of ending hostilities; (3) the appointment of a commission of officers to supervise on the spot the cessation of hostilities, secure the maintenance of the status quo, or execute some other provisional arrangement, pending a settlement of the dispute; and (4) the establishment of a commission to examine the facts, and make a report with recommendations for a solution of the dispute.

In cases where hostilities threatened but had not yet broken out and the Council needed more facts to enable it to assist the parties in reaching a peaceful solution, it could constitute a commission of enquiry to make an on-the-spot study and report, as it did in the Aaland Islands case.

The Council, in making a distinction between separating the combatants and mediating a settlement, frequently found it necessary to lay down zones of demarcation. A commission of military officers was used to see that these zones were observed. A different commission was appointed for the task of investigating the causes of the dispute and making recommendations for a settlement. In the Greek-Bulgarian dispute, the commissions worked together.

Article 11, rather than Articles 15 and 16, was the preferred basis for League peace-observation action because, under it, preventive and conservatory measures could be taken immediately without first having to establish difficult assumptions, such as whether the covenant had been violated or war had been resorted to. For example, in the dispute between Japan and China in 1931 over Manchuria, neither country ever "declared war" despite the fact that Japan had committed aggression against and occupied a vast area of China. Consequently, the "resort to war" basis for sanctions action under Article 16 never arose in this case.[4]

The League succeeded in preventing war and restoring peace whenever the great powers were in accord, particularly when Great Britain and France agreed on the action to take. Thus, with the exception of the Vilna case, where France was unwilling to put pressure on Poland, all efforts of the Council to maintain peace from 1920 to 1930 were measurably successful. After 1930, when other great powers—Japan, Italy, Germany, and Russia—began their aggressive actions, the League proved to be unequal to the task of maintaining or restoring peace. Even the support of the United States for the League's efforts to restrain Japan and Italy

[4] See W. W. Willoughby, *The Sino-Japanese Controversy and the League of Nations* (Baltimore: The Johns Hopkins Press, 1935), p. 38.

was insufficient. The United States could not effectually participate in applying Articles 11, 15, and 16 of the Covenant, to which it was not a party.

Commissions of Enquiry or fact-finding missions were customarily used by the League Council, operating under Article 11, both as a means of allaying the tensions of active hostilities and procuring impartial and trustworthy information on the causes of the controversy and as a basis for settlement. The salient features of the Council's experience in their creation and use are summarized below. [5]

1. The Council took the initiative in setting down the powers and duties and designating the personnel of each commission. The commissions were selected by and composed of neutrals. In no case were nationals of the disputant country appointed. [6] Names were usually proposed by the Council's rapporteur who was a disinterested party speaking for a Committee of Three. He would also propose the terms of reference. The disputants were usually asked whether they had any objections.

2. League commissions were usually requested by the Council to suggest a solution as well as to investigate the facts.

3. The commissions usually enjoyed unrestricted movement in the territories of the disputants. But in one instance, the commission functioned when movement was restricted to one side. [7]

4. Care was taken to appoint commissioners who had experience, eminence, and varied technical and professional qualifications.

5. Five members, rather than three, was regarded as the most suitable or ideal number. Secretariat and other expert officials were attached to the commissions as needed. For example, there were some twenty-one experts with the Lytton Commission in Manchuria in addition to its five members. Commissions could thus set up subcommittees for simultaneous investigation.

6. Members of League commissions, being appointed and paid by the League, acted in an individual capacity. Persons were

[5] This experience is set out in greater detail in the separate case studies annexed hereto, especially involving disputes between: Sweden and Finland, 1920; Yugoslavia and Albania, 1921; Allied Powers and Lithuania (Memel), 1923; Great Britain and Turkey, 1923; Greece and Bulgaria, 1925.

[6] Before 1920 such commissions were customarily established by each disputant designating one or two persons, and those so designated choosing another. See provisions of 1907 Hague Convention.

[7] Yugoslavia did not grant the commission the right of travel in its territory in 1921 during its border dispute with Albania.

generally chosen from disinterested countries. They did not take "instructions" from their respective governments, and indeed, their governments could not know what was contained in their reports since publication and distribution were made by the League immediately on receipt of an agreed typescript copy. Whether Fascist and Communist governments after 1931 would have permitted their nationals such freedom from governmental controls, or whether such freedom is enjoyed by Soviet officials operating under the United Nations today, is a question of some significance.

7. The Council, with only slight modifications, adopted the reports of its Commissions of Enquiry, together with recommendations contained therein. And until the Manchurian case of 1931, the disputants, even if sometimes reluctantly, accepted the unanimous judgment of the Council based on the thorough and impartial array of facts.

Japan was the first of the great powers to reject wholly the report of a Commission of Enquiry. When the report was adopted by the Assembly, the Japanese delegate walked out of the chamber, and later his country withdrew from the League. Thus, in 1932, the final breakdown of the League began, and thereafter it was defied successively by Germany, Italy, and Russia.

1

THE AALAND ISLANDS CONTROVERSY, 1920

Until 1809, when Napoleon forced Sweden to hand over Finland and the Aaland Islands to Russia, as a penalty for having taken the wrong side in the war, this territory belonged to Sweden. Then Russia ruled the province as one administrative unit until 1917. In 1918, Finland declared its independence, and Sweden, among other states, formally recognized Finnish sovereignty. At that time, Sweden made no reservations concerning the Aaland Islands.

The 300 islands constituting the Aaland archipelago had a population of about 27,000 in 1920. Most of the islands are geographically nearer to Sweden than to Finland, and 95 percent of the people are of Swedish culture and language. The islands have strategic importance because they command the entrance to the Gulf of Bothnia.

The Aalander agitation for reunion with Sweden became increasingly active in 1918–1919, and public opinion in Sweden began to support the separatist movement. In June 1920, the Finnish Government landed troops on the islands to offset this pro-Swedish agitation.

The Aalanders asked for self-determination and, in fact, had conducted an unofficial plebiscite which resulted in a large majority opting for Swedish annexation. The Finnish Government insisted that its sovereignty had to be maintained. This forced Sweden's hand, and it seemed that war was imminent. The issue, therefore, was whether Sweden or Finland should have sovereignty over the Aaland Islands.

THE CASE BEFORE THE LEAGUE OF NATIONS COUNCIL

Great Britain brought the matter before the League Council by invoking Article 11 (2) of the Covenant which declared it "to be the friendly right of each member of the League to bring to the attention of the Assembly or the Council any circumstance . . . affecting international relations which threatens . . . international peace."[1] The Council took up the matter in July 1920. Both Sweden and Finland appointed delegates to present their respective cases, Sweden as a member of the League, and Finland under Article 17 as a nonmember involved in a dispute.

The Finnish delegate argued that the case was a purely internal matter and therefore fell outside the competence of the Council. He also recalled that Sweden had made no reservation in regard to the Aaland Islands when Finnish independence was recognized in January 1918.

The Swedish delegate did not make a specific claim for annexation but held that the dispute should be settled by a plebiscite, in accordance with the principle of self-determination. He denied the Finnish contention that the Council was not competent to deal with the situation, since it had become a threat to the peace and was no longer a purely domestic question.

The Council decided that since its competence was challenged, this question had to be determined first. Accordingly, a committee of three eminent jurists was appointed to advise the Council on the questions: According to international law, did the question of the Aaland Islands fall wholly within the jurisdiction of Finland? Were international obligations regarding the demilitarization of the Islands still in force?[2] Both the Swedish and Finnish delegates agreed, somewhat reluctantly, that their governments would accept the report of the committee of jurists and would desist from any action which might aggravate the situation while the question was *sub judice*.

[1] The UN Charter has a similar provision in Article 35.

[2] The Treaty of Paris of 1856 had stipulated that the Aaland Islands should not be fortified or any military establishment maintained thereon.

The jurists took two months to give their opinion that the question was not purely domestic and that the Council had authority to recommend any solution it might deem wise and expedient; and that the non-fortification treaty of 1856 was still in force.[3]

The two-month delay and the undertaking not to aggravate the situation were regarded by many observers as having defused the explosive situation. The further time required to investigate the facts through an on-the-spot Commission of Enquiry, appointed after the jurists' report on the Council's competence, was regarded as a "cooling-off process" which would make the League's decision more acceptable.

INVESTIGATION BY THE COMMISSION OF ENQUIRY

The Commission of Enquiry appointed on September 20, 1920, consisted of: Baron Beyens, former Belgian Foreign Minister; Felix Colonder, former President of Switzerland; Abram I. Elkus, former United States Ambassador to Turkey. O. L. Milmore and E. M. Nielsen were appointed as the commission's secretaries. The commission was empowered "to make a thorough study of all the points involved taking into full acount the legitimate interests of every party to the dispute" and to report its findings to the Council.

It should be noted that the Council itself selected the members of the commission; that the persons appointed were individuals of eminence and recognized attainment; that they were all persons whose nationality made them disinterested in the case; and that they were answerable only to the Council, not to their respective governments. The commission spent six weeks visiting Sweden, Finland, and the Aaland Islands and completed its report in April 1921.

In their comprehensive report,[4] the commissioners went into the history of the relations between the Islands and Finland over the last hundred years, showing how it had been governed as a separate administrative unit with a large degree of local autonomy. The essential provisions of the report may be summarized as follows:

1. Finland was to continue to have sovereignty over the Aaland Islands.

2. Finland should guarantee the protection of the Aalanders in their political rights and agree that the archipelago should be neutralized and not fortified.[5]

[3] See "Report of International Committee of Jurists," League of Nations, *Official Journal*, Special Supplement No. 3 (October 1920).

[4] *Report of Commission of Rapporteurs on Aaland Islands Question*, April 16, 1921; Council Doc. B. 7. 21/68/106.

[5] These guarantees were undertaken by Finland. It was held inadmissible for the Aalanders to have direct access to the Council or the Court.

3. Finland should guarantee autonomy to the Aaland Islands with the preservation of the Swedish language in the schools, the rights of private property, and, within reasonable limits, the admission of newcomers to the franchise.

4. Finland, the Aaland Islands, and Sweden should cooperate in executing these guarantees, and if their efforts failed, the Council would suggest the measures to be followed. In any case, the Council would supervise the enforcement of the measures adopted.

5. Finland should guarantee that the neutralized Aaland Islands should never become a source of danger in a military sense to Sweden nor to any other interested power, and the Council should take steps toward the revision of the Treaty of 1856 to give it a broader basis in conformity with suggestions already made by Sweden in a draft convention.[6]

It now remained for the Council to decide what it would do with the commission's report. The Swedish delegate and influential member of the Council, Hjalmar Branting, refused to admit that Finnish sovereignty had been proved, and cited the report of the committee of jurists which had been appointed by the Council. The Finnish delegate was not pleased with the guarantees for the Swedish minority which the report recommended, holding that these were unnecessary. Nevertheless, on June 24, 1921, the Council approved the essentials of the report and the Swedish and Finnish delegates accepted the Council decision in "cool Scandinavian honesty."

EVALUATION

The case of the Aaland Islands dispute was brought before the League Council by a third party before it had reached a stage that would have made settlement more difficult. The Council, after establishing its competence by a judicial opinion, acted promptly in naming a Commission of Enquiry and endowing it with broad terms of reference. The dispatch with which the commission carried out its investigation and drew up its report enabled the Council to make a decision before the situation got out of hand. In addition to these important factors of timing, the recognized prestige and impartiality of the commissioners made the acceptance of its report likely.

Both the commission and the Council, by refusing Sweden's request for a plebiscite, established practical limits to the principle of self-determination —a principle which, if applied to all the minorities in Europe, would have created instability and chaos on the new postwar map.

[6] John S. Bassett, *The League of Nations* (New York: Longmans, Green & Co., 1928), p. 66. A special convention guaranteeing the non-fortification and neutralization of the Islands was drawn up and ratified on Jan. 19, 1922 by Germany, Denmark, Estonia, Finland, France, Great Britain, Italy, Latvia, Poland, and Sweden.

The protection of the Aaland minority, guaranteed by the League decision, proved in later years to be a valuable *via media* between the assertion of unqualified national sovereignty on the one hand and the disintegrating force of rampant self-determination on the other.

The disputants' calm acceptance of a decision uncongenial to either of them set an example that raised the prestige and authority of the League in dealing with the disputes that were to follow. Many League successes stemmed from this original case.

2

CONFLICT BETWEEN LITHUANIA AND POLAND, 1920

Both Poland and Lithuania, though separate peoples, had been tributaries of Russia until the end of World War I, when the Supreme Allied Council set the provisional boundaries of the two states in such a way that the town and province of Vilna were left to Lithuania. Poland was still at war with Russia and at that time did not contest the award, considering it to be only provisional.

The Russians pushed the Poles back almost to Warsaw, and occupied Vilna on the way without serious Lithuanian resistance. A Polish counteroffensive drove the Russians eastward and out of Vilna, which the Lithuanians promptly reoccupied. Russia, now weakened, made a separate treaty with Lithuania giving Vilna to that country. This so incensed the Poles that hostilities with Lithuania were only averted because the Russian danger had not yet been quelled.

Instead of making war on Lithuania, on September 5, 1920, Poland requested the League, under Article 11, to intervene to prevent war.[1] Ignace Paderewski presented the case for Poland, and Augustinas Voldemar spoke for Lithuania. Paderewski, believing war could not be averted if the two armies occupied the disputed area, proposed that the Lithuanian forces withdraw. This request was refused.

The Council, through its rapporteur, Paul Hymans of Belgium, tried to find some less drastic solution on which both sides could agree. A provisional solution, with M. Hymans acting as mediator, provided that both

[1] *Minutes of Ninth Session of Council of the League of Nations, September 16, 1920.*

sides would withdraw from the disputed area pending a determination of the boundary, and the Council would name a commission to visit the region and see that the agreement was kept.

A MILITARY COMMISSION OF CONTROL

The Military Commission was appointed by a Council committee, consisting of Leon Bourgeois, the President of the Council, and the Japanese and Spanish Ambassadors. The composition of the committee was also reflected in the military commission: Colonel Chardigny (French), chairman; Colonel Herce (Spanish); Major Keenan (British); Colonel Vergera (Italian); Captain Yamanaki (Japanese). The commission's terms of reference were defined in the provisional solution as expressed by the Council resolution of September 20, 1920. The Council appealed to the Governments of Lithuania and Poland to take "measures to prevent hostile acts between their troops." It proposed that the Lithuanian Government adopt as a provisional demarcation line, "the frontier fixed by the Supreme Council of the Allies in its declaration of the 8th December, 1919, and . . . to withdraw its troops from the territory to the west of this line"; and that the Government of Poland, reserving its territorial rights, "respect during the war . . . now in progress between Poland and the Government of the Soviets, the neutrality of the territory occupied by Lithuania . . . east of the line of demarcation . . . provided that respect for this neutrality be also secured from the Soviet authorities by Lithuania." If the Lithuanian and Polish Governments accepted the provisional arrangement, the Council would appoint a commission with the duty "of ensuring on the spot the strict observation by the interested parties of the obligations arising from this agreement."[2]

The Military Commission arrived two weeks later and induced each state to move its forces four miles back from the provisional boundary known as the Curzon Line. On October 7, 1920, both states accepted a formal agreement recognizing this arrangement.

This hopeful situation suddenly changed when the Russian forces collapsed, and the military party gained control of the Government of Poland. On October 12, 1920, Russia and Poland negotiated the Treaty of Riga whereby Russia ceded to Poland the territory, including Vilna, that it had ceded to Lithuania only three months before.

Before either the agreement of October 7 or the treaty of October 12 could come into effect, Polish General Lucjan Zeligowski, apparently without the authority of the Polish Government, led a band of irregular soldiers

---

[2] League of Nations, *Official Journal*, I: No. 7 (October 1920), p. 398.

into Vilna on October 9 and set up his authority there. Although the Warsaw Government verbally disavowed Zeligowski, it said it would resist any attempt to drive him out of Vilna pending a plebiscite to determine the city's wishes. More irregulars joined the rebel general and military supplies were received in large quantities from Poland. Fighting continued on a considerable scale between the Lithuanians and the Zeligowski troops, who wanted to extend their control to include Kovno.

The Military Commission succeeded in obtaining an armistice and establishing a neutral zone (150 miles long and 10 miles wide) between them. At the same time, the commission maintained a second neutral zone 60 miles long and 8 miles wide between the regular Polish Army and the Lithuanian forces. Within these two areas no civil or military authority existed.

NEW SITUATION BEFORE THE LEAGUE COUNCIL

In these circumstances, the League was confronted with a new situation that defied any peaceful solution. The Polish representative, Simon Askenazy, argued that the Treaty of Riga with Russia made the provisional boundary permanent, and it only remained for a plebiscite to determine the future of Vilna. The Council could not accept this argument and insisted that Poland's previous pledge to respect the neutrality of the disputed region was still binding. The Council did not object to a plebiscite in Vilna, but insisted on two conditions: (1) it would have to be conducted under League supervision, and (2) it would have to be executed without the presence of General Zeligowski. Further, the Council would control the railroads in the area and have the right to disarm or remove all military forces there.

Lithuania accepted the proposal for a plebiscite. The Polish representative claimed that most of Zeligowski's troops were citizens of Vilna and would vote in a plebiscite. The Polish authorities never claimed responsibility for Zeligowski's action, but they continued to protect and provision him. Eventually, they gave him full recognition and accepted the fruits of his illegal action.

In December 1920, the Council set up a Civil Plebiscite Commission, composed of representatives of Belgium, France, Great Britain, Italy, and Spain, which was sent to Vilna to take over the situation. An international force of 1,500 men from nations not represented on the Council was organized by Marshal Ferdinand Foch.[3] General Jozef Pilsudski pledged

[3] See *Minutes of the Eleventh Session of Council of the League of Nations, November −14 December 18, 1920.*

that Zeligowski's forces would leave the city as soon as the international force entered.

At this juncture, the Lithuanian representative on the Council objected to the international force on the ground that Lithuania's treaty with Russia of July 1920 provided that "no foreign troops would be allowed to enter or remain on Lithuanian territory." The Council President said that this point, if valid, should have been raised before. It was assumed that the Lithuanian objection could be based only on fear of the plebiscite's outcome since Lithuania had already favored arbitration.

The commission to supervise the plebiscite and the international force were ready to start at the end of December 1920. Lithuania still gave no assurance that it would carry out its part of the agreement. By January 21, 1921, no reply having been received, the Council requested one within ten days. When the reply came, Lithuania raised new points, especially concerning the area to be covered by the plebiscite.

The Council in March 1921, through President Bourgeois, criticized both Lithuania and Poland for causing many delays and interposing many difficulties in carrying out the plebiscite arrangements to which both had agreed. Some members of the Council were ready to give up the case, but most wished to make another effort at adjustment. A conference with the two states was called for April 20, 1921, to overcome what Arthur Balfour called "a scandal to civilization." He proposed that the two representatives meet with the Council's rapporteur, M. Hymans, and resolve "not to separate until an agreement was reached." [4]

The two parties met in Brussels with M. Hymans from April 20 to June 3, 1921. M. Hymans made a number of proposals which were unacceptable either to one party or the other. On May 20, he proposed a more drastic plan which would have divided Lithuania into two autonomous provinces: one including Vilna and the surrounding region, the other including the rest of Lithuania. The plan also provided that Poland would have free access to the sea through each. Both parties accepted the plan as a basis of discussion, but with so many reservations and conditions that the discussion failed.

Meanwhile Zeligowski and his force of over 15,000 men continued to occupy Vilna. M. Hymans, however, persisted in getting the parties together again; but on September 19, 1921, he reported failure to the Council. The Assembly, now in session, debated the issue but nothing was concluded there. On January 13, 1922, the Council decided not to renew its efforts and ordered its Military Commission of Control to withdraw from the area where it had been since October 1920. The Council, however, got both sides to recognize a neutral boundary in order to avert war.

[4] *Minutes of the Twelfth Session of Council of the League of Nations, February 21–March 4, 1921*, pp. 33–34.

At this point, the Conference of Ambassadors, which still had duties assigned by the Supreme Allied Council,[5] acknowledged the de facto situation and adjusted the boundaries in accordance with the Treaty of Riga which gave Vilna to Poland.

Thus the efforts of the League Council and its Commission of Control to settle the Vilna question in accordance with reason and the principles of the Covenant ended in failure. Outright war was averted. But Vilna went to Poland.

EVALUATION

The dispute between Poland and Lithuania arose over a genuine uncertainty about the proper location of their mutual border. In the view of the Military Commission of Control, most of the trouble might have been averted if the border had been clearly defined and delimited by the Peace Conference. [6]

The League was called in by the disputants before they resorted to war, and its Military Commission established and maintained neutral zones between the Polish and Lithuanian forces, thus preventing the outbreak of hostilities on a wider scale. After this auspicious beginning, the action of General Zeligowski and his irregulars who occupied Vilna prevented solution of the problem, making an impartial plebiscite impossible. Both the Lithuanian and Polish authorities continued to reject every compromise solution proposed by the League.

[5] When the Versailles Treaty entered into force, the peace conference was in the course of disbandment. This raised the problem of a continuing organ which would have the authority to settle current questions. The idea of the Conference of Ambassadors was approved by the Supreme Council on July 28, 1919, and was brought into being by its resolution of December 13, 1919. The Ambassadors were given the powers of the Supreme Council. These powers covered the interpretation and execution of the peace treaties with the following exceptions: (1) questions arising out of the treaty of peace with Turkey, (2) questions entrusted by them to the Reparation Commission or other permanent organs of the same nature.

The French representative presided at the sessions of the Ambassadors of Great Britain, Italy, Japan, and the United States (the principal Allied and Associated Powers). Great Britain, Italy, and Japan sat as members and the United States as an intermittent observer. These same powers were designated in the Covenant as permanent members of the League Council; however, the United States remained absent from the League.

Thus, machinery for peace observation existed with both the League of Nations and the Conference of Ambassadors. The relationship between these two organizations was far from satisfactory, and this consequently was reflected in peace-observation functions, e.g., the cases involving Vilna, Albania's frontiers, and Corfu. The existence of the two different organs was underlined when the Harding Administration came into power in March 1921. At that time, President Harding severely criticized the League and announced that the United States would resume full membership in the Conference of Ambassadors and the other organs set up to carry out the Versailles Treaty.

[6] Quoted by the Secretary-General to the Council, January 12, 1922.

The disunity of the great powers further impeded positive action. Russia was opposed to any League settlement and complicated the matter by negotiating the Treaty of Riga. Strong pro-Polish sentiments made it difficult for France to act objectively. Finally, the Conference of Ambassadors decided to recognize the de facto situation.

The greatest achievement of the League in this case was the preservation of the peace, if only because the long-drawn-out proceedings of the Council served as a cooling-off period and made the acceptance of an unjust solution easier. Lithuania, however, continued to consider itself at war with Poland until 1927 and regularly brought its complaints before the League during those years. This unsettled situation retarded the development of the League's peace-observation machinery and undoubtedly had a weakening effect on the new institution.

3

THE SAAR TERRITORY: INTERNATIONAL ADMINISTRATION AND AN INTERNATIONAL FORCE, 1920–1935

The Saar basin, which lies between France and Germany, is rich in coal and iron ore deposits. The Treaty of Versailles ceded the coal mines to France partly as payment for war damages to French mines, and partly as a credit on the reparations account of Germany.[1] The people of the Saar were German and were not disposed to accept French rule. It was therefore decided that the region should be administered by an International Governing Commission, acting under the supervision of the League of Nations Council, for a period of fifteen years after which a plebiscite would determine: (1) whether the territory was to return to Germany, (2) whether it was to become part of France, or (3) whether the League should continue to govern it.

The issue was how to maintain order in the Saar territory and after fifteen years, to provide for a plebiscite to determine the future of the territory.

[1] In 1920, there were thirty-one coal mines and five iron and steel plants, employing 104,000 workers.

THE GOVERNING COMMISSION

According to the Treaty of Versailles,[2] the Governing Commission, to be appointed by the League Council, was to consist of five members: a French citizen, a native of the Saar but not a French citizen, and three members who were not citizens of either France or Germany. They were to be appointed for one year and were eligible for reappointment. The first commission was composed of Victor Rault (French), chairman; Herr von Boch (Saarlander); M. Lambert (Belgian); Count de Moltke-Huitfeldt (Danish); Mr. R. D. Waugh (Canadian). Later, M. Morize (French) replaced M. Rault, Mr. Stephens (Canadian) replaced Mr. Waugh and was made chairman, and Sir Ernest Wilton (British) replaced M. de las Monteros (Spanish) and succeeded Mr. Stephens as chairman.

The commission appointed and recalled officials; operated and controlled railways, canals, and other public services; constituted such administrative and representative bodies as it deemed necessary; administered justice; levied taxes; in short, exercised all the powers of government subject only to the supervision of the League Council to which it rendered quarterly reports.

The inhabitants were to retain their nationality unless they chose to change it (which the French hoped many would do) and were to retain their original rights and customs, including their local assemblies, religious liberties, their schools, and their German language.

The commission was required by the Treaty of Versailles to secure the views of elected representatives of the inhabitants before changes in the laws could be made or new taxes imposed. At first, it consulted municipal and district councils. But in 1922 an Advisory Council of thirty members was elected, and a small Technical Committee of eight members was established to advise the commission. In many important matters, however, the Advisory Council was not consulted.

Because of the delicate relations existing between France and Germany, the situation called for a Governing Commission that would exercise its extensive powers with restraint and impartiality. Instead, the first chairman, M. Rault, supported by the pro-French sympathies of the Belgian and Danish members, governed the territory as if it were already French and assumed that the Saar would become French after the plebiscite. M. Rault made many important decisions without consulting his four colleagues. The Canadian and Saar members protested in vain. He tended to ignore his colleagues or treat them as subordinates instead of presiding over them as first among equals. Moreover, he placed every possible obstacle in the way of an expression of opinion by the Saarlanders themselves.[3]

[2] Articles 45–50.
[3] See F. P. Walters, *A History of the League of Nations* (London: Oxford University Press, 1952), pp. 237 ff.; John S. Bassett, *The League of Nations* (New York: Longmans, Green and Co., 1928), pp. 174, 240.

In these circumstances, the Saar member of the commission resigned before the end of the first year and requested the League Council to send investigators to look into the situation. The Council declined and decided that complaints should be channeled through the commission, which should attach its comments before bringing the complaints to the Council's attention.

In the spring of 1923, the situation in the Saar was made more difficult when France occupied the Ruhr, and the resulting embittered passions affected the entire Rhineland. The Saar miners went on a three-month strike in sympathy with their Ruhr comrades who were maintaining resistance against the French occupiers. Thirty thousand steel and railway workers were thrown out of employment in addition to 70,000 miners.

The League Council had to pay a high price for its earlier acquiescence in a "discreditable situation."[4] M. Rault, fearing the effect of a widespread strike, asked that the French garrison of 2,000 men be doubled and issued a decree for maintaining order that limited freedom of assembly and the press in terms which offended the democratic countries of the League.

The question of the Saar was debated in the British House of Commons and the British Government announced that it would demand a full inquiry. The French Government, supporting M. Rault, let it be known that it would resist such an inquiry.

When the Council met, the British representative, Lord Robert Cecil, proposed that instead of an on-the-spot inquiry, the Council should summon the chairman and the other members of the commission to answer questions and give an account of their activities. He urged the Council to investigate the following points:[5] (1) Were the members of the Governing Commission to be considered as representatives of their own states and permitted to maintain relations with them? (2) What powers should the chairman of the Governing Commission have? (3) What right had the commission to make laws without consulting the Advisory Council? (4) What was the procedure of the commission concerning protection of persons and property in the Saar?

In spite of French opposition, the Council summoned the commission, and the whole situation was aired. As a result, the chairman was requested to take no action without consulting his colleagues, and to restore normal conditions. The commission was further instructed to create a local gendarmerie and dispense with the French garrison, so hated by the Saarlanders. In this way, the Council reasserted its authority, and the tension in the Saar gradually subsided. When M. Rault's term of office as chairman expired, he was succeeded first by a Canadian, and later by the

[4] Walters, *op. cit.*, p. 240.

[5] See Minutes of the Twenty-fifth Session of Council, League of Nations, *Official Journal* (August 1923), pp. 854 ff.

British member of the commission.[6] The French garrison was finally withdrawn.

Thus the Saar after 1925 was governed by a truly international body. The League Council received periodic reports which showed that the Saar under League of Nations governance had become one of the most prosperous and quiet places in Europe. If there were grievances, any inhabitant had the right to submit petitions. After 1927, Germany, as a member of the League Council, could raise a complaint, but never did.

The population of the Saar being German, there was no doubt that in 1935 it would opt for a return to Germany. French blandishments failed to influence the Saarlanders to do otherwise. And the League, anxious to divest itself of the governing responsibility, made no effort to induce the people to prolong the status quo. But in 1933, two years before the plebiscite, the Nazi government came into power in Germany, and a return to Hitler's Germany was a quite different situation. Across the border, the Saarlanders saw beatings, murders, concentration camps, and Jew-baiting. Hitler's hostility toward the churches, in particular toward the Church of Rome, created a conflict between patriotism and conscience for the Saarlanders, many of whom were devout Catholics. Thus, the outcome of the plebiscite was no longer certain.

Hitler viewed the Saar question as a potential stumbling block; if a majority or even a sizable minority were to vote against a return to Germany, it would be a serious blow. He organized a campaign of nationalism combined with terror. The German press and radio blared out reprisals that would await anti-Nazis, Jews, and Communists after the plebiscite. A branch of the Nazi party, whose newspapers were menacing and full of blackmail, was organized in the territory.

In these circumstances, the task of the Governing Commission under its British chairman, Geoffrey Knox, became very difficult. Its members were spied upon; some of the Saar police and officials, looking ahead, were openly or secretly pro-Nazi; others feared to be loyal to the commission; magistrates were terrorized. Although the margin of safety was small, the commission stood firm for justice and the maintenance of order. It still had enough support within the territory to govern effectively. And the League, at this time, seemed willing and able to back up the commission.[7]

Aware that his threatening policy was alienating many Saarlanders, Hitler, instead of a plebiscite, which he professed would be in favor of Germany anyway, proposed that France and Germany enter into direct

[6] In 1925 the Council decided that the presidency of the commission should rotate.

[7] In the Governing Commission's report at the end of 1933, it cited a number of ordinances which had to be adopted regarding, for example, improper use of weapons, entry of persons into the territory, prohibiting the wearing of uniforms and military exercises, intimidations and threats of reprisals, forcible participation in political demonstrations, revelation of official secrets, flying of flags without authorization.

negotiations for the return of the Saar to Germany, after which there would be no further grounds for territorial conflict between them. The French, however, rejected this overture. Indeed, it would have been contrary to the treaty to have accepted it.

It was in this difficult situation that the League Council, a year before the plebiscite, began to make preparations for conducting it in a manner that would "secure the freedom, secrecy and trustworthiness of the voting," as called for in the treaty.

THE SAAR PLEBISCITE

On January 20, 1934, the League Council appointed three of its members[8] to carry on consultations and prepare a report on the organization of the plebiscite to be conducted in January 1935. The report was to be considered by the Council at its next session. The committee was instructed: "to study measures . . . to ensure . . . the regularity of the electoral proceedings"; "to . . . study . . . means of safeguarding the population against pressure of any kind and the execution of any threats likely to affect the trustworthiness of the voting"; to study suggestions of the Governing Commission regarding the maintenance of order during the plebiscite.[9]

The Council committee held many meetings and consulted many experts. The technical problems were complex. The League had no previous experience in conducting a plebiscite—certainly not under such dangerous conditions as existed in the Saar in 1935. How could public order be maintained? How could the voter speak, write, and vote without being afraid of the consequences?

The Council decided to fulfill its duties in spite of Nazi threats.[10] It had two powers which Germany feared: (1) it could postpone the plebiscite if conditions were too bad to hold it; and (2) it could define a vote in favor of the status quo as not precluding a later decision to return to Germany. Hitler did not wish to take either risk, and he reluctantly decided on a minimum of collaboration to complete the plebiscite.

In identical letters to the Council committee, both Germany and France on June 2, 1934, promised to abstain from direct or indirect pressures on the voters and from any reprisals or discrimination against any voter, later extended to any non-voter, for his part in the campaign.

On the proposal of its committee, the Council, on June 16, appointed a Plebiscite Commission to organize, direct, and supervise the plebiscite. The commission was composed of three members, M. Victor Henry (Swiss),

---

[8] Baron Aloisi (Italian), Señor Olivan (Spanish) and Señor Cantilo (Argentine).

[9] League of Nations, *Monthly Summary*, XIV: 1 (January 1934), p. 8.

[10] Minutes of the Eightieth (Extraordinary) Session of Council, League of Nations, *Official Journal*, Pt. I (June 1934); Pt. II (July 1934).

a District Commissioner; M. M. D. de Jongh (Dutch), former Burgo-
meister; M. Alan Rhode (Swedish), Head of the Legal Section of the Foreign
Affairs Ministry; a deputy, Sarah Wambaugh (American), an authority
on plebiscites and technical expert in the Tacna–Arica plebiscite; and
inspectors for each district. The commission commenced its duties on July 1.

The Council also appointed a Supreme Plebiscite Tribunal and eight
District Tribunals to deal with all disputes regarding: persons entitled to
vote; offenses covered by the plebiscite regulations; and breaches of ordinary criminal law connected with the purpose of the plebiscite and committed before, during, or after the plebiscite proceedings.

Some twenty experienced judges of Italian, Swiss, Swedish, Irish,
Norwegian, and Spanish nationality were appointed. It was provided, and
Germany agreed, that these tribunals should continue to function for one
year after the new regime was set up with full authority to hear all complaints of pressure or reprisals. The voting was fixed for January 13, 1935.

The final voting list reached nearly 540,000. Over 100,000 claims or
protests had to be examined by the tribunals. For the supervision and
counting of the vote, some 950 experienced officials were brought in from
Switzerland, the Netherlands, and Luxembourg; and a neutral chairman
was in charge of each voting center. The voting resulted in 477,000 for
union with Germany; 46,000 for the status quo; and 2,000 for union with
France. The large vote for reunion with Germany showed that Hitler's
decision to stress unity and patriotism had paid off.

The plebiscite had been conducted in full compliance with the treaty
stipulation regarding the "freedom, secrecy and trustworthiness" of the
voting. There was no disorder. The international force guarded the ballot
boxes until they were assembled and the votes counted.

The League Council, on January 15, decided that the whole territory
should be transferred to Germany on March 1, 1935. The many financial
and administrative details were completed in time, and the territory was
turned over free from debt and with a substantial sum in the treasury.

AN INTERNATIONAL FORCE

The Governing Commission had the duty to maintain law and order
in the territory, and in the highly charged conditions before and during the
plebiscite, it was evident that special precautions would be necessary.
The Nazis kept up a threatening radio campaign, and a force estimated at
16,000 men was being trained near the Saar border. Accordingly, on
December 5, the Council authorized the Governing Commission to recruit
the first truly international force that had been assembled by the League.
Great Britain contributed 1,500 officers and men; Italy, 1,300; and the
Netherlands and Sweden each 250. The commander-in-chief was Major

General Brind who had his headquarters at Saarbrucken and operated through a staff of thirty British officers and seventy-one other ranks.[11] English-speaking liaison officers were supplied by the Italian, Dutch, and Swedish contingents. The force was stationed at some twelve points throughout the territory, and sufficient transport was provided to enable 50 percent of the infantry to be moved simultaneously in an emergency. Twenty-five percent of each contingent was to be available at all times on a half-hour's notice.

Although the local Nazi leaders tried to organize a boycott, describing the force as a new army of occupation, their effort failed. The force was popular with all elements of the population.

General Brind's instructions from the League Council were that the Governing Commission was to continue to be responsible for maintaining order and that "subject to the military requirements of the situation, and without prejudice to any immediate action which may be necessary in the event of emergency," he was to comply with requests of the commission "for the intervention of the force for the purpose of maintaining or restoring order."[12]

He also received guidance from the British Army Council that the task of the Plebiscite Force was to maintain order "before, during and so long after the Plebiscite as the force may be required . . . if in the opinion of the responsible civil authority the local police forces are inadequate for the purpose."[13]

Thus the troops were employed in a military capacity and not as police. They were to come into action only at the request of the competent civil authorities, unless an exceptional emergency should arise involving danger to life or property and necessitating immediate action which, in the opinion of the local military commander, could not be adequately handled by the civil authorities present.

The nature and extent of the weapons used were matters within the discretion of the military commander receiving the request from the civil authority. Troops were commanded to act with restraint and use only that force necessary to restore order. It was no part of their duty to inflict punishment.

On the basis of his instructions, General Brind issued orders to the commanders of the national contingents for their guidance.[14] These orders were accepted by all nationalities as being in accordance with their national custom.

---

[11] See "Report by the Commander-in-Chief, International Force in the Saar." This unpublished report is available at the United Nations Library in Geneva and copies of it can be obtained on microfilm.

[12] *Ibid.*

[13] *Ibid.*

[14] *Ibid.*, Apps. I and III.

The policy was to distribute the troops so they would be rapidly available if needed, especially in the densely populated areas. In the process, however, small detachments were avoided. Their presence was made known to the population in all areas by route marches and lorry patrol. During the day of the plebiscite, the troops were "kept under cover" but close to each polling booth area. The orders were to avoid any complaint that the plebiscite was being menaced by military force. After polling had taken place, some of the troops were employed to transport the ballot boxes to a central counting place. Others were held available as a mobile reserve in the event of disorder.

When the troops first arrived in the Saar, the attitude of the population toward them was correct but frigid. But by the time of the plebiscite, a friendly attitude prevailed. General Brind felt this change was an important factor in averting disorder. The conclusion to be drawn is that such forces should be on the spot and able to overcome latent hostility some weeks before a critical issue arises.

General Brind's report contained the following conclusions:

1. The absence of serious disorder was largely due to the moral influence of the presence of troops, both as a deterrent to disorderly elements in the population and as an encouragement to the police to do their duty in difficult political circumstances.

2. One of the problems of the International Force was the absence of an adequate intelligence organization and the difficulty of obtaining reliable information. Had serious disturbances threatened or attempts to create disorder occurred, it would have been difficult to take suitable precautionary measures. General Brind recommended that in similar future situations an intelligence organization should be established in the country concerned some time before the troops arrive and before the situation reaches fever heat.

3. It was important to draw the force from countries which had no direct interest in the issue and to maintain a strictly neutral attitude at all times.

4. The composition of the force was quite satisfactory. It was made up of infantry whose mobility was secured by having enough motor vehicles available to transport 50 percent of each contingent's strength.

5. Small battalions of 300–400 men with a liberal proportion of officers were found to be suitable and would be useful for work analogous to that carried out in the Saar.

6. Armored cars and light tanks were found to be useful for patrolling outlying districts.

7. In any international force, the language question is of great importance. The Saar experience pointed out the difficulty in securing an adequate number of interpreters.

8. The civil telephone system was relied on by the Saar force. In the event of disorder, however, this would have been inadequate. Military wireless sets must be available with sufficient range to ensure direct communication at all times between force headquarters and the headquarters of the various contingents.

9. The command of the international force found that press correspondents[15] had inadequate arrangements to find out and report the true situation. Consequently, the greatest variety of false and often tendentious stories reached the outside world, some reporting incidents and troubles which never took place.

The League Council attempted to arrange a scheme for financing the four national contingents so that the extra cost of maintenance, resulting from expatriation and not covered in the budgets of the respective governments, would be established "on a basis of equality." But the different conditions of service and the inequalities in the administrative and budgetary systems of the various armies made it impossible to adhere to the principle of equality. The differences in the claims varied from twelve and a half francs per diem for British personnel to thirty-three for members of the Swedish contingent.

General Brind, in the light of this experience, recommended that in any similar situation in the future, it should be provided that no members of any contingent should suffer financial losses owing to expatriation for service under the international organization. This would include compensation for the separation of married personnel from their families, for extra wear and tear on uniforms, and for the extra cost of normal ration. The amount of such compensation required would vary from one country to another and could not, therefore, be established on the basis of equality.

The League Council had provided that each of the national contingents would be responsible for its own administration. In practice, however, force headquarters had to make arrangements for more matters than had been anticipated. It dealt with accommodations (buildings and repairs); post, telephone, and telegraph; moves by rail; civilian transport; fuel supply; local traffic regulations; leave travel facilities; ceremonial parades; and financial advice.

EVALUATION

The Saar represents the first important case of government by an international commission. The early difficulties of the Governing Commission arose from the open use of its authority in pursuit of French national policy, causing resentment among the Saarlanders. At first the League seemed to acquiesce in this misrule, but in response to protests from other

---

[15] Several hundred were sent by their agencies or newspapers.

member states, in 1925 the League Council made changes in the composition of the Governing Commission in an attempt to assure more international and impartial operation. Provision was made for the rotation of the chairmanship, for quarterly reports to the Council and for a rapporteur and a Council subcommittee to serve as liaison between the Saar Governing Commission and the League. The increasing use of advisory and technical bodies made up of people from the territory made it possible for most grievances to be resolved on the spot without frequent recourse to the League Council.

The arrangements for the 1935 plebiscite were complicated by the belligerent German Nazi presence on the border. Thus, it is significant that the Plebiscite Commission and the system of juridical tribunals were able to organize the conditions which assured the "freedom, secrecy and trustworthiness of the voting."

To assist the Governing Commission in maintaining order during the plebiscite, an international force of 3,300 officers and men was sent to the territory a month before the voting. This was the first large truly international force ever assembled, and its use proved a remarkable success. Its efficiency, discipline, and recognized neutrality made it well-received by the populace, and the peace was kept throughout this difficult period. The experience of the force brought to light several desiderata for such operations in the future.

4

ALBANIA'S TERRITORIAL DISPUTE WITH YUGOSLAVIA AND GREECE, 1921

In 1913, after the Balkan Wars, the great powers of Europe recognized Albania as a sovereign state. But World War I broke out before most of its boundaries could be established, and during the war, portions of territory claimed by Albania on the map were occupied or claimed by Serbia, Italy, and Greece.

At the war's end, in 1919, the Supreme Allied Council acknowledged the unsettled status of the region and entrusted the Conference of Ambassadors with the settlement of the Albanian boundary question. The Ambassadors procrastinated, however, and months went by without any action being taken. Meanwhile encroachment and occupation by Albania's three neighbors became more prolonged, skirmishes and violent outbreaks became more frequent, and there was danger of war in that area.

In spite of the indeterminate status of its territorial limits, Albania sought and obtained membership in the League of Nations in December 1920. In April 1921,[1] and again in June, Albania appealed to the League Council, according to the terms of Articles 11 and 15, to settle its frontiers and free its territory from foreign occupation. The Greek and Yugoslav representatives asserted that only the Conference of Ambassadors had the authority to deal with this question. The great powers on the Council accepted this view, but urged the Conference of Ambassadors to act without delay and requested the parties meanwhile to refrain from any acts of aggression.[2]

The Conference of Ambassadors again delayed, and Albania brought its case before the League Assembly in September 1921. In the Assembly debates, a number of members expressed resentment that so dangerous a situation had been allowed to continue. Reports of fighting and skirmishing arrived continuously, and the numbers of dead and wounded were listed daily in the newspapers. Under increasing pressure from the members of the League, the Council on October 6 appointed a Commission of Enquiry to report on the disturbances and to supervise the execution of the decision of the Conference of Ambassadors regarding the location of the frontiers.[3]

Climaxing a period of activity and infiltration on Albania's northern border was an invasion by Yugoslav troops in early October. In reply to Albania's accusations of aggression, Yugoslavia stated that this action was taken by an Albanian force which constituted the legal government of Albania as opposed to the Tirana Government. At this point, Lloyd George of Great Britain called for a special session of the Council to discuss the application of economic sanctions to Yugoslavia. Before the Council met, however, the Conference of Ambassadors on November 9, 1921, announced its long-awaited decision on the Albanian frontiers, declaring them to be those originally laid down in 1913, with three minor rectifications in favor of Yugoslavia.[4] Since the delimitation of the 1913 frontiers had never been carried out on the spot, the Ambassadors dispatched a Delimitation Commission of four members to survey the disputed boundaries. Yugoslavia announced that in order to avoid further danger, it would accept the Ambassadors' decision and withdraw its troops to the frontier laid down by them. Albania also accepted the decision.

[1] In this appeal Albania claimed that 140 villages had been pillaged and partially destroyed, that the Serbian attack had resulted in the death of 738 Albanians, and that 40,000 Albanians had been forced to evacuate the devastated regions. League of Nations, *Official Journal*, II: 5 and 6 (July–August 1921), p. 474.

[2] League of Nations, *Official Journal* (1921), p. 725.

[3] The Commission of Enquiry was sent to Albania in November 1921 and continued its task until April 1923, when it made its final report. *Ibid.* (May 1923).

[4] *Ibid.*, p. 1194.

On November 18, 1921, the Conference of Ambassadors informed the Governments of Yugoslavia and Albania, in identical letters, that a demarcation zone some twenty-five miles wide should be established from which all troops should be withdrawn. The purpose of this action was to give the Delimitation Commission liberty of action in fixing the frontier, and to prevent any clashes of troops. Detailed maps and descriptions accompanied the letters. The Ambassadors at the same time informed the President of the League Council of their decision to establish a demarcation zone and suggested that the Commission of Enquiry, then on its way to Albania, be given supplementary terms of reference to the effect that if it concluded that "an infringement of the regulations of this supplementary decision has been committed, this Commission should immediately inform the Delimitation Commission," which would proceed at once to Albania, to estimate the situation "regarding the position of the interested parties with respect to the demarcation zone."[5]

THE COMMISSION OF ENQUIRY

The Commission of Enquiry arrived at the frontier on November 19 with instructions from the Council to see that the Yugoslav evacuation and the Albanian reoccupation were carried out peaceably. On December 20, the commission informed the Council that the evacuation had been completed.

The members of the commission were Major Jens Christian Meinich (Norway), Col. Charles Schaefer (Luxembourg), Prof. M. Sederholm (Finland), and M. de Pourtales, secretary.

Under the terms of reference, the commission was to "keep the Council informed of the retirement of both the Serb-Croat-Slovene and Albanian troops from the provisional zone of demarcation," to "keep in touch with the Delimitation Commission . . . and . . . place itself at the disposal of the local authorities to assist in carrying out the evacuation so as to avoid incidents"; to see that "no outside assistance is given in support of a local movement which might disturb internal peace in Albania";[6] and to "examine and submit to the Council measures to end the present disturbances and to prevent their recurrence."[7]

The commission's recommendations went far beyond the elimination of foreign elements, establishing principles leading to the viability of Albania as an independent nation. Albania as a newly independent country had a

---

[5] *Ibid.*, pp. 1210–11.

[6] This referred especially to Greek elements supporting pro-Greek agitators in the border town of Koritza, the area called Northern Epirus.

[7] Minutes of the Fifteenth Session of the Council, November 16–Novenber 19, 1921, League of Nations, *Official Journal* (December 1921), p. 1193.

population sharply divided between Moslems and Christians. It was necessary to cement the people into a coordinated state, and financial and economic assistance were required to stabilize a workable social and constitutional order.

In carrying out its task of ending disturbances, the commission recommended, and the Council approved, that the League aid the Albanian Government in obtaining experts to assist in making the reforms required for better administration and economic development. The commission was convinced that the interference of Albania's neighbors could best be thwarted by foregoing an active foreign policy and setting its own house in order politically and economically. The general lawlessness which prevailed had created a situation bordering on chaos, and the commission considered its duty was to help bring about reforms. Only then would foreign capital be attracted and revenues realized to establish a stable government. [8]

The Commission of Enquiry also reported on the mineral, forest, and agricultural resources of the country which, if properly developed, would furnish a sufficient basis for a stable and independent country and advised the King in developing such a program. The commission considered, and the Council agreed, that its mandate was broad enough to cover these fields of activity.

EVALUATION

Much valuable time was lost in negotiating this border dispute as a result of unclear jurisdictional responsibilities between the Conference of Ambassadors, entrusted by the Supreme Allied Council with settling Albanian boundaries, and the League of Nations Council, charged with the duty of maintaining peace and protecting the territorial integrity of its members. Consequently, the League Commission of Enquiry did not arrive on the scene until six months after the initial request, and in the intervening period continuous skirmishing cost many lives. The invasion of Albania by Yugoslav troops was halted only after the British Government urged the Council to apply economic sanctions against the aggressor.

The commission's terms of reference were clear. Its task was to oversee and report on the withdrawal of troops, to prevent outside assistance from being given to local movements, and to submit to the Council measures to end the disturbances and prevent their recurrence. Of special interest in this case was the establishment of a broad demarcation zone from which all troops were excluded. This zone was precisely laid out on large-scale army maps, which facilitated the task of the commission in supervising the withdrawal of troops. The commission also cooperated with the Delimitation Commission in order to determine whether there was any infringement

[8] See Commission of Enquiry, *Final Report*, Doc. C. 259 (1923), VII.

of the Council's decision. Thus the Conference of Ambassadors and the League were able to work together to secure a lasting solution to the dispute.

An historian of this period states that "there can be little doubt that Albania owed her survival as an independent state to the action of the League."[9]

5

—◆—

PARTITION OF UPPER SILESIA, 1921

Both Poland and Germany wanted Upper Silesia, a region of 4,000 square miles, inhabited by 2.5 million people, with great mineral and industrial wealth, included within their respective borders. Their claims were based on historical and ethnographic grounds.

The Paris Peace Conference in 1919 heard the claims of both sides and decided that the dispute should be settled by a plebiscite. Accordingly, an Interallied Commission was set up, supported by an international force, to ascertain the wishes of the inhabitants. The result was to be reported by districts to the Supreme Allied Council, which would settle the boundary in accordance with the wishes of the people "and with consideration for the geographical and economic conditions of the inhabitants."

THE PLEBISCITE

The Interallied Plebiscite Commission was headed by a French general with an English and an Italian member. They reached the scene accompanied by an international army of 11,500 French and 2,000 Italian troops. France was known to be sympathetic to Poland, and the Poles were confident of the result of a plebiscite. There was so much fraternizing between the French troops and the Polish elements of the population that as the day of voting drew near, four British battalions arrived to give the army more of an international character.

The plebiscite held on March 20, 1921, gave 716,000 votes to Germany; 471,000 to Poland. The Germans carried thirteen out of seventeen administrative districts. When the surprised Poles saw the results, they claimed that

[9] Walters, *op. cit.*, p. 161.

the four districts which they carried should go at once to Poland. Germany held that the majority of the districts should determine the fate of the entire region.

In the dispute following the plebiscite and with the example of rebel General Lucien Zeligowski in Vilna before them, the Poles raised an irregular army under General Adalbert Korfanty and overran a large part of Upper Silesia. This caused the Germans to form armed bands, holding themselves in readiness to meet an attack. The Interallied Commission began to fall apart when the French showed sympathy for the Polish side. Thus a dangerous outbreak was pending, with England and Italy supporting Germany and France supporting Poland. The four British battalions had already left, but Lloyd George sent six battalions back to the scene. The commission, seeing a danger, recovered its authority and the Korfanty irregulars were disbanded at the end of June.

In August, the Supreme Allied Council attempted to fix the boundary according to the plebiscite results, but keeping other factors in mind as well. However, after a four-day deadlock, the Council handed the affair over to the League of Nations. The issue before the League was how to draw the frontier so that the rich resources and intermingled population of Upper Silesia would be divided in a way to terminate the bitter dispute between Germany and Poland.

ACTION BY THE COUNCIL OF THE LEAGUE

The Council accepted the mandate from the Supreme Allied Council and called an extraordinary session for August 29, under the Presidency of Viscount Ishii of Japan who had studied the Silesian problem. He presented a plan to the Council which became the basis for a solution acceptable to both the Council and the parties to the dispute. The Ishii plan was further studied and developed by a committee of four representatives of the Council—Belgium, Brazil, China, and Spain—who were helped, as needed, by experts and members of the Secretariat.

The plan worked out by the four members was unanimously adopted by the Council on October 12, 1921. The first part of the plan provided that the disputed area should be so divided as to give each side a share of the mineral deposits and the proportion of the population reflected in the plebiscite. The second part provided that for fifteen years the public utilities would continue to operate for the whole area and with uniform rates; the German mark would be the standard of value; the raw materials and half-finished products would go from one zone to the other free of duty; and the inhabitants would be free to cross from one zone to the other. A Mixed Commission and a Court of Arbitration would reside in Upper Silesia to smooth out difficulties and settle disputes. Each organ would be composed of an equal number of Germans and Poles, with a neutral chairman appointed by the League. In addition, a convention for promoting economic harmony between Germany and Poland was prepared by a commission under the presidency of M. Calonder, former President of the Swiss Confederation.

This complicated but thorough plan advanced by the League was not popular with either Germany or Poland. The territorial clauses pleased neither disputant. But in a short time the plan was working well, and in a few years, it became recognized as one of the most successful achievements of the League.

EVALUATION

The Interallied Plebiscite Commission in Upper Silesia was so composed as to cast doubt on its impartiality, as its French chairman was openly pro-Polish. In addition, the national components of the international force were not properly balanced; most of the soldiers were French, and other troops had to be brought in before the voting in order to give the force a more international character.

After a majority in the plebiscite opted for German nationality, the commission's authority deteriorated, and an acceptable solution was found only when the case came before the League Council, where persons of greater detachment and objectivity were brought into the operation. Viscount Ishii, the Japanese member of the Council, brought forward a plan which became the basis for a solution. The fact that he was far removed from the immediate scene illustrated the advantages of geographical detachment, a factor not neglected in later League cases.

The success of the League in this case helped to offset the Vilna debacle and considerably enhanced the League's prestige.

6

—◆—

CORFU: DISPUTE BETWEEN GREECE AND ITALY, 1923

On August 27, 1923, General Enrico Tellini, the Italian member of the commission delimiting the frontier between Albania and Greece, and four Italian subordinates were murdered while on the Greek side of the frontier. This situation grew out of the long-delayed unfinished business of the Peace Conference of 1919. The Conference of Ambassadors had been assigned the task of delimiting the frontiers of Albania, which involved territorial claims of Yugoslavia, Greece, and Italy. The Ambassadors were slow starting and the Delimitation Commission, appointed by them, composed of French, British, and Italian members, was slowly pursuing its task on the southeast border of Albania in the summer of 1923 when the incident occurred.

Responsibility for action was divided between the Conference of Ambassadors and the newly-formed League of Nations Council. The Council had peace-observation responsibilities toward its members, which included Greece, Albania, and the members of the Conference of Ambassadors—Great Britain, France, and Italy. Not only was there an unclear and divided jurisdiction between the Council and the Conference of Ambassadors, but the respective British and French representatives on them were different persons who frequently did not take the same positions. Thus, there was confusion and contradiction.

Benito Mussolini had taken over the Italian Government in 1922. His ideas for restoring Italian glory and prestige through military prowess and territorial expansion made him impatient and disdainful of the League Council. His truculent oratory in Rome made it almost impossible for the Italian representatives in Geneva—old line diplomats and statesmen—to follow any consistent line.

Mussolini demanded that Greece, whose complicity had not been proved: make humiliating apologies; inquire into and report on the circumstances of the crime within five days and do it in the presence of an Italian military attaché; execute all guilty persons (they could never be caught); and pay fifty million lire to the Italian Government.

Greece conceded most of the Italian demands but refused the financial penalty until an inquiry should prove Greek responsibility for the crime, either through direct involvement or negligence. Greece also offered to submit the question to the League and undertook to accept its decisions.

This qualified acceptance of Italy's ultimatum did not satisfy Mussolini, who ordered a powerful Italian squadron to occupy Corfu, after a bombardment which killed or wounded a number of the inhabitants, including some refugees who had fled from Asia Minor.

In these circumstances, Greece invoked Articles 12 and 15 of the Covenant requiring the Council to make a full investigation of the case as a basis to effect a settlement. At the same time, Greece received a demand from the Conference of Ambassadors protesting the murder of one of their agents and requesting Greece to make an immediate inquiry.

The circumstances in this dispute were not favorable to effective action by the League Council. So many errors of judgment and interpretation were made that one historian referred to this case as the "darkest spot in the history of the League."[1] The case, however, is instructive in showing what *not* to do in a similar situation.

[1] Bassett, *op. cit.*, p. 201.

ACTION BY THE LEAGUE

Members of the League Assembly, particularly the smaller states, were shocked and indignant at the brutal attack by a great power on a small country, especially as there was no proof that Greece was responsible for the murders. The smaller states were unwilling to entrust the case to the exclusive jurisdiction of the Conference of Ambassadors of which Italy was a principal member. Mussolini considered Italy's national honor to be involved, and he precluded the question being considered by either the Conference of Ambassadors or the Council. The Italian representative to the League, in arguing against the League's competence and in favor of the Conference of Ambassadors' jurisdiction, had already contradicted Mussolini's view of the competence of neither. However, the Council rejected the Italian view and held that nothing could take away the right and duty of the Council acting as enjoined by the Covenant.

Mussolini announced that if the case were considered by the Council, Italy would withdraw from the League and continue to occupy Corfu. With the rising tide of world-wide public resentment against Italy, however, he conceded that the case might be dealt with by the Ambassadors. France supported the Italian view on this point, apparently hoping to receive in exchange Italian support for its new policy of occupying the Ruhr.

After establishing its right to consider the case, the Council agreed, on grounds of expediency, to adjourn for a few days while the Conference of Ambassadors considered its responsibilities in the matter.

ACTION BY CONFERENCE OF AMBASSADORS

The conference requested Greece to investigate the facts. The findings were to be submitted to the conference, which was to be allowed to impose penalties. Greece consented to the request, invited the Ambassadors to conduct an inquiry both on the Greek and Albanian sides of the frontier, and consented to accept the conclusions reached by such an inquiry. Greece thus found itself in the embarrassing position of having agreed to accept the conclusions and findings of both the Council and the Conference of Ambassadors. To relieve its embarrassment, Greece suggested that the Council should "appoint a certain number of neutral representatives to take part in the inquiry."[2] This, however, was not done.

The rank and file of the League were not willing to see the League's competence and authority flouted and were distrustful of the Conference of Ambassadors. Under their pressure, the states who were members of

[2] Minutes of the Twenty-sixth Session of the Council, League of Nations, *Official Journal*, IV: 11 (November 1923), p. 1289.

both the conference and the League Council arranged the inquiry so that neither organization's competence would be questioned. A plan was worked out, and presented by the Spanish member of the Council, which required Greece to apologize not to Italy but to the Delimitation Commission whose chairman, the Italian member, had been killed. While the investigation was being made and possible penalties determined, Greece was to deposit fifty million lire in a Swiss bank for eventual payment to the injured party. The exact amount was to be determined by the Permanent Court at The Hague.

Although these terms came close to admitting Italy's demands, the Italian member of the Council refused to discuss them. And the other members of the Council, mostly in silence and without vote, permitted the chairman to say they were approved. They were communicated, together with a record of the meeting, to the Conference of Ambassadors. Greece, thus spared further embarrassment, hastened to accept the terms. The Greek member had suggested some compromises to the Council which further explained the acceptability of the terms.

The Assembly, however, was not satisfied with the situation. War seemed to be averted, but Corfu was still under Italian occupation, and no date had been fixed for its evacuation. More disturbing to many members was the apparent weakening of the Council whose competence had been questioned, and which in effect had not prevented a strong power from trampling on a weaker neighbor.

THE COMMISSION OF ENQUIRY

The Conference of Ambassadors set up a Commission of Enquiry consisting of British, French, Japanese, and Italian members. A proposal that the investigation should take place without the presence of an Italian was defeated because the Italian representative threatened to obstruct the effort. No neutrals were nominated by the Council. The character of the commission, therefore, was regarded as far from impartial. It was instructed to collect the evidence and report to the Ambassadors within five days.

On September 22, the commission made a preliminary report to the effect that the crime was planned and carried out with such care and precision that it could only be regarded as a political crime; and the inquiry made by the Greek authorities after the crime showed "several instances of negligence," but the facts ascertained were "not sufficiently complete and decisive" to enable the commissioners to decide on the Greek Government's responsibility. [3]

[3] The Italian member of the commission, while signing this report, made an additional report in which he fixed serious responsibility on Greece.

Nevertheless, on receiving this report, the Conference of Ambassadors decided that there was enough evidence to justify giving Italy fifty million lire. This it did on September 26, without waiting for the opinion from the Permanent Court on the amount.

The next day Italy evacuated Corfu. Public opinion accepted the award of the money to Italy as the Conference's way of getting Italy out of Corfu.

EVALUATION

The long delay in dealing with the unsettled frontier between Albania and Greece created an increasingly tense, difficult, and dangerous situation. The Conference of Ambassadors handled the whole affair in a highly subjective manner. Two members of the Conference, Italy and France, were not disinterested and were indeed suspect not only by Albania and Greece, but by many other members of the League. Thus the composition of the Delimitation Commission aroused resentment that, along with inadequate security arrangements, led to the assassination of the Italian member, which gave rise to serious consequences.

The composition of the Commission of Enquiry sent out by the Ambassadors created suspicion among the members of the League and led to a report that was regarded as biased in favor of one party to the dispute. The five-day time limit imposed for the preliminary report further jeopardized its validity. Failure to add a judicial aspect to the inquiry by the use of the Permanent Court to assess the indemnity made the final verdict appear to be subject to Italian pressure.

Greece made the mistake of appealing to both jurisdictions simultaneously, the League Council and the Conference of Ambassadors. Both had responsibilities in the case, but had the League been able to act alone, the case might have been more impartially settled.

It was generally considered that the peace-observation function of the League was weakened by the way in which this case was handled. For a time, the danger of a retrograde step in international law existed, recognizing "that states are responsible for outrages committed within their territory" even when no negligence or complicity has been proved. The small states in the Assembly debate, especially the Latin American countries, together with England and Sweden in the Council, rejected this thesis. The League members also rejected the Italian contention that a state has the right to occupy territory to bring an adversary to terms.

The League of Nations was not used to the extent intended by the Covenant, primarily because of the prior involvement of the Conference of Ambassadors. However, there was no doubt that the almost universal condemnation of Italy, expressed in public Council and Assembly debates, had the effect of causing Mussolini to withdraw from Corfu.

7

—•—

THE QUESTION OF MEMEL, 1919–1924

The port of Memel, taken from Germany in 1919 and placed temporarily under Allied sovereignty, was intended to be turned over to Lithuania and to serve as a commercial outlet for Poland as well. The Allied Conference of Ambassadors, which was still in existence five years after the end of the war, drew up a draft convention for Memel which was not acceptable to Lithuania because it gave Poland a role in the future administration of the port. In January 1923, Lithuania took forcible possession of the town, with its German population, and refused to share its administration with Poland. This aroused the strong opposition of both Poland and Germany and circumvented a settlement by the Allies.

The Lithuanian coup took place when some of the Allies, particularly France and Poland, hinted that Memel might be made into a Free City like Danzig. Poland's successful seizure of Vilna provided a precedent for the Lithuanian action.

The governments represented in the Conference of Ambassadors brought the Memel situation to the attention of the League Council in September 1923 under Article 11 (2) of the Covenant. The task before the League was: to provide a status for the disputed port that would satisfy the interests of Lithuania and Poland; and to protect the German population, who would become Lithuanian subjects, from injustice and inequality.

THE COMMISSION OF ENQUIRY

The Council met on December 15, 1923, and decided that a fresh start should be made to settle the question. Its first step was to appoint a Commission of Enquiry whose three members were chosen from countries that had no direct concern in the terms of the settlement. Norman Davis, former U.S. Under Secretary of State, was chairman; A. G. Kroller, member of the Dutch Economic Council of the Ministry of Foreign Affairs and M. Hoernell, member of the Swedish Academy of Technical Science, were named as members. Mr. Davis was appointed by the Council. M. Kroller and M. Hoernell were appointed by the chairman of the League Committee for Communications and Transit because the questions at issue concerned mainly the organization of the port of Memel.

The Council requested the commission to make a comprehensive study of the draft conventions submitted on both sides, of all existing factors that might further the solution of the problem; and to make recommendations to the Council regarding the Statute of Memel.[1] The commission first met on February 5, 1924. It visited the capitals of Lithuania and Poland and the Memel area and prepared its report for a meeting of the Council on March 12.

With minor amendments, considerable portions of the draft convention prepared by the Conference of Ambassadors were accepted by the commission. These provisions exacted a promise from the Lithuanians that the Poles should have free and equal rights with all other users of the port, and that no obstacle would be placed on the floating of timber, the main Polish export through Memel, down the Niemen River. The work of the commission was, therefore, partly fact-finding and partly mediatory.

The settlement of the Memel question was in the form of a convention to be agreed on by Lithuania and the Principal Allied Powers. The report pointed out that the Allied Powers, in separating Memel from Germany and making it a part of Lithuania, had done so with the intention that the port should serve the entire hinterland, including the whole of the Niemen basin, which took in a large area of Poland.

The principal problem was to provide an administration of the port that would protect the rights of Poland and other users while respecting Lithuanian sovereignty. For this purpose, three annexes on the Statute of Memel and the port and on the freedom of transit on the Niemen River were attached to the general convention.

The convention laid down the conditions by which the Principal Allies were to transfer Memel to Lithuania: the right of former German nationals to opt for Lithuanian nationality; the protection to be given to minorities; and the private and corporate rights of foreign nationals in Memel.

The Statute of Memel stipulated that the territory was to be an autonomous unit and governed "on democratic principles," with a governor appointed by the Lithuanian President, a legislature elected by universal suffrage, and an executive directorate of five persons, citizens of the territory. The official languages were to be both Lithuanian and German.

The Port of Memel was to be considered as "a port of international concern" whose administration, operation, upkeep and development were to be entrusted to a harbor board of three persons, thus solving the problem of Polish participation: one representing Lithuanian economic interests, one the economic interests of the territory, and a third member, appointed by the chairman of the League's Committee on Communications and Transit, to give special attention to international economic interests served by the port. The harbor board was to make an annual report to the League Committee on Communications and Transit.

[1] League of Nations, *Monthly Summary*, III: 12 (December 1923), p. 308.

The convention provided that any member of the League Council was entitled to draw attention to any infraction of the convention. In the event that differences arose over questions of law or fact concerning these provisions, they were to be referred for decision to the Permanent Court of International Justice from which there would be no appeal.

ACTION BY THE LEAGUE COUNCIL

The League Council and the Principal Allied Powers and Lithuania, as parties to the convention, accepted the report of the Commission of Enquiry in March 1924. Poland, which was not a member of the Council, wished to see certain provisions of the convention modified, but no changes were made. The convention was signed by the parties on May 8, 1924, and came into force in August 1925.

In the years after 1925, many quarrels arose over the territory between Lithuania and Germany. The Germans could not easily reconcile themselves to separation from their homeland and rule by what they regarded as an inferior race. Many complaints were laid before the League Council as alleged infractions of the Memel Statute, but the real conflict lay deeper. After 1936 Hitler openly declared that one of his objectives was the return of Memel to the Reich, and he made no further appeals to the League.

The convention remained the basis of government for Memel until March 1939 when Germany reoccupied the territory without resistance by Lithuania or the western powers.

EVALUATION

The status of the port of Memel was left undetermined from 1919 to 1923 while the Conference of Ambassadors delayed its ultimate transfer to Lithuania. Again in this case, the League could take action only after the conference had relinquished its jurisdiction.

The Commission of Enquiry, when finally set up, was composed of competent and impartial persons who in a period of about five weeks were able to devise an acceptable solution. The commission's report concentrated on the technical aspects of the problem, concerning the efficient administration of the port. This emphasis was justified by the outcome. Once the practical, economic interests of the port's users were assured, the political arrangements were more readily accepted.

The chairman of the commission stated to the Council that this case gave evidence of what could be done by the League that could not otherwise be accomplished.

8

THE MOSUL AFFAIR: FRONTIER DISPUTE BETWEEN TURKEY AND IRAQ, 1924–1925

Iraq, with British encouragement, broke away from Turkey in 1914 when the latter announced its support of Germany at the beginning of World War I. After the war, the Supreme Allied Council made Iraq a class A mandate, with Great Britain as mandatory, and its independence was recognized provisionally. Shortly after Emir Faisal was crowned King of Iraq, the Turks began to stir up trouble in the northwest sections of the country, especially in the vilayet of Mosul where many of the Kurdish tribes were friendly toward Turkey. Mosul comprised an area of 29,000 square miles with a mixed population of over 300,000 Kurds, Turks, Arabs, Christians, and Jews. Believed to be rich in oil, the territory was economically important. In 1923, British and Iraqi forces broke the resistance of these tribes to Iraqi rule, and order was restored in Mosul.

The Allies were meanwhile negotiating a treaty of peace with Turkey at Lausanne, but no agreement could be reached on the future of Mosul. Therefore, it was stipulated in the treaty that "the frontier between Iraq and Turkey should be laid down" by Great Britain and Turkey, but if they could not agree within nine months, the dispute should be referred to the Council of the League.[1] This was done in August 1924.

The issue before the Council was to determine whether the province of Mosul should become a part of Turkey or remain attached to Iraq. The disputants were Great Britain, acting as mandatory for Iraq, and Turkey.

THE CASE BEFORE THE COUNCIL

Great Britain and Turkey presented their cases to the League Council in September 1924. The British case rested chiefly on strategic grounds. Great Britain held that the whole province of Mosul should be governed by Iraq, which would make the northwest border run along the ridge of the high mountains and thus provide a more defendable frontier. If this were not done, armed forces would have to be maintained by each nation, and the prospect of renewed quarrels, if not war, on that frontier would be great.

[1] Treaty of Lausanne, Article 3 (2).

The Turkish claim was based on the positions held after the fighting in October 1918, when the British were holding a line that gave them only half of Mosul. The Turks called that the status quo line whereas the British General announced a line far to the north of the one held, therefore placing most of the vilayet in British-controlled territory. The Turks were exhausted at the end of the fighting and fell back of the armistice line.

After the war, the British organized the administration of the whole vilayet, and in 1923, King Faisal included it in the area of his civil administration. The Turks had never agreed to this arrangement and in their negotiations demanded the entire vilayet of Mosul.

The case was thus laid before the Council by Great Britain, and on September 25 the rapporteur, the Swedish delegate Hjalmar Branting, made his report. As had become the practice, he asked each representative of the parties if he would unconditionally accept the Council's decision, and each answered in the affirmative. A difference arose, however, between the two parties regarding whether the task was to fix the boundary between Turkey and Iraq, as the British held, or to decide to whom Mosul should belong, as the Turks held. The British view was accepted, and the Council appointed a commission to study the situation. Each side undertook not to disturb the status quo in the interim. However, each held a different view of the area covered by the status quo. There were minor clashes and loss of life in some areas resulting from the conflicting views of responsibility for the maintenance of order. Thus the Council had to determine where the status quo line should be drawn. A meeting of the Council was held for that purpose, and a temporary line of demarcation was drawn. Each side promised that none of its troops or civil agents would cross the demarcation line. In these circumstances, the Commission of Enquiry set out to accomplish its task.

THE COMMISSION OF ENQUIRY

In appointing commissions of enquiry, the Council tried to avoid any individual who might be suspected of partiality, either on personal grounds or grounds of nationality. In the Mosul case, since the area in dispute was supposed to be rich in oil, the Council was also careful not to include nationals from any countries which might have oil interests. The three members of the commission to visit Mosul, appointed on October 31, 1924, were M. de Wiersen, Swedish Minister, Chairman; Count Paul Teleki, geographer and former Hungarian Prime Minister; and Colonel Paulis, retired Belgian Army Officer.

The commission was charged with the duty of collecting facts and data required to fulfill its mission, and to give the Council information and suggestions which might help it to reach a decision, "giving due consideration to existing documents and to the views expressed by the interested parties both as regards the procedure and the substance of the question." It was also to make on-the-spot investigations.[2]

In accordance with these terms of reference, the commission, unlike previous Commissions of Enquiry, requested each side to appoint an assessor with expert assistants and interpreters to accompany its investigations. This innovation did not prove to be an altogether happy one and was not repeated until the Manchurian case in 1931.

The commission began its investigation in November 1924 by interviewing members of the British Government in London, then went to Ankara to get the Turkish view. It visited Baghdad, and from there it went to the vilayet of Mosul, visiting all parts of the area by plane, automobile, horseback, and on foot. They also examined economic and social conditions.

Turkey had proposed, and Great Britain opposed, the holding of a plebiscite. Consequently, the commission made a special effort to get the views of the leaders and people. It found that sentiment was not favorable to either side and that the Kurdish majority favored independence. But, if a choice were required, a majority of the population seemed to favor incorporation into Iraq, provided the mandate under Great Britain were continued for another twenty-five years.

The commission was authorized by its terms of reference "to avail itself of the services of advisers appointed respectively by each of the Governments concerned." Turkey appointed an assessor and an adviser who were natives of Mosul and so active in the Turkish cause that they had previously found it advisable to leave the country. When the commission and the assessors reached Baghdad, the assessors were separated from the party and lodged in quarters enclosed by barbed wire and outside the town wall. The British High Commissioner explained that because of their unpopularity, he could not be responsible for their safety in Baghdad. At the commissioners' request the two men were permitted to join them in Baghdad, but they were kept close to their quarters while in the city. The commission considered Turkey ill-advised to appoint such persons to accompany them, but once appointed, they insisted that these persons should have the privileges their position demanded.

In Mosul, where the assessors were popular, they were allowed to go about freely. But street demonstrations around them led to counterdemonstrations, and the British administrator told the commissioners that to assure their safety, he would have to establish police supervision of their movements and request the Turkish assessor not to wear his uniform. The outraged commissioners requested that they be given "no visible police protection," and that the protection of the Turkish assessor be assured so that he could assemble his witnesses to be brought before the commission.

[2] Minutes of the Thirtieth Session of the Council, League of Nations, *Official Journal* (October 1924).

The British High Commissioner came from Baghdad and charged that the commission had employed armed pro-Turk escorts, and that natives employed as interpreters were, in fact, pro-Turk political agitators; that the form of inquiry used threatened the authority of the British and Iraqi governments throughout the disputed area; and that the intended plan of the commissioners to separate and visit different parts of the vilayet was improper since some of them might be prejudiced and unable to make a balanced report. Such a plan to conduct a divided inquiry, he hinted, might cause the British Government to make an appeal against the report.

The chairman of the Commission of Enquiry rejected these charges and said that the Council had given the commission power to adopt its own procedure. Therefore, it was inadmissible to reopen this question. The commission proceeded with its investigation, and there was no further disturbance. The visits to the town took place without incidents, and after completing its work on the spot, the commission went to Geneva to write its report.

The commission recommended that the provisional line known as the "Brussels Line"[3] should be fixed as the frontier between Turkey and Iraq. Therefore, practically all of the vilayet would go to Iraq, but the commission conditioned this on the twenty-five year continuation of the mandate, and if this were refused, all but a small sector would go to Turkey.

This recommendation was not agreeable to Turkey, Iraq, or Great Britain. The Arabs of Iraq believed they were capable of self-government and did not favor continuation of the mandate. Great Britain and Iraq, however, accepted this condition on the understanding that the mandate would continue only until Iraq became a member of the League, which it did in 1931.

Both Turkey and Iraq (Great Britain) had agreed earlier to accept the conclusions of the commission on the frontier question. In the meantime, a new Turkish delegate to the League Council, Tewfik Rüstü Bey, had been named. He cleverly interposed many legal objections and asserted that the Council had no power to decide the question without the consent of both parties. This, of course, was contrary to the position taken by the preceding Turkish delegate.

The Council, anxious to avoid any charge that it might be exceeding its powers, decided to refer the question to the Permanent Court of International Justice for an advisory opinion. The Court met in extraordinary session, and a month later gave an opinion that the decision to be taken required a unanimous vote. The parties to the issue would take part in the voting, but their votes would not be counted in ascertaining unanimity. The Court also held that such a decision by the Council, taken in virtue

[3] Drawn by the Council in Brussels in October 1924 to end disagreement over the meaning of status quo.

of Article 3 of the Treaty of Lausanne, would be binding on the parties and would constitute a definitive determination of the frontier. The delay involved in this reference to the Court created increased uncertainty in Mosul itself where the situation on the provisional frontier was already unstable. Turkey was removing families north of the Brussels Line and sending troops into the area. In September 1924, at the request of the British Government, the Council sent a League representative to the spot whose duty was to deal with any incidents on the provisional frontier line. He, together with two League assistants, remained on the spot until the affair was completed. Iraq gave him a friendly reception, but the Turks refused to permit him to cross the Brussels Line. Nevertheless, peace reigned in the area during his presence.

On December 16, 1925, the Council endorsed the recommendations of its Commission of Enquiry, deciding that the definitive frontier should be along the Brussels Line. The Council also requested Iraq to accept the commission's suggestions for establishing harmony with Turkey, and to see that the Kurds had the privileges in the schools and local government recommended by the commission. Great Britain accepted the decision at once. Turkey joined Great Britain and Iraq in signing a treaty in June 1926 by which the new frontier was declared to be "definitive and inviolable."

Thus, after twenty-two months, a hotly contested territorial dispute was successfully brought to an end, with the Council, the Commission of Enquiry, a special representative on the spot, and the Permanent Court of International Justice contributing to the result.

EVALUATION

The processes of League justice in this case were long drawn out, and the frequent delays served to aggravate the situation further. Each step taken by the League was contested by one or both parties. The Turkish Government could not have been unaware that its choice of assessors was most unwise and would lead only to trouble. On the British side, the action of the British administrator in his constant interference with the commission's work was equally inadmissible. In short, the lack of cooperation between the two parties can be held responsible for most of the time lost in this dispute.

The entire weight of League machinery, including the Permanent Court, had to be brought to bear on the disputants before an agreement could be signed. In the face of these obstacles, the League's success was remarkable indeed.

9

---•◆•---

THE GREEK-BULGARIAN CRISIS, 1925

On October 19, 1925, shots were exchanged between the Bulgarian and Greek sentries on a troubled frontier where incidents had frequently occurred before. One Bulgarian sentry was killed, and, according to Greece, a Greek officer carrying a white flag of truce was killed. Prolonged firing and a movement of troops ensued. Both sides were angry, and the Greek Government, instead of laying its case before the League, decided to invade Bulgaria on a thirty-kilometer front. Greece claimed that Bulgarian troops had crossed the Greek frontier at another point. The reports were conflicting, but it appeared that a Balkan war was in the making.

On October 23, in a telegram to the Secretary-General of the League, the Bulgarian Government invoked Articles 10 and 11 of the Covenant and requested an immediate meeting of the League Council. Meanwhile, instructions had been given to the Bulgarian Military Command not to offer resistance to the advancing Greek troops.

On the same date, the Secretary-General, acting under one of the rare powers given to him by the Covenant,[1] summoned an extraordinary session of the Council for October 26 in Paris. Aristide Briand, in his capacity as President of the Council, but on his own authority, took the unprecedented action of sending identical telegrams to both governments reminding them of their solemn Covenant obligations "not to resort to war" and exhorting them to stop all military movements and to withdraw their troops behind their respective frontiers. M. Briand's telegram was sent to all members of the League as well as the press.[2] Later, it was found that

[1] Article 11 (1).

[2] The telegram read as follows:
"Acting President of the Council to the Greek and Bulgarian Governments.
The Secretary-General, acting under Article 11, has convoked special meeting of Council on Monday next in Paris. The Council at that meeting will examine whole question with representatives Bulgarian and Greek Governments. Meantime, I know my colleagues would wish me to remind the two Governments of solemn obligations undertaken by them as Members of the League of Nations under Article 12 of the Covenant not to resort to war and of grave consequences which Covenant lays down for breaches thereof. I therefore exhort the two Governments to give immediate instructions that, pending consideration dispute by Council, not only no further military movements shall be undertaken but that troops shall at once retire behind their respective frontiers. BRIAND." League of Nations, Minutes of the Thirty-sixth (Extraordinary) Session of the Council, *Official Journal*, VI: 11, Pt. 2 (November 1925), pp. 1696–97.

this telegram played a decisive role in the course of events, for the message was dispatched by the Athens Government to the scene of hostilities just two and one-half hours before the Greek army was scheduled to launch an attack with over 1,000 men.

The Council convened with the Greek and Bulgarian representatives present at the meeting. The task before the Council was: to bring about a cessation of hostilities between Greece and Bulgaria, and subsequently to institute an inquiry on the spot in order to ascertain the facts and responsibilities, prevent further violence, and if necessary fix the amount of reparations due.

CESSATION OF HOSTILITIES

The Council approved the President's action calling for a cessation of hostilities, which had ceased as a result of the President's appeal. The situation was still tense, however, and some skirmishing was going on. Moreover, it was not clear that steps were being taken to retire the forces behind their frontiers. The Council requested the representatives of both states to inform it within twenty-four hours that orders had been given to their troops to withdraw behind their frontiers and to inform it within sixty hours that all troops had been so withdrawn.

To oversee the withdrawal, the Council requested the French, British, and Italian Governments to send military officers to the spot and to report to the Council. Immediately these three governments sent their military attachés in Belgrade to the scene. On October 29, the military officers confirmed that the Greek and Bulgarian Governments had given withdrawal orders to their commanders and that the orders were being carried out. While they were still available, the Council requested the military attachés to remain and investigate the incidents giving rise to the trouble and to make their information available to the Commission of Enquiry.

The Council refused to listen to any arguments, explanations, or justifications by the Greek or Bulgarian representatives until it was assured that the fighting had ceased. The Greek representative at several points had started to defend his country's action in terms of "legitimate defense," but M. Briand interrupted to say that it was essential that such ideas should not take root in the minds of League members and become a kind of jurisprudence. He elaborated this view in a statement which was approved by all the members of the Council:

> Under the pretext of legitimate defence disputes might arise which, though limited in extent, were extremely unfortunate owing to the damage they entailed. These disputes, once they had broken out, might assume such proportions that the Government, which started them under a feeling of legitimate defence, would be no longer able to control them.

The League of Nations, through its Council, and through all the methods of conciliation which were at its disposal, offered the nations a means of avoiding such deplorable events. The nations had only to appeal to the Council. It had been shown that the criticisms which had been brought against the League of Nations to the effect that its machinery was cumbersome and that it found it difficult to take action in circumstances which required an urgent solution, were unjustified. It had been proved that a nation which appealed to the League, when it felt that its existence was threatened, could be sure that the Council would be at its post ready to undertake its work of conciliation.[3]

THE COMMISSION OF ENQUIRY

Only after it was assured that hostilities had ceased did the Council appoint a commission to establish the facts, prevent further violence, and make recommendations for fixing responsibility. Under the terms of reference the commission was to establish the facts and supply material for the determination of responsibility and indemnities or reparation. It was also requested to suggest measures to the Council which, in its opinion, would eliminate the causes of such incidents and prevent their recurrence.[4]

The members of the commission were: Sir Horace Rumbold, British Ambassador to Spain, Chairman; General Serriguy, France; General Ferrario, Italy; M. Drooglever Fortuyn, Member of the Dutch Parliament; and M. de Adlercreutz, Swedish Minister at The Hague. The military attachés had already overseen the separation of the fighting contingents and confirmed the fact of their withdrawal to positions behind their respective frontiers. They were knowledgeable of the facts of the situation on the spot and were therefore invaluable to the commission in determining responsibilities. The commission was, in effect, composed of eight individuals of whom five had military competence, while the others had political and diplomatic experience.

Perhaps the most significant factor in the success of this inquiry was the speed of the operation. The fighting was "nipped in the bud" by the military attachés before it got fully under way. The commission itself was on the scene within two weeks and completed its work, including visits to the two capitals, within three weeks. The Council had set a time limit for the submission of its report. The report contained a factual survey of the incident, a determination of respective responsibilities and indemnities, and recommendations of a military and political character for limiting the effects of incidents on a frontier where there were grievances and discontent on both sides, and for preventing such incidents in the future.

The report was considered by the Council a few days after its completion, and within two weeks the Council took final action by adopting, with slight

---

[3] League of Nations, *Monthly Summary*, V: 10 (October 1925), p. 259.
[4] *Ibid.*, V: 12 (December 1925), p. 327.

modification, the principal recommendations of the commission. The two parties, somewhat reluctantly, accepted the Council's verdict. Thus the whole affair was settled by December 15, less than two months after the Bulgarian Government had brought the question before the League. The President of the Council said that this happy result averted what might have been a conflict threatening peace not only in the Balkans but throughout Europe.

The commission accepted only the Greek Government's indemnity claim for the captain who was killed while advancing under the white flag. It rejected all other claims made by the Greek Government.

The commission held the Greek Government responsible for the expenses, losses, and sufferings of the Bulgarian people and government caused by the invasion of Greek troops and fixed the indemnity at approximately $215,000. [5]

The commission recommended three. types of measures.

1. Measures to Prevent Incidents. On a frontier where there had been recurrent tragedies resulting from an unsettled population of refugees who lived under unfulfilled exchange agreements, the commission recommended reorganizing the frontier guards and maintaining posts at a greater distance from the frontier. Neutral officers were to ensure the execution of these measures on parallel lines.

2. Measures to Limit the Effects of Incidents. The commission proposed a conciliation commission composed of a Greek officer, a Bulgarian officer, two neutral officers and a chairman selected from persons in the area engaged in League work.

3. Measures to Enable Prompt Action. Since communication speed proved to be an essential factor, and since other similar incidents might occur there or elsewhere, the commission recommended that special facilities for communications and transit be granted to governments and the League Secretariat in the event of a war threat.

The commission considered that much of the underlying tension in the area resulted from unfulfilled refugee exchange agreements which made the populations sullen and discontented on both sides of the frontier. It recommended that liquidation of property claims should proceed much more rapidly.

DECISION OF THE LEAGUE COUNCIL

The Council on December 14, 1925, accepted the recommendation of the commission on the financial indemnity the Greek Government should pay and recommended that it be paid within two months. It accepted with

[5] *Ibid.*, converted at the 1925 rate of 4s.1.3d/$1, courtesy of the British Information Service.

slight modifications the military and political recommendations of the commission. The Swedish Government supplied the neutral officers of the proposed conciliation commission, and the Council appointed its chairman. The Greek and Bulgarian Governments undertook to hasten the liquidation of the respective refugee property claims and to report their progress to the Council.

In summing up the case for the League Council, Sir Austen Chamberlain, rapporteur, made a statement concerning a government's assumed justification for resorting to military action, which was regarded as further extending states' obligations to abandon self-help. He said:

> The fact that the Greek Government acted without premeditation, under the impression produced by information received from the frontier post and exaggerated in transmission to Athens, has not escaped our attention. But, even if this information has been accurate, the Greek Government would not have been justified in directing the military operations which it caused to be undertaken. . . . We believe that all the members of the Council will share our view in favour of the broad principle that where territory is violated without sufficient cause reparation is due, even if at the time of the occurrence it was believed by the Party committing the act of violation that circumstances justified the action. We believe this to be a principle which all members of the League of Nations will wish to uphold and which both Bulgaria and Greece would wish to support, even if they had not already accepted in advance, as in fact they did explicitly accept at Paris, whatever decision the Council might reach on this point. [6]

EVALUATION

The promptness with which the League acted in this case was the main factor in its success in halting a potential Balkan war. The acting president's appeal, sent on his own authority before the Council could gather, set a precedent for future appeals, urging disputants to cease fighting and to wait for League action to establish justice.

The Council separated the two aspects of the case, cessation of hostilities and settlement of the dispute, and refused to hear the arguments of the two parties until they had agreed to cease hostilities. Military observers were sent to the scene immediately, arriving within twenty-four hours, to observe and report on the Council's demand for the withdrawal of forces.

Eminent political, diplomatic, and military figures were chosen to compose the Commission of Enquiry, selected and financed by the League Council. The three military attachés were able to work closely with the commission and to give it the advantage of their earlier arrival at the frontier.

[6] *Ibid.*, p. 330.

The Council, by rejecting the plea of "legitimate defence," strengthened its authority, making it clear that the League would not condone any unilateral act of force, no matter how justly provoked. The action of the Council an'd the Commission of Enquiry in this case has come to be regarded by many commentators as the "classic example" of the best way to make observation and fact-finding machinery produce positive results.

10

THE MANCHURIAN CONFLICT, 1931–1933

Prior to the Japanese aggression in Manchuria in September 1931, the clash of interests between China and Japan had led to a series of disputes concerning Japanese rights and functions. Japan sought a broader economic base for trade and commerce and regarded Manchuria, because of its location and resources, as a natural outlet for its energies. Japan's obvious aim was to control the political and economic development of Manchuria, either by influence or, if necessary, by annexation.

China's aim was to maintain sovereignty and authority over this area, but the country was weakened by civil war, and its effective power to resist Japanese determination by force was inadequate.

Over the years, Japan had built up by force, threats, and bribes a network of treaties with China, the extent and validity of which were uncertain; and Japan and China gave them different interpretations. One of these treaties gave the right to maintain forces within the prescribed limits of the South Manchuria Railway Zone (a Japanese possession). These forces had been progressively increased, and on September 18, 1931, apparently without the sanction of the Japanese Cabinet,[1] the military launched an aggression outside the railway zone on Mukden, Ant'ung, and other places, driving out the ineffective Chinese garrisons, which put up little resistance, and causing many casualties. The alleged reason for the action was that the Chinese had sabotaged the South Manchurian Railway.

The immediate issue was how to deal with the aggression of Japanese armed forces in Chinese territory outside the railway zone which Japanese

[1] Henry L. Stimson, *The Far Eastern Crisis* (New York: Harper, for the Council on Foreign Relations, 1936), pp. 34, 82. See also Y. C. Maxon, *Control of Japanese Foreign Policy: A Study of Civil-Military Rivalry, 1930–1945* (Berkeley: University of California Press, 1957), Chap. 4.

forces were permitted by treaty to control. The fundamental issue was how to prevent Japan from wresting control over the whole of Manchuria from China.

THE MATTER BEFORE THE LEAGUE COUNCIL

News of the fighting reached the League of Nations on September 19. Two days later the Chinese Ambassador in Geneva reported that the fighting was spreading, and he called on the Council, under Article 11, "to take such action as it deemed wise and effectual to maintain the peace." Thus, the League was confronted with the most serious and most complex problem that had come before it.

The Japanese and Chinese representatives on the Council had little factual information. The Japanese Prime Minister and Foreign Minister, though indignant at the army's behavior, felt obliged to defend the action to the outside world. They sent reports to Geneva promising prompt withdrawal of the troops. Without denying the League's competence, they insisted that the first step should be direct negotiations between China and Japan, with the Council being kept informed of progress but not participating in the talks.

General Chiang Kai-shek called on the Chinese nation to remain calm, ordered the army in Manchuria not to resist, and stated that the matter had been placed before the League of Nations and that justice would be done. The Chinese Ambassador told the Council that events had become increasingly grave and that the Council should act with speed. He also declared that China would accept, in advance, whatever decision the Council would make.

The Japanese Ambassador, playing for time, asked for a short adjournment as he had not yet received full instructions. He stressed the importance of Manchuria to Japan and recalled the many broken promises of China over the treaties.

The Council reluctantly agreed to give Japan time to receive instructions, but called on both sides to prevent the situation from worsening. It also decided to keep the United States officially informed of its proceedings. The tension in Geneva was shared in Washington where the Japanese aggression was seen to be a threat to basic American policies—the integrity of China, the Kellogg Pact, the Washington treaties, and the stability of the Far East. Secretary of State, Henry L. Stimson, seemed desirous of supporting the League efforts, and indeed, did much to encourage the Council.[2] But joint action was difficult since the United States shared neither the rights nor the duties of the League powers.

Had the Council acted as it had in the Greek-Bulgarian case, that is, organized a Commission of Enquiry, composed of persons already near the

_____
[2] See Stimson, *op. cit.*, p. 41.

scene who could proceed without delay to the area and report to the Council, the problem of the inadequate Chinese and Japanese reports, which were often contradictory, would have been eliminated. China urged that such a commission should be sent, but Japan opposed it. The Council, however, would have organized a commission over Japanese opposition if the United States had been prepared to cooperate. Appeals on this proposal were made to both President Herbert Hoover and Secretary Stimson.[3] Stimson felt that the idea was premature and that such a commission would make it harder for the civil authorities in Tokyo to impose their will on the army, a view which was not justified by events.[4] He urged the Council to abandon this plan in favor of continued direct negotiations between China and Japan. This appeared to stiffen the Japanese attitude both in Geneva and Tokyo.[5]

On September 25, the Japanese Ambassador reported to the Council that the Japanese forces were only defending themselves against Chinese attacks; that Japan had no territorial designs; that most of its troops were already being withdrawn within the railway zone as fast as the safety of Japanese nationals was assured; that his government was anxious to have direct negotiations with China; and that the Council would do well not to intervene. The Chinese Ambassador said that China could guarantee the safety of Japanese lives and property but would negotiate only when the Japanese troops were withdrawn within the railway zone.

The Council, at this point, had no reason to disbelieve the Japanese assurances, which were promptly accepted. Thus more time was given for direct negotiations to succeed, and the Council decided to meet again in two weeks unless the situation were cleared up in the meantime.

But the situation, instead of clearing up, became worse. The Japanese army was not withdrawing but was advancing. Japanese General Honjo was warning the population to have nothing to do with the Chinese authorities and to yield to Japanese military occupation. The Japanese Government in Tokyo declared that General Honjo's statement was unauthorized and that the bombing of Chinchow was deplored.

However, it now made the withdrawal of troops conditional not only on the safety of Japanese nationals but also on agreement to certain principles which would govern relations between the two countries.

U.S. ENCOURAGEMENT OF COUNCIL ACTION

It was now apparent, three weeks after the fighting started, that Japan was bent on extending the conflict. The Council was called to meet again on October 13, with French Foreign Minister Aristide Briand in the chair.

---

[3] The appeals were made by Norman Davis, who was in Geneva on other business.
[4] See Stimson, *op. cit.*, p. 43.
[5] Walters, *op. cit.*, p. 473.

The United States Government also had lost confidence in the Japanese desire or ability to restrict the conflict. Accordingly, Secretary Stimson sent a message to the Secretary-General of the League stating that: "it is most desirable that the League in no way relax its vigilance . . . [or] fail to assert all the pressure and authority within its competence towards regulating the action of China and Japan. . . . The American Government acting independently through its diplomatic representatives will endeavor to reinforce what the League does." [6]

The Council, on the proposal of M. Briand, invited the United States to participate in its proceedings, since the Kellogg Pact was involved as well as the Covenant. The Japanese delegate opposed M. Briand's proposal on constitutional grounds fearing that United States participation might strengthen action by the Council. He demanded that the Permanent Court of International Justice or a committee of jurists should give an opinion on the constitutional issues involved. But the Council, unwilling to consider further delays, decided that the question was one of procedure which could be decided by a majority vote. It voted 13 to 1 to invite the United States. The invitation was promptly accepted, and on October 16 Prentiss Gilbert, American Consul in Geneva, took his place at the Council table.

The United States representative, according to his instructions, could not join in formulating any Council action under the Covenant, but could only give moral support and counsel on the method of bringing public opinion to bear on preventing a breach of Article 2 of the Kellogg Pact. [7] Mr. Gilbert's participation in both secret and public meetings reflected these instructions; he was present but could take no effective part in the discussions.

The Council, after six days of discussion in which the United States representative played a disappointing role, adopted a resolution on October 24, calling for: (1) Japan to withdraw its troops without further delay and complete the withdrawal by the meeting of the Council three weeks later, and (2) the parties to begin direct negotiations when withdrawal was completed. Japan refused to accept either stipulation and voted against the resolution. The League had previously decided that action under Article 11 required the consent of all members of the Council, not excluding the member whose action it sought to control.

When the Council met again on November 16, the situation was worse. Japan was in the grip of war fever. Troop trains surrounded by cheering crowds were leaving, and the area of occupation was rapidly extending.

[6] Stimson, *op. cit.*, p. 52.

[7] Mr. Gilbert's instructions from Secretary Stimson were: "You are authorized to participate in the discussions of the Council when they relate to the possible application of the Kellogg-Briand Pact to which treaty the United States is a party. You are expected to report the result of such discussions to the Department for its determination as to possible action. If you are present at the discussion of any other aspect of the Chinese-Japanese dispute, it must be only as an observer and auditor." Stimson, *op. cit.*, p. 65.

Manchuria, 1931–1933 57

The revenues of Manchuria were diverted into Japanese hands, and Japanese control was extended over the whole of Manchuria and beyond.

Instead of having an American representative sitting at the Council table, the United States Government, in deference to anti-League sentiment at home, kept in touch by diplomatic methods and sent Ambassador Charles Dawes, a noted opponent of the League, to the Council. Dawes attended no sessions but remained in his hotel and received accounts of the proceedings through members of the Secretariat and the press.

Now the Council was faced with the choice of confessing that it was unable to control the course of events or invoking Article 15, which envisaged the use of sanctions. [8] Secretary Stimson, at this time, announced that the United States Government was convinced the matter could be settled without resort to military action. Moreover, the other great powers were preoccupied with economic depression, and the growing threat from Hitler, so sanctions were not considered feasible.

THE COMMISSION OF ENQUIRY

At this point, over two months after the beginning of the conflict, the Japanese delegate suggested that the League send a Commission of Enquiry to investigate the situation both in Manchuria and China. Such a commission seemed to be the only hope, and it might exert a moderating influence. Accordingly, the Council set up a commission and defined its terms of reference. The Japanese delegate disputed nearly every point in these terms, and it took nearly three weeks of painful and humiliating negotiation to agree on a text. It was not until December 10, almost three months after the initial aggression, that the Council settled the details of a resolution to send a commission to the Far East and to define its task. The United States announced its support of this resolution, in particular the sending of a Commission of Enquiry.

The commission's task, as defined in the terms of reference, was held by many of the smaller members of the League to be inadequate and even inconsistent with the Covenant. The commission was only to study and report on the circumstances which threatened peace and good relations between China and Japan. It was given no power to control military movements or to initiate negotiations between the parties. It was not asked to make recommendations for settling the dispute. Many delegates expressed misgivings that the Council's decision seemed, by its omissions, to

[8] On November 19, however, Stimson had informed Dawes that if the Council decided on sanctions, its action would be overwhelmingly supported by public opinion in America, and the U.S. Government would not interfere. (See U.S. Department of State, *Foreign Relations of the United States, 1931*, Vol. I [Washington: Government Printing Office, 1946], pp. 498 ff.) But it is not apparent that Dawes made any use of this message. See Walters, *op. cit.*, p. 479.

condone military occupation of Chinese territory and the results achieved by force. Briand, as President of the Council, stressed the point that no state, whatever its grievances, could seek redress by other than peaceful means.

The terms of reference of the commission were as follows: to make on-the-spot investigations and report to the Council; the Governments of China and of Japan each to nominate one assessor to assist the commission; the two governments to assist the Commission in obtaining information; if the two parties should initiate any negotiations, they would not be within the scope of the terms of reference of the commission, nor could the commission interfere with the military arrangements of either party; the appointment and deliberation of the commission should not prejudice the undertaking by the Japanese Government regarding withdrawal of the Japanese troops within the railway zone.[9]

The members of the Commission of Enquiry (known as the Lytton Commission) were selected by the President of the Council and approved by the two parties. The five members approved by the Council on January 14, 1932, were:

The Rt. Hon. The Earl of Lytton (British), Chairman, who had had many years of experience in the East as Governor of Bengal and as Viceroy and acting Governor-General of India.

H. E. Count Aldrovandi (Italian), who was a diplomat of wide experience and had been chief of Cabinet for the Italian Minister of Foreign Affairs.

General de Division Henri Claudel (French), who had foreign service in West Africa and other colonies of France and was a member of the Higher Council of War.

Major-General Frank Ross McCoy (American), who had served in the Philippines and was familiar with Japan and China through many visits to those countries. He had been the head of the American Relief Mission to Japan on the occasion of the earthquake of 1923. He had also rendered important foreign service as supervisor of the presidential election in Nicaragua in 1928 and as chairman of the Commission of Enquiry and Conciliation between Bolivia and Paraguay in 1929.

H. E. Dr. Heinrich Schnee (German), who had had executive and diplomatic experience in foreign countries. He had been a member of the Reichstag as well as the German Colonial Office.

The governments of Japan and China appointed as their assessors: H. E. Mr. Isaburo Yoshida, Japanese Ambassador to Turkey and H. E. Dr. V. K. Wellington Koo, a former Prime Minister and former Minister for Foreign Affairs of China.

The Secretary-General of the League designated M. Robert Haas, Director in the Secretariat of the League, to act as Secretary of the Commission.

[9] League of Nations, *Appeal by the Chinese Government: Report of the Commission of Enquiry*, No. C663 M 320 (Geneva: October 1, 1932), p. 6. Hereafter cited as Lytton Commission *Report*.

The commission sailed by steamer from Le Havre on February 3, 1932; arrived in Tokyo February 29; then visited Shanghai, Nanking, Peiping, and Manchuria between March 14 and July 20, 1932; and completed its unanimous report on September 4, 1932, almost nine months after its appointment. This slow-moving pace was disheartening for China and "embarrassing and even discreditable to the Council," especially as Japanese aggression and expansion were actively continuing.[10] The Chinese resented the fact that the commission did not proceed directly to Manchuria over the Trans-Siberian Railway, much the quickest route. By the time it arrived in Manchuria, Japan had subjugated all of the area and declared that the new entity, called "Manchukuo," was henceforth an independent state. The Japanese navy, not to be outdone by the army, launched an attack on Shanghai from the International Settlement, in disregard of the approaching visit of the commission and the opinion of the civilized world. A more energetic and faster program by the commission might have had no effect on the course of events, but an impression of ineffectiveness and vacillation was unfortunate. Although the commission's final report was regarded as outstanding, thorough, and comprehensive, it could not compensate for these delays.

The Japanese attack on Shanghai in February 1932 called for special action by the Council. China, on January 29, had requested that the matter be transferred from the Council to the Assembly, and considered under Article 15, which called for a full investigation of the dispute with the possibility of sanctions.

To get the facts promptly on the Shanghai situation, a Consular Committee was set up, with the agreement of the powers concerned, consisting of the American, British, French, German, Italian, and Norwegian Consuls in Shanghai, and with Robert Haas of the League Secretariat as secretary. The Consular Committee sent four reports to the Council, which were useful as sources of impartial information.

The Chinese armies in and around Shanghai fought heroically, and the Japanese withdrew with a loss estimated at 24,000 soldiers. When the Lytton Commission reached Shanghai on March 14, the fighting was over, but the negotiations for an armistice were proving difficult. The Lytton Commission did not continue the work of the Consular Committee but went on to Manchuria.

The commission signed its report in Peiping on September 4, 1932, and the lengthy document (139 pages and 12 maps) was dispatched to Geneva for translation, printing, and publication on October 2. It was processed and distributed to the press simultaneously in Geneva, Washington, London and the other world capitals.

The report, Henry Stimson said:

... became at once and remains today [1936] the outstanding impartial authority upon the subjects which it covers. Five eminent citizens of the five great

[10] Walters, *op. cit.*, p. 483.

powers, had collected and studied the evidence and reached a unanimous conclusion as to the facts of and consequent responsibility for a bitterly complicated controversy between two other great powers. Furthermore, this was accomplished in a case where their judgment . . . might be made the basis of political action under the organization of the League against a great nation. Such a report was not only momentous; it was unprecedented.[11]

COMMISSION FINDINGS AND RECOMMENDATIONS

The effect of the report was a vindication of China on all fundamental issues. The commission concluded that the operations of the Japanese army could not be regarded as measures of legitimate self-defense. And it considered that the so-called "State" of Manchukuo was based on Japanese bayonets and was not on a genuine and spontaneous independence movement.

The commission did not minimize the fact that China was "a nation in evolution, showing evidence of transition in all aspects of its national life. Political upheavals, civil wars, social and economic unrest, with the resulting weakness of the Central Government, have been the characteristics of China since the Revolution of 1911."[12] It admitted that the rights and interests of Japan were seriously affected by the weakness of authority of the Central Government of China. But it found that the people of Manchuria were overwhelmingly Chinese and did not wish to be separated from China. The commission rejected the Japanese claim that China was not an organized state but a disorganized people in the throes of anarchy, and that, therefore, treaties like the Covenant, the Kellogg Pact, and the Nine-Power Treaty of 1922 could not really be observed with respect to China.

The commission held that a mere restoration of the *status quo ante* would be no solution, a point which many League members found hard to accept because it seemed to recognize that gains might be made by resort to force. The commission, however, meant to say that Manchuria, while remaining under Chinese sovereignty, should have an autonomous status with a government whose stability would ensure an economic development advantageous to both China and Japan, and to Russia and other outside powers as well.

The ten principles to which the commission felt a satisfactory solution should conform were:

1. The solution should be compatible with the interests of both China and Japan.

2. The interests of Russia should also be recognized and safeguarded.

---

[11] Stimson, *op. cit.*, pp. 207–8.
[12] Lytton Commission *Report*, p. 13.

3. The solution must conform to the provisions of the Covenant, the Kellogg Pact, and the Nine-Power Treaty.

4. Japan's interests in Manchuria should be recognized.

5. New treaties between China and Japan should be established restating clearly the respective rights, interests, and responsibilities of both countries.

6. Provision should be made for the effective settlement of future disputes between the two countries.

7. Manchuria should have an autonomous and stable government consistent with the sovereignty and integrity of China.

8. Adequate internal order and security against external aggression should be provided by the withdrawal of armed forces and setting up of an effective gendarmerie.

9. Economic rapprochement between China and Japan should be encouraged by a new commercial treaty.

10. There should be international cooperation in Chinese reconstruction and assistance in modernizing the state.

The commission recommended that the League Council should invite China and Japan to discuss their dispute along the lines of the ten principles. Then, an Advisory Conference to help in establishing an autonomous regime in Manchuria should be summoned, consisting of representatives of China and Japan and two delegations representing the Chinese and Japanese communities in Manchuria, with the assistance of neutral observers agreed to by the parties. Differences might be referred to the League Council for settlement. Simultaneously, the respective rights and interests should be discussed separately, with the help of neutral observers, and the result of these discussions should be embodied in four separate instruments:

1. A Declaration by the Government of China constituting a special administration for the Three Eastern Provinces, in the terms recommended by the Advisory Conference;

2. A Sino-Japanese Treaty dealing with Japanese interests;

3. A Sino-Japanese Treaty of Conciliation and Arbitration, Non-Aggression and Mutual Assistance;

4. A Sino-Japanese Commercial Treaty.[13]

CONSIDERATION OF COMMISSION REPORT BY THE COUNCIL AND THE ASSEMBLY

The report was widely hailed for its thoroughness and far-reaching proposals. It soon became clear that the League and the United States would base their future policies on its findings.

[13] Lytton Commission *Report*, p. 133.

The Council met on November 21, 1932, expecting to consider the report briefly and to pass it on to the Assembly which, under Article 15, was now in charge of the question.[14] The Japanese delegate, however, attacked the report and, in effect, rejected it. He reiterated the previous arguments: that China was incapable of maintaining order and stability; that Japan had to act in self-defense, as other nations had done. The Chinese delegate rested his case on the findings and recommendations of the report, thereby indicating his acceptance.

On February 24, 1933, the Assembly adopted a resolution accepting the principles and recommendations of the Lytton Commission; inviting the parties to negotiate a settlement of the dispute on this basis with the help of a negotiating committee of fourteen members; and calling on all League members not to recognize the regime in Manchuria either de jure or de facto.[15] China voted for, Siam abstained, and Japan voted against it. When the voting was completed, the Japanese delegate stated that only Japan's policy could guarantee peace in the Far East. He thereupon walked out of the Assembly meeting.

Secretary Stimson issued a statement on February 25, endorsing the conclusions and recommendations for a settlement adopted by the Assembly. And the new Roosevelt administration a few days later also accepted, with the usual reservations, participation in the work of the negotiating committee.

On March 27, 1933, Japan announced its decision to resign from the League. The decision became effective on March 27, 1935. From 1935 until the Second World War Japan continued to control the affairs of "Manchukuo." The war brought about Japanese withdrawal, and Chinese administration was restored in the area where it remains subject to the terms of the Treaty of Friendship and Alliance Between the Republic of China and the U.S.S.R. of August 14, 1945.

EVALUATION

The Manchurian conflict was by far the most difficult, complex, and unpromising case which had come before the League. The immediate incidents of September 18, 1931, grew out of decades of controversy between China and Japan, and League intervention came much too late. China, or a third party, should have drawn the League's attention to the threatening situation much earlier if the effort were to succeed.

The treaties, imposed by a strong, stable Japanese Government on a weak China in the throes of revolution with its attendant instability and

[14] Japan had requested six weeks (from the time of publication) to study the report and prepare its observation. Hence the delay until November 21.
[15] League of Nations, *Monthly Summary*, XIII (February 1933), p. 22.

divided governmental authorities, were ambiguous and constantly the subject of dispute and misunderstanding. There was no clear-cut agreement about rights, frontiers, duties, and responsibilities. Though Japan denied the intention to annex Manchuria, there was no doubt that the military party in Japan believed that Manchuria, in fact, should belong to Japan. But the West, especially Secretary Stimson, believed that the liberal party headed by Foreign Minister Shidehara should be given a chance to hold the military in line. Mainly for this reason, the League's usual fact-finding operations were not put into action at a propitious time.

Had the United States agreed, the League would have sent a Commission of Enquiry to the spot within a week after the outbreak of hostilities on September 18, 1931. The failure of the United States to back the League at this juncture was a principal cause of the delay. The Lytton Commission, with an American member suggested by the State Department,[16] was constituted three months after hostilities had started and did not get to the scene until some seven months later. In fact, it was constituted only after a Japanese initiative. The commission took the slowest means of ocean and rail travel, going westward via New York, the Pacific, and Tokyo. It could have arrived in Manchuria much sooner via the Trans-Siberian Railway.

Both China and Japan cooperated by appointing "assessors" to assist and granting the commission unlimited access to places, organizations, and persons.

The commission itself was composed of experienced and influential persons. The commissioners were drawn from the five great powers and were, consequently, all westerners; the individuals selected were considered to be detached and impartial. They did not function in a representative capacity, and their governments had access to the report only after it was published. The advisers and supporting staff of the commission were an outstanding group of experts and officials.

The terms of reference of the commission were general and regarded by certain League members as inadequate. It was not a mediatory or negotiating body. It could only look, inquire, and report. In the eyes of some delegations, it appeared to condone a *fait accompli*. The terms of reference were restricted and very likely reflected a compromise following consultation with Japan's representative on the Council. The report, nevertheless, was one of the most thorough, formidable, and constructive which had ever been made by a Commission of Enquiry.

Neither the competence of the commission, the quality of its report, nor any other factors of this inquiry, were sufficient to secure a favorable settlement of the Manchurian dispute, and unfortunately one of the League's most thoughtful and informed decisions was to remain inoperative. The weight of League disapproval fell on Japan, yet it was undeterred in its aggressive policy and defied the organization with immediate impunity.

[16] Stimson, *op. cit.*, p. 81.

Why did the League fail in this crucial instance? One cause was the time allowed to elapse between the initial appeal and the appearance of League representatives on the scene. The promptness which had proved so effective in the Greek-Bulgarian case was not applied here. The unexpressed assumption of League action and precedent was the good faith of the conflicting parties, the universal preference for peaceful settlement. In cases where hostilities were the result of some misunderstanding, the League had been measurably effective. In the face of unprincipled, premeditated aggression, the scope of action granted by Article 16 of the Covenant was great, but until 1931, the League had not employed such sanctions. The nonrecognition of Manchukuo was the only sanction invoked at the end.

The Manchurian conflict was an example of a strong, expanding nation bordered by an economically wealthy but politically chaotic state. The disintegration in China was so complete that Japanese investments in Manchuria were threatened by the civil disorder. The result was foreseeable. The Japanese civilian government hesitated but could not control the military which was determined to achieve its objectives. Nothing could stop the Japanese army but the united, determined opposition of the world backed by armed force, and this was the ultimate step which neither the League members nor the United States was prepared to take at that time.

11
—•—

THE CONFLICT BETWEEN COLOMBIA AND PERU OVER LETICIA, 1932–1935

The Leticia Trapezium is an area of about 4,000 square miles between the Putumayo River on the north and the Amazon on the south. As part of a general frontier settlement, it had been ceded by Peru to Colombia by a treaty in 1922. But the inhabitants had not been consulted, and many of them continued to feel attached to Peru. The latter did not ratify the treaty until 1928.

The territory was important to Colombia because it gave it direct access to the Amazon. It was also important to Peru because its large trans-Andean eastern province of Loreto depended on the Amazon for its outlet and did not favor the appearance of a new Amazonian power. It was the Peruvians of Loreto who invaded Leticia "on their own authority." The

Peruvian Government, though disavowing the action, felt it necessary for patriotic reasons to come to their support when Colombian forces were organized to reoccupy Leticia instead of negotiating a settlement.

Brazil, which also borders on Leticia, offered to mediate the dispute. It was proposed that Leticia be turned over by the occupying Peruvians to a Brazilian unit while the mediation was in process. Colombia accepted the proposal, but Peru, in effect, rejected it by attaching numerous conditions. Meanwhile, the Peruvians occupied other points farther north.

ACTION BY THE COUNCIL OF THE LEAGUE

On January 14, the President of the Council of the League of Nations, in accordance with precedent, sent telegrams to the two parties asking them to refrain from any action likely to aggravate the situation. The Council asked the committee, composed of representatives of the Irish Free State, Spain, and Guatemala that was already dealing with the Bolivia-Paraguay case,[1] to follow this dispute and report to the Council. On January 24, with the respective forces still advancing, the Council sent messages to the two parties asking Peru not to intervene on Colombian territory and requesting Colombia to exercise restraint and clemency "in restoring order."[2]

The United States informed the League Secretary-General that, as a signatory to the Kellogg Pact, it had been invited by Colombia to intervene. It indicated readiness to support the Brazilian mediation proposal "as a pacific and honorable way to settle the dispute."[3] The United States and Brazil asked the two parties to meet in Rio to examine the treaty of 1922 and find a formula for settlement.

The Brazilian mediation effort was unsuccessful. On February 18, Colombia asked the League Council to convene on the basis of Article 15. Peru informed the Council that it could not be present, but the Council proceeded. The Committee of Three was asked to try to negotiate a settlement in accordance with Article 15, paragraph 3. The United States informed the League that it fully supported this effort and had so informed both parties.

The committee, on March 1, reported to the Council that it had proposed to the two parties that: during their direct negotiations a League Commission should take charge of the administration of the territory; Peruvian forces should evacuate the territory entirely; and Colombian forces should be placed at the disposal of the commission as international forces.

[1] For an account of the Chaco dispute see pp. 94 ff.
[2] League of Nations, *Monthly Summary*, XIII: 1 (January 1933), p. 21.
[3] *Ibid.*

Colombia accepted. Peru rejected the proposal, but made a counter-proposal that order should be maintained by the population itself. The committee held that it could not recommend this counterproposal to the Council.

Mediation under Article 15, paragraph 3 having failed, the Council decided on March 8 to invoke paragraph 4. The Committee of Three was requested to draw up a report on the facts and to make recommendations "deemed just and proper in regard thereto."

An Advisory Committee of thirteen states had been appointed at a previous meeting of the Council on March 18 "to watch the situation, assist the Council in the performance of its duties under Article 4, paragraph 4, and help the Members of the League for the same purpose to concert their action and their attitude among themselves and with non-Member States." [4]

The United States and Brazil were invited "to collaborate in its work." The United States indicated that it was prepared to cooperate and appointed Hugh Wilson, United States Minister in Berne, to participate without voting in the work of the Advisory Committee. The United States deemed it necessary to exercise an independent judgment on proposals or measures that the Advisory Committee might recommend.

At this point, it appeared that war was imminent. Colombian ships on the Putumayo River were fired on from the Peruvian bank and bombed from the air. Peruvian forces were being strengthened. Colombian forces captured a fort on the Peruvian side of the river. Four Peruvian ships of war were sent through the Panama Canal into the Atlantic and ordered to join Peruvian forces at Iquitos. Colombia was increasing its naval forces with two destroyers newly built in a British shipyard. The Colombian Legation in Lima was sacked by a mob.

The Advisory Committee of the Council was summoned, and members of the League at whose ports the Peruvian ships might call were requested to refuse supplies. But the messages arrived too late. Moreover, there was no precedent for refusing supplies in such circumstances.

AN ADMINISTRATIVE COMMISSION FOR LETICIA

On March 18, the Committee of Three made its report under Article 15, paragraph 4, and recommended that: (1) an Administrative Commission go to the territory within thirty days to maintain order and administer the area; (2) the Peruvian forces withdraw immediately on the arrival of the commission; (3) the commission call on military forces of its own selection to assist in maintaining order; (4) the commission's term of office be one year; (5) the disputing parties negotiate, and the Council lend its good offices at the request of either party; (6) Colombia defray the expenses of

---

[4] *Ibid.*, XIII: 3 (March 1933), p. 72.

the commission; (7) on acceptance of these proposals, both governments order cessation of hostilities, and all military forces of each country remain within its frontiers. [5]

Colombia accepted these proposals. The Peruvian delegate, however, asked the Council not to adopt the report but to open an inquiry with a view to collecting supplementary information. When the Council decided to vote without further delay, the Peruvian delegate left the Council table. The report was adopted unanimously, the votes of the parties not being counted under Article 15, paragraph 4.

On April 30, the President of Peru was assassinated. It soon became clear that public opinion in Peru did not favor the drift toward war. The new President let it be known that Peru would favor the League Council's recommendations, which it had rejected previously. Accordingly, at a special meeting of the Council on May 25, 1933, the representatives of both Colombia and Peru and the Secretary-General of the League signed the agreement embodying the proposals adopted earlier by the Council. Thus the way was opened to send an Administrative Commission to Leticia to take charge of the territory for a period of one year.

In accordance with the agreement signed by the parties, the commission to administer Leticia was appointed by the Advisory Committee, in collaboration with the Secretary-General. It was composed of: Colonel Arthur Brown (American), Commander A. L. Basto (Brazilian), Captain Francisco Iglesias (Spaniard), and Armando Mencia (League Secretariat, as secretary). When Colonel Brown was appointed Judge Advocate General of the United States Army, he was replaced by Major-General E. B. Winans. The terms of reference of the commission were those recommended by the Committee of Three on March 18.

The commission arrived in Leticia on June 23. The Peruvian commander carried out his orders to surrender the territory, and his forces withdrew on the same day. At the same time, Colombian forces evacuated the Peruvian post which they had occupied. For the first time in its history, a League flag was hoisted, indicating that the League was temporarily exercising governmental authority over the Leticia Trapezium.

For a year the commission and its staff [6] took charge of an area that had been partly destroyed, where sanitary conditions were most primitive, and where malaria and other diseases were rife. A year later, when it handed the territory over to the Colombian authorities, the damaged property and sanitary facilities had been repaired, a dispensary, three schools, and a hospital had been built, and the population of the town had increased

[5] As summarized in the Report of Advisory Committee, May 25, 1933. Minutes of Seventy-third Session of the Council, League of Nations, *Official Journal*, XIV: 7, Pt. 2 (July 1933), pp. 944–45.

[6] A garrison of seventy-five men and officers assisted the commission. Their services were efficient, and their discipline and conduct were such that no incidents occurred between them and the population.

fourfold. No crime of violence had taken place while the commission was there.

Meanwhile, the two parties were negotiating an agreement in Rio, which was concluded only a few weeks before the commission left the territory, but not ratified until September of the following year. The agreement states: "Both parties agreed to recognize: (a) that the Treaty of March 24th 1922, between Colombia and Peru, is in force; and (b) that, in virtue of that Treaty, the territory known as the 'Leticia Trapezium' forms part of the territory of the Republic of Colombia."[7]

EVALUATION

War was narrowly averted in this South American boundary dispute, as national prestige and economic interests were at stake. The League quickly took action, charging the Council rapporteurs to make recommendations for a peaceful settlement. With the assassination of Peru's recalcitrant president, the ensuing changes in government resulted in a more propitious climate for a settlement of the case.

An unusual aspect of this case was the use of an Administrative Commission to take over administration of the territory in the interim period between Peruvian and Colombian occupation. The main duty of the commission was military: to prevent further fighting between the parties. Its work was a complete success. The constructive work done by the commission in restoring war-damaged property and in building sanitary, educational, and health facilities made its presence appreciated by the population. In short, the commission played an important transitional role in helping Peru get out of a difficult situation without too much loss of face and in reconstructing amicable relations in the potentially explosive area.

12

ITALO-ETHIOPIAN WAR, 1934–1936

In 1915, when Italy was hesitating to enter World War I on the side of the Allies, Great Britain and France promised to grant it equitable compensation for any colonial possessions they might acquire at the expense of Germany.[1] But in 1918, President Wilson insisted that there should be

---

[7] League of Nations, *Monthly Summary*, XIV: 8 (August 1934), p. 186.

[1] Treaty of London, April 1915.

no territorial gains made by any of the Allies. Most of the German African colonies therefore became mandates of either Great Britain or France, which could only administer the territories.[2] Italy, however, did not secure any German territory to administer. The Allies apparently felt that they were under no obligation to fulfill their 1915 pledge, since they did not make any "sovereign" gains under the mandates system.[3] Moreover, none of the German colonies were contiguous to Italian colonial holdings, as they were to British and French possessions.

From 1918 on, particularly after Mussolini came into power in 1922, Italy felt aggrieved at this exclusion. The Italian colonies in North and East Africa were poor lands, unfit to take care of Italy's surplus population while Ethiopia, which lay between the Italian colonies of Eritrea and Somaliland, was believed to have rich mineral resources and was known to have vast fertile areas. These could open up important economic and territorial possibilities for Italy.[4]

In 1933, Mussolini began to prepare for a war of aggression on Ethiopia to expand Italy's colonial territories.[5] On December 5, 1934, a clash took place at Wal-Wal on the Ethiopia-Somaliland border in which some one hundred Ethiopians and thirty Italian native troops were killed. As the incident took place on a disputed frontier, Ethiopia proposed to submit the matter to arbitration. Italy, however, demanded that the Ethiopian Governor of Harrar proceed to Wal-Wal and, in the presence of Italian and Ethiopian troops, make a formal apology and salute the Italian flag. The Italian Government also demanded that a heavy indemnity be paid for the Italian losses.[6]

Ethiopia did not comply with this demand, and on December 15, 1934, called the League's attention to the gravity of the situation. On January 3, 1935, the Emperor reported to the League the massing of Italian troops

[2] Belgium was made mandatory over part of German East Africa, and the Union of South Africa became mandatory over German Southwest Africa.

[3] Partly to assuage Italian resentment in getting no mandates to administer, an Italian, the Marquis Theodoli, was named Chairman of the Permanent Mandates Commission, an international supervisory body, a post to which he was successively reappointed until the demise of the League.

[4] In 1926, the British and Italian Governments negotiated an agreement for promoting their respective interests in Ethiopia. Italy was to have exclusive economic influence in Western Ethiopia and along a 1,000 mile railway connecting Eritrea and Somaliland. Britain was to secure control of the Blue Nile between Lake Isana and the Sudan. The agreement was only communicated to Ethiopia afterward. When the Emperor submitted the matter to the League as incompatible with its independence, the agreement was promptly dropped.

[5] See Emilio de Bono, *Anno XIII: The Conquest of Empire* (London: Cresset Press, 1937), pp. 13–17.

[6] Later, however, Italy agreed to arbitrate the Wal-Wal matter in accord with its 1928 treaty with Ethiopia. The arbitrators found that neither side was responsible for the incident.

and requested the Council to take measures to safeguard the peace. Would the Council be able and willing to defend a weak member against the aggressive designs of a more powerful state?

ACTION AND INACTION OF THE LEAGUE

The Council took up the matter in January 1935. For some months, the League confined its efforts to conciliation and arbitration, and the parties were urged to settle their differences by direct negotiation. It soon became apparent that such negotiations could succeed only if Ethiopia capitulated.

At the same time, Great Britain and France, operating outside the Council, were carrying on conversations with Italy. All three countries were members of the League, territorial neighbors of Ethiopia, and had been parties to the Three-Power Treaty of 1926 outlining respective zones of influence in Ethiopia. All had experienced frontier difficulties and could sympathize with the other's problems in Africa. Moreover, in 1935 Hitler's increasing aggressiveness gave Mussolini a chance to play on French and British hopes for cooperation in Europe.

This dual procedure, which finally led to the disastrous Hoare-Laval plan, created easy opportunities for Mussolini to confuse his opposition and delay the imposition of effective sanctions until it was too late.

Although the Wal-Wal incident was on the way to arbitration, it became clear to the Council between March and September 1935 that the issue went far beyond a frontier incident and that Italy was preparing for a showdown involving complete annexation of Ethiopia. Arms and men were going in increasing numbers to the Italian East African colonies, and large numbers of Italian laborers were building roads, docks, and other installations.

Ethiopian appeals to the Council became more and more urgent. In May 1935, the Council heard an Ethiopian account of the massing of Italian troops in Eritrea, but the Italian delegate replied that no government can permit interference with another government's deployment of troops within its own territory.

In the face of an increasing Italian military build-up and anti-Ethiopian press and radio campaign in Italy alleging Ethiopian threats, Ethiopia asked that the Council appoint neutral observers to go to Ethiopia and inspect the frontier districts and report to the Council.[7] No action was taken on this request.

In August 1935, the Council decided that, with the worsening situation, it would undertake "a general examination of the relations between Italy and Ethiopia." At the same meeting, the British representative announced that France and Great Britain were negotiating with Italy to settle the

_____

[7] League of Nations, *Monthly Summary*, XV: 6 (1935), p. 146.

dispute. In September, the British delegate informed the Council that their suggestions had been rejected by Italy. It was obvious that the tension between the two countries had become dangerous.

On September 4, Italy presented a memorandum to the League that revealed the Italian view and showed why every effort at peaceful settlement had failed. It enumerated a series of alleged Ethiopian outrages and injustices against Italian officials and subjects, raids across frontiers, and disregard of agreements and declared Ethiopia to be a barbarous state whose signature could not be trusted. In view of Ethiopia's backward condition and aggressive behavior, Italy could no longer sit with that country on an equal basis in the League. [8]

The conditions in Ethiopia were known to be backward; there were unruly tribes, and vestiges of slavery still existed. But these conditions were known at the time Ethiopia was admitted to the League in 1923. Members of the Council pointed out that this did not give Italy the right to commit aggression, nor did it permit members of the League to repudiate their international obligations by disregarding the Covenant.

The issue was now seen as a conflict between Italy and the League. A defeat of the League would be catastrophic. Messages of loyalty and support came in from many governments and from labor and church organizations all over the world.

AN ADVISORY CORPS

On September 6, the Council appointed a committee of five—the United Kingdom, France, Spain, Poland, and Turkey—to make another effort to settle the conflict peacefully. [9] Recognizing the need for reforms in Ethiopia, which would help to remove some of the Italian grievances, the committee drew up a plan of collective international assistance to Ethiopia that called for a corps of outside advisers and specialists to assist the Ethiopian Government. [10]

The advisory corps was: (1) to organize a corps of police and gendarmerie which would be responsible for suppressing slavery, regulating the carrying of arms by persons not belonging to the army or police, policing centers with large European populations, ensuring security in agricultural areas, and maintaining order in the frontier areas; (2) to assist in promoting the economic development of the country; (3) to advise in drawing up a state

[8] See League of Nations, "Council Report on the Dispute Between Italy and Ethiopia," *Monthly Summary*, Supplement, XV: 10 (1935), p. 285. Hereafter cited as *Council Report*, October 1935.

[9] This was originally to be the usual committee of three rapporteurs, but, recognizing the special concern of Britain and France, the Council added them to make a committee of five.

[10] *Council Report* (October 1935), Annex I.

budget and in assessing and collecting taxes; (4) to advise in the reorganization and operation of other public services such as justice, education, and
public health. A principal adviser, appointed by the League Council subject
to the Emperor's approval, was to head each of these public services.

The principal advisers were to be the link with the League. Together,
they were to form a commission. The presiding member would also act as
"delegate" of the League. The delegate of the commission was to report
periodically to the League and the Emperor, who in turn was to communicate his observations of the report to the League Council. The plan was to
be reviewed by the Council at the end of five years, but no limitation was
placed on the plan's duration.

Ethiopia accepted the advisory corps proposal as a basis for negotiations;
Italy rejected the plan because "it did not take into account the rights and
vital interests of Italy." Thus conciliation failed, and the Council's next
step under Article 15 was to draft a formal statement of the facts together
with recommendations for settlement of the dispute.

On September 25, 1935, the Emperor of Ethiopia again requested "the
dispatch of impartial observers to establish the facts in regard to any
aggression or other incident that might occur in order to fix responsibility
therefor."[11] The Council committee replied on September 26 that it was
considering the Emperor's request and examining whether the circumstances would permit the observers to discharge their mission. But events
moved swiftly to military action, and no observers were ever sent.

On October 3, Italy invaded Ethiopia. Settlement of the dispute became
overshadowed by the need to take a position on the Italian invasion.
Was the war begun in disregard of the Covenant? The Council decided
that it was, and, in effect, thereby approved the application of sanctions.[12]

In Mussolini's view a "colonial operation" was different from a European
war on the plane of ethics and on the plane of expediency. In the "colonial
operation," civilization was pushing back barbarism. Therefore, the
principles of the Covenant should not apply in the same way. "We find it
monstrous that a nation [Great Britain] which dominates the world refuses
to us a wretched plot of ground in the African sun."[13]

Two days later, the Assembly met and approved the Council report.
It recommended that members of the League should set up a committee
to coordinate the application of sanctions.[14]

---

[11] A. J. Toynbee, ed., *Survey of International Affairs, 1935* (London: Oxford University
Press, 1936), II, p. 198.

[12] In a letter from Geneva to his constituents, Mr. Eden said "the real issue is whether
or not the League can prove itself an effective instrument in this dispute, and whether
its members are prepared to respect and uphold the Covenant . . . The present dispute
is a test case." *Ibid.*, p. 201.

[13] Interview with Mussolini, London *Times*, Oct. 4, 1935.

[14] The President ruled that the application of sanctions was not a matter for the
Assembly as such but for the individual members of the League.

WORK OF THE SANCTIONS CONFERENCE

From October 10 to 19, the Sanctions Conference, composed of fifty members, devised four groups of sanctions: (1) prohibiting export of all arms, ammunition, and implements of war to Italy, and lifting all restrictions on such exports to Ethiopia; (2) stopping all loans and credits to Italy; (3) prohibiting imports from Italy; (4) prohibiting specified exports to Italy such as tin, aluminum, and manganese, but not oil.[15] Members of the League agreed to put these measures into force within a matter of days.

On October 26, the U.S. Secretary of State was informed of the action taken by the Sanctions Conference, and the United States was invited to collaborate. Secretary Hull replied that the United States was "deeply interested" in preventing war and promoting the sanctity of treaties. In view of the Italo-Ethiopian dispute, the United States, wishing to discourage war but not to be involved in it, had taken independent and affirmative action to embargo arms, munitions, and implements of war to both belligerents.[16]

At the November 2 meeting of the Sanctions Conference, the Canadian representative suggested that the prohibited exports to Italy should include oil, coal, iron, and steel. These, of course, were the commodities of decisive importance; without them Italy had little chance of continuing the war. Instead, it was decided to consult the governments before reaching definite conclusions. The threat of an oil embargo remained, however. Sir Samuel Hoare and Pierre Laval, who had not attended regularly, came to the meeting and proclaimed that their countries would apply the sanctions in full. But, they added, Great Britain and France still hoped to find a basis for agreement through their conversations with Italy. Neither country would do anything behind the back of the League or inconsistent with the Covenant, and they would report to the Council if a basis for settlement could be found.

In the first month of war, the well-equipped Italian forces, fighting the Ethiopian Army equipped with spears and javelins, penetrated some forty miles into Ethiopian territory. But the hardest terrain was still ahead, and the rainy season was not far away. An oil sanction could be fatal to Italy if applied in time.

In these circumstances, Mussolini appealed to Laval for help threatening that Italy would leave the League, turn to Hitler, or even bomb the French Riviera. Laval asked for and obtained a two-week delay for the next meeting of the Sanctions Conference. Having hinted that Mussolini was

---

[15] League of Nations, *Monthly Summary*, XV: 10 (October 1935), pp. 254–55.

[16] The United States not being a member of the League did not participate in declaring Italy the aggressor. The embargo on arms and implements of war to both belligerents fell most heavily on Ethiopia.

desperate and might even wage war on the British Empire, Laval persuaded Sir Samuel Hoare to help complete a new plan of conciliation which might satisfy Italy's ambitions.[17] Little was left for Hoare to do but endorse the plan.[18] Laval hoped to persuade the Emperor of Ethiopia to accept it.

HOARE-LAVAL PLAN

Under the Hoare-Laval plan, the southern half of the country (160,000 square miles) was to be made into "a zone of economic expansion and settlement" where Italy would have exclusive economic rights and unlimited rights of immigration and settlement. While nominally under Ethiopian sovereignty and administration, it would be controlled by Italians acting in the name of the League. The plan was laid before the Italian and Ethiopian Governments on December 10 and presented to the League Council on December 18.

In Addis Ababa, Great Britain, the United States, and the smaller countries, reaction to the plan was violent and immediate. It was widely criticized as nothing less than a reward for aggression offered to Mussolini in the name of the League. Mussolini, who by now was determined to get the whole of Ethiopia without conditions, said Italy would not allow itself to be tricked. Consequently, he never sent a reply to Paris or London.

The plan delayed the extension of sanctions, which was what its authors had intended. When the Council met on December 18, the plan was dead, and no member gave it any support. In Great Britain, the Baldwin government was accused by its own supporters and public opinion of having broken faith with the League. Baldwin withdrew his approval of the plan and called for the resignation of his Foreign Secretary. A few weeks later the Laval government fell.

The Sanctions Committee, dispirited with the delays caused by the Hoare-Laval proposal, did not press for the oil sanction, which had been approved in principle. Instead, it hoped that the other sanctions would slow down the Italian advance until the rains came. But Italy resorted to poison gas which was sprayed over the retreating army and the countryside. In February, the Italians won two important battles over a virtually helpless Ethiopian Army. On May 6, 1936, the Italian armies were in Addis Ababa; victory over Ethiopia was complete; and Mussolini announced

[17] Walters, *op. cit.*, pp. 667–68.

[18] There was a steep rise in the flow of American oil to Italy, a flow which the President had no legal power to stop. This fact is said to have greatly influenced Sir Samuel Hoare to fall in with Laval in sponsoring the plan. Laval's motive for proposing the plan was the likelihood of an oil sanction being adopted. See Toynbee, *op. cit.*, pp. 243–44, 278–79.

that civilization had triumphed over barbarism and that Ethiopia was irrevocably Italian.[19]

On May 11, the League Council met in regular session with the Ethiopian question one of the items on its agenda. The Italian representative declared at the opening of the session that Ethiopia no longer existed, and therefore there should be no such question on the agenda, and no so-called Ethiopian representative should be admitted to the Council table. The Council, however, treated the Ethiopian representative as before, and the Italian delegate was ordered by Mussolini to return to Rome. The Council gave itself a month to consider the effects of annexation and informed the League members that sanctions should continue in the meantime.

SANCTIONS REVOKED

Some members held that the League should accept defeat rather than continue down the forsaken road of collective security. Others held that a victim's inability to keep up the fight did not affect the moral and legal obligations of League members. Moreover, the pressure on the Italian economy was already severe. If the existing sanctions were continued long enough, the aggressor would be forced to give up his conquest.

A meeting of the League Assembly was convoked for June 30 to discuss the question of sanctions. It appeared certain that sanctions would be maintained with the new Blum government in France, Anthony Eden as Foreign Secretary in Great Britain, and the pro-sanctionist Scandinavian and neutral states favoring their continuation. But without consulting Eden, Neville Chamberlain, Chancellor of the Exchequer, made a speech prior to June 30 in which he said that it would be "the very midsummer of madness" to continue sanctions.[20] It was assumed abroad that this was the official British opinion, and the sanctions front began to collapse. When the Assembly met on June 30, the smaller states who faithfully, and at some risk, were participating in the sanctions felt that they had been let down by the great powers, and that they could no longer look on the League as a protection against aggression.

In this gloomy atmosphere, Emperor Haile Selassie made his famous address to the Assembly on July 1, 1936. With infinite dignity, he made an overwhelming indictment of Italy's unjustifiable aggression, the gas attacks which poisoned food and water and killed or maimed all on whom the gas fell, the disappointed hopes of help from the League, and the despair of his people who were compelled to fight without weapons.

[19] Addis Ababa capitulated to the British in World War II on April 6, 1941, and all of Italian East Africa was under British control by December 1941.

[20] Walters, *op. cit.*, p. 683.

"If a strong government finds that it can, with impunity, destroy a weak people, then the hour has struck for that weak people to appeal to the League of Nations to give its judgment in all freedom. God and History will remember your judgment." The Emperor concluded, "Representatives of the world, I have come to Geneva to discharge in your midst the most painful of the duties of the head of a State. What answer am I to take back to my people?"[21]

The Assembly had no answer to give to the Emperor. Only two delegations, South Africa and New Zealand, urged the maintenance of sanctions. All the others considered sanctions to be useless and hopeless. Accordingly, sanctions were abandoned on July 16, 1936.

In September 1936, the regular session of the Assembly had to decide whether to seat an Ethiopian delegation. If it were seated, Italy would leave the League. France and Great Britain supported a report from the credentials committee finding the credentials of the Ethiopian delegation, issued by a chief of state without actual authority, as insufficient. The majority of League members, however, rejected the British-French view as dishonorable. The Ethiopian delegation was seated, and the Italian delegation returned to Rome. Shortly thereafter the German-Italian Pact established the Berlin-Rome Axis.

EVALUATION

From the beginning of this dispute, it was clear that Great Britain and France were unwilling to take any action that would seriously offend Italy. They felt that Italy had been unfairly refused African territorial gains after World War I and was justified in wishing to extend its meager holdings. They also hoped that Italy would continue to join them in checking Hitler's aggressive designs in Europe. Thus, at every turn, they impeded effective action by the League until it was too late. Throughout the summer of 1935, they postponed sending observers in the hope they could settle the dispute outside the League. These delaying tactics culminated in the humiliating Hoare-Laval plan. Once more it was demonstrated that without the cooperation of the major powers, the League was severely handicapped.

An interesting feature of this case was the advisory corps proposed by the Committee of Five. The Emperor's power would have been reduced to nominal sovereignty, while an international group of specialists virtually took over the administration of his country. This proposal for internationally sponsored tutelage of a backward country, though accepted by Ethiopia, was rejected by Italy and was never put into operation.

[21] League of Nations, *Monthly Summary*, XVI: 6 (June 1936), pp. 157–58.

As the dispute dragged on, it became clear that Italy would accept nothing less than the seizure of Ethiopia. Its consistent opposition to any proposal which left Ethiopia with effective sovereignty was similar to the Japanese performance in Manchuria.

The use of poison gas by a white European country on a dark-skinned African people caused violent reaction in the form of racial disturbances in a number of places. In Geneva, the Haitian delegate spoke eloquently for his race, and the Ethiopians became the martyred champions of Negroes throughout the world.

When sanctions were instituted, they were not the most effective ones that could have been selected. The imposition of an oil sanction against Italy or the closing of the Suez Canal could have stopped the Italian aggression in a matter of weeks. Closing the Canal was never suggested, and the oil sanction, though adopted in principle, was not put into effect. Such sanctions as were imposed were lifted soon after the conquest became an accomplished fact. They had been insulting to Italy but were not seriously damaging. The insistence on continuing to seat the Haile Selassie delegation at the League may have assuaged the collective conscience, but it merely alienated Italy without giving any real help to Ethiopia.

This performance of the League was watched with dismay by the smaller nations. Words spoken in an earlier debate now seemed ominous: "Great or small, strong or weak, near or far, white or coloured, let us never forget that one day we may be somebody's Ethiopia." [22] The reaction of world public opinion was critical and indignant. If the League could not stop the aggressor nations, who could? Failure to apply the Covenant first in Asia and then in Africa was soon to make it equally impotent in Europe.

13

——◆——

EVALUATION OF LEAGUE EXPERIENCE
IN PEACE OBSERVATION

Although each situation or dispute which arose during the League period is different from any other, there are lessons to be drawn from this experience which may serve as guidelines for further perfecting the use of peace observation as an instrumentality.

---

[22] By Alfred Nemours, delegate from Haiti. Walters, *op. cit.*, p. 653.

In 1920, the overriding political objective of European governments was the maintenance of political stability in the face of the many new boundaries hastily or temporarily drawn by the Peace Conference. Rival territorial claims and inevitable minority demands existed all the way from the Aaland Islands deep into the Balkans, and even into the disintegrated Turkish Empire in the Middle East.

With the adjournment of the Peace Conference, and the dilatoriness of the successor Conference of Ambassadors, these threatening problems fell on the League of Nations Council at its first meetings. The Wilsonian concept of letting such problems be settled through self-determination appealed to many. But on closer examination, it was seen that its general application would create as many problems as it would solve. Moreover, it might weaken the newly established state system of Europe and undermine the basis and influence of the League itself. Self-determination was therefore rejected in the first case where it might have seemed just to use it, but the legitimate claims of dissident minorities could not be overlooked, and a widespread system of guarantees came to be adopted.

Minority guarantees and supervised plebiscites, as in the cases of Upper Silesia and the Saar, came to be integral parts of peace observation. Where boundaries needed to be delimited as on the borders of Albania, and between Turkey and Iraq, special assignments were given to commissions acting on behalf of the Council. In each case, an international agency assisted in bringing about political stability, which was the objective.

Until one or more of the great powers interfered with or completely defied the Council's agency, the organizational arrangements set up and especially adapted in each case between 1920 and 1930 were measurably effective.

The terms of reference were generally precise yet broad enough to enable the commissions to deal with unforeseen matters. Interim reports were usually made, and final reports were generally accompanied with recommendations. The reports invariably began with a clarifying historical background. The most elaborate report ever made by a League Commission, that of the Lytton Commission on Manchuria, had no effect on the war but was held by most governments, including the United States, as offering a just and reasonable basis for a settlement.

A study of the composition of League Commissions of Enquiry shows that they were drawn less on the basis of nationality than of competence. Participants were appointed by, supported by, and responsible to, the League Council. They did not function in a representative capacity and did not, as far as is known, act on instructions of their respective governments. (This is also true today of certain United Nations Commissions such as Trusteeship Council Visiting Missions.) Ideological differences, of course, were not so great in the first ten years of the League period. The Lytton Commission whose five members were drawn from the five great western powers was criticized in some quarters for departing from the previous practice.

The problem of financing Commissions of Enquiry and auxiliary agencies never ceased to be a vexing one to the League. Different systems of paying these expenses were employed in an attempt to bypass the already strained budget. The budget presented in October 1920 set aside 200,000 gold francs for "Unforeseen Expenses—Special Commissions of Enquiry, etc." In the Albanian border dispute, the Secretary-General added 100,000 gold francs to the budget for the fourth fiscal year to cover the cost of the Commission of Enquiry. This method of financing ran the League into the red, and a new policy was formulated, that of making the parties to the dispute pay the expenses. In the Saar plebiscite, the operation was supported by France, Germany, and the Saar Governing Commission in 5:5:1 shares. The base salaries of the members of the international force were paid by the contributing governments (the United Kingdom, Italy, the Netherlands, and Sweden) while the differential was defrayed by the plebiscite fund mentioned above. Recognizing these problems, the Convention to Improve the Means of Preventing War included the proviso that the costs of enquiries be paid by the parties to the dispute, in line with the policy then followed by the League.[1]

The League Council had had few precedents to guide it and therefore had to build from the experiences of previous cases those methods which would be practical and avoid those that proved ineffective. Certain specific factors run through the cases that can be identified for purposes of future planning.

THE TIME FACTOR

The speed with which the Council was able to intervene in a case was very important. In the Aaland Islands case, the Council on the initiative of a third party took up the matter before hostilities had begun, and in the Greek-Bulgarian case, the President of the Council took action, backed by the Council itself, in a matter of hours after hostilities had begun. On the other hand, the cases of Vilna, Manchuria, and Mosul proved to be more difficult since there were too many delays before the League Council was able to organize a peace-observation activity and get it on the scene. In the Manchurian case, the Lytton Commission of Enquiry did not reach the area until five months after hostilities were under way.

COOPERATION OF THE PARTIES

The cooperation of both parties was an important factor in getting positive results. Such cooperation, even though given reluctantly at times, was

[1] See Appendix that follows.

present in the Aaland Islands, the Greek-Bulgarian, and the Memel cases, each of which was brought to a successful conclusion. In the Aaland Islands case, the two Scandinavian countries involved could be expected to be amenable to legal and peaceful procedures. In certain other cases, such respect for law did not and does not today exist in the same degree. In the Corfu, Manchurian, and Ethiopian cases, for example, there was open defiance of League Council action. However, some headway was made in the Albanian border cases when only one country, Albania, was responsive while the other parties, Yugoslavia and Greece, were in opposition. When neither party cooperates, the position is difficult.

AGREEMENT OF THE GREAT POWERS

When the great powers on the League Council were in agreement on the action to take, the outcome was generally positive. And the more so when the smaller or elected members of the Council also went along with the plans. Thus, in the Aaland Islands and Greek-Bulgarian cases, there was unanimity in the Council. In the Vilna case, which dragged out to an indifferent result, France's alliance with Poland tended to hamper the Council's action. Likewise in the Corfu and Ethiopian cases, there was evident, though understandable, lack of great power-agreement to make the intervention succeed. In the Ethiopian case, the discussions outside the Council of France and Great Britain with Italy tended to negate the Council's plans for any form of peace observation disliked by Italy.

QUALITY OF OBSERVERS

A study of the Commissions of Enquiry set up by the League of Nations during the period under review shows that great care was exercised in their selection. When this was not the case, perhaps for political reasons, as for example in appointing a non-neutral French chairman to the Governing Commission of the Saar, there was trouble until the Council reorganized the commission to give it a more disinterested quality. The principle of impartiality was also observed, to a large extent, in supplying the commissions with staffs made up of international officials drawn from the League Secretariat or from outside sources. For example, in the Manchurian conflict, it would be difficult to find a more eminent and competent group than was assembled on the Lytton Commission.

INTERNATIONAL STATUS OF COMMISSION MEMBERS

Nearly all League Commissions of Enquiry and auxiliary commissions were composed of eminent persons who did not act as representatives of their governments. Most of them were former ambassadors, statesmen, soldiers, lawyers, or other experts, usually drawn from countries detached from the situation dealt with. They were often chosen from nationals of smaller countries whose detachment and disinterestedness could be assumed. However, in the case of the Lytton Commission, the five members were nationals of Great Britain, United States, France, Italy, and Germany. There was some criticism that they were all westerners and that several of their countries were directly concerned in the dispute. The members, however, apparently did not consult their governments before making their report. Therefore, the report did not necessarily reflect the official policy of their respective governments.

USE OF ASSESSORS

In two cases in the League's experience (Mosul and Manchuria) assessors were appointed who were nationals of the two disputing countries. Their function was to serve as liaison for the commission and facilitate its contacts. In neither case did the use of such assessors prove good. In the Mosul case, the presence of the Turkish member, in fact, tended to stir up the Iraqi people and caused disturbances that hampered the commission's work. In both cases, there was some difficulty about granting access to the assessor as a representative of the antagonist government.

USE OF AUXILIARY COMMISSIONS OR AGENCIES

Auxiliary commissions, particularly military groups or judicial bodies, were used by the League to assist Commissions of Enquiry where they would be helpful. In the Vilna case, a military commission succeeded in setting up neutral zones between the contending armies. In the Greek-Bulgarian case, three military attachés were on the scene within hours to oversee the cease-fire and disengagement operations. In the Saar, an international force of 3,300 men maintained order while a plebiscite was being conducted under the authority of the League's Governing Commission. Also in the Saar case, a judicial tribunal, with subordinate panels made up of outside persons, was available to assure the trustworthiness of the voting and to listen to any complaints regarding irregularities. In the Aaland Islands case, a judicial opinion was given by a committee of three jurists dealing with the question of the League's competence which was being contested by Finland. It may be concluded, therefore, that such auxiliary bodies were helpful in bringing about conditions in which the Commission of Enquiry could carry out its task.

NATURE OF TERMS OF REFERENCE

In most cases, the League of Nations Council laid down detailed terms of reference to be followed by its appointed Commissions of Enquiry. In the majority of cases, these terms included making recommendations for a solution of the dispute and fixing indemnities deemed to be proper. An exception to the rule of precise instructions was that of the Lytton Commission in Manchuria. Here the terms were so general that a number of countries felt that the omission to request withdrawal of the Japanese troops to their original positions meant that the Council was condoning a *fait accompli* and accepting the Japanese aggression. Whether more precise terms would have been helpful in the existing circumstances is open to doubt.

SEPARATION OF CESSATION OF HOSTILITIES FROM SETTLEMENT

The classic example of the Greek-Bulgarian case showed that the League Council considered it a duty to stop hostilities first, regardless of the merits and to look into the settlement of the case afterwards. The party which, even if on the defensive, refused to respond to the League's request to cease hostilities was in danger of being considered the aggressor. Aristide Briand as President of the Council refused to permit arguments of the parties based on "legitimate defense" on the ground that this might give a pretext for any country to resort to force without using the peace-observation machinery which the League provided. The Council was unanimous in supporting this point of view, and it was indeed referred to as "the new jurisprudence." While it was not always possible to make a clear distinction, this principle never ceased to be prominent in League discussions dealing with control and prevention of war.

EFFECTS OF SIMULTANEOUS THREATS

It is perhaps obvious that it is more difficult to deal with several threats occurring at the same time than with one at a time. In the Corfu case, it was apparent that France, which was planning the occupation of the Ruhr, needed and wanted Italian support, and in both the Manchurian and Ethiopian cases, the Hitlerian threat in Europe caused many countries to hesitate to take action in Asia or Africa when they were preoccupied with formidable threats nearer at hand. In such circumstances, it is obvious that the outbreak of aggressive action in several places would make it more difficult if not impossible, for the international organization to take desirable and necessary action.

APPENDIX:

CONVENTION TO IMPROVE
THE MEANS OF PREVENTING WAR, 1931

*(An Attempt by the League of Nations To Codify the Experience Gained
from 1921 to 1931 in Using Commissions of Enquiry)*

In September 1931 the League adopted the Convention to Improve the Means of Preventing War, based on ten years' experience in setting up and using Commissions of Enquiry in some ten cases coming before the League. The Convention had been prepared by the Committee on Arbitration and Security of the Preparatory Commission on Disarmament and was based on suggestions originally put forward by the German delegation in 1928. It never received the ten ratifications necessary to enter into force.

The Convention represented a further development of Article 11 in that it considered the prevention of hostilities in political disputes by conciliation instead of the use of collective force and sanctions after hostilities were already under way. It was designed to correct a weakness in the Covenant as it made the decisions of the Council under Article 11 legally binding.[1]

Accompanying the Convention was a carefully drafted protocol embodying executive regulations as to the composition and working of Commissions of Inspection. These regulations were not drawn up in the abstract but were the result of practical experience gained from the various cases running from the Aaland Islands case (1921) up to but not including the Manchurian case (1931).

The salient points of the Convention and accompanying executive regulations may be summarized as follows:[2]

ACTION IN SITUATIONS SHORT OF WAR

1. The High Contracting Parties, in the event of a dispute between them, undertake to apply the conservatory measures recommended by the Council and aimed to prevent an aggravation of the dispute.
2. If the forces of one of the parties enters the territory or territorial waters of the other, or enters a demilitarized zone laid down by agreement, the Council may prescribe measures to ensure their evacuation, and the High Contracting Parties undertake promptly to carry out such measures.

[1] J. T. Shotwell and Marina Salvin, *Lessons on Security and Disarmament from the History of the League of Nations* (New York: King's Crown Press, 1949), p. 44.

[2] League of Nations, Conference on the Reduction and Limitation of Armaments, *Conference Documents* (IX Disarmament, 1935. IX), II.

3. If a threat of war develops from the foregoing circumstances, the Council may fix lines which must not be passed by land, naval or air forces, and the High Contracting Parties undertake to comply with the Council's recommendations. Such lines should, if possible, be fixed by agreement with the parties. The High Contracting Parties undertake to take precautions to prevent incidents.

4. The Council shall, if it thinks fit or if one of the parties so requests, "appoint commissioners for the sole purpose of verifying on the spot the execution of the conservatory measures . . . recommended by the Council," under the foregoing conditions. The High Contracting Parties undertake to afford these commissioners every facility to perform their duties.

Regulations Under Article 4 of the Convention to Improve the Means of Preventing War, Particularly in Reference to the Composition and Working of the Commissions of Inspection

1. Constitution of Commissions
   a) The commissioners shall be appointed by the Council with the approval of the states of which they are nationals. They shall *not* be nationals of the parties to the dispute.
   b) Unless otherwise decided by the Council, the Commission shall include the same number of each nationality.
   c) The Council shall appoint the President of the Commission. The Commission may be divided into several sections each of which shall consist of not less than three members of different nationalities. If a section consists entirely of military officers, the senior member of the highest rank shall preside.

2. Work of the Commission
   a) The role of the Commission shall be to verify on the spot the execution of the measures recommended by the Council. (Convention Article 4)
   b) The commissioners shall have the right to visit any point to which they may have to proceed in execution of their mission, and remain there as long as may be necessary. They shall have the right to move about freely, and remain within the withdrawal zone lines fixed by the Council.
   c) On land, the commissioners shall have the right to enter and remain in such military establishments as are within the fixed zones; on sea, they may go on board ships passing through a fixed zone; with reference to aircraft, they may establish lookout posts at the frontiers or in the fixed zones. On request of a party, commissioners may accompany land, sea, or air forces moving near a fixed zone, to assure they have not entered the zone.
   d) Commissioners shall enjoy diplomatic privileges and immunities. They shall also be provided with League identity papers.

3. Facilities to be Accorded to Commissions
   a) The parties to which a mission is sent shall take the necessary measures to enable the commissioners to discharge their duties. They shall see that the public authorities and the population place no obstacle of any kind in the way of the work of the Commission. They shall give the latter all assistance in their power in order to facilitate the accomplishment of its mission. They shall, more particularly, appoint one or more officials who shall be at the constant disposal of the Commission. Such officials shall be provided with written instructions giving them full powers to call for the assistance of the civil and military authorities.

b) The parties shall afford the commissioners any protection that may be asked by them. They shall provide, at the commissioners' expense, all necessary facilities for transport and accommodation.

4. Reports of Commissions
   a) The President of the Commission shall keep the Council informed of its activities, and, in particular, of any infraction of the measures recommended by the Council.
   b) The Council shall be immediately informed of any difficulty which might arise between any of the parties to the dispute and the Commission.
   c) On the conclusion of the mission, the President of the Commission shall submit a report, together with any dissenting opinions in the event of disagreement.

5. Secretariat and Financial Provisions
   a) The Secretary-General shall organize and make available to the Commission such secretariat as the Council may consider necessary. They shall enjoy the same diplomatic privileges and immunities as the commissioners.
   b) The allowance granted to the commissioners shall be fixed by the Council on the advice of the Secretary-General. Unless otherwise decided by the Council, the expenses attaching to such Commissions shall be borne by the parties to the dispute.

During the debate on the Japanese action in Manchuria, M. Munch of Denmark expressed the belief that the Convention would yet be ratified in time to be employed in this case where it was so apropos.[3] His belief turned out to be unjustified. By the time the Convention was open to signature in late September 1931, the League had lost the impetus to expand its powers, particularly as concerned the agreement of disputing parties to Council action in their dispute. Whereas the Convention would have obligated all signatories to obey any Council decisions under Article 11, the temper of the League was inclining in the other direction—towards requirement of unanimity, including the agreement of the disputants.[4]

[3] League of Nations, *Monthly Summary*, XII: 3 (March 1932), p. 86.
[4] Walters, *op. cit.*, p. 462.

CASES UNDER INTER-AMERICAN ORGANIZATIONS AND PROCEDURES

————————•——————————

PREFATORY NOTE

THE ORIGINS OF THE PRESENT INTER-AMERICAN SYSTEM FOR THE maintenance of international peace can be traced back to the early nineteenth century when most of the Latin American republics won their independence from Spain. As weak countries facing a hostile Europe, they sought to band together for their mutual protection. As early as 1826, Simón Bolívar called a conference of Spanish-American republics at Panama where a treaty of confederation was drafted. It provided for mutual guarantees, the establishment of a representative assembly, and procedures for the settlement of their disputes by peaceful means. Political chaos following disruptive wars of independence prevented these efforts from being put into practice.

In 1889, the United States convoked the First International Conference of American States in Washington, setting in motion a series of conferences which have continued. At the conclusion of this conference in April 1890, the permanent international agency that has developed into the present Organization of American States was established.

The first phase in the development of inter-American peace and security procedures, from 1890 to 1936, was characterized by efforts to devise juridical procedures for the peaceful settlement of inter-American disputes. During this period, which culminated in the Inter-American Conference for the Maintenance of Peace at Buenos Aires in 1936, some twelve general treaties were signed dealing with pacific settlement procedures, as well as a large number of special local treaties. These treaties reflected two Latin American biases: an emphasis on the use of peaceful procedures rather than collective action for the settlement of international disputes; and a proclivity toward juridical formulas as the means for achieving this end. The effectiveness of these treaties even in theory was limited. None was ratified by all the American states, and most of them lacked several ratifications. Only once was the system established by these treaties successfully applied to a dispute.

The period 1890–1936 also saw the struggle between the Latin American countries and the United States over the intervention issue. The hostility toward the United States for its interventionist policy of the early twentieth century impeded the development of any intimate association in peace observation. Although the United States accepted the principle of nonintervention in Latin American terms in 1933, the latent fear of United States power has continued to restrict the delegation of authority to an international agency that the Latin American countries believe may be dominated by the United States in its own political interests.

The second phase of the development of peace-observation procedures was from 1936 to 1948. In this period, the emphasis shifted from juridical formulas to the principle of consultation and the use of collective measures. The period culminated in the conclusion of the two treaties: the Inter-American Treaty of Reciprocal Assistance (Treaty of Rio de Janeiro), 1947, and the Charter of the Organization of American States, 1948.

At the Bogotá Conference in 1948, concurrently with the Charter of the OAS, the American Treaty of Pacific Settlement, known as the Pact of Bogotá, was drafted. Its purpose was to replace the numerous earlier treaties with one consolidated instrument of pacific settlement. The treaty sets forth procedures to be followed, beginning with good offices and progressing through mediation, investigation and conciliation, and judicial settlement to compulsory arbitration. Parties are permitted to select any one of these procedures in the first instance, but if that procedure fails, they are required to go as far as necessary toward a final arbitration. However, because of the requirement of compulsory arbitration if other procedures fail, and other controversial items, as of 1964, the Pact of Bogotá had been ratified by only nine governments.[1] The United States has not ratified it, and of the larger Latin American countries, only Mexico has become a party.

INTER–AMERICAN PEACE COMMITTEE

A more constructive move in this field is represented by the Inter-American Peace Committee, which has exercised important

[1] Costa Rica, Dominican Republic, El Salvador, Haiti, Honduras, Mexico, Nicaragua, Panama, and Uruguay.

peace-observation functions. The committee was established by Resolution XIV of the Second Meeting of Foreign Ministers in 1940, which recommended that the Governing Board of the Pan American Union: [2] "organize . . . a committee of representatives of five countries which shall have the duty of keeping constant vigilance to insure that States between which any dispute exists or may arise . . . may solve it as quickly as possible, and of suggesting . . . measures and steps which may be conducive to a settlement." [3] The committee is an autonomous body directly responsible to the Meeting of Foreign Ministers.

The Inter-American Peace Committee was not installed for eight years. Shortly after the Bogotá conference of 1948, the Dominican Republic presented to it a complaint against the Government of Cuba. Since its installation in July 1948, the committee has considered some fourteen cases, and it has made a major contribution to the peaceful solution of controversies among the American states. The five original members of the committee were two from the north (Mexico and the United States), two from the south (Argentina and Brazil) and one from the central area (Cuba). When its statutes were revised in 1956, provision was made for a regular rotation of members, one new government being elected each year for a term of five years.

The basic authority of the Inter-American Peace Committee is the vague statement in the resolution of 1940. Its function is merely to bring parties together and suggest procedures to them. In its first statutes, which the committee drafted, it interpreted its authority as enabling it to consider any case brought before it whether by a party to a dispute or by another member state. In 1956, the statutes were changed, and the committee was prohibited from considering any dispute unless brought before it by a party to the controversy, and unless the other party or parties agreed that the committee consider the matter. In its report to the Fifth Meeting of Foreign Ministers in 1959, the committee pointed out that since the adoption of its new statutes no further cases had been brought before it, [4] reflecting the fact that the requirement of prior consent of all parties

[2] The Governing Board of the Pan American Union was, in the Charter of the OAS, converted into the present Council of the Organization.

[3] Carnegie Endowment for International Peace, ed., *International Conferences of American States*, First Supplement 1933–1940 (Washington: Carnegie, 1940), p. 360.

[4] Inter-American Peace Committee, *Report to the Fifth Meeting of Consultation of Ministers of Foreign Affairs* (Washington: Pan American Union, 1959).

had made it too easy for any government facing charges to block communication.

In 1959, the Fifth Meeting of Foreign Ministers, faced with the need for doing something about the turbulent situation in the Caribbean following the Castro revolution in Cuba, assigned additional functions to the Peace Committee and solely in conjunction therewith restored to it the authority to act on its own initiative without the prior consent of the governments concerned. Resolution IV of the Santiago Meeting requested the committee to study and report on the problems of international tension in the Caribbean. The nature of this assignment departed substantially from the traditional function the Peace Committee had previously exercised.

INTER–AMERICAN COLLECTIVE SECURITY SYSTEM: TREATY OF RIO DE JANEIRO

The collective security system of the OAS, based on consultation and the adoption of collective measures to prevent or repel aggression, rests primarily on the Treaty of Rio de Janeiro, although the Charter of the OAS contains supplementary provisions in regard thereto. Drafted two years after the Charter of the United Nations, the Treaty of Rio was designed to relate juridically to the UN document. Thus a distinction is made between procedures for dealing with armed attacks under the right of self-defense, recognized in Article 51 of the UN Charter, and those regarding other forms of aggression or threats to the peace which relate more directly to Articles 52 and 53 of the UN Charter. The central obligations of the treaty in regard to both types of cases are set forth in Articles 3 and 6 respectively.

Article 3 of the Rio Treaty has never been invoked. The salient paragraphs of it state that:[5] (1) " an armed attack by any State against an American State shall be considered as an attack against all the American States," and each contracting party "undertakes to assist in meeting the attack in the exercise of the inherent right of individual or collective self-defense recognized by Article 51" of the UN Charter; (2) "on the request of the State or States directly attacked and until the decision of the Organ of Consultation of the

[5] Inter-American Conference for the Maintenance of Continental Peace and Security, *Report on the Results of the Conference* (Washington: Pan American Union, 1947), p. 62. Hereafter cited as Rio Treaty.

Inter-American System," each contracting party may determine the measures "it may individually take in fulfillment of [its] obligation . . . and in accordance with the principle of continental solidarity." The Organ of Consultation shall meet without delay to examine those measures and to agree upon "the measures of a collective character that should be taken."

Even though several of the cases considered under the Rio Treaty have in fact involved armed conflict, the OAS governments have preferred not to invoke the provision for automatic and immediate assistance, but to rely on Article 6 which emphasizes prior consultation and collective measures. This article reads:

> If the inviolability or the integrity of the territory or the sovereignty or political independence of any American State should be affected by an aggression which is not an armed attack or by an extra-continental or intra-continental conflict, or by any other fact or situation that might endanger the peace of America, the Organ of Consultation shall meet immediately . . . to agree on the measures which must be taken . . . to assist the victim of the aggression or . . . which should be taken for the common defense and for the maintenance of the peace and security of the Continent. [6]

The Organ of Consultation referred to was defined in the Charter of the OAS as the Meeting of Consultation of Ministers of Foreign Affairs, [7] which can be convoked to serve as the organ under the Rio Treaty or for other purposes. Moreover, foreseeing the need for rapid action, which should not be deferred until the physical convening of the Meeting of Foreign Ministers, the Rio Treaty provides in Article 12 that the Governing Board of the Pan American Union (now the Council of the OAS) "may act provisionally as an organ of consultation" until the Meeting of Foreign Ministers takes place. This article is the only authorization which the Council has to take cognizance of the substance of a dispute between American states or to deal with problems of aggression from an extra-continental source. Most of the cases in which the Rio Treaty has been invoked have been dealt with by the Council under this grant of power,

---

[6] Rio Treaty, p. 63.

[7] The Meeting of Consultation of Ministers of Foreign Affairs is a regular organ of the OAS whose function, as stated in Article 39, is "to consider problems of an urgent nature and of common interest to the American States, and to serve as the Organ of Consultation." When convoked "to serve as the Organ of Consultation" it derives its powers from, and is governed by, the Rio Treaty. When convoked under the first clause, the Meeting of Consultation may take cognizance of almost any urgent problem, but its decisions cannot involve taking sanctions nor are they binding on states which do not agree.

which has proved to be the most important single basis for peace-observation work by the OAS.

Requests to invoke the Rio Treaty are submitted to the Council, which must then decide whether the prima facie evidence warrants convocation of the Organ of Consultation. [8] The Council has decided on occasions that it has no power to conduct even a preliminary investigation of charges except under the authority of the Rio Treaty, by calling a meeting of foreign ministers and then acting provisionally under Article 12. Once a meeting of foreign ministers is convoked (even though the date and place may not be fixed), the Council has usually appointed a committee to investigate the facts of the charges in the field and submit a report. In the majority of cases, such action by the Council has set in motion a series of peace-observation activities, often coupled with informal mediation, which has successfully brought the conflict to a close and made the Meeting of Foreign Ministers unnecessary. In only two cases under the Rio Treaty has a formal Meeting of Consultation of Ministers of Foreign Affairs taken place.

The investigating committees of the Council acting provisionally as the Organ of Consultation under the Rio Treaty usually have consisted of five members of the Council, selected by the chairman on an *ad hoc* basis in accordance with the authority given to him in each case. A small civilian secretariat has been provided by the Pan American Union. The terms of reference for such committees have usually been "to investigate and report," sometimes with recommendations. The committees have interpreted their mission with considerable flexibility, depending on the nature of the case and character of the individuals comprising the committees.

There is no provision in the inter-American collective security system outlined above for any permanent military agency. The Inter-American Defense Board, established in 1942, is a planning and advisory agency without command functions, and dedicated to plans for hemisphere defense against extra-continental aggression. Such military arrangements as have been set up in connection with the maintenance of peace within the hemisphere have been of an *ad hoc* nature and have been terminated as soon as possible. Military advisers appointed in this way have, however, played a vital role in peace-observation activities.

[8] Voting in the Organ of Consultation, pursuant to Articles 17 and 18 of the Rio Treaty, is by two-thirds vote, excluding parties directly interested. Voting within the investigating committees, as within the Inter-American Peace Committee, is by majority.

INTER–AMERICAN SYSTEM AND THE
UNITED NATIONS

The relationship of the OAS to the UN is based primarily on the provisions of the pertinent treaties of both the regional and world systems; it has been greatly affected, however, by interpretations and actions that have developed the underlying treaty provisions in ways hardly foreseen by the original drafters.

Both the Charter of the OAS and the Rio Treaty expressly recognize the primacy of the United Nations Charter. Article 102 of the OAS pact states: "None of the provisions of this Charter shall be construed as impairing the rights and obligations of the Member States under the Charter of the United Nations." [9] Article 10 of the Rio Treaty is virtually identical.

However, in Article 2 of the Rio Treaty

> . . . the High Contracting Parties undertake to submit every controversy which may arise between them to methods of peaceful settlement and to endeavor to settle any such controversy among themselves by means of the procedures in force in the Inter-American System before referring it to the General Assembly or the Security Council of the United Nations. [10]

A similar self-limiting provision appears in Article 21 of the OAS Charter with respect to pacific settlement, although mention of the General Assembly is there omitted. Two questions arise here with respect to Articles 33 and 52 of the UN Charter: (1) Have the parties to the Rio Treaty given up their right to take a dispute with another American state directly to the United Nations? (2) Are the organs of the United Nations, especially the Security Council, enjoined from taking cognizance of an Inter-American dispute until the OAS shall have had an opportunity to settle it?

These questions were raised in connection with the Guatemalan (1954), the Dominican Republic (1960), and the Cuban cases (1960 and later). In no case was a formal juridical pronouncement made on the basic questions mentioned above. In each case, however, important precedents were set in support of the thesis that while no state can be denied a hearing in the United Nations, in cases of disputes between members of the OAS, a reasonable opportunity should be given to the regional agency to settle them before they are acted on by the world organization.

[9] OAS, *Annals of the OAS*, I: 1 (Washington: Pan American Union, 1949), p. 85.
[10] Rio Treaty, p. 62.

Another question closely related to peace observation arises in connection with Article 53 of the United Nations Charter which states that: "no enforcement action shall be taken under regional arrangements or by regional agencies without the authorization of the Security Council." The main question is one of definition: What constitutes "enforcement action" requiring the authorization of the Security Council? Are any sanctions, such as the rupture of diplomatic relations or interruption of commerce, to be construed as "enforcement action," or are only those measures involving the use of force to be considered in this category? In the Dominican Republic case of 1960, the OAS adopted sanctions short of the use of force without authorization of the Security Council (even though the Soviet Union sought to have the Council grant such authority) thus giving implicit support to the more restricted interpretation of the term "enforcement action."

Article 5 of the Rio Treaty provides for keeping the Security Council informed of "activities undertaken or in contemplation" for the purpose of maintaining inter–American peace and security, and this requirement has been faithfully observed.

SPECIAL CHARACTERISTICS OF PEACE OBSERVATION IN LATIN AMERICA

Peace observation in the Organization of American States reflects both the cultural characteristics and the history of Latin America. Though there are wide differences in the racial background of the countries of Latin America, all except Haiti reflect the Spanish-Portuguese heritage: a strong emphasis on individualism, personal dignity, honor, and courtesy. Government in the Hispanic tradition is mainly a matter of personal relationship between the leader and the individual. This applies even to international government.

The reluctance to say anything that might offend the pride of others was, in some early cases of peace observation, carried to such an extreme that the meager records fail to disclose what the issue was. Reference is made merely to "certain differences." Many of the cases conclude with the signing of a "pact of friendship."

Peace observation in other geographic areas has developed along with peace-keeping. There has never been a peace-keeping operation in Latin America. The reason may be composite. Except for the

Haitian-Dominican conflicts, there have been no strong racial hatreds in the Latin American area. The Latin Americans are nearly all Catholic, and they have no history of religious conflict. Even the national animosities, which sometimes exist, are rarely virulent. Perhaps in only a single area are there passionate hatreds: those of democratic peoples for a neighboring dictatorship. Even there, it is a personal rather than an international matter. Peace observers in other areas have sometimes given their lives to carry out their mission. But there is no case in Latin America of a peace observer coming under fire and being killed.

1

THE CHACO DISPUTE BETWEEN BOLIVIA AND PARAGUAY, 1928–1929 AND 1932–1935

In 1878, President Rutherford B. Hayes in a dispute between Argentina and Paraguay over Central Chaco awarded to Paraguay the territory between the Pilcomayo and Verde Rivers, stating no western boundary.[1] Subsequent to this award, Bolivia claimed the whole northern Chaco, including the area awarded to Paraguay, on the ground that the Spanish Audiencia of Charcas (Bolivia) had always exercised jurisdiction down to the west bank of the Paraguay River. Bolivia lost its outlet to the Pacific Ocean to Chile in 1883. The Pilcomayo River and from it to the Atlantic Ocean, then, remained the only feasible outlet for Bolivia to the sea. Paraguay, however, claimed the Chaco Boreal on the alleged grounds of settlement, occupation, and control from the time of the original province of Paraguay. Matters thus smoldered between Bolivia and Paraguay for many decades. Treaties were signed in 1879, 1887, and 1894 but were never ratified. In 1907, both countries agreed to arbitrate title to some 50,000 square miles, but the President of Argentina would not serve as umpire.[2] At the end of 1928, Paraguayan troops seized and destroyed a

[1] Gordon Ireland, *Boundaries, Possessions, and Conflicts in South America* (Cambridge: Harvard University Press, 1938), pp. 32, 33.

[2] Graham H. Stuart, *Latin America and the United States*, 5th ed. (New York: Appleton-Century-Crofts, 1955), p. 367.

Bolivian advance post in territory claimed by both countries; Bolivia captured a Paraguayan post 225 miles northwest of Asunción; and diplomatic relations between the two countries were ruptured.

Twice the Chaco dispute flared into open war, in 1928 and again in 1932. The fighting in the earlier phase was stopped in 1929 through the use of a special commission of investigation and conciliation (the McCoy Commission) under the good offices of the International Conference of American States on Conciliation and Arbitration, then meeting in Washington. The more violent fighting in 1932 did not terminate until 1935. In the second phase, the American states suspended their efforts, and a League of Nations commission took over the case. Peace was finally restored through a Chaco Peace Conference, consisting of the two parties and six American republics, including the United States. In each phase, the basic issue was whether Paraguay or Bolivia should have sovereignty over the Chaco Boreal.

THE COMMISSION OF INVESTIGATION AND CONCILIATION

Armed hostilities between Paraguay and Bolivia broke out three days before the opening of the International Conference of American States on Conciliation and Arbitration, and diplomatic relations were ruptured. Nevertheless, on the opening day, the representatives of Bolivia and Paraguay joined in the unanimous resolution of the conference urging the parties to adjust their differences peaceably.[3] The efforts of a special committee led to the signature of a protocol on January 3, 1929, by representatives of Bolivia and Paraguay, which was attached to the Final Act of the Conference.[4] This protocol is a sort of charter for the Commission of Investigation and Conciliation which was set up. The commission was formed by representatives of the two countries plus delegates appointed by the Governments of the United States, Mexico, Colombia, Uruguay, and Cuba.

The commission was to investigate "and determine . . . which of the parties has brought about a change in the peaceful relations between the two countries." It was to establish its own procedures and terminate its work in six months. It had authority to conciliate, but if this were not possible, it was to report "the results of its investigation and the effortr made to settle the incident."

[3] *Bulletin of the Pan American Union*, LXIII (1929), p. 124. Hereafter cited as PAU, *Bulletin* LXIII.

[4] PAU, *Bulletin* LXIII, p. 125. See also: Notacion Carnegie Para La Paz Internacional, *Conferencias Internacionales Americanas, 1889–1936* (Washington: Carnegie Endowment, 1938), p. 585. The protocol is not available in English in Carnegie publications.

An important limitation in the authority of the commission was that it did "not include nor affect the territorial question, as contended by Bolivia, and of boundaries, as contended by Paraguay, which exists between both countries, nor does it include or affect the agreements in force between them."

General Frank R. McCoy, often a "troubleshooter" for the U.S. Government in this period, was the American member and chairman of the commission. The other members were Manuel Marquez Sterling, Cuba; Fernando Gonzalez Roa, Mexico; Raimundo Rivas, Colombia; General Guillermo Ruprecht, Uruguay. Bolivia had two representatives: David Alvestegui and Enrique Finot; the Paraguayan representatives were Enrique Bordenave and Francisco C. Chaves. It is understood that Argentina had been offered a place, but that country, "preferring to work alone," refused to serve, and thus Uruguay was named.[5]

The U.S. Secretary of State, Frank B. Kellogg, opened the first meeting of the commission at the Pan American Union in Washington on March 13, 1929.[6] The first success of the commission was the repatriation of prisoners, of the Paraguayan nationals on June 30 and the Bolivian nationals on July 9.[7]

Even before this phase of the work was over, however, the commission moved for an amplification of its authority. On June 28, 1929, General McCoy asked Bolivian and Paraguayan delegations to authorize the commission to prepare plans for a settlement of the fundamental question between them.[8] The Bolivians accepted with the understanding that the proposals should have only unofficial and informal character. The Paraguayans accepted with a reservation "of all the views in the memorials it presented." These were so vast that the representative would not mention them in detail.

General McCoy reported to the U.S. Secretary of State the successful termination of the first two functions of the commission—repatriation of nationals and conciliation on September 21, 1929.[9] He then stated that the commission had prepared a plan for the settlement of the fundamental question with the unofficial advice of geographic, economic, and other experts, but the plan failed to satisfy either country, and the commission abandoned the effort. Efforts to prepare a plan for arbitral settlement were worked on but were similarly inconclusive. With the report to the Secretary of State, the commission terminated its work.

[5] Ireland, *op. cit.*, p. 73.

[6] The minutes of the plenary sessions and a great many documents of the commission are published in *Proceedings of the Commission of Inquiry and Conciliation, Bolivia and Paraguay* (Baltimore: Sun Book and Job Printing Co., 1929).

[7] PAU, *Bulletin* LXIII, p. 759.

[8] PAU, *Bulletin* LXIII, p. 755.

[9] PAU, *Bulletin* LXIII, p. 1078.

EVALUATION OF THE COMMISSION

The facts presented above are the clearest answer to the charge that the Pan American mechanisms are ineffective or, when effective, do not get down to basic solutions. This commission merely restored the *status quo ante.* It achieved the return of seized forts and of prisoners, mutual forgiveness, and the resumption of diplomatic relations; but the basic issue, sovereignty over the Chaco, remained unsolved. In postponing war for another three years, however, it rendered good service.

The lesson of this experience is that the peace mechanism may be a good one and the personnel in charge of it excellent, but if the parties are too hostile to use it, it will be ineffective; if they are willing to use it only in part, it will be only partly effective.

THE LEAGUE OF NATIONS COMMISSION

General Frank McCoy was concluding his work on the Commission of Investigation and Conciliation in 1929 at about the same time that General John J. Pershing was finishing his settlement of the Pacific coast Tacna-Arica dispute, in which Tacna was awarded to Peru and Arica to Chile. The latter award dashed Bolivia's hopes of regaining a port on the Pacific and stimulated its desire for an outlet to the Atlantic via the Paraguay and the Plata.

A miniature arms race then ensued between Paraguay, small and poor, and larger and more populous Bolivia, which, though poor, had some wealthy citizens, such as the Patiño family. Bolivian forces had been training since 1911 under a German mission headed by Colonel Hans Kundt,[10] who was to lead the Bolivian forces in the coming war. A French military mission instructed Paraguayan forces from 1926 to 1930, and it was then followed by an Argentine mission. From 1926 to 1932, Paraguay spent nearly five million dollars on arms and gunboats.[11] Bolivian penetration roads and new forts began to appear in the disputed zone. By the end of 1932, full-scale war between Paraguay and Bolivia had broken out.[12]

The outbreak of hostilities was first brought to the attention of the Council of the League of Nations by the Bolivian delegate on July 21, 1932. He charged Paraguay with aggression at Lake Chuquisaca and remarked on the coincidence that Paraguay at once withdrew from the "Commission of Neutrals" at Washington, which had been negotiating with a view to the conclusion of a nonaggression pact between Bolivia and Paraguay.[13]

[10] Kundt acted as Chief of the General Staff in 1911–1914, 1921–1926, and 1929–1930.

[11] David H. Zook, *The Conduct of the Chaco War* (New York: Bookman Associates, 1961), p. 63.

[12] *Ibid.*, p. 78.

[13] The neutrals were the United States, Colombia, Cuba, Mexico, and Uruguay. League of Nations, *Monthly Summary*, XII: 8 and 9 (August and September 1932), p. 259.

The Paraguayan delegate replied that the Bolivians had launched the aggression 100 kilometers to the southwest of Lake Chuquisaca, and the post there had since been retaken. Bolivia, he said, had constructed ten new forts in the Chaco. Paraguay had, in fact, withdrawn from the "Commission of Neutrals" but had since returned.

Efforts to adjust the dispute by the President of the League Council, M. Matos of Guatemala, the members of the Pan American Union, and the five American "neutrals," joined by representatives of the ABCP powers —Argentina, Brazil, Chile, and Peru—failed. By November 1932, the Paraguayan offensive had pushed back the Bolivian line fifty-six miles in the north and fifty miles in the west.[14] This first of the three Paraguayan offensives during the Chaco War was halted by the Bolivians at the end of 1932. Paraguay declared war on Bolivia on May 10, 1933, and Bolivia appealed to the League of Nations.

THE COUNCIL OF THE LEAGUE OF NATIONS

The Council of the League of Nations met in extraordinary session on May 15, 1933, to consider the situation. It shortly received a report from a Committee of Three, which recommended that the two governments confide the settlement of the dispute to an impartial authority, which would study the problem and fix the frontier. The Council decided to send to the spot a commission which would supervise the cessation of hostilities, prepare an agreement for arbitration, and report on the facts in dispute. Paraguay accepted unconditionally; Bolivia informed the League's Committee of Three that, in its opinion, "the plan drawn up would not restore peace at an early date." It was opposed to the idea that the territory in dispute be delimited by preliminary arbitration, which it considered "would be futile."[15]

The Council of the League met on July 3, 1933, to consider the report of the Committee of Three on terms of reference of its commission to be sent to the spot. The Council approved the constitution of the Commission of Enquiry and instructed the Secretary-General to make the necessary financial arrangements.

The Bolivian representative presented his country's objection to a cessation of hostilities not accompanied by an arbitration agreement. Since it was conducting a war at a distance of 2,000 kilometers, such a suspension would be adverse to its interests.[16]

---

[14] Ireland, *op. cit.*, p. 76.

[15] League of Nations, *Monthly Summary*, XIII: 5 (May 1933), p. 107.

[16] League of Nations, *Monthly Summary*, XIII: 7 (July 1933), p. 164.

The terms of reference,[17] required the commission to negotiate an agreement for the cessation of hostilities; to prepare an agreement for arbitration; to make an inquiry on all the circumstances of the dispute, including the part which the two parties had taken; and to report to the Council. Shortly after the Council of the League approved these terms, General Hans Kundt with 25,000 troops started the first great Bolivian offensive at Fort Nanawa.

On July 19, 1933, the Commission of Enquiry was constituted under the chairmanship of the Spanish ambassador in Mexico, His Excellency Julio Alvarez del Vayo. The British member was Brigadier General Alexander B. Robertson; General Henri Freydenberg was the French member. Others were Count Luigi Aldrovandi (Italy), a former member of the League of Nations Commission of Enquiry for the Far East; Major G. R. Rivera Flandes (Mexico), former Director of the Geographic Section at the Ministry of War. Later, the Secretary-General made available his legal adviser, J. A. Buero (Uruguay), assisted by M. Henri Vigier (France), Counsellor in the Political Section of the League Secretariat. It is understood that the United States declined an invitation to serve on this Commission of Enquiry.

The commission started inauspiciously with both Bolivia and Paraguay recommending that their four neighboring states, the ABCP group, should act on the Council's behalf for the purpose of settling the dispute. The Paraguayan Government maintained that the League Commission would require considerable time for its studies, whereas the neighbors were already well informed. The Bolivian Government replied that "it had requested wide terms of reference with full liberty of initiation and action."[18]

On August 3, the League Council, while displaying a cooperative attitude to the ABCP countries, resolved that the League of Nations remained seized of the question. The European members of the League Commission embarked on October 19 and 20 for Montevideo, and, after a brief stop at Rio, where they learned that the ABCP group had retired from the field on October 1,[19] they arrived in Montevideo on November 3, 1933. The Bolivian representative threatened to ignore the work of the commission if its powers were not defined as Bolivia understood them.[20] The Committee of Three replied that the terms of reference had been fixed by the unanimous action of the Council on July 3, including the Bolivian representative, and rejected the Bolivian argument.

When the Commission of Enquiry started to work in Montevideo, the Bolivian minister to Uruguay insisted that if the commission could not

[17] Approved by the League Council, *ibid.*, p. 156. Text appears in *ibid.*, XIII: 5, p. 107.

[18] *Ibid.*, XIII: 7, p. 164.

[19] *Ibid.*, XIII: 11 (November 1933), p. 252.

[20] *Ibid.*, XIII: 10 (October 1933), p. 212.

achieve a direct solution, it should delimit the zone that was to be the subject of arbitration. Provided the action of the commission was exercised within these limits, Bolivia "agreed to participate and to appoint its representatives for this purpose."[21] The commission replied that it would do its whole duty as set forth in its terms of reference of July 3.

The commission left Montevideo on November 11 and spent two weeks in Paraguay visiting the Chaco, then departed on December 1 for Bolivia and returned to Montevideo on December 23, 1933. While in Bolivia, the members were not permitted to visit the Chaco, but they arranged a truce during the Christmas season. During December, most of the Bolivian Army was surrounded by Paraguayan troops, and on December 11, 8,000 men surrendered. General Kundt was dismissed. At the close of 1933, Bolivia had only 7,000 men in the field. Of 77,000 Bolivians shipped to the Chaco, 10,000 were prisoners, 14,000 were dead, 32,000 were evacuated as sick or wounded, 8,000 were in the communications zone, and 6,000 deserted to Argentina.[22]

The truce obtained by the League commission proved unavailing. Bolivia, in defeat, was still unwilling to consent to security guarantees without a prior agreement on arbitration; Paraguay wished to impose a victor's peace. Both parties used the time to regroup forces.

The Seventh International Conference of American States meeting at Montevideo did little but wring its hands over the Chaco War. U.S. Secreaty of State Cordell Hull told the heads of all delegations on his arrival that the League of Nations commission then visiting Bolivia and Paraguay was the only body with an authoritative mandate in the dispute. Telegrams were received from the presidents of Argentina, Brazil, Chile, Colombia, Mexico, Peru, and the United States, urging the conference to do everything possible to end the Chaco War. The conference adopted a resolution on peace in the Chaco that seemed to promise support for an eventual League Commission solution.[23]

The final effort of the League commission was to draft a treaty of peace on March 4, 1934. It contained the following points:[24] (1) Bolivian troops were to retire to the Villa Montes-Robero Line; (2) Paraguayan troops to retire to the Paraguay River; (3) each army to be reduced to 5,000 men in three months; (4) lower Pilcomayo region to be patrolled by Paraguayan police; (5) upper Pilcomayo region to be patrolled by Bolivian police; (6) neutral zone of forty miles to be policed as provided by League Council;

[21] *Ibid.*, XIII: 11, p. 252.

[22] Zook, *op. cit.*, pp. 167, 174.

[23] U.S. Delegation to the 7th International Conference of American States, *Report to the Conference* (Washington: Government Printing Office, 1934), pp. 12, 14, 262.

[24] League of Nations, *Official Journal*, 15th Year (1934), pp. 242–71, 748–867, 1530–1611.

(7) war prisoners to be repatriated; (8) Permanent Court of International Justice to give final judgment on the frontier between the two countries. Both the Bolivian and Paraguayan Government rejected the commission's draft treaty.[25]

Through the spring of 1934, the Paraguayans continued their offensive while the Bolivians refilled their depleted divisions. The League Commission left Montevideo on March 14, "leaving the situation practically unchanged."[26]

The Chaco commission's report to the League Council was made on May 11. The commission did not take as a basis of its draft treaty a prior Paraguayan proposal for the total demilitarization of the Chaco under international supervision, because Paraguay wished to police the entire area, including parts its armies had not reached—an impossible condition. Despite military reverses, Bolivia would not accept such a basis for the demilitarization of the Chaco.

The League Commission felt that Bolivia should accept President Hayes' award of 1878, covering those areas of the Chaco opposite its chief towns, and that Paraguay ought to accept the Treaty of Petropolis of 1903, under which Brazil ceded to Bolivia those parts of the Chaco north of Bahia Negra and thus gave Bolivia an area of the Paraguay River from which it would have access to the sea.

The commission also dealt with questions of violations of international law. It regarded decisions on this point as prejudicing its main objective, the restoration of peace, since the allegations on both sides tended to separate the parties more widely. It refused to consider charges of mistreatment of prisoners of war, as being beyond its authority.

The League had already been considering the dispute for a year; it dealt ineffectually with the problem for another year before the Chaco Peace Conference took over and ultimately achieved a peace. However, the League of Nations was not wholly ineffective in this case. One of the recommendations of the Commission of Enquiry related to an arms embargo and particularly to the strict control over the arms transit by neighboring countries. The British delegate at the Council took up this point,[27] and gradually such an embargo went into effect, although Chile interpreted its treaty with Bolivia as forbidding it. At the request of President Franklin D. Roosevelt, the U.S. Congress passed legislation empowering the President to prohibit the sale of arms and munitions in the United States.[28] On the day he signed the act, the President invoked it against shipments to both Bolivia and Paraguay.

[25] League of Nations, *Monthly Summary*, XIV: 3 (March 1934), p. 68.
[26] Ireland, *op. cit.*, p. 83.
[27] League of Nations, *Monthly Summary*, XIV: 5 (May 1934), p. 105
[28] 48 Stat. 811, 1744 (1934.)

THE LEAGUE ASSEMBLY AND THE CHACO
PEACE CONFERENCE

Two years after the outbreak of hostilities, that is, on May 31, 1934, Bolivia appealed to the League of Nations under Article 15 of the Covenant, and the Assembly of the League was called on to make recommendations. This it did in a report of November 24, 1934, which followed generally the recommendations of the Commission of Enquiry.

The Assembly set up a committee of five states—Argentina, Brazil, Chile, Peru and Uruguay—to achieve a settlement. The United States accepted an invitation to participate with this group. The Assembly yielded the field of action to the six states, assembled as the Chaco Peace Conference at Montevideo. This conference was under the auspices of the League, having been authorized by a special meeting of the Assembly. Paraguay withdrew from the League of Nations in February 1935.

Against the background of continued Paraguayan military success, the Chaco Peace Conference continued its work until a peace protocol between Paraguay and Bolivia was signed at Buenos Aires on June 12, 1935. This was the first big step toward peace, since demobilization of the contending armies and exchange of prisoners followed. Three years of difficult negotiations ensued before a territorial settlement was reached. The parties' original demands were so extreme as to seem irreconcilable, but changes of government in Bolivia, Paraguay, and Argentina brought new personnel and new bargaining positions to the conference table. On June 21, 1938, a treaty of peace, friendship, and boundaries was signed. This agreement provided for arbitration by the presidents of the six mediator republics. It was ratified on behalf of both parties, and the arbitral award was handed down in October. By the end of 1938, the military commission of the Chaco Peace Conference declared that each side's territory had been delivered in accordance with the award. Despite the doctrine of non-recognition of territorial gains made by force of arms, Paraguay had won the Chaco.

EVALUATION OF THE LEAGUE OF NATIONS COMMISSION

The unhappy experiences of the Commission of Investigation and Conciliation of the American States and the League Commission of Enquiry on the Chaco has prompted one writer to declare:

> Not only was the Chaco War not prevented by either the inter-American peace procedures or by the League of Nations, but it is probably true that the termination of the war was not hastened by any of the mediatory efforts indicated. Indeed, the efforts of the peace-makers seem to have contributed to the delay of the peace. At any rate, the war came to an end only when one of the belligerents had won its objectives and the other was too exhausted to

continue the struggle. To cap the sorry spectacle, the peace was concluded largely on the terms of the victor nation. Confidence in the inter–American security system descended to a new low.[29]

Such a sweeping condemnation is as unfair to the League of Nations Commission as it is to the Commission of Investigation and Conciliation.

As stated above, the League's Commission started inauspiciously, as the two contestants suggested that the commission step aside in favor of the ABCP powers, who were more familiar with the situation. Obviously this move rankled, for the commission in its final report wrote:

> It is essential that the system of interventions from many quarters should come to an end–that there should no longer be a doorway through which the parties can leave one procedure for another and experiment with a fresh formula when the negotiations take a turn unsatisfactory to them.[30]

The first point of this commission's experience is that the use of two jurisdictions without proper coordination renders peace efforts more difficult. The second point is that where a commission of inquiry has conciliation and fact-finding functions, the requirement to fix responsibility on one of the parties for alleged misconduct may impair the possibility of conciliation. The third lesson of the League Commission experience is identical with that of General McCoy's Commission: however sound the peace mechanism and competent the people in charge, the success of the mission hangs principally on the cooperation of the parties to the dispute.

2

THE HAITIAN–DOMINICAN REPUBLIC DISPUTE, 1937

In early October 1937, Dominican soldiers massacred hundreds or possibly thousands[1] of Haitian migratory laborers who were crossing the border in search of the seasonal cane-cutting work. The Haitian Government requested the Dominican Government to investigate. The Dominican

[29] John Lloyd Mecham, *The United States and Inter-American Security, 1889–1960* (Austin: The University of Texas Press, 1961), p. 159.
[30] League of Nations, *Monthly Summary*, XIV: 5, p. 105.
[1] Mecham, *op. cit.*, p. 175.

Government announced that it had begun an investigation to determine responsibility and apply appropriate penalties to those who were guilty.[2]

On November 12, 1937, the president of Haiti requested the presidents of Cuba, Mexico, and the United States to use their good offices to bring about a settlement. On December 14, following a series of conferences, the Government of Haiti invoked the Gondra Treaty[3] and the General Convention of Inter-American Conciliation. The Gondra Treaty required both parties to agree to use its provisions. In this case, the only case in which that treaty was ever used, the Dominican Government agreed, and both parties named their representatives.

The issue was whether the Government of the Dominican Republic bore any responsibility for the massacre of the Haitian laborers.

THE COMMISSION OF INQUIRY AND CONCILIATION

The records of the Commission of Inquiry and Conciliation are scanty, and the only terms of reference apparently were those contained in the treaties themselves. The General Convention of Inter-American Conciliation added the conciliation function to the investigation functions provided for by the Gondra Treaty.[4] The terms of reference laid down in Article 6 of the Conciliation Convention provide:

> It shall undertake a conscientious and impartial examination of the questions which are the subject of the controversy, shall set forth in a report the results of its proceedings, and shall propose to the Parties the bases of a settlement for the equitable solution of the controversy.

Both the Gondra Treaty and the Inter-American Conciliation Convention provided that each party would bear its own expenses and a proportionate share of the general expenses of the commission.

Under Article 3 of the General Convention, the two permanent commissions established at Washington and Montevideo under the Gondra Treaty could exercise conciliatory functions "either on their own motion when it appears there is a prospect of disturbance of peaceful relations, or at the request of a party to dispute." A term of six months is fixed for the conciliatory function unless extended by the parties to the jurisdiction.

[2] *Bulletin of the Pan American Union*, LXXII: 3 (March 1938), p. 152. Hereafter cited as PAU, *Bulletin* LXXII.

[3] Treaty to Avoid or Prevent Conflicts Between the American States, 1923.

[4] The text of the General Convention appears in *Treaties, Conventions, International Acts, Protocols, and Agreements Between the United States of America and Other Powers*, Vol. IV (Washington: Government Printing Office, 1938), pp. 4764–67. The Gondra Treaty is in the same volume, pp. 4691–95. For a history and analysis of the Gondra Treaty see Mecham, *op. cit.*, pp. 98–100.

The permanent commission at Washington under the Gondra Treaty consisted of the three Latin American diplomatic representatives longest accredited there. They were Dr. Adrían Recinos, Minister of Guatemala; Señor don Manuel de Freyre y Santander, Ambassador of Peru; and Dr. Felipe A. Espil, Ambassador of Argentina. They met on December 15, 1937. On December 27, the Government of the Dominican Republic appointed its representatives, Señor Andrés Pastoriza and Señor Manuel de Jesús Troncoso de la Concha. The Haitian representatives were M. Abel Legér, and the American, Hoffman Philip, a former U.S. Ambassador to Chile.

The commission reached agreement by the end of January 1938. While the Dominican Government accepted no official responsibility for the acts, it agreed to pay an indemnity of $750,000, one third to be paid in cash and the remainder in five annual installments of $100,000 each. It also agreed to continue judicial procedures to punish those guilty. It stated that, among its other objectives, it wished "to avoid the regrettable situation created by the return in mass to Haitian territory of persons of Haitian nationality who lived in Dominican territory." [5] In other words, it did not wish to lose its supply of cheap labor.

The initial sum of $250,000 paid was on February 28, 1938, but the first of the annual installments was not paid when due. The Dominican Government claimed that this was an accidental omission in its budget. By a compromise reached in February 1939, the Haitian Government settled for $275,000 in cash in place of the $500,000 balance paid in installments. This amount was paid. [6]

EVALUATION

It has been said that the nine treaties of the Inter-American System providing for direct negotiation, good offices, mediation, investigation, conciliation, and arbitration are primarily bilateral in character although they may be multilateral in form. These are to be distinguished from the Rio Defense Treaty, the OAS Charter, and the Inter-American Peace committee which are essentially collective.

> The distinction is that in the case of the former it is left primarily to the parties to the dispute to elect the procedure and to apply it, whereas in the latter category, and particularly in the case of the Organ of Consultation either in the form of Foreign Ministers or of the Council of the Organization, a community effort is involved. [7]

[5] PAU, *Bulletin* LXXII: 3, pp. 153–56.

[6] Ireland, *op. cit.*, p. 68.

[7] The Honorable William Sanders, Assistant Secretary-General of the OAS, "Trends and Developments of the OAS," address before the District of Columbia Political Science Association, Nov. 14, 1962.

In this case, with the interventions of the presidents of Cuba, Mexico, and the United States, something of a "community effort" is involved, beyond the literal scope of the treaty. The case illustrates the point that the prewar bilateral treaties and the multilateral treaties of an essentially bilateral character in the Inter-American System were of limited value as instruments for the peaceful settlement of international disputes. In contrast, the postwar inter-American peace-keeping machinery has demonstrated flexibility and adequacy to meet changing situations.

As a leading authority, Professor J. Lloyd Mecham has written, however: "It would be a great mistake . . . to predicate the efficacy of a security system . . . on the purely technical perfection of the peace machinery, for the machinery is merely the means to an end. The essential of the problem is the will of the member states to peace."[8]

In the prewar period, the terms "inquiry" or "investigation," are used loosely; they connote questions addressed to governments. Present-day use in the OAS usually involves on-the-spot investigations at the scene of alleged incidents, frequently with interrogation of witnesses and other first-hand methods of fact-finding.

3
———◆———

THE COSTA RICAN AND NICARAGUAN CASES, 1948–1949 AND 1955

Most of the small countries of the Caribbean area have been politically unstable since their independence. They are predominantly one-crop agricultural countries, illiteracy is widespread, and great numbers of the people exist under primitive conditions.

Shortly after World War II, some of the countries, after overthrowing their dictator rulers, began to develop democratic processes of government. Costa Rica was one of these. José Figueres led a successful revolution of pro-democratic forces against the government of conservatives supported by Communists. The conservative-Communist coalition had been aided by General Anastasio Somoza, who presided over the neighboring police state of Nicaragua. His regime was the target of frequent plots by political enemies living in exile. Many of the exiles were associated with the Caribbean

---

[8] Mecham, *op. cit.*, p. 76.

Legion, whose aim was to liberate Nicaragua, the Dominican Republic, and other countries. Anti-Figueres Costa Ricans had fled to Nicaragua, where they plotted their return to power.

There was little evidence of a vested interest of any world power in this situation. The United States was concerned because, for many decades, it had sought to promote political stability as a basis for economic growth, and it had supported the adoption of the Inter-American Treaty of Reciprocal Assistance (the Rio Treaty) by the American Republics as a measure of hemisphere defense. Both of the conflicts between Costa Rica and Nicaragua were brought before the OAS under that treaty, the 1948–1949 case being the first to be considered under it.

THE 1948–1949 CONFLICT

On December 11, 1948, the Costa Rican ambassador to the Organization of American States charged that the Government of Nicaragua was guilty of violating Article 6 of the Rio Treaty by supporting an invasion of Costa Rica. He requested the chairman to convoke the Council of the OAS to act as the Provisional Organ of Consultation under Article 12.[1]

The Council met on December 12 but adjourned for two days to study the problem. At that time, the Nicaraguan Government denied that it was involved in the hostilities and described the situation as an "internal conflict of Costa Rica." When the Council met on December 14, the Costa Rican ambassador again accused the Government of Nicaragua of having violated the territorial integrity of Costa Rica by aiding a conspiracy to overthrow the Costa Rican Government.

The Nicaraguan ambassador again rejected the charges and raised two significant points. His government opposed the application of the Rio Treaty to the present case because it was not one of "grave danger and undeniable emergency" for which the treaty's consultation system was intended. Furthermore, he accused the governments of Costa Rica and Guatemala of harboring bands of revolutionaries such as the Caribbean Legion, whose activities were a threat to the peace. The Nicaraguan Government therefore urged the Council, without establishing itself as a Provisional Organ of Consultation under the Rio Treaty, to appoint a committee of information to visit the scene and to study the facts and their antecedents.[2]

The Council decided that it could not investigate the situation without setting itself up as Provisional Organ of Consultation and that it could not

[1] Pan American Union, *Applications of the Inter-American Treaty of Reciprocal Assistance, 1948–1956* (Washington: Pan American Union, 1957), p. 19. Hereafter cited as PAU, *Applications.*

[2] PAU, *Applications,* p. 20.

do the latter without first convoking a meeting of the organ itself. It therefore passed a resolution which provided that a Meeting of Consultation of Ministers of Foreign Affairs, the date of which was not set, should be called to study the situation; to set itself up as Provisional Organ of Consultation; to appoint a committee to investigate on the spot the facts and their antecedents; and to request the cooperation of all the American governments and the Secretary General of the Organization of American States. [3]

Acting under authority of the resolution, the chairman, Ambassador Enrique V. Corominas of Argentina, appointed representatives of Brazil, Colombia, Mexico, Peru, and the United States to the investigating committee. The Government of Peru declined to permit its representatives to serve, as Costa Rica had not recognized Peru's recently established military government. The four other countries were represented by their ambassadors on the Council.

THE COMMITTEE OF INFORMATION

The basic terms of reference of the Committee of Information set forth in the resolution were: "to investigate on the spot the facts denounced and their antecedents." In informing the members of the committee of their appointment, however, Chairman Corominas expanded and interpreted the strict terms of reference. He referred to the establishment by the Council of an "Information and Study Committee" to examine the situation between the two countries, its causes and background, "and also," he added, "of those other situations related to such problems that might threaten the peace and security of the hemisphere." [4] This broadened the committee's terms of reference substantially, and it may be inferred that the inclusion of this language was not unrelated to the wishes of the Nicaraguan Government to bring into consideration bits of recent history which would tend to stress the internal political factors in Costa Rica responsible for the hostilities and to implicate President Figueres in the purposes of the Caribbean Legion.

The chairman went on to state (presumably on his own authority) that the Provisional Organ of Consultation thought the committee should meet without delay, appoint its chairman, and adopt the measures it deemed necessary for the performance of its duties, and that the committee might consider taking a technical staff to serve as advisers and consultants. The chairman of the Council added the important words: "It is understood that, after the committee has gathered the material required to reach its decision, it will provide the Organ of Consultation with its suggestions as

[3] For the operative paragraphs of resolution of Dec. 14, 1948, see PAU, *Applications*, p. 22.

[4] PAU, *Applications*, p. 22.

to the methods, proposals, or recommendations that it believes should be adopted, not only as a matter of necessity, but also as a matter of urgency." [5]

This strengthening of the committee's terms of reference proved to be important to its performance, as well as to other committees which followed it, and leaned heavily on the precedents set in this instance. The committee's position was further strengthened by the fact that both parties had supported the designation of a committee, and were therefore bound to cooperate with the mission.

The Committee of Information acted quickly. The resolution by the Council of the OAS to constitute itself a Provisional Organ of Consultation and appoint a fact-finding committee was taken on December 14; invitations to the four ambassadors were extended on December 15; and they, with their staffs, left Washington on December 16.

The four ambassadors and their advisers were: José María Bello, Brazil, General Gervasio Duncan, military adviser; Silvio Villegas, Colombia, General Francisco Tamayo, military adviser, Dr. Jaime López Mosquera, civil adviser; Paul C. Daniels, United States, Colonel T. Alfonso Sapia-Bosch, military adviser, W. Tapley Bennett, Jr., civil adviser; Luis Quintanilla, Mexico, Mr. Manuel González, civil adviser. Santiago Ortiz was secretary of the committee; Miguel Aranguren and Carlos E. Urrutia, assistants to the secretary; Hernane Tavares da Sa, representative of the Department of Information of the Pan American Union. [6]

Ambassador Luis Quintanilla of Mexico was elected chairman of the committee. He had represented Mexico in Washington and at other diplomatic posts, and was a recognized authority on Latin America, the OAS, and the United Nations. Paul C. Daniels, the U.S. member, had served for many years in Latin American affairs and was well-known in Central America.

The Committee of Information arrived in San José, Costa Rica, on December 17. The ambassadors visited their respective embassies, called on the president of Costa Rica and other officials, interrogated prisoners, and men allegedly associated with the Caribbean Legion. The investigations included a visit to the province of Guanacasta where most of the hostilities had taken place.

On December 20 the committee flew to Managua. The members of the committee visited their respective embassies there and called on the president and other Nicaraguan officials. After two days of investigation, the committee returned to Washington. It had spent five days in its investigations. It presented its report to the Provisional Organ of Consultation on December 24, 1948, the day after its return. The committee found that: (1) there was no doubt that the Nicaraguan Government had failed to prevent revolutionary activities organized in their country by Costa Ricans

---

[5] PAU, *Applications*, p. 23.
[6] PAU, *Applications*, p. 23.

against the Government of Costa Rica;[7] (2) after December 10, the Nicaraguan Government began to take measures to prevent the rebels from continuing to receive aid from Nicaragua; (3) there was no proof of participation by the armed forces of Nicaragua in the revolt, although some members of the Nicaraguan military might have given technical aid; (4) the committee knew of no contact between the armed forces of Nicaragua and Costa Rica; (5) according to certain Costa Ricans, the failure to carry out the amnesty measure led to the resort to desperate and violent measures by political adversaries of the Figueres government;[8] (6) for many months before the invasion, the Costa Rican Government gave material and moral help to the Caribbean Legion.

The same day, December 24, the Provisional Organ of Consultation approved the text of a resolution submitted by the Committee of Information which: (1) called on both governments to immediately abstain from any hostile act toward each other; (2) stated that the Nicaraguan Government should have taken adequate measures to prevent the development in Nicaragua of revolutionary activities against the Government of Costa Rica, and to prevent the departure from its territory of an expeditionary force against Costa Rica; (3) declared that the Costa Rican Government should take measures to rid its territories of groups organized on a military basis and conspiring against the security of Nicaragua and other republics.

The Council acting provisionally as the Organ of Consultation then requested both governments to "faithfully observe the principles and rules of non-intervention and solidarity contained in various inter-American instruments signed by them" and resolved to "continue in consultation" until positive assurances should be received from both governments that they would act accordingly.[9]

The Costa Rican minister of foreign affairs accepted the basic resolution on December 28, but expressed the hope that the Council acting provisionally as the Organ of Consultation would apply sanctions against Nicaragua and reserved the right so to petition. So far as that portion of the resolution specifying that Costa Rica should prevent groups from conspiring on its territory against the Government of Nicaragua, the note stated that this had already been done and invited verification by the Inter-American Commission of Military Experts.

The address by the Costa Rican ambassador to the Council that same day was not so cordial. He stated that the Government of Costa Rica did not acquiesce in the resolution and criticized it on the ground that it placed "responsibility on Nicaragua for events which have already taken place and prejudges Costa Rica for events that have not occurred and that the Government of Costa Rica has guaranteed will not occur."

[7] PAU, *Applications*, pp. 26–27.

[8] The reference is to an internal political amnesty declared by the victorious party in Costa Rica following the revolution of 1948.

[9] PAU, *Applications*, p. 28.

The Nicaraguan minister of foreign affairs in a simple note reasserted his government's innocence, expressed agreement with the resolutions of the Provisional Organ of Consultations and gave cordial assurances of further cooperation.[10]

THE INTER-AMERICAN COMMISSION OF MILITARY EXPERTS

The Council acting provisionally as the Organ of Consultation recognized that some observation procedure was needed to ensure that its recommendations were carried out. It therefore established an Inter-American Commission of Military Experts of five members, to go to Costa Rica and Nicaragua to aid in the effective fulfillment of the resolution. The military advisers nominated by the four members of the Committee of Information were named to the Military Commission, and Colonel Carlos M. Bobeda of Paraguay was added as a fifth member. Theirs was truly a "peace-observation" function.

As in the case of the original information committee, Chairman Corominas of the Council again interpreted and clarified the terms of reference of the Commission of Military Experts. He asked the commission to seek the faithful application by both Nicaragua and Costa Rica of the provisions of the Inter-American Convention on the Duties and Rights of States in the Event of Civil Strife,[11] which was binding on both governments. He dealt with the prevention of military movements aimed at overthrowing other governments, and stated that the commission should not only furnish information to the Provisional Organ concerning measures taken by both governments, but should "also help to apply the aforesaid measures."[12] The chairman of the Council said that both governments had given assurances of complete cooperation in the work of the Commission of Military Experts.

At this point, the political representatives in the Council, acting provisionally as the Organ of Consultation, worked with the parties to bring about a pact of amity which would terminate the controversy. The Commission of Military Experts went to Central America to observe, report on, and assist the governments of the two countries to adopt measures recommended by the Council in its resolution of December 24.

The first members of the commission arrived in San José on December 30, 1948. They carried out a similar program in each country. They obtained information on measures taken to prevent endangering the peace, visited border areas to observe the situation, and interviewed various groups.

[10] PAU, *Applications*, pp. 31–35.
[11] Adopted at the Sixth International Conference of American States, Havana, 1928.
[12] PAU, *Applications*, p. 30.

A resolution authorizing the governments of Costa Rica and Nicaragua to set up mixed commissions to deal with border control problems was adopted by the Provisional Organ of Consultation on January 26, 1949, but there is no record of a mixed commission being established.

At the end of January the Commission of Military Experts returned to Washington and submitted a report to the Council acting provisionally as the Organ of Consultation. The report indicated that the steps taken by both the Costa Rican and the Nicaraguan Governments had adequately complied with the Council's resolution of December 24, 1948.[13] The military experts pointed out, however, that although satisfactory measures had been adopted by each government, their effectiveness would depend on the spirit in which they were carried out. This was related to the political antagonism and distrust which continued to exist between the two governments. Therefore, the problem and its solution were basically within the political and not the military field.

The Council acting provisionally as the Organ of Consultation had, in fact, been attending to the political factors. A special committee consisting of representatives of El Salvador, Mexico, the United States, Costa Rica, and Nicaragua was appointed to draft a pact of amity to be signed by the two parties. This agreement pledged the two governments to abide by their obligations to refrain from intervention in each other's affairs, and to work out a further agreement for the effective application of the provisions of the Convention on the Duties and Rights of States in the Event of Civil Strife. The controversy was terminated by the signature of the pact of amity by the two parties in the presence of the Council on February 24, 1949.[14] A final resolution was adopted ending the activities of the Council as Provisional Organ of Consultation, and terminating the Inter-American Commission of Military Experts.

EVALUATION

An evaluation of this performance of the OAS must take into account that this was the first case under the Treaty of Rio de Janeiro, which had entered into force only eight days before the Costa Rican ambassador lodged his complaint with the chairman of the Council. The Council, therefore, had not only to deal with the facts in this case, but had to work out new procedures.

Despite the lack of precedent, the Council acted with speed, common sense, initiative, and vigor. The prompt appearance on the scene of the Committee of Information and the period of observation by the Military Commission appeared to have a calming effect on both sides.

[13] PAU, *Applications*, pp. 39–47.
[14] The text appears in PAU, *Applications*, pp. 48–51.

The Council set a precedent by constituting itself as a Provisional Organ of Consultation, and working out the system whereby the date for the Meeting of Consultation of the Ministers of Foreign Affairs was left open while the Council dealt with the problem provisionally in' the hope—which proved to be justified—that a Meeting of Ministers of Foreign Affairs would prove unnecessary. This important precedent has served well in several cases. However, the basic decision involved also created problems for the OAS in subsequent cases.

In this case, the OAS approached the problem essentially from the traditional Latin American standpoint of seeking a peaceful settlement rather than resorting to punitive or enforcement measures authorized in the treaty. The Council recognized in its basic resolution of December 14 that both parties had some legitimate complaint that should be taken into account. The report of the Committee of Information aimed at attributing blame to both parties as a basis for urging them to take steps necessary to restore peaceful relations between them. The final conclusion of the pact of amity would seem to justify this approach, even though the failure of the two governments properly to implement the pledges made in the pact resulted in a renewed outbreak of hostilities six years later.

The procedures and mechanisms adopted by the Council to deal with this case seem to have been flexible and adapted to the immediate situation. The terms of reference for both the Committee of Information and the Inter-American Commission of Military Experts were broad, leaving considerable discretion to the members. The fact that they performed their tasks satisfactorily is a testimony to the high caliber and good judgment of the individuals who were appointed to the two missions. The *ad hoc* nature of the missions also made it easy to abolish them as soon as the situation warranted, returning responsibility for the maintenance of peace to the two interested governments .It also limited the expense involved. The air transportation provided by the United States was helpful in this situation where the financial costs had not been provided for in advance.

THE 1955 CONFLICT

The second case between Costa Rica and Nicaragua was a repetition of the first, involving ideological differences between the two governments, plotting and counter-plotting of political exiles, and the personal animosities of the two heads of state, President José Figueres of Costa Rica and General Anastasio Somoza, the Nicaraguan dictator. Costa Rica charged in the OAS Council that the Government of Nicaragua was plotting to overthrow the Costa Rican Government, and in fact reported that its territory had been invaded by "military forces proceeding from abroad." Again the Council acted as Provisional Organ of Consultation and authorized the chairman of the Investigating Committee to make an on-the-spot investigation and report.

THE INVESTIGATING COMMITTEE

Representatives of Brazil, Ecuador, Mexico, Paraguay, and the United States served as members of the committee. As in the 1948–1949 case, Ambassador Luis Quintanilla of Mexico, who was familiar with the job to be done, was chairman. The Investigating Committee organized its own Committee of Military Experts, members of which were detailed by the governments represented on the committee. It initiated aerial reconnaissance.

A new element in the case was the Costa Rican request to the OAS Council for military aid. The committee reported that its observation planes had encountered rebel-piloted planes over Costa Rica, and stated further that Costa Rica did not have the aircraft or other arms necessary to defend itself. The Council adopted a resolution under which the United States expedited the sale of four P-51 combat planes to the Costa Rican Government. These planes gave Costa Rica control of its air space and turned the tide of military advantage in its favor. The United States Caribbean Defense Command gave essential support to the military observers. Close liaison was established between them, and supplies, services, and communications were made available to the committee.

The Council requested the Investigating Committee to prepare and put into effect, in consulation with the two governments involved, a plan for effective surveillance of the common frontier of the two countries. The committee had virtually established such a system of surveillance through its military observation posts and aerial surveillance. The committee also obtained agreement of the two governments to establish a security zone on both sides of the border from which troops of each government would be excluded except with permission of the OAS military observers. An air corridor was established which was to be patrolled by aircraft of the committee. The case was concluded on January 9, 1956, by the signing of a new bilateral agreement on political exiles.

EVALUATION

This case was one of the outstanding successes of the Inter-American collective security system. The Council acted promptly, vigorously, and effectively. The Investigating Committee deserves major credit for bringing the conflict to a successful close and laying the basis for a long-term settlement between the two countries. Two major innovations were the use of pacific observation flights and the institution of a security zone to prevent armed clashes between the forces of the two states. The case illustrates that the avoidance of detailed terms of reference, the appointment of competent and respected men, and their prompt arrival on the spot are important to success. The threat of sanctions was also a major factor in the success of the OAS in this case.

4

HAITIAN–DOMINICAN REPUBLIC DISPUTE, 1949

In February 1949, Haiti reported to the Council of the Organization of American States that "certain grave acts" had created a situation that could endanger the peace between Haiti and the Dominican Republic.[1] The "acts" referred to were the efforts of a former Haitian Army officer, Colonel Astrel Roland, who appeared to have obtained collaboration of certain Dominican officials in a plot to overthrow the Government of Haiti. The Haitian Government had requested the Dominican Government not to grant asylum to Colonel Roland. Nevertheless, the Colonel had reached the Dominican Republic.

On February 8, the Haitian note stated, Colonel Roland had made a radio broadcast in French that was considered insulting to the Haitian president. The Haitian Government had protested to the Dominican Government, but the offensive radio campaign had been resumed by Colonel Roland on February 10.

Following the statement by the Haitian ambassador, the representative of the Dominican Government replied that his government had not been previously informed of the serious charge brought against it.[2] He demanded proof of the alleged participation of the Dominican officials in a subversive plot, and he defended the right of the Dominican Republic to grant asylum to Colonel Roland. He contended that Colonel Roland was stating his private opinions over a private radio station. He complained that the Government of Haiti had called for the convocation of an Organ of Consultation without any effort at bilateral negotiations, and he argued that the Rio Treaty was not intended to be applied to such vague and questionable situations.

[1] PAU, *Applications*, pp. 61, 62.
[2] PAU, *Applications*, pp. 63–67.

The issue before the Council was two-fold: Did the facts alleged by the Haitian Government implicate the Government of the Dominican Republic in Colonel Roland's subversive activities? If so, did the situation affect "the inviolability or the integrity of the territory or the sovereignty or political independence" of Haiti and "endanger the peace of America" within the meaning of Article 6 of the Rio Treaty?

CONSIDERATION BY THE OAS COUNCIL

After hearing the representatives of the two countries on February 16, the Council adjourned for one week to consider the matter. There was considerable doubt that Haiti's case warranted invocation of the Rio Treaty and the calling of a Meeting of Foreign Ministers. There were suggestions that the Haitian complaint would more properly be considered by the Inter-American Peace Committee.[3] The Council met again on February 23, and the representatives of the two countries indicated their readiness to follow some procedure of peaceful settlement. The Council refused to convoke the Organ of Consultation and expressed the hope that good relations between Haiti and the Dominican Republic would be strengthened, and friendship between the two nations thus deepened.[4]

In the Haitian case, the Council displayed a commendable reluctance to throw the whole machinery of collective security into action in circumstances that did not clearly meet the requirements of Article 6 of the Rio Treaty. The Council was unwilling to become involved in an internal political dispute under the guise of an international controversy. The case demonstrated that, while any member of the OAS may bring charges against another member state under the Rio Treaty, the Council must determine whether the circumstances warrant recourse to the treaty, or whether the parties can be guided into the paths of peaceful settlement.

CONSIDERATION BY THE INTER-AMERICAN
PEACE COMMITTEE

Apparently following the suggestions made informally by various representatives of American states, the Haitian Government brought their complaint before the Inter-American Committee on Methods for the Peaceful Solution of Conflicts. It was considered by the committee on March 24, one month after the Council had decided to refrain from invoking the Rio Treaty.

[3] Minutes of the Meeting of the Council, Feb. 16, 1949, OAS Doc. C-a-18/49. (The committee was then known as the Inter-American Committee on Methods for the Peaceful Solution of Conflicts.)
[4] PAU, *Applications*, p. 63.

The records of the Peace Committee's deliberations are almost non-existent. The final report[5] on this case, however, indicates that the committee appointed a delegation of three members (Argentina, Mexico, and the United States) who went to Port-au-Prince and Ciudad Trujillo from May 29 to June 4. The delegation performed essentially a mediation, rather than a fact-finding, function. A joint declaration was signed by representatives of both governments and by members of the Peace Committee on June 9, 1949. The essence of the commitment undertaken by the two governments is in Article 2 which states: "That they do not and will not tolerate in their respective territories the activities of any individuals, groups, or parties, national or foreign, that have as their object the disturbance of the domestic peace of either of the two neighboring Republics or of any other friendly Nation."[6]

EVALUATION

The efforts of the Peace Committee, following Haiti's unsuccessful attempt to invoke the Rio Treaty smoothed over the immediate crisis between the two countries and resulted in an outward adherence to principles of international law as opposed to violent or subversive action. The case demonstrated the value of the Inter-American Peace Committee to handle less serious conflicts between states. It showed that the committee could influence the disputing parties through the personal visit of a delegation to the highest officials of the two governments. The calm established by the Peace Committee's action was of short duration, however, since the underlying causes of tension between the two countries remained unresolved.

5

CARIBBEAN CASES, 1949–1950

Tension between the Dominican Republic and Haiti was relaxed only temporarily by the efforts of the Inter-American Peace Committee. The general situation in the Caribbean continued to deteriorate in 1949 and 1950. At the heart of the problem were the subversive activities of political exiles

[5] "Segundo Informe de la Comisión Interamericana de Paz," in *Décima Conferencia Interamericana, Actas y Documentos*, Vol. II (Washington: Pan American Union, 1958).

[6] Inter-American Peace Committee, *Report to the Fifth Meeting of Consultation of Ministers of Foreign Affairs* (Washington: Pan American Union, 1959), Doc. 5, App. A, Part II, p. 33.

who sought the aid of other countries in the Caribbean area in overthrowing the governments from which they had fled. A growing clandestine
traffic in war-surplus arms was one manifestation of this situation.[1] The
most striking single event was probably the abortive attempt by an invasion
force to use illicitly obtained former U.S. military aircraft, originating from
Guatemala and the United States, to overthrow the Dominican Government. Only one of the planes reached its destination, where all fifteen
members of the expedition were either killed or captured.[2]

The politically, economically, and socially underdeveloped countries of
the Caribbean area presented in extreme form the basic political dichotomy
found throughout most of Latin America: a formal dedication to the
principles of representative democracy in theory and the widespread
departure from these principles in practice. In 1950, the Dominican
Republic was the epitome of the Latin American military dictatorship
which operated through a hollow façade of democratic procedure. Nicaragua, Honduras, and Venezuela were ruled by similar, if less absolute,
regimes. On the other hand, Cuba was, at the time, governed by a liberal
though corrupt government which professed its adherence to democracy.
In Guatemala, the administration of President Juan José Arevalo was
pressing forward with a program of economic and social reform that included a strong opposition to dictatorships. Costa Rica was also a democratic government following the successful revolution led by José Figueres.
Thus the Caribbean area was split between two international factions
based on bitterly conflicting political practices, the parties to each faction
seeing in the other's existence a constant threat to their political integrity.

CONSIDERATION BY THE INTER-AMERICAN
PEACE COMMITTEE

The United States proposed that the Inter-American Peace Committee
take an initiative[3] under its basic statute (Resolution XIV of the Second
Meeting of Foreign Ministers) "of keeping constant vigilance to insure
that States between which any dispute exists or arises . . . may solve it as
quickly as possible, and of suggesting . . . the measures and steps which
may be conducive to a settlement."[4] Other members of the committee

[1] Leonard Pomercy, "The International Trade and Traffic in Arms," U.S. Department of State, *Bulletin*, Vol. 22 (1950), p. 357.

[2] There is a discrepancy in available records as to whether one or two planes reached
Luperon. See Pomercy, *op. cit.*, which refers to two planes, and "United States Memorandum Submitted to the Inter-American Peace Committee," *ibid.*, Vol. 21 (1949),
p. 453, which mentions only one.

[3] Recollection of John C. Dreier, who was at that time alternate to Ambassador Paul
Daniels, U.S. member of the committee.

[4] *Reports on the Second Meeting of the Ministers of Foreign Affairs of the American Republics*
(Washington: Pan American Union, 1940), p. 34.

maintained that it could only act on the request of an American government. The issue was evaded by having it recorded that the committee took up consideration of the problem at the request of the United States. Even so, Mexico and Argentina were doubtful whether the committee could consider a general situation not involving a specific dispute between states. [5]

The committee on August 3, 1949 requested information or suggestions that the governments on the Council of the OAS wished to offer "for the better understanding of the situation." Eight governments sent observations and information to the committee, [6] of which only the United States text is available. [7]

Secretary of State Dean Acheson described the situation prevailing in the Caribbean as "repugnant to the entire fabric of the Inter-American System" and stated that the United States would be derelict in its duty if it did not "condemn it in strongest terms." The Secretary then declared, "Aggression or plotting against any nation of this hemisphere is of concern to us. . . . We shall use our strongest efforts, in keeping with our international commitments, to oppose it and to defend the peace of the hemisphere." [8]

The Peace Committee made no effort to conduct field investigations. However, after considering the replies received from the various governments, it issued a report stating that it believed its duty was "limited to the solemn reaffirmation of certain standards and principles that are basic for American peace and solidarity." It set forth fourteen generalized points emphasizing the importance of nonintervention, and the complete ratification and strict enforcement of various treaties incorporating this rule.

If there had been any hope that the gentle reminders by the Peace Committee or the warnings of the Secretary of State of the obligations of the American republics to settle disputes peacefully and avoid intervention in each other's affairs would have any beneficial effect, such hopes were short-lived. The situation in the Caribbean continued in turmoil and the peace-observation efforts of the Peace Committee were transferred to the Council of the OAS under the Treaty of Rio de Janeiro.

EVALUATION

The willingness of governments to use the Peace Committee, an essential element in whatever success it has enjoyed, [9] was lacking in this case, which

---

[5] Inter-American Peace Committee, *Report to the Fifth Meeting of Consultation of Ministers of Foreign Affairs* (Washington: Pan American Union, 1959), pp. 16–17.

[6] Costa Rica, Cuba, Dominican Republic, Guatemala, Haiti, Nicaragua, United States, Venezuela.

[7] U.S. Department of State, *Bulletin*, Vol. 21 (1949), p. 453.

[8] *Ibid.*, p. 463.

[9] *Ibid.*, p. 990.

the United States rather than a party involved had initiated. Mere consideration of the problem by the committee in Washington and the enunciation of generalities was all that the committee felt it was authorized to do. Its efforts were ineffective. The initiative of the United States was a praiseworthy attempt to get the multilateral machinery of the OAS to take up an obviously threatening situation before it became violent. The result demonstrated, however, that the Peace Committee, in the absence of a specific case submitted by the parties and lacking any powers of investigation, could not be expected to fill such a role.

CONSIDERATION UNDER THE TREATY OF RIO DE JANEIRO

On January 3, 1950, the Haitian ambassador to the OAS asked the Council to convoke the Organ of Consultation immediately under Articles 6 and 8 of the Treaty of Rio de Janeiro to adopt security and defense measures against the threat to the peace by the Dominican Republic. According to the Haitian note, the Dominican Government had violated the joint declaration signed before the Peace Committee on June 9, 1949. It had permitted Colonel Astrel Roland to resume his subversive activities and had also plotted to assassinate Haitian officials and use the resulting chaos to cover an invasion of Haiti by Dominican forces under Trujillo's new war powers. Since these plans affected the inviolability of the territory, the sovereignty, and the political independence of Haiti, application of the Rio Treaty was justified. However, if the Council was not convinced of this, the Haitian Government requested that a Meeting of Consultation of Ministers of Foreign Affairs be called under Articles 39 and 40 of the Charter of the OAS.[10]

The Council met on January 6 and heard a further statement from the Haitian ambassador and a reply from the representative of the Dominican Republic. The latter rejected the Haitian charges and asked that the Organ of Consultation be convoked under the Rio Treaty to consider a series of plots and threats aimed at overthrowing the Dominican Government. These, he said, had been hatched with the connivance of the governments of Cuba, Guatemala, Haiti, and Venezuela.

The Council decided that sufficient evidence had been presented to warrant the action requested. The Council constituted itself provisionally as the Organ of Consultation and established a committee to conduct an on-the-spot investigation. The committee was composed of the five OAS Council representatives, Bolivia, Colombia, Ecuador, United States, and

[10] PAU, *Applications*, pp. 71–74.

Uruguay.[11] Their powers and attributes were fixed by the Organ of Consultation. The membership of the committee reflected the general criteria of geographical distribution, impartiality, and size of states. Notable is the absence of any of the small states of the Central American and Caribbean area, a fact attributable to the widespread tendency of all states in the area to align themselves with either the pro- or anti-dictatorial factions.

The terms of reference were spelled out in detail, in contrast to the vague terms given to the Information Committee in the Costa Rica-Nicaragua case in 1949. The Council authorized the committee to investigate the facts and their antecedents referred to in the Haitian and Dominican notes of January 3 and 6 respectively; authorized it to hear witnesses, take depositions, and avail itself of any other sources of information it considered pertinent; directed it to hold meetings in Washington to hear representatives of the parties and other witnesses; authorized it to decide on its own itinerary for travel, "giving prior notice thereof to the respective governments"; and instructed the committee to prepare reports covering both the facts and conclusions developed in its investigations. Meetings of the committee were to be private. The committee was also authorized to elect its chairman and establish its procedures. The expenses of members of the committee (but not their advisers) were to be paid by the Pan American Union, which also provided a secretariat.[12]

The committee investigated from January 12 to March 13, starting in Washington and continuing in the Caribbean area. It obtained testimony principally from officials of the governments concerned, including the former chargé d'affaires of the Dominican Embassy in Port-au-Prince who had been personally involved in some of the plotting. In Haiti, the Dominican Republic, Cuba, and Guatemala, the committee interviewed not only officials of the respective governments but a number of exiles, prisoners, and other individuals implicated in the incidents and plots to which the two notes referred. From February 15 to March 13, when they returned to Washington, the committee analyzed the evidence they had assembled and prepared a detailed report of the facts uncovered and conclusions reached. The report constitutes a thorough and convincing exposition of the web of plots and counterplots, of propaganda campaigns, of illicit arms traffic, of the organization of revolutionary expeditions, and of the involvement of government officials in virtually all of these activities.[13]

The committee found that the Dominican Government had violated the provisions of the joint declaration of June 9, 1949; that certain Dominican officials, including one person known to be close to Generalissimo Trujillo, not only tolerated, but aided, the conspiracy organized by Colonel Roland to overthrow the Haitian Government.[14]

[11] PAU, *Applications*, pp. 81–82.
[12] PAU, *Applications*, pp. 85–86.
[13] PAU, *Applications*, pp. 87–123.
[14] PAU, *Applications*, p. 109.

On the subject of the complaints of the Dominican Government against Haiti, Cuba, and Guatemala, the committee found that the Haitian Government had not been involved in anti-Dominican plots. It found, however, that both Cuban and Guatemalan officials had participated in plots against the Dominican Government.[15]

The committee then considered the underlying tensions in the Caribbean: the limitations of the Havana Convention of 1928 on the Duties and Rights of States in the Event of Civil Strife, which established certain obligations directly related to the problems under consideration; the increased number of political exiles whose activities lay at the center of the international troubles; the lack of effective democracy in some countries; the excessive armaments acquired by certain governments; and the need for a continuing committee of the Organ of Consultation to assure the fulfillment of its recommendations by the governments concerned. Such a Special Committee of five members was established by the Council.[16]

After considering the Investigating Committee's report, the Council, acting provisionally as the Organ of Consultation, adopted five resolutions proposed by the committee. Resolutions I and II declared that the actions of the Dominican Government in one case and the Cuban and Guatemalan Governments in the other were contrary to principles of the Inter-American System. The governments were urged to take steps to assure that these principles were henceforth observed.[17] Other resolutions called for studies by the OAS of measures to stimulate the effective exercise of democracy, to strengthen the Havana Convention of 1928 and to improve the regimen controlling the activities of political exiles.[18]

As its final act on April 8, the Council terminated its action as Provisional Organ of Consultation, canceling the convocation of the Meeting of Foreign Ministers and leaving the matter in the hands of its Special Committee.[19] No effort was made to punish the delinquent governments beyond administering a verbal admonition in politely worded resolutions. In fact, the resolutions of the Council abound with exhortations urging the several governments involved in the dispute to make every effort to re-establish not only formal but friendly relations on the basis of stricter common adherence to the principles and obligations of the OAS.

[15] PAU, *Applications*, pp. 111, 115.

[16] PAU, *Applications*, pp. 121–23, 128. The same five members who had constituted the Investigating Committee were appointed to the new body which took the name of the Special Committee for the Caribbean.

[17] These steps principally concerned the prevention of interventionist activities within their territories, the avoidance of systematic and hostile propaganda directed against other governments, and the solution of various specific points of controversy by bilateral negotiations.

[18] PAU, *Applications*, pp. 124–30.

[19] PAU, *Applications*, p. 135.

WORK OF THE SPECIAL COMMITTEE FOR THE CARIBBEAN

The Special Committee was established by the Council acting provisionally as the Organ of Consultation, a body which was considered juridically distinct from the Council exercising its normal functions under the Charter of the OAS. The Council formally terminated its action in this capacity and reverted to its normal position, in which it could no longer take cognizance of political disputes. Yet the Special Committee continued in existence, even though its parent body had disappeared, and was authorized to consider important political questions that were beyond the competence of the Council itself. It was for this reason that the committee was instructed to report not to the Council but to the governments through the General Secretariat of the OAS. This anomaly has a bearing on certain later situations that confronted the OAS when there was need for important follow-up work to observe and report on compliance with decisions of the Organ of Consultation.

Between April 1950 and May 1951, the Special Committee held meetings with the parties to the controversies, received reports and statements from the governments involved, and submitted three reports to the governments of the Organization of American States. The reports stated that several governments had initiated measures that had helped to establish good will among the countries concerned; relations among the countries of the Caribbean had improved;[20] in regard to the Haitian-Dominican case, diplomatic relations had been re-established and the two chiefs of state had agreed to work out measures to regulate the political, economic, and social relations between the two countries. In regard to the case involving the Dominican Republic, Cuba, and Guatemala, the governments had taken additional steps in accordance with the recommendations of the Organ of Consultation.

EVALUATION

In this second case under the Rio Treaty, the OAS again acted with promptness and vigor. It acted more effectively in the immediate issue of investigating and airing the charges and countercharges that had built up emotional tensions threatening war than in the deeper, underlying causes of the tensions between governments of differing political complexion. The uncovering and publishing of information concerning the widespread extra-legal activities by virtually all governments concerned, and the frank assignment of blame, had the effect of deflating the whole movement of political subversion on both sides.

[20] PAU, *Applications*, p. 145.

A progressive improvement in the situation began to take place almost as soon as the OAS had taken cognizance of the two complaints. This development may be laid to the following factors: (1) two conflicting states felt themselves victims of indirect aggression, and both saw in the OAS an instrument that would be useful in bringing such activities to an end; (2) the OAS under the Rio Treaty had the power to send an investigating committee into troubled areas; (3) behind the always courteous and formal recognition of national sovereignty lay the power of the OAS to resort to the sanctions of the treaty; and (4) the consequent calming effect of the "presence" of an OAS committee in the troubled areas. Also important was the OAS policy of promoting the restoration of friendly relations rather than meting out punishment. The high qualifications of the individuals who composed the Investigating Committee enabled it to do an excellent job. The Special Committee established by the Council further promoted the compliance of the governments involved with the recommendations of the Organ of Consultation. A somewhat less successful performance was registered by the OAS with respect to resolving the underlying problems responsible for the immediate conflicts. Here, too, credit must be given for progress made.

The basic problem of political instability and the inevitable international conflicts which arise in connection with the existence of dictatorial governments in Latin America remain unresolved. Nothing of tangible value resulted from the studies initiated under the resolutions of April 8, 1950, on how to promote democracy in Latin America without violating the principle of nonintervention. Yet, as a result of the recommendations of the Organ of Consultation, the Havana Convention of 1928 was strengthened by the approval of a protocol in 1957. The system for controlling the activities of political exiles was also greatly improved by the adoption at the Tenth Inter-American Conference (1954) of two new conventions on the subject.

6

SITUATION IN GUATEMALA, 1954

Guatemala, the second largest and most populous of the coffee and banana producing countries of Central America, is an underdeveloped country. Its three million people are predominantly Indian; poverty, disease, and illiteracy are widespread. The wealthy upper class is very small, their wealth consisting mainly of land held in large estates. Government, since the overthrow of Spanish rule in 1823, has usually meant the rule of one personal leader, or *caudillo*, after another. The last such *caudillo* was General Jorge Ubico, whose dictatorial rule lasted from 1931 to 1944. While coffee is the most important single product, economic activity in Guatemala was long dominated by the United Fruit Company.[1]

With the overthrow of the Ubico dictatorship and the inauguration in 1945 of Juan José Arévalo as president, a period of fundamental social revolution began in Guatemala. Arévalo "abolished forced labor and promulgated an advanced Labor Code, laid plans for the breakup of large landholdings, created a Social Security institute, reorganized the army in the direction of less authoritarianism, made several educational improvements, and under his stimulus the Indians began to participate in government."[2] This program led him into conflict with established interests, including United States businesses. Misunderstanding in neighboring states also developed over his tolerance of Communists in government posts.

His successor, Colonel Jacobo Arbenz, carried the program of social revolution further. The most controversial measure of his administration was the Agrarian Reform Law of 1952 under which large tracts belonging to the United Fruit Company were expropriated. Confiscatory measures of doubtful legality were also taken against the railway system, which was largely owned by outside interests.[3] Moreover, Communist influence in the government grew until members of the legalized Communist party and their fellow travelers, despite their small number in proportion to the total population and their few official positions, virtually dominated governmental policy in several strategic areas, including foreign affairs.[4]

The growing use of Guatemala as a base for Communist subversion in Central America increasingly concerned the United States and Guatemala's neighbors. Guatemalan envoys to other Latin American countries disseminated propaganda, inspired labor disturbances, and encouraged revolutionary groups.[5]

Although the United States Government sought to protect its citizens and private interests from arbitrary and confiscatory seizure of property without adequate compensation, its principal worry was the growing Communist

---

[1] For a study of economic development and Communist policy in Guatemala, see: Theodore Geiger, *Communism vs. Progress in Guatemala*, Planning Pamphlet No. 85 (Washington: National Planning Association, 1953).

[2] Lewis Hanke, *Mexico and the Caribbean* (Princeton: D. Van Nostrand, 1959), p. 16.

[3] John D. Martz, *Central America: the Crisis and the Challenge* (Chapel Hill: University of North Carolina Press, 1959), pp. 49–50.

[4] Ronald M. Schneider, *Communism in Guatemala, 1944–1954* (New York: Praeger, 1959), Chap. 8, *passim*, and pp. 294–96.

[5] *Communist Aggression in Latin America*, Hearings before the Sub-committee on Latin America of the Select Committee on Communist Aggression, 83 Cong., 2 sess. (1954). (Hereafter cited as *Communist Aggression*, Hearings.) See also: Schneider, *op. cit.*, pp. 297–98.

influence in this Central American state.[6] The Guatemalan Government rejected the charges of Communist influence, describing them as merely a smoke-screen for the opposition of the United States to all social change and its desire to protect entrenched economic interests.

Against this background, the Tenth Inter-American Conference met at Caracas in March 1954. Secretary of State John Foster Dulles led the campaign to obtain an anti-Communist resolution from that conference. Despite intense opposition from the Guatemalan delegation and reluctance on the part of two other delegations, a resolution was adopted 17 to 1, with Guatemala opposing and Argentina and Mexico abstaining:

> That the domination or control of the political institutions of any American State by the international communist movement, extending to this Hemisphere the political system of an extra-continental power, would constitute a threat to the sovereignty and political independence of the American States, endangering the peace of America, and would call for a Meeting of Consultation to consider the adoption of appropriate action in accordance with existing treaties.[7]

The general assumption was that the Caracas resolution was aimed specifically at Guatemala, but no action was taken pursuant to it in the OAS. A number of the Latin American governments continued to dismiss the Communist threat to hemisphere security as unimportant. Then on May 15, 1954, a shipment of 15,000 cases of Czech arms arrived in Puerto Barrios, Guatemala, aboard a Swedish steamship, the Alfhem, coming from Stettin, Poland. The four Central American governments of El Salvador, Honduras, Nicaragua, and Costa Rica requested the U.S. State Department to participate in joint measures against the introduction of further arms into the area.[8] The United States responded by entering into special military and arms agreements with Honduras and Nicaragua[9] and pressed discussions with other Latin American governments regarding possible action through the OAS.

Opposition to the Arbenz regime both in and outside of Guatemala began to intensify. The secret police of Guatemala launched a campaign of terror, with arrests, imprisonment, torture, and murder of opposition leaders. Outside the country, opposition groups began to coalesce around Colonel Castillo Armas who set up his headquarters in neighboring Hónduras and openly proclaimed his intention of leading a revolutionary

---

[6] See, for example, Assistant Secretary of State John M. Cabot, "Inter-American Cooperation and Hemisphere Solidarity," U.S. Department of State, *Bulletin*, Vol. 29 (1953), pp. 555–56; and Secretary of State John Foster Dulles, "International Unity," *ibid.*, Vol. 30 (1954), pp. 938–39.

[7] Tenth Inter-American Conference, Resolution XCIII, *Final Act* (Caracas: Ministry of Foreign Affairs of the Republic of Venezuela, 1957), p. 121.

[8] Testimony of Ambassador John E. Peurifoy, *Communist Aggression*, Hearings, p. 120.

[9] Mecham, *op. cit.*, p. 446.

movement. By early June, it was clear that an international conflict was in the making.[10] On June 18, Castillo Armas moved across the border with a few hundred men.

GUATEMALAN APPEAL TO UN SECURITY COUNCIL AND THE INTER-AMERICAN PEACE COMMITTEE

On June 19, 1954, the Guatemalan minister of foreign affairs, Guillermo Toriello, asked the Security Council "to take the measures necessary to prevent the disruption of peace and international security in this part of Central America and also to put a stop to the aggression in progress against Guatemala."[11] He complained of repeated dropping of propaganda and arms in Guatemala by aircraft from Honduras and Nicaragua. Moreover, despite protests to the Government of Honduras, an expeditionary force from Honduras had captured the Guatemalan frontier port of El Florido and advanced about fifteen kilometers into Guatemalan territory. He charged the United States with false reports about recent arms acquisitions by Guatemala and with a policy of encircling and boycotting Guatemala. He said the facts cited proved that aggression had been perpetrated by the Governments of Honduras and Nicaragua "at the instigation of certain foreign monopolies whose interests have been affected by the progressive policies of my Government." There is no doubt that by "foreign monopolies" the foreign minister meant U.S. business interests, in particular, the United Fruit Company. The item was placed on the provisional agenda of the Security Council for discussion on June 20, and representatives of Guatemala, Honduras, and Nicaragua were invited to take part.

Guatemala also appealed to the chairman of the Inter-American Peace Committee, Ambassador Luis Quintanilla, on June 19, "to avert a threat to the peace of the American continent." It alleged violations by the governments of Nicaragua and Honduras of the principle of nonintervention and of the sovereignty of Guatemala.[12]

The Inter-American Peace Committee transmitted copies of the Guatemalan note to the ambassadors of Honduras and Nicaragua. By midnight June 19, Chairman Quintanilla received an urgent telephone call from Toriello requesting the Inter-American Peace Committee to depart for Guatemala the next morning, or at the latest on the 21st. The request was suspended and then canceled as the case had been submitted to the Security Council, which was taking cognizance of the Guatemalan complaint.[13]

[10] Schneider, *op. cit.*, pp. 305–11.
[11] UN Security Council, *Official Records*, Ninth Year, Supplement for April, May, and June 1954, S/3232.
[12] Inter-American Peace Committee, *Report to the Fifth Meeting of Consultation of Ministers of Foreign Affairs* (Washington: Pan American Union, 1959), p. 57. Hereafter cited as IAPC, *Fifth Meeting*.
[13] IAPC, *Fifth Meeting*, p. 58.

Guatemala did not bring its case before the OAS under the Treaty of Rio de Janeiro as might have been expected. It may have felt that political pressures by the opponents, particularly the United States, would render such an appeal unavailing. However, the OAS would have given Guatemala an inter-American platform from which to appeal for sympathy and to arouse public opinion in the other Latin American countries. Guatemala's failure to do so may be attributed to two factors: (1) it might have weakened its appeal to the Security Council (which Guatemala obviously preferred because of the Soviet Union's presence) on jurisdictional grounds, which in fact proved to be its undoing; (2) Guatemala was technically not a party to the Treaty of Rio, since its ratification had not yet been deposited.[14] Foreign Minister Toriello subsequently cited this fact as having legally prevented Guatemala from appealing to the OAS.[15] Consideration of the Guatemalan problem in the OAS under the Rio Treaty came later at the initiative of other countries, and for a different purpose.

Discussion in the Security Council, June 20

In his argument before the Security Council on June 20, the Guatemalan representative repeated his country's charges against the United Fruit Company, the United States, Honduras, and Nicaragua and made two requests: (1) that an observation commission be sent to Guatemala to investigate, and on the basis of its report, the Council should call on Honduras and Nicaragua to apprehend the exiles and mercenaries who were invading Guatemala and whose bases were in Nicaragua and Honduras; (2) that "an observation commission of the Council be constituted in Guatemala, and in other countries if necessary, to verify the fact that the countries accused by Guatemala had connived at the invasion."[16] He concluded by declaring that the Guatemalan Government declined to allow the OAS and the Inter-American Peace Committee to concern themselves with the situation.

The representatives of Honduras and Nicaragua urged that the matter be settled in the OAS. The Brazilian and Colombian members of the Security Council introduced a resolution[17] referring the Guatemalan complaint to the OAS and prepared an additional paragraph to the proposed resolution, calling for the immediate cessation of bloodshed.

[14] Guatemala had ratified the Rio Treaty with a reservation regarding its claims to British Honduras. This reservation was, according to inter-American legal procedures, submitted to the other ratifying parties, who did not accept it. Guatemala then withdrew its instrument of ratification.

[15] Guillermo Toriello, *La Batalla de Guatemala* (Santiago de Chile, Editorial Universitaria, S.A., 1955), pp. 116–17.

[16] UN General Assembly, *Official Records*, Ninth Session, Supplement No. 2, A/2712, p. 49. Hereafter cited as A/2712.

[17] UN Secretary Council, S/3236 Rev. 1, June 20, 1954.

When the New Zealand representative urged referral to the OAS, the Guatemalan representative stated the position of Guatemala on jurisdiction. He asserted that Article 33 of the UN Charter, requiring parties to a dispute first to seek solution by peaceful means, and Article 52 on regional arrangements were inapplicable. Guatemala had no dispute with any nation. What was involved was aggression, hence Articles 34, 35, and 39 governed and gave his government an unchallenged right to appeal to the Security Council.

A debate on the issue took place between Soviet Ambassador Tsarapkin and U.S. Ambassador Lodge. The Soviet delegate stated that there was a clear case of aggression against Guatemala by neighboring states. Guatemala, which could be crossed in a day's march, might well be overcome while the case was being considered in the OAS, an organization under the domination of the United States.[18]

Ambassador Lodge replied that the case should first be handled by the OAS, as originally requested by Guatemala. "The information available to the United States strongly suggested that the situation did not involve aggression, but a revolt of Guatemalans by Guatemalans." He characterized the allegation of armed intervention as "an unspeakable libel" and "flatly untrue."

The issue was clear: should the Council approve the draft Brazilian-Colombian resolution referring the case to the OAS? The vote was 10 in favor and 1 against. The resolution thus failed to be approved because of Russia's sixtieth veto. A French amendment calling for immediate cessation of bloodshed was passed unanimously as a separate resolution.

The upshot of the Security Council's consideration was inaction on the Guatemalan request for the dispatch of an investigative mission and an implied policy of permitting the OAS to exercise initial jurisdiction over an inter-American dispute. The Security Council took up the Guatemalan case once more on July 25, but in the meantime the spotlight had shifted to the Inter-American Peace Committee.

Action of the Inter-American Peace Committee

On June 22, 1954, the day after the Government of Guatemala canceled its initial request for an investigation by the Inter-American Peace Committee, the Honduran ambassador at Washington sent a note to the chairman stating his government's belief that, although Guatemala had withdrawn its complaint against Honduras, "it is absolutely necessary to define responsibilities in a conflict in which continental peace is being disturbed."[19]

A meeting was held on June 23 to hear the proposal of the Nicaraguan ambassador, seconded by the Honduran ambassador, that a special fact-finding subcommittee be designated to visit Guatemala, Honduras, and

[18] A/2712, p. 50.
[19] IAPC, *Fifth Meeting*, p. 60.

Nicaragua immediately. The Peace Committee asked the Guatemalan Government, in effect, whether it would be welcome.

The Guatemalan Government first declined to have the Inter-American Peace Committee intervene,[20] but on June 26 stated that since the Security Council "has postponed consideration of the aforesaid case until it should receive a report from the Inter-American Peace Committee the Government of Guatemala . . . places at the disposal of the Inter-American Peace Committee and of the Subcommittee of Information that it appoints, all the facilities within its power."[21]

On June 27, the chairman of the Peace Committee informed the Guatemalan chargé that the Inter-American Peace Committee would set itself up as a Subcommittee of Information. It would depart June 28 and remain three days each in Guatemala, Honduras, and Nicaragua. The committee consisted of Ambassador Luis Quintanilla of Mexico (chairman), Ambassador Gonzalo Güell of Cuba, Ambassador Fernando Lobo of Brazil, Ambassador José Carlos Vittone of Argentina, and Ambassador Paul C. Daniels of the United States. All were accompanied by staff, generally including a military adviser.

The Arbenz government was ousted on June 27 and 28, and the committee delayed its departure. On June 30, the new ruling junta in Guatemala requested the committee to refrain from intervening in the situation. On July 2, after consulting the authorities of all three governments, the committee announced that the controversy between them had ceased to exist.[22] Thus ended the Inter-American Peace Committee's efforts.

UN Security Council Meeting, June 25

On June 25, two days before the overthrow of Colonel Arbenz, and while the Peace Committee was still corresponding with Guatemala, the UN Security Council held the second of its two meetings on the Guatemalan complaint. It was convened at the request of the Soviet and Guatemalan representatives. The issue was whether the Security Council would adopt the provisional agenda including the case of Guatemala.

The Brazilian representative opposed the adoption of the agenda and stated that he had unofficial information that the Guatemalan Government had withdrawn its prior objections and would now receive the Inter-American Peace Committee.[23]

The Soviet representative demanded that the Guatemalan representative be invited to attend the meeting even before the agenda was adopted. His challenge was rejected by a vote of 10 to 1. The Colombian delegate

[20] IAPC, *Fifth Meeting*, p. 62.
[21] IAPC, *Fifth Meeting*, p. 63.
[22] IAPC, *Fifth Meeting*, p. 69–70.
[23] A/2712, p. 51.

supported the Brazilian position. The British and French delegates agreed that the OAS initiative should be allowed to proceed, but abstained on the narrow issue. In the final vote, the motion to adopt the agenda was defeated 5 to 4 with 2 abstentions. Voting for were Denmark, Lebanon, New Zealand, and the U.S.S.R. Voting against, and hence in effect leaving the case in the hands of the OAS, were the United States, Brazil, China, Colombia, and Turkey. The United Kingdom and France abstained. Here, six days after its first appeal, ended the Guatemalan Government's effort to have its complaint dealt with in the Security Council, where it had a powerful Russian friend with a veto.

CONSIDERATION IN THE COUNCIL OF THE OAS

Since the delivery of Czech arms to Guatemala, various Latin American countries and the United States had been discussing possible OAS measures to cope with the growing Communist influence in Guatemala and neighboring countries. It was not until mid-1954, however, that negotiations reached the point of an agreement among a substantial number of countries to convoke a Meeting of Foreign Ministers to serve as the Organ of Consultation under the Rio Treaty. On June 26, representatives of ten countries[24] requested the Council of the OAS to convoke a Meeting of Consultation under Articles 6 and 11 of the Rio Treaty to consider "a situation which they believe endangers the peace of America and affects the sovereignty and political independence of the American States," and which had risen from the "demonstrated intervention of the international communist movement in the Republic of Guatemala."[25]

The Council met to consider the request on June 28, the day that the Peace Committee set off on its abortive trip to Central America and the day after the first of the changes had taken place in the Government of Guatemala that ultimately replaced Arbenz with Castillo Armas. No Guatemalan representative attended the Council's meeting, probably due to the confused situation within that government. The representatives of Ecuador and Uruguay led a fight to amend the ten-power proposal by shifting the emphasis from "the intervention of international communism in Guatemala" to the "situation created by the recent events in Guatemala," with attention to the expected report of the Inter-American Peace Committee.[26] These efforts failed, however, and the Council adopted a resolution convoking the Organ of Consultation "for the purpose of considering all aspects of the danger to the peace and security of the

[24] Brazil, Costa Rica, Cuba, Dominican Republic, Haiti, Honduras, Nicaragua, Panama, Peru, and the United States.

[25] PAU, *Applications*, pp. 151–52.

[26] Minutes of Meeting of OAS Council, June 28, 1954, OAS Doc. C-a-153 Corr.

continent resulting from the penetration of the political institutions of Guatemala by the international communist movement, and the measures which it is desirable to take."[27] The meeting was set for July 7 at Rio de Janeiro.

Meanwhile, events were moving swiftly inside Guatemala, and the Council met again on July 2 to review the situation. The chairman announced that the president of El Salvador had informed him that Lieutenant Colonel Elfego Monzón, president of the military junta of Guatemala, and Colonel Castillo Armas had agreed to establish a provisional government in Guatemala, and that hostilities in that country had been brought to an end. With the main reason for its concern with the Guatemalan situation eliminated by the victory of the Castillo Armas forces, the Council voted to postpone *sine die* the Meeting of Consultation convoked on June 28.[28] This terminated the action of the OAS under the Rio Treaty with regard to the Guatemalan Communist threat.

EVALUATION

The significance of the Guatemalan situation of 1954 is that no peace observation was carried out by any international organization, despite the fact that the situation was of a kind that called for such action and that initiatives were taken in three international bodies[29] to get activities under way. The factors responsible for this confusion and inertia were organizational, procedural, and political.

From the procedural and organizational viewpoint, while the fact that Guatemala was not a party to the Rio Treaty may have limited its ability to turn to the most appropriate OAS body, the Organ of Consultation under that treaty, there is convincing evidence that the controlling factor was its conviction that the United Nations was a better forum for its case, and that this position hardened as the matter unfolded. Guatemala may have had a legitimate concern in having recourse to the Peace Committee, as the only regional body available, but its initial vacillation between concentrating on the UN or obtaining the concurrent intervention of the Peace Committee made it difficult for either to act vigorously. Moreover, it should be pointed out that the Peace Committee was not the only regional agency available to Guatemala. It could have invoked Article 39 of the

---

[27] PAU, *Applications*, p. 153.

[28] PAU, *Applications*, pp. 154–55.

[29] The reference is to Guatemala's appeal to the UN Security Council and the Inter-American Peace Committee, and the request of June 26 by ten states to the OAS. In the latter case, although the objective was different, had the projected Meeting of Consultation been held, some form of peace observation would no doubt have been adopted.

OAS Charter, which provides that the Ministers of Foreign Affairs shall meet in consultation either as the Organ of Consultation under the Rio Treaty or "to consider problems of an urgent nature and of common interest to the American States." Meetings of the latter type have been held on three occasions to consider situations arising from international tensions. One of these was convened prior to the time the Charter entered into effect, pursuant to Resolution XL of the Bogotá Conference which provided that: "The agencies that have hitherto functioned as organs of the system of the Union of American Republics shall immediately adopt the nomenclature and provisions established in the Charter of the Organization of American States."[30]

The uncertainty of the jurisdictional issue between the United Nations and the OAS was a further obstacle to the prompt initiation of peace-observation activities. A seeming conflict existed between the right of all members of the United Nations to appeal to the Security Council in cases of aggression or threats to the peace on the one hand, and the duty of members of the OAS on the other hand to resort to that agency in the first instance. For political reasons, the debate in the Security Council was therefore focused on a procedural question regarding jurisdiction rather than on the facts of the case or how to undertake peace observation promptly and effectively. The Guatemalan case did not settle the issue of jurisdiction, but the decisions taken in this instance tipped the balance toward giving priority to the regional organization in considering a dispute between its members.

The fact was, of course, that the Guatemalan situation, although couched in terms of a conflict between Guatemala and its neighbors, Honduras and Nicaragua, with the United States being charged with complicity in the aggressive acts, was in fact a small facet of the cold war, and thus involved directly the political interests of the two great world powers, the United States and the Soviet Union. The political interest of the Soviet Union was to bring the issue before the Security Council where it could use its influence for some positive action or veto any decisions to which it might object.

The political interest of the United States was to the contrary. Since the ultimate objective of the United States was the liquidation of Communist domination in Guatemala, more support could be expected for that objective in the OAS than in the United Nations, in particular in the OAS Council, coming soon after the March 1954 resolution (XCIII) of the Tenth Inter-American Conference. This resolution called for consultation in the event of the domination or control of the political institutions of any American state by the international Communist movement. The jurisdictional issue—of giving the OAS at least priority—obtained the support of key Latin American countries in the United Nations, in line with the

[30] Novena Conferencia Internacional Americana, *Actas y Documentos* (Bogotá: Ministerio de Relaciones Exteriores, 1953), pp. 308-9.

well-known position of Latin America on the relationship between the regional and the international organization. The Latin Americans had been the principal champions at San Francisco of freeing regional action from the veto in the Security Council as much as possible.

The conclusion must be drawn, therefore, that the Guatemalan situation of 1954 which, but for the Communist issue, would have been a minor controversy between small Central American countries, became embroiled in great power politics, with the result that timely action by either the OAS or the UN was frustrated.

The tactics of the United States in this case were in large degree determined by the difficulties which were encountered in attempting to get effective action by the OAS on the Communist threat to hemisphere security which the situation of Guatemala presented. Had the projected Meeting of Foreign Ministers been held on July 7, 1954, as provided for in the Council's resolution of June 28, the ability and willingness of the members of the OAS to take effective action in such a situation would have been put to the test. As it was, the rapid success of Castillo Armas set this test aside, and it remained for the problem to be posed again several years later under far more serious circumstances in the case of Cuba.

7

REQUEST OF THE GOVERNMENT OF ECUADOR, 1955

The boundary dispute between Ecuador and Peru dates from colonial times and has been a source of tension between these two countries, and in inter-American relations generally, for years. In the enthusiasm of wartime solidarity, Ecuador and Peru signed a Protocol of Peace, Friendship and Boundaries at Rio de Janeiro on January 29, 1942, setting up a formula whereby the boundary was to be settled and marked. Four mediating powers, Argentina, Brazil, Chile, and the United States, signed the Protocol as guarantors, and any dispute or doubt concerning its execution was to be settled by the parties with the assistance of the four guarantors. [1]

The protocol gave the largest share of the disputed area to Peru, which had recently seized large portions of it by force. Public opinion in Ecuador resented the settlement, despite the government's approval, and ultimately forced the resignation of the foreign minister who had signed it. Repeated border incidents kept the issue alive. When technical difficulties were

---

[1] For text of Protocol, see U.S. Department of State, *Bulletin*, Vol. 6 (1942), pp. 194–96.

encountered in applying the terms of the protocol, Ecuador began to challenge the validity of the agreement, and sought to reopen the entire problem in one international forum or another.

On September 8, 1955, the Ecuadoran ambassador to the OAS requested a special meeting of the Council, charging that Peru, in disregard of its inter-American commitments, was massing troops on the border to attack Ecuador. The Ecuadoran Government, therefore, requested a Meeting of Consultation under Article 6 of the Inter-American Treaty of Reciprocal Assistance. [2]

The Government of Ecuador had also submitted this situation to the four guarantor governments of the boundary protocol and the representatives of these powers were meeting to consider it in Rio de Janeiro. The Council, therefore, confined itself to expressing satisfaction at the prompt action of the guarantor powers and requesting information with regard to developments. The four powers appointed a commission of military attachés in Quito and Lima to look into the situation. After reconnoitering the area by land and air, the commission reported that it had seen nothing abnormal. On September 26, the Ecuadoran representative again addressed the Council, stating that, thanks to the prompt action of the four guarantor powers and the interest displayed by the OAS Council, the feared attack had been avoided. His government, therefore, withdrew its request for a Meeting of Consultation under the Rio Treaty. [3]

Reference to this incident is included in this study because a request was made in the first instance for consideration of the situation under the Rio Treaty. However, since the protocol of 1942 contained special provisions regarding the settlement of disputes under it, the Council wisely decided not to inject itself into the case. The peace observations of the guarantor powers effectively quieted the situation.

8

—◆—

HONDURAN–NICARAGUAN DISPUTE, 1957

The boundary between Honduras on the north and Nicaragua on the south is where Central America thickens and juts out into the Caribbean like a knee. The territory, disputed since colonial times, is like a knee-cap between Rió Coco and Rió Bodega.

In 1906 the dispute had been submitted to arbitration by the King of Spain, who decided that the boundary should follow the course of the

[2] PAU, *Applications*, pp. 227–28.
[3] PAU, *Applications*, pp. 235–34.

Coco River, thus awarding most of the disputed territory to Honduras.[1] Nicaragua refused to accept the award on various legal technicalities.

Except for the "Postage Stamp War" of 1937, hostilities were largely averted, but the dispute dragged on for many decades. Both countries signed the Rio Treaty with reservations in regard to this dispute.[2]

Early in 1957, the Government of Honduras took steps to organize the administration of the disputed area, including some sections over which Nicaragua had been exercising de facto control. Nicaragua strengthened its forces in those sections. In April, the Honduran ambassador to the OAS requested a meeting of the Council of the OAS to convoke the Organ of Consultation under the Rio Treaty in order to deal with new "aggression of the Government of Nicaragua."[3] He charged Nicaragua with repeated violations of Honduran territory.

There was no direct interest of any third power in the Honduran-Nicaraguan controversy. The only concern of the United States was to see that the OAS collective security system worked as speedily and efficiently as possible in restoring peace to Central America and ultimately eliminating the border issue as a source of conflict.

The Council met in early May to consider the complaint and hear the representatives of Honduras and Nicaragua. It was clear that, in view of the disagreement on where the boundary lay, the aggressor could not be immediately determined. Each government charged aggression by the other and invoked the Rio Treaty. The Council passed a resolution applying the Rio Treaty in the usual manner and proceeded to act provisionally as Organ of Consultation. It authorized the chairman "to appoint a committee to investigate on the ground the pertinent facts and their antecedents and to submit a report thereon."[4] The resolution also made the usual appeal for cooperation to all member states of the OAS and called on the two parties to abstain from any acts that might aggravate the situation.

THE INVESTIGATING COMMITTEE

Chairman Fernando Lobo of the Council named the representatives of Argentina, Bolivia, Mexico, Panama, and the United States to the

[1] For a map showing the conflicting claims and arbitral award, see Inter-American Peace Committee, *Report to the Eighth Meeting of Consultation of Ministers of Foreign Affairs*, OEA/Ser. L/III CIP/1/62 (Washington: Pan American Union, 1962), App. II, p. 19.

[2] Mecham, *op. cit.*, pp. 173–74.

[3] Unión Panamericana, *Aplicaciones del Tratado Interamericano de Asistencia Recíproca, 1948–1960* (Washington: Pan American Union, 1960), pp. 219–20. The records of cases under the Rio Treaty from this one forward are available only in this Spanish edition, hereafter cited as *Aplicaciones del Tratado*, with proper years. Translations into English are by the author.

[4] *Aplicaciones del Tratado, 1948–1960*, p. 231.

committee. Ambassador Ricardo Arias Espinosa, a former president of Panama, was elected chairman of the committee, and the veteran trouble-shooter, Luis Quintanilla, vice-chairman.[5] No attempt was made to spell out the terms of reference of the committee. The committee recognized that its function was to investigate the immediate conflict and possibil-ities of terminating it, without attempting to enter into the tricky legal substance of the long-standing dispute over the boundary and the validity of the King of Spain's award. Since both governments had reserved their legal position on this issue in ratifying the Rio Treaty, the committee had to adhere to a strict impartiality with respect to the legal controversy.

Arriving in Tegucigalpa, Honduras, on May 4 in a plane made available by the United States Caribbean Defense Command at Panama, the com-mittee, accompanied by political and military advisers, was greeted with an emotional demonstration of nationalistic fervor by the local people. To put a stop to the fighting and to the mobilization of further forces, the committee sought to obtain an agreement between the parties for a cease-fire but found that in existing circumstances no agreement was possible between the two governments. The committee then drafted separate but identical agreements for a cease-fire between each government and the committee. After discussions with the Honduran authorities on May 4 and a trip to Managua for the same purpose the next day, two such agreements were signed and went into effect on May 5. The agree-ments provided for a cease-fire, a promise by each government to abstain from acts of any kind that would aggravate the situation, and the prepara-tion by the committee of a troop-withdrawal plan within four days, subject to the approval of each government. The cease-fire agreements reserved the legal position of each government in regard to the boundary question.

Having achieved a cease-fire, the committee heard statements from both governments regarding their legal claims to the border area, despite the committee's desire to refrain from becoming involved in this aspect of the problem; received and investigated numerous complaints from both sides regarding alleged violations of the cease-fire agreements; and prepared the plans for troop withdrawals to be presented to both governments within the four-day limit established in the cease-fire agreements of May 5. The five titular members of the committee stayed together, commuting between Tegucigalpa and Managua as necessary, but assigned advisers to remain in charge of offices in each capital to serve as channels of com-munication and contact with the respective governments.

To attend to the last two of the functions mentioned above, the com-mittee on May 6 established a Committee of Military Advisers under the command of the ranking military officer, Col. Alphonse A. Greene (United

---

[5] The other members were Eduardo Augusto García, Argentina; John C. Dreier, United States; Mario V. Guzmán Galarza, Bolivia.

States), and notified the two governments of this fact, requesting their collaboration with the military group. In view of the number of complaints of cease-fire violations received from both governments requiring verification, the committee requested the Council to recommend that member governments [6] assign additional military officers of a rank no higher than colonel to serve with the Committee of Military Advisers. Four more governments responded to the Council's resolution adopted for this purpose, increasing the military group to seventeen officers from nine countries. [7] Considerable logistic support was provided by the United States Caribbean Defense Command. The rough, mountainous terrain and prevalence of cloudy weather made field observation difficult, and most of it had to be carried out on the ground rather than by air.

The Committee of Military Advisers also drafted the plan of troop withdrawal for the approval of the Investigating Committee and the two governments. The tactic of drawing up separate agreements was again adopted. Each government was requested to approve a plan applying solely to its forces within its territory, but each was shown the corresponding plan presented to the other government.

The troop withdrawal plans involved three features. (1) Regular and auxiliary forces of each country were to be withdrawn to specific bases a safe distance from the frontier (usually their regular bases), with the exception of normal border guards which had been stationed along the border prior to January 1, 1957. (2) Volunteer troops and other recent inductees were to be disarmed and demobilized. (3) Tactical aircraft were to be kept out of a designated frontier area, and government transport planes could fly there only with the approval of the Committee of Military Advisers. Detailed execution of the plan by the respective governments was to be under the supervision of the military committee. [8]

A special complication was encountered in the Nicaraguan plan, because the Guardia Nacional of Nicaragua included not only military forces but a number of auxiliary groups of nonmilitary character such as immigration officers and local police, whose continued presence in the frontier area was considered necessary to the normal conduct of civil government. In order to obtain the agreement of the Nicaraguan Government to the plan, without antagonizing the Honduran authorities, the committee sent identical notes to each government saying that, in carrying out the plan of troop withdrawal, the committee would "take into account insofar as reasonable and possible, the need of maintaining in the area involved, such military personnel as might be desirable and indispensable for the

[6] *Aplicaciones del Tratado, 1948–1960*, pp. 246–47.
[7] Argentina, Bolivia, Chile, Ecuador, Mexico, Panama, Paraguay, United States, and Venezuela. *Aplicaciones del Tratado, 1948–1960*, p. 257.
[8] *Aplicaciones del Tratado, 1948–1960*, pp. 262, 263, 265.

exercise of administrative functions."[9] This statement accorded some discretion to the Committee of Military Advisers supervising the withdrawal.

Although the committee and its military group had made extraordinary efforts to devise a troop withdrawal plan that would be effective and yet interfere to the minimum degree with the requirements of each government for protecting its legal position as well as the security of its territory, long arguments were needed before both governments agreed. Working day and night, the committee succeeded, and both plans went into effect on May 10.

With its immediate aim—a cessation of hostilities—accomplished, the committee left for Washington the same day, leaving its military advisers in the area along with a political adviser as its direct representative. The committee's report to the Council contained a brief narrative of activities and its conclusions and recommendations.[10]

The first conclusion of the Investigating Committee states that the case involved an especially complex situation which, because of disagreement over the boundary, did not permit the members of the Investigating Committee to determine responsibility for aggression. The second conclusion, contrary to Nicaraguan claims, was that both Honduras and Nicaragua had exercised control over various places in the disputed territory.

Stating that it had no competence to judge the legal questions which divided the governments, the Investigating Committee recommended to the Council that it establish an *Ad Hoc* Committee of the Council to conciliate the parties. It pointed out that both were signatories of the American Treaty of Pacific Settlement (Pact of Bogotá) and urged that if various other procedures failed to solve the dispute, the proper organ for a solution would be the International Court of Justice.

The Council followed the recommendations of the Investigating Committee. Moreover, the *Ad Hoc* Committee, which was appointed to carry out the task, consisted of the same ambassadors who had constituted the Investigating Committee, and it was authorized to continue to use the services of the Committee of Military Advisers in the field.

The Council meetings establishing the *Ad Hoc* Committee and recommending urgent efforts by the parties to reach a definitive settlement were held on May 17 and 24, 1957.[11] The committee held some fifteen sessions in an effort to bring the parties together. In a candid report to the Council on June 14, 1957, it stated that it "entrusted to Ambassador Luis Quintanilla, the Vice-Chairman, the task of bringing together—at his residence—the Representatives of Honduras and Nicaragua" to formulate the basis of an agreement. Ambassador Quintanilla and his Argentine

[9] *Aplicaciones del Tratado, 1948–1960*, pp. 266–67.
[10] *Aplicaciones del Tratado, 1948–1960*, pp. 250–68.
[11] *Aplicaciones del Tratado, 1948–1960*, pp. 268, 270, 271.

colleague, acting as a subcommittee, later traveled to Managua and Tegucigalpa and obtained signatures to an agreement from both the military junta of Honduras and the president of Nicaragua to submit the dispute to the International Court of Justice.[12]

Members of the *Ad Hoc* Committee may have feared that the judgment of the International Court might not be carried out promptly, for the agreement contained the proviso that, if one party should fail to comply with the decision of the Court, the other party would, before appealing to the UN Security Council, request a Meeting of Consultation of Ministers of Foreign Affairs, as provided for in the Pact of Bogotá.

While pursuing the objective of bringing about an agreement for the settlement of the legal question of the boundary, the *Ad Hoc* Committee was also aware of the necessity for keeping the situation along the border calm. The nature of the problem, coupled with the rough terrain and the presence of bands of undisciplined irregulars, made possible minor incidents that at any time might complicate the fundamental task. Nevertheless, since it would take at least two years to obtain a decision from the International Court, it did not seem desirable to maintain the OAS Committee of Military Advisers on the scene merely to hear and investigate such occasional charges and counter-charges as might be made. The *Ad Hoc* Committee, therefore, obtained the cooperation of the two governments in setting up a Honduran-Nicaraguan Mixed Military Commission to take over the functions of investigation and observation that had been exercised by the OAS military committee.[13] The latter was thereafter disbanded and responsibility for policing the border was returned to the two parties.

On June 27, 1957, the Council of the OAS canceled the Meeting of Foreign Ministers and dissolved itself as the Provisional Organ.[14]

EVALUATION

This case was another example of prompt, effective action by the OAS through the use of an Investigating Committee with considerable discretionary authority. The handling of the case again demonstrated the value of having high-caliber men of broad experience serve on the mission, and of selecting them from countries which have no direct interest in the issues involved nor political sympathies with either side. The case further showed the importance of divorcing the immediate task of terminating hostilities from the long-range task of working out a peaceful settlement, which in the eyes of the OAS is always the ultimate desideratum. For the former task, the availability of a small but highly competent and impartial

[12] *Aplicaciones del Tratado, 1948–1960*, pp. 274, 291.
[13] *Aplicaciones del Tratado, 1948–1960*, p. 290.
[14] *Aplicaciones del Tratado, 1948–1960*, p. 291.

group of military officers was essential. Without their technical and professional knowledge, the achievement of a plan for withdrawal of troops might well have been impossible. Finally, the continuation of political efforts at conciliation, before the powers of the Rio Treaty were relinquished, again demonstrated the interrelationship between actual or potential enforcement action and the achievement of a peaceful settlement.

9

—•—

THREE CARIBBEAN CASES IN 1959

The triumph of the Castro revolution in Cuba on January 1, 1959, ushered in a new era of political upheavals in the Caribbean area with international complications. Even before the July 26 revolution in Cuba was fully consolidated, the Castro forces began to foment their particular brand of revolution in other Caribbean countries. Of the several attempts made in the first six months of the regime, Panama was the first. Nicaragua under the Somoza family and the Dominican Republic under Generalissimo Trujillo were next.

At this period, Castro had a great deal of public support in the Western Hemisphere. Although the mass trials and killings in Cuba shocked public opinion, he had not yet expropriated Cuban and American properties or publicly insulted the United States Government. About the time this case was heard, he was in the Press Club in Washington proclaiming friendship for the United States and denying Communist affiliation. He was probably at the zenith of his popular support both in Cuba and in the Western Hemisphere—the personification of the movement for social and political reform that was evident in varying degrees in all Latin American countries. Latin American diplomats tended to think of Castro as "a good boy, if somewhat impulsive." Having an eye to the substantial Castro following in all their countries, they had no desire to oppose him publicly.

THE SITUATION OF PANAMA, 1959

On April 27, 1959, Ambassador Ricardo Arias of Panama, who had been chairman of the Investigating and *Ad Hoc* Committees in the preceding application of the Rio Treaty, charged in the OAS Council that his country had been invaded "by forces composed almost entirely of foreign elements." He demanded the immediate convocation of an Organ of

Consultation under Article 6 of the Rio Defense Treaty.[1] He stated that on April 15 the Government of Panama had learned that eighty to one hundred armed men would invade Panama from Cuba. The Panamanian Government communicated these reports to the chargé of Cuba and invoked Article 1 of the Convention on Duties and Rights of States in the Event of Civil Strife, signed at Havana in 1928. The Cuban Government gave assurances that steps would be taken to prevent such a movement. Nevertheless, on April 25, the vessel Majaré arrived on the Atlantic coast of Panama with eighty armed men of whom three were captured. They declared that they had sailed from Batabanó, Cuba, on April 19, and that two other vessels with armed reinforcements were expected to join them shortly.[2]

The Panamanian Government preferred no charges against the Government of Cuba—an indication of the reluctance of the Latin American community to attack or antagonize the popular Castro government. In the Council debate, the Cuban representative condemned the invasion, saying that it was not supported by his government and was contrary to the non-interventionist and prodemocratic sentiments of the Cuban revolutionary regime.

On April 28, the Council convoked the Organ of Consultation and constituted itself as a provisional Organ. It authorized the appointment of a committee "to investigate, on the spot, the pertinent facts and submit a report thereon." It called on "any government that has reason to believe that there are persons in zones under its jurisdiction" participating in activities against the territorial integrity of Panama "to use all means to prevent such activities." The Council also anticipated certain needs of the committee by asking the member governments of the OAS to provide planes for peaceful observation flights and by recommending favorable attention to requests of Panama for defensive armaments.[3]

The committee included: Ambassador Fernando Lobo of Brazil, chairman; Ambassador John C. Dreier of the United States, vice-chairman; Ambassador Juan Plate of Paraguay; Ambassador César Barros Hurtado of Argentina; and Minister Jorge Hazera of Costa Rica. All but the Costa Rican member were accompanied by military advisers.

The issue was clear even though the parties to the case were not formally identified: Had Panama been the victim of armed aggression from abroad?

The Investigating Committee

As was the general rule in the OAS, there were no detailed terms of reference for the Investigating Committee. The committee was merely instructed to investigate the pertinent facts on the spot and render a report.

---

[1] *Aplicaciones del Tratado, 1948–1960*, p. 316.
[2] *Aplicaciones del Tratado, 1948–1960*, p. 297.
[3] *Aplicaciones del Tratado, 1948–1960*, pp. 301–02.

The committee left for Panama on April 28, 1959, and consulted with high officials of the Panamanian Government. Two Cuban officers had been sent to Panama by the Cuban Government and had gone to Nombre de Dios to dissuade the expedition from its purposes. They brought back word that the expedition would surrender if it was permitted to return to Cuba immediately with all its equipment. This the Panamanian Government refused to do.

The committee interrogated the four prisoners—three Cuban and one Panamanian. Then, on April 30, it sent its military advisers and the two Cuban officers to Nombre de Dios to bring the expedition leader, César Vega, and two companions to Albrook Air Base in the Canal Zone. The committee advised them to accept the government's terms of unconditional surrender in view of the unanimous condemnation of their misguided venture by all the American republics.

The leaders of the expedition were convinced by the committee, and on May 1 Juan Plate and Jorge Hazera, plus some military advisers, witnessed the surrender of the invading force and the deposit of their arms. The chairman also visited the prisoners in Panama City on May 3 to verify their nationality.

Meanwhile, the Cuban Government had informed the chairman of the OAS Council that since April 28 (when the first OAS resolution was passed) no expedition had sailed, or could sail, from Cuba because of the vigilance of the Cuban authorities. [4]

Persistent rumors of additional invasion forces en route to Panama, and repeated appeals of the Panamanian Government, however, led the committee to establish a naval patrol of the Caribbean waters adjacent to the Panamanian coast, in addition to the air patrol already in effect. It requested the Council to ask that the governments assign naval vessels in addition to aircraft. The Council acceded, and on May 1 a naval patrol was instituted with vessels provided by the United States and Colombia. Other governments made various offers of assistance. Command over the vessels was nominally exercised by the Military Advisers of the Investigating Committee, but actually was carried out through the Commanding General, U.S. Caribbean Defense Command, with whom the committee made arrangements to that end.

The Council's resolution of April 30, responding to the committee's request for naval vessels, made clear that their duty was merely to observe and identify vessels within the meaning of the term "peaceful observation" and the norms of international law. [5] Under the prodding of the Panamanian Government, which feared that mere observation and identification would leave any invading force free to proceed to its destination, the committee requested the Council to authorize the vessels participating in the

[4] *Aplicaciones del Tratado, 1948–1960*, p. 311.
[5] *Aplicaciones del Tratado, 1948–1960*, p. 322.

patrol to "detain" suspicious vessels encountered within Panamanian "jurisdictional waters" with the authority and at the request of the Panamanian Government. The members of the Council and their governments were concerned that such authorization would constitute a possibility of infringing on the freedom of the seas and touching on the subject of what constituted "jurisdictional waters." The Council therefore denied giving the authorization to the committee, and recommended that the governments participating in the naval patrol reach agreement with the Government of Panama for the above-mentioned purpose. [6]

One further step was taken by the Investigating Committee to strengthen its naval patrol. The committee was informed of reports that two vessels flying the Guatemalan flag might be carrying the suspected second invasion force from Cuba. It therefore requested the Guatemalan Government, which had offered its cooperation, to assign two officials to accompany the naval patrol vessels, who, if a suspicious Guatemalan ship were encountered and identified, could in the name of the Guatemalan Government dissuade it from its purpose. Replying to the committee's request, the Guatemalan Government said that it had checked its sources of information, was satisfied that no Guatemalan vessels were involved or present in the area, and that the assignment of the officials was therefore unnecessary. [7]

By this time, the original rebel force had surrendered, and no signs of the rumored reinforcements had been discovered. The committee returned to Washington on May 4. On the same day, the observation patrols were terminated, and the military advisers wound up their business and departed on May 5. [8]

The committee submitted a report to the Council on June 9, in which it related its activities and stated its conclusions and recommendations. [9] It declared that Panama had been the victim of an invasion proceeding

---

[6] *Aplicaciones del Tratado, 1948–1960*, pp. 322–23.

[7] *Aplicaciones del Tratado, 1948–1960*, pp. 312, 326.

[8] *Aplicaciones del Tratado, 1948–1960*, p. 313.

[9] The delay in submitting the report was, according to one member of the committee, due primarily to the concern of some of the members over the fate of the Cuban "invaders" whom they had induced to surrender to the Panamanian authorities. This action had been taken on the understanding, never explicitly stated, that once the Cubans had been subjected to Panamanian jurisdiction, they would be quickly released. As it turned out, the Panamanian Government had different ideas, and a long-drawn-out legal proceeding ensued. Although any official concern on the part of the OAS committee with the administration of justice by the sovereign state of Panama was, of course, out of order, some members of the committee felt that if they threatened to include reference to the supposed understanding in the report, it would induce the Panamanian Government to release the prisoners more quickly. This tactic, for various reasons, did not work, and the report was finally issued while the Cubans were still in the Panama jail. The matter was ultimately resolved by direct negotiations between the Cuban and Panamanian Governments. The delay in Council action may also be attributed in part to the fact that on June 2 the Council became involved in another case—that of Nicaragua.

from abroad, creating a situation within the scope of Article 6 of the Rio Treaty; but the situation had been liquidated due in large measure to "the prompt and effective action of the Organization of American States." It urged the Council to remind the governments of the need to enforce more effectively the provisions of the Havana Convention of 1928 and recommended the cancellation of the convocation of the Organ of Consultation under the Rio Treaty. The Council acted in accordance with these suggestions on June 18, 1959.

Evaluation

The Panama case of 1959 might be described as an example of effective, though routine, action by the Council under the Rio Treaty, with comic-opera overtones. It is hard to imagine a similar situation developing anywhere else in the Western Hemisphere. Nor is it easy to justify invoking the entire machinery of collective security under the Rio Treaty for an incident of such minor proportions, particularly in the absence of any charge against another state.

However, the case had significance from the legal and procedural standpoints. The silence of the committee and the Council in regard to the negligence of the Cuban Government in allowing such an expedition to take off demonstrated the reluctance of the Latin American countries to incur popular disfavor by criticizing the Castro revolutionary government. This factor had far more serious consequences in later situations. The novel feature of peace observation in the Panama incident was that it involved the first effort to organize a collective naval patrol under OAS direction. The member governments of the OAS, however, were not willing to give the Investigating Committee authority to detain vessels even in Panamanian waters with the authority of the Panamanian Government—let alone on the high seas—primarily because of the controversial legal issues involved. The same problem would have to be faced again under far more serious circumstances in the Cuban missile crisis of 1962.

THE SITUATION OF NICARAGUA, 1959

On June 2, 1959, the Nicaraguan ambassador, Guillermo Sevilla Sacasa, asked the chairman of the OAS Council, Ambassador Gonzalo Escudero of Ecuador, to convoke a meeting of Foreign Ministers as an Organ of Consultation under the Rio Treaty to consider a charge that Nicaragua had been invaded with airplanes and arms from Costa Rica. His government had also learned that three barge loads of armed revolutionaries were approaching Nicaragua by sea.[10]

[10] *Aplicaciones del Tratado, 1948–1960*, p. 362.

The Council met the following day and Ambassador Sevilla Sacasa presented the case. As in the case of Panama, Nicaragua did not accuse any particular government of contributing to the alleged aggression. In fact, the ambassador complimented the Costa Rican Government and President Echandi for efforts to prevent illegal projects against the Nicaraguan state from being hatched in Costa Rica. Little enthusiasm was generated in the Council, however, on behalf of the unpopular Government of Nicaragua, now headed by the son of the assassinated Anastasio Somoza. In this session and in the second, held on June 4, opposition to any action by the OAS was strongly voiced by the Cuban and Venezuelan delegates, who argued that the whole incident was part of an internal political struggle against the Somoza family dictatorship and that the exiles had every right to return to their native land for whatever purposes they might have.[11]

Further information appeared to be needed so that the Council could judge whether an act falling within the scope of Article 6 of the Rio Treaty had taken place. Precedent put the Council in a dilemma: it could not send an investigating committee into the field without first invoking the Rio Treaty and acting provisionally as the Organ of Consultation, yet it wished more information to determine whether the facts warranted the convocation of the Organ. Representatives of Colombia and Uruguay argued that the Council was warranted in obtaining information on its own account before taking the decision to invoke the treaty, but this view was not supported by the majority.[12]

Unwilling to reject the Nicaraguan appeal out of hand in view of the recent precedent of the Panama case, the Council on June 4 convoked the Organ of Consultation and appointed a committee to gather information so the Council might be in a position to decide on the measures it might be advisable to take. The resolution did "not imply in any way a pre-judgment of the nature of the facts, nor intervention in the affairs of a member state."[13]

The committee's terms of reference were limited, compared with the flexible grants of authority given to investigating committees in most of the previous cases under the Rio Treaty. The efficient Nicaraguan National Guard had already overcome the invaders, there were no hostilities to be terminated, nor was there any immediate threat of international conflict to be averted. The committee's sole function, therefore, was to assemble information on what had gone on, and report to the Council, which had indicated that it would reserve judgment and refrain from further action until the committee had reported.

The members of the Council appointed to the committee were Ambassador Julio Lacarte (Uruguay), chairman; Ambassador Vicente Sánchez

---

[11] Minutes of Meeting of OAS Council, June 4, 1959, OAS Doc. C-a-321, pp. 10–19.

[12] *Ibid.*, pp. 38–39.

[13] *Aplicaciones del Tratado, 1948–1960*, p. 363.

Gavito (Mexico), vice-chairman; Ambassador John C. Dreier (United States); and Minister L. Haddock Lobo (Brazil). There were no military advisers, and the staff was much smaller than usual.

The question was whether Nicaraguan territory had been violated by an action falling within the terms of Article 6 of the Treaty of Rio de Janeiro.

Work of the Information Committee

The committee did not leave for Nicaragua until ten days after it was constituted on June 4. It sent telegrams to thirteen member governments of the OAS in the Caribbean region to make reports on the events described by Nicaragua. Replies with offers of cooperation were received from all but the Dominican Republic.[14] The lapse of ten days to accomplish this exchange indicates the unenthusiastic attitude of the committee toward its task, and particularly its desire to avoid being used to bolster the Somoza government against its internal foes.

From June 15 to 19, the committee was in Honduras and Costa Rica interviewing the Honduran and Costa Rican presidents and other officials and the captured rebels. Students demonstated against the committee,[15] believing it to be serving the interests of the Somoza government. The committee was shown arms of Italian, United States, and Dominican manufacture taken from the invaders, and received a statement from Costa Rican University students criticizing the Council's action in convoking the Organ of Consultation in this case. An important development was the visit of Dr. Enrique Lacayo Farfán, chief of the Nicaraguan Revolutionary Movement, to the committee.

By coincidence, the day before the committee arrived in San José, Costa Rican authorities had discovered an encampment of Nicaraguan rebels, with large quantities of arms and ammunition, at Punta Llorona, a remote point on the Costa Rican Pacific coast. Some of the arms had apparently come from Cuba. The committee witnessed the measures taken by President Echandi to disarm and disperse this rebel force, despite the sympathies for them openly displayed by several important members of the political opposition in Costa Rica.

The committee returned to Washington on June 24 and reported that: (1) A group of 110 individuals left Punta Llorona, Costa Rica, on May 31 in a privately owned Costa Rican airplane. The first flight brought them to Los Mojones, Nicaragua, and the second to Sierra Azul. (2) The group was organized in Costa Rica without the knowledge of the government but with the aid of Costa Rican elements. (3) Some expedition leaders had been

[14] The reply of the Dominican Republic was received after the committee had left for Central America.

[15] *Aplicaciones del Tratado, 1948–1960*, p. 349.

to Cuba and solicited aid from the Cuban Government, which was not given, the leaders thought, because of ideological differences with the Cubans. (4) All expedition members were captured, but none was killed by Nicaraguan forces. (5) There was no verification of the rumors of barges coming from Mexico. (6) In addition to the 110-man force mentioned above, there was the Nicaraguan Revolutionary Movement in Costa Rica, headed by Dr. Lacayo Farfán, and a force of undetermined size had been discovered at Punta Llorona and broken up by the Costa Rican Government. (7) The Honduran-Nicaraguan Joint Military Commission was a good agency, but the Nicaraguans believed it could have done a better job of preventing infiltration from Honduras into Nicaragua. (8) Most of the arms used in the invasion were bought on the Costa Rican black market. "There were indications . . . that at least some of these armaments came directly or indirectly from Cuba." (9) According to the Honduran-Nicaraguan Joint Military Commission, there were in Honduras seventy men of various nationalities with arms of Dominican and U.S. manufacture who proposed to invade Nicaragua. The Government of Honduras had taken some of them prisoner and intended to stop the remainder from entering Nicaragua.[16]

The lengthy report of the committee, dated June 26, 1959, ended with the finding of facts summarized above. In view of its limited terms of reference, it refrained from drawing conclusions or making recommendations for the Council to act upon.

On June 28, the Council heard the committee's report. The reaction is described by the U.S. member as follows:

> On hearing the committee's report, the Council, in a lackluster session fully reflecting the members' distaste for the whole affair, adopted a tepid resolution canceling the invocation of the Rio Treaty and piously recommending that the member governments "strengthen the measures designed to maintain peace, observing the principle of non-intervention."[17]

On July 16, although the case had been closed, the committee issued an additional report which dealt especially, but not exclusively, with indications of Cuban collaboration with Nicaraguan revolutionaries.[18] Of great interest was the information concerning legends and marks visible in photographs of the arms seized by the Costa Rican Government at Punta Llorona indicating their Cuban origin. Documents were also included showing the personal interest of one of Fidel Castro's closest collaborators,

[16] *Aplicaciones del Tratado, 1948–1960*, pp. 360–61.

[17] John C. Dreier, *The Organization of American States and the Hemisphere Crisis* (New York: Harper & Row, for the Council on Foreign Relations, 1962), pp. 69–70.

[18] "Additional Report of the Committee . . . Acting in the Case of Nicaragua," etc., OAS Doc. C-i-419, Add. Rev. 2.

Ernesto ("Che") Guevara, in helping certain Nicaraguan revolutionaries who had strong Communist connections. Some of this information was provided to the committee by the United States Government, since it dealt with a naturalized U.S. citizen active in these affairs.

Evaluation

The results of the field investigations of the committee in this case justified the cautious attitude of the Council on hearing the Nicaraguan complaint. The immediate threat to the Nicaraguan Government, arising from the invasions of May 31 and June 1, had already been eliminated by the Nicaraguan National Guard. The potential threat from the second expedition discovered in Punta Llorona, Costa Rica, had been dissipated by the prompt action of Costa Rican authorities. All these threats involved only Nicaraguan exiles and a few private Costa Rican sympathizers.

The committee had not discovered official collaboration of any government in the organization or supply of these revolutionary expeditions. On the contrary, both the Costa Rican and Honduran Governments had adopted correct attitudes toward these movements, although in Honduras some evidence of a less than zealous enforcement of international legal obligations was noted.[19] The situation remained, therefore, essentially an internal political problem of Nicaragua, where the continuing power of the Somoza family resulted in a series of plots and conspiracies organized, necessarily, outside of Nicaraguan territory. The Castro revolution in Cuba had created a new and more favorable atmosphere for the prosecution of such revolutionary plans. No positive evidence was uncovered of Cuban governmental support to the expeditions that were the subject of the original Nicaraguan complaint, even though documents were obtained indicating the personal interest of Guevara in other Nicaraguan revolutionary plans.

From the standpoint of peace observation in the OAS, the case illustrated: (1) An unpopular government might use the collective security system of the Rio Treaty to protect the political status quo by confusing internal political unrest with international aggression or intervention. (2) The invocation of the Rio Treaty before the facts have been clarified tends to detract prestige and popular support from the international peace machinery. There seems no way to avoid this so long as the Council follows its policy of refusing to obtain the facts until *after* it convokes the Organ of Consultation. (3) The functioning of the OAS peace-observation system is severely handicapped when prevailing emotions and political sympathies are aroused against the government appealing for assistance. (4) The discreet and careful job of the committee named by the Council to study this case was helpful in airing causes of international tension in the area

[19] *Aplicaciones del Tratado, 1948–1960*, p. 354.

and emphasizing the need for governments to observe their international obligations for nonintervention in good faith.

PETITION OF THE DOMINICAN REPUBLIC, 1959

Following the investigations in Panama in May 1959 and in Nicaragua in June, the Dominican ambassador to the OAS, Virgilio Díaz Ordóñez, on July 2 charged the Governments of Cuba and Venezuela with supporting two invasions in June against the Dominican Republic. He called for a Meeting of Consultation of Ministers of Foreign Affairs under the Rio Defense Treaty.[20] The Cuban and Venezuelan ambassadors to the OAS rejected the charges and opposed the convocation of an organ of consultation. The Haitian delegation proposed that the Council establish an investigating committee without prejudice to the consideration by the Council of the Dominican request for the invocation of the Rio Treaty.[21] The two invasions complained of had been mounted in Cuba and had been wiped out by the efficient Dominican military forces. In the process, the Dominican Government gathered considerable evidence on the origin and composition of the expeditions.[22]

The issue was whether to investigate the charges of the Dominican Government as a situation falling within Article 6 of the Rio Treaty.

The hostility between the Dominican dictator, Generalissimo Trujillo, and his neighbors and the revulsion created in other countries by the brutality of the Dominican police state toward its own citizens were so great that virtually no one would come to the support of the Dominican dictatorship.

The OAS Council

If, in the Nicaraguan case, the Council of the OAS lacked enthusiasm, in this case it refused to act at all. The Council first postponed consideration of the Dominican request, as well as of a Haitian proposal for the establishment of an investigating committee prior to acting on the Dominican motion.[23] At the meeting of the Council on July 6, the Haitian delegate asked for a Meeting of Consultation under Article 39 of the OAS Charter. Again the Council postponed action, this time to July 10. The U.S. representative later wrote that at this time "a complete breakdown of the OAS security system was only narrowly averted."[24]

[20] *Aplicaciones del Tratado, 1948–1960*, p. 387.

[21] *Aplicaciones del Tratado, 1948–1960*, p. 388.

[22] Dreier, *op. cit.*, pp. 70–71. No evidence of Venezuelan complicity was ever produced, although Castro's support of the abortive invasions later became a matter of public knowledge—despite Cuban denials in the Council.

[23] *Aplicaciones del Tratado, 1948–1960*, p. 388.

[24] Dreier, *op. cit.*, p. 70.

At the July 19 session of the Council, the representatives of Brazil, Chile, the United States, and Peru formally proposed a Meeting of Consultation of Ministers of Foreign Affairs under Articles 39 and 40 of the Charter "to consider the grave situation which exists in the Caribbean."[25] Such a meeting would, of course, have no enforcement powers as would be the case under the Rio Treaty. The Dominican representative agreed to the extent of stating that his government had decided to "leave without effect" his note of July 2 so fas as concerned invocation of the Rio Treaty.

The Cuban and Venezuelan representatives opposed the convocation of a Meeting of Consultation, since it might be considered to be in response to the Dominican request, and obtained a temporary postponement of the consideration of the four-power proposal.

On July 13, the four-power proposal was approved. As a result there was held in Santiago, Chile, from August 12 to 18, 1959, the Fifth Meeting of Consultation of Ministers of Foreign Affairs.[26] What happened at Santiago is outside the purview of this case, but will be discussed in the activities of the Inter-American Peace Committee whose role was profoundly affected by the decisions of the Santiago Conference.[27]

Evaluation

Why was an investigating committee not set up when the Government of the Dominican Republic had every right to it, and the circumstances warranted such action? The answer seems to be that political considerations may render a treaty inapplicable in practice. In this case, the majority of OAS governments would do nothing that their people might consider as aiding a hated dictator against those who sought to overthrow him, even if it meant violating an international obligation.

10

—•—

VENEZUELAN–DOMINICAN REPUBLIC CASE, 1960

The Fifth Meeting of Consultation of Ministers of Foreign Affairs under the OAS Charter met at Santiago, Chile, in August 1959, to consider the problem of tensions in the Caribbean with a view to restoring peace and security in the area. Tensions, however, continued to mount. The antagonism between the Dominican Republic and Venezuela, heightened by the

[25] *Aplicaciones del Tratado, 1948–1960*, p. 389.
[26] *Aplicaciones del Tratado, 1948–1960*, p. 390.
[27] See pp. 194–95.

personal emnity between Generalissimo Trujillo and President Betancourt, caused the relations of these two countries to reach a crisis.

At a meeting of the Council of the OAS on June 6, 1960, the Venezuelan ambassador requested the immediate convocation of an Organ of Consultation under Article 6 of the Rio Treaty because of acts of intervention and aggression culminating in the attempt to assassinate President Betancourt.[1]

On July 8, with the unanimous approval of the members entitled to vote, the council resolved to convoke a Meeting of Foreign Ministers, to constitute itself a Provisional Organ of Consultation, and to appoint an investigating committee. The committee consisted of Ambassador Erasmo de la Guardia of Panama, chairman; Ambassador Emilio Donato del Carril of Argentina; Ambassador Vicente Sánchez Gavito of Mexico; Ambassador Carlos A. Clulow of Uruguay; and the alternate U.S. representative to the OAS, Henry C. Reed.[2]

The issue was whether the Dominican Government was implicated in the attempted assassination of the president of Venezuela and other acts that would constitute aggression under the Treaty of Rio de Janeiro.

THE INVESTIGATING COMMITTEE

The committee's terms of reference were the customary sentence of the Council's resolution: "to investigate the alleged acts and their antecedents and to submit a report thereon."

The committee spent four days in Caracas. Its report, dated August 8, 1960, was transmitted to the members of the Council for reference to their governments and subsequently was submitted to the Sixth Meeting of Ministers of Foreign Affairs at San José, Costa Rica. This report is one of the best submitted by investigating committees of the OAS. It is not merely a chronological account of the committee's activities, but is divided into sections according to subject matter and has conclusions for each of the three substantive sections.[3]

The Investigating Committee found that: the Dominican Republic had contrived to make possible the leaflet-throwing expedition in Venezuelan territory on November 19, 1959;[4] that the Dominican Government had

[1] *Aplicaciones del Tratado, 1948–1960*, p. 393.

[2] *Aplicaciones del Tratado, 1948–1960*, p. 395. This is at the end of the volume. A supplement for 1960 and 1961 follows. The supplement is available only in Spanish and will be referred to herein as *Aplicaciones, Suplemento*.

[3] *Aplicaciones, Suplemento*, pp. 21 *et seq.*

[4] This part of the report deals with the same set of facts which constitutes the case on "Subversive Leaflets Against the Government of Venezuela, 1959" in the Inter-American Peace Committee section. See pp. 195 ff.

issued diplomatic passports to Venezuelans hostile to the Government of Venezuela and had requested Colombian diplomatic visas for these persons; that the attempt on the life of the president of Venezuela was part of a plot to overthrow the government and that those implicated in the plot received moral and material aid from high officials of the Dominican Government. This aid consisted principally of facilitating travel to and residence in the Dominican Republic and of providing equipment.

The committee had interrogated a number of the Venezuelan participants in the attempt on President Betancourt's life. The only rebuttal by the Dominican minister of foreign affairs to a subcommittee of the Investigating Committee, which had gone to the Dominican Republic, was to the effect that the witnesses who implicated the Dominican officials must have been "brainwashed." [5]

Shortly after the Investigating Committee returned from Venezuela, the Council of the OAS set August 16 in San José, Costa Rica for the Sixth Meeting of Ministers of Foreign Affairs to serve as the Organ of Consulation in application of the Rio Treaty. [6]

At this meeting, U.S. Secretary of State Christian Herter paid tribute to "the thoroughness, impartiality and high sense of responsibility" of the Investigating Committee and declared its conclusions to be well-founded. He linked the committee's report with that of the Inter-American Peace Committee of June 6, 1960, which found international tensions in the Caribbean to be aggravated by flagrant violations of human rights by the Dominican Republic. [7] He argued for the establishment of a special committee of the Sixth Meeting to supervise and assure free elections in the Dominican Republic, as a means of attacking the aggressive attitude of the Dominican Government at its source.

The majority of Latin American delegates at San José would have been happy to see a democratic government established in the Dominican Republic, but they were reluctant to make the OAS responsible for the measures that such an effort would require. [8] In the conflict between promotion of democracy and nonintervention, nonintervention won. Punitive sanctions were imposed on the Dominican Republic pursuant to Articles 6 and 8 of the Rio Defense Treaty, but no explicit provisions were adopted to encourage a democratization of that country.

The Sixth Meeting condemned the Government of the Dominican Republic for acts of aggression against Venezuela which culminated in the attempt on the life of the president. It called for breaking diplomatic relations and economic sanctions, beginning with an immediate arms embargo.

[5] *Aplicaciones, Suplemento,* p. 26.
[6] *Aplicaciones, Suplemento,* p. 10.
[7] U.S. Department of State, *Bulletin,* Vol. 43 (1960), p. 355.
[8] Dreier, *op. cit.,* p. 99.

The OAS Council was authorized to "study the possibility and desirability" of extending the embargo to other articles. The resolution authorized the Council to terminate the sanctions when the Dominican Government should "cease to constitute a danger to the peace and security of America." [9]

The sequel to the Sixth Meeting of Foreign Ministers constitutes one of the most interesting episodes in the development of peace-observation activities by the OAS in view of the important assignment given to the Council. Two purposes were involved in the decisions of the Meeting of Consultation. On the surface, the purpose of the sanctions was to force the Dominican Government to change its international policy and forego further aggressive, interventionist activities. An unspoken purpose, however, was to bring about a change in the Trujillo dictatorship on the ground that, so long as the Generalissimo remained in power, the basic attitude of the Dominican Republic toward peace and security would not change. This purpose remained unspoken because any outright recognition thereof would be attacked as intervention in the internal affairs of that country.

The Council on September 21, 1960, appointed a special committee to carry out the assignments of the San José meeting. The committee reported to the Council on December 19 that it could detect "no change in the attitude of the Government of the Dominican Republic toward the fundamental principles of the inter-American System." It said that lifting the sanctions could not be justified, and recommended instead an extension to petroleum and petroleum products, and to trucks and spare parts. The Council approved this recommendation on January 4, 1961. [10]

On May 30, 1961, Generalissimo Trujillo was assassinated, and a new era in Dominican history began. The Council was faced with a serious decision in the exercise of its peace-observation functions: it could write off the whole matter by lifting the sanctions, on the ground that the death of the dictator had eliminated the source of Dominican aggressiveness; or it could use its power to help bring about an orderly transition to a democratic system in the republic.

The Special Committee, somewhat cautiously, took the latter course. It dispatched a subcommittee to the Dominican Republic in mid-June and again in September to observe the situation developing there, as various factions began to jockey for power, but the committee withheld judgment. During this period, groups in the Dominican Republic tried to organize political parties and to formulate a plan for establishing a broadly representative provisional regime that would oversee the transition to a constitutionally elected government. The exclusion of the Trujillo family

[9] *Aplicaciones, Suplemento*, p. 14.

[10] *Aplicaciones, Suplemento*, pp. 16, 17.

and others closely associated with them was an essential but difficult step in this process. Apparently, believing that the situation was so delicate and involved so great a danger of Castro intervention that responsibility for it could not be left solely in the hands of the OAS Council, the United States sent a special emissary to Santo Domingo in an effort to promote a satisfactory political pact among the various factions. The United States put on a demonstration of naval force off the coast near the capital to make clear its opposition to the Trujillos' return to power.

The OAS Special Committee continued to play a role in the situation. In November, its subcommittee visited the island again. It then recommended that the sanctions against the Dominican Republic be lifted, inasmuch as that government had "ceased to constitute a danger to the peace and security of America." This the Council did on January 4, 1962.[11]

The most interesting feature of the subcommittee's reports on their trips to Santo Domingo is the broad scope of their inquiry. It is clear that the members of the committee did not confine themselves to a narrow view of their task. They "not only talked with government officials, but with leaders of government and opposition parties; the reports to the Council covered not only foreign policy of the Dominican Government but the political situation in that country, including inter-party negotiations, the progress of 'democratization,' the plans for free elections, and other outright political subjects."[12] The subcommittee thus interpreted in broad terms the peace-observation function given to it as a result of the resolution of the Sixth Meeting of Foreign Ministers and gave attention to the deeper and unspoken purpose of that action.

EVALUATION

The work of the Investigating Committee in this case merited the high praise given it by the Secretary of State. Its investigation was thorough, and its precise and objectively phrased conclusions were based on convincing evidence.

The second feature of this case marks a departure in OAS peace-observation work in that it assigned the responsibility for observing and judging the performance of the Dominican Government to the Council, which was no longer "acting provisionally" for the Meeting of Consultation. The establishment of this precedent was in response to practical necessity and was perhaps facilitated by the overwhelming desire of Latin American countries

[11] *Aplicaciones, Suplemento*, p. 20.

[12] John C. Dreier, "The Council of the OAS: Performance and Potential," *Journal of Inter-American Studies*, V (July 1963), pp. 308–9.

to press down on the Trujillo dictatorship. The case is also the first and, to date, the only time that the OAS attempted to use peace observation to influence an internal political situation, even though there was no explicit recognition of this purpose because of Latin American sentiment against intervention. The action of the Council in this respect was very cautious, since the members were conscious of the delicate ground on which they were treading, as the political situation in the Dominican Republic "deteriorated . . . to the point where it called for a larger measure of firmness than the OAS was prepared to provide" in order to avoid a "drift into chaos, Castroism, or another military dictatorship."[13]

11

———◆———

REQUEST OF COLOMBIA ON THE CUBAN SITUATION, 1962

The Colombian ambassador on the OAS Council on November 14, 1961, requested the convocation of a Meeting of Ministers of Foreign Affairs on January 10, 1962, in accordance with Article 6 of the Rio Treaty, to consider threats to the peace of the hemisphere that might arise from Communist intervention, and to determine what measures to take concerning them. The request was approved by a resolution of the Council of December 4, 1961, and the place of convocation was fixed as Punta del Este, Uruguay, by a resolution of December 22, 1961.

Thus there came about the noteworthy Eighth Meeting of Consultation of Ministers of Foreign Affairs at Punta del Este from January 22 to 31, 1962, resulting in the exclusion of Cuba from the Inter-American System.[1]

This case did not involve the use of peace observation but is listed here as being an application of the Rio Treaty. Insofar as it has a bearing on the Cuban Missile Case, 1962, the Punta del Este Conference is briefly discussed in the section on the background of that case.

[13] Dreier, *Organization of American States*, pp. 100, 101.

[1] Octava Reunión de Consulta de Ministros de Relaciones Exteriores, *Actas y Documentos* (Washington: Unión Panamericana, 1963), OEA/Ser. F/III.8.

12

CUBAN MISSILE CRISIS, 1962

The direct confrontation between the United States and the Soviet Union which took place in the Cuban missile crisis of October 1962 may prove to be the most significant event of the second half of the twentieth century. Its implications for the future of the human race go far beyond the scope of this study.

The problems for the United States created by the Castro revolution in Cuba concerned bilateral issues related to the seizure of American properties and other acts reflecting an increasingly bitter anti-U.S. policy on the part of the Castro regime; the efforts of the Castro regime to export its revolutionary, anti-U.S. program to other Latin American countries, which if successful would *inter alia* undermine the structure of the Inter-American System; and the growth of Communist influence in the Castro government and the development of close collaboration between Cuba and the Soviet Union, with both political and military implications.

From the beginning, United States officials were concerned over the influence of known Communists and Communist sympathizers in the Castro regime. The visit to Cuba of Soviet Deputy Premier Anastas Mikoyan in February 1960, however, highlighted for the first time the growing collaboration between the two governments. In June and July several leading Cubans visited Moscow, and Soviet and Chinese Communists made statements in support of the Castro regime, including Chairman Khrushchev who said: "Figuratively speaking, if need be, Soviet artillerymen can support the Cuban people with their rocket fire, should the aggressive forces in the Pentagon dare to start intervention against Cuba." [1]

Viewing the problem at this time primarily in hemisphere terms, the United States sought to arouse the Latin American countries to the growing Communist subversion of Cuba. The Latin American governments, however, for political reasons, feared taking a strong critical stand against the popular Castro revolution. Some of them discounted the extent of Communist infiltration as well as its danger to the peace and security of the hemisphere. Nonintervention and self-determination were the slogans under which they maintained a policy of seeing no evil in the Cuban

[1] *New York Times*, July 10, 1960, p. 2.

problem. Powerful political forces sympathizing with the stated objectives of the Cuban revolution in virtually every Latin American country supported the position taken in OAS councils.

The United States first attempted to call attention to the Communist danger in Cuba in the Inter-American Peace Committee. This committee had been instructed by the Fifth Meeting of Consultation of Ministers of Foreign Affairs in 1959 to make a study of international tensions in the Caribbean.[2] Seeking to have the committee consider the Communist problem in this connection, the United States submitted to it a memorandum of August 1, 1960, entitled "Responsibilities of the Cuban Government for Increased International Tensions in the Hemisphere," which included a section on "The Cuban Government and Sino-Soviet Communism."[3] The committee, however, was primarily concerned with the problems associated with the Dominican Republic, and its report to the Meeting of Foreign Ministers merely transmitted the memorandum as an appendix without comment.

The Seventh Meeting of Foreign Ministers was called to consider the problem of Communist intervention in Cuba, but it took only mild and circumlocutory action thereon. The Declaration of San José condemned extracontinental intervention in the Americas and "the attempt of the Sino-Soviet Powers to make use of the political, economic, or social situation of any American state,"[4] but it made no direct criticism of Cuba, nor did it take positive action to check the growth of Communist influence there.

Unsuccessful in promoting collective action through the OAS, the United States turned to other approaches. Support for anti-Castro Cuban exiles increased, culminating in the disastrous Bay of Pigs invasion of April 1961. The Alliance for Progress, launched by President Kennedy in March as a refinement of the Latin American social development program initiated by President Eisenhower in 1960, was to some degree designed to strengthen the United States' political position in Latin America in the face of the Castro-Communist alliance.

The new economic and social policy of the Alliance for Progress and the increasingly clear evidence of Castro's adherence to the Communist bloc led the Eighth Meeting of Consultation of Ministers of Foreign Affairs, meeting as the Organ of Consultation under the Rio Treaty on January 3, 1962, for the first time to face up to the problem of Castroism. The meeting declared that adherence by any state to Marxism-Leninism was incompatible with the Inter-American System, and that the Castro government

[2] This assignment and the work of the Peace Committee pursuant thereto are discussed more fully in the section on the Inter-American Peace Committee. See pp. 190 ff.

[3] Inter-American Peace Committee, *Report to the Seventh Meeting of Consultation of Ministers of Foreign Affairs*, Doc. CIP-6-60 (Washington: Pan American Union, 1960), App. J.

[4] Seventh Meeting of Consultation of Ministers of Foreign Affairs, *Final Act*, OEA/Ser. C/II.7 (Washington: Pan American Union, 1960), p. 4.

was therefore excluded from participation therein.[5] The fact that six Latin American countries, including the three largest, Argentina, Brazil, and Mexico, abstained from voting in favor of the exclusion (although they favored the general principle of incompatibility) revealed how strong noninterventionist sentiment continued to be. The meeting at Punta del Este also set up a new Special Consultative Committee on security matters to advise the member governments on problems of Communist aggression and subversion;[6] but no means could be agreed upon of bringing pressure to bear on the Cuban Government to alter its Communist orientation or of obtaining first-hand evidence of what was going on in the island republic.

In the summer of 1962, following the two-week visit of Cuban Defense Minister Raúl Castro to Moscow, the world became aware of a large military buildup by the Soviet Union in Cuba. Thousands of Russian personnel, classified as technicians, arrived in ships bringing cargoes that were unloaded at night under strict security precautions. The United States had initiated surveillance of Cuba from the air, and as late as September 4 and 13, President Kennedy reported that there was no evidence of organized combat forces in Cuba from any Soviet bloc country, or of the existence in Cuba of any offensive missiles. He stated that if it were otherwise, the gravest issues would arise.[7]

The increasing concern of the Latin American governments at these developments was reflected in the statement of American foreign ministers meeting informally at Washington, October 2 and 3, to the effect that the intervention of the Sino-Soviet bloc in Cuba called for "special and urgent attention" and a readiness to consider "measures beyond those already authorized" if the situation so required.[8]

On October 22, the nation and the world were shocked by President Kennedy's radio and television broadcast saying that within the past week unmistakable evidence had established the fact that a series of offensive missile sites was in preparation in Cuba. The missiles were of two kinds: those of medium range, capable of carrying a nuclear warhead for a distance of 1,000 miles, which could strike at Washington, the Panama Canal, Mexico City, and other centers of the southeastern United States and Central America; and other missiles of double that range, which would bring the area between Hudson Bay on the north and Lima, Peru, on the south within range. In addition, jet bombers capable of carrying nuclear weapons were being uncrated in Cuba. Denouncing this vast buildup, which had been accomplished in secrecy and deception, President Kennedy stated unilateral and collective steps to cope with the situation. These were:

1. A strict quarantine against all offensive military equipment under shipment to Cuba.

---

[5] Eighth Meeting of Consultation of Ministers of Foreign Affairs, Resolution VI, *Final Act*, OEA/Ser. C/II.8 (Washington: Pan American Union, 1962).

[6] *Ibid.*, Resolution II.

[7] U.S. Department of State, *Bulletin*, Vol. 47 (1962), pp. 450, 481–82.

[8] *Ibid.*, p. 599.

2. Increased surveillance of Cuba.

3. A policy of regarding any nuclear attack from Cuba "against any nation in the Western hemisphere as an attack by the Soviet Union on the United States, requiring a full retaliatory response upon the Soviet Union."

4. The reinforcement of Guantánamo and evacuation of dependents, and a standby alert for other units.

5. A call for an OAS Organ of Consultation Meeting, invoking Articles 6 and 8 of the Rio Treaty.

6. A call for an emergency meeting of the UN Security Council to pass a resolution requiring the prompt dismantling and withdrawal of all offensive weapons in Cuba, under supervision of UN observers, before the quarantine would be lifted.

7. A call on Chairman Khrushchev "to halt this clandestine, reckless and provocative threat to world peace." [9]

The week of October 22 to October 28, 1962, when Chairman Khrushchev agreed to dismantle and withdraw the missiles, is one of the most fateful periods of recent history. The tense drama was enacted in three theaters: the communications system between the White House and the Kremlin; the Council of the Organization of American States; and the Security Council and the Secretary-General of the United Nations. Fact-finding and observation were important subjects of consideration in all three phases.

KENNEDY-KHRUSHCHEV NEGOTIATIONS

Ten letters were exchanged between the American and Soviet heads of state from October 22 to October 28, five in each direction. The crisis was resolved by a letter of October 26, 1962, from Chairman Khrushchev to President Kennedy (which has never been made public) and by President Kennedy's reply of October 28, 1962. In essence, the bargain was "no missiles" in exchange for "no quarantine and no invasion." Between these two letters there was another letter from Chairman Khrushchev to President Kennedy, dated October 27 and commonly known as the "Turkey letter," because it offered to dismantle bases in Cuba in return for the dismantling of U.S. bases in Turkey. President Kennedy made public the fact that he had inconsistent and conflicting proposals before him, but he resolved the question by ignoring the "Turkey letter" in his reply of October 28. The essence of the agreement is contained in the following quotation:

> As I read your letter, the key elements of your proposals—which seem generally acceptable as I understand them—are as follows:
> 1. You would agree to remove these weapons systems from Cuba under appropriate United Nations observation and supervision; and undertake,

[9] *Ibid.*, pp. 715–20.

with suitable safeguards, to halt the further introduction of such weapons systems into Cuba.

2. We, on our part, would agree–upon the establishment of adequate arrangements through the United Nations to ensure the carrying out and continuation of these commitments–(a) to remove promptly the quarantine measures now in effect and (b) to give assurances against an invasion of Cuba.

I am confident that other nations of the Western Hemisphere would be prepared to do likewise. [10]

ACTION IN THE ORGANIZATION OF AMERICAN STATES

Immediately after the President's radio and television speech of October 22, Assistant Secretary of State Edwin M. Martin gave the Latin American ambassadors a private briefing on the situation and the course of action which the United States proposed, and requested an emergency meeting of the Council of the OAS under the Rio Treaty.

The Council met the following morning. The United States, represented by the Secretary of State, requested the immediate convocation of the Organ of Consultation under the Rio Treaty and the adoption by the Council, acting provisionally, of a resolution, based on Articles 6 and 8 of the Treaty, authorizing extreme measures. The Latin American governments responded by unanimously adopting a resolution calling for the immediate dismantling and withdrawal from Cuba of all offensive weapons and recommended to the member states that they:

> Take all measures, individually and collectively, including the use of armed force . . . to ensure that the Government of Cuba cannot continue to receive from the Sino-Soviet powers military material and related supplies which may threaten the peace and security of the Continent and to prevent the missiles in Cuba with offensive capability from ever becoming an active threat to the peace and security of the Continent. [11]

The resolution also expressed the hope that the UN Security Council would "dispatch United Nations observers to Cuba at the earliest possible moment."

The United States had made clear that it was determined to institute the quarantine of Cuba in any event. Adoption of the OAS resolution, however, converted what would otherwise have been a unilateral move of self-defense into a collective measure.

The OAS resolution of October 23, 1962, also served as a multilateral basis for the continued air surveillance of Cuba by the United States,

[10] *Ibid.*, pp. 745–46.
[11] Pan American Union, Council of the OAS Acting Provisionally as Organ of Consultation, Council Series OEA/Ser. G/V, C-d-1024 Rev., Oct. 23, 1962.

although for technical reasons actual participation therein by Latin American countries was not practicable.

Twelve Latin American countries (Argentina, Colombia, Costa Rica, Dominican Republic, Ecuador, El Salvador, Guatemala, Haiti, Honduras, Nicaragua, Panama, and Venezuela) offered to provide military assistance and port facilities to aid in the operation.[12] Several offers included naval units, posing the need for coordinating forces. On November 9, on the recommendation of the Council acting provisionally as Organ of Consultation, Argentina, the Dominican Republic, and the United States notified the Council that an inter-American combined quarantine force had been established into which they were integrating their respective naval units. The officers of the participating navies would be placed on the staff of the Commander of the Combined Quarantine Force.[13]

EVENTS AT THE UNITED NATIONS

The Cuban and U.S. permanent representatives to the Security Council on October 22 requested the Council to consider the Cuban situation. A similar Soviet request followed on October 23. On the same day, the Council of the OAS adopted its resolution, and President Kennedy, invoking it, ordered the quarantine to go into force on October 24.

On October 24, Acting Secretary-General U Thant proposed to President Kennedy and Chairman Khrushchev a two- or three-week suspension of action. "This involves," he stated, "on the one hand the voluntary suspension of all arms shipments to Cuba, and also the voluntary suspension of the quarantine measures involving the searching of ships bound for Cuba."[14] The Secretary-General sent a second message to President Kennedy on October 25 asking "U.S. vessels in the Caribbean to do everything possible to avoid direct confrontation with Soviet ships." He addressed Chairman Khrushchev similarly and asked that Soviet ships on the way to Cuba "stay away from the interception area."[15] Both sides agreed promptly.

On the 26th, the Secretary-General in a letter to Premier Castro asked him to suspend construction on missile bases during negotiations. Castro responded the next day, accepting the proposal provided "the U.S. Government desists from threats and aggressive actions against Cuba, including the naval blockade of our country."[16] This, indeed, was Castro's

[12] A. G. Mezerik, ed., *Cuba and the United States* (New York: International Review Service, 1963), II, p. 89.

[13] *United States Participation in the United Nations: Report to the Congress for the Year 1962* (Washington: Government Printing Office, 1963), p. 106.

[14] *New York Times*, Oct. 25, 1962, p. 23.

[15] *Ibid.*, Oct. 27, 1962, p. 8. United Nations, *Yearbook of the United Nations, 1962* (New York: Columbia University Press, 1964), p. 109.

[16] The entire exchange is in the *New York Times*, Oct. 28, 1962, p. 31.

method of operation: to agree in principle and place unacceptable conditions on the agreement. That attitude was responsible for the later collapse of all the inspection and verification proposals.

POST-CRISIS NEGOTIATIONS UNDER THE UNITED NATIONS

The post-crisis period is that period between the Kennedy-Khrushchev agreement of October 27-28, 1962, and January 7, 1963, which was the date when U.S. Ambassador Adlai Stevenson and Soviet First Deputy Foreign Minister V. Kuznetsov stated that a degree of understanding on the Cuban missile crisis had been reached which rendered it unnecessary "for this item to occupy further the attention of the Security Council at this time."[17] The subject matter of the negotiations was the kind of inspection, if any, to be used to verify the dismantling and withdrawal of the offensive weapons then in Cuba, and to assure the halting of further introduction of such weapon systems into Cuba.

In addition to UN observation and supervision, three other methods were discussed: (1) inspection by the Red Cross; (2) inspection by neutralist ambassadors; and (3) denuclearization of Latin America.

The genesis of the last-named was in an offer by President Joao Goulart of Brazil on October 29, 1962, to approach the United States, Cuba, and the Soviet Union to find a constructive solution that would guarantee the self-determination and nuclear disarmament of Cuba. A resolution sponsored by Brazil, Bolivia, and Chile was introduced into the Political Committee of the UN General Assembly, calling on all member states to consider Africa and Latin America as denuclearized zones and recommending that the countries in these areas agree: "neither to receive nor to manufacture nuclear weapons . . . to dispose forthwith of any nuclear weapons or nuclear delivery vehicles which may now be in territory under their jurisdiction and to make provision for such verification of these arrangements as would insure that they are in fact being observed."[18]

The strategy of the Soviet bloc countries (including Cuba) was to approve the denuclearization of Latin America but to attach impossible conditions, such as the removal of bases in Guantánamo Bay, the Panama Canal, and Puerto Rico. Since the Cuban crisis lasted beyond the closing of the Seventeenth General Assembly, the UN postponed voting on the draft until the next session.

The idea of denuclearizing Latin America gained impetus through the declaration of April 29, 1963, signed by the presidents of Bolivia, Brazil, Chile, Ecuador, and Mexico.[19] Under this declaration, the Latin American

[17] UN Security Council, S/5227, Jan. 7, 1963, p. 1.
[18] UN General Assembly, A/C.1/L.312/Rev. 2, Nov. 15, 1962.
[19] UN General Assembly, A/5415.

states were to sign a multilateral agreement whereby their countries would undertake not to manufacture, receive, store, or test nuclear weapons or nuclear launching devices.

A resolution to study the idea was approved in the General Assembly on November 27, 1963, by a vote of 91 to 0 with 15 abstentions.[20] The Soviet bloc and Cuba were among those abstaining. To make the position of the United States "crystal clear," Ambassador Charles Stelle said: "If the states of Latin America work out an agreement to establish a nuclear free zone which meets the criteria my Government believes necessary, the U.S. will respect the agreement."[21]

In the same statement Ambassador Stelle repeated Ambassador Stevenson's earlier charge: "The representative of Cuba has excused himself from support of the draft resolution before us, which is broadly supported by other Latin American States, by enumerating certain conditions, which, as well he knows, are unacceptable."

Use of the International Committee of the Red Cross as an inspection agency was suggested to the Secretary-General by the Soviet Government on October 29. The suggestion was that if Castro refused on-site inspection by the UN, the inspection could be accomplished either by using the non-aligned members of the diplomatic corps at Havana or a corps of Red Cross inspectors.[22]

On October 30 and 31, the Secretary-General conferred with Castro about inspection. UN Under-Secretaries Omar Loufti and Dr. Tavares de Sá, and the UN Military Adviser, Brigadier I. J. Rikhye, accompanied the Secretary-General to Havana. During this period, both the quarantine and air surveillance were lifted.[23]

Castro took the position that inspection either by the UN or the International Committee of the Red Cross was "an act of humiliation and violation of Cuban sovereignty." He asked why the United States could not accept a Soviet public statement that the weapons were out of Cuba, when Cuba had to accept a U.S. public statement that it would not invade Cuba. The talks ended without agreement, and the U.S. quarantine and air surveillance were resumed on November 1.

The idea of using neutralist ambassadors as inspectors was submitted to the Secretary-General as a joint Soviet-Cuban proposal on November 13. U Thant did not favor it, however, and it was not even forwarded to the U.S. delegation to the United Nations.

[20] UN Press Release GA/2910, Dec. 17, 1963, Part II, p. 6.

[21] U.S. Mission to the UN, Press Release No. 4310, Nov. 19, 1963.

[22] The account of the progress of Red Cross and nonaligned ambassadors inspection is taken from Robert Crane, "The Cuban Crisis: A Strategic Analysis of American and Soviet Policy," *Orbis*, VI (Winter 1963), which in turn is based on press accounts, largely the *New York Times*.

[23] David L. Larson, ed., *The "Cuban Crisis" of 1962, Selected Documents and Chronology* (Boston: Houghton Mifflin, 1963), p. 321.

Because of the difficulties with Castro, Chairman Khrushchev sent First Deputy Prime Minister Anastas Mikoyan to Havana. Prior to his arrival on November 2, Castro anticipated the visit by publicly declaring that Cuba would submit to no inspection or verification of any kind. This statement was repeated in his letter of November 15 to the Secretary-General. He concluded by warning that he would have any U.S. planes over Cuba shot down to the extent Cuban fire power could do so. By this uncompromising stand, Castro salved his wounded ego, but he was revealed as head of a satellite state, not consulted by his master on the removal of the weapons.

The United States was committed to on-site inspection by the UN from the beginning of the crisis, but it was soon indicated that this policy was not rigid. On November 2, President Kennedy said in a brief address:

> The United States intends to follow closely the completion of this work through a variety of means, including aerial surveillance, until such time as an equally satisfactory international means of verification is effected.
>
> While the quarantine remains in effect, we are hopeful that adequate procedures can be developed for international inspection of Cuba-bound cargoes. The International Committee of the Red Cross, in our view, would be an appropriate agent in this matter. [24]

The International Red Cross announced that it would be glad to extend its "good offices" provided the United States, the Soviet Union, and Cuba agreed. On November 7, Red Cross representative Paul Ruegger and the Secretary-General discussed the proposed methods of inspection. Since Mikoyan had been unable to change Castro on inspection, the Soviet Union set the following conditions for Red Cross inspection: that it cover only inspection of ship cargoes bound from Cuba; that it be applied only to Soviet or Soviet-chartered ships; that Swiss Army technicians be assigned to the Red Cross to replace not only the U.S. quarantine, but the U.S. "alongside eyeball inspection." The negotiations broke down, and on November 12, 1962, the *Journal de Genève* announced that the International Committee of the Red Cross was no longer interested. [25]

All of the foregoing inspection proposals—Red Cross, neutralist ambassadors, and denuclearized Latin America—were discussed as substitutes or alternatives for the UN on-site inspection in Cuba accepted by President Kennedy and Chairman Khrushchev in the basic agreement of October 27 and 28, 1962. Castro made UN inspection unacceptable by five conditions: (1) cessation of the economic blockade and pressure; (2) cessation of "subversive" activities; (3) cessation of "piratical" attacks from the United States and Puerto Rico; (4) cessation of the violation of Cuban air space and territorial waters; and (5) withdrawal of the United States from the

[24] U.S. Department of State, *Bulletin*, Vol. 47 (1962), p. 762.
[25] Crane, *op. cit.*, p. 551.

Guantánamo Naval Base. Neither the Secretary-General nor Mikoyan could budge Castro from the conditions he imposed on his acceptance of UN inspection, and he repeated his demand for the surrender of Guantánamo in a message directly to Khrushchev on November 7.

It has been said that the U.S. policy on inspection was "fluid and flexible" and aimed at achieving "maximum security with minimum risk."[26] The only inspection achieved was unilateral and consisted of intensive U.S. aerial surveillance and "alongside eyeball inspection" at sea.

EVALUATION

The Cuban missile crisis, in which two superpowers were in direct conflict, does not offer any useful precedent with respect to the exercise of observation and verification functions by international organizations, since neither the OAS nor the UN was given the opportunity to perform such functions. It can be adduced that the threat of nuclear conflict between the United States and the Soviet Union was faced and dissipated by direct negotiations between the two heads of state, while the rest of the world was unable to play any effective role. The facts demonstrate, however, that both the OAS and the UN played important roles in providing the political and extra-party context within which these direct negotiations developed.

The final conclusion on the respective contributions of the OAS and the UN depends, thus, on whether one expects that the action of international organizations can, at this stage of development, be definitive or simply complementary in conflicts like the Cuban crisis.

In this case, which involved a direct military threat to the hemisphere, the OAS gave the United States an international decision under which it could justify, on both legal and political grounds, its acts of surveillance on the sea and in the air, which were undertaken in collaboration, if only token in character, with other members of the OAS.

The United Nations provided a forum for marginal discussion both private and public, supporting the direct negotiations between the two heads of state. Thus the UN introduced important if intangible elements of restraint and provided a brake on precipitous actions and a moral and psychological environment favorable to face saving on the part of the Russians.

The case also demonstrated that the OAS as a regional agency was not an appropriate vehicle for dealing with the situation involving the conflict between the two superpowers. This was inherent in its nature as a regional international organization. The OAS did, however, give powerful political underpinning to the United States reaction by its demonstration of hemisphere solidarity at a decisive moment in the crisis; it offered the Russians

---

[26] Crane, *op. cit.*, pp. 549–52.

and the world evidence that the stand taken by the United States was supported by the Latin American states and did not constitute an arbitrary power move on the part of the United States. In its resolution of October 23, the OAS gave the United States authority to invade Cuba if necessary. The use of this authority was contingent on United States willingness to court the danger of a nuclear conflict with the Soviet Union—a factor beyond the scope of the OAS to judge, but which necessarily involved the fate of the other members. They too had a direct stake in, if not a direct responsibility for, waging such a conflict.

While the Security Council of the United Nations was impotent to act in a decisive way in the absence of agreement between the two superpowers, the Secretary-General provided the third-party initiative that at another critical moment eased tensions in providing a temporary hope for the establishment of a UN observation system.

In the last analysis, it was the political leverage exercised by a small power, Cuba, that was responsible for frustrating a more conclusive role by the United Nations. Castro's adamant refusal to accept what Khrushchev had agreed to forced the latter to choose between backing up his one Western Hemisphere ally or losing face in the Communist world.

13

HAITIAN–DOMINICAN REPUBLIC DISPUTE, 1963

The perennial hostility between the Dominican Republic and Haiti continued even after the assassination, on May 31, 1961, of the Dominican dictator, Generalissimo Trujillo, whose oppressive regime had for so long been a source of tension in the Caribbean. Juan Bosch had been chosen president of the republic in a free and fair election. In the meantime, President Francois Duvalier of Haiti had extended his period of office in an election of doubtful validity and had been showing increasing evidence of establishing a police dictatorship at his end of the island.

On April 28, 1963, the Dominican Republic requested an immediate convocation of the Council of the OAS alleging many acts by the Haitian Government that endangered the peace and security of the hemisphere. Chief among them was the forcible entrance and occupation of the Dominican Embassy at Port-au-Prince by Haitian police. The new, democratically elected government of the Dominican Republic informed the Haitian

Government that in view of the seriousness of the acts the Dominican Government expected that within 24 hours the Government of Haiti would give evidence of a "rectification of its conduct toward the Dominican Republic."[1] It was reported that the Dominican Army had been mobilized along the frontier.

The Haitian representative countered with charges that the Dominican Republic was preparing military aggression against Haiti. He requested an organ of consultation under Articles 39 and 40 of the Charter "to take cognizance of the indescribable aggression that the Government of the Dominican Republic plans to undertake within 24 hours." A motion to convoke a Meeting of the Organ of Consultation under the Rio Treaty was introduced by the chairman of the Council.[2]

The immediate issue was whether the acts charged by the Dominican Republic fell within the terms of Article 6 of the Rio Treaty. The subsequent substantive issues would be whether acts of agression had in fact taken place, by whom they had been carried out, and what measures, if any, should be taken by the OAS to fulfill the purposes of the Rio Treaty.

The OAS Council in its second meeting on the case, April 28, 1963, constituted itself provisionally as the Organ of Consultation and authorized the chairman "to appoint a committee of five members to make an on-the-spot study of the events denounced by the Dominican Republic . . . and submit a report thereon."[3]

THE INVESTIGATING COMMITTEE

The committee comprised: Alberto Zuleta Angel, chairman, and Santiago Salazar Santos (Colombia); Emilio Sarmiento Caruncho (Bolivia); Enrique Gajárdo Villarroel (Chile); Gonzalo Escudero (Ecuador); and Francisco Roberto Lima (El Salvador). It left Washington within twenty-four hours of its appointment, arrived at Port-au-Prince on April 30, and interviewed the Haitian minister of foreign affairs, René Chalmers. At the outset, the chairman stated the committee's view of its jurisdiction, namely, to investigate the events denounced by the Dominican Republic. Hence, at this point, there was only one issue. The Haitian foreign minister nevertheless insisted on pressing a series of charges, including one that the Dominican Government was exterminating the Haitian colony in the Dominican Republic.

The committee consulted with the dean of the diplomatic corps to work out the problems of the peaceful departure of Dominican diplomats and

---

[1] OAS Council, *First Report of the Special Committee*, OEA/Ser. G/IV, C-1-608, May 13, 1963, p. 1. Hereafter cited as *First Report*.

[2] Under Article 13 any party to the Rio Treaty may request such action.

[3] *First Report*, p. 3.

the transfer to another embassy of Haitian asylees who had taken refuge in the Dominican Embassy in Port-au-Prince. The committee left for Santo Domingo on May 2, 1963, and, in conversations, the Dominican Government charged: (1) the unlawful entry of the Dominican Embassy by Haitian police; (2) the presence in Haiti of members of the Trujillo family who were a danger to Dominican security; (3) disregard by Haiti of inter-American treaties on asylum; (4) keeping the asylees in a state of anxiety and refusal to issue safe conducts to all; and (5) a plot to assassinate President Bosch.

The committee adhered to the strict interpretation of its function, but the chairman conveyed to the Dominican foreign minister the substance of the charges by the Government of Haiti, emphasizing that he did so purely for purposes of information. [4]

After hearing an oral report from the members of the committee who had returned to Washington on May 8, the Council of the OAS, acting provisionally as Organ of Consultation, enlarged the terms of reference of the Investigating Committee "to authorize [it] to make an on-the-spot study of the situation existing between Haiti and the Dominican Republic and to offer the parties their services for the purpose of finding a prompt solution to the conflict and to ward off the threats to the peace and security of the area." [5]

This was the first time that the Council enlarged the terms of reference of an investigating committee under the Rio Treaty to give it explicit mediation or conciliation functions. Entrusted with new powers, on May 13, 1963, the Investigating Committee left Washington again for the Dominican Republic and Haiti. The Assistant Secretary-General of the OAS, Dr. William Sanders, accompanied the committee at its request. The mission remained in Santo Domingo and Haiti from May 13 to May 23.

The committee dealt with a series of charges, countercharges, recriminations and contradictory testimony, all embittered by the injection of the racial issue on the Haitian side and the Dominican Government's repugnance toward the Duvalier "tyranny." The issues previously raised were the focus of major attention: the Dominican mobilization on the frontier; the menacing attitude of Haitian authorities towards diplomatic missions which had admitted asylees; the presence in each country of political exiles from the other who were considered dangerous plotters. It sent two members on an inspection tour of the Dominican border area to verify the withdrawal of troops. Aided by the committee's mediation, several of the Haitian asylees in diplomatic missions were permitted to leave the country, thus somewhat relaxing the tension associated with this problem. Progress toward any genuine conciliation between the parties was, however, minimal.

[4] *First Report*, p. 8.
[5] *First Report*, p. 16.

The Investigating Committee's second written report to the Council dealt first with "facts and events denounced by the Government of the Dominican Republic," reporting that:[6] (1) There had been an illegal entry of the chancery of the Dominican Embassy in Port-au-Prince by two Haitian police. (2) There were members of the Trujillo family in Haiti dangerous to Dominican security (and the committee named them). (3) While the Government of Haiti might not be guilty of disregard of inter-American treaties on asylum, in the interest of peace, the Haitian Government should be less rigid in this matter. (4) The Investigating Committee found no evidence of a plot to assassinate President Juan Bosch. (5) At the time the Investigating Committee was making its first visit, another agency of the regional system, the Inter-American Commission on Human Rights, sent a request to visit Haiti which the Government of Haiti refused. The Haitian foreign minister, in replying to the observations of the Investigating Committee, reaffirmed his government's adherence to the principles of respect for human rights but felt that any interference by the Human Rights Commission would be an intervention in the internal affairs of Haiti.

With respect to the facts and events denounced by the Government of Haiti, the Investigating Committee found that: (1) As to the charge that one of the goals of Dominican policy was the extermination of the Haitian colony in the Dominican Republic, the committee had heard conflicting evidence and decided that it was a matter to be investigated by the judicial authorities of the respective countries. (2) With respect to the Dominican Republic's giving asylum to enemies of the Government of Haiti and permission to carry on hostile activities, the reverse charge had also been made, and the committee said that both governments should be more careful to carry out their international responsibilities in this respect. (3) The committee took cognizance of publicly expressed insults by Dominican officials of President Duvalier and other Haitian officials. (4) It was unable to verify charges of the violation of Haitian air space by Dominican aircraft. (5) It believed that Dominican troop concentrations had been dispersed and that only normal border guards remained.

The recommendations by the Investigating Committee in support of these findings, made on June 10, 1963, were largely exhortations to the two governments to take various steps in accordance with their international obligations. They were adopted by the Council on July 16, 1963. The Council did not terminate its action as Provisional Organ of Consultation.

The third phase of this case was initiated by an abortive invasion of Haiti on August 5, 1963, allegedly led by the Haitian General Leon Cantave from the Dominican Republic, to which he had fled when the invasion collapsed. The Haitian representative to the OAS complained to the Investigating Committee. In reply, on August 13, the Dominican representative gave the flight numbers of the airplanes which had brought

[6] OAS Council, *Second Report of the Committee of the Council Acting Provisionally as Organ of Consultation*, etc., OEA/Ser. G/IV, C-1-624, June 10, 1963, pp. 8–19.

General Cantave from New York to Santo Domingo to July 1 and had taken him back to New York on July 14. The Dominican Government denied that he had been in the Dominican Republic on the date of the alleged invasion or subsequently. It also denied aiding the rebels in any way.

On August 17, the Haitian foreign minister told the committee that another invasion of Haiti had been mounted on August 15 and offered proof of the complicity of the Dominican Government.

The committee (lacking the Bolivian member) remained in Haitian or Dominican territory from August 22 to the end of the month. It investigated the places of the alleged invasion, interrogated witnesses, and examined arms and vehicles. While it found that the invasions had been mounted from Dominican territory, there was nothing to prove complicity by the Dominican Government.[7]

Reviewing the recent Dominican-Haitian difficulties, the committee tried to find an acceptable formula of conciliation between the two governments. Since they had broken diplomatic relations, the committee, after conversations in each capital, drafted two unilateral declarations which, they suggested, could be issued simultaneously by the respective governments and subsequently endorsed in a resolution of the Council acting provisionally as Organ of Consultation. The proposed drafts expressed the determination of the respective governments to apply appropriate international agreements with respect to the specific problems of exiles and asylees and to accept the supervision of the frontier by the OAS so long as conditions so required. The Dominican Government agreed to adopt this procedure, provided the Haitian Government also agreed. The latter first indicated a favorable attitude but then attempted to bring its complaints before the United Nations Security Council, and finally rejected any possibility of agreeing to the declarations.

The committee's report contains a review of its efforts, and a detailed refutation of many complaints and alleged misstatements contained in the Haitian document. It concluded its report by stating that the recommendations made in its second report were an adequate basis for the solution of the outstanding problems between the two countries and expressing the hope that they would resort to bilateral negotiations to that end. The case was thus left hanging in mid-air.

EVALUATION

This is typical of the problems presented to the OAS as a result of the chronic tensions between the two republics occupying the island of Hispaniola. It was compounded of political hostility and racial antagonism

---

[7] Consejo de la OEA, *Tercer Informe de la Comisión del Consejo de la OEA actuando provisionalmente como Organo de Consulta*, etc., OEA/Ser. G/VI, C/INF-359, 12 novembre 1963, p. 38.

against a background of basic instability. The action of the OAS was effective, by the prompt dispatch of an investigating committee, in calming the atmosphere in both countries and leading both governments to take measures that would overcome the major obstacles to the maintenance of peaceful, if not cordial, relations. In this sense, the Investigating Committee played a role similar to that of the Inter-American Peace Committee, since the issues dealt more with intangible matters of aggressive and suspicious attitudes than with concrete acts, so that it was impossible to fix the blame on either party. The Council, having invoked the Rio Treaty, found it necessary to continue to use its power as provisional organ in view of the somewhat inconclusive results of its peace-making efforts and the recurring incidents between the two governments. At this writing, the case is still on the books of the Council. The experience confirms the likelihood of continued difficulties between the two countries.

14

—•—

RIO LAUCA DISPUTE BETWEEN
BOLIVIA AND CHILE, 1962

The Rio Lauca dispute between Bolivia and Chile involves the application of the Rio Defense Pact, but it is not one in which peace observation was carried out. There are, nonetheless, lessons to be learned from this failure to implement peace observation.

The Rio Lauca rises in northern Chile and after flowing for some 100 kilometers in Chile and receiving water from entirely Chilean tributaries, enters Bolivia where it flows for 250 kilometers before losing itself in a salt lake, Lake Coipasa.

As far back as 1939, the Government of Bolivia learned of Chilean intentions to divert waters of the Rio Lauca for the irrigation of the Azapa Valley in Arica, the northernmost province of Chile. Both countries had approved without reservation the Declaration on the Industrial and Agricultural Use of International Rivers, drawn up by the Seventh International Conference of American States held at Montevideo in 1933.[1] Under Article 7 of that declaration, a state planning to use the waters of international rivers is required to give notice to other riparian states, and

---

[1] The text of this Declaration LXXIII is in *Report of the Delegates of the OAS to the Seventh International Conference of American States, Montevideo, Uruguay,* Dec. 3–26, 1933 (Washington: Government Printing Office), p. 267.

under Article 8 provision was made for a Mixed Technical Commission from both sides to pass judgment on the case. Mixed Technical Commissions were established for the Rio Lauca in 1949 and in 1960.

On April 14, 1962, the Bolivian representative in a note to the Chairman of the Council of the OAS alleged the immediate threat of aggression by Chile by diverting the waters of the Rio Lauca. He asserted that the Mixed Technical Commission, in August 1949, had signed a document stating that the information supplied by the Chilean Government on the proposed diversion was insufficient.

The dispute came to a head at the end of 1961 when the Chilean Government proceeded to make test diversions. Bolivia objected; Chile responded by offering to conduct bilateral negotiations. Bolivia accepted provided the works were stopped. Chile refused this latter condition, and on March 21, 1962, announced that it would begin to use the waters of the Rio Lauca in the first days of April. A second and third offer to initiate bilateral negotiations were similarly rejected or unanswered.

On April 18, 1962, the Bolivian representative asked for an extraordinary session of the Council to hear the case. Four sessions of the Council then took place pursuant to the Rio Defense Pact. [2]

The issue was whether Chile was committing an act of aggression against Bolivia and diverting waters from the Rio Lauca, an international river.

The Chilean reply was circulated to the Council before the first session in the form of an address made on April 18, 1962, in Chile by the Chilean minister of foreign affairs. Chile alleged that Bolivia had never made formal objections to the diversion works in the 22 years during which the matter was pending. Chile refused to accept the condition imposed on bilateral negotiations because this condition put into the hands of Bolivia the possibility of endless delay. Here, indeed, was the crux of the Chilean defense.

Chile would not accept the latest Bolivian proposal for procedure under the Montevideo Declaration of Use of International Rivers. This would require a new description of the proposed works, three months for a Bolivian reply, designation of another Mixed Commission, a six months' wait for its conclusion, then pass to bilateral renegotiation without terms, and beyond that to a conciliation process. Had this proposal been accepted, Chile would run the risk of further delay, perhaps of years. [3]

DECISION OF THE OAS COUNCIL

On May 24, 1962, the OAS Council passed a resolution omitting any reference to the charge of aggression made against Chile and refraining from setting up an Investigating Committee.

[2] *Aplicaciones del Tratado, 1960–1964,* p. 80.
[3] *Aplicaciones del Tratado, 1960–1964,* p. 85.

The resolution expressed the hope that the two countries would resume normal diplomatic relations.[4] In bland terms, equating the two parties, the Council called on both governments to choose one of the methods of peaceful settlement open to them and suggesting the Pact of Bogotá, which both had signed, as the proper procedure.

REACTION OF THE PARTIES

While stating that the resolution was acceptable, the Bolivian Government would agree to resumption of diplomatic relations provided Chile would desist from using the waters of the Rio Lauca. Meanwhile, Bolivia would continue the interruption of diplomatic relations as the only means of protest open to it.[5]

The Bolivian representative in the Council had responded the day after the passage of the resolution. The Chilean delegation took over a month. In essence, the Chilean Government rejected diplomatic procedure and mediation as a means of settlement of the case but would accept judicial settlement or arbitration.[6]

The Bolivian Government insisted that mediation was the appropriate means of settlement but would agree to submit the case to the Permanent Court of International Justice, always provided that Chile refrained from using the waters of the Rio Lauca.[7]

The last word on the part of the Chilean Government, on August 1, 1962, rejected the condition imposed by Bolivia on the offer of judicial settlement or arbitration.

On five separate occasions, from about the middle of 1962 to the middle of 1963, the Bolivian Government wrote to the President concerning the Rio Lauca dispute. With respect to Bolivia's request for the convocation of an Organ of Consultation, the OAS Council abstained from any reply; it rested on the resolution of May 24, 1962.[8]

The Bolivian reaction was to boycott the meetings of the Council of the OAS, except for participation in the consideration of the Venezuelan-Cuban case of 1964, and continued to maintain this boycott until January 21, 1965, when the Bolivian representative resumed his place after a change of government in La Paz.

EVALUATION

Since the resolution of May 24, 1962, left the parties in the position in which they had found themselves, it was tantamount to a denial of the

[4] *Aplicaciones del Tratado, 1960–1964,* p. 89.
[5] *Aplicaciones del Tratado, 1960–1964,* p. 90.
[6] *Aplicaciones del Tratado, 1960–1964,* p. 92.
[7] *Aplicaciones del Tratado, 1960–1964,* p. 93.
[8] *Aplicaciones del Tratado, 1960–1964,* p. 100.

Bolivian charge that Chile had committed aggression in diverting waters of the Rio Lauca.

The omission of the creation of an Investigating Committee to find the facts, as is generally done, may be taken as an indication that the Council was not of the opinion that Bolivia had made out a prima facie case.

This interpretation has been confirmed by personal conversations with persons who were close to the controversy. In general, the Council members felt that Bolivia was a relatively backward country unwilling or unable to develop the international river, and unwilling to see its more advanced neighbor do so. The Council members refused to use the OAS machinery to aid the Bolivian position.

15

VENEZUELAN–CUBAN DISPUTE, 1963–1964

Castro had tried to overthrow, in turn, the Governments of Panama, Nicaragua, the Dominican Republic, and Haiti. The expeditions to accomplish these objectives were launched or aided by Castro in 1959, his first year in office. All of them were unsuccessful. Thereafter Castro turned to subversion, a less direct method of overthrowing non-Communist governments. Venezuela, rich, nearby with heavy U.S. petroleum investments there and with a substantial Communist opposition, became a prime target of Castro Communism.[1]

When Castro came to power on January 1, 1959, Romulo Betancourt was already President-elect of Venezuela. He was then in the interior of the country and was surprised to learn that Castro, who he had never met, was coming to Caracas to participate in a mass meeting with Betancourt's recent principal opponent in the election, Rear Admiral Larrazabal. Betancourt extended his tour to stay out of Caracas but returned, at Castro's request, to meet him. The story of that meeting and of the subsequent steps from cool correctness to open hostility is contained in President Betancourt's statement to the OAS Investigating Committee on December 9, 1963.[2]

At the first meeting, Castro put to President Betancourt what the former termed "the master plan against the Gringos," which consisted of

[1] *Aplicaciones del Tratado, 1960–1964*, p. 183.
[2] *Aplicaciones del Tratado, 1960–1964*, p. 197.

the Government of Venezuela lending to the Government of Cuba 300 million dollars. President Betancourt refused this, as he did the ensuing request for 300 million dollars' worth of petroleum products.

By October 1959, "a veritable airline bridge" was established between Venezuelan Communists and Havana. In October, President Betancourt telephoned the Foreign Minister of Cuba to say that a projected visit to Venezuela by Che Guevara and Raúl Castro was unacceptable.

During the summer of 1960, in connection with Trujillo's attempt to assassinate President Betancourt, Cuban comment provoked an energetic protest by the President. Meanwhile the political refugee problem at the Venezuelan Embassy in Havana became acute. Nearby houses were rented to accommodate the 500 to 600 asylees.

The incident which resulted in the breaking of relations was Venezuela's support of the Commission on Human Rights of the OAS when it asked for a cessation of the mass executions in Cuba. The Cuban reply, through the minister of foreign affairs, was that the U.S. Department of State and CIA "dictated the genuflecting statements of the Government of President Betancourt." Venezuela transferred the asylees to the Mexican Embassy and broke relations. From that moment, Castro fomented seditious uprisings and terrorism against the Venezuelan Government.

On November 29, 1963, the Venezuelan representative on the Council of the OAS sent the chairman a note requesting an immediate convocation of the Organ of Consultation under Article 6 of the Rio Defense Pact to consider measures to be taken against Cuba for acts of intervention and aggression against Venezuela.[3]

The issue was whether the Government of Cuba was guilty of intervention and aggression against Venezuela.

A special meeting of the OAS Council was held on December 3, 1963, and the Venezuelan representative concentrated his charges on the finding of a large amount of military equipment hidden on the Venezuelan coast at a place called Maccama and with respect to which the Venezuelan Government claimed to have ample proof of Cuban origin.

THE INVESTIGATING COMMITTEE

The OAS Council, acting provisionally as Organ of Consultation, approved a resolution "to authorize the Chairman of the Council of the Organization to appoint a committee to investigate and report on the acts denounced by Venezuela at the meeting of the Council held this morning."

This single sentence constituted the terms of reference of the committee.[4] The chairman appointed as members of the committee: Argentina, Colombia, Costa Rica, the United States, and Uruguay.

[3] *Aplicaciones del Tratado, 1960–1964*, p. 183.
[4] *Aplicaciones del Tratado, 1960–1964*, p. 184.

The committee met the next day and elected as chairman Ambassador Rodolfo A. Weidmann of Argentina. The other committee members were Ambassador Alfredo Vázquez Carrizosa of Colombia, Ambassador Gonzalo J. Facio of Costa Rica, and Ward P. Allen of the United States. The Uruguayan representative on the OAS Council, Emilio N. Oribe, attended this meeting and announced that he would be replaced by a special representative, Félix Polleri Carrió, Uruguayan Ambassador to Panama.

The committee established precedent at its first meeting by asking for two technical experts from the staff of the Inter-American Defense Board. The Board appointed Colonel Fernando Izurieta Molina and Colonel Juan Giró Tapper. The Colombian, Costa Rican, and Argentine delegations had their own military advisers. Four experienced secretariat officers were supplied by the Pan American Union from the office of the Juridical Adviser.

The committee remained in Venezuela for one week, from December 8 to 15. On the second day, it heard the statement of President Betancourt referred to above. Thereafter, the committee heard Venezuelan Government witnesses describe the circumstances under which the arms were found and observed chemical experiments designed to reveal characteristics of the arms. For several days, the military advisers made technical examinations. These officers and the representatives of the United States and Uruguay also visited the site where the arms were found and interrogated civil and military authorities and residents.

To support the charge of subversion, representatives of the Venezuelan Government produced tapes of radio propaganda from Havana and produced one Venezuelan who had gone through several months of guerrilla training in Cuba.

The chairman and the representatives of Colombia and Costa Rica and the representatives of the United States and Uruguay, together with the military and secretariat staff, returned to Washington in mid-December 1963. Their report to the Council was rendered on February 18, 1964.[5]

The conclusions of the committee report fully substantiated the charges made by the Venezuelan Government. A chapter of the report is entitled "Opportunity Offered to the Government of Cuba to Present Its Defense." The committee on January 24, 1964, sent a note to the Cuban Government inviting it to present a statement, in writing if it so desired. By cable on February 3, 1964, the Government of Cuba answered that "it neither recognizes, admits nor accepts the jurisdiction of the OAS" and made statements condemnatory of the Organization and its members, whereupon the committee unanimously ignored the receipt of the communication.[6]

---

[5] *Aplicaciones del Tratado, 1960–1964*, p. 192. The photographs of the arms appear in OEA/Ser. G/IV, C-1.658, Feb. 18, 1964.

[6] *Aplicaciones del Tratado, 1960–1964*, p. 213.

On June 26, 1964, the OAS Council resolved to convoke the Ninth Meeting of Consultation of Ministers of Foreign Affairs to be held at the headquarters of the OAS on July 21, 1964. It elected as chairman the minister of foreign affairs of Brazil, Vasso Leitão da Cunha. The meeting concluded on July 26 and produced three substantive documents: (1) Resolution on Application of Measures to the Present Government of Cuba, (2) a Declaration to the People of Cuba, and (3) a Declaration on Regional and Economic Coordination.[7]

The Resolution on Application of Measures to the Present Government of Cuba begins with a declaration that the acts verified by the Investigating Committee constitute an aggression and intervention by Cuba in the internal affairs of Venezuela that affects all the member states. The present Government of Cuba is condemned for these acts.

The third paragraph, invoking Articles 6 and 8 of the Rio Defense Pact, imposes the following sanctions on the Government of Cuba:

a. That the governments of the American states not maintain diplomatic or consular relations with the Government of Cuba;
b. That the governments of the American states suspend all their trade, whether direct or indirect, with Cuba except in foodstuffs, medicines, and medical equipment that may be sent to Cuba for humanitarian reasons; and
c. That the governments of the American states suspend all sea transportation between their countries and Cuba, except for such transport as may be necessary for reasons of a humanitarian nature.

Following the precedent established when sanctions were voted against the dictator Trujillo, the OAS Council was authorized to discontinue the sanctions when the Government of Cuba shall have ceased to constitute a danger to the peace and security of the hemisphere.

In the fifth paragraph, the Government of Cuba is warned that if it should persist in acts of aggression or intervention, the member states preserve their essential rights of self-defense to resort to armed force, either individually or collectively until such time as the Organ of Consultation takes measures to guarantee the peace and security of the hemisphere.

The Declaration to the People of Cuba expressed profound concern for their fate and the hope that they would soon liberate themselves from the tyranny of the Communist regime.

The Declaration on Regional and International Economic Coordination was another endorsement of the aims and purposes of the Alliance for Progress.

There were two statements by the Chilean and Mexican delegations, respectively, appended to the Final Act of the Ninth Meeting. The Chilean delegation declared that it abstained from voting on paragraphs 1 and 2

[7] OAS Official Records, OEA/Ser.F/11.9 (English), Doc. 48, Rev. 2, p. 4, entitled "Final Act of the 9th Meeting of Consultation of Ministers of Foreign Affairs."

of the resolution (breaking relations and prohibiting trade with Cuba) because it did not consider the acts of the Government of Cuba to be "aggression." It voted against paragraph 3 (which cut off trade) and paragraph 5 (which warned Cuba of the right of self-defense) on the ground that these paragraphs were not compatible with Article 51 of the Charter of the United Nations and Article 3 of the Rio Defense Pact. The Chilean Government also abstained on the Declaration to the Cuban People, although agreeing with its basic content, because it deemed such an exhortation to be intervention.[8] The Mexican delegation was less forthright in its reservations. It, also, objected to the third paragraph on the ground that it was incompatible with Articles 3 and 10 of the Rio Defense Pact.[9]

At the time of the termination of the ninth meeting, Cuba had diplomatic relations only with Mexico, Chile, Bolivia, and Uruguay in the western hemisphere. According to the Rio Defense Pact (Article 17), the Organ of Consultation takes its decision by a two-thirds vote of all the signatory states that have ratified the treaty. Under Article 20, the decision on sanctions is binding on all signatory states, except that no state is required to use armed force without its consent.

By the end of 1964, all governments in the Western Hemisphere had broken off diplomatic relations with Cuba, except Mexico.

EVALUATION

Seen in relation to the earlier OAS peace observation cases involving Castro, the case shows the increasing awareness of the danger of Castro to the hemisphere and the movement of all the Latin American governments except Mexico from a position of benevolent regard for Castro to one of condemnation.

The Mexican position must be understood in the light of historical perspective. Little more than 100 years ago, the United States took by force one-third of Mexican national territory. Accordingly, the doctrine of nonintervention has been exalted by the Mexican Government over all other doctrines in the Inter-American System. This attitude is not a doctrinaire one; it reflects the widespread attitude of the Mexican people. Also, in part, it reflects the favorable attitude toward Castro taken by the Mexican left.

The use of weaponry specialists from the staff of the Inter-American Defense Board was an excellent idea. The Final Report of the Group of Military Advisers, which included the Argentine naval attaché, may be regarded as a model for peace observers who have occasion to identify the origin and intended use of clandestine shipments of guerrilla-type weapons.

---

[8] *Ibid.*, p. 11.
[9] *Ibid.*, p. 11.

16

---♦---

THE PANAMA CANAL DISPUTE
UNITED STATES AND PANAMA, 1964

On January 9, 1964, the American public was shocked to learn that some hundreds of rioting Panamanians had invaded the Panama Canal Zone to fly the Panamanian flag over Balboa High School, where students had insisted on flying the United States flag. The Canal Zone police, unable to cope with the mob, had called in U.S. troops. A number of civilians and soldiers were killed and some hundreds wounded. Demonstrations at the border and in other parts of Panama continued for several days and considerable property was destroyed. Panama charged the United States with aggression, broke off diplomatic relations, and appealed the case to the OAS and the United Nations.

In June 1962, when President Chiari visited President Kennedy at Washington, agreement had been reached that "their representatives will arrange for the flying of Panamanian flags in an appropriate way in the Canal Zone."[1] Pursuant to this agreement in principle, announcement was made that the flag of Panama would be flown together with the flag of the United States on land in the Canal Zone where the U.S. flag is flown by civilian authorities. The action of the Balboa High School students was thus seemingly contrary to international agreement.

The flag incident and previous incidents like it must be seen in the light of the history of United States relations with Panama. Since the beginning of the Panama Canal in 1903, those relations have largely concerned the Canal Zone. They are based on the Hay-Bunau Varilla Convention of November 18, 1903, under Article 2 of which "the Republic of Panama grants to the United States in perpetuity the use, occupation and control of a zone of land . . . for the construction, maintenance, operation, sanitation and protection of said Canal of the width of ten miles." Under Article 3 of the treaty, Panama grants to the United States "all the rights, power and authority within the zone . . . which the United States would possess and exercise if it were the sovereign of the territory within which said lands and waters are located to the entire exclusion of the exercise by the Republic of Panama of any such sovereign rights, power or authority."

---

[1] U.S. Department of State, *Bulletin*, Vol. 47 (1962), p. 82.

The Panama Canal Zone, so described, comprises about 650 square miles of territory. About 36,000 American personnel, civilian and military, together with about 11,000 Panamanians, reside in the zone to operate and protect the Canal. These are called Zonians. The executive power in the zone is exercised by a Governor, appointed by the President of the United States, and the Zone Government is under the supervision of the U.S. Secretary of the Army. The U.S. Congress exercises the legislative power, and the judicial power is under a District Court forming part of the U.S. Federal Judicial System. The Canal, and its operation, is Panama's most valuable economic asset; nearly $100 million is spent there annually in addition to the direct revenue paid to Panama. This has been increased several times and in 1964 amounted to nearly $2 million.

THE BASIC ISSUES

Differences between the two countries arose almost from the beginning over the interpretation of the two articles quoted above, particularly the concepts and scope of "sovereignty" and the rights held "in perpetuity." Panama has insisted on a limited interpretation of sovereignty, that is, one restricted to the overall purpose of the convention—the construction, operation, and protection of the Canal. It denied that the United States had the right to establish custom houses, tariffs, and post offices in the Zone, on the ground that these activities were not connected with the construction and operation of the Canal. On the other hand, the United States has maintained the right under the convention to exercise these attributes of sovereignty to the exclusion of Panama.

Grievances of an economic and social nature have also been the subject of complaint by the Panamanians. Some of these were adjusted in modifications of the 1903 treaty made in 1936, 1942, 1947, and 1955.

Thus, early in the Roosevelt administration, negotiations were begun with Panama that culminated in a "General Treaty of Friendship and Cooperation" signed March 2, 1936, and ratified three years later.[2] The United States gave up the right to acquire additional new lands in Panama, and the right to intervene to maintain law and order in Panama and Colon. It renounced the U.S. guarantee of Panamanian independence and limited its exclusive commercial rights in the Zone.

In 1950, pursuant to a convention between the United States and Panama regarding the Colon Corridor and certain other corridors through the Canal Zone,[3] the United States granted a corridor through the Zone to connect Colon with the rest of Panama and made certain other corridors

[2] 53 Stat. 1807.
[3] TIAS, 3180.

for the new Byrd-Roosevelt transisthmian highway which crossed both Zone and Panamanian territory.

Major changes were made by the treaty of mutual understanding and cooperation signed January 25, 1955, whereby the annuity was raised from $430,200 to about $1.9 million annually.[4] The United States also gave up the right to enforce sanitary measures in Panama and Colon and agreed to certain measures desired by Panama concerning Panamanian labor and commercial opportunities within the Zone. It also agreed to build a bridge across the canal, the cost of which was approximately $20 million.[5] The present annuity payment is deemed by Panama to be grossly inadequate compensation for its "greatest natural resource," its geographical position.

The Panamanian Academy of International Law, at the time of the Suez Canal crisis, pointed out that in the years before 1956, the annual payment was no more than that paid before 1903 to Colombia for the transisthmian railway concession alone. "The Academy pointed out by contrast that at the time of the nationalization of the assets of the Suez Canal Co. in Egypt that Company was paying 7% of its gross profits to the Egyptian Government."[6]

The gross revenues of the Panama Canal Company for fiscal 1963 were over $103 million and the net revenues only $2.3 million.[7] While gross revenues continue to mount owing to the increasing use of the Canal, net revenues have been declining, largely owing to higher wage rates paid to Panamanians. It would be a mistake, however, to assume that the Panamanian Academy would be satisfied with 7 percent of gross revenues which means roughly $7 million instead of the present $2 million. Since nationalization of the Suez Canal Company, the Egyptian Government has been receiving not only the 7 percent royalty but an additional sum in taxes. Some prominent Americans, for example, Milton Eisenhower, President of The Johns Hopkins University, have recently spoken in favor of increased payments to Panama in the form of royalties on gross revenues.[8]

The issue concerning jobs and wages of Panamanian employees is set against a background that does not redound favorably to the United States. Starting with the construction of the Canal, U.S. employees were put on the "gold roll" and native employees on the "silver roll." Up to 1946, rest

---

[4] TIAS, 3297. It is interesting to note that the increase in annuity from $430 thousand to about $1.9 million effected by the 1955 treaty is paid out of Department of State appropriations and not out of revenues of the Canal.

[5] Richard Reeve Baxter and Doris Carroll, *The Panama Canal* (New York: The Association of the Bar of the City of New York, 1964), p. 24.

[6] Baxter and Carroll, *op. cit.*, p. 35.

[7] Panama Canal Company, *Annual Report of the Panama Canal Company and the Canal Zone Government, Fiscal Year Ended June 30, 1963*.

[8] Milton S. Eisenhower, *The Wine Is Bitter: The United States and Latin America* (Garden City, New York: Doubleday, 1963).

rooms, drinking fountains, and even post office windows were segregated by the sign "gold" or "silver" above the accommodations.

Under a so-called "Memorandum of Understanding Reached" appended to the 1955 treaty, the United States was committed to seek congressional legislation that would embody the principle that the basic wage for any given wage level will be the same whether an employee is a citizen of the United States or of the Republic of Panama. Overseas pay and tax differentials would still continue for the U.S. citizen, and he would get greater annual leave benefits and travel allowances to permit periodic vacations in the United States.

These principles were not enacted into law until 1959, and while partial satisfaction has been achieved with adoption of the principle of equal pay for equal work, the Panamanian objective is now to obtain more of the higher paying jobs. Between 1959 and 1962, the number of employees not U.S. citizens in the higher paid positions increased by 417 percent, but when President Chiari visited President Kennedy in 1962, equal employment opportunities were still an issue.[9]

The problem of Panamanian participation in the Canal Zone market is long and involved but follows much the same pattern as the issue concerning equal employment opportunities. When the Canal was built in the swamps and jungle of the isthmus, it was unavoidable that the Canal Company should go into a vast range of commercial activities: provision of housing and food for employees, provision of ship stores to transiting vessels, etc. In his instructions to Secretary of War Taft in 1904, President Theodore Roosevelt stated that the United States did not seek to exercise any greater governmental functions than necessary. "Least of all do we desire to interfere with the business and prosperity of the people of Panama."[10]

Nevertheless, commercial activities on the part of the Canal Company seem to have expanded after 1904 because, as Secretary Taft told a Senate Committee: "After a sudden influx of laborers, the merchants of the zone were apparently quite short of provisions, or else they attempted to make a corner upon them."[11]

Abuses of commissary privileges continued, and the first step in their prevention came with President Franklin Roosevelt's agreement for the United States to exercise vigilance to prevent contraband trade in commissary articles, to prohibit sale of "tourist" goods for disposal to ships in transit, and to regulate other sales to ships in transit.[12] The treaty of 1936 went somewhat further along the same lines, but the basic principle remained that the United States should not manufacture or process any

[9] Baxter and Carroll, *op. cit.*, p. 37.

[10] U.S. House Committee on Foreign Affairs, *Report on United States Relations with Panama*, 86 Cong. 2 Sess. (1960), p. 22.

[11] *Ibid.*, p. 23.

[12] *Ibid.*, p. 24.

article available in satisfactory quantities, quality, and at reasonable prices in the Republic of Panama.

In addition, commissary privileges were restricted to those resident in the Zone, and the United States agreed to withdraw, with a few exceptions, from selling supplies to ships in transit.

The "third-country purchases" problem is a special variant of the problem of Panamanian access to the Zone market. It had long been the practice of the Canal Zone agencies to buy supplies in the cheapest world market, for example, meat from Australia or New Zealand, textiles from Europe, luxury goods from the Orient. The Panamanians felt that it was wrong to permit these imports if Panamanian industry could supply similar products on a fairly competitive basis.

Item 8 of the understanding attached to the 1955 treaty provided that the Zone agencies would acquire items for sale either from U.S. or Panamanian sources unless, in certain instances, it is not feasible to do so.

Later the dispute centered around the word "feasible" and further concessions were made such as, for example, a limit of $50 on luxury items. Corollary efforts by the Zone authorities reinforced the ban on third-country purchases, such as sending technicians to Panamanian farm cooperatives to bring up the quality of Panamanian beef offered for sale.

Substantial as are the three categories of economic problems sketched above, it is in the political realm that passions run highest, and the flag issue is the symbol of the dispute. It is an outrage to Panamanian nationalism that "the attributes of sovereignty" were transferred in perpetuity by an infant republic to the colossus of the North. The typically colonial attitudes of the Zonians—those North Americans who have lived for two or three generations in the Zone—have exacerbated the relationship.

During the 1955 treaty negotiations, Panama tried to obtain a concession that ships transiting the canal should fly the Panamanian as well as the U.S. flag. This concession was refused on the ground that "we did not want to leave one grain of evidence that could a hundred years hence be interpreted as implying any admission by the United States that we possess and exercise anything less than 100 per cent of the rights of sovereignty in this area."[13]

On November 3, 1959, Panama's independence day, mobs led by rabble rousers lined up at the border of the Canal Zone intending to plant the Panamanian flag in the Zone.

> With Panamanian National Guardsmen conspicuously absent from the scene, the Governor of the Canal Zone was forced to call for U.S. Armed Forces to help quell the ensuing violence. In the Republic of Panama on the same day rioters lowered the American flag at the U.S. Chancery and tore it to shreds.[14]

[13] Testimony of Assistant Secretary of State Henry Holland, in U.S. House Committee on Foreign Relations, *Report on United States Relations with Panama*, p. 20.
[14] *Ibid.*, p. 2.

On the 28th, mobs again tried to break into the Zone, but this time were dispersed by Panamanian Guardsmen working along with U.S. troops. Thirty people were injured.

All this happened during a recess of the U.S. Congress. When Congress reconvened in January 1960, the House Committee on Foreign Affairs learned that the Department of State had under consideration a Panamanian Government request that the Panamanian flag be flown in the Canal Zone and that it was likely that the request would be granted.[15] The Subcommittee on Inter-American Affairs held meetings and heard testimony and agreed to a resolution that the traditional interpretations of the treaties of 1903, 1936, and 1955, with special reference to matters concerning territorial sovereignty, should be made only pursuant to treaty. This resolution was approved by the House by a vote of 381 to 12.

Nevertheless in 1960, the Eisenhower administration directed that the Panamanian flag be flown in a single place in the Canal Zone, that is, the Shaler Triangle opposite the Panamanian Legislative Palace. Pursuant to the Kennedy-Chiari communiqué of June 1962, following President Chiari's visit to Washington, Ambassador Joseph Farland and Major General Robert Fleming held meetings for over a year with Dr. Galileo Salis, Panamanian Foreign Minister, and Dr. Octavio Fabrega, former Foreign Minister.

These special representatives announced the principle in January 1963 that the flag of Panama would be flown side by side with the U.S. flag on land in the Canal Zone whenever the U.S. flag was flown by civilian authorities.[16] The flags were flown, in fact, at the Canal Zone Administration building in Balboa Heights and in Cristobal, but in view of the impracticability of erecting dual flagpoles at all of the sites in the Zone, the number of sites was reduced.

Many other points at issue were settled, such as the recognition of exequaturs issued to foreign consuls in the Zone and labor problems relating to Panamanians working in the Zone. This work stopped in July 1963 because Panama considered it was dealing only with peripheral problems and not with the critical issue of exercise of sovereignty in perpetuity.

The Zone residents felt intensely about the flag issue, and the majority seemed to prefer that no flags be flown rather than both flags.[17] The action by U.S. students to fly the American flag alone at Balboa High School no doubt reflected the view of Zonian parents. The equal determination of the Panamanian students to fly the Panamanian flag led directly to the tragic events of January 9, 1964.

[15] *Ibid.,* p. 2.
[16] U.S. Department of State, *Bulletin,* Vol. 48 (1963), p. 171.
[17] *Washington Post,* Jan. 19, 1964, p. A14.

CASE BEFORE THE UNITED NATIONS AND THE OAS

The day after the outbreak of the incidents, and while the disturbances were still in progress, Panama requested an urgent meeting of the UN Security Council. On the same day, a meeting of the Inter-American Peace Committee of the OAS took place at the request of the United States and Panama to consider the situation.

At both meetings the delegate of Panama charged aggression against Panama by armed forces of the United States quartered in the Panama Canal Zone. Before the Security Council, he made a series of charges against the United States, particularly with failure to carry out the flag agreement, placing the blame for the rioting and bloodshed on the Americans.

Ambassador Stevenson, deploring the tragic and needless loss of life, and regretting this blot on the long record of friendship, rejected categorically the charge of American aggression. The Panamanian delegate's knowledge of the facts could be no better than his, Stevenson said. Moreover, at the meeting in Washington that afternoon of the Inter-American Peace Committee, both governments agreed that a committee should "go to Panama immediately to ascertain the facts." President Johnson had telephoned to President Chiari that afternoon, and both agreed there had to be a stop to violence in the Zone. U.S. authorities were instructed to do everything possible to restore and maintain peace and order. The United States was ready through direct discussions with the Panamanian Government to try to resolve such differences as may exist. In these circumstances, and as the Inter-American Peace Committee was about to leave for Panama, Ambassador Stevenson believed that the problem should continue to be pursued in the regional forum in accordance with the charter.

The delegate from Brazil spoke favorably of the speedy action taken by the regional agency and its ability to handle the situation. He believed that the Security Council should remain seized of the matter, and suggested that the President of the Council should address an appeal to the two parties to exercise restraint. This was agreed to and the Council adjourned. It has not taken up the matter since.

As both the United States and Panama had consented, the Inter-American Peace Committee decided to "study the case and go to Panama . . . to investigate the situation and recommend measures for the settlement of the dispute."[18] The Council of the OAS designated Chile to take the place of the United States on the five-state Inter-American Peace Committee during consideration of the dispute.[19] Other members of the committee were Argentina, Colombia, the Dominican Republic, and Venezuela, the

[18] UN Security Council, S/5511, Jan. 11, 1964.

[19] This action took place in conformity with Article 11 of the Statutes of the Inter-American Peace Committee.

presiding country.[20] The primary concern of the committee was to re-establish and maintain order in Panama. Therefore, it left immediately to carry out on-the-spot activities designed to accomplish this end. Through the initiative of the committee, a Mixed Commission on Cooperation was established, composed of one member of the IAPC, acting as chairman, and one civilian and one military representative of each of the parties. The efforts of the Mixed Commission and the IAPC helped to solve certain problems relating to immediate sources of friction, such as the display of Panamanian and United States flags in the Canal Zone and the free passage of persons and vehicles.

In a press release of January 15, the committee noted that the parties agreed to accept its invitation to re-establish diplomatic relations and "to begin formal discussions which will be initiated thirty (30) days after diplomatic relations are re-established, by means of representatives who will have sufficient powers to discuss without limitations all existing matters of any nature which may affect the relations between the United States and Panama."[21]

This January accord broke down, however, due to different interpretations of it given by the two parties. The stumbling-block to any further progress by the Inter-American Peace Committee appeared to be the insistence of Panama to initiate negotiations to conclude a new treaty with the United States concerning the Panama Canal.

Although the on-the-spot intervention of the Inter-American Peace Committee was swift, the reaction of the parties to the IAPC suggestion of January 15 did not come until almost two and a half months later, and only after the convocation of the Organ of Consultation under the Rio Treaty.

Panama, in a note of January 28, 1964, reiterated its previous request of January 9 to invoke the Rio Treaty. It stated that "since the friendly intervention of the Inter-American Peace Committee has ceased . . . the convocation of the Organ of Consultation continues to be urgent and undeferable."[22]

In two special meetings of the Council, January 31 and February 4, the positions of the United States and Panama were fully aired. Both countries agreed to a full investigation of the facts, the United States preferring the IAPC as the appropriate organ for such an investigation and Panama insisting on an investigating committee of the Organ of Consultation.[23]

---

[20] The members were: Enrique Tejera París, Venezuela; Alfredo Vázquez Carrizosa, Colombia; José Antonio Bonilla Atiles, Dominican Republic; Rodolfo A. Weidmann, Argentina; and Manuel Trucco, Chile.

[21] UN Security Council, S/5520, Jan. 21, 1964.

[22] Council of the OAS, OEA/Ser.G/V, C-d-1189 (English), Jan. 29, 1964.

[23] See Council of OAS, OEA/Ser. G/V, C-d-1191 of Jan. 31, 1964, and OEA/Ser. G/V C-d-1196 of Feb. 4, 1964.

On February 4, 1964, a resolution was adopted by the Council to act provisionally as Organ of Consultation under the Rio Treaty. A general committee of all members of the OAS Council, with the exception of the two disputants, was formed to:

> . . . investigate . . . the acts that occurred in Panama on January 9 and 10, 1964 . . . and submit a report to the Organ of Consultation on the matter and on the efforts . . . of the United States and Panama . . . to find a solution to the dispute . . . to assist the parties in their search for a fair solution. . . .[24]

A delegation of the general committee left for Panama on February 11. The five-nation delegation included Ilmar Penna Marinho, Brazil; Gonzalo J. Facio, Costa Rica; Vicente Sánchez Gavito, Mexico; Emilio N. Oribe, Uruguay; and Chairman Juan I. Plate, Paraguay. During their stay in Panama, from February 11 to February 18, the members carried out the duties conferred on the general committee by the February 7 resolution.[25]

On its return to Washington, the five-member subcommittee continued to work for an acceptable joint declaration by the United States and Panama that would initiate a solution to the causes of conflict relative to the Panama Canal. On March 15, without waiting for interpretive statements by Presidents Johnson and Chiari, the delegation made public the text of a joint declaration to which both the United States and Panama had unofficially agreed.[26] However, President Johnson, in an extemporaneous departure from his prepared speech of March 16 on the Alliance for Progress, stated that there had been "no genuine meeting of the minds."[27]

The delegation reported its findings of the past month to a closed session of the general committee on March 17, 1964, as well as the failure of the joint declaration to enter into force due to "circumstances that arose shortly after it was published that were connected primarily to the interpretation . . . given to certain terms contained therein."[28]

At this juncture, the responsibility to carry on discussions with the parties in order to arrive at a solution to the problem was placed with the Chairman of the general committee, Ambassador Juan Bautista de Lavalle (also Chairman of the OAS Council), and the five-member delegation was relieved of any further duties.

On April 3, 1964, the two Governments agreed to a Joint Declaration under which they decided:

1. To re-establish diplomatic relations.

[24] See Council of the OAS, OEA/Ser.G/III, C-sa-534, Feb. 7, 1964.
[25] *Ibid.*
[26] OAS, Information Service, News Release of March 15, 1964.
[27] *New York Times*, March 17, 1964.
[28] OAS Official Records, OEA/Ser.D/III.15 (English), p. 5.

2. To designate without delay Special Ambassadors with sufficient powers to seek the prompt elimination of the causes of conflict between the two countries, without limitations or preconditions of any kind.

3. That therefore the Ambassadors designated will begin immediately the necessary procedures with the objective of reaching a just and fair agreement which would be subject to the constitutional processes of each country.

PROPOSALS FOR A NEW CANAL AND A NEW TREATY

Between April and December 1964, every effort by the representatives of the two countries to reach a just and fair agreement failed on the question whether the 1903 treaty should be revised and on what pre-conditions, if any.

But in an announcement on December 19, 1964, President Johnson said the United States had decided that plans should be undertaken to build a new sea-level canal somewhere across the isthmus to take care of increasing traffic. He indicated that there were four possible sites—in Panama, Colombia, Costa Rica, and Nicaragua—and that the United States will negotiate with each country where surveys will be undertaken. With this vast program in mind, the United States will propose to Panama "the negotiation of an entirely new treaty on the existing Panama Canal." He said the new treaty should recognize the sovereignty of Panama. It must retain the "rights necessary for effective operation and protection of the canal and should provide for its own termination." The old treaty should continue "until new agreement is reached." Congress had authorized $17 million for surveys to be made on all possible routes.

Thus, the first real step was taken toward ending the sixty-year controversy over sovereignty and rights in perpetuity. President Robles of Panama called the announcement "a transcendental public statement of policy" which will remove the main Panamanian grievances. His representatives on the negotiating committee in Washington were recalled for consultation.

With this announcement, President Johnson, in effect, liquidated the dispute with Panama. It left the leftist demonstrators and anti-Americans chagrined. As long as the site is in doubt, Panama can hardly afford to let them have free rein. Presumably, one element in the choice of site will be the stability of the area.

17

---•---

CASES UNDER THE INTER–AMERICAN PEACE COMMITTEE

The Inter-American Peace Committee exercises a function quite distinct from that of the Organ of Consultation under the Rio Treaty. Essentially, the committee extends a rudimentary form of good offices to parties in conflict when they choose to avail themselves of its services. It cannot compel, nor can it hand down judgments of fact or law. Its procedures are informal and normally confidential, so that few records of its hearings exist. The cases that have been brought before the Inter-American Peace Committee are discussed below.[1]

SITUATION BETWEEN CUBA AND THE DOMINICAN REPUBLIC, 1951[2]

The situation between Cuba and the Dominican Republic, known informally as the case of the Quetzal, was one of the outstanding successes of the Inter-American Peace Committee. It is an example of the unique character of so many of the inter-American disputes brought before OAS organs during the 1950's and of the way in which they were handled.

The animosity between Cuba and the Dominican Republic has become a diplomatic tradition in the Caribbean, and the case of the Quetzal was but one act in a continuing drama in which the same characters appear

[1] The case on the situation between Haiti and the Dominican Republic, 1949, is discussed on pp. 115 ff. The case on the situation in the Caribbean in 1949 under the Inter-American Peace Committee is discussed in connection with the action subsequently taken, pp. 117 ff. The case under the Inter-American Peace Committee, titled "Controversy Between Guatemala, Honduras, and Nicaragua, 1954," is discussed with the cases under the Rio Treaty under the title "Situation in Guatemala, 1954," pp. 124 ff.

[2] The accessible official records provide virtually no information on the substance of this case or the process by which a settlement was reached. The committee's formal report merely gives the text of a declaration signed on Christmas Day, 1951, by both parties, who in characteristically florid language avowed their devotion to inter-American principles and friendly relations. The brief discussion below is based on unpublished, personal notes made at the time by one of the participants.

again and again. The specific issues at any one time are linked with a history of plots, conspiracies, and mutual recriminations. The present case erupted when Generalissimo Trujillo was in power in the Dominican Republic, and a liberal, left-wing government ruled in Havana, both of them giving various degrees of support to the political exiles and refugees from the other country.

The Quetzal, a former U.S. Navy landing craft, had been bought by a leading Dominican revolutionary, Miguel Angel Ramirez, who used the vessel in various anti-Trujillo adventures, including the abortive "Cayo Confites" expedition of 1947.[3] At that time, the Cuban Government seized the vessel and all other equipment assembled for the expedition. In 1951, however, the Cuban courts ordered the Quetzal stripped of its armaments and returned to its former owner. Ramirez outfitted the boat for commercial use and obtained a provisional Guatemalan registry. On July 25, 1951, the Quetzal, captained by a Dominican revolutionary and manned by a crew of Guatemalans, Cubans, and one other Dominican, sailed from a Cuban port for Livingston, Guatemala. The ship was either seized by the Dominican Navy or, as was afterwards made to appear, had been voluntarily surrendered by the Dominican captain. The Dominican courts convicted Cuban and Guatemalan crew members of crimes against the Dominican state and sentenced them to twenty years at hard labor. The two Dominicans were released.

The Cuban Government protested the imprisonment of the Cuban sailors and demanded their freedom on the ground that the Quetzal had been illegally seized and that the Dominican courts therefore had no jurisdiction over the crew. Failing to obtain satisfaction, on November 26, 1951, Cuba brought the dispute before the Inter-American Peace Committee. The issue, therefore, was whether the Dominican courts had jurisdiction over the Cuban members of the crew of this vessel.

The Peace Committee requested that the Dominican Government agree to the committee's intervention. The Dominican Government agreed, provided opportunity were given to present Dominican complaints against Cuba, particularly the charge that the latter had violated inter-American agreements by returning the Quetzal to Ramirez, the revolutionary.

Both governments informed the committee that their foreign ministers would represent them. The committee feared that a public debate by two top officials would only aggravate the tension, and consulted with them informally in an effort to find some basis for a conciliation. These efforts were unproductive, so the committee held a formal meeting on December 21, at which the two foreign ministers stated their cases. The committee continued to hold informal sessions with the two foreign ministers at the

---

[3] Details in the report of the investigating committee in the Caribbean situation of 1950. See *Aplicaciones del Tratado Interamericano de Asistencia Recíproca, 1948–1960*, pp. 101–4.

Cuban or the Dominican Embassy in Washington, or at the residence of the Peace Committee chairman, Ambassador Luis Quintanilla of Mexico.

During these conversations, it became clear that Cuba was mainly interested in the release of the Cuban seamen. The Dominican Government did not object to having the jurisdictional question brought before the International Court of Justice, but it insisted on bringing Cuba into court, not only for having restored the Quetzal to Ramirez, but also in connection with the "Cayo Confites" expedition of 1947.

The Peace Committee prepared a draft formula for an agreement on methods of resolving the dispute, covering three points: (1) the immediate release of the Cuban seamen, presumably by a pardon to avoid the legal issue; (2) the submission of the two justiciable issues to the International Court; and (3) a mutual pledge of nonintervention and restoration of normal relations. The formula was accepted in principle, but was rejected primarily because the parties could not agree on the scope of the case that the Dominican Government was to bring before the Court. Three times the committee revised the draft only to have it rejected.

The mediation efforts were complicated when the Dominican Government pardoned the Guatemalan crew members, but not the Cubans. In Havana, demands for breaking relations and other reprisals against the Dominican Republic were reported. The committee forestalled precipitate action by the Cubans and made clear to the Dominicans that their action, which they had been urged not to take, left them no alternative but to release the Cubans as well. Assurances to this effect were obtained.

When the fourth draft of an agreement was turned down, the chairman of the committee, Ambassador Quintanilla, suggested that since the Cuban Government would not agree to have the "Cayo Confites" matter brought before the Court, and the Dominican Government would not, in those circumstances, allow the Quetzal case to be adjudicated, all reference to either case be eliminated, and an agreement be issued with mutual promises of good behavior and restitution of diplomatic representatives. Since the Cuban sailors were now being released, no reference to them would be necessary. The proposal was accepted by both parties.

The simple agreement, which appears in the committee's final report, was signed at a ceremonial session of the Peace Committee, held in the Pan American Union on Christmas Day. Both governments expressed their satisfaction over the resolution of the incident and, in appreciation of the committee's efforts, decorated the four participating members. [4]

The Quetzal case illustrates the informal methods often used by the Inter-American Peace Committee. The negotiations were personal. The role of Ambassador Quintanilla was particularly outstanding in his imagi-

---

[4] The fifth member was Cuba which, as a party to the dispute, had withdrawn from the committee during consideration of the case.

native seizure of the psychological moment in which to introduce his formula to drop the whole matter. As a result, Cuba obtained the release of its seamen. The Dominican Government, which, it appears, had blundered in seizing the Quetzal, by skillful negotiation in the committee obtained an acceptable way out. The Peace Committee gave both parties a neutral ground on which to negotiate without loss of face, and served as a catalyst to bring about a mutually satisfactory resolution.

SITUATION BETWEEN COLOMBIA AND PERU, 1953–1954

In a note from the Colombian minister of foreign affairs dated November 17, 1953, the services of the Inter-American Peace Committee were requested in finding a solution to the dispute with Peru over the asylum of Victor Raúl Haya de la Torre in the Colombian Embassy in Lima.

The Peruvian Government declined the committee's offer of assistance; hence under its statutes, it could not function. The members of the committee signed a document which urged bilateral negotiations.[5] Fact-finding was not involved. Haya de la Torre had already been confined in the Colombian Embassy for almost five years.

In 1950 the International Court of Justice ruled that, according to agreements in force between the two countries, Colombia was not required to surrender the asylee to the Peruvian Government as the latter demanded, but neither was Peru required to give him a safe-conduct out of the country as Colombia claimed. The matter was thus left for political negotiation, and on April 6, 1954, during the Tenth Inter-American Conference at Caracas, the two governments announced their agreement on procedure whereby Haya de la Torre was allowed to leave the country. Whether the efforts of Colombia to bring the dispute before the Peace Committee had anything to do with the ultimate agreement is a matter of conjecture; it is more likely that the settlement was motivated by a desire to present a picture of harmonious solidarity at the Caracas Conference.

SITUATION BETWEEN THE DOMINICAN REPUBLIC AND CUBA, 1956

This case was another resulting from recurring antagonisms between these two countries. At this time, Cuba was governed by General Batista, who had ousted the previous left-wing regime, thus showing that Cuban-Dominican controversies continued even when their political systems were

[5] Inter-American Peace Committee, *Report to the Fifth Meeting of Consultation of Ministers of Foreign Affairs*, Doc. 5 (Washington: Pan American Union, 1959), p. 46. Hereafter cited as IAPC, *Fifth Meeting*.

fundamentally at odds. The issues involved in this dispute were minor and involved the usual activities of exiles, public recriminations, and insults. The committee made repeated efforts to help the two parties settle the immediate issues, but found it impossible to do more than urge a resumption of bilateral negotiations to that end. [6]

INVASION OF HAITI, 1959

The Fifth Meeting of Consultation of Ministers of Foreign Affairs at Santiago, Chile, in 1959 gave a new and special assignment to the Inter-American Peace Committee: to study the problems of international tension in the Caribbean. [7] In carrying out this assignment, the committee was authorized to exercise its own initiative without requiring the prior consent of all parties to a dispute, as called for in its Statutes of 1956.

On August 31, 1959, the Haitian representative on the Council of the OAS requested the Peace Committee to investigate the invasion of his country on August 13 by a band of Haitian and Cuban nationals who had sailed from Cuba. [8] The Cuban Government stated that it had not been able to prevent the expedition, thus causing the Haitian Government to fear a repetition of the incident. No formal charges, however, were made against the Cuban Government.

In view of the absence of any recognized intergovernmental dispute, the committee looked on the Haitian complaint as one item in its general study of Caribbean tensions. A subcommittee visited Haiti and the Dominican Republic but could not obtain permission to visit Cuba. [9] It heard the views of the Haitian Government concerning the invasion incident and other complaints about activities of Cuban diplomats in Port-au-Prince which were considered to be intervention in Haiti's internal affairs. It also interviewed five prisoners of Cuban nationality, the sole survivors of the invading force, who showed little understanding of the nature and purpose of the venture in which they were involved.

In a report issued several months later, the Peace Committee stated that "although the Government of Haiti expressed serious concern over the possibility of another" invasion, none had occurred, due "to the failure of the invasion" and "to the interest shown by the pertinent organs of the Organization in the appeal made to them by the Government of Haiti." [10]

[6] IAPC, *Fifth Meeting*, p. 73.

[7] See above, pp. 117 ff.

[8] Inter-American Peace Committee, *Report to the Seventh Meeting of Consultation of Ministers of Foreign Affairs*, OEA/Ser. F/II.7 (Washington: Pan American Union, 1960). pp. 3–5. Hereafter cited as IAPC, *Seventh Meeting*.

[9] IAPC, *Seventh Meeting*, p. 8.

[10] IAPC, *Seventh Meeting*, p. 5.

The Peace Committee was unable to make a full investigation of the Haitian invasion because it failed to obtain permission to visit Cuba. Consideration of this case by the committee was valuable chiefly for the evidence it gave of the concern of the OAS over incidents of this character and for the opportunity it offered to show the OAS "presence" in the Caribbean area, which, it was hoped, would have a calming effect on the tense situation there.

SUBVERSIVE LEAFLETS AGAINST
THE GOVERNMENT OF VENEZUELA, 1959

In November 1959, three months after the Santiago Meeting enlarged the powers of the Inter-American Peace Committee, Venezuela complained to the committee that a plane of U.S. registry, piloted by two Cuban citizens, had dropped leaflets over the island of Curaçao, urging the Venezuelan Army to revolt against its government. The leaflets were intended for a Venezuelan city, but they had been dropped over Curaçao by mistake. The plane, which had departed from Miami and stopped in Nassau and Ciudad Trujillo, had subsequently made a forced landing in Aruba. There, the persons on board were arrested by the Dutch authorities.

The Venezuelan representative, who was a member of the Inter-American Peace Committee, abstained from the committee's deliberations as his government was a party to the dispute.

Had the Dominican Government, or high officials thereof, connived at an attempt to violate Venezuelan sovereignty and arouse rebellion? The Inter-American Peace Committee took cognizance of the case under Resolution IV of Santiago. It took statements made to the Dutch and U.S. authorities by the U.S. pilots who had flown the plane from Miami to Ciudad Trujillo, and from Cuban citizens who had flown it from the Dominican Republic to Aruba. The committee found that the loading of the plane with leaflets and the arrangements for the flight from Ciudad Trujillo to Aruba "could not have been carried out without the connivance of the Dominican authorities."[11]

The committee could not visit Cuba; and it is not recorded whether it sought to visit the Dominican Republic. Its findings rested on information obtained from the Governments of the United States, Venezuela, and the Netherlands. Though brief, they seem quite correct, and in the circumstances, the committee could not have done more.

[11] IAPC, *Seventh Meeting*, p. 6.

THE CASE OF ECUADOR AND THE
DOMINICAN REPUBLIC, 1960

This case is one of a series in 1959–1960 which reflected the unremitting hostility between the Dominican dictator, Trujillo, and President Betancourt of Venezuela and his political allies. As a result of harsh measures taken by the Dominican Government, thirteen Dominican nationals had taken diplomatic asylum in the Venezuelan Embassy in Santo Domingo. When Venezuela broke relations with the Trujillo government, the Ecuadoran Embassy took over responsibility for Venezuelan affairs, occupied the building previously housing the Venezuelan Embassy, and placed the Ecuadoran coat-of-arms over the door. The Ecuadoran Embassy then requested safe-conduct for the diplomatic asylees in accordance with accepted Latin American custom and agreement. The Trujillo regime not only refused to permit the asylees to leave the country, but adopted a series of harrassing tactics against the Ecuadoran Embassy on the grounds that its occupancy and protection of the former Venezuelan Embassy was not acceptable.

The Ecuadoran representative on the OAS Council, Ambassador Gonzalo Escudero, in February 1960, requested the good offices of the Inter-American Peace Committee in this dispute. The issues were whether the Dominican Government had violated international law by denying essential facilities to the Ecuadoran Embassy, and whether the Dominican Government could rightfully refuse safe-conduct to the Dominican asylees. The services denied the Ecuadoran Embassy were the unrestricted access to light, telephone, and food supplies. Moreover, ditches had been dug in front of the building to obstruct access, and the place had been subjected to twenty-four hour vigilance; the right to place a shield or flag of the Embassy on the building was also denied. [12]

The Ecuadoran complaint invoked both the regular statutes of the Inter-American Peace Committee and the enlarged powers to investigate tensions in the Caribbean conferred by Resolution IV of the Fifth Meeting of Foreign Ministers. Thus a question of procedure arose at the outset.

In March 1960, the Dominican representative in the OAS Council stated that he recognized the competence of the committee in accordance with its statutes but not on the basis of Resolution IV of the Santiago Meeting; [13] and that his government would accept the services of the committee with respect to the situation of the Ecuadoran Embassy but not with respect to the question of the asylees, since his government had denounced the Latin American Conventions on Diplomatic Asylum.

[12] IAPC, *Seventh Meeting*, App. C, p. 8.
[13] IAPC, *Seventh Meeting*, App. C, p. 1.

The Inter-American Peace Committee, under the chairmanship of U.S. Ambassador John C. Dreier, dodged the jurisdictional issue. It stated that:

> It had decided not to enter into the substance of doctrinary questions that might give rise to difficulties and, therefore, it preferred not to express an opinion on that occasion as to whether its jurisdiction was governed by the Statutes or by Resolution IV; nevertheless, it did not believe it feasible to separate the problem of the presence of Dominican nationals in the Ecuadoran Embassy in Ciudad Trujillo from that of the situation of the aforesaid Diplomatic Mission, inasmuch as it was convinced that the former was exercising a determining influence on the latter situation. The authority to make pronouncements on legal questions, such as the effect of the denunciation of the Conventions on Diplomatic Asylum by the Government of the Dominican Republic, it felt justified in hoping that the Dominican Government would not make an insuperable obstacle of its reservations. [14]

The dispute over jurisdiction and the failure of the committee to seek a resolution of it did not affect the ultimate outcome of the case. The Dominican Government even withheld its agreement to the consideration of the case, which the statutes of the Peace Committee required.

After a series of exploratory talks with the Dominican ambassador to the OAS, the committee, on March 18, formally inquired whether his government would consent to the committee's taking action on the case. The Dominican Government replied on March 25 that it believed the case could be dealt with directly between the two parties and "without the mediation of an international organization being essential for this purpose." [15] The Ecuadoran representative stated that bilateral efforts for eight months had been futile, and he insisted that the committee use every means in its power to achieve a settlement.

The Dominican representative informed the committee on March 21 that an agreement had been reached between the Dominican Government and the Brazilian Embassy resulting in the safe exit of some Dominican asylees. This agreement was specifically stated not to establish a precedent.

On March 30, the committee transmitted to both parties a draft of a joint declaration, the essential part of which guaranteed safe-conduct for the asylees. It added that "the Government of Ecuador will not permit the . . . Dominican nationals to carry out, during their stay in Ecuador, acts contrary to the applicable provisions of inter-American treaties now in force," that is, efforts to overthrow the Dominican Government. [16]

The Dominican Government responded that the Dominican nationals, not under prosecution or sentences, could leave the Ecuadoran Embassy

[14] IAPC, *Seventh Meeting*, App. C, pp. 1–2.
[15] IAPC, *Seventh Meeting*, App. C, pp. 2, 15.
[16] IAPC, *Seventh Meeting*, App. C, p. 3.

and return to their customary life in the Dominican Republic.[17] The next day it reiterated its refusal to accept the competence of the committee.

The Ecuadoran representative accepted the Peace Committee's proposal but rejected the Dominican formula. Accordingly, the Peace Committee reported to the OAS Council that it had failed to solve the dispute. In a footnote to its report the committee expressed its concern over the lack of cooperation of the Dominican Republic.

In reporting to the OAS its failure to solve this dispute, the Peace Committee stated that it would continue to consider the case in connection with the study of tensions in the Caribbean which it had been instructed to undertake by the Fifth Meeting of Foreign Ministers.[18] This was a thinly veiled insinuation that the committee would be looking further into the question of the relationship between international tensions and the denial of human rights in the Dominican Republic. The committee's efforts and findings in regard to the Dominican asylees contributed to the growing antagonism toward the Dominican dictator, both inside and outside of his country—antagonism which was soon to prove fatal to him.

VIOLATION OF HUMAN RIGHTS
IN THE DOMINICAN REPUBLIC, 1960

Three political currents helped to bring before the Inter-American Peace Committee in February 1960 the question of the violation of human rights in the Dominican Republic: (1) the initiative of Venezuela which felt under constant menace of aggression so long as the dictatorship of Trujillo continued; (2) support for anti-Trujillo moves from other Latin American republics that applauded the downfall of dictatorships in Venezuela and Cuba and considered Trujillo an extreme manifestation of this chronic Latin American malady; (3) the departure of the United States in 1959 from its strict noninterventionist attitude by joining in condemning dictatorships of all kinds. The United States realized that no progress toward curbing Communist dictatorship could be made in Latin America unless strong measures were also taken against the military-type dictatorship symbolized by Trujillo.[19] Anti-Trujillo sentiment was further outraged in January 1960 when the Dominican police discovered a plot against the dictator and retaliated with a series of mass arrests, imprisonment, torture, and killings.

The Venezuelan complaint invoked Resolution IV of the Fifth Meeting of Ministers of Foreign Affairs, which requested the Inter-American Peace Committee to study international tensions and the relation thereto of the violation of human rights and denial of representative democracy. The

[17] IAPC, *Seventh Meeting*, App. C, p. 3.
[18] IAPC, *Seventh Meeting*, App. C, p. 5.
[19] Dreier, *The Organization of American States and the Hemisphere Crisis, op. cit.*, pp. 97–98.

subject of Venezuela's request was, therefore, clearly within the competence of the committee.

The chairman of the Committee was U.S. Ambassador John C. Dreier. Other members were Salvadoran Ambassador Hector David Castro, Mexican Ambassador Vicente Sánchez Gavito, and Uruguayan Ambassador Carlos A. Clulow. Since Venezuela was a party at issue, the Council designated Colombia as a substitute, which was represented by Minister Santiago Salazar Santos.

The issue before the committee was whether violations of human rights in the Dominican Republic were contributing to international tensions in the Caribbean.

The committee first requested information from member states of the OAS other than the two parties. It then conferred informally in late February with the Dominican ambassador to the OAS, Virgilio Díaz Ordóñez, and attempted to obtain information on the recent events in his country and to secure permission to visit it. On March 8, the ambassador told the committee his government would not consent to its proposed visit.

The basis for the committee's consideration of human rights and representative democracy in the Dominican Republic stemmed from its duty to provide a report on the relation of these matters to international tensions. The committee, however, was concerned over the plight of persons, reported to be over 1,000, who had been arrested and imprisoned in the recent anti-Trujillo plot. The Dominican ambassador maintained that such reports were exaggerated, that the number of arrests had been only 222, and that many, particularly the women, had been promptly released.[20]

The Dominican ambassador was known to the committee as an unusually able diplomat, whose personal influence on the Trujillo regime would be one of moderation. In his conversations, he referred to the custom of issuing amnesties to prisoners on Easter and suggested that the committee carry out its study in general terms rather than with reference to any particular country. The possibility of amnesty for political prisoners was also suggested by the February 28 Pastoral Letter of the Dominican Bishops. Since the committee wished to avoid any step which might adversely affect the prisoners, it withheld its report on the situation in the Dominican Republic until after the Easter holiday. Instead it issued on April 14 its "Special Report on the Relationship Between Violations of Human Rights or the Non-Exercise of Representative Democracy and the Political Tensions that Affect the Peace of the Hemisphere." This report treated the problem in general terms and mentioned no one country.[21]

The committee, however, gathered as much information as it could regarding the situation in the Dominican Republic. It obtained information from interviews with escaped refugees from the Trujillo regime and other

[20] IAPC, *Seventh Meeting*, App. D, pp. 3–4.
[21] IAPC, *Seventh Meeting*, App. D, p. 4 and App. E.

individuals who had recently been in the Dominican Republic, and from reports made available by member governments of the OAS.

When Easter passed and the hoped-for amnesty did not materialize, the committee drafted its report on the case presented by Venezuela. It found that there were flagrant violations of human rights in the Dominican Republic, including "the denial of free speech and assembly, arbitrary arrests, cruel and inhuman treatment of political prisoners, and the use of intimidation and terror as political weapons." These conditions increased international tensions in the Caribbean as Dominicans sought asylum abroad where they organized activities aimed at the overthrow of Trujillo. These, in turn, led to demands for international action to curb the excesses of the dictatorship, and to the retaliation of the Dominican Government by counterrevolutionary activities of Dominican agents abroad.[22]

The performance of the Inter-American Peace Committee in this case must be judged from three different standpoints.

First, so far as the specific Venezuelan charge was concerned, the committee did a creditable job in investigating the violations of human rights and pointing out their effect on international tensions.

Second, the committee's general report on the relation between violations of human rights and international tensions appears to have served a political purpose far removed from the committee's basic purpose of helping governments settle disputes.

Third, it is questionable whether it was wise for the Fifth Meeting of Foreign Ministers to have assigned responsibilities of this character to the Inter-American Peace Committee. At the Santiago Meeting, because of opposition to establishing a new committee to carry out the observation and study functions embodied in Resolution IV, the Peace Committee was assigned this function. This effort to camouflage the purpose of calming the turbulent Caribbean during the early Castro era, however, was not entirely successful. The Peace Committee was given insufficient power and too vague a directive to deal realistically with the Castro problem, and its role and performance was confused in the public mind by the belief that it was equipped to carry out this large task. Only in regard to the Dominican Republic did the committee contribute in some measure to the special and essentially political objective assigned to it.

REQUEST OF THE GOVERNMENT OF NICARAGUA (BOUNDARY DISPUTE), 1961

As indicated in the case dealing with the Honduras-Nicaragua Boundary conflict of 1957, the two countries agreed to submit their controversy to

[22] IAPC, *Seventh Meeting*, App. D, pp. 5–7.

the International Court of Justice.[23] On November 18, 1960, the Court issued an opinion that recognized the jurisdiction of Honduras over a large territory in which Nicaragua had been exercising de facto control. Both parties accepted the decision. Differences arose over how it was to be carried out. Transfer to Honduras of areas in which Nicaraguan settlements had been established involved many problems, and on February 15, 1961, Nicaragua asked for the services of the Inter-American Peace Committee in suggesting methods to settle the differences. The Nicaraguan ambassador to the OAS emphasized that his government was firmly resolved to carry out the decision fully.[24]

In accordance with its statutes, the committee first informed the Honduran Government of the Nicaraguan initiative and asked whether Honduras would accept the committee's services in the matter. At first, the Honduran Government replied that it would accept the intervention of the Peace Committee only on the condition that the Nicaraguan Government first withdraw all its military, civil, and administrative authorities from territory now recognized as Honduran. By skillful negotiation, the committee had this impossible condition withdrawn, thus opening the door to formal consideration of the issues.[25]

The question posed for the Peace Committee was how to devise a formula under which the two governments could carry out the Court's decision.

After discussions with both sides, the Peace Committee drafted a "Basis of Arrangement" that provided for the immediate withdrawal of the Nicaraguan authorities from the territory now part of Honduras and the establishment of a Mixed Commission made up of one representative from each party with Ambassador Sánchez Gavito of Mexico as chairman. A staff for the commission would be provided by the OAS. The commission was to assure a free choice to all inhabitants of the affected territory to move to Nicaragua or to remain in their present locations; to supervise the orderly relocation of those wishing to move; to fix the boundary in the two sectors which the award of 1960 had left unclear; and to supervise the demarcation on the ground of the entire line. The Peace Committee itself would remain available for assisting the parties in resolving any other questions that did not come within the scope of the Mixed Commission's responsibilities.[26]

Both governments agreed to the "Basis of Arrangement." On March 21 the Peace Committee, accompanied by high officials of both governments, flew over the Coco River area and supervised the installation of the Mixed

---

[23] See above, Rio Treaty Case, pp. 139 ff.

[24] Inter-American Peace Committee, *Report to the Eighth Meeting of Consultation of Ministers of Foreign Affairs*, OEA/Ser. L/III, Pt. I, App. 2 (Washington: Pan American Union, 1962), p. 2. Hereafter cited as IAPC, *Eighth Meeting*.

[25] IAPC, *Eighth Meeting*, p. 4.

[26] IAPC, *Eighth Meeting*, p. 7.

Commission at its headquarters in the territory.[27] This action terminated the active participation of the Peace Committee in the case.

The Mixed Commission set about its main tasks of supervising the withdrawal of Nicaraguan authorities, the relocation of persons, and of settling the boundary in the two areas of uncertainty. By mid-April, the last of the Nicaraguan authorities had withdrawn. By the middle of May, about 4,000 people had been moved from an area of about 8,700 kilometers under the watchful eyes of the commission's staff and with the cooperation of the two governments.[28]

Two areas were involved in the final definition of the boundary. One, at the mouth of the Coco River, was settled without difficulty; but conflicting claims and opinions arose over the area of Teotecacinte, at the western end of the disputed line. It was agreed to leave the decision to the chairman who handed down his opinion on August 5, 1961, thus bringing the ancient boundary dispute to an end.[29] The satisfaction of both governments with the undertaking was indicated by their both conferring decorations on Ambassador Sánchez Gavito.

This case is one of the outstanding successes of the Inter-American Peace Committee. A vast area was transferred to Honduras from Nicaragua, 4,000 individuals were removed, and the boundary was fixed. Respect built up for the OAS and its peace-keeping machinery and the basic willingness of the parties to use the machinery contributed to the committee's success.

The leadership and vigor of Mexican Ambassador Vicente Sánchez Gavito marked him as a worthy successor to his compatriot Ambassador Luis Quintanilla. This successful operation was carried out by a Peace Committee composed entirely of Latin Americans.

A unique feature in this case was the use of the Mixed Commission, consisting of representatives of both parties and a neutral OAS chairman with a large staff of advisers and assistants recruited by the Organization. This proved to be a good way to handle the highly technical job of boundary fixing and marking as well as supervising the transfer of population.

REQUEST OF THE GOVERNMENT OF MEXICO (GUATEMALAN DISPUTE), 1961

Ambassador Vicente Sánchez Gavito[30] of Mexico, on June 2, 1961, informed the Inter-American Peace Committee that the Government of

[27] IAPC, *Eighth Meeting*, p. 9.
[28] IAPC, *Eighth Meeting*, pp. 12–13.
[29] IAPC, *Eighth Meeting*, p. 16.
[30] Ambassador Sánchez Gavito was serving at the time as chairman but stepped down from that position for the purposes of this case which involved his government.

Guatemala had charged that communist troops were being trained "in Mexican territory, adjacent to the Guatemalan border on lands leased or owned by ex-President Lázara Cárdenas . . . for an invasion into Guatemalan territory in the immediate future." Raúl Castro, chief of Cuban Armed Forces, had arrived in Mexico to inspect the invader troops. Ex-President Cárdenas was also reviewing these troops, and on May 30, the Communist former President of Guatemala Jacobo Arbenz Guzmán said that Guatemala would soon be invaded by land, sea, and air.[31]

Mexico denied the charges, and requested the Inter-American Peace Committee to proceed immediately to Mexico on a fact-finding mission. Mexico also complained that the Government of Guatemala failed in courtesy in not bringing the matter first to the attention of the Mexican Government. What importance should be attached to the indirect charges aired by Guatemala, and how should Mexico's request for an investigation be handled?

Only five weeks earlier, an ill-fated expedition based in Nicaragua and Guatemala had been launched in the Bay of Pigs area of Cuba. It was understandable that the Government of Guatemala expected trouble following a visit by Major Raúl Castro to Mexico where pro-Castro sentiment was strong.

The Inter-American Peace Committee responded to the Mexican request by meeting the same day, June 2, 1961, and decided that it was competent to act under Resolution IV of the Fifth Meeting at Santiago.

The acting chairman invited the Guatemalan representative to supply "complementary data" to the allegations contained in the message to the Secretary-General. The Guatemalan representative declined to do so, saying he had nothing to add to statements already made.

Accordingly, the Inter-American Peace Committee concluded on June 5, 1961, that there was no doubt whatever "concerning the manner in which the Government of Mexico is fulfilling its international obligations" and that consequently it was not necessary for the committee to go to Mexico to investigate the facts.[32]

REQUEST OF THE GOVERNMENT OF PERU (HUMAN RIGHTS IN CUBA), 1961

In November 1961, Peru requested the Inter-American Peace Committee to investigate the denial of human rights and the pursuance of Communist policies by the Government of Cuba. This action by Peru was one in a series of efforts to bring before the OAS the question of Communism in Cuba and Cuban-directed subversion in other countries. In 1960, the

[31] IAPC, *Eighth Meeting*, p. 18.
[32] IAPC, *Eighth Meeting*, p. 21.

United States had submitted material on Communist influence in Cuba to the Inter-American Peace Committee in connection with its study of international tensions in the Caribbean, but no real examination of the problem had been carried out at that time. The Seventh Meeting of Consultation of Ministers of Foreign Affairs, held in San José, Costa Rica, in August 1960, condemned Sino-Soviet intervention in the hemisphere but failed to mention Cuba by name. During 1961, evidence of Cuban-inspired subversion was uncovered in other Latin American countries. Thus concern over Communism in Cuba began to spread among Latin American countries, and the formerly passive, noninterventionist attitude of some gave way to demands for action by the OAS. Certain of the larger states, however, continued to resist any such move.

Peru, in October 1961, requested the OAS Council to convoke the Organ of Consultation under the Rio Treaty to consider the situation in Cuba; but in accordance with a resolution of the OAS Council, Peru brought the case before the Inter-American Peace Committee, under its broad powers to investigate international tensions in the Caribbean.

Peru asked the committee to examine the following facts: (1) acts of force by the ruling regime of Cuba against citizens and foreigners including executions, imprisonments, physical maltreatment, and confiscations; (2) action of international Communism in the countries of America and incorporation of the Cuban Government into the Sino-Soviet bloc; (3) Communist infiltration by the Government of Cuba into the other countries of America, making use of diplomatic officers, official missions, and secret agents, for the purpose of instigating subversion against legally constituted governments and democratic institutions.[33]

The issue before the committee was whether the Government of Cuba was guilty of the charges leveled by the Government of Peru.

The committee invited the Cuban representative to attend a meeting on November 29. He declined, on the basis that representatives of El Salvador, Venezuela, Colombia, and the United States, as the Inter-American Peace Committee, were not competent to deal with the question because official acts of these governments showed them to be hostile to Cuba and thus unable to judge the situation impartially.[34] A request by the committee to visit Cuba was similarly rejected. The Cuban reply contained language injurious to the OAS, the committee, and its member states, and the committee unanimously declared the note unacceptable.[35]

Despite the lack of access and cooperation, the committee went ahead with its study. It assembled documents, interrogated exiles, consulted the

---

[33] IAPC, *Eighth Meeting*, p. 22.

[34] The other member of the committee was Uruguay, not mentioned in the Cuban note. El Salvador, Venezuela, and the United States had already broken diplomatic relations with Cuba at this time.

[35] IAPC, *Eighth Meeting*, pp. 25–26.

governments of other American states, and issued a report that constituted a severe indictment of the Cuban Government.[36]

The committee presented substantial evidence showing the identification of the Government of Cuba with Marxist-Leninist ideology and socialism of the Soviet type, and the widespread violation of human rights and democratic principles. Acceptance by Cuba of Soviet military aid was similarly documented. It admitted that the facts were difficult to verify, but found that the Government of Cuba was guilty of instigating subversion and revolution against the constitutional governments and democratic traditions of America. Cases were cited in which other American governments had declared Cuban diplomatic representatives *personae non gratae* on account of their intervention in internal affairs.

The committee concluded by pointing out that the alignment of Cuba with the Soviet bloc, the adoption of Marxist-Leninist ideology and politics, and the violation of human rights conflicted directly with basic principles of the Inter-American System.

The committee found the facts and reported them in forthright language. There was no effort to gloss over unpleasant situations as is so often the case in the documents emanating from inter-American deliberations. The member countries of the Peace Committee were Colombia, El Salvador, the United States, Uruguay, and Venezuela, all of which were represented by their ambassadors to the OAS. With the exception of Uruguay, these countries favored stronger action on the Cuban problem through the OAS, and Uruguay's representative was of that opinion also. For the first time, Mexico was not a member of the committee, having completed its term the previous year. Its absence is significant in the light of the strong language adopted in the committee's report.

Following the Peace Committee's report, and Colombia's proposal to convoke the Organ of Consultation under the Rio Treaty on the Cuban problem, the Eighth Meeting of Consultation of Ministers of Foreign Affairs was held at Punta del Este, Uruguay, in January 1962. At this conference, the main political doctrine used to justify the exclusion of Cuba from the Inter-American System was the incompatibility of Marxism-Leninism with the principles of that system.[37] Thus the Peace Committee's report on the Peruvian request laid the groundwork for the more vigorous action taken under the Rio Treaty at Punta del Este.

[36] IAPC, *Eighth Meeting*, pp. 27, 45.

[37] Eighth Meeting of Consultation of Ministers of Foreign Affairs, Resolution IV, *Final Act*, OEA/Ser. C/II.8 (Washington: Pan American Union, 1962).

18

—•—

EVALUATION OF THE PEACE–OBSERVATION EXPERIENCE OF THE ORGANIZATION OF AMERICAN STATES

The peace-observation activities of the OAS have dealt primarily with intra-hemisphere situations threatening the peace, although some attention has been given to disputes or controversies involving extra-hemisphere powers, notably in the Cuban missile crisis. With regard to the intra-hemisphere disputes the OAS serves as a collective security system for the maintenance of peace and security: in regard to the disputes involving extra-continental powers, the OAS (under the Rio Treaty) assumes the character of a defensive alliance.

Most of the cases examined have involved the small countries of Central America and the Caribbean, an area noted for its political instability and backward economic and social conditions. These disputes have ranged from minor incidents, involving little more than public arguments and recriminations, to hostilities. Four cases (two involving Costa Rica and Nicaragua, the Honduras-Nicaragua case, and the Guatemalan situation) involved armed conflict of serious proportions.

The causes of these disputes may be summarized as follows: Political activities of exiles, especially, but not exclusively, associated with the existence of harsh dictatorships, have constituted the major cause. Refugees from oppressive or otherwise unacceptable governments have maintained a continuing series of plots to overthrow those governments unsympathetic to the refugees' political views. These conflicts have in some cases been exacerbated by the existence of strong personal animosities between heads of states. Territorial disputes have also caused international conflict, primarily in cases where disagreements over boundaries have existed since colonial times. Racial antagonism, compounded with political differences, has served as a contributing cause in the bad relations between the Dominican Republic and Haiti. Communist subversion has been a major factor in the cases involving Cuba and Guatemala.

While some cases brought before OAS organs have involved specific incidents of aggression, many have been recurrent outbursts of chronic situations of tension between certain countries (as, for example, the

Dominican Republic and Haiti, or Cuba and the Dominican Republic). The larger Latin American countries have generally been less seriously affected by political and territorial problems that have plagued the small Caribbean-Central American states and have appeared to be better able to resolve any disputes by direct negotiation, without resort to international agencies. [1]

PERSISTENCE OF CAUSATIVE PROBLEMS

In estimating the future needs for peace-observation machinery in the Latin American area, consideration should be given to the degree to which the problems responsible for creating international controversies persist.

The problem of the activities of political exiles is undergoing some change. On the whole, despite the continued recurrence of military governments, the harsh, personal dictatorships of the traditional type are disappearing. The increasing international concern with the problems of human rights and popular government and the pressures for economic and social, as well as political, reform in all Latin American countries have tended to soften the character of authoritarian governments even when established by military force. [2] Pressures for economic development also tend to make governments less interested in dabbling in the internal political affairs of their neighbors—an interest that the effective OAS opposition to such ventures has also tended to dull. A gradual lessening of the activities of political exiles as a cause of international tensions in the traditional sense may therefore be expected.

An exception to the foregoing statement is Cuba, which constitutes the most highly organized police state in Latin American history, from which a large number of refugees have fled and seek support from other governments, including the United States. In view of the military strength of the Castro regime, the problem involves primarily the activities of underground groups which seek to overthrow Castro and whose ability to persist is highly speculative.

The problem of exiles, moreover, is but one facet of the deeper problem of political and social instability that continues to assail most Latin American countries and that cannot fail to have a deleterious and weakening effect on the structure of international relations. Despite a diminution in the problem of exiles, the long-range problem of the delayed maturation of the Latin American polities remains as a factor contributing to international conflicts.

[1] For example, in 1963 Argentina and Chile settled a minor but long-standing boundary dispute by direct negotiation.

[2] Recent military governments established in Argentina, Brazil, Ecuador, Guatemala, and Peru are examples.

Turning to the problem of territorial disputes, with the settlement of the Honduran-Nicaraguan boundary in 1961, only one major territorial dispute remains between American republics: that of Ecuador and Peru. A potential dispute exists between Guatemala and Mexico over the Mexican border with Belize (British Honduras) should Guatemala ever achieve its ambition of reincorporating that territory within its national boundaries. Other boundary problems involve either small and unimportant bits of territory that are not likely to promote serious international controversy, or are concerned with European powers and therefore outside the scope of the OAS.

Racial antagonisms will probably continue to contribute to tensions between Haiti and the Dominican Republic. The future relations of these countries and their need to resort to international agencies for the consideration of their disputes will depend, however, primarily on their achievement of political maturity and social stability. In the meantime, the unsettled political situation and the chronic antagonisms in these two states will no doubt create future occasions for international peace-observation activities, as they have in the past.

While the traditional causes of conflicts requiring peace observation through the OAS are declining, the problem of Communist subversion and aggression has risen. This problem must be viewed in two aspects: (1) Communist subversion initiated and directed primarily from the Soviet Union or China in countries other than Cuba, where Communist control has been established; and (2) that involving activities fomented and supported primarily by Cuba. The OAS would be more directly concerned with the latter because of Cuba's position inside the hemisphere.

Prior to December 1963 no peace observation of any significance had been carried out through the OAS with regard to the problem of Communist subversion in the Americas, as in neither the Guatemalan incident of 1954 nor the Cuban problem since 1960 could any effective procedure be designed or agreed upon. A major reason for this—aside from the political inhibitions that have been described elsewhere—was that Communist subversion was in both cases carried on with the cooperation, or at least the tolerance, of the two Latin American governments involved.

What may well be encountered increasingly, however, is the tactic of Cuban support of guerrilla activities in other Latin American countries. The governments that are the targets of such activities may seek the support of the OAS in investigating the Cuban instigation of these activities and fixing responsibility. This was in fact done in the Venezuelan-Cuban case of 1963–1964. The Special Consultative Committee on Security against Communist aggression established by the Eighth Meeting of Foreign Ministers was motivated in part by the recognition of this problem; however, no government has yet called on that agency for consultative or investigative work, and its future role is somewhat in doubt.

CASES INVOLVING EXTRA-CONTINENTAL POWERS

As indicated earlier, the function of the OAS with respect to an international conflict between American states and an outside power changes to that of an alliance under the Treaty of Rio de Janeiro. Peace observation or other functions of peaceful settlement are not appropriate to the regional organization in such cases, since European governments would not be likely to accept peace observation by an agency of which they are not members. It will be recalled that the OAS in its resolution of October 23, 1962, called for United Nations inspection in Cuba to verify the withdrawal of offensive weapons by the Soviet Union. Communist subversion and indirect aggression involving the Sino-Soviet powers will probably continue to be the most likely cause of international conflicts between American and extra-hemisphere powers. Unlike the problem of Cuban-directed subversion discussed above, the subject of Soviet- or Chinese-directed subversion would remain largely outside the sphere of OAS peace-observation work, however important the action of the regional system might be from a defense standpoint.

Another possible source of conflict with extra-continental powers is the existing territorial disputes between American and European powers. They concern mainly the problems of British Honduras (Great Britain and Guatemala), the Falkland Islands (Great Britain and Argentina) and the boundary between Venezuela and British Guiana. Here, again, except in the unlikely case of outright aggression, the exercise of international responsibilities for peace observation would properly belong to the United Nations rather than the OAS.

ADAPTATION OF THE OAS SYSTEM TO REGIONAL CHARACTERISTICS

Experience supports the view that a major reason for the existence and strength of the OAS is the opportunity it gives to the Latin American countries to deal with their international disputes in their own way. These states are intensely proud of the international system they have created together with the United States. They resent and oppose any intrusion of nonmember countries into their domestic or foreign affairs, feeling that such action would not only constitute improper intervention, but might involve the imposition of procedures that would clash with their own methods and traditions.

Basically, the Latin American states as a group share a desire to settle their disputes by peaceful means. Individual states may depart from this principle in specific situations, but the weight of the Latin American community is normally on the side of pacific settlement. The use of force, even in accordance with treaty provisions, is viewed as the least desirable recourse. This approach is supported by appeal to long-established principles that the Latin American countries have developed as guides for their international conduct and that evoke a strong emotional response among both governments and the public. The principle of peaceful settlement is one of these. Another is the principle of nonintervention, which has particular relevance to the many international disputes related to internal political situations. An extraordinary respect for the sovereignty of all governments, a high regard for the niceties of protocol, and a desire to work out "face-saving" formulas are characteristic of the Latin American way. Sentiment plays an important part in appeals to erring governments. These considerations in practice, if not in theory, lead to flexible procedures, and also give opportunity for the exercise of personal influence on the part of mediators. All these factors are found in the histories of the individual cases examined in this study. Perhaps the element of flexibility is best illustrated by the varied manner in which the investigating committees have carried out their tasks, and by the improvised arrangements for the participation of military personnel when needed.

Although the Latin American governments are deeply committed to their regional system, they have shown due respect for their obligations under the United Nations Charter and have recognized its supreme responsibility for the maintenance of international peace and security should the regional system fail, or should cases arise involving non-American states.

ADEQUACY OF REGIONAL MACHINERY

Viewed from the structural and procedural standpoint, the peace-observation machinery available to the member states of the OAS is ample. Its ineffectiveness in some situations has been due more to emotional and political factors than to deficiencies in organization.

The basic obligations and procedures related to peace observation in the American states are set forth in three treaties: the Charter of the OAS; the Treaty of Rio de Janeiro; and the Pact of Bogotá. Of these only the last has proved ineffectual. Half of the signatories have not ratified it. In due course, a renegotiation of an Inter-American treaty of pacific settlement seems to be called for, but in the meantime the procedures set forth in the Pact of Bogotá are available for the use of any government that so desires, whether or not it has ratified the treaty.

In the Meeting of Consultation of Ministers of Foreign Affairs (under the Charter or as Organ of Consultation under the Rio Treaty), in the Council and in the Inter-American Peace Committee, the OAS has three agencies that meet most of the requirements for effective peace observation. Improvements could be made in the Council and the Peace Committee, however, and some such improvements are in fact coming about by decisions taken under the stress of practical necessity. Assignments given the Council by the Meeting of Foreign Ministers in connection with the Dominican Republic case (1960) and the Cuban case (1962) have already increased its responsibilities and effectiveness in the peace-observation field. The Peace Committee, given what seems excessive responsibility by the Fifth Meeting of Foreign Ministers in the Caribbean situation, requires a reconsideration of its permanent authority. The problems associated with these two organs are not, however, fundamental in nature. [3]

The peace-observation activities of the OAS have generally been entrusted to well-qualified individuals, a factor which the personal nature of negotiations makes particularly important. Most of the men participating in investigating committees have been their countries' ambassadors to the OAS, often to the United States as well, and many have brought outstanding abilities and long experience to their task. In contrast to the United Nations, the OAS has not given the Secretary-General any significant role in carrying out peace observation aside from staffing functions.

ROLE OF THE UNITED STATES

The participation of the United States in the peace-observation activities of the OAS has been important. It has brought to these activities potential power and political influence that have added to the weight and the seriousness with which recommendations and negotiations were attended to by countries involved in disputes. In any political action, the element of power is essential, and in the inter-American community power is, for good or ill, concentrated in the hands of the United States. This is not to suggest that the OAS security system is a tool which the United States can manipulate at will; the frustrations which this country encountered in dealing with the Cuban situation through the OAS prior to the 1962 missile crisis proves the contrary. It does suggest, however, that while the Latin American countries have largely determined the structure and procedures of the inter-American security system, its effective use still requires the application of a greater power than the Latin American countries can bring to the task themselves, and here it is necessary to turn to the United States. This is a factor of which sophisticated Latin American statesmen are keenly, if tacitly, aware, and it should never be forgotten in projecting plans for future peace-observation or peace-keeping activities through the regional system.

[3] For a more detailed discussion of these problems and suggested solutions, see Dreier, *The Organization of American States and the Hemisphere Crisis, op. cit.*, pp. 125–27; and by the same author, "The Council of the OAS: Performance and Potential," *Journal of Inter-American Studies*, V (July 1963).

On an operational level, the participation of the United States is important to OAS peace-observation work because of the logistic support it has given to investigating committees. On more than one occasion, access to remote areas has been provided by U.S. Government aircraft, and when large groups of military officers were engaged in field observation, their transportation, communication, and maintenance have depended on the contribution or loan of United States equipment and supplies. In addition, the U.S. military establishment has provided the fuel and maintenance needed by those of other countries. Since all the conflicts in which the OAS needed such support took place in the Central American-Caribbean area, U.S. bases in Puerto Rico and the Canal Zone were readily accessible.

RELIABILITY OF THE OAS SYSTEM

The adequate and well-adapted machinery of the OAS, backed in most cases by both official and public opinion in Latin America and the United States, has turned in an effective and useful record in peace observation. Yet the performance of this machinery has been influenced by several intangible factors that must be recognized in any evaluation. Some of the intangible factors favorably influencing the attitude of the OAS member states have been referred to above. Note must also be taken of those that have unfavorably affected the capacity of the OAS.

A major factor in the operation of the regional machinery is that the governments and their articulate public sectors tend to become overwhelmed in a given situation by emotional considerations that powerfully affect their political actions. For example, the strong noninterventionist feeling, particularly the fear of U.S. intervention, has served to inhibit, even prohibit, positive action by the OAS. Cuba is the outstanding example. The outpouring of revolutionary fervor following Castro's victory was another instance of how a widespread Latin American emotional attitude affected the ability of the OAS to function with respect to Cuba. Part of this revolutionary fervor took the form of intense anti-dictator sentiment. In 1959, this was responsible for the unwillingness of the OAS to invoke the Rio Treaty on behalf of Trujillo, and in 1960, it made the member states eager to impose sanctions on the Dominican Government over which the Generalissimo presided. It was, however, a similar wave of emotional response to the military threat of Soviet missiles in Cuba that enabled the OAS to take the rapid and dramatic decisions in support of the United States proposals on October 23, 1962.

In contrast with these emotional factors, political considerations of a more mundane sort—the playing of politics for individual national advantage—have not seriously affected the OAS peace-observation procedures. Important decisions on peace-observation proposals have generally been adopted unaminously or by overwhelming majorities. Nor have the investigating committees on the whole been divided by political differences among their members. The major political division that exists at this time in the OAS with respect to collective security is between the majority and the small minority (though the latter includes some of the larger countries) that has opposed what they consider intervention in internal Cuban affairs. This opposition reflects the domestic politics of the countries making up the minority groups and is more akin to the emotional factors mentioned above than to what can properly be considered international politics.

Mention should also be made of the tendency of some governments to bring minor problems or transitory controversies before the OAS without having considered sufficiently the possibility of solving them through direct negotiation. This tendency is particularly evident in unstable governments, which see in the appeal to the regional system a means of propping up their weak stance. The Council has shown a commendable discretion in refusing to invoke the Rio Treaty machinery for issues that can be settled without recourse to this powerful instrument.

Two basic questions arise in evaluating the OAS peace-observation history. How effective would the OAS be in a serious conflict between two major Latin American countries? And, secondly, how would the system function in a case brought against the United States? To these questions, no definite answers can be given in the absence of a test case. As has been indicated earlier, however, the likelihood of a conflict involving the larger Latin American countries is greatly reduced by the absence among them of the problems which have caused conflicts between the smaller ones, and by the tendency of the larger powers, at least since World War II and the establishment of the OAS collective security system, to settle their disputes by direct negotiation. Moreover, the larger countries of Latin America, especially Brazil, Mexico, Chile, and Colombia, have taken a leading role in establishing collective security systems both in the OAS and in the United Nations, while Argentina has proved to be a reliable supporter. Their use of force in an international dispute would, therefore, conflict with their well-established policy and international standing. The only foreseeable cause for such an eventuality seems to be the successful domination of one of the Latin American countries by Soviet- or Chinese-inspired Communism.

In a case involving the United States, it seems obvious that the effective use of OAS peace-observation machinery would depend entirely on the willingness of the United States to accept such a procedure. Present United States policy seems to favor such a position so long as vital security interests of this country are not unduly jeopardized thereby.

IMPLICATIONS FOR THE FUTURE OF
UNITED NATIONS PEACE OBSERVATION

From the standpoint of United States policy with reference to future peace-observation activities in international organizations, the experience of the OAS suggests the following conclusions.

1. The system of peace-observation activities developed in the OAS has demonstrated its usefulness in dealing with most disputes among Latin American states. It has effectively drawn on regional traditions and has developed procedures in keeping with the cultural and political customs prevailing among these countries. While the record of the OAS leaves room for improvement, it justifies a continued reliance on it for peace observation and mediation in intra-American controversies. This policy would respond to the desire of the Latin American countries to handle their problems in their own way and would favor the U.S. objective of opposing the intervention of non-American powers—particularly those antagonistic to the United States—in intra-hemisphere relations. A policy of continued reliance on the regional agency need not conflict with the recognition of the ultimate responsibility of the United Nations should the OAS prove incapable of effective action in any given case. Nor should the possibility of improving the OAS machinery be neglected.

2. The United States should continue to participate actively in the activities of the OAS if it is to succeed, and be prepared to assume a major share of the practical burden of such work. There is no substitute for power, and, under present conditions in the Western Hemisphere, only the United States can bring the necessary power to bear on serious conflicts, even though collective procedures are used for that purpose.

3. The peace-observation capacity of the OAS is severely limited in disputes involving non-American states. Should the dispute be with a non-American government such as the United Kingdom, which is normally ready to seek legal and pacific solutions, the proper forum is the United Nations. A more difficult problem is posed in the case of a conflict with Communist powers which seek to strike at the vital interests of the United States and whose controversy with a Latin American country would be governed by that purpose. When the conflict reaches the point of presenting a military threat, the OAS may serve a valuable purpose for the United States as a defensive alliance, distinct from its function of peace observation. In situations where the extra-continental Communist power limits itself to political subversion, enlisting the aid of nationals of the target country, the OAS tends to be inhibited by its extreme concern for nonintervention. This poses for the United States the difficult choice between compromising with the negative attitude of the OAS or accepting the political liabilities inherent in the adoption of unilateral action without OAS backing. In any event, if political tension between the United States and the Soviet Union should

reach the point where the latter agrees to have recourse to some international peace-observation procedure, the proper agency would be the United Nations rather than the regional system.

4. One final question deserves attention: To what extent can the experience and methods of the OAS be transplanted to other regions? Certainly the causes of international disputes which have been encountered in Latin America are found elsewhere, particularly among the newer states of Africa and Asia where political instability, territorial disputes, racial antagonisms, and Communist subversion are common features of the scene. Yet any attempt to rely in other portions of the globe on regional procedures modeled on those of the OAS would overlook two fundamental factors. One is the long tradition of cooperation among Latin American countries and their attachment to certain common ideas and policies which are rooted in their history. Such a foundation, which plays a vital part in the OAS record, is not found in any other regional grouping to any comparable extent. Moreover, the success of the OAS system has depended on the active participation of a major world power, the United States, which has been willing to support the principles and procedures of the regional system and lend its weight to their effective application. No parallel to such a situation exists elsewhere in the world, except for the different and special case of the British Commonwealth. It seems, therefore, that on other continents, the newer states would have to work out regional systems in their own way, profiting by the OAS experience where it is relevant, but drawing primarily on their own cultural and political heritage as the Latin American countries have done for themselves.

MAJOR CASES
UNDER THE UNITED NATIONS

PREFATORY NOTE

A<small>RTICLE</small> 33 OF THE UNITED NATIONS CHARTER PROVIDES THAT the parties to any dispute likely to endanger the maintenance of international peace shall first seek a solution by peaceful means of their own choice. In the majority of the cases discussed in this section, peace observation, when it took place, was under the auspices of an organ of the United Nations. However, in conjunction with the UN cases, a few situations are also considered where the parties in attempting to settle the controversies by means of their own choice, pursuant to Article 33, set up special international arrangements for peace observation.

UNITED NATIONS CHARTER RESOURCES
FOR PEACE OBSERVATION

The Security Council

The Security Council has "primary responsibility for the maintenance of international peace and security." Members agreed "that in carrying out its duties under this responsibility, the Security Council acts on their behalf" (Article 24). Under Article 34, the Security Council has authority to "investigate any dispute, or any situation which might lead to international friction or give rise to a dispute." Under this article, peace observation may be a resource for the future but has little relevance for the past. It has been used only once. However, both Soviet and U.S. legal authorities agree that a decision to investigate under this article is legally binding on all United Nations members.

Under Article 36, the Security Council may "recommend appropriate procedures or methods of adjustment." If the Security Council deems that continuance of the dispute is likely to endanger the maintenance of international peace and security, under Article 37 it may "recommend such terms of settlement as it may consider appropriate." Therefore, the Security Council may recommend peace observation either as a procedure or as a term of settlement. The scope of such peace observation would be far wider than a decision under Article 34. However, the decision would merely be a recommendation, not binding on any of the parties, and peace observation to be effective would need agreement of the parties. Furthermore, such a decision could be vetoed by any permanent member of the Security Council not a party to the dispute. Practically all peace observation under the Security Council has been pursuant to and limited by these Charter provisions.

Under Articles 40 and 41 in Chapter VII, if the Security Council has determined the existence of a threat to the peace, breach of the peace or act of aggression, it may order various types of measures not involving the use of armed force either to prevent the aggravation of the situation or to give effect to its decisions. Under these articles, the Security Council could set up such peace-observation machinery as it wished. All members of the United Nations would be required to carry out the Security Council decisions. Since this action comes under Chapter VII of the Charter, it would require the concurrence of all the permanent members of the Council. The Security Council has only twice, in the Palestine and Korean cases, made the determination under Article 39 of the existence of a threat to the peace, breach of the peace, or act of aggression which is a necessary preliminary to action under Articles 40 and 41. As brought out in the discussion of the Palestine case, the Security Council never related any of its actions directed toward peace observation to Chapter VII. Therefore peace observation depended on the consent of the parties. In the Korean situation, the Soviet Union was absent from the Council and therefore did not veto the action. The Korean action at that time did not involve peace observation but rather repelling aggression. Thus the Security Council has never used its powers under Chapter VII to obtain peace observation. Again this is a resource that might be used in the future.

Under Article 29, one of a group of articles coming under the rubric "procedure," the Security Council may establish such subsidiary organs as it deems necessary for the performance of its functions. The establishment of a subsidiary organ would thus not be subject to the great power veto. On two occasions, a limited amount of peace observation was attempted under this article.

In 1948, the Soviet Union voted against a resolution under Article 29 to set up a subcommittee to study at headquarters the available material on the Communist take-over in Czechoslovakia. Since a satellite representative was, at the time, President of the Security Council, the Soviet Union was able to sustain its negative vote as a veto using the so-called double veto machinery to prove that the resolution was not procedural. A number of years later, when a Western representative was President of the Security Council, the same procedures were used to uphold a subcommittee appointed to study the situation in Southeast Asia. While this device can probably be used to avoid a great power veto for a restricted kind of peace observation, it probably could not be used to obtain on-the-spot inspection and is of minor importance.

The General Assembly

Articles 11 and 12 of the Charter give to the General Assembly authority to discuss any question relating to the maintenance of international peace and security brought before it in accordance with Charter procedures. It can make recommendations with regard to any such questions to the states concerned, to the Security Council, or to both, subject to the limitation that the Assembly may not make recommendations with regard to any situation while the Security Council is exercising the functions assigned to it. The decision to remove a matter from the Security Council is a procedural decision and therefore not subject to the great power veto. Under Article 14, the Assembly may recommend measures for the peaceful adjustment of any situation regardless of origin that it deems likely to impair the general welfare or friendly relations among nations.

The authority of the Assembly to make recommendations on matters affecting the maintenance of international peace and on the peaceful adjustment of such matters presumably includes the authority to recommend the use of peace-observation measures. Therefore as a practical matter, two-thirds of the General Assembly can initiate peace observation. However, the General Assembly decision can go no farther than to recommend peace observation to the parties with the instituting of peace observation depending on consent from one or both parties to permit the mission to operate. All of the General Assembly measures relating to peace observation have stemmed either from Article 11 or Article 14 or both.

The Secretary-General

Under Article 99 the Secretary-General may bring to the attention of the Security Council any matter that in his opinion may threaten the maintenance of international peace and security. The Secretary-General has taken the position that in order to carry out his functions under this article, it may be necessary for him to dispatch personnel from the Secretariat to disturbed areas to determine whether a particular matter threatens the maintenance of international peace and security sufficiently to justify his bringing it to the attention of the Security Council. Such a mission might have substantial functions that could be described as peace observation. However, the peace observation would have only the limited objective of determining whether the matter was a threat to the peace. It could not be used except by agreement of the parties to adjust the controversy.

In short, while a considerable number of Charter provisions permit peace observation with the consent of the parties and in some instances without such consent, as a practical matter the most important peace-observation missions have been authorized either by the Security Council under Article 36 or Article 37 or both, or by the General Assembly under Article 11 or Article 14 or both. Under all of these articles, peace observation can only be instituted through recommendation which is not binding on the parties.

USE OF PEACE OBSERVATION BY THE UNITED NATIONS

Four separate trends can be identified in the use of peace observation since the United Nations began in January 1946.

1. The founding fathers of the United Nations contemplated that the Security Council would have the primary responsibility for dealing with matters involving the maintenance of international peace and security. Therefore, in the first years of the United Nations when peace observation was required, the Security Council was called on to authorize it and to set up the necessary machinery. With the intensification of the cold war in 1947 and 1948, the Soviet Union began to use its veto to prevent the establishment of peace-observation machinery in instances where the Western powers believed it was advisable and to cripple the exercise of

peace-observation functions in areas where it had already been authorized. This use (or abuse) of the veto by the Soviet Union led to the second phase of peace observation.

2. Commencing in 1948, the Western powers began to propose peace observation in the General Assembly in cases where the Security Council could not set up the machinery because of Soviet opposition. The peace observation in the Balkan area was transferred from the Security Council to the General Assembly when the Soviet Union began to obstruct the Western proposals in the Security Council. The peace-observation machinery in Korea was set up by the General Assembly.

3. Commencing about 1952, the Western powers began to find the peace-observation efforts of the General Assembly almost as unsatisfactory as those of the Security Council. The increase in the number of members in the Assembly made it difficult to establish machinery that could function effectively. At the same time, an apparent diminution of the cold war (the spirit of Camp David) resulted in efforts to set up peace-observation machinery in disturbed areas as a result of East-West agreements outside the United Nations. For example, the committee set up to obtain the evacuation of Chinese Nationalist troops from Burma was independent of the United Nations though it was carrying out a UN recommendation. Other examples are the Neutral Nations Supervisory Commission, set up as part of the Korean Armistice Agreement, and the International Control Commissions in Southeast Asia. The "troika" personnel arrangements in Southeast Asia and the even less satisfactory Korean arrangements made the operations generally ineffective.

4. In recent years, all peace-observation and peace-keeping missions have used exclusively the facilities of the Secretary- General. This has taken place whether the organ authorizing the peace observation was the Security Council or the General Assembly. The Secretary-General has a great deal of experience and know-how from the numerous peace-observation missions, some of which have lasted for many years. By 1956, when the hostilities commenced in the Suez, he was capable of organizing and dispatching to the scene of hostilities a force of some 6,000 within a few weeks. Furthermore, the direction and support of all the United Nations peace-observation missions operating in the late 1950's contrasted favorably with the frustrations of the missions operating through special arrangements. In the case of Jordan and Yemen, at least a portion of the original initiative for peace observation stemmed from the

Secretary-General himself with subsequent confirmation by either the Security Council or the Assembly.

The recent peace-observation missions have relied almost entirely on personnel from states other than the great powers. The Secretary-General has always insisted that peace observation be carried out with the consent of both parties. The missions report to the United Nations through the Secretary-General, with a theoretical independent right of access to the UN organs authorizing the missions. This present pattern has been far more effective than anything in the past, and for the immediate future seems likely to be the sole pattern of peace observation except, of course, in instances where the controversies are dealt with by regional organizations.

In the following sections, twelve cases in which the United Nations has conducted full-scale peace-observation operations are discussed in detail. Eleven other cases in which peace observation was requested but never fully carried out by the United Nations are included, and three other cases where peace observation took place as a result of special multinational arrangements are considered. The lines between types or categories of cases in a few instances are not sharply defined. For purposes of this study, several cases have been considered as one which might have been divided into two or more.

1

———◆———

THE INDEPENDENCE AND TERRITORIAL INTEGRITY OF GREECE

Immediately preceding World War II, the King of Greece established a semi-fascist dictatorship under General John Metaxas, a royalist. This act made the monarchy a symbol of the extreme right. As a result, when the Axis occupied Greece in 1941 and the King established a government in exile, he had little support in Greece.[1] The underground resistance movement, under the leadership of the Communist party, organized a National Liberation Front (EAM) of six leftist parties and a guerrilla band known

[1] The historical narrative is largely drawn from Winifred N. Hadsel, "American Policy Toward Greece," *Foreign Policy Reports*, XXIII (Sept. 1, 1947), pp. 150–53.

as ELAS. In the early war years, Great Britain supported EAM-ELAS. Beginning in 1943, however, the British supported a rival guerrilla group, the EDES, under non-Communist leadership. At the same time, the small, well-trained Greek Army was purged of Communists.

At the end of the war, the country was left in effect with two national governments and two military forces: the non-Communist government in exile supported by the Greek Army, the British troops, and the EDES; the Communist EAM supported by ELAS. A Government of National Unity was established on May 17, 1944, to which all factions pledged allegiance. The efforts of the Communist groups to take over the government led to civil war, however, and resulted in the destruction of ELAS as a fighting force in December 1944. The Communists urged the remnants of the underground to wage guerrilla warfare in the north of Greece where they could receive assistance from the Communist regimes in Albania, Bulgaria, and Yugoslavia.

In January 1946, the Soviet Union charged in the Security Council that the presence of British troops constituted interference with the internal affairs of Greece, with possible grave consequences for the maintenance of international peace. The President of the Security Council merely noted the statements made during the debate.[2]

On August 24, 1946, the Ukrainian representative brought before the Security Council a complaint concerning incidents along the Greek-Albanian frontier. By that time, the Communist guerrilla forces in the north were receiving assistance from the Communist neighbors of Greece. Accordingly, the United States proposed that an investigating commission look into the border incidents along the whole northern border of Greece. The Soviet Union vetoed the resolution.[3]

On December 3, 1946, the Greek Government charged in the Security Council that Albania, Bulgaria, and Yugoslavia were assisting the guerrilla forces in northern Greece. The United States proposed, and this time the Soviet Union did not veto the proposal, that a commission be established to conduct an investigation in northern Greece, Albania, Bulgaria, and Yugoslavia to determine the causes and nature of the border violations.

Early in 1947, the commission was formed and went to the Balkans. When the commission reported, however, the Soviet Union disagreed with its recommendations and vetoed three Security Council resolutions based on them. A United States proposal that the General Assembly make recommendations concerning the situation was also vetoed. The United States then obtained the removal of the item from the Security Council agenda in order to permit the General Assembly to consider the matter.[4]

[2] *United States Participation in the United Nations, Report by the President to the Congress for the Year 1946* (Washington: Government Printing Office, 1947), p. 36.
[3] *Ibid.*
[4] *Ibid., 1947*, pp. 19–21. Hereafter cited as *1947 President's Report.*

The General Assembly, at its second regular session in 1947, established an eleven-nation United Nations Special Committee on the Balkans (UNSCOB) to investigate the border situation and report to the Assembly. The Soviet Union and Poland challenged the legality of the committee and declined to serve as members. The remaining nine members served on the committee for four years until its dissolution in 1951.[5]

By 1951, the situation along the northern borders of Greece had greatly improved. This was partly due to the rift between Yugoslavia and the Cominform, after which Yugoslavia no longer assisted the guerrillas. Since Greece believed that the presence of United Nations observers was helpful, most of the functions of UNSCOB were transferred in 1952 to the Peace Observation Commission (POC), organized pursuant to the Uniting for Peace Resolution. The POC was located at United Nations headquarters in New York, and at the request of the Greek Government, it established a Balkan Subcommission over Soviet objection. Six observers and a small secretariat were dispatched to Greece. These arrangements continued through 1954.

TERMS OF REFERENCE

THE COMMISSION OF INVESTIGATION

The Commission of Investigation was established by the Security Council under a resolution of December 19, 1946,[6] providing that: "the Security Council under Article 34 of the Charter establish a Commission of Investigation to ascertain the facts relating to the alleged border violations along the frontier between Greece on the one hand and Albania, Bulgaria and Yugoslavia on the other." The members of the commission were the eleven states represented on the Security Council. The Council requested the Secretary-General to provide staff and assistance to the commission. The commission was to investigate conditions in Greece, Albania, Bulgaria, and Yugoslavia and report to the Security Council. It met in Athens and Salonika from January 29 to March 24, 1947, and in Sofia, Bulgaria and Belgrade, Yugoslavia from March 26 until April 2. It dispatched teams to the border to study incidents and conditions.

In the first week of April, the commission went to Geneva to prepare its report.[7] The United States suggested that it leave a "border team" in

---

[5] *1947 President's Report*, pp. 21–23.

[6] UN Security Council, *Official Records*, First Year, Second Series, No. 28, 86th and 87th meetings, Dec. 19, 1946, pp. 700–1.

[7] See: Harry N. Howard, *The United Nations and the Problem of Greece* (Washington: Government Printing Office, 1947), pp. 3–7.

Greece, but the Soviet Union objected. The United States thereupon proposed and the Security Council adopted a resolution directing the commission to "maintain in the area concerned a subsidiary group composed of a representative of each of the members of the commission. [8]

On April 30, the commission set up a subsidiary group with "authority to perform its functions in northern Greece and in other parts of Greece, Bulgaria, and Yugoslavia." [9] Despite the Security Council resolution, Yugoslavia and Albania declined to cooperate with the group, and Bulgaria indicated that its cooperation would be established for each individual case. Therefore, in effect, the work of the subsidiary group took place solely on the Greek side of the border.

As previously mentioned, the Soviet Union opposed the commission's report and vetoed three resolutions intended to implement it. The United States, therefore, on September 15, 1947, proposed that the Greek question be removed from the Security Council agenda. This being a procedural matter, the veto was not involved. The proposal was adopted by the Security Council, with the Soviet Union and Poland opposing. This action terminated the commission [10] and brought the matter before the General Assembly.

UNITED NATIONS SPECIAL COMMITTEE ON THE BALKANS

The United Nations Special Committee on the Balkans (UNSCOB), created by a General Assembly resolution of October 21, 1947, was to carry on most of the functions of the former Commission of Investigation. [11] The resolution called on the states involved "to cooperate in the settlement of their disputes by peaceful means, and to establish normal diplomatic and good neighborly relations among themselves"; to provide "machinery for the regulation and control of their common frontiers and for the pacific settlement of frontier incidents and disputes"; and to cooperate in the settlement of refugee problems.

The resolution recommended cooperation of the four governments and the committee and authorized the committee to recommend convening a special session of the General Assembly. The committee was composed of representatives of Australia, Brazil, China, France, Mexico, the Netherlands, Pakistan, the United Kingdom, and the United States, with "seats being held open for Poland and the Union of Soviet Socialist Republics." The principal headquarters were in Salonika. With the cooperation of the

[8] UN Security Council, *Official Records*, Second Year, No. 37, 130th and 131st meetings, Apr. 18, 1947, pp. 799–800.
[9] *Ibid.*, Supplement No. 11, S/337, p. 1.
[10] *1947 President's Report*, p. 21.
[11] UN General Assembly, Res. 109 (II), Oct. 21, 1947.

four governments concerned, the committee was to "perform its functions in such places and in the territories of the four States concerned as it may deem appropriate." The committee could establish its own procedures and name subcommittees, and was to report to the General Assembly. It would remain in existence pending a new decision of the General Assembly. Of particular interest was the provision that the Secretary-General should supply staff for the committee and "enter into a standing arrangement with each of the four Governments concerned to assure the Special Committee, so far as it may find it necessary to exercise its functions within their territories, of full freedom of movement and all necessary facilities for the performance of its functions," the first step toward status agreements.

UNSCOB's terms of reference were considerably broader than those of the Commission of Investigation. The Soviet Union had contended with some justification that its terms of reference were exhausted once it had found the situation likely to endanger international peace and security.[12] UNSCOB was instructed to use its good offices to settle disputed matters, as well as to observe the maintenance of peace. Its authority to operate within the territories of the four governments, while depending on the consent of the governments, went far beyond conducting hearings and listening to witnesses.

The Third General Assembly on November 27, 1948, continued UNSCOB with virtually the same terms of reference.[13] The Assembly resolution added to the previous resolution: (1) a condemnation of Bulgaria, Albania, and Yugoslavia; (2) a recommendation to all members of the United Nations and to all other states that their governments refrain from any action designed to assist directly or through any other government any armed group fighting against the Greek Government; (3) an authorization to UNSCOB to consult with the Interim Committee; (4) an authorization "to utilize the services and good offices of one or more persons whether or not members of the Special Committee." In other respects, the resolution confirmed the terms of reference of the previous resolution. It also called on the four governments "to renew the previously operative conventions for the settlement of frontier questions or to conclude new ones, and also to settle the problem of refugees."[14] It also dealt with the question of Greek children within the territories of other states.

A resolution adopted by the First Committee on November 11, 1948, asked the President of the General Assembly, the Secretary-General, the chairman, and rapporteur of the First Committee "to act in the capacity of conciliators . . . to explore the possibilities of reaching agreement

[12] Leland M. Goodrich and Anne P. Simons, *The United Nations and the Maintenance of International Peace and Security* (Washington: Brookings Institution, 1955), p. 178.

[13] UN General Assembly, Res. 193 (III), Nov. 27, 1948.

[14] This referred to the League of Nations case in connection with the Greek-Bulgarian border.

amongst themselves as to the methods and procedures to be adopted with a view to resolving present differences between them."[15] This conciliation effort made some headway but eventually failed.

By the time the Fourth General Assembly, 1950, began to consider the problem, the Yugoslav Government, as a result of its controversy with the Soviet Union, closed its frontiers to guerrillas.[16] The General Assembly resolution of November 18, 1949,[17] continued UNSCOB. The only new point in its terms of reference was that the General Assembly noted statements of Albania, Bulgaria, and Yugoslavia that Greek guerrillas entering their territories had been disarmed and called on the states to permit UNSCOB "or other appropriate international agency" to verify the fact. The resolution contained slightly more specific language on the subjects of restoration of diplomatic relations and repatriation of refugees.

The Fifth General Assembly noted an improvement in the situation on the northern frontiers of Greece and continued UNSCOB,[18] and the Sixth General Assembly in 1952 terminated the committee.

THE PEACE OBSERVATION COMMISSION (POC) AND THE BALKAN SUBCOMMISSION

UNSCOB indicated to the General Assembly in the fall of 1951 that the character of the problem had changed, and that UNSCOB was no longer necessary. It was discontinued on December 7, 1951. The Greek delegate, in the *Ad Hoc* Political Committee of the Assembly, then requested the General Assembly to continue its vigilance through use of the Peace Observation Commission which had been established under the Uniting for Peace Resolution of 1950.[19] The Assembly, on December 7, 1951, requested the POC to establish a Balkan subcommission composed of not less than three or more than five members with its seat at United Nations headquarters in New York.[20] The subcommission had authority to send observers "to any area of international tensions in the Balkans on the request of any State or States concerned, but only to the territory of States consenting thereto;" "to visit any area in which observation . . . is being conducted;" and to report to the Peace Observation Commission and the

[15] UN General Assembly, A/C.1/385.

[16] Harry N. Howard, "Greek Question in the Fourth General Assembly of the United Nations," U.S. Department of State, *Bulletin*, Vol. 22 (1950), p. 307.

[17] UN General Assembly, Res. 288 (IV) A and B.

[18] *United States Participation in the United Nations, Report by the President to the Congress for the Year 1951* (Washington: Government Printing Office, 1952), pp. 304–5.

[19] UN General Assembly, *Ad Hoc* Political Committee, A/AC.53/L2.

[20] UN General Assembly, Res. 508 (VI) A and B, Dec. 7, 1951.

Secretary-General. The functions of the POC and its subcommission, unlike those of UNSCOB, were limited to peace observation, and the subcommission, by reporting to the Secretary-General as well as the POC, could in effect bypass the POC.

On January 23, 1952, over the opposition of the Soviet Union, the POC appointed a subcommission of five members—Colombia, France, Pakistan, Sweden, and the United States—with terms of reference as set forth in the General Assembly resolution. The Greek Government, on the same day, requested the immediate dispatch of observers to its frontier areas,[21] and the subcommission responded affirmatively. The Secretary-General was requested to continue the services of six UNSCOB observers until the new observers arrived in Greece.[22] The terms of reference of the Balkan subcommission thereafter remained unchanged.

ORGANIZATION

THE COMMISSION OF INVESTIGATION

The commission consisted of eleven delegates, mostly with the rank of minister, and a secretariat of twenty-seven persons furnished by the United Nations Secretary-General. The personnel included a press officer, a photographer, administrative officers, interpreters, secretaries, verbatim reporters, and stenographers. In general, the United Nations Secretariat, as compared to the country delegations, furnished more services in the Balkan operation than in the operations going on at the same time in Indonesia, Korea, and even Palestine. The personnel in the eleven delegations totaled fifty-six.

In addition to the delegations and United Nations Secretariat personnel, each of the four states where the border disturbances were taking place provided liaison officers: Bulgaria, thirteen including three military liaison officers; Greece, thirteen including four military liaison officers; and Yugoslavia, seventeen including four military liaison officers.[23]

The chief activity of the Commission of Investigation was to hear witnesses. As a part of this activity, investigating teams, at times as many as seven, traveled throughout Greece and occasionally visited Yugoslavia, Bulgaria, and Albania. They made thirty-three investigations. The composition and activity of the teams varied considerably. For example, the

[21] UN General Assembly, Peace Observation Commission, Balkan Subcommission, A/CN.7/SC.1/1.

[22] *Ibid.*, A/CN.7/SC.1/2.

[23] UN Security Council, *Official Records*, Second Year, Special Supplement No. 2, S/360, Annex I, Vol. II, pp. 255–58. Hereafter cited as S/360.

personnel of Team 1, which was very active, totaled twenty-two including the chairman from the United Nations Secretariat and held twenty-five meetings. In contrast, Team 2, which was set up specifically to interview the Greek guerrilla leader Markos, had twenty-one members and met only twice. A third team, the largest, with thirty-eight members, met only three times in Alexandropolis.

The commission was in Athens from January 29 until February 18, 1947. From February 25 to March 22, its activities were centered in Salonika with the entire commission going to the border between March 15 and March 22 (and entering Yugoslavia) to investigate specific incidents which had previously occurred in various sectors. The commission went to Sofia on March 26, to Belgrade on March 30, and to Geneva on April 7 to prepare its report. It returned to New York to attend the Security Council meetings in June and July.

The subsidiary group established on April 30 had its headquarters in Salonika. Albania, Bulgaria, and Yugoslavia declined to cooperate with the group. Therefore its on-the-spot investigations were confined to the Greek side of the border. The group consisted of one representative from each of the members of the commission with a staff not exceeding one.[24] Within its limited authority, it acted without instruction from the delegations in Geneva. In effect, the group reported through the United Nations Secretary-General. Thus, without particular authority from the Security Council, a novel organizational pattern began to emerge where the observers along the boundary represented the United Nations rather than their respective states. This pattern continued under UNSCOB, even though the delegates were generally close at hand, either in Athens or Salonika. It remains the organizational pattern of peace observation presently prevailing under the United Nations.

The Soviet Union contended that the establishment of the subsidiary group went beyond the terms of the Security Council resolution creating the commission. The Soviet bloc declined to cooperate with the group, a position that continued after the abolition of the Commission of Investigation and the creation of UNSCOB.

The twenty-seven personnel from the United Nations Secretariat were divided between Geneva, where the commission was preparing its report, the Athens headquarters, and the Salonika offices of the subsidiary group. Each delegation was generally responsible for its own expenses. The United Nations Secretariat personnel were paid from the UN budget. Since the Commission of Investigation never had any observer groups stationed on the border and in the main listened to witnesses in cities, the special problems of logistic support of peace-observation groups did not arise.

---

[24] Howard, *The United Nations and the Problem of Greece*, p. 9.

UNITED NATIONS SPECIAL COMMITTEE ON THE BALKANS

Despite the increased functions of UNSCOB, the initial budgetary committee estimate provided for a secretariat of only twenty-five members plus eight locally recruited. The initial budgetary provision called for expenditures of $72,840 in 1947 and $538,600 in 1948.[25]

The first formal meetings of UNSCOB took place in Paris in November 1947. By December 1, it had established its headquarters in Salonika where it remained, although occasionally it held meetings in Athens and prepared its first report in Geneva.

Five observation posts were established on the border,[26] each consisting of four observers from the delegations and six auxiliary personnel from the United Nations Secretariat. All mobile equipment was loaned by delegations, principally the United States. Each group was also loaned radio equipment to permit communication with the central station in Salonika,[27] and miscellaneous equipment. UNSCOB headquarters in Salonika consisted of three administrative officers, four radio operators, one précis writer, three interpreters, one auto mechanic, and one radio repairman. The United States loaned the committee four aircraft and their crews.[28]

The observers were paid by the respective governments and were given a United Nations per diem of $3.50 for maintenance. The United Nations Secretariat furnished food, but the individual personnel paid for it. Gasoline and oil were drawn from army stocks and reimbursed by the United Nations. Greek, British, and American military authorities furnished maps.[29] Signal equipment was loaned to UNSCOB largely by the United States.

The annual costs of the field teams coming from the United Nations budget were $313,410 plus subsistence allowances of $102,060.[30] As pointed out, the United Nations budget did not cover transportation and communications equipment, medical or custodial services, and other major items.

UNSCOB operations showed expenditures of $602,841 for 1948, which was over the initial budgetary provision. For fiscal 1949, the General Assembly approved expenditures of $508,200 for the headquarters and $750,000 for the observation groups. A supplemental appropriation of $89,100 was also approved for the transportation and per diems of alternate representatives.[31]

[25] UN General Assembly, A/415 (mimeo.), Oct. 18, 1947.

[26] UN General Assembly, *Official Records*, Third Session, Supplement No. 8, A/574, p. 3.

[27] See: Table of Organization and Equipment, UN General Assembly, A/521/Corr. 1 (mimeo.), Feb. 9, 1948, pp. 2–3. Hereafter cited as A/521/Corr. 1.

[28] UN General Assembly, A/521 (mimeo.), Jan. 9, 1948, p. 33.

[29] A/521/Corr. 1, p. 4.

[30] *Ibid.*

[31] U.S. Department of State, "The Problem of Greece in the Third Session of the General Assembly," *Documents and State Papers*, I: 10 (January 1949), pp. 591–92.

Largely because of improved conditions on the Greek border, the United Nations appropriation for the fiscal year 1950 was reduced to $850,000, plus $50,000 for assisting the repatriation of Greek children.[32] For fiscal 1951, the estimate was $525,000, plus $50,000 for the repatriation of Greek children. This further reduction was also due to the improved situation.[33] These expenditures are low because they do not include compensation and lodging for the delegations except for the members assigned to observation posts, nor do they include the most expensive items of logistic support.

THE POC AND THE BALKAN SUBCOMMISSION

By the time that the Balkan Subcommission took over the work of UNSCOB, the disorders on the border had largely disappeared. The Balkan Subcommission with headquarters in New York consisted of five members. In response to the Greek request, it dispatched to the border six observers, one from each of the members of the subcommission and a principal observer from the United Kingdom. The supporting secretariat personnel was small.

PERFORMANCE

COMMISSION OF INVESTIGATION

Of the thirty-three field investigations conducted by the observation teams organized by the commission, thirteen were engaged almost exclusively in interrogation of witnesses. Five involved also investigations of refugee or prisoner-of-war camps on both sides of the border. Twelve were direct investigations of border incidents, and the remaining three were directed toward establishing the fact of help to the Greek guerrillas from across the border.[34]

In addition to its investigating teams, the Commission of Investigation had a committee of experts to plan its work. This was indispensable because of the volume of communications addressed to the commission. The committee examined these communications and determined which should be submitted to the commission. It also selected and scheduled witnesses to be heard. Two drafting committees were also established to prepare the commission's report to the Security Council.

[32] Harry N. Howard, "Greek Question in the Fourth General Assembly of the United Nations," U.S. Department of State, *Bulletin*, Vol. 22 (March 1950), p. 370.

[33] Harry N. Howard, "The Greek Question in the Fifth Session of the General Assembly of the United Nations," U.S. Department of State, *Bulletin*, Vol. 24 (1951), p. 345. Hereafter cited as Howard, "Greek Question in Fifth Session."

[34] S/360, p. 12.

The most voluminous sources of information were the four governments. For example, the Greek liaison officer, Mr. Kyrou, presented the so-called "Greek White Book" which narrated border incidents in two volumes. The liaison representative of Albania charged Greece with 172 frontier violations from December 1944 to the end of 1946. In all of these incidents, however, only six persons were killed, sixteen wounded, and two captured, and some animals were lost. The Communist-dominated coalition of Greek political parties (EAM) and other leftist organizations also presented testimony; and a number of Greek citizens, formerly associated with the Greek Communist Party, testified to the programs carried on in Yugoslavia, Bulgaria, and Albania to assist the Greek guerrillas. The Soviet and Polish representatives visited Markos, the chief of the Greek guerrillas, privately, and attempted to insert in the commission documentation a report of their interview with him; but the commission declined to receive the evidence except as a private communication from the Soviet delegate.

The issues before the commission have been classified by a member of the United States delegation as:[35] charges by Greece that Albania, Bulgaria, and Yugoslavia were supporting the guerrilla movement in Greece; that the neighboring countries were interfering in the internal affairs of Greece with the aim of detaching from Greece parts of its territories (Aegean Macedonia and Western Thrace); of provocation of border incidents by Albania, Bulgaria, and Yugoslavia; Albanian, Bulgarian, and Yugoslav contentions that the Greek regime was responsible for a state of civil war in Greece and for the disturbances in the northern districts; that the Greek Government was conducting a policy of provocation toward them by maintaining quislings in Greek territory and by their subversive activities with respect to Albania, Bulgaria, and Yugoslavia; and that the Greek Government was conducting an expansionist foreign policy which was a provocation to them.

It will be obvious that the bulk of the evidence on all these points consisted of witnesses' statements, with each side contending that the witnesses on the other side were lying or were forced to testify as they did. Occasionally, however, the actions of the delegates themselves corroborated some of the testimony to which they were objecting. For example, while the Yugoslav and Bulgarian Governments denied the Greek charge that they were aiming to detach Aegean Macedonia and Western Thrace from Greece, the Bulgarian representative on the commission stated that Bulgaria would never give up its claim to Western Thrace.

The evidence of witnesses concerning border incidents, assistance to the guerrillas, and asylum to escaping guerrillas, was corroborated by on-the-spot investigations that took place long after the incidents. The evidence concerning political refugees in Greece from Yugoslavia, Bulgaria, and Albania was corroborated through field investigation of the camps where

[35] Howard, *The United Nations and the Problem of Greece*, pp. 17–19.

the refugees were held. The commission found that they were receiving excellent treatment.

After the commission adjourned to Geneva, the subsidiary group investigated a number of incidents on the Greek frontiers but was not permitted to cross the frontier even when the neighbors of Greece had requested the investigation. The bulk of the evidence presented to the subsidiary group was also in the form of testimony of witnesses. However, the testimony was reinforced by observation of the border itself from the Greek side.

The commission in its report reached conclusions the general purport of which was "that the three northern neighbors of Greece had encouraged, assisted, trained, and supplied the Greek guerrillas in their armed activities against the Greek Government."[36] The commission recognized that the Yugoslav support of the guerrillas was greater than that furnished by Albania and Bulgaria. The report also dealt with conditions in Greece arising from the problems of economic rehabilitation after the Greek liberation. The French delegate objected to some of the commission's conclusions but supported its proposals based on the conclusions. The Soviet and Polish delegations objected to both the conclusions and the proposals.

The commission report proposed that:[37] (1) Albania, Bulgaria, Greece, and Yugoslavia do their utmost to establish good neighborly relations and to refrain from supporting elements aiming at the overthrow of the lawful governments of those countries; the states concerned should take all possible measures to deprive guerrilla bands of aid or protection; (2) the Security Council should recommend border conventions along the lines of a previously existing Greek-Bulgarian convention; (3) the Security Council should establish a commission or a single commissioner to investigate frontier violations, hear complaints, use its good offices, make studies and investigations, and report to the Security Council.

The report also dealt with the question of international supervision of refugees and agreements for the voluntary transfer of minorities. The Soviet veto in the Security Council led to the abolition of the commission and the transfer of the problem to the General Assembly.

UNITED NATIONS SPECIAL COMMITTEE ON THE BALKANS

As heretofore pointed out, UNSCOB, in addition to functions of peace observation, was entrusted with substantial functions of good offices and mediation. The original resolution called on Albania, Bulgaria, Yugoslavia, and Greece to establish normal diplomatic and good-neighborly relations,

[36] *Ibid.*, pp. 23–24.
[37] S/360, I, pp. 248–51.

to establish frontier conventions, to cooperate in the settlement of refugee problems, and to study the practicability of concluding agreements for the voluntary transfer of minorities. UNSCOB was established to observe the compliance of the four governments with these recommendations and to assist them in their implementation.

In addition the General Assembly had recommended "the pacific settlement of frontier incidents and disputes," with UNSCOB observing compliance with this recommendation, which was pure peace observation.[38] For UNSCOB to carry on any functions of good offices or mediation would require the cooperation of both sides. Albania, Bulgaria, and Yugoslavia made it clear in the General Assembly that they considered UNSCOB an illegal organization because its establishment violated the principle of unanimity among the permanent members of the Security Council in connection with peace-keeping.[39] UNSCOB, as soon as it was organized, requested the cooperation of the four governments but received a reply only from Greece.

Despite the failure of Albania, Yugoslavia, and Bulgaria to cooperate, there was no complete blackout of communications comparable to that which took place on the border between North and South Korea. Yugoslavia continued diplomatic relations with Greece and addressed eleven complaints of border violations to the Government of Greece.[40] Albania made more than one hundred charges of border violations by Greece in communications to the United Nations Secretary-General, "presented solely for the information of the Secretary-General of the United Nations and of public opinion."[41] Bulgaria also addressed a number of complaints of border violations to the Secretary-General and, even though there were no diplomatic relations with Greece, engaged in direct talks with the Greek Government on the resumption of diplomatic relations.

All of the complaints received by the Secretary-General from Albania and Bulgaria were referred to UNSCOB which examined them even though they had not been sent directly to the committee.[42] In one instance (the so-called Evros incident), Bulgaria permitted UNSCOB to conduct an investigation on Bulgarian soil, but denied that this indicated any change in its policy of contesting the legality of UNSCOB. The UNSCOB decision in that case was objective and favored neither Greece nor Bulgaria.

[38] U.S. State Department, "United Nations Special Committee on the Balkans; Report to the Third Session of the General Assembly," *Documents and State Papers*, I: 6 (September 1948), p. 377. Hereafter cited as "Report to 3rd Session."

[39] Harry N. Howard, "United Nations Special Committee on the Balkans: Comment on the Report of the Special Committee to the Third Session of the General Assembly," *Documents and State Papers*, I: 6 (September 1948), p. 364. Hereafter cited as Howard, "Comment on Report to 3rd Session."

[40] "Report to 3rd Session," p. 382.

[41] Howard, "Comment on Report to 3rd Session," p. 367.

[42] "Report to 3rd Session," p. 398.

UNSCOB, in its first annual report, June 30, 1948, concluded that its good offices functions had failed.[43] The Third General Assembly in 1948 appointed a conciliation committee in an endeavor to reach a pacific settlement of existing differences between Greece and its northern neighbors. This committee made some progress toward reaching an agreement for resumption of diplomatic relations and for establishing frontier treaties. The effort was renewed by a new conciliation committee appointed during the Fourth General Assembly in 1949. However, the work of the conciliation committee was overtaken by events—the split between Yugoslavia and the Cominform. Due to the existence of these conciliation committees, UNSCOB's role in good offices or conciliation was minimal after 1948.

The main role of UNSCOB, of course, was observation of the frontier. When it became apparent at the outset that the committee would not be permitted to function in Bulgaria, Albania, or Yugoslavia, it organized itself to conduct the observations solely from the Greek side of the frontier. The first annual report of UNSCOB explained its method of performing this function. It divided its observation functions into two classes: (1) support by Greece's northern neighbors of the Greek guerrilla movement, and (2) the situation on the northern frontier.

UNSCOB cited four types of support of the Greek guerrilla movement and indicated its method of dealing with the situation. (1) In regard to the proclamation of a provisional Greek Government by the Greek guerrilla leader Markos, UNSCOB pointed out the dangers that would arise if Greece's northern neighbors formally recognized the Markos government. No formal recognition took place, probably partly because of UNSCOB's strong position.[44] (2) The Balkan Action Committees had been established in Greece's northern neighbors to raise funds and supplies to assist the Greek guerrillas. UNSCOB established this fact largely through monitoring broadcasts which proved, for example, that levies were being made for a portion of wages to finance the guerrilla activities. These broadcasts were reinforced by testimony from students escaping from the Communist countries and by reports from the observation teams of continuous flows of supplies to the guerrillas. (3) Through monitoring techniques, UNSCOB established that the "Free Greece" radio station of Markos was located in Yugoslavia. The monitoring disclosed constant inciting of the Greek people to revolt against their government. For example, a proclamation of the Greek Communist Party issued on January 23, 1951, stated: "If in 1946-49 the Democratic Army of Greece had won, our troubles would now be over and we should today have been under the warm aegis of the Soviet Union, exactly the same as the other people's democracies."[45] (4) UNSCOB established the removal and retention of Greek children in Yugoslavia,

---

[43] "Report to 3rd Session," p. 377.

[44] "Report to 3rd Session," p. 392.

[45] Howard, "The Greek Question in the Fifth Session," p. 398.

Bulgaria, and Albania by interviewing parents; by monitoring statements of the "Free Greece" radio and Belgrade radio appeals for contributions to the Yugoslavian Red Cross to take care of the children; and by circulating a questionnaire in Greece to establish a census.

The previous category of incidents related to activities at some distance from the northern frontiers. On the frontier itself, Greece had charged that the guerrillas were receiving military training in Yugoslavia, Albania, and Bulgaria, and that wounded guerrillas were being hospitalized north of the Greek border. The Albanian complaints against Greece included some seventy flights of Greek planes over Albanian territory and firing of shots from Greece to Albania.

The observation groups set up by UNSCOB obtained information by touring as much of their areas as feasible; by visiting the frontier whenever possible; and by interrogating witnesses. They were hampered in their work by the presence of mines and general disorder. They made fifty-eight reports, but there could be no continuous observation of the frontier.[46]

On the Albanian frontier, the observation groups reported no signs of good neighborly relations. Through interrogation of witnesses, the groups obtained considerable information concerning guerrilla support from Albania. One witness testified that the guerrillas had been instructed to avoid crossing the border when United Nations teams were in the neighborhood. The observation teams also saw firing from across the border. Furthermore, the fact that there were few wounded prisoners as a result of Greek activities indicated to the observers that the wounded were being hospitalized on the other side of the border. After studying the terrain, the military observers pointed out that the logistic support of the guerrillas was impossible except from Albania.

On the Yugoslav frontier, the testimony of witnesses concerning large crossings of the border was corroborated by observing guerrillas crossing and recrossing and by evidence of the crossings, such as "mule track traces." As on the Albanian border, the observers witnessed firing from across the Yugoslav border. Interrogations at refugee camps operated at two points in Yugoslavia could be compared with the findings of the Committee of Investigation when it visited these camps in the previous year. As on the Albanian frontier, there was no evidence of good neighborly relations.

In contrast, on the Bulgarian frontier, where the terrain was far less rugged, there were some frontier relations. Meetings took place between Greek and Bulgarian officials, and, as pointed out in connection with one incident at Evros, UNSCOB was invited to investigate on the Bulgarian side of the frontier. The observers saw border crossings and watched actions against the guerrillas. In one instance, the observers saw Greek soldiers

[46] "Report to 3rd Session," p 398.

cross the Bulgarian frontier to prevent the movement of a large amount of supplies from Greece to sanctuary in Bulgaria. [47]

The first report shows clearly that considerable peace observation can be effected even though access is granted only on one side of a boundary line. The information which UNSCOB obtained permitted conclusions that "good neighborly relations between Greece and her northern neighbors do not exist"; that "the Greek guerrillas have received aid and assistance from Albania, Bulgaria, and Yugoslavia; that they have been furnished with war material and other supplies from those countries; that they have been allowed to use the territories of Albania, Bulgaria, and Yugoslavia for tactical operations." [48]

The second report of UNSCOB is largely a repetition of the first except for the fact that after the Greek Army victory near Konitza over the guerrillas infiltrating from Albania, the bulk of the guerrilla forces withdrew into the adjacent countries. By 1950, the Yugoslav Government, following its conflict with the Cominform, had closed the border and ceased to give assistance to the guerrillas. The third UNSCOB report in 1950 stated that the Greek-Yugoslav border region had remained quiet. This split the remaining area of guerrilla activities into two widely separated sections since the Yugoslav section of the border lay between the Albanian section and the Bulgarian section. The General Assembly in 1950 renewed UNSCOB at the request of Greece. However, UNSCOB was authorized to recommend its own dissolution prior to the fall of 1951 if conditions permitted. Its report for the period ending August 15, 1951, recommended its own abolition and replacement by the POC and stated: "During the past twelve months, the guerrillas have not ventured to undertake any specifically military operations against the Greek Army." [49]

The pattern of external aid to the guerrillas was different, and guerrillas re-entering Greece were instructed to avoid open clashes with the Greek Government. [50] Therefore, this report was mainly concerned with such matters as refugees, frontier markings, and broad support of the Communist efforts from countries such as Rumania and Czechoslovakia which did not border Greece.

THE POC AND THE BALKAN SUBCOMMISSION

The General Assembly by resolution of December 7, 1951, discontinued UNSCOB after sixty days. Another resolution requested the POC to establish a Balkan Subcommission. The Balkan Subcommission was

[47] "Report to 3rd Session," pp. 404, 405.
[48] "Report to 3rd Session," p. 406.
[49] UN General Assembly, *Official Records*, Sixth Session, Supplement No. 11, A/1857, p. 11. Hereafter cited as A/1857.
[50] A/1857, p. 20.

authorized to dispatch observers to any area in the Balkans. Its jurisdiction, however, was limited to peace observation. The Greek Government requested and the Balkan Subcommission obtained six observers, who went to Greece.

During the discussions in the *Ad Hoc* Political Committee of the General Assembly in November, Mr. Lopez, the Philippine delegate, asked whether the members of the subcommission were individuals or states and requested a definition of the relation of the subcommission to the POC.[51] The questions were never answered during the General Assembly.

As pointed out, the observers were requested to report to the Balkan Subcommission and to the Secretary-General for the information of members. The Secretary-General's report to the Eighth Session of the General Assembly noted that the observers sent four special reports on incidents, all in July and August 1952, to the Balkan Subcommission, which had "taken note of the various reports from the observers," and had "not found it necessary to report to the Peace Observation Commission."[52] The Greek question was never on the agenda of the General Assembly after 1951, and the only way in which these reports reached the membership of the United Nations was through the report of the Secretary-General.

The report of the Secretary-General for the year July 1, 1953–June 30, 1954, indicated only one serious border incident for that period.[53] It also pointed out that a Greek-Bulgarian boundary commission had been set up to deal with disputes on that border. At the suggestion of Greece, on December 21, 1953, the number of observers on the Greek-Bulgarian boundary was reduced to three, and on May 28, 1954, the subcommission approved the discontinuance of the observer group. This reduced the subcommission to a purely paper organization which probably still exists, since there is no indication of its abolition.[54]

EVALUATION

In 1946, Greece was in a political turmoil. Its economy was impoverished and its political integrity was threatened by guerrilla activities that were receiving assistance from its northern neighbors. By 1951, Greece was beginning to prosper. The political situation had been stabilized, and the threats from guerrilla activities had almost disappeared. A variety of factors undoubtedly contributed to this improvement: (1) the strengthening of the

[51] UN General Assembly, *Ad Hoc* Political Committee, *Official Records*, Sixth Session, p. 14.

[52] UN General Assembly, *Official Records*, Eighth Session, Supplement No. 1, A/2404, p. 49.

[53] UN General Assembly, *Official Records*, Ninth Session, Supplement No. 1, A/2663, p. 29.

[54] For the general problem of the use of the POC see pp. 226–27.

economic situation under the Truman plan; (2) the strengthening of the Greek military forces with assistance from the United States so that Greece was able to achieve military victory in 1948 over the guerrilla forces along the Albanian border near Konitza; (3) the impasse between the Soviet Union and Yugoslavia, which resulted in Yugoslavia's closing the border and denying further assistance to the guerrilla forces; (4) possibly a broad change in Soviet policies after 1948 as the Soviet Union seemed to be less concerned with an immediate take-over of Western Europe and more alarmed at deviations from the pristine purity of Communist doctrine in Communist groups outside the Soviet Union.

Although all these factors contributed to the successful outcome, the UN peace-observation operations were an important factor. The best proof of this is that Greece insisted on the continuation of UNSCOB for one year after the Western powers had expressed doubt whether UNSCOB was any longer necessary. Furthermore, when UNSCOB was dissolved, Greece supported the assignment of its responsibilities to a subcommission of the POC and immediately requested and obtained POC observers.

Evolution of Peace Observation in Greece

The original Security Council Commission of Investigation in which the Soviet Union and Poland participated was primarily interested in examining witnesses and hearing testimony. Indeed, it first began sitting in Athens and only later moved to Salonika where it would be closer to the area of the disorders. Even in its travels to Yugoslavia, Bulgaria, and Albania and to all parts of Greece, its main activity was to hear witnesses. Only in the last month, March 1947, before the commission moved to Geneva to write its report, did it begin investigating certain border incidents. The subsidiary group which remained in Greece placed greater emphasis on investigations.

When the Soviet Union in the Security Council vetoed efforts to continue the work of the Commission of Investigation, the General Assembly created UNSCOB which faced a different situation from that which had confronted the Security Council Commission of Investigation. The General Assembly had anticipated a situation where the Soviet Union and the Communist neighbors of Greece would refuse to cooperate and therefore provided for peace observation from one side of the border.

Mediation

UNSCOB, unlike the Commission of Investigation, had authority from the General Assembly to use its good offices and mediate between the parties. The mediation failed because Albania, Bulgaria, and Yugoslavia refused to cooperate. However, informal Greek-Bulgarian discussions of the substantive problems dividing them continued even during the most tense periods, notwithstanding the fact that no formal diplomatic relations existed between the two countries. Diplomatic relations continued between Greece and Yugoslavia with formal exchanges that resulted in Yugoslavia's closing the border to the guerrillas after the impasse between Yugoslavia and the Soviet Union. Only Albania declined to negotiate with Greece.

The Third and Fourth General Assembly set up conciliation groups headed by the President of the Assembly in an attempt to narrow some of the substantive differences. The efforts almost succeeded with Bulgaria and Yugoslavia, and both reached a certain degree of agreement with Greece. No progress, however, was made in solving the differences between Albania and Greece, and Yugoslavia and Bulgaria insisted that no agreement could take effect unless it included Albania. The Soviet-Yugoslav impasse resulted in improved relations between Greece and Yugoslavia and eliminated the urgency of solving the differences between Greece on the one hand and Albania and Bulgaria on the other.

UNSCOB encouraged bilateral discussions between Greece and its northern neighbors and refrained from pressing conciliation or mediation in view of the greater opportunities for successful conciliation either through direct negotiations or use of the conciliation group in the General Assembly.

General Conciliatory Approach of UNSCOB

The moderate attitude shown by UNSCOB in the exercise of its functions of conciliation extended to peace observation. UNSCOB, even though rebuffed by the northern neighbors of Greece, continued its efforts to communicate with them. The committee received indirectly from the Secretary-General the complaints against Greece made by Albania and Bulgaria directly to the Secretary-General. UNSCOB attempted to investigate these complaints even though Albania and Bulgaria denied the validity of the committee.[55] UNSCOB criticized the Greek Government and military authorities where such criticism seemed warranted, though, of course, the UNSCOB attitude toward Greece was most friendly and its reports laudatory.

Techniques of Peace Observation

Confronted with the problem of peace observation from one side of the border, UNSCOB developed techniques of peace observation which went far beyond the concept of the Commission of Investigation of confining itself to interrogation of witnesses. In addition to interrogations, it monitored the radio broadcasts both of the "Free Greece" station and of Yugoslav, Bulgarian, and Albanian stations. It established through

---

[55] Yugoslav complaints were made directly to Greece and never reached UNSCOB.

monitoring techniques the fact that the "Free Greece" station was operating from Yugoslavia. It visited the frontier as frequently as possible and observed whether good neighborly relations existed. It examined captured weapons and also conditions on the border to determine the extent and nature of logistic support. It witnessed firing from across the border and occasionally movement of individuals in both directions across the border. On account of the nature of the terrain and the danger of land mines, UNSCOB could not maintain continuous surveillance of the border. However, it developed techniques that made it possible to reach conclusions. The UNSCOB experience contributed much toward understanding the potentials and the limitations of small observation groups stationed near a frontier.

Logistic Support

In 1947, the United Nations Secretary-General had had little experience in organizing and supporting peace-observation missions. The problem was less acute in connection with the Commission of Investigation, which was stationed in large cities and took only occasional trips as a large group to the border areas. Transportation was furnished by the countries the commission visited.

When UNSCOB established permanent observer missions, the logistics problem immediately emerged. The United Nations secretariat in Greece was relatively small and most of the expenses of the delegates and their supporting personnel were borne by the respective states rather than by the United Nations. The United Nations had to rely on contributions from states (which, as a practical matter, meant the United States) for means of transportation, for radio communications systems, and for other major items of support.

Even at the start, the UN Secretary-General realized the advantage of using the United Nations flag and other United Nations identification symbols. Gradually, the United Nations assumed a greater proportion of the logistics burden, which included furnishing some supplies and reimbursing the delegations for travel expenses. However, during the UNSCOB operation the major items of supply came from the United States and the largest expense of the mission, salaries of personnel, was borne by the delegations. While the arrangements worked out satisfactorily, they could scarcely set a precedent, since in many areas the United States would not be in a position to furnish with ease the type of support that was required in Greece.

Structure of Peace-Observation Groups

The Commission of Investigation, UNSCOB, and the POC were all groups in which the members were states. Thus, the delegates were under instructions from their governments, and the official actions of the group, in theory at least, represented the attitudes of the governments. This was of some importance during the deliberations of the Commission of Investigation where the most important decision was the content of the report. Extensive debates and compromises were required to produce a report on which only the Soviet Union and Poland disagreed.

In UNSCOB, the use of a commission of instructed delegates caused less trouble. In the first place, the Soviet Union and Poland declined to occupy their seats. While the preparation of reports still required government instructions to the delegates, this phase of UNSCOB was far less significant. The most important activities of UNSCOB were the operations of the observer teams. The members of these teams acted as individuals and seldom called for instructions from their governments. Their reports went to UNSCOB and were generally included as attachments to the UNSCOB report without any detailed analysis or comment.

The shift from a pattern of a group of instructed delegates to a group of individuals became even more apparent when UNSCOB turned its functions over to the POC. The POC formed a subcommission of five states which at the request of the Greek Government dispatched six observers to Greece. The observers reported both to the Secretary-General and to the POC. In fact, the reports of the observers were circulated directly by the General Assembly to the UN members, in effect insulating the observers from both the POC and its subcommission.

Quality of Delegates

An important factor in the success of peace observation in the Greek case was the high quality of delegations. The initial United States group, for example, included outstanding individuals such as Mark Ethridge, Harding Bancroft, Cyril Black, and Harry Howard. The initial delegations developed a tradition of dedication and moderation that continued through the period of peace observation.

Terms of Reference

Finally, an advantageous factor was the clear and well-thought-out terms of reference of UNSCOB. The United Nations General Assembly foresaw two possible methods of operation: (1) observation on both sides of the line and mediation if the northern neighbors of Greece cooperated; (2) observation on one side of the line if the cooperation of the northern neighbors of Greece did not materialize. Thus, in sharp contrast to the situation in Korea, the functions of UNSCOB were always clearly defined, and its authority was adequate to permit an outstanding achievement.

2

·•·——

THE PROBLEM OF PALESTINE

After World War I, Palestine was placed under a League of Nations mandate with Great Britain as the mandatory power. Over the years, Great Britain tried unsuccessfully to get the Arabs and Jews in Palestine to agree on their future, but conflicting views between them made a settlement impossible. One of the purposes of the mandate was "the establishment of a Jewish national home, with the necessary safeguards for the civil and religious rights of all the country's inhabitants irrespective of origin or religion."[1] The main purpose of this, as well as other mandates, was to prepare the area for eventual self-government.

The British Government brought the problem of Palestine before the United Nations on April 2, 1947, and it has been continuously before the Organization since that date. During this time, some ten United Nations committees, groups, or authorized individuals have been given or assumed responsibilities having some relation to peace observation and fact-finding. The functions performed by most of these groups turned out to be different from and generally more extensive than those visualized at the time of their formation. Peace observation and fact-finding have been divided among a number of groups with varying terms of reference. Furthermore, there has generally been no time limit on performance. Only rarely is the more usual pattern of international observation present—a committee with a specific and limited function to be performed within a limited period of time.

In April 1949, Great Britain requested the Secretary-General to place the problem on the agenda of the next regular session of the General Assembly and to appoint a special committee to consider it.[2]

On November 29, 1947, the United Nations General Assembly, acting on the report of the Special Committee, recommended the partition of Palestine into an Arab state and a Jewish state, with an international trusteeship for Jerusalem and economic union of all Palestine. A commission was established to implement the General Assembly recommendations.[3]

---

[1] Trygve Lie, *In the Cause of Peace* (New York: Macmillan, 1954), p. 159.
[2] *United States Participation in the United Nations, Report by the President to the Congress for the Year 1947* (Washington: Government Printing Office, 1948), p. 43.
[3] UN General Assembly, Res. 181(II)A, Nov. 29, 1947. Hereafter cited as Res. 181(II)A.

The Arab states refused to accept the recommendations of the General Assembly and indicated their intention to use force to prevent their implementation. The United Nations Security Council then passed a resolution calling for a truce between the Jewish and Arab communities, and established a Truce Commission in Palestine composed of Belgium, France, and the United States; Syria refused to serve. [4] In addition, the General Assembly appointed a United Nations Mediator, with functions overlapping those of the Truce Commission, to promote a peaceful adjustment of the situation. [5]

The British mandate for Palestine expired on May 15, 1948, and the Provisional Government of Israel immediately proclaimed independence. Hostilities broke out with armed forces from the neighboring Arab states invading Palestine. The United Nations Security Council obtained a four-week cease-fire and enlarged the authority of the UN Mediator to supervise its observance. [6]

Hostilities were resumed when the cease-fire expired. Thereupon, on July 15, 1948, the Security Council found a threat to the peace under Article 39 of the United Nations Charter and ordered the parties involved to desist from further military action. [7] Nevertheless sporadic military action continued. The UN Mediator, Count Bernadotte, who was murdered on the day before his proposals were submitted to the UN, suggested certain adjustments of the partition plan. Security Council action culminated in a resolution of November 16, calling on the parties directly involved in the conflict to seek agreement, with a view to an immediate armistice, including the delineation of permanent armistice demarcation lines. [8]

On December 11, 1948, at the end of its regular session, the General Assembly established a Conciliation Commission (consisting of France, Turkey, and the United States) to assume the functions of mediation formerly assigned to the Mediator, and in addition, at the request of the Security Council, any functions assigned by the Council to the Mediator or Truce Commission. [9]

[4] UN Security Council, Resolution adopted at the 287th meeting, April 23, 1948, S/727. Hereafter cited as S/727.

[5] UN General Assembly, Res. 186, May 14, 1948. Hereafter cited as Res. 186.

[6] UN Security Council, Resolution adopted at the 310th meeting, May 29, 1948, S/801. Hereafter cited as S/801.

[7] UN Security Council, Resolution adopted at the 338th meeting, July 15, 1948, S/902. Hereafter cited as S/902.

[8] UN Security Council, Resolution adopted at the 381st meeting, Nov. 16, 1948, S/1080. Hereafter cited as S/1080.

[9] UN General Assembly, Res. 194 (III), Dec. 11, 1948. Hereafter cited as Res. 194 (III). During the first six months of 1948, a large portion of the Arab population of the areas of Palestine under Jewish occupation had fled to the neighboring Arab states where they led a miserable existence as refugees. The General Assembly by resolution provided funds to alleviate their condition and requested the Secretary-General to appoint a UN Director of Relief for Palestine Refugees. Res. 212 (III), Nov. 19, 1948. The General Assembly has continued ever since to provide relief for the refugees. This activity is only remotely related to peace observation.

Pursuant to the Security Council resolution of November 16, 1948, referred to above, negotiations for an armistice were commenced early in 1949 between Israel and the four Arab states bordering on Israel—Egypt, Jordan, Lebanon, and Syria. These negotiations conducted under the chairmanship of the UN Acting Mediator resulted in four separate armistice agreements:[10] with Egypt, February 24, 1949; Lebanon, March 23, 1949; Jordan, April 3, 1949; and Syria, July 20, 1949. Each agreement provided for a Mixed Armistice Commission to supervise the truce, to delimit the armistice lines, and to provide for withdrawal and reduction of forces. In each commission an equal number of members is chosen by each side and a chairman is designated by the Chief-of-Staff of the United Nations Truce Supervision Organization.

The armistice having been attained, the Security Council, on August 11, 1949, terminated the functions of the Mediator.[11] The UN Secretary-General was also requested to arrange for the continued service of such personnel of the Truce Supervision Organization as might be required to observe and maintain the cease-fire and to perform the functions assigned to the personnel by the four armistice agreements. The Chief-of-Staff of the Truce Supervision Organization was to inform the Security Council on the observance of the cease-fire and the armistice and keep the Conciliation Commission informed of matters affecting its work.

On October 29, 1956, the Israeli armed forces invaded Egypt. When a United States resolution in the Security Council to terminate the hostilities was vetoed by France and Great Britain, the Security Council called for a special session of the General Assembly and transferred the problem to the Assembly.

Resolutions of the General Assembly on November 4 and 7 established the United Nations Emergency Force (UNEF).[12] The first contingents entered Egypt on November 14 with the consent of the Egyptian Government.[13] UNEF was never permitted to enter Israeli territory. It occupied the Suez Canal areas when the British and French troops were withdrawn and replaced the Israeli troops as they withdrew toward their border. UNEF, in turn, moved eastward toward the Israeli border as the Egyptian

---

[10] UN Security Council, *Official Records*, Fourth Year, Special Supplement No. 3, S/1264/Rev. 1; Special Supplement No. 4, S/1296/Rev. 1; Special Supplement No. 1, S/1302/Rev. 1; Special Supplement No. 2, S/1353/Rev. 1. Hereafter cited as S/1353/Rev. 1.

[11] UN Security Council, Resolution adopted at the 437th meeting, Aug. 11, 1949, S/1376. Hereafter cited as S/1376.

[12] UN General Assembly, Res. 998 (ES–I), Nov. 4, 1956. Hereafter cited as Res. 998 (ES–I). UN General Assembly, Res. 1001 (ES–I), Nov. 7, 1956. Hereafter cited as Res. 1001 (ES–I).

[13] *United States Participation in the United Nations, Report by the President to the Congress for the Year 1956* (Washington: Government Printing Office, 1957), p. 55. Hereafter cited as *1956 President's Report*.

authorities assumed governmental responsibilities. By the end of March 1957, UNEF was deployed along the Egyptian side of the armistice line, where it still remains, to prevent border incursions and to remove the tension that heretofore prevailed along this line.

In view of the complex machinery dealing with the Palestine problem, the analysis that follows of UN operations in Palestine is divided into three periods.

The first period from April 2, 1947, to the completion of the armistice agreements on July 20, 1949, was a period of improvisation. The United Nations erected specific machinery to meet specific emergencies: the Palestine Commission, the Truce Commission, the UN Mediator, the Palestine Conciliation Commission, the United Nations Director of Relief for Palestine Refugees. None of these groups had peace observation as its primary function, but all were required to carry on some peace-observation and fact-finding functions.

During the second period, from July 20, 1949, until the establishment of the United Nations Emergency Force on November 7, 1956, the peace-observation functions in the main passed to the four Mixed Armistice Commissions (MAC's); the UN Truce Supervision Organization furnishing services and personnel to the Mixed Armistice Commissions; the Chief-of-Staff of the UN Truce Supervision Organization, who in addition to acting as the Chief of UNTSO was given liaison functions with the United Nations; and the Palestine Conciliation Commission (PCC). However, UNTSO has in fact practically no relationship with the PCC, and the PCC, concerned primarily with mediation and a long-term peace settlement, has played only a minor role in peace observation. The sole relation of the Director of Relief for Refugees to peace observation is in the logistical field.

The organization of peace observation during the third period, from November 7, 1956, to the present, after the Israeli invasion of Egypt, is the same as during the second period with the one exception that along the Egyptian demarcation line UNEF prevented the types of incidents which were dealt with primarily by the MAC's along the other demarcation lines.

The Problem from April 2, 1947, to July 1949

THE SPECIAL COMMITTEE ON PALESTINE

As stated above, on April 2, 1947, the United Kingdom requested a special session of the General Assembly to constitute and instruct a Special Committee to prepare for the consideration of the problem of Palestine at the next regular session of the General Assembly.[14]

---

[14] UN General Assembly, A/364/Add. 1, Sept. 9, 1947, p. 1.

Terms of Reference

The General Assembly on May 15, 1947, established a Special Committee on Palestine (UNSCOP), consisting of representatives of Canada, Czechoslovakia, Iran, the Netherlands, Peru, Sweden, Uruguay, Guatemala, and Yugoslavia. The committee was given wide powers to ascertain facts, and to investigate issues relevant to the problem of Palestine, and to submit appropriate proposals for solution of the problem.[15] The committee was instructed to "give most careful consideration to the religious interests in Palestine of Islam, Judaism, and Christianity." The General Assembly at the same time called on all governments and peoples, and particularly the inhabitants of Palestine, to refrain from the threat or use of force or any other action that might be prejudicial to an early settlement.

Organization

To service the committee, the Secretary-General designated a secretariat of fifty-seven members headed by an Assistant Secretary-General of the United Nations.[16]

Performance

UNSCOP had no substantial functions directly related to peace observation. Furthermore, since Great Britain as the mandatory authority was primarily responsible for maintaining order, the maintenance of peace had not yet become an acute problem. The committee's performance is of interest merely in foreshadowing the political problems and limitations of later groups.

The committee met for the first time on May 26, 1947, and submitted its final report on August 31, 1947. It spent only six weeks in Palestine, traveling throughout the country and interviewing representatives of the Jewish agency. It also met in Beirut and Geneva and visited displaced persons' camps in Germany and Austria. The Arab Higher Committee representing the Arabs of Palestine declined to collaborate with the committee. Representatives of the Arab states presented their views in Beirut, Lebanon, but did not appear before the committee in Palestine.[17] On September 1, 1947, the committee presented to the General Assembly a report containing majority and minority plans for solving the Palestine problem. The Arab states objected to both plans. The Jewish Agency with ostensible reluctance accepted the majority plan for partitioning Palestine into Jewish and Arab states. Over the objection of all the Arab states, the General Assembly, by a

[15] UN General Assembly, A/364, Sept. 3, 1947, pp. 4–5. Hereafter cited as A/364.
[16] A/364, p. 6.
[17] A/364, pp. 8, 10.

two-thirds majority, adopted a plan based on the majority report.[18] The Soviet Union and the United States both supported the General Assembly resolution of November 29, 1947.

Evaluation

From the standpoint of peace observation and the fact-finding incidental to peace observation, the operations of the Special Committee on Palestine might be characterized as an educational prelude. The Arabs of Palestine refused to cooperate, and the Arab states restricted their cooperation to the presentation of their views at committee meetings outside Palestine. The problems of maintaining security and preventing violence had not arisen since Great Britain as the mandatory power was responsible for security.

THE UNITED NATIONS COMMISSION FOR PALESTINE

The General Assembly resolution of November 29, 1947, proposed the partition of Palestine with economic union and set up the United Nations Commission for Palestine consisting of one representative from each of the five member states: Bolivia, Czechoslovakia, Denmark, Panama, and the Philippines.[19]

Terms of Reference

The administration of Palestine was to be turned over progressively to the United Nations Commission for Palestine as the mandatory power. The United Kingdom withdrew its armed forces. The commission was to establish the frontiers of the Jewish and Arab states in Palestine and the city of Jerusalem, in accordance with the General Assembly recommendations. After consulting democratic parties and public organizations of the Arab and Jewish states, the commission was to establish in each state a provisional council of government under the general direction of the commission. The commission was to report to the Security Council if by April 1, 1948, the provisional councils could not be established or could not perform their functions.[20] The resolution suggested the establishment of armed militias to maintain order and described the transfer of governmental functions from the provisional councils to provisional governments. The commission was to assist in establishing an economic union between the two states as soon as possible. The measures taken by the commission

[18] For text of this report, see Res. 181 (II)A.

[19] Res. 181 (II)A.

[20] Since the mandate was to terminate on May 15, 1948, the governments would have to be functioning by that date.

within the recommendations of the Assembly were to become immediately effective unless the commission previously received contrary instructions from the Security Council.[21]

Organization

In the first week of December 1947, the Secretary-General of the United Nations set up a commission secretariat in New York, choosing Ralph Bunche as the principal secretary. The commission assembled for its first meeting at Lake Success on January 9, 1948, to elect its officers and adopt provisional rules of procedure. It held sixty-five meetings, all in the United States, between January 9 and April 10. All the meetings except the first were private.[22]

Performance

The commission invited representatives of the Arab Higher Committee, the Jewish Agency, and Great Britain to sit with it. On January 18, 1948, the Arab Committee refused to recognize the validity of the United Nations action and therefore declined the invitation.[23] Violence broke out in Palestine, and the commission, in its first special report to the Security Council on February 16, 1948, stated that 869 persons had been killed and 1,909 wounded between November 30 and February 1.[24]

Despite the provision of the General Assembly resolution for "progressive" turning over of authority from the mandatory to the commission, Great Britain did not "regard favourably any proposal by the commission to proceed to Palestine earlier than two weeks before the date of the termination of the Mandate."[25] The British likewise refused to permit the formation of militias or frontier demarcation.[26]

The commission was convinced that no other step could be taken under the General Assembly resolution to improve the security situation in Palestine. Accordingly, it referred to the Security Council "the problem of providing that armed assistance which alone would enable the commission to discharge its responsibilities on the termination of the Mandate."[27]

The Security Council never provided such armed assistance. In the latter part of March, the United States representative proposed to the Security Council that the Palestine Commission suspend its efforts. A temporary

[21] Res. 181 (II)A.
[22] UN General Assembly, A/532, April 10, 1948, p. 4. Hereafter cited as A/532.
[23] A/532, p. 6.
[24] UN Security Council, S/676 and attached document A/AC.21/9, Feb. 16, 1948, p. 5. Hereafter cited as S/676.
[25] A/532, p. 8.
[26] S/676, pp. 10, 15.
[27] A/532, p. 1.

UN trusteeship for Palestine under the UN Trusteeship Council was proposed on termination of the mandate. The trusteeship was viewed as a means of maintaining order and permitting an eventual political settlement. The United States representative took the legal position of doubtful validity that the United Nations lacked the power to enforce a political settlement.

A special session of the General Assembly convened on April 16, 1948, but failed to approve a trusteeship or any alternative arrangement.

As a result of the Security Council resolution of April 23[28] and a "last-minute" General Assembly resolution on May 14,[29] the day before the expiration of the mandate, some of the responsibilities of the UN Commission for Palestine—including peace observation and fact-finding—passed to other units. Thus, the UN Commission for Palestine was relieved of further responsibility.

Evaluation

The United Nations Commission for Palestine had substantial responsibilities for on-the-spot peace observation and fact-finding incidental to its main function of providing a transition from the British mandate to the political and economic status proposed in the General Assembly resolution of November 29, 1947. Except for a small advance party, which proceeded to Jerusalem early in March and stayed there until May 1 as guests of the British, the commission never got to Palestine. The extent of on-the-spot observation was negligible.[30]

The chief reasons for the failure of the commission to carry out its functions were: (1) the opposition of the Arabs; (2) the unwillingness of the United Kingdom as mandatory power to permit the commission to operate in the manner contemplated by the Assembly resolution; (3) the failure of the Security Council to provide the military force to carry out the General Assembly program. In this instance, the Soviet Union supported and the United States and the United Kingdom opposed Council action to provide such military force.

THE TRUCE COMMISSION IN PALESTINE AND THE UNITED NATIONS MEDIATOR FOR PALESTINE

By April 1948, it was apparent that the United Nations Commission for Palestine would not succeed in taking over the executive authority from the mandatory power and transferring it peaceably to Jewish and Arab states

[28] S/727.
[29] Res. 186.
[30] A/532, p. 12.

and a regime for Jerusalem. During the early months of 1948, the Jewish Agency perfected plans for assuming authority and establishing a provisional government over the portion of Palestine assigned to the Jewish state. Considerable liaison took place between the Jewish Agency and the Truce Commission. The planning of the Arab Higher Committee was primarily military. It set up local national committees in all the Arab towns in Palestine and in some of its villages; these were primarily for fund-raising and military recruitment.[31] Only in the last hours before the termination of the mandate did the Higher Committee request Arab civil servants of the Palestine government to carry on their duties and report to the local national committee. Meantime internal disorders continued, and the flight of numerous Arab inhabitants from their homes added to the confusion.

Terms of Reference

The United Nations, confronted with the imminent breakdown of all government and law and order, established two emergency units to deal with immediate problems. (1) The Security Council on April 17 called on all organizations in Palestine—particularly the Arab Higher Committee and the Jewish Agency—to cease all military activities and acts of violence, to refrain from bringing military personnel or war material into the country and from carrying on political activity that might prejudice the rights, claims, or position of either community.[32] The Council established a Truce Commission composed of the representatives of three of the four states having career consuls in Jerusalem (Belgium, France, and the United States). Syria, the fourth state, refused to serve.[33] The Truce Commission immediately sought to arrange for a cease-fire in Jerusalem and to investigate rumors of Arab invasion. (2) Meanwhile, the General Assembly established the office of United Nations Mediator in Palestine. The Mediator (Count Bernadotte) was empowered to work with local authorities to arrange for the operation of essential services, to assure the protection of the Holy Places, and to provide a peaceful adjustment of the future situation of Palestine.[34] The same resolution terminated the Palestine Commission.

On May 22, 1948, the Security Council issued a cease-fire order,[35] which it reaffirmed on May 29, calling for a cessation of all acts of armed force for a period of four weeks during which no additional military personnel

[31] Jacob C. Hurewitz, *The Struggle for Palestine* (New York: W. W. Norton & Co., 1950), pp. 313, 309.

[32] S/723.

[33] S/727.

[34] Res. 186.

[35] UN Security Council, Resolution adopted at the 302nd meeting, May 22, 1948, S/773.

should be trained, mobilized, or introduced into the district. Responsibility of supervising these provisions was given to both the Truce Commission and the United Nations Mediator who were to be aided by military observers.[36]

When military operations resumed after thirty days, the Security Council determined that the Palestine situation constituted a threat to the peace within the meaning of Article 39 of the UN Charter. Subsequently, pursuant to Article 40, the parties were ordered to desist from further military action.[37] On August 19, the Security Council reaffirmed the truce.[38]

In the meantime, Count Bernadotte recommended certain changes in the Palestine partition plan in a report dated September 16.[39] Two days later he was assassinated.

On October 19, the Security Council passed a resolution to strengthen the truce supervision by guaranteeing free access to the observers.[40] When Israel undertook a general offensive in the Negeb in October, the Security Council issued a fourth cease-fire order on November 4 and called on the Acting Mediator to establish provisional lines beyond which no movement of troops was to take place. The parties should seek to agree on permanent truce lines, and if they failed to agree, permanent lines and neutral zones should be established by the Acting Mediator.[41] This order led to the armistice negotiations commencing early in 1949.

On December 11, 1948, the General Assembly, in accordance with one of Count Bernadotte's recommendations, established the Palestine Conciliation Commission (PCC), consisting of France, Turkey, and the United States, to take over the original functions of the Mediator as stated in the General Assembly resolution of May 14. On the request of the Security Council, the PCC could also undertake any of the functions conferred by the Council on the Mediator.[42]

Thus, during the period from late April until December 1948, both the Mediator and the Truce Commission had concurrent responsibility from the Security Council in implementing the cease-fire. The General Assembly gave the Mediator additional responsibilities not related to peace observation, and the Security Council gave him the responsibility for demarking truce lines.

[36] S/801.
[37] S/902.
[38] UN Security Council, Resolution adopted at the 354th meeting, Aug. 19, 1948, S/981.
[39] UN Security Council, S/1025, Oct. 5, 1948. Hereafter cited as S/1025.
[40] UN Security Council, Resolution adopted at the 367th meeting, Oct. 19, 1948, S/1045. Hereafter cited as S/1045.
[41] S/1080.
[42] Res. 194 (III).

Organization

The career consuls in Jerusalem were appointed to the commission because they were on the spot and were acquainted with the situation. Not until May 11 was a staff assembled, which consisted of four persons furnished by the United Nations Secretariat, including a principal secretary and a military adviser. These individuals were transferred to the staff of the Mediator after his appointment thus denuding the Truce Commission staff and creating a lack of personnel once again.[43] In practice, however, the responsibilities of the Truce Commission for the cease-fire were confined to Jerusalem where they were assisted by staff from the Mediator.[44]

To observe the first truce (June 11–July 9), the Mediator arranged with the states making up the Truce Commission to furnish fifty-one observers. The United States also supplied some seventy technicians. Count Bernadotte's country, Sweden, supplied five colonels to aid him. The UN Secretary-General supplied fifty-one guards.[45]

To observe the second truce, commencing July 18, the members of the Truce Commission supplied 682 military personnel. France, the United Kingdom, and the United States supplied the communications equipment.[46] The Mediator issued instructions on the role of the observers, the procedures for dealing with breaches of the truce, and the administrative organization of the operation.[47]

Prior to the first truce, alternative procedures for obtaining personnel had been suggested. The Arabs suggested using International Red Cross personnel. A second proposal called for personnel supplied by the Secretary-General. The Soviet Union wanted to obtain personnel from all Security Council states members (except Syria) rather than confine the personnel to members of the Truce Commission.

The first truce resulted from an agreement between the Arabs and the Israelis. The second truce and subsequent cease-fires resulted from Security Council orders, implemented by instructions to the Mediator. The General Assembly never gave any instructions to the Mediator, and after his assassination did not even confirm the Security Council designation of Ralph Bunche as Acting Mediator.

Performance

In the field of peace observation the function of the Mediator (and in Jerusalem, the Truce Commission) was to determine whether the Jews

[43] UN Security Council, S/915, July 25, 1948.

[44] UN Security Council, S/888, July 12, 1948. Hereafter cited as S/888.

[45] S/888 and S/1025.

[46] Larry Leonard, "The United Nations and Palestine," *International Conciliation*, No. 454 (October 1949), p. 694.

[47] UN Security Council, S/928, July 28, 1948. Hereafter cited as S/928.

and Arabs were observing the truce and cease-fire terms laid down by the Security Council.

Both Arabs and Jews were ordered to: cease acts of violence; refrain from encouraging the entry into Palestine of fighting personnel; refrain from importing weapons and war materiel; refrain from activities which might gain military advantage from violation of the truce; and refrain from action endangering the safety of the Holy Places. Supervision of the truce thus required observation of the fighting lines as well as transportation and communication lines. The area included all of Palestine and all of the neighboring Arab states.

The Mediator's first instruction to the observers included the following:

> Fundamental objective of terms of truce is to ensure to fullest extent possible that no military advantage will accure to either side as a result of application of truce. Observer is entitled to demand that acts contrary to terms of truce be not committed or be rectified but has no power to enforce such demands and must rely largely upon his ability to settle disputes locally by direct approaches to local commanders and authorities and where possible by bringing the commanders and authorities together. [48]

During the first truce, Palestine was divided into five areas, each under a commanding officer with its own headquarters and observation posts.

Area	Headquarters	Observation Posts
Western	Tel Aviv	3
Jerusalem	Jerusalem	1 (mobile)
Central	Ramallah	4
Southern	Gaza	2
Northern	Afrula (later Nazareth)	1

Observers were also stationed in Damascus, Beirut, Bennt Jbail, Amman, Baghdad, Egyptian ports, and Cyprus. [49]

For the period of the second truce, observer groups were attached to each of the Arab and Israeli armies: 127 observers were in Israel, 79 in Jerusalem, 40 in the Arab areas of Palestine, and 69 in the Arab states. These did not include Secretariat personnel. [50]

The activities of the observers were directed by a Chief-of-Staff acting on behalf of the Mediator and assisted by a Central Truce Supervision Board consisting of a senior officer from each member of the Truce Commission together with the Chief-of-Staff's political adviser. After the death

[48] S/928, p. 1.
[49] S/1025.
[50] UN General Assembly, A/648, Sept. 18, 1948, Pt. 2, p. 14. Hereafter cited as A/648.

of Count Bernadotte, the Swedish Chief-of-Staff and his political adviser were replaced by officials of the UN Secretariat of American nationality.

The observers had full right of access to all military positions and the right to inspect all transportation. They were entitled to armed protection and safe conduct.[51] When disputes or violations occurred, the observers notified the local commanders and through direct negotiation tried to bring them together. Complaints of violations were investigated by observers on the spot or by special teams of investigators. Witnesses were heard and other data collected. Serious complaints were referred to the Central Truce Supervision Board or to the Mediator who in turn brought the most important incidents to the attention of the Security Council. The parties occasionally brought complaints directly to the Security Council.[52]

During the first truce, 500 complaints of truce violations were registered with the Mediator. Under the second truce, there were 300. Most of the complaints were either without substance or exaggerated.[53] During the first truce, the Mediator referred three serious complaints to the Security Council, and the Acting Mediator referred twelve to the Security Council during the second truce. The Mediator frequently called on the Security Council for interpretation of his authority, for additional authority, and to consider his suggestions for settlement of the Palestine problem.[54]

Evaluation

The Mediator and the Truce Commission operated under a number of unfavorable circumstances: antagonism between Arabs and Jews was extreme; in Arab Palestine, organized government broke down completely after May 15, 1948; the boundaries between Arab Palestine and Jewish Palestine were uncertain and constantly changing; and the situation of the Arab refugees increased tensions and invariably led to truce violations.

On the other hand, several factors were favorable to their work: (1) After July 15, when the Security Council determined the existence of a threat to the peace, the Mediator and Truce Commission were in a position to request compulsory sanctions if either side failed to cooperate. The existence of this possibility inevitably eased their tasks in maintaining order. (2) In the Security Council, both the Soviet Union and the United States were supporting the efforts of the Mediator and the Truce Commission to maintain order. (3) The Mediator and the Truce Commission during most of the period had competent staff and excellent logistic arrangements, due primarily to their ability to draw on the members of the Truce Commission (the United States, Belgium, and France) for personnel and supplies.

[51] S/1045.
[52] Leonard, *op. cit.*, p. 703.
[53] A/648, p. 9.
[54] Leonard, *op. cit.*, p. 707.

Although it might have been politically advantageous to rely on the Secretariat personnel, this was not feasible. The Russians recognized this and went no further than to suggest that personnel be furnished from all members of the Security Council except Syria. (4) The peace-observation function, the accomplishment of an armistice, had a terminal date, which would not be too far in the future. The importance of this factor is stressed in Count Bernadotte's report of September 16, 1948, which contains the following statement:

> The truce is not an end in itself. Its purpose is to prepare the way for a peaceful settlement. There is a period during which the potential for constructive action, which flows from the fact that a truce has been achieved by international intervention, is at a maximum. If, however, there appears no prospect of relieving the existing tension by some arrangement which holds concrete promise of peace, the machinery of truce supervision will in time lose its effectiveness and become an object of cynicism. If this period of maximum tendency to forego military action as a means of achieving a desired settlement is not seized, the advantage gained by international intervention may well be lost. [55]

(5) The Mediator and Truce Commission had adequate powers for effective peace observation: the unlimited right of access to Arab Palestine, Israel, and the neighboring Arab states; the right to inspect all transportation; excellent lines of communication both with the area and UN headquarters; the right to examine witnesses and collect data; and safe conduct and military protection.

From the outset, the Mediator and the Truce Commission were confronted by practically all of the problems inherent in complex peace-observation situations; demarcation of boundary lines, establishment of demilitarized zones, infiltration, establishment of contacts between opposing field commands, establishment of procedures for dealing with violations of a cease-fire, demining, transfer of prisoners, protection of minority groups. Furthermore, after July 1948, the available personnel and supplies, though far from sufficient, allowed some effort to deal with these problems. This was in contrast to the situation in Indonesia where only the most urgent tasks could be carried forward. The Mediator, for example, was able to establish fixed observation posts at crucial points and have contingents located in all of the Arab capitals. Thus the Palestine operations in this period furnished the maximum information concerning the problems and requirements of peace observation.

It is difficult to estimate whether the assignment to the Mediator of functions beyond peace observation aided or hindered peace observation. The Mediator's function of seeking an armistice with demarcated armistice lines seems so closely related to peace observation that it would be difficult to separate the functions. On the other hand, the longer-range objective

[55] A/648, Pt. 2, p. 26.

of mediation—suggesting a settlement of the Palestine problem—might well have been entrusted to a different group. Probably Bernadotte's assassination resulted from the conviction of the more violent Israeli factions that his plan of settlement would supersede and destroy the partition plan.[56] The greatest strength of a peace observer group rests in recognition by both sides of the objectivity of the group. Functions such as suggesting long-term settlements of political problems are bound to raise greater controversy than peace-observation functions, and thus detract from the image of objectivity.

Dividing functions between the Truce Commission and the Mediator did no harm. Without the Truce Commission, the Mediator would have found it difficult to assemble an adequate staff. On the other hand, the Truce Commission members lacked both the prestige and stature of the Mediator. Few jurisdictional conflicts arose primarily because the Truce Commission, located in Jerusalem, confined its activities to Jerusalem. The problems arising in Jerusalem were, for the most part, different from those in other parts of Palestine.

The best criterion of the relative success of the operation was that during the period from May 1948 to August 1949 the Mediator referred only fifteen major violations to the Security Council. Despite some limitations of time and personnel, the peace-observation groups clearly contributed to reducing the number of truce violations and limiting the adverse consequences of the violations that took place.

The Problem under the Armistice, July 1949–November 1956

THE MIXED ARMISTICE COMMISSIONS (MAC'S), THE UNITED NATIONS TRUCE SUPERVISION ORGANIZATION (UNTSO), THE CHIEF-OF-STAFF OF UNTSO

On July 20, 1949, the last of the four armistice agreements was signed between Israel and Syria.[57] On August 11, the Security Council relieved the Acting Mediator of further responsibilities and abolished his office. The functions of the Truce Commission expired when the truce was replaced by an armistice, and the commission ceased all activities. It was never formally abolished. The United Nations Truce Supervision Organization (UNTSO), recruited originally for the Truce Commission and assigned to the Mediator, continued in existence and was requested to furnish the personnel and services needed to observe and maintain the cease-fire and to perform the functions assigned by the Mixed Armistice

---

[56] UN Security Council, S/863, July 3, 1948, and S/870, July 8, 1948.
[57] UN Security Council, S/1353, July 20, 1949, and S/1353/Add. 1.

Agreements. The Chief-of-Staff of UNTSO was requested to inform the Security Council of the observance of the cease-fire and armistice and keep the Palestine Conciliation Commission apprised of matters affecting its work. The conclusion of the armistice agreements and demarcation of armistice lines diminished the scope of peace observation.

Terms of Reference

The terms of reference of the four MAC's, UNTSO, and the Chief-of-Staff of UNTSO are derived from: (1) the Security Council resolution of November 16, 1948, calling for the establishment of an armistice; (2) the Four Mixed Armistice Agreements; (3) the Security Council resolution of August 11, 1949, relieving the Acting Mediator of responsibilities.

The Security Council resolution of November 16, 1948, called on the parties to negotiate an armistice either directly or through the Acting Mediator. Each armistice agreement established an armistice line and provided for withdrawal of troops behind that line. The agreements affirmed certain general principles previously stated in Security Council resolutions, such as the right of each party to its security and freedom from fear of attack (Article 1). The agreements contained three general principles for their implementation: (1) no military or political advantage should be gained under the truce; (2) no changes in military positions should be made by either side after the armistice; and (3) the provisions of the armistices are dictated by purely military considerations.

The agreements set up Mixed Armistice Commissions, composed of three or five members—an equal number appointed by each of the parties with a chairman designated by the Chief-of-Staff of the United Nations Truce Supervision Organization. The MAC's could employ observers from either state or from UNTSO. The observers from UNTSO were to remain under the command of the UNTSO Chief-of-Staff. The agreements provide procedures for taking action on complaints from either side. There is also provision for appeals to a Special Committee headed by the Chief-of-Staff and one member from each side.

The Security Council resolution of August 11, 1949,[58] (1) reaffirmed the previous cease-fire order "bearing in mind that the several Armistice Agreements . . . provide for their supervision by the Parties themselves, relies upon the Parties to ensure the continued application and observance of these agreements"; (2) discharged the Acting Mediator of further responsibilities; (3) noted the provisions of the Mixed Armistice Agreements establishing the MAC's; (4) requested the Secretary-General to arrange for the continued service of such personnel of UNTSO as needed to observe and maintain the cease-fire, and to assist the parties to the Armistice Agreements in supervising the application and observance of the terms of

[58] S/1376.

those agreements, "with particular regard to the desires of the Parties as expressed in the relevant articles of the Agreements"; and (5) requested the Chief-of-Staff to report to the Security Council on the observance of the cease-fire and to keep the Palestine Conciliation Commission informed of matters affecting the commission's work.

It is obvious that the peace-observation functions granted to the MAC's, UNTSO, and the Chief-of Staff were far less than those held by the Mediator and the Truce Commission. To some extent, this was inevitable. The existence of armistice lines meant that the chief activity of peace observation would be directed to detecting violations of those lines.

With the passing of time, however, certain interpretations were given to the Mixed Armistice Agreements and the August 11 resolution.[59] (1) The jurisdiction of the MAC's was confined to the consideration of violations of the armistice agreements that had already taken place and had been brought to the attention of the MAC's by one of the parties. (2) The functions of UNTSO were limited to providing personnel and services to the MAC's. (3) The functions of the Chief-of-Staff were limited to acting as or designating the chairman of the MAC's, acting as chairman of the Special Committee, and reporting to the Security Council.

If the consideration by the MAC's of violations *after* they had taken place was insufficient to maintain the cease-fire, the only recourse was to the Security Council for further authority. Furthermore, while the armistice agreements look forward to "restoration of peace in Palestine," and the Security Council resolution of August 11 spoke of "the final settlement of all questions outstanding," no provision was made to deal with the situation in the event that these hopes failed to materialize.

Organization

During the second truce, UNTSO, with headquarters in Jerusalem, supplied 682 military personnel most of whom were from the United States, France, and Belgium. When the armistice agreements were concluded, the peace-observation function diminished. The embargo on military shipments and entry of military personnel into Palestine as well as the supervision of transportation lines ended. With the demarcation of armistice lines, the chief function of peace observation became the prevention of incursions by either side beyond the armistice lines. In addition, UNTSO was given specific functions in connection with the demilitarized zones adjoining Jerusalem: Mount Scopus, The Mount of Olives, the Latrun Pumping Station, Government House, which became UNTSO headquarters, etc.[60]

---

[59] These generalizations would not hold true for the special roles of the Chiefs-of-Staff in the demilitarized zones.

[60] E. H. Hutchison, *Violent Truce* (London: John Calder, 1956), p. 21.

The Mixed Armistice Agreement with Jordan varied from the other agreements by setting up a Special Committee to deal with these problems. Nevertheless, the peace-observation functions were to be far less extensive under the armistice than they had been under the truce. Furthermore, the Security Council on August 11 had reiterated that the United Nations was relying primarily on the parties themselves to ensure observance of the armistice. Therefore, the number of observers was gradually reduced to between forty and fifty.[61]

Although most officer personnel originally came from Belgium, the United States, and France, since 1953, officers have been recruited on a broader basis—from Denmark, Sweden, Canada, New Zealand, and other countries.

The observers had to be spread quite thin. For example, in 1952 during a period of high tension, there were only five observers in addition to the Chief of the MAC attached to the Jordan MAC where the boundary exceeds 300 miles.[62] As a result, the MAC's, whose headquarters were on or near the respective borders, mainly devoted themselves to investigating incidents where one or both parties filed complaints. Peace observation, therefore, was mostly confined to action after the fact. The complaints, especially to the Israel-Jordan MAC, were too numerous to permit investigation of any but the most serious cases. In May 1953, the backlog of unsettled complaints before the Israel-Jordan MAC was 1,500. By April 1955, the docket stood at 2,150.[63]

Despite the limited numbers of observers, it became apparent that in the areas where most of the incidents occurred, the cease-fire could be best assured through stationing observers at fixed posts on both sides of the line. The Chiefs-of-Staff claimed this right on the basis of the provisions of the Security Council resolution of August 11, 1949, granting UNTSO jurisdiction over observance of the cease-fire. Israel objected to this, claiming that the sole authority of the Chief-of-Staff and of UNTSO was derived from the Mixed Armistice Agreements. The Arabs also objected on occasion, though less frequently than the Israelis who consistently took the position that the truce supervisors' right to freedom of movement was confined to the investigation of complaints brought before the MAC's. Usually, after some wrangling, the observers were permitted to go wherever they wished.[64]

Performance

The central fact of this period of peace observation in Palestine is that tension increased rather than diminished, resulting ultimately in the

[61] Eedson L. M. Burns, *Between Arab and Israeli* (New York: Obolensky, 1963), p. 27.
[62] Hutchison, *op. cit.*, p. 11.
[63] Burns, *op. cit.*, p. 41.
[64] *Ibid.*, pp. 54–56.

collapse of the armistice when the Israelis invaded Egypt on October 29, 1956. It may be assumed that the failure to maintain peace resulted primarily from the political facts underlying the conflict. This study is not intended to analyze the political facts but rather to point out how UN peace observation affected the conflict. Therefore, only those incidents and situations are considered where the powers or limitations of the peace-observation structure strongly affected performance, either favorably or adversely. As the problems confronting the four MAC's varied greatly, the best way to evaluate the performance of the entire peace-observation machinery is through an analysis of the problems of the respective MAC's and the methods of meeting those problems.

The Israel-Lebanon MAC. General Eedson L. M. Burns decribed the Lebanese operation as follows: "UNTSO had few difficulties in connection with the General Armistice Agreement between Israel and Lebanon. In fact the Israel-Lebanon MAC worked as it had been intended all MAC's should." [65] It met at periodic intervals and seldom had difficult complaints to deal with. The reason General Burns gives for this favorable situation is that the armistice demarcation line "was the prewar frontier between Palestine and Lebanon, and so was generally accepted by the inhabitants, and was not a galling invitation like the ADL's [Armistice Demarcation Lines] around the Gaza strip and the West Bank in Jordan." As a further reason, General Burns cites "the length to which . . . [the Lebanese] would go to appease Israeli aggressiveness." [66]

Walter Eytan of the Israeli Foreign Office accounts for the relative quiet of the Lebanese border as follows:

> The relatively small number of "incidents" on the Lebanese border was due to Lebanon's desire for a quiet life. Much of the little trouble there was arose from ordinary petty crime or the smuggling which is endemic along land frontiers in most parts of the world. Had Egypt and Jordan shown as peaceable a disposition, most of the strife on their borders could have been averted. [67]

This "peaceable disposition," however, did not prevent the Israelis from applying mildly a policy of "retaliation" when minor incidents occurred.

Additional factors that may account for the relatively peaceable disposition of the Lebanese are the religious and racial pattern of the country where a large sector of the population is not Moslem. During the period from 1949 to 1956, political changes in Lebanon did not materially affect the enforcement of the armistice agreements.

The Israel-Syria MAC. In two respects the Israel-Syria boundary was as favorable for peace observation as the Israel-Lebanon boundary. First,

---

[65] *Ibid.*, p. 120.

[66] *Ibid.*, p. 122.

[67] Walter Eytan, *The First Ten Years* (London: Weidenfeld and Nicolson, 1958), p. 102.

the boundary was only about twenty miles long, and second, in the main it followed the pre-World War II frontier of Palestine.

Other factors were less favorable. Along the Syrian border, unlike other areas, the Syrian troops at the time of the cease-fire were occupying territory awarded to Israel under the 1947 partition plan. The Syrian armistice was delayed fifteen weeks by the negotiations concerning these relatively small areas.[68] Article V of the armistice agreement provided for "separating the armed forces of the two Parties in such manner as to minimize the possibility of friction and incident, while providing for gradual restoration of normal civilian life in the area of the Demilitarized Zone."[69] The same article provided for the exclusion of the armed forces of both Syria and Israel from the areas where the armistice demarcation line does not correspond to the international boundary between Syria and Palestine, and stated that the chairman of the MAC "shall be responsible for the full implementation of this article."[70]

These ambiguous provisions led to three interpretations:

1. The Israeli Government took the position that Israel had full sovereignty in the demilitarized zone subject only to its commitment not to introduce its military forces into the zone. Furthermore, the chairman of the MAC (the Chief-of-Staff) rather than the MAC had jurisdiction over incidents involving the zone. The Israeli boycott of the Syrian MAC was justified by the inclusion in the agenda of matters involving the zone.

2. The Syrian Government took the position that it could claim that any Israeli activities were in violation of the provisions for restoration of normal life in the zone and also the general principle in the armistice agreement that neither side should gain a military or political advantage. Therefore *any* activities in the zone required Syrian consent.

3. The Chiefs-of-Staff who were chairmen of the MAC, Generals William Riley, Byron V. Leary, and Carl C. Von Horn, took the position that the chairman of the MAC could determine whether the activity violated the armistice agreement, subject to review by the Security Council. The MAC was "almost wholly preoccupied with questions relating to the demilitarized zone."[71]

A further cause of frustration was that a part of the boundary ran a few feet from the shore of Lake Tiberias, which created a temptation on both sides to shoot at ships on the lake. Also the demilitarized zones included

[68] Jacob C. Hurewitz, "The Israeli-Syrian Crisis in the Light of the Arab-Israel Armistice System," *International Organization*, V: 3 (August 1959), p. 467. Hereafter cited as Hurewitz, "Israeli-Syrian Crisis."

[69] S/1353/Rev. 1, p. 3.

[70] S/1353/Rev. 1, p. 4.

[71] Hurewitz, "Israeli-Syrian Crisis," p. 468. For recent discussion see Fred J. Khouri, "Friction and Conflict on the Israeli-Syrian Frontier," *The Middle Eastern Journal*, XVII (Winter 1963), p. 14.

two Israeli kibbutzes which were east of Lake Tiberias and almost completely surrounded by Syria and Jordan.

In contrast to the Lebanese-Israeli relations, the political situation between Syria and Israel always remained tense. Syria was the last of the four neighboring states to agree to an armistice. The very weakness of the government encouraged intransigent and fanatic positions and prevented compromises.[72]

The number of incidents, doubtless because of geographic conditions, was far less than on the Egyptian or Jordanian borders, but the incidents that occurred were serious.

On February 14, 1951, Syria complained to the MAC concerning dredging operations conducted by an Israeli company in the demilitarized zone with the objective of draining the Huleh Marsh area. The Chief-of-Staff of UNTSO recommended that the operation cease until the MAC could deal with the problem. The company refused to cease operations, and fights broke out in the demilitarized zones. The normal handling of this matter through the MAC was not possible since Israel declined to participate because the problem involved the demilitarized zone, and also because of the alleged bias of the UN chairman. Israel also denied the authority of the Chief-of-Staff and UNTSO in the demilitarized zones.[73]

On May 8, 1951, the Security Council at the request of the Chief-of-Staff ordered a cease-fire, reaffirmed the provisions of the armistice agreement relating to the responsibilities of the chairman of the MAC, and called on the parties to participate in the meetings of the MAC. The resolution also had specific findings on this dispute. Both Israel and Syria consented to the resolution, but Israel continued to decline to participate in the MAC meetings. However, Israel permitted UNTSO to have some freedom of movement in the demilitarized zone.

While the Security Council resolution disposed of the immediate problem, it did not clarify the authority of the MAC's or UNTSO so as to prevent future challenges to their jurisdiction. Furthermore, the Security Council settlement of this case was possible only because of Soviet abstention.

Three years later, in 1953, Israel proposed to divert part of the water of the Jordan River from a location in the demilitarized zone for a power project. The Chief-of-Staff of the MAC took the position that the diversion project changed the nature of the zone in such a manner as to alter the value of the zone to Syria. Israel again denied the jurisdiction of the Chief-of-Staff and continued the project. When the matter was brought to the Security Council, the United States strongly supported the findings

---

[72] Eytan, *op. cit.*, p. 43. Burns, *op. cit.*, p. 110.

[73] *United States Participation in the United Nations, Report by the President to the Congress for the Year 1951* (Washington: Government Printing Office, 1952), p. 115. Hereafter cited as *1951 President's Report.*

of the Chief-of-Staff. Syria, however, took the extreme position that no undertakings could be carried on in the demilitarized zone without the consent of Syria. The Soviet Union supported Syria and vetoed a United States sponsored Security Council resolution stopping the diversion project and calling on the parties to abide by the decisions of the Chief-of-Staff. Despite the failure of the Security Council to act, Israel stopped the project after the United States indicated that economic aid would cease unless Israel obeyed the order.[74]

From the standpoint of this study, the significance of these two incidents is that they show the relationship between the limited and ambiguous terms of reference of the peace-observation machinery and its effectiveness. In the earlier episode, Israel both denied the jurisdiction of the Chief-of-Staff and UNTSO and declined for technical jurisdictional reasons to participate in the MAC. The specific problem could be resolved only by the Security Council. In the later episode, even though the MAC was generally supporting Syria, Syria denied its jurisdiction and denied the right of Israel to take any action in the demilitarized zones without its consent. The Security Council could not resolve this issue because by 1954 the Palestine problem had become part of the cold war, with the Soviet Union using its veto to support the Arab position.

After January 1954, the Syrian border remained relatively quiet until December 1955. On December 11, several companies of Israeli troops crossed the demarcation line and attacked Syrian military posts. The Syrian casualties were fifty-six killed, nine wounded, and thirty-two missing. In this instance, since Israel was found to be at fault, the Security Council without fear of a Soviet veto was in a position to take effective action on receipt of the report from the Chief-of-Staff.[75]

It is significant that an operation involving several hundred Israeli soldiers could take place with no warning. General Burns on the night of the raid wrote in his diary after all-day negotiations with the Israeli Government: "Maybe Israel is preparing something." One reason for this situation was that after 1951 "the Mixed Armistice Commission machinery no longer operated as between Israel and Syria,"[76] because Israel declined to participate, and no machinery short of the Security Council could reactivate the MAC without the agreement of both parties.

The Israel-Jordan MAC. The main incidents occurring on the Lebanese and Syrian borders could be summarized because they were relatively few. But on the Jordanian and Egyptian borders there were literally thousands of incidents, several of which demonstrate both the effectiveness and the limitations of the MAC's.

[74] Burns, *op. cit.*, p. 11.
[75] *1956 President's Report*, p. 37.
[76] Burns, *op. cit.*, pp. 107, 114.

During most of the period from 1949 to 1956, the political tension between Jordan and Israel was far less than between Syria or Egypt and Israel. Israel had always recognized the sincere efforts of King Abdullah to convert the armistice into a peace.[77] Even after his assassination in July 1951, the policies of the government remained unchanged. General Sir John B. Glubb, a responsible and effective British soldier, continued as Commander of the Arab Legion until March 1956. General Burns notes the sincere efforts of General Glubb and other government leaders to prevent infiltration of Israel.[78]

Furthermore, the interests of Jordan were frequently in conflict with those of the other Arab states. Jordan had occupied the old city of Jerusalem and what remained of Arab Palestine when the British departure in May 1946 created a governmental vacuum. The other Arab states would have preferred an independent Arab Palestine and an international regime for Jerusalem.

The vast number of border incidents arose more from the artificial nature of the boundary than from political tension. The boundary line frequently divided villages from the fields which supported their populations, from their sources of water, and even from their cemeteries. There never had been an international boundary line in this area. The line was 300 miles long, and the Jordan-Israeli Armistice, in addition to demarcation of boundaries, covered issues such as the status of Mount Scopus, access to the Holy Places in the old city of Jerusalem, and the use of the cemetery on the Mount of Olives. Despite the directives in the Armistice Agreement for immediate tentative arrangements on these issues, practically no progress has been made in fifteen years.

There have been, however, a number of periods of relative quiet along the demarcation line: 1950, when the enforcement of the truce was generally effective in all parts of Palestine;[79] February through April 1952, when all complaints were handled by the local Israeli and Jordanian commanders;[80] from October 1954 through 1955 when Israel returned to the MAC after the relief of Commander E. H. Hutchison, whom it accused of bias as chairman of the Mixed Armistice Commission.[81]

Commander Hutchison's detailed descriptions of on-the-spot investigations show how much can be accomplished to ascertain the facts as long as the interested parties allow the observers to investigate and do not try to conceal the evidence.[82]

[77] Eytan, *op. cit.*, p. 41.

[78] Burns, *op. cit.*, p. 48.

[79] *United States Participation in the United Nations, Report by the President to the Congress for the Year 1950* (Washington: Government Printing Office, 1951), p. 72.

[80] Hutchison, *op. cit.*, p. 18.

[81] Burns, *op. cit.*, pp. 41, 47.

[82] For example, "Investigation of Bedouin Raids," Hutchison, *op. cit.*, Chap. IX.

In 1955, when Israel and Jordan were apparently less belligerent than at any other time, the casualties on the Jordanian front were one-ninth as large as on the much shorter Egyptian front. They were one-third as large as in 1956, when the policies on both sides became more aggressive. [83]

The Israel-Egypt MAC. Although the boundary between Israel and Egypt was in part an artificial one, it was much easier to police than the Israeli-Jordanian line. During the 1948 hostilities, Egyptian forces had occupied the Gaza Strip, an area about twenty-five miles long and five miles wide along the Mediterranean Sea at the southern end of Palestine. South of the Gaza Strip, the boundary, which for at least a century has been an international boundary, runs through the Sinai desert. Two main roads lead through the Sinai Peninsula to Suez: the first along the Mediterranean Sea; the second some fifteen miles south, leading to Beersheba in Israel. This latter road crosses into Israel through a demilitarized zone just beyond which is the small Israeli town of El Auja. At its southern end, the boundary reaches the Gulf of Aqaba, so close to the Israeli port of Elath that, until 1956, Egyptian military installations were able to prevent Israeli use of the port.

The area requiring close observation was in the main confined to the twenty-five miles of the Gaza Strip, the El Auja demilitarized zone, and the military installations near Elath. Theoretically, therefore, the Israel-Egypt MAC had an easier task than the Israel-Jordan MAC. Moreover, the Israelis never boycotted the Israel-Egypt MAC, which continued to function during the entire period. Nevertheless, the casualties on both sides of the Egyptian frontier were much greater than in any other area, and the most important violations of the armistice took place there.

Several factors helped to account for these violations. The presence of some 200,000 Palestine Arab refugees in the Gaza Strip created a situation which was bound to lead to border incidents. The Egyptians, unlike the Jordanians, made no effort to stop raids into Israel, probably because of the political situation in Egypt. Beginning in 1955, the Egyptians apparently encouraged and organized raiding parties, proceeding not only from Egypt but also from Jordan.

The most important Israeli accusations of violations of the armistice agreement, preventing Israeli ships from going through the Suez Canal or entering the Israeli port of Elath, were beyond the jurisdiction of the MAC. The tensions on the Egyptian frontier grew continuously worse culminating in the Israeli invasion of Egypt in October 1956.

Incidents Affecting Peace Observation. The relationship between the limited terms of reference of the MAC's and their effectiveness is illustrated most dramatically in "the barrel incident." This incident itself was of no great importance and at the time it occurred attracted more amusement than concern.

[83] Burns, *op. cit.*, p. 47.

The Special Committee designated in the Israel-Jordan Armistice Agreement was responsible for enforcing the 1948 agreements to maintain free movement of traffic to Mount Scopus, a Jewish enclave within territory occupied by Jordan. The committee was never able to work out arrangements for satisfactory use of the facilities. However, agreements were worked out for convoys from Israel to furnish supplies to the Jewish occupants of Mount Scopus, subject to inspection by UNTSO to assure that no military supplies were being transferred.

On June 4, 1952, the UN guards, while inspecting a convoy in the "no man's land" area, found that a test rod struck a metal object in the center of an oil drum. The UN observer ordered the drum removed from the truck and attempted to open it. The Israelis thereupon rolled the truck back into Israel and demanded the return of the barrel.

The significant feature of this incident was the Israeli claim that by withdrawing the convoy, they deprived the MAC and UNTSO of the authority to inspect the barrel. General Riley, the Chief of UNTSO, after stating his belief that there was "extrinsic" matter in the barrel, returned it to the Israelis. Thus, the Israelis received apparent support for their contention that peace observation, except for the established procedures of bringing complaints to the MAC's, depended on agreement of the parties. UNTSO or the Chief-of-Staff could take no independent initiatives.

The Israeli policy of "retaliation" and the motivation behind it must be analyzed in order to draw a conclusion on the relation of this policy to the limitations of the peace-observation machinery. The policy did not stem solely from the weakness of the UN peace-observation effort. If the peace-observation effort had been more effective, however, the Government of Israel would have lost its rationale for the policy.

This policy of "retaliation" is described and justified by Walter Eytan, Director-General of the Israeli Foreign Office, as follows:

> In the end, Israel had no alternative but to hit back. It will always be debated whether the means she chose were the best. They did not help her in the eyes of world opinion, which disliked "reprisals," specially when they appeared indiscriminate. But what was the alternative? Protest to the MAC's? This was done times without number, to no effect. All the Commissions could do was to establish guilt and censure the guilty. They could not take preventive or even deterrent action. The night after a Commission's meeting, the raids would start again, setting off anew the futile round of accusation, investigation, discussion and censure. Might Israel not have complained to the Security Council? This was not possible over the heads of the MAC's and would . . . have been fruitless. Nor was it possible to patrol or police every yard of a long demarcation line, much of it in difficult terrain. If "infiltration" could not be prevented, it must be attacked at its source—on the other side of the line. . . . There was much pressure on the security authorities by the villagers themselves, who asked for nothing better than to be allowed to take law into their own

hands and attack the attackers. But the Government was never willing to countenance a "thieves in the night" policy. . . . But any action that was decided upon would be taken by its own forces—it could not be left to the private initiative of the victims. [84]

Thus, Eytan has stated in a completely forthright manner the deliberate decision of the Israeli Government to violate the armistice agreements, which forbid reprisals. Moreover, he has related the Israeli decision to the limited effectiveness of the armistice machinery, that is, the MAC's could not take deterrent action.

Perhaps Eytan was not equally forthright in relating the policy of retaliation solely to the motive of deterring the Arabs from raids into Israel. In 1956, evidence captured by the Israelis in Egypt made it clear that the Egyptian Government was deliberately organizing the so-called Fedayeen raids into Israel, which were causing great loss of life. [85] However, the reprisals took place against Jordan as well as Egypt, despite the fact that while Glubb remained as commander of the Arab Legion, he was probably doing everything in his power to prevent raids from Jordan, and was relatively successful. [86]

One of the most vicious reprisals, described earlier, took place against Syria where there was practically no infiltration. This particular incident took place when Jordan and Egypt were showing interest in Eric Johnston's proposals for the use of the Jordan River to benefit both the Israelis and the Arabs. This might have been a first step toward a peaceful adjustment of the Palestine problem. The Syrian politicians, more fanatic than the Jordan and Egyptian leaders, were just beginning to evince an interest in the proposals when the incident near Lake Tiberias destroyed all possibility of agreement.

General Burns points out that the policy of retaliation received its chief support in Israel from General Dayan and Prime Minister Ben Gurion. Mr. Moshe Sharett and other civilian leaders had many reservations. Burns suggests that one Israeli motive may have been to win peace through a policy of force. [87] Some Israeli leaders, in the early stages of Israel's life, had been revolutionaries all their lives and, like some of the early Russian revolutionaries, may have been temperamentally incapable of a policy of peace through compromise or even of permitting tensions to simmer. The policy of retaliation, regardless of its wisdom, may have reflected these characteristics.

Performance of the peace-observation machinery also was adversely affected by the Israeli boycott of the Mixed Armistice Commissions. It has been pointed out that Israel boycotted the Israel-Jordan MAC from

[84] Eytan, *op. cit.*, pp. 99–100.
[85] Burns, *op. cit.*, p. 62.
[86] *Ibid.*, p. 60.
[87] *Ibid.*, p. 65.

December 1953 to October 1954, when Commander Hutchison was chairman. This permitted the accumulation of 1,500 unsettled claims.[88]

In April 1951, Israel notified the Chief-of-Staff of UNTSO that it would not participate in the Israel-Syria MAC meetings because the agenda included matters affecting the demilitarized zones, and Israel could no longer rely on the impartiality of the chairman. Israel did not return to the MAC even after a new chairman was appointed and a Security Council resolution called on the parties to attend all meetings and to respect the chairman's rulings.[89]

These incidents point to an organizational shortcoming. The theory that the armistice and its enforcement depended on agreement of the parties enabled one party to paralyze the armistice machinery by refusing to participate. Only the Security Council could call on the parties to return to the commission, and Israel at times disregarded the Security Council. It was a short procedural step to the Israeli note of October 5, 1956, stating that Israel would not permit UN observers to investigate incidents occurring within Israel.[90]

In the latter part of 1955 and in early 1956, with the armistice rapidly disintegrating, General Burns as Chief-of-Staff of UNTSO took the initiative in attempting to devise methods for reducing the violations of the armistice agreements.

In the fall of 1955, the place of greatest tension was the demilitarized zone near El Auja on the Egyptian border. The United Nations Secretary-General endorsed a three-point plan to separate the parties: (1) UNTSO should mark the international frontier along the extent of the El Auja demilitarized zone; (2) Egypt should withdraw all its posts which encroached in the demilitarized zone; (3) Israel should withdraw from the demilitarized zone all troops in excess of the number present before the most recent series of incidents. Even such a light initiative toward maintaining peace could not be taken by UNTSO without agreement of both Egypt and Israel. This was not obtained.[91]

Along the Gaza Strip, where much blood was being shed, both Israel and Egypt agreed that UN military observers should be stationed on both sides of the line. Despite the emergency, Israel insisted that the stipulation should be ratified by the MAC. "The purpose of this stipulation was presumably to avoid admitting that UNTSO, independently of decisions by the MAC, could have authority to 'observe the cease-fire' as ordered by the Security Council in its August 11, 1949 resolution and at other times."[92]

[88] *Ibid.*, p. 41.
[89] *1951 President's Report*, p. 115.
[90] Burns, *op. cit.*, p. 172.
[91] *Ibid.*, p. 98.
[92] *Ibid.*, p. 148.

The Secretary-General (Hammarskjold) was fully aware of all the modalities of the problem. To meet this issue, he attempted to obtain a general cease-fire stemming directly from the Security Council, "different in character from previous cease-fires dependent upon local agreements." The general cease-fire would express "a recognition in this particular situation of the obligation to observe a fundamental principle of the Charter."[93] This presumably would have reversed the line of authority for enforcement of the armistice. Instead of stemming from the MAC's and moving directly to the Security Council, it would have run from the Security Council through the Chief-of-Staff who in turn would have supervised the MAC's.

Doubtless because of the emergency, the Security Council unanimously adopted a series of resolutions calling on the parties to put into effect the measures suggested by the Secretary-General for preventing border incidents, and confirming the importance of free movement by the UN observers.[94]

Nevertheless the border violations continued, and tensions increased. This clarification of the authority of the Chief-of-Staff and UNTSO to take initiatives to maintain the cease-fire independently of the MAC's came too late. With both Egypt and Israel deliberately flouting the armistice, the peace-observation machinery functioning since the armistice in 1949 was no longer adequate to carry out its tasks.[95] The Israeli invasion of Egypt marked its final failure. Not only had the machinery proved inadequate to maintain the armistice, it had not even given notice of the Israeli mobilization in an area where observers were stationed. Despite the constant increase in tensions, the Israeli invasion was a complete surprise to the Chief-of- Staff, to the Israel-Egypt MAC and to the UNTSO observers. General Burns candidly writes:

> I must confess that prior to October 28 the reports of the mobilization did not excite me greatly. During my term as Chief of Staff UNTSO the Israelis had several times mobilized a portion of their reserves, usually followed by reports from the U.S. military attaché at Tel Aviv that the situation was dangerous and war a possibility. So, on this occasion, I thought that it was just a repetition of previous false alarms. UNMO's in the Beersheba area had reported increased activity of the Israeli troops in the area, but not to a degree that pointed to an immediate Israeli attack,[96]

[93] UN Security Council, S/3594, May 2, 1956.

[94] See: UN Security Council, Resolution adopted at the 722nd meeting, April 4, 1956, S/3575; Resolution adopted at the 728th meeting, June 4, 1956, S/3605.

[95] See the following Chief-of-Staff Reports: UN Security Council S/3638, Aug. 21, 1956; S/3670, Oct. 13, 1956; S/3685, Oct. 18, 1956.

[96] Burns, *op. cit.*, pp. 177, 178.

Evaluation

It is suggested that the following factors, most of which are interrelated, played a major role in the successes and failures of the truce supervision efforts during this period: (1) character of the boundary; (2) intentions of the parties; (3) the time element; (4) limitations in terms of reference; (5) relation to mediation; (6) organization; and (7) the refugee problem.

Character of the Boundary. As pointed out, the Israel-Lebanon boundary was a well-established international frontier. The Israel-Syria boundary, except for a very small distance, also was an international frontier and generally followed water courses and other geographical features. The Israel-Jordan boundary was artificial and drawn without logic, for example, separating villages from the agricultural fields on which they depended and from their water supplies. As might be anticipated, the boundaries with Lebanon and Syria were relatively easy to police and incidents of infiltration were few. There were practically no incidents of any importance on the Lebanon boundary, and the serious incidents on the Syrian boundary, in practically all cases, resulted from political motivations unrelated to the day-to-day problems of truce supervision. Practically all the incidents on the Syrian frontier took place in the demilitarized zones where the truce demarcation line did not follow the boundary. The serious breaches of the armistice leading to its ultimate collapse in October 1956 took place along the Jordan and Egypt boundaries, which were artificial. However, other factors played a large role in causing these serious incidents.

Intentions of the Parties. It seems clear that both the Israelis and the Lebanese desired to prevent violence along the frontier. The Israeli policy of retaliation, resorted to in other areas, never appeared in any major degree along this boundary. The combination of a natural boundary and good intentions on both sides resulted in an effective truce, with a minimum of truce-supervision machinery.

The various Syrian regimes showed far greater hostility toward Israel during most of this period than the Lebanese or the Jordanians. This may have resulted from the weakness of the regimes, which ultimately led to Syria being temporarily absorbed in the United Arab Republic. Hostility to Israel throughout this period was a device to increase the popularity of regimes beset by political and economic problems. The Israeli irrigation efforts, which aroused great antagonism and some violence, took place along this boundary.

The most flagrant violation of the armistice by Israel, its policy of retaliation, also took place here. The magnitude of the Israeli attack on Syrian military posts in December 1955 dwarfed the claimed Syrian incursions and may have indicated Israeli motives far beyond maintaining its own security. Despite the extreme tension between Syria and Israel, the number of casualties on both sides of this frontier, except for the major incident in 1955, was relatively small. During most of this period, Israel stayed away from plenary sessions of the MAC, thus handicapping truce supervision, but allowed UNTSO to send observers to the boundary. The relative effectiveness of truce supervision along this boundary seems to indicate that the nature of the boundary is a greater factor in determining the effectiveness of truce supervision than the intentions of the parties.

This conclusion is strengthened by the situation along the Jordan frontier where the consensus is that Jordan, until the overthrow of General Glubb in March 1956, made strong efforts to prevent the infiltration of Arabs into Israel across its boundary. Even afterwards, the Jordanian Government was far less hostile to Israel than Syria or Egypt. The reason was partly because of the strong British influence in Jordan and partly because of the differences between Jordan and the other Arab countries, arising from the Jordanian occupation of the Old City of Jerusalem and most of the Arab portion of Palestine. The large number of incidents and casualties along this frontier indicate that despite the efforts of the Jordan Government to avoid incidents, truce supervision is difficult along an unfavorable boundary.

The greatest number of casualties took place along the Egyptian frontier in 1955 and 1956. This reflected the fact that both Egypt and Israel were deliberately violating the armistice—Egypt through planning and subsidizing the Fedayeen raids, some of them staged from Jordan, and Israel through its policy of retaliation.

Even with good intentions on both sides, effective truce supervision along an artificial boundary is difficult to obtain; and even with bad intentions and lack of cooperation, a certain measure of effectiveness in truce supervision can be obtained along a natural boundary. Where there is a combination of an artificial boundary and the desire of both sides to flout the armistice, any effective truce supervision—even advance warning of massive violations—is doomed.

The Time Element. The most effective truce supervision took place from two to four years after the armistice commenced. The truce supervision machinery, originally intended to last only a year, had had time to be perfected, and during this period there was still some hope of moving from an armistice to peace. Beginning in 1954, conditions began to deteriorate, and they grew progressively worse in 1955 and 1956.

Without passing judgment on the policies of the Israeli and the Arab governments, which led to this deterioration, there seems to be some relation between the length of time of the armistice and the adoption of policies which led to renewed hostilities. The Egyptian policy of encouraging raids into Israel did not develop until after the failure of Eric Johnston's mission, which would have been a tangible step towards peace. The Israeli policy of retaliation leading to the Israeli invasion of Egypt in 1956 may have been influenced by Israeli impatience with an armistice that was not winning peace. Likewise, the most flagrant Israeli and Egyptian inter-ference with access to critical areas did not become acute until 1954, after the failure of the Johnston mission.

The Palestine experience during this period seems to indicate that if an armistice lasts too long without turning into a peace, the prestige of the international organization conducting the truce supervision erodes. The parties show less respect for the international authority and deliberately flout the armistice. Violence increases and ultimately, as in this case, the armistice breaks down.

Limitations in Terms of Reference. It seems clear that the truce-supervision effort was adversely affected by the limited terms of reference of UNTSO and the Chief-of-Staff. The Security Council never granted to the Chief-of-Staff or to UNTSO authority over truce supervision beyond a vague directive to maintain the truce. (This was in contrast to the broad authority of the Mediator prior to the armistice.) Therefore, the Israelis, and to a lesser degree the Arabs, were in a position to claim that truce supervision was limited to investigation of incidents brought to the atten-tion of the MAC's *after* they had occurred.

The contention was made that the sole role of the Chief-of-Staff was to furnish an organization to support the MAC's and to act as liaison to the Security Council. Without the consent of both parties, the Chief-of-Staff could not on his own authority take general steps to strengthen the armi-stice, for example, to station observers in strategic places. Any such meas-ures, in the absence of agreement of the parties, depended on a decision of the Security Council. The Security Council was deluged with reports of incidents from Israel and the Arab states, which it could not investigate. The absence of any intermediate authority between the MAC's and the Security Council thus paralyzed the entire operation. In addition to the problem of bringing such details to a high-level international organization two thousand miles away, the possibility of an objective decision of the Security Council disappeared when the Soviet Union decided, in 1954 and 1955, to make the Palestine problem an issue in the cold war, with the Soviet Union siding with the Arabs.

The evidence of the adverse effects on truce supervision of the limited terms of reference of the Chief-of-Staff and UNTSO is found in the numer-ous contentions of lack of jurisdiction made by both Arabs and Israelis—more by Israelis than by the Arabs; and in the futile efforts of General Burns, a highly competent Chief-of-Staff, immediately prior to the collapse of the armistice, to obtain the consent of both the Arabs and the Israelis to establishing procedures that would diminish the possibility of armistice violations.

Despite these limitations, UNTSO and the Chief-of-Staff performed indispensable functions. They arranged cease-fires. For example, once shooting had started, neither side would ask for a cease-fire for fear of appearing to be weaker. Without the presence of UNTSO to make the initiative to call for simultaneous cease-fires, there would have been no one to perform this vital role. They presented unbiased reports to the United Nations Security Council as a basis for its resolutions. They acted as a trip wire, so to speak, to limit the activities of both parties.

Relation to Mediation. It is difficult to determine whether the truce supervision would have been more effective had the truce supervision organization been responsible for mediation too. Mediation proposals are likely to be more controversial than efforts to avoid violence. As a result, if the functions of mediation and peace observation are combined, the peace observers are more likely to be accused of lack of objectivity, and, as in the case of Bernadotte, assassinated. On the other hand, because of the close relation between the effectiveness of truce supervision and the hope of an ultimate peace, the truce supervision organization is likely to be more active in promoting an ultimate settlement than a group such as the PCC sitting in New York with functions confined solely to mediation. Furthermore, the limited usefulness of the PCC made it difficult to attract personnel capable of carrying out an active and constructive program.

Organization. The experience in Palestine seems to indicate that an operative structure, though illogical, will function effectively if able and devoted individuals serve. This experience also shows that a small group can be reasonably effective even under the most difficult conditions if both parties wish the effort to succeed. Local investigations of the violations uncovered the true facts in most instances. However, where the desire to have an effective armistice is lacking, there is little that can be done by a small group. For example, the small group of observers could not detect in advance the most massive breaches of the armistice, including the full-scale invasion of Egypt, which must have required weeks of advance planning and preparation.

The Refugee Problem. In analyzing the results of truce supervision in this period, the importance of the unsolved problem of the Arab refugees must be emphasized. Much of the infiltration of Israel, leading to its policy of retaliation, was by Arab refugees. The Arab states consistently declined to discuss a peace settlement until the refugee problem was solved. The refugees' plight was the visible means of continuing Arab hostility to Israel and was used by Arab governments to distract their people from political embarrassments and economic distress. The refugee problem was the most important cause of the failure of efforts to transform the armistice to a peace settlement.

THE PALESTINE CONCILIATION COMMISSION (PCC)

The Palestine Conciliation Commission is not and never has been a peace-observation group. During the period prior to the Armistice, the UN Mediator had had both peace-observation and mediatory functions, the latter derived from General Assembly resolutions and the former from Security Council resolutions. The Mediator's plan for a solution of the Palestine problem called for progress from a truce to an armistice and then to a settlement, and for adjustments of the partition plan. The report proposed forming a Conciliation Commission to perform both functions.[97]

Terms of Reference

On December 11, 1948, the General Assembly established a Palestine Conciliation Commission,[98] consisting of France, Turkey, and the United States, to assume the function given to the Mediator by the General Assembly resolution of May 14, 1948,[99] relating to mediation, and to undertake on the request of the Security Council any of the functions assigned to the Mediator or the Truce Commission by the resolutions of the Council.[100] These functions included the peace-observation activities of the Mediator. However, the Security Council never requested the PCC to assume any of these functions, and the commission continues to operate within the framework of its original terms of reference.

Organization

The PCC first met in Geneva on January 17, 1949, and before February 1 had established headquarters and a small secretariat in Jerusalem.

Performance

From 1949 to 1951 the chief activities of the PCC, in addition to major political negotiations, were directed toward developing a permanent international regime for the Jerusalem area, and working out a settlement of the refugee problem. The commission met in Lausanne, Beirut, Paris, and New York, as well as in London. In 1949, the PCC submitted its proposals on Jerusalem to the General Assembly. The Assembly failed to support the proposals and requested the Trusteeship Council to prepare an international trusteeship agreement for Jerusalem.[101] The major effort to work out a political settlement, in 1951, was unsuccessful.[102]

[97] S/1025.

[98] Res. 194 (III).

[99] Res. 186.

[100] This would include the functions enumerated in S/727 of April 23, 1948; S/773 of May 22, 1948; and S/801 of May 29, 1948.

[101] *United States Participation in the United Nations, Report by the President to the Congress for the Year 1949* (Washington: Government Printing Office, 1950), p. 45.

[102] *1951 President's Report*, p. 112.

Beginning in 1951, the PCC devoted itself, with some success, to more limited tasks concerning the Arab refugees from Palestine. It sought release of accounts that had been blocked in Israeli banks and undertook the task of listing the real and personal properties left behind in Israel. After July 1952, the main activities of the PCC took place in New York. The United States representative to the United Nations or his deputies represented the United States on the PCC. The major effort for a long-term settlement in 1954—Ambassador Eric Johnston's attempt to obtain agreement on a program for using the waters of the Jordan River—was independent of the PCC. The program was developed by the United Nations Relief and Works Agency with Eric Johnston acting as the personal representative of the U.S. President. After 1956, the PCC assumed some additional functions but not in the area of peace observation.

The most significant recent activity of the Palestine Conciliation Commission was its appointment in August 1961 of Joseph E. Johnson as its special representative to visit the Middle East "to explore with the host governments and with Israel practical means of seeking progress in the Palestine Arab Refugee Problem."[103] Any solution of the refugee problem would have profound implications for all other Palestine problems. Mr. Johnson submitted a plan to the interested states which would have moved the Palestine problem, including its peace-observation aspects, off dead center. Neither side, however, was prepared to accept the plan, and Mr. Johnson resigned in January 1963.[104]

Evaluation

The relation of the PCC to the peace-observation function may be summarized as follows:

1. The Acting Mediator (Ralph Bunche) originally proposed that the PCC be responsible for peace observation and that UNTSO be subordinate to the PCC.[105] He changed his position later and advocated a separation of the mediation and truce-supervision functions because of a basic conflict between the two functions. Truce-supervision decisions could appear objective much more easily than recommendations for long-range settlements. Bunche may also have been influenced by Israeli opposition to "administrative or executive functions" for the PCC, as well as by Soviet

---

[103] UN General Assembly, Seventeenth Session, *Official Records*, Supplement No. 1 (A/5201).

[104] UN General Assembly, Eighteenth Session, *Official Records*, Supplement No. 1 (A/5501).

[105] UN General Assembly, *Official Records*, Third Session, First Committee, p. 771. Hereafter cited as Third Session, First Committee.

proposals to abolish UNTSO.[106] This separation of the mediation and truce-supervision functions accounts for the failure of the Security Council to grant the PCC the authority it had previously given to the Mediator. The fact that truce-supervision functions were in "no man's land" after the abolition of the office of the Mediator led to jurisdictional objections, particularly by Israel. These objections in turn hindered the MAC's work.

2. The limited jurisdiction of the PCC may have hindered its work. For example, in February 1950, Egypt requested that Arab refugees in the Gaza area be permitted to return to their farms in a nearby Israeli-occupied area. The PCC proposed a negotiating formula to Egypt and Israel. Israel rejected the proposal on the ground that it was within the jurisdiction of the MAC rather than the PCC.

3. The composition of the PCC probably played an important role in introducing the cold war into the Palestine problem. The Soviet Union had objected to the composition of the PCC (France, Turkey, and the United States) and had suggested a broader membership including Poland.[107] "By frustrating Soviet moves and agreeing to membership in the Committee, the United States implicitly had accepted responsibility for the conciliation effort, more especially since neither France nor Turkey could effectively have resisted determined policy decisions taken in Washington."[108]

4. The decision of the PCC in 1951 to limit itself to the narrow problems of Arab refugees' blocked accounts in Israel and compensation for property losses was, in effect, temporary abandonment of any effort to convert the armistice into a peace. Regardless of the justification for such a decision, it affected the truce supervision adversely by indefinitely postponing the transition from armistice to peace. It probably encouraged the elements, both in Israel and the Arab countries, who preferred a resumption of the war to a continuation of the armistice.

5. The lack of progress toward a political settlement had adversely affected the truce supervision. At the same time, the ineffectiveness of the truce supervision was one element hindering mediation efforts. However, the most effective mediation effort—the attempt to obtain division of the Jordan River's waters—was made in 1954 after the armistice had started to deteriorate. The failure of this effort was quickly followed by the collapse of the armistice.

6. The mission of Joseph E. Johnson to solve the refugee problem was a constructive step. Its failure emphasized that the political situation was still not ripe for a compromise solution of any substantial phase of the Palestine problem.

[106] J. C. Hurewitz, "United Nations Conciliation Commission for Palestine," *International Organization*, VII (November 1953), pp. 490, 495. Hereafter cited as Hurewitz, "Conciliation Commission."

[107] Third Session, First Committee, pp. 772, 829.

[108] Hurewitz, "Conciliation Commission," p. 492.

The Problem from November 7, 1956, to the Present

THE UNITED NATIONS EMERGENCY FORCE (UNEF)

On October 29, 1956, the Israeli armed forces, as a climax to the mounting tensions, invaded Egypt. The Israeli Government had expelled UN personnel from the El Auja demilitarized zone and disregarded an order from the Chief-of-Staff for a cease-fire and withdrawal of forces from Egypt, thus repudiating the armistice. On October 30, 1956, the United Kingdom representative informed the Security Council that the United Kingdom and France had called on Egypt and Israel to cease warlike actions and to withdraw their forces to a distance ten miles from the Suez Canal. The United Kingdom and France then attempted to seize the Canal and the Egyptians sank ships in it, blocking it for navigation. The United Kingdom and France vetoed a Security Council resolution calling on Israel to withdraw its forces from Egypt. Thereupon, with the approval of the United States and the Soviet Union, the Security Council called an emergency session of the General Assembly, where there was no veto, to deal with the problem. [109]

The General Assembly was confronted with two main problems: reopening the canal and restoring the armistice.

Apparently, all members of the General Assembly agreed that the best way to stop the fighting and thereafter to permit the restoration of navigation in the Suez Canal was to place a military force in the area between the Israeli and Egyptian forces. The British and French suggested that their forces, which were already occupying a part of the Suez, be used. This was objectionable to Egypt and to the majority of the General Assembly members who regarded the British and French as aggressors.

The Soviet Union in the Security Council called for the withdrawal of British, French, and Israeli forces and for all member states—in particular the United States and the Soviet Union—to give assistance to Egypt if the troops were not withdrawn. This proposal was objectionable not only to the United States but to most UN members, who wished neither United States nor Soviet troops in the area. [110] The third proposal was for the formation of a United Nations Emergency Force with contingents coming from states other than the permanent members of the Security Council. Such forces would enter Egyptian territory with the consent of the Egyptian Government to obtain a cease-fire, to replace troops other than those of Egypt, to arrange for reopening the Suez Canal, and to restore the armistice. On November 4, the General Assembly adopted this proposal and both parties thereupon agreed to a cease-fire. [111] On November 5 and 6,

---

[109] *1956 President's Report*, pp. 47–48, 49–50.

[110] Burns, *op. cit.*, p. 89.

[111] Res. 998 (ES-I).

the Assembly adopted two additional resolutions detailing the organization and terms of reference of UNEF, generally as suggested in the reports of the Secretary-General.[112]

A cease-fire had been achieved immediately after the adoption of the November 4 resolution. The first UNEF forces were airlifted to Egypt on November 15. By March 8, 1957, all Israeli, French, and English troops had withdrawn and thereafter the Egyptian Government took over the full administration of the area.[113] UNEF was ultimately deployed on the Egyptian side of the boundary between Egypt and Israel and became a part of the truce-supervision and peace-observation machinery. This analysis is concerned solely with the role of UNEF in performance of the latter function.

Terms of Reference

UNEF did not supersede the existing truce-supervision machinery (the MAC's, UNTSO, the Chief-of-Staff), which continued to operate with unchanged terms of reference on the Jordanian, Lebanese, and Syrian boundaries.

Along the Egyptian boundary both the MAC and UNEF theoretically continued to have functions:

> UNEF . . . is . . . to direct and administer the cessation of hostilities . . . secure and supervise the withdrawal of forces, and seek observance of the provisions of the General Armistice Agreement between Egypt and Israel. . . . UNEF has a wider and different role to play in the Middle East than has the Truce Supervision Organization. It is a police and patrol force rather than an observer corps.
> To prevent duplications in their tasks, however, arrangements were made for the Egypt-Israel Mixed Armistice Commission to be placed under the operational control of UNEF's Commander. The legal status of both organs remains unchanged.[114]

The Israeli Government has taken a different position, claiming that the armistice agreement between Israel and Egypt is no longer valid and therefore the MAC no longer exists. Neither Egypt nor the Secretary-General has accepted the Israeli position.[115]

The Israeli Government, in accordance with its position, has lodged complaints with UNEF rather than with the MAC. As a practical matter,

[112] UN General Assembly, Res. 1000 (ES-I), adopted Nov. 5, 1956; Res. 1001 (ES-I).

[113] UN General Assembly, Twelfth Session, *Official Records*, Supplement No. 1, A/3594, p. 23.

[114] Gabriella Rosner, *The United Nations Emergency Force* (New York: Columbia University Press, 1963), pp. 71, 98.

[115] UN General Assembly, Twelfth Session, *Official Records*, Supplement No. 1, A3594, p. 21.

this has not hampered truce supervision since either the MAC or UNEF could act on Israeli complaints.

The Israeli position would raise problems if Egypt should file a complaint requiring investigation on the Israeli side of the border. Even before the establishment of UNEF, Prime Minister Ben Gurion took the position that "on no account will Israel agree to the stationing of a foreign force, no matter how called, in her territory, or in any of the areas occupied by her."[116] Since Israel has never consented to UNEF's presence in Israel, an investigation in Israel would have to be made by the MAC, which Israel no longer recognizes. However, the problem has not yet arisen.

The truce-supervision functions of UNEF are defined in the General Assembly resolution of November 7, 1956, which "concurs in the definition of the functions of the force as stated in paragraph 12 of the Secretary-General's report,"[117] as follows:

> In the General Assembly resolution the terms of reference are . . . "to secure the cessation of hostilities in accordance with all the terms" of the resolution of 2 November, 1956. This resolution urges that "all parties now involved in hostilities in the area agree to an immediate cease-fire and as part thereof halt the movement of military forces and arms into the area;" and also "urges the parties to the Armistice Agreements promptly to withdraw all forces behind the armistice lines, to desist from raids across armistice lines into neighboring territory, and to observe scrupulously the provisions of the Armistice Agreements." These two provisions combined indicate that the functions of the United Nations force would be, when a cease-fire is being established, to enter Egyptian territory with the consent of the Egyptian Government, in order to help maintain quiet during and after the withdrawal of non-Egyptian troops, and to secure compliance with the other terms established in the resolution of 2 November, 1956. The force obviously should have no rights other than those necessary for the execution of its functions, in cooperation with local authorities. It would be more than an observers' corps, but in no way a military force temporarily controlling the territory in which it is stationed; nor, moreover, should the force have military functions exceeding those necessary to secure peaceful conditions on the assumption that the parties to the conflict take all necessary steps for compliance with the recommendations of the General Assembly. Its functions can, on this basis, be assumed to cover an area extending roughly from the Suez Canal to the armistice demarcation lines, established in the Armistice Agreement between Egypt and Israel.[118]

As stated previously, this study is concerned only with the UNEF role in peace observation, which is related to its function to "help maintain quiet . . . after the withdrawal of non-Egyptian troops."

[116] *Aide-Mémoire* of Ben Gurion, Jan. 23, 1957.
[117] E. Lauterpacht, *The UN Emergency Force: Basic Documents* (New York: Praeger, 1960), p. 2.
[118] *Ibid.*, pp. 14–15.

The Secretary-General seeks to interpret the terms of reference of UNEF in such a manner as to correct the limitations and inadequacies of the truce-supervision machinery. One of the chief limitations, as heretofore pointed out, was that in the absence of specific Security Council directives, which were rarely feasible, the functioning of the MAC's depended on consent of the parties, which in turn depended on the pressure exerted on them by the great powers to cooperate with the MAC's. The Secretary-General recognized that "functioning, as it would, on the basis of a decision reached under the terms of the resolution 'Uniting for Peace,' the force, if established, would be limited in its operations to the extent that consent of the parties concerned is required under generally recognized international law." The General Assembly "could not request the force to be *stationed* or *operate* on the territory of a given country without the consent of the Government of that country."[119]

The Secretary-General immediately obtained the consent of Egypt to stationing of the force in Egypt. By February 7, 1957, within two months after the establishment of the force and while Egypt still desired and needed the force to regain control of the Sinai Peninsula and the Gaza Strip, the United Nations had worked out an agreement with Egypt concerning the status of UNEF, which assured that Egypt could not legally hamper or harass UNEF in its activities. For example, the agreement specifically provides: "The Government of Egypt recognizes the right of the Force and its members to freedom of movement across armistice demarcation lines and other military lines in the performance of the functions of the Force and the official duties of its members." The agreement entered into force on "the date of the arrival of the first element of the force in Egypt, and shall remain in force until the departure of the Force from Egypt."[120] Egypt, therefore, could not alter the agreement unilaterally or terminate it so long as the force remains. There is some question whether Egypt could even obtain the removal of the force without UN consent. In short, the Egyptian consent to UNEF is sufficiently broad so that UNEF, in contrast to the MAC's and UNTSO, has not been hampered with claims of lack of jurisdiction, objections to personnel, or refusal of access.

The United Nations recognized the need to insulate the Arab-Israeli dispute from the cold war. The PCC, consisting of Turkey, France, and the United States, could with some justification be accused of a Western orientation, as could the personnel of UNTSO recruited originally from Belgium, France, and the United States. On the recommendation of the Secretary-General, the General Assembly avoided this problem in establishing UNEF. The resolution of November 5 provides for the recruitment of officers "who shall be nationals of countries other than those having permanent membership in the Security Council." The resolution of

[119] *Ibid.*, p. 13.
[120] *Ibid.*, pp. 20 ff.

November 7 establishes an Advisory Committee of representatives from Brazil, Canada, Ceylon, Colombia, India, Norway, and Pakistan.[121]

One of the prime weaknesses of the truce-supervision machinery was the absence of a chain of command from the MAC's to the United Nations. The General Assembly had granted to the Chief-of-Staff the authority to recruit and direct the UNTSO staff, to furnish personnel for the MAC's, and to act as liaison with the United Nations. It had contemplated that the Security Council would grant additional powers to the Chief-of-Staff, but this never materialized. Consequently, the Chief-of-Staff could do nothing to improve the effectiveness of truce supervision without agreement of the parties, which was generally impossible to obtain, or the Security Council's decisions on individual incidents brought to its attention—an ineffective, clumsy mechanism.

The General Assembly avoided this situation in establishing UNEF by: (1) establishing a United Nations Command; (2) delineating its functions; (3) providing a high-level Advisory Committee of representatives of states to report to the UN Command; (4) authorizing the Secretary-General "to issue all regulations and instructions which may be essential to the effective functioning of the Force, following consultation with the Committee aforementioned"; (5) authorizing the Advisory Committee to request the convening of the General Assembly "whenever matters arise which, in its opinion, are of such urgency and importance as to require consideration by the General Assembly itself."[122]

Organization

During the entire period, the organization of the MAC's operating along the Lebanese, Syrian, and Jordanian borders remained substantially the same as before the invasion of Egypt. The Israeli-Egyptian MAC was temporarily placed under UNEF operational control.

The resolution establishing UNEF appointed Major-General E. L. M. Burns, the Chief-of-Staff of UNTSO, as Chief of the Command and authorized him to recruit immediately from UNTSO a limited number of officers, nationals of countries other than the permanent members of the Security Council. The remaining officers and troops would be furnished as a result of negotiations between the Commander and states other than permanent members of the Council.

General Burns had recommended that the force be strong enough so "that it would be in no danger of being thrust aside, pushed out, or ignored as the UN Military Observers had been in Palestine—mainly by the Israelis, but on occasion by the other parties." He believed that the forces

[121] *Ibid.*, pp. 1–3.
[122] *Ibid.*, pp. 1, 29, 3

should be of division size and that contingents should not be less than battalion size.[123]

In March 1957, when the General Assembly adjourned, the total strength of the force was 6,073 with 5,795 in Egypt. Ten countries provided contingents varying in size from 1,272 to 330.[124] As of May 1964, the national contingents were approximately as follows: Indians, 1,900; Canadians, 900; Brazilians, 630; Danes, 560; Norwegians, 500; Yugoslavs, 730. UNEF was equipped with light and automatic weapons, jeeps, armored carriers, and observation and communications equipment. The cost has amounted to approximately $17,250,000 per year, of which $9,000,000 is paid to governments for the extra and extraordinary costs of providing contingents. The United States has contributed approximately 45 percent of the costs. The extra costs vary among contributing states from approximately $20 per month per soldier for Indian troops, to $100 for Brazilian and Canadian troops, to $400 for Yugoslav troops. Major items of expense are allowances, costs of personnel rotation, maintenance of vehicles, rations, and international staff salaries. The individual contingents pay the basic salaries of their members.

Under the regulations,

> The United Nations Emergency Force is a subsidiary organ of the United Nations consisting of the United Nations Command . . . and all military personnel placed under the United Nations Command by Member States. The members of the Force, although remaining in their national service, are, during the period of their assignment to the Force, international personnel under the authority of the United Nations and subject to the instructions of the Commander through the chain of command. The functions of the Force are exclusively international and members of the Force shall discharge these functions and regulate their conduct with the interest of the United Nations only in view.[125]

The Commander has full authority over the force, which flies the UN flag.

The intention of the General Assembly to have a UN force, operating independently of states, and particularly of the great powers, was not completely realized. The evacuation of dependents of UNTSO personnel was largely handled by the U.S. Navy. The transportation of the first UN military observers to Suez was in a British warship. The advance parties of UNEF were transported to the staging area near Naples in U.S. military aircraft on a nonreimbursable basis, and to Egypt in Canadian military transport planes. The heavy equipment was airlifted in Canadian planes. Canada also provided the signal corps and most of the technical services. Logistic support at the outset came from the U.S. Navy.[126] Munitions have

[123] Burns, *op. cit.*, p. 188.
[124] *1956 President's Report*, p. 70.
[125] Lauterpacht, *op. cit.*, p. 37.
[126] Burns, *op. cit.*, pp. 183, 195, 202, 214, 218.

never been a major problem because of the Secretary-General's directive that troops may fire only in self-defense, which includes resisting efforts to prevent the troops' withdrawal from positions.

The UN international radio network, after being expanded to include UNEF stations at Naples and in the Suez, provided adequate communications facilities.[127] Ultimately, UNEF procured its own supplies and, as early as December, established an air transport and reconnaissance unit, using Canadian equipment and personnel. UNEF has its own engineer, shop repair, and medical personnel.[128]

The organizational arrangements point out clearly some of the limitations of an international force. Although the force is "in no way a military force temporarily controlling the territory in which it is stationed" and has no "military functions exceeding those necessary to secure peaceful conditions *on the assumption that the parties to the conflict take all necessary steps for compliance with the recommendations of the General Assembly*,"[129] UNEF, particularly in its early stages, depended on assistance from states.

Performance[130]

The bulk of UNEF is deployed along the demarcation line and international frontier, approximately 145 miles. Along the demarcation line (Gaza Strip) are a series of intervisible observation posts each manned during the day by two men. There are seventy posts in twenty-five miles. Any observation post can obtain additional support from the section headquarters within ten to fifteen minutes, and it is always provided during harvest season or at other times when local inhabitants might be tempted to cross the frontier. At night, the observation posts are withdrawn, and mobile patrols are organized varying in strength from five to seven men.

Along the international frontier, constant control and observation is maintained in only a few troublesome areas. In some places, there are daily patrols. In others, there is aerial reconnaissance. Land patrols are undertaken only two or three times a week. Canadian troops and vehicles patrol the first twenty-eight miles, and Yugoslav vehicles and airplanes patrol the remainder, which is desert.

The Straits of Tiran leading to the Israeli port of Elath are under constant observation from Sharm el Sheikh where forty-three Swedish troops and nine Canadians are stationed. The contingent responsible for observing the Straits has purely peace-observation functions in contrast to the mixture of peace observation and peace-keeping in other sectors.

[127] *Ibid.*, p. 219.
[128] Rosner, *op. cit.*, p. 122.
[129] Lauterpacht, *op. cit.*, pp. 14–15. Italics added.
[130] The best description of the method of operation of UNEF is in Rosner, *op. cit.*, pp. 100–1.

There seems to be general agreement that this method of operation has been highly successful with incidents largely confined to minor violations, no different in degree or type from the problems encountered by domestic police.[131] In the Gaza Strip, especially at crop time, thieves cross the border from the Egyptian side. Occasionally children cross the border either as runaways or for adventure. Few Israelis attempt to cross to Egypt, and these are generally criminals in flight, occasional Orthodox Jewish religious fanatics, or the mad and half mad. There was one Israeli-Arab love match. The individuals are generally apprehended and returned. General Burns points out that, at the outset, he requested assistance from the Egyptian authorities in preventing infiltration and that the latter not only accepted his suggestions but publicized them and took adequate steps to inform the Gaza population.

General Burns' estimate of the success of the operation is that UNEF has worked very well. During the four and a half years after the force was formed, the frontiers were quiet. The General Assembly voted each year to continue the force, and many delegations view its continuation as essential.[132]

The Annual Reports of the Secretary-General to the United Nations[133] and the reports of the U.S. President to the Congress[134] conclude that the force has been generally effective.

While Israel refuses to recognize UNTSO on this border, five to seven UNTSO observers remain, supplementing UNEF. Since the United Arab Republic correctly refused to recognize UNEF as supplementing UNTSO, the channel of communications on border incidents and exchange of prisoners is Israel-UNEF-UNTSO-U.A.R.

As stated above, the Chief-of-Staff, UNTSO, and the MAC's continue to have full responsibility for truce supervision along the other boundaries. The Lebanese boundary has remained almost completely free of incidents. The headquarters of the MAC is in Beirut, with one out-station at sea and one on land. There are five UN observers. The MAC meets once a month and never takes a vote. The situation along the Syrian border during much of the period after 1956 was not propitious for peaceful conditions. In 1958, Syria became a part of the United Arab Republic and did not resume its status as an independent state until 1961. The MAC had not met in regular plenary sessions since 1951 because of Israeli refusal to attend the meetings. However, Israel allowed UNTSO and the Chief-of-Staff to have access to the border regions. Despite these unfavorable circumstances, only six complaints of incidents along the border during the period were serious enough to reach the Security Council.

[131] *Ibid.*, p. 103.

[132] Burns, *op. cit.*, pp. 274, 280.

[133] UN General Assembly, *Official Records*, Thirteenth Session, Supplement No. 1, A/3844, p. 11.

[134] *United States Participation in the United Nations, Report by the President to the Congress for the Year 1959* (Washington: Government Printing Office, 1960), p. 56.

The first case did not involve violence. The second was a complaint by Israel made to the Security Council in December 1958, and a counter-complaint by the U.A.R. The Security Council took no formal action, but the President of the Council pointed out that the incidents could have been dealt with under the armistice agreements and called on the parties to cooperate with UNTSO and the Chief-of-Staff.[135] The third case involved a series of incidents in the demilitarized zone climaxed by an Israeli raid on an Arab village in 1960. In this case, the report of the UN Chief-of-Staff reviewed fully the jurisdictional controversies concerning the authority of the MAC in the demilitarized zones.[136]

The fourth and most important case involved fighting in the Lake Tiberias area on March 16 and 17, 1962. The Secretary-General without any reference to the MAC, which had not been meeting in plenary session for years, attempted to obtain the agreement of the parties to a series of measures: (1) the establishment of an additional observation post in Syria; Syria agreed; (2) a UN patrol boat on Lake Tiberias which is Israeli territory; Israel refused to agree but permitted the establishment of observation posts in Israel, a request which it had refused in 1956; (3) increased visits by UN military observers to the demilitarized zone and defensive areas; both parties agreed.

The Security Council resolution terminating the consideration of this incident endorsed the measures recommended by the Chief-of-Staff for strengthening the Truce Supervision Organization in its task of maintaining and restoring the peace and of detecting and deterring future incidents and called on the Israeli and Syrian authorities to assist the Chief-of-Staff in their early implementation.[137] The resolution also called for observance of the cease-fire and the General Armistice Agreement, and for reactivating the Mixed Armistice Commission. Despite the Security Council resolution, the MAC still does not meet, and the backlog of complaints amounts to 23,500.

This Security Council resolution went far, granting authority to the Chief-of-Staff to take action in advance of incidents and to strengthen the truce-supervision machinery and operations, independent of any agreed decisions by the MAC. It thus remedied the prime defect in the terms of reference for the MAC-UNTSO peace-observation activities. In short, the Chief-of-Staff obtained increased independent powers.

Possibly as a result of this increased authority, when the next serious violence occurred, Israel brought the matter to the Security Council instead of retaliating.[138] Israel also submitted a list of 93 minor incidents

[135] *Ibid., 1958* (Washington: Government Printing Office, 1959), pp. 66–67. Hereafter cited as *1958 President's Report.*
[136] UN Security Council, S/4270, Feb. 23, 1960.
[137] UN Security Council, Resolution adopted at the 1,006th meeting, April 9, 1962, S/5111.
[138] UN Security Council, S/5394, Aug. 21, 1963.

which had occurred since December 1962.[139] Syria made a counter-complaint alleging Israeli shooting but no casualties.[140] A draft resolution criticizing Syria was vetoed by the Soviet Union.[141]

The most recent case considered by the Security Council in November and December 1964 involved a series of incidents in the Tel-El-Qadi area along the armistice demarcation line between Israel and Syria.[142] On October 23, 1964, Israel notified the chairman of the Israel-Syria MAC that it intended to reconstruct a track and parallel drainage ditch on the Israeli side of the armistice demarcation line (ADL) and that an accurate survey by Israel would precede the construction. The chairman reminded the Israeli delegate that UNTSO, in 1963, had surveyed the western part of the track, but the survey had not extended as far as Tel-El-Qadi.[143] When the work on the track got past the surveyed portion of the ADL, the Syrians claimed encroachment on their territories. A series of firings from both sides of the ADL resulted in considerable loss of life and property damage to both parties, particularly to Syria.

The Syrians brought the matter to the attention of the Security Council on November 13, 1964, and supported a resolution introduced by Morocco condemning Israel for the incidents and calling on the parties to participate fully in the meetings of the MAC.[144] A United States and United Kingdom compromise resolution deplored the military action and loss of life and called on the parties to participate fully in the MAC meetings and cooperate in completing the UN survey of the armistice demarcation line.[145] The Soviet Union vetoed the U.S.-U.K. resolution, and the Moroccan resolution failed to receive seven votes.

The headquarters of the Israel-Syria MAC is in Damascus. There are four out-stations in Israeli territory and six in Syrian territory. Sixty-three military observers and observers of at least two nationalities are stationed at each post to avoid charges of favoritism.

Despite the fact that the MAC does not meet, resulting in a growing backlog of incidents, the cease-fire orders are generally effective, since both sides accept UN orders transmitted across the border.

However, the Tel-El-Qadi incidents demonstrate two defects in the UNTSO machinery. First, UNTSO continues to operate on the fallacy that nothing can be done without the consent of the adversaries. Any Israeli encroachments were merely a matter of a few meters.[146] The slight effort required for completion of the UNTSO survey would resolve the

[139] UN Security Council, S/5396, Aug. 22, 1963.
[140] UN Security Council, S/5395, Aug. 21, 1963.
[141] UN Security Council, S/5407, Aug. 29, 1963.
[142] UN Security Council, S/6061, Nov. 24, 1964, p. 1. Hereafter cited as S/6061.
[143] S/6061, pp. 5–6.
[144] UN Security Council, S/6085/Rev. 1, Dec. 5, 1964.
[145] UN Security Council, S/6113, Dec. 17, 1964.
[146] S/6061, p. 8.

issues of fact. This action should not depend on obtaining the consent of the parties.

Second, the Israeli refusal to attend meetings of the MAC has prevented MAC findings of fact that when published would establish to the world which party was at fault.

Political conditions along the Jordanian border were more favorable. The MAC continued to function. Furthermore, after the formation of the U.A.R., the Jordanian Government feared an Egyptian-inspired revolution to absorb Jordan into the U.A.R. and even brought a complaint against the U.A.R. to the attention of the Security Council.[147] This situation furnished added incentive to Jordan to avoid incidents along the Israeli frontier.

The headquarters of the Israel-Jordan MAC is in Jerusalem, and there are six outposts near the line. In addition, there are intermittent patrols along routes set by Jordan. Thirty-five military observers are attached to this MAC.

Jordan, during this period, brought two complaints against Israel but neither involved violent incidents. One concerned an Israeli afforestation in the no-man's land along the road to Jerusalem, and the other an Israeli military parade in Jerusalem.[148]

The former case involved a situation not directly covered in the armistice agreements. It is significant that the Security Council, rather than requesting the parties to agree on a solution, directed the Chief-of-Staff to conduct a survey and called on the parties to cooperate with the Chief-of-Staff and in the MAC in carrying out the recommendations of the Chief-of-Staff.[149] This action represented a limited step in the direction of giving the Chief-of-Staff authority to carry out the armistice agreements independently of the action in the MAC.

The success of UNEF on the Egyptian front probably contributed to the relatively quiet conditions on other fronts. Much of the violence along the Jordanian border prior to November 1956 had been instigated by Egypt from the Gaza Strip. This was no longer possible with UNEF patrolling the border. However, an equally important factor in discouraging violations along other borders may have been the strong stand of the United Nations against violence, reflected not only in the establishment and support of UNEF but in dealing with the few minor incidents brought to the attention of the Security Council during this period.

The proposed actions of the Arab states to divert the resources of the Jordan River before reaching Israeli territory have not yet come before UNTSO or the MAC's. The most significant diversion of waters would be in Lebanon and would therefore be within the jurisdiction of the Israel-Lebanon MAC, which has always functioned effectively.

[147] *1958 President's Report*, p. 79.
[148] UN Security Council, S/4777, April 1, 1961.
[149] *1958 President's Report*, p. 65.

As far back as 1953, the United States and the United Kingdom had proposed that hydraulic engineers be made available to assist in settling the dispute. A revival of such a proposal in the context of consideration of the dispute by the Israel-Lebanon MAC might be timely.

Evaluation

As indicated in the preceding section, the establishment of UNEF not only practically eliminated violent breaches of the armistice on the Israeli-Egyptian front but also resulted in a situation where the truce supervision was vastly improved on the remaining boundaries. In the following section, some main factors which led to the improvement of truce supervision and several factors where the present relatively favorable situation might be improved are discussed.

A Positive International Program. The experience after the Israeli invasion of the Sinai Peninsula shows clearly the beneficial results of positive international action to restore peace. The chief specific action was the establishment of UNEF. However, the willingness of the Security Council and General Assembly to take new positive positions was reflected in their treatment of the relatively few incidents on other boundaries, which were brought to their attention after 1956. It seems certain the international concern for maintaining the armistice, and a willingness to take positive action in connection with violent breaches, influenced all the countries in the area to pursue more peaceful policies. Thus, the long chain of incident, retaliation, and counterretaliation was broken.

Separation of Hostile Forces. Prior to the invasion of Suez, the Chief-of-Staff had attempted to separate the Israeli and Egyptian forces in the more crucial areas by seeking agreement on establishing a series of permanent patrol posts on both sides of the boundaries and even on building a fence. His efforts failed. The United Nations Emergency Force, after completing its preliminary duties of supervising the evacuation of troops from the Suez and the Sinai Peninsula and making arrangements for reopening the Suez Canal to navigation, was deployed along the Egyptian side of the armistice demarcation line and international boundary line separating Israel from Egypt. It succeeded in its sole important duty of preventing infiltration over the line. This success, however, required a force of 5,000 and an annual expenditure of approximately $17,250,000 to patrol a frontier less than 200 miles long, more than half of which ran through a roadless and sparsely settled desert. Furthermore, General Burns recognized that the cooperation of both the Egyptian and Israeli Governments was a major factor in obtaining even this success. The cost and difficulty of this method of truce supervision militates against its use in larger areas where conditions are more complex.

Military Cooperation. The military organization of UNEF disclosed what had already appeared in the operation of the MAC's, that cooperation between the military leaders of the Arabs and of the Israelis is easier than among the civilian leaders. In the period before UNEF, the most effective enforcement always took place when the MAC's were able to delegate the adjustment of incidents to the commanders in the field along both sides of the demarcation line. UNEF had little difficulty in obtaining cooperation from both the Israeli and Egyptian military personnel. This probably arises from the fact that both Arab and Israeli military leaders had gone through parallel military training programs, usually with the British. Their viewpoints on strictly military matters therefore tended to coincide, and this led to understanding in other areas.

International Forces. The Secretary-General, at the time UNEF was established, pointed out three possible procedures for establishing and deploying an international force in the area: (1) call on an individual or state to carry on the venture; (2) establish a United Nations command entrusted to a single state and call on other states to furnish contingents to that command—the pattern used in Korea; (3) establish a United Nations command under the direction of the UN Secretary-General with individual states contributing contingents to that command.

The Secretary-General recommended and the General Assembly adopted the third procedure. The Secretary-General had broad discretion in choosing the countries from which contingents would be accepted. The sole limitation imposed by the Assembly was that no contingents should come from the permanent members of the Security Council. This is, of course, the antithesis of the so-called "Article 43 Forces" envisaged in the United Nations Charter where the permanent members of the Security Council were to furnish substantially all the contingents. Because of the peculiar circumstances of this situation, the Secretary-General did not request contingents from other nations in the area, such as Turkey or Greece. The contingents came mainly from distant countries with a relatively small interest in the political problems of Palestine. It should be noted that when the Secretary-General set up his force in the Congo, he attempted to obtain as many contingents as possible from neighboring states with the greatest interest in the problem of restoring peace in the Congo. It seems clear that both decisions were politically correct and therefore that it is not possible to lay down in advance a definite rule on the states participating in any United Nations force.

As previously pointed out, even though the military involvement of UNEF was minimal—the forces could fire only in self-defense—a completely self-sufficient United Nations operation could not be developed. Fortunately, General Burns, a capable Canadian officer, was in the area as the Chief-of-Staff of UNTSO and therefore could set about immediately to build UNEF. Especially in the early stages, he had to rely on Canadian assistance to organize and supply the force. In some cases, even available Canadian assistance was insufficient. He had to use the assistance, on a nonreimbursable basis, of the United States despite the policy of the General Assembly that UNEF should be independent of great powers. Thus, even where a nucleus already existed for a United Nations force and where its military functions were limited, UNEF depended somewhat on the backstopping of specific states.

Improvisation versus Advance Planning. The Secretary-General made clear that UNEF was being established pursuant to the policy set forth in the "Uniting for Peace" Resolution of the General Assembly. He made full use of the recommendations of the Collective Measures Committee and additional studies which he had made of the specific situation in Palestine. As a result of this advance planning, he notably improved on the improvised setup which prevailed between the armistice and November 1956.

1. Much of the improvisation in the earlier period resulted from the unwillingness of the Security Council in this case to take mandatory action to deal with threats to the peace and breaches of the peace under Chapter VII of the Charter. The alternative was to work out all arrangements through agreement of the parties. The Secretary-General, when UNEF was formed, accepted this alternative, but immediately, when the Egyptians needed UNEF, worked out a detailed agreement with Egypt which permitted the force to operate effectively. The only way the Egyptians could have avoided this agreement would have been to eliminate UNEF altogether, and there was some doubt whether they could do this without the consent of the General Assembly. Thus, through adequate advance planning UNEF avoided one of the situations which had constantly plagued the MAC's, the Chief-of-Staff, and UNTSO.

2. The second organizational defect of the truce-supervision effort in the earlier period was the absence of any established chain of command. The Israelis and occasionally the Arabs had taken the position that all authority stemmed from the MAC's. The Chief-of-Staff and UNTSO were relegated to furnishing personnel and services for the MAC's and acting as liaison to the Security Council. Thus there was no method of reinforcing the MAC's decisions short of calling for a decision of the UN Security Council in New York.

The Secretary-General avoided this weakness by establishing immediately a United Nations Command consisting of the commanding officer reporting to the Secretary-General and an Advisory Committee consisting of representatives of some of the states providing contingents for the force. Thus the Commander of UNEF had a clear line of authority over the operating officers, and could augment the moral force of his decisions through submitting them to the Advisory Committee and to the Secretary-General. In all but the most extraordinary situations, UNEF could act without referring matters to the Security Council or the General Assembly in New York. In fact, the only matters ever referred to a UN organ were the annual reports and the requests for budget.

3. In the arrangements for organizing the force, the Secretary-General and the Commander-in-Chief followed closely the recommendations of the Collective Measures Committee, and it is generally agreed that this resulted in expeditious activation of the force and efficient operation.

Terminal Date of Program. Perhaps the greatest weakness of the UNEF effort was the failure to work out methods for terminating the program and reinstituting the MAC or an equivalent forum providing face-to-face consultation. The reports of the Secretary-General stressed that the force was an emergency force but set no time limit on its duration. Furthermore, the objective of the force went no further than to restore the status quo ante when political tensions were already so great that the armistice had collapsed. It was probably not possible to limit the length of life of UNEF in advance, although the Soviet Union advocated this position. However, it would have been helpful if the program had included a new and thorough effort to reduce the basic tensions behind the collapse of the armistice. This position, however, would have been contrary to the Arab viewpoint which was that Israel had breached the armistice and therefore the United Nations should limit itself to punishing Israel and restoring the status quo ante.

The apparent theory of the Secretary-General was that if the armistice could be maintained, time would improve the basic underlying conditions. This is a questionable theory. It is true that the lapse of time has replaced Ben Gurion with a prime minister and government that seem more cooperative. Lapsed time may also have increased the awareness of the neighbors of Egypt of the imperialist designs of Nasser. However, Nasser's influence in the Arab world today may be even stronger than in 1956. In other respects, lapse of time has done little to change the basic situation. The refugee problem continues with little or no desire either on the part of the Arab states or the refugees themselves to take practical steps for its improvement. Neither Israel nor the Arab states were willing to support the recent unbiased and constructive recommendations of Dr. Johnson to the PCC to ameliorate the situation. Meanwhile, military strength on both sides has increased. Each report of the Secretary-General stresses that the departure of UNEF might result in a vast deterioration of conditions of law and order. While this may be partly a manifestation of Parkinson's law, it is nevertheless probably a correct evaluation. Thus having once established a force of 5,000 with an annual expenditure of some $20,000,000, the United Nations does not know how to disestablish it.

EVALUATION OF THE PALESTINE OPERATION, 1947–1964

The Palestine controversy has continued for seventeen years with no solution in sight. During all that period, the chief political factors have remained relatively constant: Arab-Israeli hostility and intransigence, and the constant irritant of the Arab refugees. The relationships among the Arab states have varied, as have the relationships of the Arab states and, to a lesser extent, Israel to the great powers.

The institutional and organizational arrangements have changed so greatly that it is difficult to find generalizations on peace observation that carry through the entire operation. Nevertheless, some deductions may be drawn from this experience.

The Palestine situation is the prime example of the difficulty involved in restraining violence when prospects of a political settlement are dim or nonexistent. The effectiveness of the relatively simple machinery of UN peace observation depends primarily on the moral prestige of the United Nations. The Palestine experience in 1948 showed that a UN peace-observation mission numbering less than 1,000 could greatly reduce violence in the area, and that after the armistice, a far smaller peace-observation group working with both sides could be reasonably effective. However, the prestige of a UN mission erodes as time passes with no progress toward a political settlement. Even after considerable erosion of prestige, the peace-observation machinery continues to restrain if not eliminate violence and plays a fundamental role in ordering cease-fires and assisting in restoring some semblance of an orderly border after breaches of the peace.

The vastly more complex and expensive peace-keeping machinery of UNEF was able to restore order after 1956. The very size of the peace-keeping force makes it less dependent on prestige in its task of maintaining order. However, the question arises whether its authority also will not erode over a period of years. Furthermore, the United Nations may not give financial support to such extensive and costly machinery for an indefinite length of time, or extend a similar operation to the other borders of Palestine.

There is no simple answer to the basic problem of restraining violence when the controversy causing the violence seems unsolvable. However, in at least three respects, the efforts to solve the Palestine problem have settled into modalities which have seemed to aggravate rather than moderate the long-range negotiating atmosphere: (1) Some of the boundaries are artificial and ill-suited for a peaceful area. (2) The terms of reference of the MAC's, the Chief-of-Staff, and UNTSO and the relationship among them are vague and inadequate. (3) The mediation function, entrusted to a Western-oriented group located in New York, is practically dormant. Reviving the group through broadening its international representation and increasing its activities might conceivably produce some success.

For many years there has scarcely been a discussion of minor boundary adjustments or of changing the PCC. Recently, the Security Council has moved slightly in the direction of strengthening the authority of the Chief-of-Staff. The only major change since the 1949 armistice has been the establishment of UNEF.

The Palestine operations, however, have been of value to the United Nations in guiding its course on other problems involving both peace observation and peace-keeping. For example: (1) UNTSO furnished the initial staff for UN headquarters, for UNEF, the United Nations Operation in the Congo, and the United Nations Yemen Observation Mission; (2) the UNTSO operations have furnished the pattern for logistic arrangements used in other areas; (3) the line of authority from the Security Council to military observers, which the Secretary-General advocated but never obtained for UNTSO, became the pattern for UN missions in other areas and also for UNEF.

Palestine and Kashmir are the two areas in which it became apparent at an early stage that the peace observation would need to continue indefinitely. This situation raises both the organizational problems of maintaining a lengthy operation and the political and bureaucratic problems of how to terminate the operations. Palestine is the extreme case of an operation anchored at dead center. The fear of upsetting the precarious balances which prevent open warfare results in an inertia, where efforts for progress are snuffed out because of the possiblity of retrogression. This is unfortunate since good organizational change may be easier to obtain than substantive adjustments and might contribute materially to relaxation of tensions in the area.

3

THE PROBLEMS RELATING TO INDONESIAN INDEPENDENCE[1]

In July 1945, the Anglo-American Chiefs-of-Staff gave military jurisdiction over Indonesia to the South East Asia Command (SEAC) under the leadership of Admiral Lord Louis Mountbatten. After the surrender, the SEAC was to repatriate the Japanese forces, numbering 283,000; liberate the 100,000 allied prisoners of war; and maintain order until the territories could be restored to their respective authorities.[2] However, the first SEAC troops, numbering only 1000, did not land in Java until September 29, and did not occupy the key Java cities until October and November.

[1] This study deals with UN peace observation in Indonesia in the period from July 31, 1947, through April 3, 1951. It considers other aspects of the United Nations operations only to the extent necessary for an understanding of the peace-observation activities.

[2] Alastair M. Taylor, *Indonesian Independence and the United Nations* (Ithaca: Cornell University Press, 1960), p. 6.

On August 15, 1945, when Japan surrendered, Japanese forces occupied all of Indonesia. Two days later, the two leaders of the independence movement, Sukarno and Hatta, proclaimed the independence of Indonesia and commenced steps to set up a government and a national army. Between August and November, the leaders of the Republic of Indonesia had the opportunity to consolidate their position in Java and Sumatra (though not in the other islands) with the result that, even after the landing of SEAC troops, they continued to control most of these islands except for enclaves surrounding the chief cities.

During the war, the Dutch queen had called for the postwar reconstruction of Indonesia "on the solid foundation of complete partnership" with the Netherlands.[3] At the end of the war, the Dutch were initially unwilling to negotiate with Sukarno whom they regarded as a Japanese agent and collaborator. By November, however, with British urging, the Netherland's representative, Van Mook, commenced negotiations with Sukarno's Prime Minister, Sjahrir, the most moderate of the leaders of the Indonesian Republic.

The negotiations had not made much progress by January 21, 1946, when the Ukrainian Soviet Socialist Republic complained in the Security Council that the British were using their troops and also Japanese troops to wage war against the Indonesian people.[4] It seems clear that this Soviet tactic had little to do with the situation in Indonesia, but merely represented a Soviet countermove to the Iranian complaint against the presence of Soviet troops in northern Iran. The Ukrainian resolution to establish a Commission of Inquiry received support only from the Soviet bloc. After it was defeated, the President of the Security Council declared the matter closed.[5] The sole result of the Security Council discussion was that the Soviet Union emerged as a champion of Asian nationalism.

After much stormy negotiation between the Netherlands and the Republic of Indonesia, an agreement was initialed on November 15, 1946, known as the Linggadjati Agreement. The agreement called not only for a truce but for "the rapid formation of a sovereign democratic State on a federal basis to be called the United States of Indonesia"[6] (U.S.I.), composed of the Republic of Indonesia, Borneo, and the Great East. The agreement was formally signed on March 25, 1947, even though at that time both the Netherlands and the Republic of Indonesia had conditioned their approval on conflicting interpretations.

---

[3] This was a policy statement broadcast from London on Dec. 6, 1942.

[4] UN Security Council, *Official Records*, First Year, First Series, Supplement No. 1, Annex 4. Letter from Mr. D. Manuilsky, Head of the Delegation of the Ukrainian SSR to Mr. J. N. O. Makin, President of the Security Council.

[5] UN Security Council, *Official Records*, First Year, First Series, 18th meeting, Feb. 13, 1946, pp. 256–63.

[6] For the text of the Linggadjati Agreement see: *Documents on International Affairs, 1947–48* (London: Oxford University Press, 1952), pp. 739–42.

The controversy and military action on both sides which led to the United Nations establishing "peace observation" and "good offices" machinery arose from the attempted implementation of the Linggadjati Agreement. The United Nations was not concerned with establishing a goal of Indonesian independence, since this had already been decided at Linggadjati. It was concerned only with the transition from the existing situation to independence and the maintenance of peace during that transition period.

The Security Council met again on July 31, 1947, to consider the Indonesian problem. Dutch forces had launched a "police action" in Java and Sumatra following the breakdown of negotiations to implement the Linggadjati Agreement. On August 25, 1947, the Council called on its members with career consuls in Batavia (Djakarta) to report on the Indonesian situation and established a Good Offices Committee to assist the parties in working out a cease-fire.[7] On November 1, the Council again called for a cease-fire and requested the Good Offices Committee to assist the parties in bringing this about.[8] At the same time, the Council requested the Consular Commission to put its military observers at the disposal of the Good Offices Committee. The Security Council retained jurisdiction over the problem.

Negotiations continued between the parties assisted by the Good Offices Committee and resulted in a truce agreement, the "Renville Agreement," on January 19, 1948.[9] However, the relations between the Netherlands and the Republic began to deteriorate in the summer of 1948, culminating in a second Dutch "police action" on December 19, 1948.

The matter was immediately brought to the attention of the Security Council.[10] On January 28, 1949, the Security Council called for the restoration of the Republican government to Djogjakarta and speedy implementation of the provisions of the Renville Agreement calling for the establishment of an independent United States of Indonesia.[11] It reconstituted the Good Offices Committee as the United Nations Commission for Indonesia (UNCI). The UNCI played an active role in the successful negotiations leading to the "Round Table Agreements" for the formation of the U.S.I. on November 21, 1949, and transfer of sovereignty to the

[7] UN Security Council, Resolutions adopted at the 194th meeting, Aug. 25, 1947, S/525, Pts. I and II. Hereafter cited as S/525.

[8] UN Security Council, Resolution adopted at the 219th meeting, Nov. 1, 1947, S/594. Hereafter cited as S/594.

[9] Signed on board the U.S. naval vessel *Renville*. For text see: UN Security Council, *Official Records*, Third Year, Special Supplement No. 1, App. XI.

[10] UN Security Council, Resolution adopted at the 392nd meeting, Dec. 24, 1948, S/1150. Hereafter cited as S/1150.

[11] UN Security Council, Resolution adopted at the 406th meeting, Jan. 28, 1949, S/1234. Hereafter cited as S/1234.

U.S.I. on December 27, 1949.[12] After that date, the commission offered its assistance in disturbances in the South Moluccas, but in the main was inactive. On April 3, 1951, it reported to the Security Council that there were no items left on its agenda and adjourned *sine die*.[13] Thus, the United Nations peace-observation functions, which were closely related to other functions such as "good offices," "mediation," and "arbitration" began on August 25, 1947, and in the main ended on December 27, 1949.

In general, the United Nations peace-observation functions were ancillary to the main objective of obtaining an independent United States of Indonesia. The terms of reference, and to a much greater degree the tasks of peace observation, varied to conform to the changing requirements of the "good offices," "mediation," and "arbitration" functions intended to lead to an independent United States of Indonesia. In the usual pattern of peace observation, the observers have precise functions that continue with little change for long periods of time (for example, in Kashmir). Contrary to this usual pattern, the tasks of the peace observers in Indonesia and also their instructions were constantly changing. This leads to a complex narrative in sections dealing with terms of reference and performance.

TERMS OF REFERENCE

The terms of reference of the United Nations machinery with peace-observation functions were, indeed, complex and in a continual state of flux, because of the numerous directives issued by the Security Council. These directives should be considered in detail, because the Netherlands used them to create jurisdictional confusion, which was to hinder peace observation activities, and because they account for the frequent changes in the character of the peace-observation activities.

On August 1, 1947, the Security Council called on the parties to cease hostilities, to settle their disputes by arbitration or other peaceful means, and to keep the Security Council informed.[14] Security Council resolutions of August 25, 1947, set forth the bases for two groups with peace-observation tasks, the Consular Commission and the Good Offices Committee (GOC).

THE CONSULAR COMMISSION AND THE GOOD OFFICES COMMITTEE, AUGUST 1947–DECEMBER 1948

In the first resolution of August 25, the Security Council noted that "the Netherlands Government intends immediately to request the career consuls stationed in Batavia jointly to report on the present situation in

---

[12] For the text of the Round Table Agreements see: UN Security Council, *Official Records*, Fourth Year, Special Supplement No. 6, Apps., S/1417/Add. 1.

[13] UN Security Council, *Official Records*, Sixth Year, Special Supplement No. 1, S/2087, p. 29. Hereafter cited as S/2087.

[14] UN Security Council, Resolution adopted at the 173rd meeting, Aug. 1, 1947, S/459.

the Republic of Indonesia." The Council requested members with career consuls in Batavia to report to the Security Council on the situation in Indonesia, such as the observance of the cease-fire orders and the conditions prevailing in areas under military occupation or from which armed forces in occupation might be withdrawn by agreement between the parties. The Council requested the parties to grant to the Consular Commission "all facilities necessary for the effective fulfillment of their mission."[15]

The Consular Commission reported to the Security Council during September and October that their cease-fire order was not fully effective and that neither side was attempting to reach agreement.[16] Thus, the commission fulfilled its original mission.

On November 1, 1947, after having discussed the Commission reports, the Security Council requested it to make its services available to the GOC.[17]

At this time, the GOC was just beginning to function and the Consular Commission, having carried out its original mission, was given the new mission of being the eyes and ears of the Good Offices Committee. Thus, the Commission's jurisdiction after November 1, 1947, was limited to the jurisdiction of the GOC.

In the second resolution of August 25, the Security Council established the Good Offices Committee, "consisting of three members of the Council, each party selecting one, and the third to be designated by the two so selected."[18] The states on the committee, "if the parties so request to assist in the settlement of the dispute," were Australia (chosen by the Republic of Indonesia), Belgium (chosen by the Netherlands), and the United States. The Security Council resolution of October 3 provided that the Secretary-General "act as convener of the Committee of Three and arrange for the organization of its work" and that "the Committee of Three . . . proceed to exercise its functions with the utmost dispatch."[19]

Shortly after the GOC arrived at Batavia, the Security Council, on November 1, 1947, (1) called on the parties to consult either directly or through the Committee of Good Offices to give effect to the cease-fire resolution, (2) requested the GOC "to assist the parties in reaching agreement on an arrangement which will ensure the observance of the cease-fire resolution," and (3) requested the commission to place its military observers at the disposal of the GOC. The Security Council in addition interpreted the term "cease-fire" as used in the Council resolution of August 1.[20]

[15] S/525, Pt. I.

[16] UN Security Council, S/573 (mimeo.), Sept. 24, 1947; S/581 (mimeo.), Oct. 11, 1947; and S/586 which appears in *Official Records*, Second Year, Special Supplement No. 4. Hereafter cited as S/586.

[17] S/594.

[18] S/525, Pt. II.

[19] UN Security Council, Resolution adopted at the 207th meeting, Oct. 3, 1947, S/574.

[20] S/594.

The jurisdiction of the Committee of Good Offices was enlarged on February 28, 1948, as a result of Security Council directives "to pay particular attention to the political developments in Western Java and Madura and to report to the Council thereon."[21] Also, on July 6, 1948, the Security Council resolved that the President of the Council cable the Good Offices Committee for an early report on "restrictions on the domestic and international trade of Indonesia, and the reasons for the delay" in implementing Article 6 of the Truce Agreement.[22]

On July 29, 1948, the Security Council called on the parties with the assistance of the GOC to observe "both the military and economic articles of the Renville Truce Agreement and to implement . . . the Twelve Renville Political Principles and the Six Additional Principles.[23] There were no further Security Council directives until December 28, 1948.

In summary, during the period from August 25, 1947, to December 28, 1948, under the terms of reference of the Consular Commission and the GOC, the peace-observation activities in Indonesia consisted of: (1) A series of reports by the Consular Commission direct to the Security Council, the final one being dated October 14, 1947, on the observance of the cease-fire orders and the conditions prevailing in areas under military occupation. (2) Services made available by the Consular Commission and its military observers after November 1, 1947, to assist the Good Offices Committee in discharging its duties: of ensuring the observance of the cease-fire including the agreement of each party not to extend its control over territory not occupied by it on August 1, 1947; of observing the political developments in Western Java and Madura; of determining the reasons for delay in implementing the agreements for self-determination by the Indonesian people and the political principles contained in the Renville Truce Agreement.

THE CONSULAR COMMISSION AND UNCI,
DECEMBER 1948–DECEMBER 1949

After the second Dutch "police action," during which the Dutch captured Djogjakarta and imprisoned Sukarno, Hatta, and other Indonesian political leaders, the Security Council ordered a cease-fire and the immediate release of the political prisoners.[24] The Council also requested the Consular Commission, on December 28, to report to the Security Council on the situation in Indonesia, covering the observance of the cease-fire orders and the conditions prevailing in areas under military occupation or

[21] UN Security Council, Resolution adopted at the 259th meeting, Feb. 28, 1948, S/689.

[22] UN Security Council, Resolution adopted at the 329th meeting, July 6, 1948.

[23] UN Security Council, Resolution adopted at the 342nd meeting, July 29, 1948, S/931.

[24] S/1150.

from which armed forces in occupation might be withdrawn.[25] Under this directive, the Consular Commission reported directly to the Security Council, once again raising its jurisdictional relationship to the Good Offices Committee.

The Security Council transferred to UNCI all the functions of the GOC and assigned to it the additional function of assisting the parties in implementing the December 24 resolution. The resolution required:[26] discontinuance of military operations by the Netherlands and cessation of guerrilla warfare by the Republic of Indonesia; release of political prisoners by the Dutch and furnishing facilities by the Dutch to the Republic of Indonesia "for communication and consultation with all persons in Indonesia"; holding elections which UNCI would observe; restoration of the civil administration of the Government of the Republic of Indonesia; agreed arrangements for temporary retention of some Netherlands forces to assist in the maintenance of law and order.

All of these functions related directly to peace observation. They were far less important than the detailed provisions of the resolution relating to negotiations between the Dutch and the Indonesians for the establishment of the United States of Indonesia. These latter provisions, which were not directly related to peace observation, vastly increased the role of the UNCI in the negotiations. Though compulsory arbitration is perhaps too strong a description for this new role as stated in the Security Council resolution, in effect the UNCI decisions had to be accepted because of the dire international consequences if they were rejected.

The Consular Commission was requested to provide military observers and other staff and facilities to UNCI to enable it "to carry out its duties under the Council's resolutions of December 24, 1948 and December 28, 1948 as well as under the present resolution and shall temporarily suspend other activities."[27] Thus, for a very short time, the Consular Commission was given the task of reporting directly to the Security Council on the situation in Indonesia. After January 28, 1949, the UNCI had greatly expanded functions requiring peace observation, which would continue to be carried on by the Consular Commission on behalf of the UNCI.[28]

ORGANIZATION

The Good Offices Committee and the Consular Commission were established simultaneously on August 25, 1947. The terms of reference of

[25] UN Security Council, Resolution adopted at the 394th meeting, Dec. 28, 1948, S/1165.

[26] S/1234.

[27] S/1234.

[28] The expanded functions of the UNCI, however, were in the political field. "In the military sphere," according to Taylor, "its apparatus . . . functioned continuously and effectively from the autumn of 1947 until the terminal date." *Op. cit.*, p. 40.

the GOC never established whether its members were acting as individuals, as representatives of their governments, or as agents of the Security Council.[29] The secretariat, of course, reported to the Security Council.

The Consular Commission, which was responsible for peace observation consisted of the six Consul Generals in Batavia (China, France, and the United Kingdom in addition to the Consul Generals of the three members of the Good Offices Committee). At its first meeting, the staff consisted of two military attachés, a secretary, and a press officer.[30] Each member of the Consular Commission requested his government to furnish military observers, and by the end of September, twenty-five additional military observers had been assigned to the commission (Australia 4, Belgium 2, China 4, France 3, United Kingdom 4, United States 8).[31]

In carrying out its first function of reporting to the Security Council on the situation in Indonesia and observance of the cease-fire, the commission made seven extensive field trips in September 1947. Teams of two participated in each of these trips except the field trip to Republican headquarters in Djogjakarta where four observers participated. In addition, the military observers made numerous shorter trips.[32] As has been noted, the Consular Commission was merely reporting on the observation of the cease-fire at this time, and had no duties in connection with the implementation of the cease-fire.

Between September 1947 and January 1948 the Good Offices Committee devoted itself largely to working out the terms of a truce. By January 1948, when the Consular Commission's military observers were required to supervise the implementation of the Renville Agreement, their number had dropped to fifteen. The GOC requested additional officers.[33]

After the Renville Truce Agreement, the GOC created four subcommittees to supervise its implementation. The security subcommittee dealt with all the problems related to peace observation.[34] It established a pool of military assistants under the direction of a Military Executive Board (MEX) composed of the senior military assistants (senior observer officers) of the members of the GOC, acting as a body and without regard to rank. The senior military assistants of China, France, and the United Kingdom (which were not members of the GOC) attended the meetings of the MEX and the security subcommittee as observers. However, directives to observers from countries other than the three represented on the GOC were subject to the approval of the Consul General concerned "since an oath of

[29] *Ibid.*, p. 419.

[30] S/586, p. 1.

[31] S/586, p. 1.

[32] S/586, p. 3.

[33] Taylor, *op. cit.*, p. 424.

[34] UN Security Council, *Official Records*, Third Year, Supplement for June 1948, S/787, p. 44. Hereafter cited as S/787.

allegiance taken by these officers precludes their accepting orders from any but military and civilian authorities of their own country."[35]

The number of military observers during the first quarter of 1948 reached a peak of fifty-five (Australia 15, Belgium 4, United States 15, China 5, France 6, United Kingdom 10). On April 30, there were forty-seven.[36]

During this period of rapid implementation of the truce, until June 1948, military observers were mainly in contact with the local commanders on both sides, who with the help of the military observers reached agreement on the specific steps to implement the truce.[37] Procedures, which will be discussed in the section on performance, were set up to deal with violations. The observers were mainly deployed in nine teams along the "status quo" line between the Dutch and Indonesians.

Shortly before the second Dutch "police action" in December 1948, the Dutch required most of the observers to return to Batavia.[38] However, a part of the Good Offices Committee, along with a number of military observers, were in the Republican areas when the second Dutch "police action" commenced.[39] The military observers returned to the field on January 7, 1949, and, during the next two weeks, gathered information which led to two Interim Reports[40] and a more definitive report analyzing the military situation.[41] During the early part of 1949, however, the Netherlands did not permit the military observers to observe areas on the Dutch side of the former "status quo" line, on the ground that this would be "observation of internal security" which was beyond the jurisdiction of the UNCI.[42] Not until May 27 did the Dutch permit observation behind the Dutch lines.

With the completion of the agreement for restoration of Djogjakarta to the Indonesian Republic in June 1949, the functions and the organization of the military observers again changed. Six teams of military observers took positions between the Netherlands and Republican forces during the period of withdrawal.[43]

[35] S/787, p. 57.

[36] S/787.

[37] S/787, p. 58.

[38] UN Security Council, *Official Records*, Fourth Year, Supplement for January 1949, S/1189, p. 6. Hereafter cited as S/1189.

[39] UN Security Council, *Official Records*, Third Year, Supplement for December 1948, S/1129/Add. 1, p. 224. Hereafter cited as S/1129/Add. 1.

[40] UN Security Council, *Official Records*, Fourth Year, Supplement for January 1949, S/1212 and S/1213. Hereafter cited as S/1212 or S/1213.

[41] UN Security Council, *Official Records*, Fourth Year, Supplement for January 1949, S/1223. Hereafter cited as S/1223.

[42] UN Security Council, *Official Records*, Fourth Year, Supplement for March 1949, S/1270, p. 18. Hereafter cited as S/1270.

[43] UN Security Council, *Official Records*, Fourth Year, Special Supplement No. 5, S/1373, p. 13. Hereafter cited as S/1373.

The final phase of peace-observation activities commenced with the adoption of three important documents in August 1949: (1) the Cease-Hostilities Order, (2) the Joint Proclamation, and (3) the Regulations Governing the Implementation of the Agreement to Cease Hostilities. The UNCI was given responsibilities in implementing these agreements, including the function of serving on the Central Joint Board and local joint committees to work out detailed arrangements at the local government level. Four such committees were established in Sumatra and nine in Java, all of them including military observers.[44]

The final major duty of peace observation (as specified in the Round Table Agreements) was to observe the demobilization and repatriation of Netherlands troops, and the absorption of some of those of Indonesian origin into the Indonesian armed forces. Seventeen assembly areas were set up near ports in Sumatra, Java, Madura, Riouw, Bangka, and Billiton, and mobile observer teams were located where the territorial commands were established. These teams could go anywhere where observation was required. As the assembly areas closed down, the military observers were withdrawn, and the number of observers reduced.[45]

By October 1950, most of the Netherlands troops had been demobilized or evacuated. When the Indonesian Government declined the offer of the UNCI to send observers to the South Moluccas to assist in obtaining a peaceful settlement of the revolt in that area, it became apparent that the need for United Nations military observers would soon end.[46]

The UNCI final report (April 3, 1951) states that all the military problems by that time had been solved.[47] On April 13, 1951, only five military observers remained, and they left Indonesia shortly thereafter.[48]

The arrangements for transportation, communication, and supplies were primitive. This was the first United Nations effort directed toward mediation and conciliation, and no United Nations machinery had been developed.[49] The use of a Consular Commission for peace observation stemmed partly from the fact that in this way it would be possible to avoid Soviet membership on the commission. However, an additional reason was that the consulates alone were able to furnish immediately transportation and communication facilities and supplies.

The Consular Commission continued to use consular facilities, as did the GOC, even after the initial operations since no United Nations lines

[44] UN Security Council, *Official Records*, Fifth Year, Special Supplement No. 1, S/1449, App. I, p. 20. Hereafter cited as S/1449.

[45] UN Security Council, *Official Records*, Sixth Year, Special Supplement No. 1, S/2087, pp. 4–5. Hereafter cited as S/2087.

[46] S/2087, pp. 26–27.

[47] S/2087, p. 29.

[48] Taylor, *op. cit.*, p. 424.

[49] Goodrich and Simons, *op. cit.*, p. 293.

of communication were established. Prior to the Renville Agreement, communication facilities for the observers in the field consisted of American portable radios and receivers, the main receiver set being in the American Consulate at Batavia. After the agreement was concluded, the Renville remained indefinitely in the Djakarta harbor. This naval communications ship became the principal line of communications for United Nations operations in Indonesia both for broadcasting and receiving.

In the early stages, both the Dutch and the Indonesians cooperated fully with the military observers in logistic arrangements, since neither party expected the other to live up to its obligations unless neutral observers were present.[50]

Theoretically, after the Renville Agreement, the observers were to spend half of their time in Dutch-controlled territory and the other half in Indonesian-controlled territory. However, the situation being very difficult in Indonesian-controlled territory, only token appearances were made, and the greater part of the information was collected from a hilltop post, Kaliurang, in the Residency of Djogjakarta.

Generally, the Netherlands furnished transportation in Netherlands-controlled territory and the Indonesians in Indonesian-controlled territory. However, the Indonesians lacked equipment of all kinds, and there was no regular United Nations channel for providing it. Probably the first, and a strange, request for United Nations equipment was a telegram from the chairman of the GOC to the President of the United Nations Security Council on June 28, 1948, asking for eighteen jeeps and spare parts.[51]

During the period of the second "police action," communications deteriorated. When the Netherlands Army seized Djogjakarta in December 1948, communications with Indonesian-held territory were uncertain. During this crucial period, two members of the GOC and a number of observers and members of the United Nations secretariat were at Kaliurang, but Ambassador H. Merle Cochran in Djakarta reported that he had not been able to communicate with them and that his only military information had been furnished by the Dutch.[52] Once the Netherlands seemed to be gaining the upper hand, they restricted the movement of the military observers despite Indonesian protests.[53]

After the second Dutch "police action" and the consequent increase in tensions, the personnel in both the UNCI and the Consular Commission as a matter of protection found it desirable to stress their connection with the United Nations. At this time, the Military Executive Board decided that

[50] S/586, p. 3.

[51] UN Security Council, *Official Records*, Third Year, Supplement for July 1948, S/929, p. 124.

[52] UN Security Council, *Official Records*, Third Year, Supplement for December 1948, S/1138, p. 287. Hereafter cited as S/1138.

[53] S/1189, p. 2.

vehicles should fly the United Nations flag and be painted blue and white, personnel should wear United Nations armbands, and in certain circumstances should be armed.[54] The board also prepared a United Nations manual for the observers, known as the "Netherlands-Indonesian Manual for the Implementatation of the Cessation of Hostilities."[55] This, however, came late, inasmuch as many of the important functions of peace observation had already been completed.

After the Round Table Agreements in November 1949, the United Nations machinery once again enjoyed the cooperation of both parties in regard to logistics. In addition to the public mail and wire services, the Central Joint Board, the local committees, and the UNCI military observers had free access to the radio signal services of the Netherlands Army as well as its mail bag services.[56]

In mid-1950, after independence and having gained the upper hand, the Indonesians declined to permit the military observers access to the South Moluccas, despite Dutch protests.[57]

During the period of the Good Offices Committee (1947–1948), the United Nations bore little of the cost for its peace-observation machinery in Indonesia. Although there was provision in the budget for special missions, the expenditures for the individual special committees and commissions existing at that time were not listed separately.

The military observers were supplied through the Consular Commission. Therefore, Australia, Belgium, the United States, China, France, and Great Britain were responsible for paying their respective observers. These expenditures were not isolated in the various government budgets.

The Dutch covered the majority of expenses incurred by the Good Offices Committee: their quarters at the Hotel des Indes in Djakarta, meals, and transportation. Thus, during this initial period United Nations headquarters was involved with only the expenses of the small United Nations secretariat which accompanied the GOC.

The Security Council resolution of January 28, 1949, requested the Consular Commission to facilitate the work of the UNCI by providing military observers. The Secretary-General was also requested to make available staff, funds, and other facilities "required by the Commission for the discharge of its functions."[58]

The United Nations financial reports for 1949–1951 indicate that, with the inception of the UNCI, the peace-observation machinery in Indonesia

[54] S/1373, pp. 28–29.
[55] S/1373, App. VIII, Pt. B.
[56] S/1449, p. 13.
[57] UN Security Council, *Official Records*, Fifth Year, Supplement for September through December 1950, S/1842, p. 79. Hereafter cited as S/1842.
[58] S/1234.

was financed, on the whole, by UN headquarters. The figures are as follows:[59]

	1949	1950	1951
Travel of representatives	34,000	41,782	—
Temporary assistance	65,000	53,767	28,857
Travel and subsistence of staff and observers	128,187	191,096	39,873 [60]
Local transportation	3,763	11,908	—
Motor vehicles purchased	12,700	—	—
Communication services	8,979	3,314	1,225
Insurance	19,385	11,085	—
Rental and maintenance of permanent equipment	—	58	—
Other	11,720	6,246	4,298
Total	$283,813	319,256	74,253

The figures indicate the relative activity of the peace-observation machinery. The 1950 figure reflects the increase in the number of observers from forty to sixty-three[61] made in the latter part of 1949. This was the highest number reached during the UN experience in Indonesia. The task of observing demobilization and repatriation of Dutch forces also occurred in 1950.

PERFORMANCE

During the three and one half years of operations of the GOC, the UNCI, and the Consular Commission, as pointed out, the peace-observation function encountered periods of intense activity and of relative quiet. The specific functions of the military observers varied considerably. This variation does not mean that the problems in maintaining a truce or cease-fire changed constantly, but rather that the group entrusted with maintaining the truce never sought to fulfill completely this function. Both the GOC and the UNCI were looking primarily toward a permanent solution through the establishment of the Republic of Indonesia. Truce supervision and peace observation in general were confined to specific activities necessary for the progress of the mediation efforts. Therefore in describing the performance of the peace-observation and truce-supervision machinery, it

[59] UN General Assembly, *Official Records*, Fifth Session, Supplement No. 6, A/1253; Sixth Session, Supplement No. 6, A/1800; and Seventh Session, Supplement No. 6, A/1223.
[60] This figure represents "Travel and Transport."
[61] Taylor, *op. cit.*, p. 424.

is important to stress both what was done and what was not done. Furthermore, any meaningful analysis of the performance requires viewing the specific activities in the perspective of the most important circumstances conditioning them. Therefore, before discussing the chief efforts related to peace observation, the favorable and unfavorable aspects of the situation in which the United Nations effort took place will be indicated.

Favorable Aspects

The United Nations mediation efforts in Indonesia during its most important phases did not constitute a "cold war" issue. Of the initial mediation group Indonesia chose Australia, the Netherlands chose Belgium, and Belgium and Australia chose the United States. The United States initially supported a resolution that would have established a truce-supervision observation group (in contrast to a mediation group) consisting of all the members of the Security Council. The resolution to establish this group was unwittingly vetoed by the French who voted against it in the belief that it would not obtain seven votes.

The substitute group consisted of the representatives of the states with permanent consular representatives in Batavia (Djakarta). In addition to the three members of the mediating group, the states with permanent consular representatives were China, the United Kingdom, and France. This group excluded the Soviet Union which protested vigorously; but it had the advantage of making available to the commission the facilities of the consulates. In view of the fantastic material shortages and confusion in postwar Indonesia, it is difficult to see how the commission could have operated except through the use of the consular facilities.

The Soviet Union did not make the Indonesian question into a cold-war issue until 1950. This apparently was a delayed reaction to the suppression by the Indonesian Republic of an attempted Communist revolution in 1948. The only effect of this belated Soviet stand was to prevent a Security Council resolution congratulating the United Nations Commission for Indonesia on obtaining agreement between the Dutch and the Indonesians for the establishment of a free and sovereign Indonesia. The implementation of the agreement did not depend on Security Council approval. At all earlier stages, the parties, as well as the United Nations agencies operating in Indonesia, could reasonably anticipate that communications to the Security Council would be considered, and where necessary the Security Council would act.

In general, the attitude of both parties toward the United Nations mediation and truce-supervision groups was correct if not always cooperative. The Good Offices Committee in early reports pointed out that the Dutch had no confidence that the Indonesians could fulfill their agreements in the absence of a neutral observer, and the Indonesians had a similar view of the Dutch. Therefore, both parties welcomed neutral observers.

Until the last six months of the peace observation, the Indonesians demonstrated the unsatisfactory conditions prevailing in the area. This was to their advantage since the Netherlands defense of its "police actions" depended on its claim to have pacified the country. The Dutch, while not welcoming them, in the main permitted the observation teams to go wherever they wished and furnished them with transportation, means of communication, and accommodations in Djakarta.

An exception took place during the month preceding the second Dutch "police action." At this time, the Dutch attempted to conceal their intentions from the military observers. After the transfer of sovereignty from the Netherlands to the Republic of Indonesia, the Indonesians became less cooperative and declined to permit the military observers to go to the South Moluccas where a rebellion was in progress against the Republic of Indonesia. Despite these exceptions, the United Nations observers met with relatively few man-made obstacles to their observation.

Another aspect favoring the United Nations efforts resulted from the fact that prior to the establishment of any United Nations machinery, the Netherlands and the Republic of Indonesia had signed the Linggadjati Agreement which outlined, to be sure in ambiguous terms, the ultimate objective of a free and sovereign United States of Indonesia with some relation to the Netherlands. Since the ultimate objective was agreed upon, the mediators could concentrate on the narrower problem of methods of achieving the objective. This factor created an atmosphere that had a great effect on the truce-supervision and peace-observation efforts. The emergence of an independent and sovereign Indonesia would automatically solve the problems of truce supervision and peace observation. Therefore, the emphasis was placed less on maintaining the truce and remedying violations than on establishing an atmosphere that would permit the mediation efforts to go forward. In other words, mediation was the prime objective. Thus, the Consular Commission concentrated on reporting to the Security Council the conditions in Indonesia and on certain specific tasks that would facilitate first a truce and then the establishment of a free and sovereign Indonesia, rather than on the more usual tasks associated with truce supervision and peace observation. As pointed out, the small number of military observers, together with the inadequacy of accommodations in the regions controlled by Indonesia, prevented observers from acting in any other manner.

The high quality of the personnel favored both mediation and peace-observation efforts. The first United States member of the GOC, Chancellor Graham of the University of North Carolina, was outstanding and effective, and the same can be said of his Australian and Belgian colleagues. The Indonesians at first believed that his successor, Ambassador Coert DuBois, an experienced United States Foreign Service Officer, had a pro-Dutch bias, but within six months they had the highest regard for him. DuBois' successor, who served until the completion of the agreements for the establishment of a free and sovereign Indonesia, was Ambassador Merle Cochran, an outstanding United States diplomat, who at one time was revered in Djakarta, though certainly not in The Hague. [62] The high calibre of the principals was reflected in their subordinate staff, both military and political. Graham, DuBois, and Cochran—the chairmen of the Good Offices Committee and the United Nations Commission for Indonesia—at crucial times made timely and constructive proposals. The final Round Table Agreement was largely the result of the patient efforts of Cochran.

Unfavorable Aspects

The most obvious unfavorable factor was the lack of experience of the United Nations. This was the first attempt of the United Nations either to mediate among states or to supervise a truce. Most other unfavorable factors stemmed from this lack of experience. The United Nations had no machinery for supplying either the personnel or the support for a United Nations group. This problem was by-passed by establishing the Good Offices Committee with only three or four members of the United Nations Secretariat to accompany it, and the Consular Commission, which used the facilities of the respective consulates.

The relationship of the GOC to the United Nations was never spelled out. Its members did not know whether they were serving as individuals, as representatives of their states, or as representatives of the Security Council. In fact, this made little practical difference. The relationship between the Consular Commission and the Good Offices Committee was also ambiguous. The Security Council on two occasions requested the Consular Commission to report directly to the Council. It also requested the commission to furnish facilities including military observers to the Good Offices Committee. Since three members of the Consular Commission were not represented on the Good Offices Committee, the military observers from those three states were not permitted to undertake missions for the GOC without approval of their Consul General. The Dutch used this jurisdictional confusion to deny access to the military observers during the crucial period immediately following the second "police action." When sovereignty was transferred to the Republic of Indonesia, the confusion became even greater since the military observers were detached from the consulates and transferred to the newly established embassies. Despite this confused picture, in practice, few problems arose because of the cooperative attitude of all of the states represented on the Consular Commission.

Another unfavorable aspect arising from the inexperience of the United Nations was the limited terms of reference of the GOC and the Consular Commission especially in the early stages, a situation that was only partially remedied with the reconstitution of the Good Offices Committee into the

[62] Most of the Indonesian public figures who thought highly of Ambassador Cochran are now either in jail or in exile.

United Nations Commission for Indonesia. The GOC had authority only to lend its good offices to the negotiators. The Netherlands took the position that any suggestions from the committee must be unanimous and could neither be considered nor made public without the consent of both the Dutch and the Indonesians. Thus, when Ambassador DuBois and his Australian colleague made suggestions in the summer of 1948 for compromising apparently irreconcilable differences which had arisen between the parties, the Dutch resented the publication of the suggestions after they had refused to consider them. This limited power of mediation carried over into the field of truce supervision and peace observation since the Netherlands contended that the Consular Commission had no authority beyond the Good Offices Committee.

The reports of the GOC and the Consular Commission on the situation in Indonesia were admirable. Their suggestions to the parties for maintaining the truce were excellent. If their suggestions were not carried out, however, the only recourse was to report to the Security Council. These jurisdictional limitations were partially removed when the Good Offices Committee was reconstituted as the United Nations Commission for Indonesia. The UNCI was permitted to act by majority vote; but no effort was made to give it authority to take action in the field in order to maintain the truce. In truce supervision, the UNCI as well as the GOC had to depend on the continuing agreement of the parties, which could be and was altered without notice.

A great obstacle to effective truce supervision, also related to the inexperience of the United Nations, was the absence of logistic support. The observers obtained some transportation from the consulates, but in the main they were dependent on the parties for transportation, supplies, and communications. Communications facilities after the arrival of the U.S.S. Renville were good. In many matters, however, the observers continued to be dependent on the parties. In general, the Netherlands army furnished assistance in Dutch-controlled territories. The Indonesians were more willing than the Dutch to facilitate the movements of the observers, but lacked the equipment. Beginning in 1949, the United Nations Secretariat furnished some supplies, which enhanced the effectiveness of the observers.

Guerrilla warfare was also unfavorable for peace observation. There never was a clear-cut demarcation line between the Dutch occupied territory and the Republican territory. The Netherlands drew an artificial line (the Van Mook line) between the Dutch front line posts; but there were tremendous pockets of resistance behind this line. When the Republic of Indonesia accepted the Van Mook line, under the Renville Truce Agreement, it withdrew 35,000 troops from these pickets.[63]

After the Netherlands repudiated the Renville Truce Agreement through the second "police action," the situation became even more confused.

[63] S/787, p. 59.

Although the Netherlands claimed that the Republic of Indonesia no longer controlled any territory, at least in the Island of Java, it was not difficult to establish that the Dutch control, at best, was limited to the principal cities and highways connecting them. The Dutch control after the police action was even less as regimes in other parts of the island, set up with Dutch assistance and originally favorable to the Netherlands, resigned as a result of the second "police action." During most of the period, the task of peace observation was to set up a line and arrange for the evacuation of forces from behind rather than to patrol an existing line.

In the context of this background, a more detailed chronological consideration of the "peace-observation" activities as they emerged will be discussed.

Peace Observation: First Tasks

The report of the Consular Commission of October 14, 1947, was in response to the Security Council resolution of August 25, 1947, calling for a report "on the situation in Indonesia" including observance of the cease-fire orders and conditions prevailing in areas under military occupation. The commission received cooperation from both sides and produced a competent report. [64]

Even at this early date, the commission grasped the basic problem of military operations in Indonesia. The Netherlands forces claimed the right to "dominate and control an area, without necessarily occupying the whole of it," even though Republican troops remained behind the Dutch lines. [65] The Netherlands further claimed that the cease-fire did not prevent them from conducting "mopping up" operations behind their lines (the Van Mook line). The Indonesians justified their attacks on Dutch posts and ships and mining of roads to prevent the "mopping up."

The commission performed an excellent service in bringing this problem to the attention of the Security Council. The Security Council did little to enlighten the situation in its resolution of November 1, 1947. This advised the parties, the GOC, and the Consular Commission that "its resolution of August 1 should be interpreted as meaning that the use of the armed forces of either party by hostile action to extend its control over territory not occupied by it on August 4, 1947, is inconsistent with the Council resolution of August 1." If it appeared that some withdrawals of armed forces might be necessary, the parties were invited "to conclude between them as soon as possible the agreements referred to in its resolution of August 25, 1947. [66]

The Consular Commission had requested statements from both the Dutch and the Indonesians of claimed violations of the cease-fire. In

[64] S/586, p. 3.
[65] S/586, pp. 5, 7.
[66] S/594.

addition to the main problem arising from the "mopping up" operations, the Indonesians alleged 811 breaches by the Dutch, including naval blockade, atrocities, arson, and plundering. The Dutch alleged 1,792 Indonesian breaches including terrorization of villages, atrocities, sabotage, kidnapping, and firing at ships.

The commission noted that it had made no detailed investigation of individual incidents, and that complete observance of the cease-fire order could not be expected. The report covered such topics as banditry, the scorched-earth policy of the Indonesians, hardships and shortages, and even concluded that practically all educated Indonesians are nationalists.

Thus, in the first stage, the Consular Commission only reported. It made no efforts to assist in maintaining or supervising the cease-fire.

Peace Observation after the Renville Truce Agreement,
November 1947–June 1948

The Security Council resolution of November 1, 1947, called on the parties to consult with each other, either directly or through the Committee of Good Offices, on the means to be employed to give effect to the cease-fire resolution and to "cease any activities or incitement to activities which contravene that resolution."[67] The Consular Commission was requested to make the services of the military observers available to the GOC.

At the first meeting of the GOC, the committee and the parties to the dispute agreed that every effort should be made to bring about an atmosphere that would increase the chances of a political settlement.[68]

The GOC received suggestions from both the Indonesians and the Dutch, and concluded that progress would best be made if the parties met with each other. At a meeting on November 12, a special committee was established by the parties to implement the Security Council resolution. The special committee laid the groundwork for the conference on the U.S.S. Renville that produced the Renville Truce Agreement signed on January 17 and January 19, 1948. The GOC had appointed six representatives including three military officers to be present at the Renville Conference.[69]

As anticipated by the previous Consular Commission report, an impasse arose in the discussions on the question of the Dutch "mopping up" operations to consolidate their forward positions.[70] After considerable negotiation, an important feature of which was a series of meetings between the GOC military advisers and the Dutch military leaders, the Renville Agreement was reached. It provided for a status quo line as set forth in a previous

[67] S/594.
[68] UN Security Council, *Official Records*, Third Year, Special Supplement No. 1, S/649, p. 4. Hereafter cited as S/649.
[69] S/649, p. 7.
[70] S/649, p. 10.

Dutch proclamation, a demilitarized zone between the status quo line and forward positions, and evacuation of troops both from the demilitarized zones and from pockets behind the status quo lines. It also provided that, on acceptance of the Truce Agreement, the GOC would place its military assistants at the disposal of both parties. These would assume, "in the first instance, responsibility for determining whether an incident requires inquiry by the higher authorities of either or both parties."[71] The military observers were increased from fifteen to a peak of fifty-five to take care of these increased functions.

In addition to the 35,000 Republican soldiers evacuated from positions on the Dutch side of the status quo line,[72] prisoners of war were released, though problems arose in distinguishing between prisoners of war, political prisoners, and criminals. At this time, the Dutch released 1,500 Indonesians, but the Indonesians found only 6 Dutch prisoners out of 185 troops who had disappeared. The evacuation of families of military personnel also commenced. The military observers from the Consular Commission sought to supervise these activities.

During this period, largely through meetings of local commanders with GOC military observers present, the delineation of the status quo line and the demilitarized zones was completed. The parties agreed in all instances except three, where the security subcommittee of the GOC made decisions that both parties accepted. The GOC in its second interim report on May 26, 1948, stated that the cease-fire during this period was generally observed.[73]

The security subcommittee also developed procedures for dealing with violations of the truce. (1) Incidents outside the demilitarized zones after completion of evacuations were not investigated unless there was prima facie evidence that the incidents were instigated by the government of the other party. In such cases, the incidents would be reported directly to the GOC. This procedure in effect stopped any investigation of the most numerous and important truce violations. (2) Military incidents in the demilitarized zones would be reported to the subcommittee by the military assistants except where settled locally by them. (3) The GOC would follow any procedures it saw fit to obtain speedy action. (4) Other incidents would be reported to the chairman of the GOC with the comments of each side and recommendations from the GOC military assistants for further GOC action.[74]

The most frequent subjects of complaints were sabotage, intimidation, reprisals, propaganda broadcasts to provoke disturbances, infiltration, subversive activities, and violations by naval and air forces.

[71] S/649, pp. 72–73.
[72] S/787, p. 59.
[73] S/787, p. 58.
[74] S/787, p. 62.

The above procedures for dealing with truce violations would have been well-founded if the observers had spent half their time in Dutch-controlled territory, and if they had been stationed in the neutral zone. However, as mentioned earlier, information concerning Indonesian-controlled territory was collected solely at Kaliurang. Theoretically it would have been easy to station observers in the neutral zone, but there were not enough observers, and since the Dutch placed the same limitations on the Consular Commission as they did on the GOC, the observers would have been unable to do much "settling."

During this period, the GOC produced three reports requiring field investigations on matters affecting the truce but not directly related to peace observation.[75] These highly competent reports all showed the existence of conditions that might endanger both the truce and an ultimate peaceful settlement.

In summary, during this period, the GOC continued its political and economic reporting and assisted or directed successful operations such as the evacuation of Indonesian troops behind the Dutch lines, the demilitarization of truce lines, and the release of prisoners of war. The GOC, however, did not develop extensive machinery either to prevent truce violations or to deal with them after they occurred.

The Deterioration of the Truce, June–December 1948

The Renville Truce Agreement dealt with a political settlement in Indonesia as well as with the observance of the cease-fire. The Security Council resolution of February 28, 1948, (1) commended the GOC for assistance given to the parties in their endeavors to reach a peaceful settlement; (2) continued its offer of good offices; and (3) requested the parties and the GOC to keep the Security Council informed of progress toward a political settlement.

The negotiations toward a political settlement, however, made no progress in March, April, or May. The Netherlands, on May 27, called a conference at Bandung on the problem of establishing the U.S.I. and invited a number of groups not associated with the Republic of Indonesia to attend. They did not ask the GOC to participate, a circumstance that the GOC reported to the Security Council.[76] Indeed, the Netherlands refused

---

[75] A report on political developments in West Java of April 21, 1948, S/729. See: UN Security Council, *Official Records*, Third Year, Supplement for June 1948, pp. 11–24; a report on political developments in Madura of May 18, 1948, S/786; UN Security Council, *Official Records*, Third Year, Supplement for June 1948, pp. 25–41; a report of restrictions on trade in Indonesia of July 24, 1948, S/919; UN Security Council, *Official Records*, Third Year, Supplement for July 1948, pp. 90–106.

[76] UN Security Council, *Official Records*, Third Year, Supplement for June 1948, S/842, pp. 91–118.

even to consider proposals for interpretation of the Renville Principles submitted by the United States and Belgian representatives on the GOC.[77] Meantime, during May, truce violations and violent incidents increased.

The third interim report of the GOC to the Security Council showed the virtual completion by the security subcommittee of its specific tasks of border delineation, release of prisoners of war, and evacuation of military personnel and families of military personnel.[78]

Violations of the truce were being investigated.[79] Some reports of the military observers showed alarming conditions, that is, the total destruction of twenty-four out of forty-seven rubber estates in East Java and the wiring of all factories with aerial bombs ready for immediate detonation.[80] However, the GOC, although fully informed of the deterioration, took no steps until after a new United States representative, Ambassador Cochran, was appointed in August. In September, he submitted a working paper with proposals for an over-all political settlement. The "Cochran plan" launched a series of negotiations that ultimately broke down with the decision of the Netherlands Government on December 3 to end negotiation and establish an interim administration on its own terms.[81]

During all this period of deteriorating relations, the GOC concentrated its activities on efforts to achieve a political settlement rather than on enlarging its peace-observation activities, which would have required a vastly increased staff. It observed erosion of the truce, but first conveyed this information to the Security Council on December 12, 1948.[82] The GOC's delay in reporting was due primarily to the fact that, visibly, the Netherlands was pursuing a moderate course, and the GOC felt that any interference might prove fatal. In effect, the Dutch concealed their intentions so well that intelligence reports did not show evidence of the second "police action" until December 6.

The Second Police Action,
December 1948–January 1949

The GOC special report to the Security Council on December 12 pointed out that the delay in achieving a political settlement had serious economic effects, intensified political tension between the parties, and resulted in an increasing strain on the truce. The GOC did not believe that the unsatisfactory level of truce enforcement could be maintained as the possibility

[77] UN Security Council, *Official Records*, Third Year, Supplement for June 1948, S/850, and S/850/Add. 1, pp. 147–50.
[78] UN Security Council, *Official Records*, Third Year, Supplement for June 1948, S/848, and S/848/Add.1, pp. 122–47, 142–43. Hereafter cited as S/848 or S/848/Add. 1.
[79] S/848/Add. 1, pp. 145–46.
[80] S/AC 10/Conf.2/C.3/20/Add. 3, Aug. 24, 1948.
[81] Taylor, *op. cit.*, pp. 142, 158.
[82] UN Security Council, *Official Records*, Third Year, Supplement for December 1948, S/1117, pp. 122–25. Hereafter cited as S/1117.

of political agreement became more remote. It could see further economic deterioration, general unrest, and social upheaval, and widespread hostilities might be the outcome. [83]

On December 19, the Netherlands terminated the Renville Truce Agreement because of claimed Indonesian violations, seized Djogjakarta, and interned the Republican leaders.

While a GOC group was in Kaliurang in the residency of Djogjakarta at the time, Cochran was unable to communicate with them or to ascertain the truth of the Netherlands claims of Indonesian violations. However, he reported immediately to the Security Council the Netherlands violation of the immunity of the Republican delegate in Djakarta and the seizure of his documents, and Dutch failure to follow procedures for terminating the Renville Agreement prescribed in Article 10 of the Agreement. [84] A further report of the GOC on December 21 confirmed and expanded the views of the earlier reports. [85]

This prompt reporting made it possible for the Security Council, despite Soviet obstruction, to fix the blame and to pass three resolutions immediately: (1) calling for a cease-fire; (2) requesting the Netherlands to release their political prisoners immediately and to report to the Security Council within 24 hours; and (3) requesting the Consular Commission to report on the situation in Indonesia. [86] Immediately after these resolutions, Cochran secured the release of the Republican delegation in Djakarta. [87]

The resolution calling on the Consular Commission to make a report directly to the Security Council as soon as possible on the situation in Indonesia created a theoretical jurisdictional problem since the military observers from the Consular Commission had been assigned to the GOC. Nevertheless, on December 31, Ambassador Cochran demanded from the Netherlands that the military observers return to their posts. He pointed out that the GOC had no firsthand information as a result of the immobilization of the observers. This jurisdictional problem would have remained theoretical, had it not been that the Dutch used the jurisdictional confusion as an excuse for preventing the military observers from returning to the field. [88]

Consequently, the Consular Commission on January 7 asked the Security Council to clarify the confusion. [89] While the clarification did not become

---

[83] S/1117, pp. 124–25.

[84] S/1129/Add. 1, p. 227.

[85] See S/1138, pp. 287–94.

[86] Resolutions S/1150 of Dec. 24, 1948; S/1164 of Dec. 28, 1948; and S/1165 of Dec. 28, 1948.

[87] UN Security Council, *Official Records*, Third Year, Supplement for December 1948, S/1166, p. 323.

[88] S/1189, pp. 6–7, 10, 15.

[89] UN Security Council, *Official Records*, Supplement for January 1949, S/1190, pp. 17–18.

official until the Security Council resolution of January 28, 1949, the Netherlands permitted the military observers to be dispatched to Java and Sumatra on January 9.[90]

By January 14, the GOC reported that the Dutch forces were insufficient to prevent guerrilla action and to maintain law and order in the towns.[91] On January 17, the GOC reported the conditions under which Sukarno, Hatta, and the other Republican leaders were imprisoned in violation of the Security Council resolution.

On January 24, a GOC analysis of the military situation reported that it was impossible to establish a cease-fire. The Netherlands Government had not established law and order in areas formerly occupied by the Republicans, and there was no Indonesian government to enforce a cease-fire.[92] These reports formed the basis for the Security Council resolution of January 28, 1949, establishing the UNCI and radically altering the entire framework for peace observation.

Implementing the Security Council Resolution of
January 28, 1949

The most important provisions of the Security Council's resolution were those indicating the procedures to carry out "the expressed objectives and desires of both parties to establish a federal, independent, and sovereign United States of Indonesia at the earliest possible date."[93] This, as stated previously, came close to compulsory arbitration. In general, the truce-supervision and peace-observation provisions were ancillary to this main objective.

These provisions called on the Republic to cease guerrilla warfare, and on the Dutch to discontinue immediately all military operations and to release all political prisoners, return the Republican officials to Djogjakarta, and permit the Republic to administer the Djogjakarta area.

The Committee of Good Offices was changed to the United Nations Commission for Indonesia with the provision that it could act by majority vote (instead of unanimously). Its functions related to peace observation were enlarged to include: (1) implementation of the January 28 resolution; (2) making recommendation to the Security Council concerning the powers and functions of any United Nations agency remaining in Indonesia to assist in implementing an agreement to establish a sovereign state; (3) observation of elections to ensure that they would be free and

---

[90] UN Security Council, *Official Records*, Supplement for January 1949, S/1193, p. 19. However, the status of the Consular Commission became even more confusing in December 1949 with the transfer of sovereignty to the Republic of Indonesia and the consequent transfer of military attachés from the consulates to the newly established embassies.

[91] S/1212, p. 49.

[92] S/1223, p. 61.

[93] S/1234.

democratic; (4) restoration at the earliest possible moment of the civil administration of the Republic, including economic measures for the proper functioning of the administration and recommendation of the extent to which Netherlands forces should remain temporarily to maintain law and order.

The Consular Commission was requested to provide "military observers and other staff and facilities" and to "temporarily suspend other activities."[94]

The UNCI report in March disclosed the failure of the Dutch to release the Indonesian leaders and return them to Djogjakarta and also the Netherlands decision on February 26 to convoke a Round Table Conference at The Hague to arrange for the rapid transfer of sovereignty to a United States of Indonesia.[95] During March and April, the main activities of the UNCI were directed toward obtaining agreement for the restoration of Indonesian leaders to Djogjakarta and for a Round Table Conference to take place immediately thereafter. These activities required a minimum of support from the Consular Commission.

On May 9, 1949, the UNCI reported agreement on the restoration of the Republic to Djogjakarta, which ushered in the next extensive operations requiring peace observation and truce supervision.[96]

After agreement on the restoration of the Republican administration, a subcommittee under the auspices of the UNCI was set up in May to make arrangements. The subcommittee was composed of representatives of the two parties and the representative of the UNCI, assisted by the commission military adviser. On May 11, agreement was reached to give opportunity to everyone to leave the Residency of Djogjakarta before the change of administration. The military observers were to assist in these arrangements. Thirty thousand persons left by June 9.[97]

The withdrawal of Dutch forces commenced on June 24 and was completed on June 30. The Sultan of Djogjakarta ordered all Republican forces to avoid contact, and no incidents occurred. During the period of the withdrawal, the military observers were organized into six teams under the supervision of the commission's military advisers, which took up positions between the Republican and Dutch forces—the first instance in which United Nations forces were used to separate antagonists.[98] Sukarno and Hatta returned to Djogjakarta on July 6.

A second subcommittee tried to work out measures to effectuate cessation of guerrilla warfare, and on June 22, agreement was reached on (1) an order to cease hostilities; (2) a joint proclamation by authorities of the

[94] S/1234.
[95] S/1270, pp. 8–29.
[96] UN Security Council, S/1320 (mimeo.).
[97] S/1373, p. 12.
[98] S/1373, p. 13.

Netherlands and the Republic of Indonesia; and (3) regulations governing implementation of cessation of hostilities and a Netherlands-Indonesian Manual.[99] The regulations provided for a Central Joint Board and local joint committees with UNCI representation. As previously pointed out, the manual prescribed United Nations insignia for the military observers, defined terms, and set forth rules for implementing the agreements.[100] Complaints were to be made to the local joint committees with appeals to the Central Joint Board. Important matters could be taken directly to the Central Joint Board.

By September 9, all the joint committees had been organized and by October 19, arrangements were completed for zones of patrol. The UNCI noted that the difficulties of implementation were generally based on interpretation of the cease-fire agreement and were solved locally. However, during this period, the Netherlands with UNCI supervision released 10,030 prisoners of war and 4,500 other prisoners and turned over 215 political prisoners to the Republic of Indonesia.[101] This phase of the activities ended on December 27, 1949, with the transfer of sovereignty from the Netherlands to the United States of Indonesia.[102]

In summary, the peace-observation machinery, after the January 28, 1949, resolution, began to function in May with the establishment of the UNCI subcommittees. Three months passed, however, before the August agreements were reached, and two more months passed before all the local joint committees were organized and the zones of patrol agreed upon. With independence scheduled for December 1949, little time was left to put the machinery into effect.

UNCI Peace-Observation Activities
after Transfer of Sovereignty

The UNCI, after the transfer of sovereignty to the Republic of Indonesia, continued to supervise the implementation of the Round Table Agreements. The most onerous remaining task was to arrange for the repatriation of the Royal Netherlands Army of 80,000, and the dissolution of the Netherlands-Indonesian Army of 65,000, mainly of Indonesian origin. It was agreed that these troops should gather in seventeen assembly areas near ports, and that United Nations military observers should be located near

[99] For regulations see S/1373, App. VIII, pp. 58–71; for Netherlands-Indonesian Manual see App. VIII.

[100] S/1373, p. 29.

[101] S/1449, pp. 1, 4, 5–8, 15.

[102] Although the Round Table Conference agreement envisioned a federated state in Indonesia, the government of the United States of Indonesia found it desirable to alter that structure in favor of a unitary state—the Republic of Indonesia. This change took place on August 17, 1950. Shortly thereafter (September 28) Indonesia was admitted to the United Nations.

the territorial command. The observers would be mobile and in a position to go wherever observation was required. By July 15, 1950, 67,000 Netherlands troops had left Indonesia; and 26,000 of the Netherlands-Indonesian troops had joined the Indonesian Army; 18,750 had been demobilized; and 3,250 had gone to the Netherlands. By October 5, the number remaining in Indonesia had been reduced to 7,000 Netherlands troops and 8,000 Netherlands-Indonesian troops, most of the latter having refused to be repatriated to Indonesia.[103] The evacuation of troops was not completed until May 1, 1951.

The UNCI was also required to supervise the plebiscites to determine the relation of the various parts of the United States of Indonesia to the Republic of Indonesia. In this task, the commission relied on information submitted to it by the parties, on its own observation, and on reports from its military observers.[104] The United Nations observers gave timely reports concerning the organization of a unitary state instead of the originally contemplated federation. Their terms of reference would not have permitted further action.

During 1950, four uprisings took place against the Indonesian Government: one in Bandung, two in Makasar, and one in Amboina in the South Moluccas. In the first Makasar incident, the United Nations military observers obtained the release of the Indonesian territorial commander who had been detained by the rebellious factions. In the second Makasar incident, United Nations military observers reported on a deputy Netherlands commander who had disappeared. In the South Moluccas incident, the UNCI attempted a far more extensive role. On April 23, 1950, a group of Netherlands-Indonesian troops seized authority and proclaimed a South Moluccas Republic. The commander of the Netherlands forces, having failed to re-establish authority, announced his refusal to consider the troops any longer as members of the Netherlands armed forces. On August 4, the UNCI offered its good offices to settle the controversy. On September 23, the Indonesian Government expressed willingness to make use of UNCI suggestions and advice, but on September 28, Republican troops landed on Amboina and fighting commenced. On October 6, the commission appealed to the Republic of Indonesia to halt military operations and to establish a cease-fire, and it offered to send military observers. The Republic of Indonesia declined the UNCI offer on the ground that UNCI intervention would encourage the rebels.[105]

The Republic of Indonesia military operation succeeded from the military standpoint. One of the results was that most of the Netherlands-Indonesian troops hailing from the South Moluccas elected to leave Indonesia and go to the Netherlands. On October 11, the UNCI reported

[103] S/2087, pp. 5, 7.
[104] S/2087, p. 3.
[105] For the UNCI report of the South Moluccas affair see S/2087, pp. 25–29.

to the Security Council "that it had exhausted all means at its disposal" and suggested that the Security Council request the Republic of Indonesia to use existing machinery for peaceful settlement.[106] The Indonesian Government apparently believed that this suggestion gave the rebel forces some status as the governing authorities of a federated area of Indonesia. The Indonesian Government had already abandoned the idea of a federation, and had established a unitary state. Accordingly, it opposed the suggestion.

The commission concluded its report of April 3, 1951, with the statement that since the military problems were solved, and no other matters were being submitted to the UNCl, it was adjourning *sine die*. This terminated the United Nations mediation and peace-observation operations in Indonesia.

EVALUATION

The Indonesian situation was the first case where the newly formed United Nations sought to mediate between two states. It was the second situation where the United Nations sought to supervise a truce and thus to establish peace-observation machinery.[107] The first comprehensive study of the United Nations efforts to maintain international peace and security (1955) included the following statement:

> There is only one case, the Indonesian question, in which the effort made by the United Nations can be considered an unqualified success. The role of the Security Council, and especially of its subsidiary organs, was unquestionably of great significance, for although a settlement might have been reached even without intervention by the Council, the action of the Council decreased the bloodshed and increased the speed with which an independent Indonesia was established.[108]

The analysis which led to this conclusion dealt primarily with the mediation efforts of the United Nations. The judgment of the United Nations effort in Indonesia as related to peace observation cannot be expressed in similarly unqualified terms. Unquestionably, the United Nations achieved a remarkably successful result. There were, however, organizational weaknesses and flaws, largely the results of inexperience, which were counterbalanced by superlative personal performances.

[106] S/1842, pp. 79–80.
[107] The first situation was along the northern Greek border.
[108] Goodrich and Simons, *op. cit.*, p. 317.

Political Reporting

The Good Offices Committee, the Consular Commission, and the UNCI produced sound and timely reports on the situation existing in Indonesia. In a sense, this reflected the background of the principals who in most instances were Foreign Service Officers accustomed to political reporting. Among the situations which these groups analyzed brilliantly and reported were: (1) the fact that the basic problem of enforcing the cease-fire arose from the absence of any clear demarcation line between the territories held by the Netherlands and those held by the Republic of Indonesia, with pockets of Indonesian troops behind the lines claimed by the Dutch; (2) the intention of the Netherlands to breach the truce through the second "police action," which Ambassador Cochran reported a week in advance, despite the Dutch denial of access of the military observers to the crucial areas; (3) the inability of the Netherlands to establish law and order after the second "police action"; and (4) the conditions of the confinement of Sukarno, Hatta, and the other revolution leaders. These were outstanding examples of successful political and military reporting.

Specific Tasks Ancillary to Mediation

The GOC, the UNCI, and the Consular Commission had great success in carrying out specific functions allotted to them, first to enforce the truce and later to implement the Round Table Agreement for a free and sovereign Indonesia. These tasks included: (1) supervising the removal of the Indonesian troops from behind the status quo line established under the Renville Agreement; (2) release of prisoners of war both after the Renville Agreement and after the Round Table Agreement; (3) separation of the Dutch and Indonesian troops at the time of the restoration of the Residency of Djogjakarta to the Indonesians and the release of Sukarno and Hatta from their confinement; (4) supervision of the evacuation of Indonesians wishing to leave the Residency of Djogjakarta after the restoration of the administration to the Republican leaders; and (5) supervision of the evacuation of Dutch troops and the disposition of troops of Indonesian origin in the Netherlands Army. All of these specific and difficult tasks were carried successfully to a conclusion without incidents.

The Combination of Mediation and Peace Observation

Since in the main the Consular Commission acted merely as the eyes and ears of the Good Offices Committee and the UNCI, the mediation and truce-supervision and peace-observation functions were in effect combined in one body. This arrangement in the circumstances of the situation in Indonesia turned out to be a happy one. Since the ultimate objectives in Indonesia had already been agreed upon under the Linggadjati Agreement, the task of mediation was limited to facilitating and implementing the agreements to carry out the objective. Truce supervision and peace observation were an integral part of the task of mediation, and therefore their combination was helpful. As will be noted, the stress on ultimate implementation of the agreements may have led to neglect of the immediate problems of maintaining a truce.

Illogical Machinery for Truce Observation

As noted above, the machinery was illogical, dictated by the political situation in the Security Council, plus the lack of any existing machinery in the United Nations for peace observation or truce supervision. This lack of logic, however, did not have adverse effects in the unusual circumstances of this case—highly qualified personnel and complete cooperation between the two groups.

Supplies, Transportation, and Communications

The absence of the United Nations facilities for supplying transportation and communication adversely affected the operations. While generally the Dutch permitted free communication, they cut off communication at the crucial moment of the second "police action." Only the high competence of Ambassador Cochran prevented a blackout of the Dutch operations during this period. The means of transportation and the supplies were limited and uncertain. Furthermore, after the second "police action" with the resulting intensification of Indonesian hatred of the Dutch and all foreigners, the safety of the military observers was in jeopardy. At this time, military observers discovered that flying the United Nations flag, wearing United Nations armbands, and identifying United Nations vehicles greatly increased their safety. This experience undoubtedly led to the development of United Nations facilities to supply other peace-observation groups.

Status of Personnel

The fact that the members of the GOC did not initially know whether they were acting in their individual capacities, as representatives of government, or as representatives of the United Nations has already been mentioned. As the operations developed, the advantages, particularly from the standpoint of security, of at least the supporting personnel having the status of United Nations employees became more and more apparent.

Absence of Machinery To Prevent Truce Violations

The greatest failure of the effort was that neither the terms of reference of the three United Nations groups operating in Indonesia nor their resources permitted them to set up machinery to prevent violations of the truce, to establish responsibility for violations, or to rectify the situation after the violations had taken place. Despite this handicap, the military observers had great achievements. At the outset, they saw that the best possibility of dealing with truce violations was to leave primary responsibility to the field officers of both parties, who frequently could reach agreement more easily than their superiors. Likewise, the military observers established channels for advising the field officers and the parties when agreements could not be obtained.

This became the usual pattern for UN peace-observation missions. However, except on specific tasks, such as the separation of Dutch and Indonesian troops at the time of the restoration of the Republic of Indonesia leaders to Djogjakarta, the military observers never had the authority nor were they in a position to prevent truce violations or to provide remedies after the violations had taken place. The prime example of the effect of this limited authority is found in the events of the second Dutch "police action." The military observers were quite sure that the Netherlands intended to repudiate the truce agreement. The logical response would have been to send a substantial number of military observers to Djogjakarta to prevent the Dutch seizure of Sukarno, Hatta, and the other Indonesian leaders. It is suggested that the Netherlands would have hesitated to use force against the United Nations observers. It is beyond the scope of this study to speculate on what the political developments might have been if the second Netherlands "police action" had not taken place.

4

THE PROBLEM OF
THE INDEPENDENCE OF KOREA

The Foreign Ministers of the United States, the United Kingdom, and the U.S.S.R., in planning the postwar settlements, never got around to agreeing on a specific program for Korea. The Cairo Declaration and the Potsdam Declaration dealt with Korea only in general terms. [1] The Foreign Ministers of the three powers (and later China) agreed in Moscow in December 1945 to set up a joint United States-Soviet Union commission to

[1] Robert E. Sherwood, *Roosevelt and Hopkins* (New York: Harper and Brothers, 1948), p. 903.

meet in Korea and, through consultation with Korean democratic parties and social organizations, to prepare for the formation of a provisional government. The Joint Commission was to consult with the provisional government and submit its proposals to the four powers for approval. The parties to the Moscow Agreement assumed that there would be a four-power trusteeship for a period of up to five years to prepare Korea for independence. Before such a trusteeship could be set up, however, fast-moving events created a pattern that has proved impossible to change.

At the time Japan surrendered in August 1945, the United States had no program for the transfer of governmental authority in Korea. On the other hand, Soviet troops, accompanied by Russian-trained Korean Communists, occupied a small part of Korea before the surrender and within two days after Japan's announcement of its willingness to surrender. It seemed probable that the Soviet armies would receive the surrender of all Japanese forces throughout Korea, and would then occupy the entire country and set up a Communist regime.

Therefore, the United States was relieved when the Soviet Union acceded to a United States suggestion that the Soviet Union receive the surrender of Japanese forces north of the 38th parallel, and the United States receive the surrender of the troops south of the 38th parallel.

In the north, the Soviet Union had a Moscow-trained Korean Communist, Kim Il Sung, to head the government, and a Communist regime was rapidly established. In the south, the United States Commander, Lieutenant General John R. Hodge, initially tried to govern through the Japanese administrators, and when this failed, he set up a United States military government.

Negotiations between the Soviet Union and the United States from 1946 through August 1947 on arrangements for a provisional government for all of Korea had little success. The main reason for disagreement between the two powers was that a popular vote would have established a non-Communist regime for all of Korea, because Korea south of the 38th parallel had two-thirds of the population of the country. Therefore, the Soviet leaders suggested formulae that would have assured the Communist domination of any Korean government: consultation only with those South Korean groups that had supported the program for a four-power trusteeship, thus eliminating the Syngman Rhee supporters; or 50 percent of the voting power in North Korea, thus assuring that one Communist elected in the south would establish a Communist majority.

When all efforts to obtain agreement in the Joint Commission failed, the United States suggested a four-power meeting to consider how the Moscow Agreement might be speedily carried out. The Soviet Union rejected this proposal, and the United States submitted the problem of Korean independence to the United Nations General Assembly in September 1947.

Over the objection of the U.S.S.R., the General Assembly established the United Nations Temporary Commission on Korea (UNTCOK) to expedite fulfillment of the program for attaining Korean independence.[2] The commission consisted of representatives from Australia, Canada, China, El Salvador, France, India, the Philippines, Syria, and the Ukrainian S.S.R. The Ukrainian government declined to serve.

A year later, the General Assembly created a new commission, the United Nations Commission on Korea (UNCOK), to continue some of the work of UNTCOK, but with different terms of reference.[3] UNCOK had seven members, representatives from Australia, China, El Salvador, France, India, the Philippines, and Syria.

The 1949 General Assembly continued UNCOK for another year with greatly changed terms of reference.[4] In fact, the operations of UNCOK in its second year were so different from the first year of operations that, in the interests of clarity, they are discussed separately. The following discussion reviews UN operations from their beginning in November 1947 until hostilities commenced on June 25, 1950, at which point peace observation ended until after the armistice.

THE UNITED NATIONS
TEMPORARY COMMISSION ON KOREA

Terms of Reference

The United Nations Temporary Commission on Korea was established by two General Assembly resolutions dated November 14, 1947. The first resolution found that the Korean question could not be "correctly and fairly resolved" without participation of elected representatives of the Korean people and established UNTCOK "to facilitate and expedite such participation and to observe that the Korean representatives are in fact duly elected by the Korean people and not mere appointees by military authorities in Korea."[5] The second designated the members of the commission and recommended "that the elections be held not later than 31 March 1948 on the basis of adult suffrage and by secret ballot . . . [and that] representatives, constituting a National Assembly . . . establish a National Government of Korea." The number of representatives from each voting area or zone should be proportionate to the population, and the elections should be under the observation of the commission.[6] The resolu-

---

[2] UN General Assembly, Res. 112 (II), Pts. A and B, adopted Nov. 14, 1947. Hereafter cited as Res. 112 (II).

[3] UN General Assembly, Res. 195 (III), Dec. 12, 1948. Hereafter cited as Res. 195 (III).

[4] UN General Assembly, Res. 293 (IV), Oct. 21, 1949. Hereafter cited as Res. 293 (IV).

[5] Res. 112 (II), Pt. A.

[6] Res. 112 (II), Pt. B.

tion outlined the next steps following the election: (1) the National Assembly should form a national government and notify the commission of its formation; (2) the national government should constitute its own national security forces, take over the functions of government from the military forces; and (3) arrange for the complete withdrawal of occupation forces from Korea as soon as practicable. The commission was to report, with its conclusions, to the General Assembly and could consult with the Interim Committee with respect to the application of the resolution in the light of developments.[7] It is clear from the above that UNTCOK's functions were primarily to act as neutral observers of elections and troop withdrawals— not to make political judgments.

When the North Koreans, dominated by the Soviet Union, declined to cooperate with UNTCOK, the commission might have reported to the General Assembly that it could not fulfill its function of facilitating "the attainment of the national independence of Korea." Instead, with ample legal authority, it sought the advice of the Interim Committee, which made a political judgment: that UNTCOK should proceed to arrange for elections in South Korea alone. This political judgment changed the character of UNTCOK which, in effect, became the adviser of one party rather than the neutral observer of both parties. UNTCOK observed the 1948 elections in South Korea and made a number of suggestions in connection with the elections which were accepted by the South Korean authorities. It reported its activities to the 1948 General Assembly.

Organization

After June 5, 1948, UNTCOK relied largely on the personnel of its national delegations to carry on the activities. The maximum number was thirty: eighteen in the delegations, twelve in the United Nations Secretariat. The largest delegation, that of France, never had more than six persons. Three of the eight delegations consisted only of the delegate. The eighteen members of delegations consisted of the eight delegates, four alternates, two advisers, and four secretary-typists. The Secretariat personnel consisted of a principal, secretary, an assistant secretary, an administrative and finance officer, two interpreters, a précis writer, three stenographers, and three persons recruited locally.[8]

UNTCOK carried on most of its work through meetings between January 12 and June 4, 1948, forty-six in Seoul and twelve in Shanghai.[9] Initially, UNTCOK organized three subcommittees: the first to study ways and means of ensuring a free atmosphere for Korea; the second to examine

[7] Res. 112 (II), Pt. B.

[8] UN General Assembly, *Official Records,* Third Session, Supplement No. 9, A/575/ Add. 4, p. 31. Hereafter cited as A/575.

[9] A/575, p. 6.

documents from Korean sources and to secure statements from Korean personalities; the third to examine the electoral laws of Korea.[10]

The organization was neither intended nor suited to perform peace-observation functions. Late in March, after the decision of the Interim Committee of the General Assembly to go ahead with elections only in South Korea, the subcommittees were abandoned. A main committee took over all functions, and on March 20, set up pre-election observation groups to observe the preparations for the elections and the elections themselves. Three groups toured Korea and interviewed the candidates for election in April. Four more groups covered most of the electoral districts to observe pre-election preparations. Their task ended April 24. During the period preceding and including election day, May 9, nine small groups observed the situation.[11]

Performance

UNTCOK organized itself on January 12, 1948. As previously pointed out, the objective of the United Nations was the attainment of national independence for Korea and the withdrawal of occupying forces. This required unification of North and South Korea. UNTCOK was established to expedite the program by arranging fair elections. UNTCOK's peace-observation activities were not to commence until preparations had been made for elections both in the north and in the south.

UNTCOK approached the U.S.S.R., whose troops were still in North Korea, the Ukraine, which was a member of UNTCOK but declined to serve, and the military authorities in North Korea.[12] All of UNTCOK's efforts in this direction, which lasted for approximately forty-five days, were unsuccessful. This might have been anticipated for a number of reasons. First, the Soviet Union had opposed bringing the problem of Korea to the General Assembly, claiming that it was part of the peace settlements which, under Article 106 of the United Nations Charter, were to be settled by the great powers. Second, both the U.S.S.R. and the Ukraine had indicated in the General Assembly that they would have nothing to do with UNTCOK. Third, the resolution establishing UNTCOK provided that it could consult with the Interim Committee of the General Assembly, a group which the Soviet Union considered illegal and was boycotting.

By February 14, UNTCOK had reached the conclusion that its efforts to deal with the North Korean authorities had failed, and the question of the next step arose. The commission had two choices: (1) it could abandon its work, on the ground that the objective of national independence for Korea was impossible to attain since the North Korean authorities had failed to cooperate; or (2) it could consult with the Interim Committee as

[10] A/575, p. 7.
[11] A/575, p. 8.
[12] A/575, pp. 24–25.

authorized by the General Assembly resolution "with respect to the application of this resolution in the light of developments." Although there was general agreement in UNTCOK on the desirability of consulting the Interim Committee, wide divergencies arose on the questions that should be submitted to the Interim Committee. [13]

In the discussions in UNTCOK, it became obvious that the Interim Committee might recommend that UNTCOK supervise elections only in South Korea. This issue was charged with dynamite. Dr. Syngman Rhee, the South Korean leader who seemed to have the greatest following, supported such a course, as did General Hodge and the American military government. They were both concerned by the disorganization in South Korea in comparison to North Korea where the Soviet Union had established a strong government using Communist-educated Koreans. However, the other most important Korean leaders—Kim Koo and Dr. Kimm Kiusic—took a different view. In particular, Dr. Kimm Kiusic, leader of the more moderate political elements in South Korea, believed that an election in the south would crystallize and make permanent the division of Korea. Australia, Canada, and India did not want an election only in the south, and Syria was lukewarm toward the idea. The other members of UNTCOK tended to favor it. The phrasing of the resolution calling for consultation with the Interim Committee anticipated a negative reaction— the Interim Committee was expected to find UNTCOK unable to carry out its aim in North Korea and advise against holding an election only in the south. Accordingly, it received the favorable votes of Australia, Canada, India, and Syria, with three negative votes and one abstention. [14]

By the time the Interim Committee met on February 19, Dr. Syngman Rhee had agreed with Kim Koo and Dr. Kimm Kiusic that one more effort would be made for a conference between the leaders of north and south. If this failed, Kim Koo and Kimm Kiusic would not oppose the idea of separate elections in South Korea. [15]

The United States was exerting strong pressures for an election in South Korea, and on February 24, it proposed a resolution to that effect in the Interim Committee. Canada and Australia continued to oppose the course advocated by the United States. The Canadian Foreign Minister, Lester Pearson, objected both because he believed the Interim Committee was incompetent to act on the problem and because he opposed separate elections in South Korea. Norway suggested a special session of the General Assembly.

In the end, the Interim Committee adopted the United States resolution. [16] Dr. Kimm Kiusic immediately resigned from the Korean Interim

---

[13] Leon Gordenker, *The United Nations and the Peaceful Unification of Korea* (The Hague: Martinus Nijhoff, 1959), p. 60.

[14] *Ibid.*, p. 63.

[15] *Ibid.*, p. 64.

[16] The vote was 34 to 2 with 11 abstentions.

Legislative Assembly expressing the fear that unification would now become impossible.[17] Detailed discussion of the action of the Interim Committee has been necessary since it had the effect of changing fundamentally the nature of UNTCOK. By this action UNTCOK acquired a specific peace-observation function—to observe the elections in South Korea. However, it was clear that UNTCOK's original functions, to mediate between north and south, arrange for national elections, and then serve as a neutral observer of the national elections, had ceased.

As pointed out previously, on March 20, UNTCOK revised its organizational structure to observe the elections. The three subcommittees had, however, performed certain functions and prepared background material that proved to be of great value.[18] Subcommittee 1, organized to devise ways and means of ensuring a free atmosphere for elections in Korea, had established a definition of the minimum requirements for a free atmosphere. It had also provided a questionnaire for use by subcommittee 2 in its inquiries concerning the existence of a free atmosphere. Subcommittee 2 had examined documents from Korean sources and, using the questionnaire, had consulted with civilian leaders on whether there was a free atmosphere in South Korea. The UNTCOK report, however, noted that the leftist leaders were either in jail, in North Korea, or refused to testify. Subcommittee 3 analyzed the electoral provisions under Korean law. The report noted that UNTCOK's sources of information concerning North Korea were limited to Pyongyang broadcasts.

From April 5 to April 24, the commission talked to officials and candidates, covered almost all of the electoral districts, and discovered that over 90 per cent of the potential voters had registered. It had no contact, however, with the extreme leftists. On April 25, it reported that a free atmosphere existed in South Korea for the election. From May 7 to May 11, it divided into groups that visited the polling places and after the election observed the opening of a representative number of ballot boxes.[19]

UNTCOK probably exerted a favorable influence at the time of the elections. The rightist groups under Syngman Rhee, which were sponsoring the election, did not control the Assembly and had to form a coalition in order to obtain a majority. Unquestionably, more groups participated in the election than would have been possible if UNTCOK had been absent. The electoral procedures which UNTCOK had recommended were generally followed and were helpful. However, both at the time and in retrospect, it is clear that the holding of national elections only in the south did nothing to promote the main objective of UNTCOK—the establishment of an independent and sovereign Korea.

[17] Gordenker, *op. cit.*, pp. 74–75.
[18] A/575, pp. 30–36.
[19] A/575, p. 38.

On May 15, all of the delegates and most of the personnel of UNTCOK went to Shanghai to prepare a report and were absent during the rest of May and the early part of June.[20] Thus UNTCOK may have lost its greatest opportunity to influence the turn of events in South Korea during the period of formation of the national government. In July and August, the South Korean Government set itself up as a complete national government for all of Korea even though elections had been held and observed only in the south.

The members of UNTCOK were in disagreement regarding whether their terms of reference would permit consultation with a government so constituted since the consultations might be deemed recognition. Although UNTCOK decided to consult with the South Korean Government by a vote of four to two with one abstention, the consultations were without substance and might be described as ceremonial.[21]

In September and October, UNTCOK met in New York to draft its report, which was submitted without recommendations. The French delegate insisted that UNTCOK proceed to Paris at United Nations expense in order to be available for questioning at the General Assembly meeting in October.

UNTCOK, in its final report, related that it had received all complaints concerning a free atmosphere for the election, violations of the electoral law, and illegal practices, and had forwarded them to the United States authorities. It also reported that "the results of the ballot of May 10, 1948 are a valid expression of the free will of the electorate in those parts of Korea which were accessible to the Commission."[22] It is clear from the UNTCOK reports that it had received no worthwhile information on public opinion in Korea as a result of its consultations and relied solely on published materials such as the election returns and the National Assembly debates.[23]

UNTCOK had been established as a temporary commission and its authority was not renewed by the 1948 General Assembly.

UNITED NATIONS COMMISSION ON KOREA, DECEMBER 1948–OCTOBER 1949

Terms of Reference

UNTCOK's report was approved by the General Assembly, which found that "there has been established a lawful government" in South Korea,

---

[20] A/575, p. 39.
[21] Gordenker, *op. cit.*, p. 138.
[22] A/575/Add. 3, p. 3.
[23] Gordenker, *op. cit.*, p. 141.

"that this Government is based on elections which were a valid expression of the free will of the electorate of that part of Korea; . . . and that this is the only such Government in Korea."[24] The General Assembly then established UNCOK "to continue the work of UNTCOK . . . and in particular to: lend its good offices to bring about the unification of Korea and the integration of all Korean security forces in accordance with the principles laid down by the General Assembly in the Resolution of 14 November 1947"; to "seek to facilitate the removal of barriers to economic, social, and other friendly intercourse caused by the division of Korea"; to "be available for observation and consultation in the further development of representative government based on the freely expressed will of the people"; and to "observe the actual withdrawal of the occupying forces and verify the fact of withdrawal when such has occurred; and for this purpose, if it so desires, request the assistance of military experts of the two occupying Powers."[25]

So long as the North Koreans declined to cooperate, of course, these functions of UNCOK were insubstantial. Therefore, its sole observation function was related to withdrawal of United States troops—not an onerous task since the United States military authorities wanted to withdraw at the earliest possible time. The first two functions were mediation functions and depended on the willingness of both the North and South Koreans to listen to mediation, a situation that never developed. Any steps by UNCOK during this period to carry out the third function would inevitably carry the inuendo that the Syngman Rhee government was not a fully developed "representative government based on the freely expressed will of the people." Its efforts thus brought it into conflict with the host government. The Rhee government, accordingly, contended that this function was intended to apply only to North Korea.[26]

The General Assembly of 1949 voted to continue UNCOK for another year and restated its functions with one significant addition that was included at the suggestion of UNCOK. The commission "shall observe and report any developments which might lead to or otherwise involve military conflict in Korea."[27] This was a substantial function in peace observation and led to UNCOK's report of the North Korean invasion of South Korea on June 25, 1950.

The resolution rephrased UNCOK's advisory function to read that the commission should "be available for observation and consultation throughout Korea in the continuing development of representative government based on the freely expressed will of the people, including elections of

[24] Res. 195 (III).
[25] Res. 195 (III).
[26] UN General Assembly, *Official Records*, Fourth Session, Supplement No. 9, A/936, p. 9. Hereafter cited as A/936.
[27] Res. 293 (IV).

national scope."[28] This eliminated the contention of the South Korean Government that the so-called advisory function applied only to North Korea, and it compelled the South Korean Government to pay some heed to UNCOK in the later period.

Organization

The UNCOK organization was similar to that of UNTCOK. There were seven delegations (Canada and the Ukraine, which had never participated in UNTCOK, were eliminated).

The delegation personnel during the first year reached a peak of fifteen: seven delegates, two alternates and six secretaries. The secretariat expanded to thirty-two: eighteen from headquarters and fourteen recruited locally. The personnel from headquarters consisted of a principal secretary, a deputy principal secretary, three assistant secretaries, one administrative officer, one assistant administrative officer, one paymaster, two interpreters, two précis writers, six typists, and one military-technical observer. Locally recruited personnel included four translator-interpreters, two corresponding secretaries, one clerk-messenger, one office machine operator, three dispatchers, and three receptionists.[29]

UNCOK set up three subcommittees: the first to study economic and social barriers caused by the division of Korea; the second to study the development of representative government everywhere in Korea; the third to work out procedures to be employed in observation and verification of the withdrawal of American forces.[30]

Thus UNCOK in its first year had no peace-observation functions other than to observe the withdrawal of the United States troops. The staff, however, took a number of observation trips including four to the 38th parallel. On April 29, 1949, a subcommittee suggested that observer teams be stationed along the border as a means of contributing to the peace and security of Korea. No action was taken, however, beyond recommending this course in the report to the General Assembly.[31]

As noted, the 1949 General Assembly requested the commission to observe and report any developments which might lead to or otherwise involve military conflict in Korea. UNCOK moved slowly to implement this decision. The General Assembly resolution was dated October 21, 1949, and not until March 25, 1950, did UNCOK request the Secretary-General to provide military observers.[32]

[28] Res. 293 (IV).

[29] UN General Assembly, *Official Records*, Fourth Session, Supplement No. 9, A/936/Add. 1, pp. 51–55. Hereafter cited as A/936/Add. 1.

[30] A/936, p. 4.

[31] A/936, pp. 18, 33.

[32] UN General Assembly, *Official Records*, Fifth Session, Supplement No. 16, A/1350, p. 14. Hereafter cited as A/1350.

In the request for observers, UNCOK suggested four observation zones with two observers in each zone. The observers would remain in the field three weeks out of four. They would use the South Korean telephone system for communicating between points along the border and for communication with Seoul headquarters. UNCOK would borrow a mobile radio unit from the United States military advisers for one of the groups stationed in a remote area. UNCOK likewise requested four jeeps marked with United Nations symbols, which would be serviced by native drivers and mechanics. A detailed but scanty list of required supplies was also provided.[33]

The Secretary-General produced two Australian military observers at the end of May. They departed almost immediately for the 38th parallel and did not return to Seoul until June 24, the day before the North Korean attack.[34] On June 27, after the attack, the United States Air Force evacuated UNCOK to Japan. Seven of the personnel returned to Pusan at the southern tip of Korea on June 30 and remained in Korea until August when UNCOK became inactive after completion of its report.[35]

Performance, December 1948–October 1949

As set forth in the section on terms of reference, UNCOK, in its first year, had four main functions: (1) to bring about the unification of Korea; (2) to facilitate the removal of barriers to economic, social, and other intercourse between north and south; (3) to be available for observation and consultation in the further development of representative government based on the freely expressed will of the people; and (4) to observe the withdrawal of the occupation forces.

It will be obvious that the first two functions depended on cooperation between the north and south. Accordingly, as soon as UNCOK was organized in February 1949, it set up a subcommittee to study the means by which unification could be promoted.[36] Dr. Rhee took the position that, under the General Assembly resolution establishing UNCOK, unification meant unification on the basis of a South Korean Government and objected to any efforts of UNCOK to contact the North Korean authorities. Nevertheless, Dr. Rhee did not object to an UNCOK request to the Soviet Government to use its good offices. When this effort failed, UNCOK embarked on a number of approaches to the North Korean authorities. For example, it sent a secretariat member to Hong Kong and Shanghai to determine whether it was possible to sail from either of those ports to North Korea with a message. A number of methods of informal approach were explored and communications dispatched.

[33] A/1350, pp. 41–42.
[34] A/1350, p. 40.
[35] A/1350, p. 30.
[36] A/936, p. 4.

All of these activities were clandestine, since the South Korean Government would have objected violently. The efforts failed, and UNCOK reported to the General Assembly that it could do nothing to achieve the unification of Korea or the removal of economic barriers between north and south. Nor could it observe the withdrawal of Soviet troops.[37]

Subcommittee 1, which also dealt with UNCOK's function of facilitating the removal of economic and social barriers between north and south, prepared an excellent report based largely on published data dealing with economic, social, and technical factors affecting the problem of Korean unification.[38] Thus the first two functions of UNCOK in its first year, because of the inability to make contact in North Korea, did not involve peace observation other than reporting political developments—a normal function of any diplomatic mission.

UNCOK's third function, being available for observation and consultation in the further development of representative government based on the freely expressed will of the people, involved UNCOK in bitter controversies with the South Korean Government. The South Korean representative in the General Assembly had interpreted this provision to apply solely to the development of representative government in the north. The South Korean election having taken place and the government having been recognized by many United Nations members, he contended there was no further reason to consider whether it was representative of and based on the freely expressed will of the people.[39]

UNCOK set up subcommittee 2 to deal with this problem. Subcommittee 2 was given the authority to consult and communicate with individuals and organizations other than the government. The South Korean Government immediately denied that UNCOK had such authority. However, subcommittee 2 did consult with a number of individuals who had to pass a Korean police guard on the way to the consultations. In response to invitations, eleven individuals testified before the subcommittee, but said nothing damaging to the South Korean Government.[40] The witnesses did not include either Kim Koo or Dr. Kimm Kiusic, who consulted informally with another subcommittee of UNCOK. These informal consultations resulted in Syngman Rhee's denunciation of Kim Koo and Dr. Kimm Kiusic as traitors and his accusations that UNCOK, through dealing with them, was strengthening the Communists.[41]

It will be obvious that in this phase of its work UNCOK did not perform any substantial peace-observation functions. In the main, it heard only the

[37] A/936, p. 11.
[38] For the report of subcommittee 1, see A/936/Add. 1, pp. 1–3.
[39] Gordenker, *op. cit.*, p. 147.
[40] For the report of subcommittee 2, see A/936/Add. 1, pp. 18–29.
[41] Gordenker, *op. cit.*, p. 156.

official line of the South Korean Government. It is possible that its controversy with the South Korean Government may have moderated some of
the Government's actions.

The fourth function of UNCOK, in this period, to observe the withdrawal
of the occupation forces, theoretically was a peace-observation function.
As pointed out, however, the United States position was to withdraw as
rapidly as possible. UNCOK observed the withdrawals and reported that
they had been completed by June 29, 1949. UNCOK had only one individual among the delegation and secretariat personnel with qualifications
to report on a military withdrawal.[42] Therefore, the function could not be
considered a substantial one. UNCOK reported that it could not verify
the Soviet contention that its troops had been withdrawn.[43] However
inadequately prepared the commission might have been to observe the
withdrawal of troops, its report added some weight to the statement of the
United States and the South Koreans that the troops had been withdrawn.
Even during this period of intense cold war, the Soviets never questioned
the withdrawal of the troops.

In addition to UNCOK's stated duties in its first year, it performed other
functions, which might be described as incidental to its main tasks: it made
a number of observation trips, four of them to the 38th parallel; it visited
the Korean Military Academy and the military installations around Seoul
and it observed several local elections. As a result of these trips, an *ad hoc*
committee of UNCOK on April 29 suggested a study to determine whether
observer teams would contribute to the peace and security of Korea. On
May 31, the *ad hoc* committee decided that it was not useful to continue the
consideration of the question in the absence of specific authority from the
General Assembly. However, UNCOK's report raised the issue of such
observation, noted the growing military strength in the north, and suggested that the continued presence of the commission in Korea was a
stabilizing factor and that its authority should be prolonged for one year.[44]
This was probably the most useful function performed by UNCOK in its
first year, and it furnished the basis for the significant activities of UNCOK
later.

Performance, November 1949–October 1950

The 1949 General Assembly voted to continue UNCOK for another year
and restated its functions with two main changes. The provision requesting
UNCOK to be available for observation and consultation in the continuing
development of a representative government based on the freely expressed
will of the people was amended to include the words "throughout Korea"

[42] *Ibid.*, p. 200.
[43] A/936, p. 11.
[44] A/936, pp. 12, 18, 34.

and to include the subject of "elections of national scope." Thus, the fundamental controversy between UNCOK and the South Korean Government was decided in favor of UNCOK. In addition, as previously stated, UNCOK was given the authority to "observe and report any developments which might lead to or otherwise involve military conflict in Korea." [45] This latter change involved considerable debate in the General Assembly. The title of the agenda item was "Peaceful Unification of Korea," and it was contended that this function related to threats of forcible unification of Korea rather than the subject under consideration.

UNCOK, in its second year, performed three main functions. First, buttressed by its additional authority, it resumed consultations on the development of representative government in Korea. It met less opposition than in the previous year possibly because of its increased authority from the General Assembly, but more probably because of the pressure exerted by the United States on the South Korean Government and the increased danger of attack from the north. In any event, when the South Korean Government proposed to postpone the elections for the National Assembly from May to November, UNCOK protested, and the South Korean Government acceded to the protest and the election was scheduled for May 30. [46]

The second function performed by UNCOK was the observation of the May 30 election. UNCOK had far fewer personnel for observation than UNTCOK had two years earlier. Unlike UNTCOK, it did not hold hearings in advance of the election, study electoral laws, or recommend changes. However, it observed elections and heard complaints that opposition candidates and their supporters had been beaten and sent to jail. [47] Before UNCOK could report its conclusions, the North Koreans attacked South Korea on June 25. Obviously, adverse conclusions after the attack would have been irrelevant and harmful to the United Nations.

The third and most significant function was directly associated with peace observation—the observation of developments which might lead to or otherwise involve military conflict in Korea. UNCOK was slow to organize its peace-observation machinery. Not until February 7, more than three months after the General Assembly resolution, did it organize a committee of the whole to consider ways of observing and reporting any developments which might lead to or otherwise involve military conflict in Korea. The information that it received consisted of: (1) evidence from qualified officials of the Republic of Korea and of the United States-Korean military group; (2) visits by members of the commission or of the secretariat to areas along the 38th parallel and other areas where the situation was considered critical; (3) examination of reports received from

[45] Res. 293 (IV).
[46] A/1350, p. 23.
[47] A/1350, p. 24.

the Government of the Republic of Korea on the extent of guerrilla activities; (4) scrutiny or monitoring broadcasts of Radio Pyongyang and examination of North Korean propaganda leaflets; and (5) dispatch of field observers for the purpose of direct observation, particularly in areas lying adjacent to the 38th parallel. UNCOK continued to move slowly. On March 2, the committee of the whole recommended that the commission employ trained field observers who would be stationed where needed in prevailing circumstances. It was not until March 25 that UNCOK requested the Secretary-General to provide eight field observers, and the first two arrived only at the end of May. The request outlined the methods of organization and the supplies that would be required. [48]

In the meantime, on May 10, UNCOK heard reports from the South Koreans of the build-up of the North Korean forces. These reports were based on the interrogation of captured North Korean soldiers, reports of intelligence agents working in the north, and reports of defecting Communists from the north. On the surface, at least, the danger of conflict did not stem entirely from the north since there were a number of statements by South Korean leaders indicating the necessity of shedding blood to achieve unification. [49]

Fortunately, the military observers embarked on a field trip to the 38th parallel shortly after their arrival, and they returned to Seoul on June 24, the day before the North Korean attack. Therefore, on June 25 at the time of the attack, the commission was able to report [50] that: "The observers reported that they had been impressed . . . by the fact that the South Korean army was organized entirely for defense . . . that there were visible no military or other supplies necessary for a large-scale attack." The commission further reported that: "The Northern regime is carrying out a well-planned concerted and full-scale invasion of South Korea. . . . South Korean forces were taken completely by surprise. . . . The invasion . . . presupposes a long-premeditated, well-prepared, and well-timed plan of aggression. . . . The objective . . . was to secure by force what could not be gained by any other means."

This report from UNCOK was of inestimable value in obtaining United Nations support for the resolutions to meet the Communist aggression, in both the Security Council and the General Assembly. It was a unanimous report subscribed to by all the members of UNCOK including India. Therefore, it undoubtedly contributed to the world-wide support of the United Nations in meeting the aggression. However, it came too late to result in advance warning of the intentions of the North Koreans even though ample evidence had been presented to UNCOK by the South Koreans in May or even earlier.

[48] A/1350, pp. 13–14, 20.
[49] A/1350, p. 28.
[50] A/1350, pp. 3–4.

UNCOK was evacuated to Japan on June 27. Seven of its members, however, including two representatives, returned to Pusan at the southernmost tip of Korea on June 30 and remained there until August. UNCOK prepared its report to the General Assembly in Tokyo and concluded with the understatement that some of its functions had been inoperative. Its most important remaining tasks were to submit the report and prepare itself to assist, should a favorable opportunity arise, in bringing about the reunification of Korea.

The 1950 General Assembly terminated UNCOK and established a new commission to take over its functions. The new commission had no peace-observation functions until the establishment of the truce three years later.

Evaluation

The three years of efforts sponsored by the United Nations to obtain the peaceful unification of Korea ended in failure. The United Nations commissions achieved neither unification nor peace. Probably Soviet intransigence would in any event have prevented a peaceful settlement of the Korean problem except through the establishment of a Communist regime throughout Korea.

While UNTCOK and UNCOK were intended to be neutral commissions, the circumstances of their establishment and continuance prevented this. The Soviet Union had originally objected to the submission of the Korean problem to the United Nations on the ground that it was part of the peace settlements and therefore should be considered by the signatories to the Four-Power Declaration of Moscow and France in accordance with Article 106 of the Charter. The Soviet Union opposed the decision of the General Assembly and stated that it would not cooperate in carrying out this decision. In particular, the Soviet Union opposed the reference in the resolution to the Interim Committee of the General Assembly which the Soviet Union considered an illegal body and was boycotting. Thus the commission from the outset became directly involved in the cold war.

When the commission arrived in Korea, it was dependent on United States military authorities for housing, transportation, communication, and practically all other facilities. The United States military authorities through their security arrangements controlled all access to the commission. The Interim Committee's decision to hold a South Korean election, whether right or wrong, resulted largely from United States insistence based on the desire of the United States military authorities to set up a civilian government in South Korea at the earliest possible moment. The leaders of the more moderate parties in Korea and half of the membership of UNTCOK disapproved of this decision. Afterwards there was constant dissension among the members of UNTCOK concealed by the commission's practice of not reporting its votes publicly. However, the existence of this dissension was known everywhere. Thus, even if UNTCOK and later

UNCOK were not considered to be instruments of the United States or the conservative South Korean groups headed by Dr. Syngman Rhee, neither were they regarded as impartial groups.

Neither UNTCOK nor UNCOK ever received adequate authority from the General Assembly to carry on the activities they were required to carry on. The original General Assembly resolution establishing UNTCOK never contemplated a situation where UNTCOK would be operating only in South Korea and therefore never defined the relationship between UNTCOK and a South Korean government. The terms of reference of UNCOK in its first year were most inadequate. The South Korean Government had to pay some regard to UNTCOK until it reported on the 1948 elections since conceivably the report might have been unfavorable— a remote possibility in view of the strong Western interest in organizing a government in South Korea at the earliest possible moment.

After UNTCOK approved the elections, however, the South Korean Government found it an inconvenience. In its first year of operations, from the fall of 1948 to the fall of 1949, it had no substantial functions and appeared to the South Korean Government merely a group that interfered with the exercise of sovereignty by that government. In the second year of operations, UNCOK received greater cooperation probably because of indications from the United States that it did not approve of the anti-United Nations attitudes of the South Koreans. The imminent threat of invasion from the north may also have changed the South Korean attitude somewhat. Furthermore, the resolution of the 1949 General Assembly clarified the terms of reference of UNCOK and gave it a substantive function of observing the military threats from North Korea. In short, both UNTCOK and UNCOK were hampered in their operations by inadequate authority.

The structure and organization of both UNTCOK and UNCOK were unsuitable for the tasks delegated to them. UNTCOK consisted of nine representatives of governments and UNCOK of seven. It was impossible for either group to act rapidly because of the necessity of obtaining instructions from their governments. When conscientious delegates, for example, the Indian delegate to UNTCOK, attempted to use their own judgment in emergencies, such as to decide whether to go ahead with an election in South Korea, they sometimes found their positions overruled by the home government.

The organizational inadequacy of UNCOK would probably have shown up even more strongly if contact had been made with the North Koreans. An agreement to establish a national government would have depended on delicate negotiations conducted with secrecy and judiciousness. Either a talented individual appointed by the United Nations Secretariat or technically qualified experts appointed either by the Secretariat or individual governments would have been better suited to conduct this type of negotiation than the political delegates of states.

The organization was unsuitable to accomplish its objectives and the quality of personnel steadily declined with the increasing frustration of the activities of UNTCOK and UNCOK. Originally, the French delegate was the renowned Paul Boncour, and there were several other delegates of ambassadorial rank. In later years, the delegates were of low rank and absented themselves for long periods from the meetings. Immediately after the elections in 1948, practically all of UNTCOK's personnel went to Shanghai to prepare a report and thus were away from Korea during the period when they might have exercised the greatest influence on the South Korean Government. In the fall of 1948, M. Boncour insisted that UNTCOK attend the General Assembly in Paris at United Nations expense, even though this served no useful purpose. The delegates from China and the Philippines never made any pretence of taking a position contrary to Dr. Syngman Rhee's.

In the main UNTCOK and UNCOK based what little peace observation they accomplished on published materials and interviews with government officials. Although some efforts were made to broaden the contacts with individuals, these efforts were not pressed far, especially when the Syngman Rhee government started imprisoning individuals who had contacted the commission.

This method of operation was inevitable in view of the limited size of the commissions and the lack of technical qualifications of most of the personnel. When UNTCOK, and UNCOK in the second year of its operations, observed elections, they used all personnel regardless of their previous training. Even then, the numbers were too few to accomplish anything except random sampling. UNCOK in its first year of operation observed the withdrawal of American troops even though there was only one individual in UNCOK with military experience. The only genuinely skillful observation of the 38th parallel immediately before the North Korean invasion in June 1950 was the work of two military observers who were assigned to the commission by the United Nations Secretariat less than a month prior to the beginning of hostilities. In short, the concept of peace observation that seemed to prevail in the commission until the end was to hold meetings, hear witnesses, and evaluate written material. The sole contact with North Korea came through listening to radio broadcasts from Pyongyang and from reading Communist literature which crossed the border.

In these adverse circumstances, the United Nations Secretariat performed its duties efficiently. A number of outstanding officers were assigned from time to time to UNTCOK and UNCOK and facilitated the preparation of the informative reports to the General Assembly. The group was always identified with the United Nations by the United Nations flag and insignia. This resulted in popular enthusiasm for the group even when the South Korean Government was hostile.

The fact that UNTCOK and UNCOK had positive achievements—ensuring reasonably free elections, moderating some of the extreme policies of the South Korean Government, determining that the North Koreans were the aggressors—is strong evidence of the desirability of the presence of representatives of an international organization in an area during a period of international tension. This is true even when the possible usefulness of the group is diminished from the outset by the conditions under which it is established and by its unsatisfactory organization and terms of reference, as was the case in Korea.

UNITED NATIONS COMMISSION FOR THE UNIFICATION AND REHABILITATION OF KOREA (UNCURK), 1950–1964

On June 25, 1950, the North Korean forces crossed the 38th parallel and invaded South Korea. Excepting for brief truces, hostilities continued until the conclusion of an armistice agreement on July 27, 1953.

The United Nations Commission on Korea (UNCOK), which had been responsible for peace observation and other functions in 1949 and 1950, filed its final report in October 1950, and the 1950 General Assembly did not continue the commission. In lieu of UNCOK, the Assembly established the United Nations Commission for the Unification and Rehabilitation of Korea:

> ... to (i) assume the functions hitherto exercised by the present United Nations Commission on Korea; (ii) represent the United Nations in bringing about the establishment of a unified, independent and democratic government of all Korea; (iii) exercise such responsibilities in connexion with relief and rehabilitation in Korea as may be determined by the General Assembly after receiving the recommendations of the Economic and Social Council. [51]

If progress had been made in the direction of a unified Korea, UNCURK would have had peace-observation functions by virtue of its succeeding to the functions of UNCOK. Theoretically, UNCURK, as the successor to UNCOK, has the authority "to observe and report any developments which might lead to or otherwise involve military conflict in Korea." However, the machinery set up under the armistice agreement has assumed this function until a settlement is reached.

The reports of UNCURK usually cover: (1) the unification of Korea; (2) withdrawal of foreign troops; (3) participation of North Korea in General Assembly discussions; and (4) international relations of South Korea and political conditions in South Korea. On the unification of Korea UNCURK's role has been limited "owing to the persistent non-acceptance of the United Nations principles and resolutions for the unification of Korea

[51] UN General Assembly, Res. 376 (V), Oct. 7, 1950. Hereafter cited as Res. 376 (V).

by the North Korean authorities."[52] On the withdrawal of troops, the Soviet Union has taken the position that "so long as there are foreign troops in the south of the Korean peninsula, Korea cannot be unified by peaceful means."[53] The United Nations position continues to be "that the United Nations forces, which were sent to Korea in accordance with resolutions of the United Nations, have in greater part already been withdrawn, and that the governments concerned are prepared to withdraw their remaining forces from Korea when the conditions for a lasting settlement laid down by the General Assembly have been fulfilled."[54] Thus an impasse exists.

The United Nations has conditioned North Korean participation in General Assembly discussions since 1961 on its acceptance of "the competence and authority of the United Nations to deal with the Korean question." The North Koreans refuse to recognize this, and thus there is another impasse.

The comments of UNCURK in its reports on international relations of and political conditions in South Korea are not invariably favorable to the South Korean Government, particularly on the substitution of military for coalition government.[55] UNCURK may be a moderating influence.

In addition to the above, UNCURK reports place great stress on the commission's function of preserving democratic institutions in Korea and in particular on the observation of elections.[56] They also deal with economic conditions in South Korea and with UNCURK's liaison with the Agent General of the United Nations Korean Reconstruction Agency (UNKRA). They invariably point out "that the armistice agreement remains in full force and has not been superseded by a proper peace settlement."[57]

None of UNCURK's activities, in view of their remote relationship both to the maintenance of order along the boundary and to the ultimate objective of a peaceful settlement, could properly be deemed peace observation. Any peace observation that has taken place since the armistice comes under the aegis of the armistice machinery.

NEUTRAL NATIONS SUPERVISORY COMMISSION (NNSC) AND MILITARY ARMISTICE COMMISSION (MAC), 1953–1964

After two years of bitter negotiations between the Commander-in-Chief of the United Nations Command on the one hand and the Supreme

[52] UN General Assembly, *Official Records*, Seventeenth Session, Supplement No. 13, A/5213, p. 1. Hereafter cited as A/5213.

[53] UN Security Council, S/5140, June 25, 1962, p. 3 (mimeo.).

[54] A/5213, p. 2.

[55] UN General Assembly, *Official Records*, Sixteenth Session, Supplement No. 13, A/4900.

[56] UN General Assembly, *Official Records*, Eighteenth Session, Supplement No. 12A, A/5512/Add. 1.

[57] A/5213, p. 3.

Commander of the Korean People's Army and the Commander of the Chinese People's Volunteers on the other, a military armistice was achieved in Korea on July 27, 1953. The agreement established a Military Armistice Commission (MAC) and a Neutral Nations Supervisory Commission (NNSC), both of which have peace-observation functions. The failure of the Geneva Conference in 1954 to establish a peace based on the agreed objective of a unified and independent Korea in no way affected the continuance of the armistice. The MAC and the NNSC have continued to the present, though their peace-observation activities today are different from those that were contemplated at the time the armistice was signed. Neither the NNSC nor the MAC was required to report regularly to the United Nations, although occasional special reports have been filed and considered by the United Nations General Assembly.

Terms of Reference

The Military Armistice Commission consists of ten senior officers:[58] five from the United Nations Command and five from the North Korean and Chinese forces. It was provided with joint observers teams, the operations of which it would direct. "The mission of the Joint Observer Teams shall be to assist the Military Armistice Commission in supervising the carrying out of the provisions of this Armistice Agreement pertaining to the Demilitarized Zone and the Han River Estuary." The MAC or, with certain restrictions, the senior member of either side was authorized to dispatch joint observer teams "to investigate violations of this Armistice Agreement reported to have occurred in the Demilitarized Zone or in the Han River Estuary."

The MAC also transmits to the commanders of the opposite sides all reports of violations of the agreement and other reports received from the NNSC. It was authorized "to request the Neutral Nations Supervisory Commission to conduct special observations and inspections at places outside the Demilitarized Zone where violations of this Armistice Agreement have been reported to have occurred." The MAC was required to report violations and also their correction to the commanders of both sides and to meet daily with provision for agreed recesses not to exceed seven days.

The NNSC consists of four senior officers: two nominated by the United Nations Command, one each from Switzerland and Sweden; two nominated by the Koreans and Chinese, one each from Czechoslovakia and Poland. Besides conducting special observations outside the demilitarized zone at the request of the MAC or the senior officer of the MAC on either side, it has the functions of conducting inspections and reporting the results

[58] For the complete text of the Korean Armistice Agreement from which the following information is taken, see U.S. Department of State, *United States Treaties and Other International Agreements Series*, No. 2782 (July 27, 1953). Hereafter cited as TIAS 2782.

to the MAC in connection with the agreements of both sides to (1) "cease the introduction into Korea of reinforcing military personnel" and (2) "cease the introduction into Korea of reinforcing combat aircraft, armoured vehicles, weapons, and ammunition." The armistice makes specific provision for the rotation of personnel and replenishing of armaments.

The NNSC was to establish twenty Neutral Nations Inspection Teams, five located at ports in South Korea and five located at ports in North Korea, and ten to be held in reserve near the headquarters of the NNSC. The NNSC was to meet daily in Panmunjom with provision for agreed recesses not exceeding seven days. The records of all meetings were to be forwarded to the MAC. The inspection teams were to make periodic reports and also special reports to the NNSC, which would send copies to the MAC. The NNSC or any member was authorized to communicate with any member of the MAC. This provision turned out to be very important.

Thus, the MAC was to have responsibility for peace observation in the demilitarized zone and for directing peace observation by the NNSC in areas outside the zone except in the ports where permanent inspection teams of the NNSC were stationed under the terms of the treaty. In effect, the NNSC has no authority except to report violations to the MAC which can "settle" them "through negotiations" and report them to the commanders of the opposing sides. The treaty provides only for ground inspection.

Organization

The MAC consists of ten senior officers, five appointed by the UN Command and five appointed by the North Korean and Chinese Communists. It was provided initially with ten joint observer teams consisting of not more than six nor less than four officers of field grade, half appointed by the UN Command and half by the Communists. The number of observer teams was reduced from time to time; at present there are four. The MAC has an extensive secretariat. However, its organizational arrangements cover all of its activities, only a small fraction of which could be deemed to be peace observation.

The armistice agreement contains detailed provisions concerning the organization of the NNSC. (1) It is composed of four senior officers, one from each of the neutral nations who "shall be permitted to use staff assistants." (2) Administrative personnel is furnished by the neutral nations. (3) The NNSC was to be initially assisted by twenty Neutral Nations Inspection Teams, ten stationed at specified ports, five in North Korea and five in South Korea, and ten mobile teams held in reserve in the vicinity of Panmunjom. (4) Each inspection team consisted of not less than four officers, preferably of field grade, two from the Swedish and Swiss contingent and two from the Polish and Czech contingent. Subteams of two officers "may be formed as circumstances require" with half either

Swedish or Swiss and half either Polish or Czech. Additional personnel were furnished either by the neutral nations or by the commanders of each side. Every eight weeks, Switzerland and Sweden rotated personnel assigned to fixed posts in designated ports because of the depressing effect of service at these posts.

Each of the four contingents consisted of ninety-five men. Four officers arrived in Korea on July 25, less than a month after the armistice. Sixty-four arrived on September 9 and the remainder shortly thereafter. The ninety-five were allocated as follows: 15–20 to the secretariat and command headquarters; 35–40 to the inspection teams located at designated ports; 30–35 to the mobile inspection teams; and 5–10 to special functions in the camp.[59]

At the first meeting of the NNSC, a secretariat was agreed on of approximately twenty-five (six for each country) to prepare meetings, make records of meetings, deal with requests of the MAC for inspections, and inform the MAC on the results of inspections. Agreement was also reached on insignia, identification cards, and all organizational problems.[60]

Each of the four states assigned three or four men to each fixed inspection post, a chief, an assistant, a secretary or interpreter, and a telegrapher. Since reports from the fixed posts were infrequent and late, the NNSC dispatched inspection teams toward the end of 1953 to determine on-the-spot activities at the fixed posts, that is, whether the instructions from the NNSC were suitable to work needs and whether the living conditions were satisfactory. The inspection was completed in eight days in the south where the inspectors traveled by helicopter, and in thirty days in the north where the railways were the sole means of transportation. The inspectors found the conditions to be satisfactory.[61]

The organization of the ten mobile groups depended on the function they were called on to perform. The first group was set up to investigate complaints both from the North Koreans and from United Nations Command concerning conditions in prison camps in South Korea. The group attempted to include personnel with legal training. The composition of the second group was different since it was called on to investigate the illegal entry of military planes into North Korea. During the period ending November 30, 1953, only four of the ten mobile teams had been used for six days. Therefore, Switzerland proposed the reduction of the number of teams to six and this was accepted.[62] Early in 1955, at the request of Switzerland and after General Assembly discussion, two stationary teams

[59] Switzerland, "Rapport du Conseil fédéral à l'Assemblée fédérale sur la participation de délégués suisses à l'exécution de la convention d'armistice conclue en Corée le 27 juillet 1953," *Feuille fédérale de la Confédération Suisse, 1955*, I, pp. 707, 711. Hereafter cited as "Rapport du Conseil fédéral."

[60] "Rapport du Conseil fédéral," pp. 711–12.

[61] "Rapport du Conseil fédéral," p. 714.

[62] "Rapport du Conseil fédéral," pp. 715–16.

were abolished in each area (North Korea and South Korea), and the size of the remaining six fixed teams was reduced by 50 percent.[63]

On May 3, 1956, the United Nations Command requested the NNSC to withdraw the fixed inspection teams from South Korean ports because the Communists were in default on their obligation not to rearm North Korea and to permit inspections to verify this result. Therefore, it was inequitable for the teams to operate in the south. On June 8, the NNSC withdrew all of its fixed teams and instructed the personnel to return to Panmunjom.[64]

Since June 1956, all that remains of the NNSC is stationed at Panmunjom: the commission itself, the secretariat, and the representatives at command headquarters. The commission continues to meet daily and adjourn in less than five minutes. For a number of years, it has not had any business to transact.

The main expenses of the NNSC (food, lodging, transport) were borne by the belligerents. This never created a problem since it was the Communist side that pressed for the continuance of the NNSC. The salaries of personnel and the cost of operational equipment are borne by the neutral nations without reimbursement as a contribution to the maintenance of international peace.[65]

Performance

The peace-observation functions of the MAC were: (1) to patrol the boundaries of the demilitarized zone and the Han River estuary; (2) to investigate incidents in the demilitarized zone at the request of either party; and (3) to request the NNSC to conduct special observations at places outside the demilitarized zone.[66] The latter function disappeared when the NNSC ceased virtually all of its activities in 1957. The MAC continues to carry on the first two functions. For example, in 1962 it investigated a fire-fight incident on the border and checked the demarcation line markers. The reports of the observation teams are classified. However, much of their content can be found in the records of the public meetings of the MAC. Since both sides apparently desire to avoid incidents in the demilitarized zone, the boundary line remained relatively tranquil.

As pointed out earlier, the NNSC was established to prevent the introduction into either North or South Korea of military personnel or weapons

[63] Jacques Freymond, "Supervising Agreements: The Korean Experience," *Foreign Affairs*, XXXVII: 3 (April 1959), p. 501.

[64] "Withdrawal of NNSC Teams from South Korea," U.S. Department of State, *Bulletin*, Vol. 34 (1956), pp. 967–71.

[65] "Rapport du Conseil fédéral," p. 738.

[66] TIAS 2782, pars. 26–28.

beyond those existing on the date of the armistice. It was to accomplish this objective in the main through three types of operations:

1. Fixed inspection teams were to be located in five ports in North Korea and five ports in South Korea. Since Korea had no substantial armaments industry of its own, presumably all armament shipments as well as all troop movements would be through these ten ports. The fixed inspection teams were to be permitted to observe all shipments coming through the ports to determine whether there were violations of the armistice agreement.

2. The North Koreans and the United Nations Command were each to give full reports on all replacements of personnel and materials to the NNSC. The headquarters group would audit these reports to obtain information pertinent to the observance of the armistice.

3. If either side suspected violations of the armistice, it could request inspections anywhere in North or South Korea to determine whether such violations had taken place. Ten mobile neutral nations inspection teams were held in reserve in Panmunjom to carry out such inspections.

The NNSC did not submit regular reports to the United Nations. The first official report of the results of peace observation was from the Swiss Council to the Swiss Federal Assembly on the participation of the Swiss delegates in the NNSC. This report, which was presented on May 5, 1955, deals with the period from the armistice on July 27, 1953, to March 1955. Much of the same ground was covered in a statement by the Swedish delegate to the First Committee of the General Assembly on December 2, 1954.[67]

The report of the Swiss Federal Council notes that on April 14, 1953, more than three months before the armistice, the Swiss Government had dispatched an *aide mémoire* to the United States Government pointing out that the Poles and Czechs were not neutral within the popular meaning of that term, but merely nonbelligerent. The *aide mémoire* further pointed out imperfections in the armistice agreement:

> Ten days' notice of commencement of the functions was not sufficient to permit the observers to station themselves to take up their work in Korea.
>
> The fixed observers would be located only in ten ports and would be unable to report on use of other ports or on airplanes entering Korea.
>
> Since the commission had four members, in the event of failure to agree there would be two commission reports.
>
> The commission would have no independent communication and transportation system.

[67] UN General Assembly, *Official Records*, Ninth Session, First Committee, 738th meeting, Dec. 2, 1954.

The United States reply on May 20 took the position that the United States would attempt to clarify some of these questions in the armistice negotiations and that the MAC would work out satisfactory procedures.[68]

Switzerland and Sweden organized their groups in advance, and the first contingent went to Tokyo in June. As previously pointed out, the first small Swiss and Swedish contingents arrived in Korea on July 25. The first meeting of the NNSC took place on August 1. While the NNSC had no difficulty in solving procedural questions, no agreement was reached on several matters important to the successful operation of the NNSC. Within the first month, it became quite clear to the Swiss and Swedish representatives that: (1) the Poles and Czechs were not neutral; (2) entries and exits of materials and personnel in North Korea were taking place outside of the five ports and therefore knowledge of these entries had to depend on the reports from North Korea; (3) the mobile inspection units could not engage in inspections unless a majority so decided; and (4) most of the demands for inspections from the United Nations Command were refused as a result of a two to two vote in the inspection teams.[69]

The Swiss delegate continued that the South Koreans desired a large amount of control and the North Koreans in contrast desired minimum control. There were occasional errors in the reports from South Korea, but these simply represented negligence in furnishing a large mass of telegrams and other reports. In South Korea, three of the fixed observation groups worked day and night (those at Pusan, Inchon, and Taegu). There were practically no shipments to the remaining two ports in South Korea. All nonmilitary shipments as well as military shipments to South Korea were declared, and the Poles and Czechs insisted on complete inspections.

In contrast, in North Korea there was minimum traffic in two ports, and none at all in the other three. General Harlan C. Parks, of the United States Air Force, in 1955 reported the construction of railways to bypass the ports. When the Swiss and Swedish delegates wished to inspect trains, they were required to announce their intention two hours in advance. When the teams arrived at the station, it was practically deserted. If a train was there, the Poles and Czechs refused to allow inspection if the station master said that it contained no military equipment. The North Koreans produced no bills of lading or other documents. Many lines of communication from Manchuria and Siberia into North Korea did not pass through the ports of entry. No air traffic was examined. In short, it was impossible at any time to apply in the north the strict procedures used in the south.[70]

[68] "Rapport du Conseil fédéral," pp. 691–92.
[69] "Rapport du Conseil fédéral," p. 713.
[70] "Rapport du Conseil fédéral," pp. 717–18.

The Swiss delegate demonstrated the inadequacy of North Korean reporting of armament movements through the following table summarizing armament movements as reported by the parties from the beginning of the armistice until the end of 1954:[71]

Type of Armament	South Korea	North Korea
Combat planes	631	0
Combat vehicles	631	7
Rifles	82,860	641
Munitions	226,000,000 rounds	56,650 rounds

General Parks, the senior member of the United Nations Command in the MAC, made a statement to the MAC summarizing the North Korean armistice violations. He quotes the senior Swiss member: "I think we have the right to ask ourselves how it is possible that an army [the North Korean] counting several hundred thousand soldiers can be logistically supported by the amount of material as shown by the figures which are being submitted to us."[72] General Parks pointed out that all airfields in North Korea were inoperative on July 27, 1953. United Nations Command radar surveillance detected continually increasing jet aircraft activity after that date, despite the North Korean reports that no aircraft had been shipped into North Korea. On September 21, 1953, this evidence was confirmed when a North Korean pilot defected and surrendered a MIG-15 to the United Nations Command. The pilot said he personally observed at least eighty combat aircraft brought into North Korea.[73]

With respect to the mobile teams, most of the requests of the United Nations Command for inspections were vetoed by Poland and Czechoslovakia. The few that took place in North Korea were unsatisfactory. On February 12, 1954, the Chinese Communists and North Koreans announced that they would not admit the mobile teams into North Korea at the request of the United Nations Command because the inquiries were based on lying complaints.[74]

In fact, on April 30, 1954, the Polish and Czech members of the NNSC filed a complaint against the United Nations Command based on a thorough study of United Nations Command reports. They accused the UN Command of over-reporting the outgoing combat material, under-reporting the incoming combat material and introducing changed types of

[71] "Rapport du Conseil fédéral," p. 723.

[72] "UN Command Cites Violations of Korean Armistice Agreement," U.S. Department of State, *Bulletin*, Vol. 33 (1955), p. 192. Hereafter cited as "UN Command Cites Violations."

[73] "UN Command Cites Violations," pp. 192–93.

[74] "Rapport du Conseil fédéral," p. 719.

aircraft. On May 4, the Swedish and Swiss members commented on the Polish and Czech contentions as follows:

> These are some of the comments the Swedish and Swiss members want to present in order to refute allegations which they consider to be a tissue of malicious fabrications, gratuitous distortions, misleading half-truths, and delusive insinuations without foundation in reality. The methods resorted to consist largely in isolating facts and figures from their proper context and in making sweeping generalizations on the basis of premises thus distorted.
>
> There is no denying that the United Nations Command has laid itself wide open to inspection and observation by the Neutral Nations Inspection Teams and has never attempted to conceal anything from the Neutral Nations Supervisory Commission not even its mistakes and clerical shortcomings.... As far as the Swedish and Swiss Members have been able to find the United Nations Command has loyally and sincerely abided by the letter and spirit of the Armistice Agreement.[75]

The situation of much inspection in South Korea and none in North Korea led to hostility by the South Koreans toward the NNSC culminating in demonstrations on July 31 against the NNSC. Ostensibly to assure the safety of its members, steps were taken by the South Koreans that reduced the freedom of movement of the inspection teams. Possibly because of the demonstrations in South Korea, the Polish and Czech members became more conciliatory after July 20, 1954, and a number of inspections took place in North Korea after that time.[76]

Nevertheless, inspections continued to be frustrated. For example, on February 21, 1955, the United Nations Command requested a mobile inspection team investigation of six airfields where it was claimed that MIG aircraft had been illegally introduced, and the Czech and Polish delegates stalled the dispatch of the inspection team for one week. Despite the concealment of aircraft during that week, eighty-eight MIG's were observed on these fields, but the Czech and Polish members vetoed requests by the Swiss and Swedish members for available documents to establish when the aircraft were brought into North Korea.

Subsequently, two defectors from North Korea described the ruses employed by the North Koreans to prevent the discovery of the violations, and these were presented by General Parks at the July 5, 1955, meeting of the MAC.

A. Your side [the Communists] flew many combat aircraft away from the inspected airfields.

B. Your side hid combat aircraft in ravines in the hills in the vicinity of the airfields and camouflaged them.

---

[75] "Excerpts from May 4 Memorandum to Korean Military Armistice Commission," U.S. Department of State, *Bulletin*, Vol. 30 (1954), p. 947.

[76] "Rapport du Conseil fédéral," pp. 722, 725.

C. Your side dismantled some of the aircraft and concealed them.

D. Your side stationed heavy guards about the hiding places and prevented inspection of these areas by the mobile inspection teams.

E. Your side arbitrarily reduced the boundaries of the airfields, thereby restricting the scope of the mobile inspection team inspection.

F. Your side prepared false testimony by long, detailed coaching of probable witnesses and by substituting politically indoctrinated higher ranking officers for lower ranking officers by switching insignias.

G. Your side delayed the assembly of newly arrived combat aircraft at Taechon by leaving them in their crates until the mobile inspection team investigations were completed. Senior Lieutenant Lee, who reads Russian, noticed the wording 'Kiev Aircraft Factory' on tags attached to one of his unit's combat aircraft. This aircraft's log book showed that the plane left the Russian factory in March 1955.[77]

As early as April 14, 1954, the Swiss and Swedish delegates had suggested to the North Koreans and the United Nations Command that the NNSC be terminated.[78] The Czech and Polish delegates as well as the Chinese Communists had opposed this request on the ground that the NNSC was a necessary part of the treaty mechanism. Again on May 4, the Swedish and Swiss delegates, as authorized in the armistice agreement, addressed a letter to General Julius Lacey, then United Nations Commander and senior member of the MAC, describing the inability of the NNSC to investigate in North Korea and requesting a reconsideration of the armistice provisions. It was suggested that three of the North Korean ports should be replaced with three railroad crossing points from Manchuria to North Korea.[79]

As indicated earlier, after consideration by the 1954 General Assembly of the situation in Korea, agreement was reached to reduce the stationary inspection teams by abolishing two in each area. Furthermore, there was a 50 percent reduction in the number of men on the remaining teams.

On January 25, 1955, an *aide mémoire* from Switzerland and Sweden suggested the abolition of the NNSC. The United States reply on March 2 said: "the Government of the United States agrees with the Government of Sweden (Switzerland) that the NNSC should be abolished." Furthermore, the United States doubted "that any useful purpose would be served by a continuance of the Neutral Nations Supervisory Commission.[80] At a

---

[77] "UN Command Cites Violations," pp. 195–96.

[78] "Rapport du Conseil fédéral," p. 740. At the 1954 Geneva Conference, General Bedell Smith, U.S. Under Secretary of State, also expressed the view that the NNSC was useless. See "U.S. Views on Communist Proposals at Geneva," U.S. Department of State, *Bulletin*, Vol. 30 (1954), p. 941.

[79] "Rapport du Conseil fédéral," pp. 720–22.

[80] "Reply to Sweden and Switzerland on Korean Supervisory Commission," U.S. Department of State, *Bulletin*, Vol. 32 (1955), p. 429.

press conference on August 16, 1955, Secretary of State Dulles stated that the NNSC was obsolete and thus reaffirmed the United States position.[81]

With the complete frustration of and the growing sentiment against the NNSC, the United Nations Command on May 31, 1956, informed the Communist Command in Korea and the NNSC of its intention to suspend the activities of the NNSC's teams in the three South Korean ports because of Communist violations of the armistice agreement. The United Nations Command justified this action on the basis that the armistice agreement was a contract including certain provisions with which the other side had failed to comply, that is, the provisions on reporting, reinforcement, and supervision.

At a meeting of the MAC on June 4, the Communist representatives attacked the United Nations Command for violations of the armistice agreement and demanded the withdrawal of the May 31 announcement. When the United Nations Command refused to withdraw the announcement, on June 5 the NNSC unanimously agreed to recommend to the MAC the provisional withdrawal of the fixed inspection teams both in North and South Korea. The Communist side in the MAC declined to accept the NNSC recommendation, but they could do nothing since the NNSC teams in South Korea were required to withdraw by June 9. The teams in North Korea returned to Panmunjom on June 10 and 11.[82]

From this point on, the activities of the NNSC were limited to recording information furnished by either side. The personnel was further reduced to reflect the more limited functions. However, there has been no further pressure either from the Communists or the United Nations Command to abolish the NNSC. The comment of the best historian of the NNSC on this situation is as follows:

> The Americans and South Koreans, no longer hampered by the presence of the Czechoslovaks and Poles and free to accelerate the modernization of their armament, now showed less haste to do away with a body which had ceased to inconvenience them and might even serve to restrain the propaganda against them by the North Koreans and Chinese. The Neutral Nations Supervisory Commission thus remains a façade, maintained only because of apprehension about the void which would occur if it were abolished.[83]

The final collapse of peace observation took place in 1957 with the decision of the United States, in its capacity as the Unified Command, to proceed with the rearmament of South Korea "in order to maintain a relative military balance in Korea and thus to preserve the stability of the

[81] "Transcript of Secretary Dulles' News Conference," U.S. Department of State, *Bulletin*, Vol. 33 (1955), p. 340.

[82] UN General Assembly, A/3167, Aug. 16, 1956, p. 6 (mimeo.).

[83] Freymond, *op. cit.*, p. 501.

armistice.[84] In the report, the United States cited the failure of the North Koreans to live up to paragraph 13(d) of the armistice agreement which required both sides to cease the introduction into Korea of reinforcing combat aircraft, armored vehicles, weapons, and ammunition with provisions for replacement of worn-out equipment. The report cited the inability of the NNSC to obtain information because of Communist obstruction. It stated specifically that the Communists had built up their air force in North Korea to more than seven hundred planes (without disclosing the source of this information). Therefore, the United Nations Command "considers that it is entitled to be relieved of corresponding obligations under . . . [paragraph 13(d)] until such time as the relative military balance has been restored and your side, by its actions, has demonstrated its willingness to comply." The report stated that "the United Nations Command does not intend to start an arms race and . . . that the replacement weapons are being deployed for defensive purposes only." Furthermore, the United Nations Command would fully observe "the cease-fire and all the provisions of the Armistice Agreement save to the extent to which it is entitled to be relieved from compliance because of Communist violations of sub-paragraph 13(d) and of those covered in its statement to the Military Armistice Commission of 31 May 1956."[85] This statement covered violations of 13(c), restriction of introduction of military personnel, as well as 13(d). Since the NNSC was established only to observe the enforcement of 13(c) and 13(d), it ceased, therefore, to have any function, but it continues to exist.

Evaluation

It is clear that the Communists completely disregarded the provisions of the armistice agreement intended to prevent the introduction of additional military strength into North Korea, and frustrated the NNSC in carrying out its functions. Nevertheless, despite Communist obstruction, the Swiss and Swedish members obtained sufficient information concerning the North Korean violations to permit reports to the United Nations on such violations. The United Nations Command, of course, had far more detailed information than the Swedish and Swiss members of the NNSC. However, the confirmation of such information from the observers of two neutral states unquestionably strengthened the United Nations Command case in the General Assembly as well as in the forums of world public opinion. On the other hand, the Communists found the existence of the NNSC useful in veiling their violations of the armistice. On the whole, it seems difficult to disagree with the previously mentioned views of General Bedell Smith and Secretary Dulles that the NNSC was useless and obsolete.

[84] UN General Assembly, A/3631, Aug. 13, 1957, p. 1 (mimeo.).
[85] *Ibid.*, p. 4.

Jacques Freymond, who has written the history of the NNSC, points out the limitations of authority which assured its failure. Paraphrasing his presentation:[86]

1. The NNSC was devoid of executive power and not concerned with the follow-up of any violations that it might observe. The follow-up rested with the MAC.

2. The NNSC was restricted in a geographical sense in that supplies to either side in violation of the armistice agreement need not come through the ten ports designated for inspection teams. The fixed teams had no freedom of movement.

3. The NNSC in North Korea and at certain times in South Korea was accompanied by body guards who restricted its movements even in the limited areas where it had access.

4. The NNSC was immobilized from within by the inability to make decisions since on all crucial issues the vote was two to two.

5. Most important, the NNSC, despite its description, was not neutral. The Polish and Czech representatives invariably supported the Communists.

Freymond derived the following lessons, again paraphrased, from the NNSC experience:[87]

1. Armistice supervision should be organized with the greatest care, and procedures should be worked out in advance to the smallest detail. This did not happen in the Korean Armistice Agreement.

2. The countries participating in peace supervision should be consulted in advance. The Swiss made useful suggestions, but the armistice agreement had already reached a point where the suggestions could not be carried out.

3. The observation teams must be assured freedom of movement with no restrictions to specified areas. The South Koreans feared espionage from the Polish and Czech members, and they as well as the North Koreans restricted movements.

4. Violations and attempts to violate the armistice by either side should be punishable. This was not provided for in the armistice agreement.

5. Reports of the inspectors should be given the widest publicity.

6. Peace supervision should be placed in the right hands. The personnel should have a political background, a knowledge of international and military affairs, and moral authority before the world. While the Swiss and Swedish personnel qualified under these criteria, this could not be claimed for the Czech and Polish personnel.

7. A corps with special training should be created. This implies advance knowledge to the participating countries of their participation. The advance notice to the members of the NNSC was entirely inadequate.

Mr. Freymond's criticisms of the NNSC cover the organizational flaws that made its failure a certainty. He does not deal, however, with the fact

[86] Freymond, *op. cit.*, p. 497.
[87] *Ibid.*, pp. 502–3.

that the United States and the United Nations Command were apparently
aware of these flaws in advance and were prepared to deal with the situation if NNSC should fail. The very fact that the Communists would suggest
as "neutral" members of the commission not only the Czechs and Poles but
also the Soviet Union was an indication that the Communists never intended the commission to be neutral. Technically speaking, Czechoslovakia, Poland, and the Soviet Union were nonbelligerents, but the
Soviet Union was in fact furnishing most of the logistic support which was
needed by the North Koreans to carry on hostilities. Admiral C. Turner
Joy, the first chief negotiator for the United Nations Command, deals with
this in great detail in his book, describing the Panmunjom negotiations:[88]

> Our concept of an armistice was that of a cease fire arranged under conditions
> precluding substantial change in the relative strengths of the opposing sides.
> . . . When Washington decided in a final effort to achieve an armistice to allow
> the Communists to build airfields in North Korea during the truce period, the
> basic premise upon which the armistice had been designed went up in a wisp
> of smoke. With that action there was no longer any chance to prevent the
> military capabilities of Communist forces in Korea from increasing in a major
> degree during the truce.

Admiral Joy implies naiveté in Washington in permitting such a development. It seems more probable that Admiral Joy was naive in attributing
naiveté to Washington.

As previously pointed out, the Swiss Government had presented an
aide mémoire to the United States on April 14, 1953, prior to the signing of
the armistice, pointing out that the Poles and Czechs were not neutral and
that other conditions made it improbable that the NNSC would function.[89]
The United States reply suggested that the United States would attempt to
clarify some of the provisions of the armistice and would attempt to work out
procedures in the MAC for resolving impasses. It is difficult to believe that
the United States really thought that the impasses could be worked out
either before the armistice or in the MAC at a later date.

The inevitable conclusion must be that the United States had made a
decision not to take the risk of bringing the hostilities to a conclusion
through driving the Communists out of Korea. Such a course certainly
would have involved bombing Communist China and the risk of broadening the Korean war into a world war. A recent writer on the Korean
situation, Gene M. Lyons, states:

> It is, of course, difficult to pin down exactly when, after the setback of
> November and December, 1950, the United States decided it was not willing
> to risk open war with Red China and possibly the Soviet Union to create a

[88] Charles Turner Joy, *How Communists Negotiate* (New York: Macmillan, 1955),
pp. 72–73.
[89] "Rapport du Conseil fédéral," p. 690.

situation which would permit the early unification of Korea. By March, 1951, however, the government in Washington seems to have been coming around to the position of consolidating the Republic of Korea behind the 38th parallel and leaving the matter of unification where it was before June 25, 1950: an ideal to be achieved through peaceful negotiation but with little chance of success within the near future. This seems clear in the reluctance of the State Department to respond to the request of the Joint Chiefs for 'political guidance' during February and March, particularly with regard to crossing the 38th parallel again.

At any rate, American policy seems clear. The United States agreed to negotiate a cease-fire arrangement, but rejected the proposal for the withdrawal of foreign troops and determined that U.S. troops would remain in Korea until a genuine peace was achieved. In point of fact, the United States thus accepted the existence of a divided Korea until such time as it was certain that a peaceful unification of the peninsula could be gained. This certainty depended on the proven good will not only of the Soviet Union but of Communist China as well. Since the United States could not be optimistic about the intentions of either, it seems reasonable to conclude that American policy now assumed the condition of a divided Korea for some time to come, at least until there was a sharp change for the better in the course of the cold war. . . .[90]

The existence of such a policy was confirmed by the readiness of the United States to rearm South Korea when it became apparent that the alternative position contained in the armistice agreement of keeping North Korea relatively disarmed had failed.

If, as seems possible, the United States and the United Nations Command were convinced that the armistice provisions against rearming North Korea would fail and that the NNSC would be ineffective, the question arises why the negotiators of Panmunjom worked so hard to obtain these provisions in the armistice agreement. When the Communists suggested fixed posts in two ports in North Korea and two ports in South Korea, why did the United Nations Command call for fixed inspection posts in ten ports in each area and after months of negotiating compromise on five? Why did the United States and the United Nations Command object to the Soviet Union as a member of the NNSC and accept Poland and Czechoslovakia which were puppets of the Soviet Union? Would it not have been much better to have accepted the Soviet Union on the Supervisory Commission and changed the name of the commission from Neutral Nations Supervisory Commission to "Non-Belligerents Supervisory Commission"? With such a changed name, the Communists would not have had as good a vehicle in the forum of world opinion for concealing their violations.

It is suggested that the United States itself was interested in having an armistice agreement that in theory at least would aim to prevent the rearmament of the Communists in North Korea. From the standpoint of

[90] Gene M. Lyons, *Military Policy and Economic Aid: The Korean Case, 1950–1953* (Columbus: Ohio State University Press, 1961), pp. 52–53, 80.

domestic politics, President Truman had found great opposition to his decision to restrain General Douglas MacArthur and General Matthew Ridgway from broadening the hostilities to include Communist China. General Eisenhower during the presidential campaign had achieved publicity through his statement that he would fly to Korea, thus assuming that his personal presence might have some effect on Communist actions.

It seems probable that the provision for peace observation through the NNSC stemmed from the desire of the United States administration (after President Eisenhower's public stand) to obtain an armistice agreement that purported to keep North Korea relatively disarmed, especially since, if the agreement failed, the United States could fall back on its major political decision to rearm South Korea and permit the continuance of a divided Korea rather than to broaden hostilities. Thus the provisions for peace observation in the Korean Armistice Agreement were probably patterned as much to meet domestic political considerations in the United States as to create an effective instrumentality for peace observation.

It is somewhat ironical that the MAC machinery which calls for the belligerents themselves to carry out peace observation in the demilitarized zone has been relatively successful despite the absence of neutral observers. The reason, of course, is that the Communists did not *wish* incidents in the zone, and therefore any incidents that took place were accidental. On the other hand, the Communists determined to violate the armistice provisions which the NNSC was to supervise. The NNSC could detect large-scale violations but could not prevent them.

The NNSC experience is and should be of the greatest value in pointing out practical problems of peace observation and factors likely to lead to the success or failure of a mission.

5

—————•—————

THE PROBLEM OF KASHMIR

Kashmir is one of 500 princely states whose status was left undetermined at the end of World War II when the subcontinent was divided into two independent nations—India and Pakistan. Most of these states chose either India or Pakistan without difficulty on the basis of geographical proximity and preponderance of Hindu or Moslem population. Kashmir was the only one of these states that theoretically might have had alternatives to joining India or Pakistan. One would have been independence, since it adjoins not only India and Pakistan, but Sinkiang, Tibet, and the Soviet Union. It has a mixed though predominantly Moslem people. It quickly became an object of contention and the scene of armed struggle, and the Kashmir problem has been before the Security Council ever since. [1]

In Kashmir, the Hindu dynasty, which after 1840 ruled the predominantly Moslem population, was never closely identified with the indigenous population. It owed its authority to British support, based on the practical premise that the alternative of Sikh rule promised even worse government. Thus the decision of the rulers in 1947 to adhere to India could not be deemed a reflection of national sentiment. The Sheik Mohammed Abdullah, a Moslem, who is the national hero of Kashmir, was in charge of the government in Kashmir at the time of the accession to India and supported this step, but maintained that the ultimate disposition would depend on the outcome of a plebiscite. [2]

Kashmir is the victim of centuries of misgovernment which continued until World War II. C. B. Birdwood wrote in 1956:

> The great sage of modern Islam, Sir Mohammed Iqbal, himself a Kashmiri, in shame and sorrow wrote of the plight of his people: "The Kashmiri has come to hug slavery to his bosom. . . . A stranger to the dignity of self, ashamed of his ego." Sir Zafrulla Khan was a little more realistic and less poetic when, before the Security Council, he said that one soldier armed with no more than a bayonet could drive 4,000 Kashmiris in whatever direction he desired. [3]

The author suggests the possibility that, under these conditions, a plebiscite would have little meaning.

Another complicating factor of the problem is that Kashmir consists of several areas with different and unrelated ethnic backgrounds. The eastern portion, part of Ladakh, is Buddhist and is controlled by India. The southern portion, Jammu and adjoining territories, is largely Hindu and is controlled by India. The large rugged northern area and a smaller western area, both under the control of Pakistan, are predominantly Moslem. Plebiscites in these areas would undoubtedly result in their remaining under their present control. Only in the vale of Kashmir, two-thirds of which is under Indian control, and the city of Poonch and its environs is a predominantly Moslem population under Indian control. However, the vale itself is by far the richest part of Kashmir, and the predominantly Moslem

---

[1] *United States Participation in The United Nations, Report by the President to the Congress for the Year 1951* (Washington: Government Printing Office, 1952), p. 102.

[2] Initially supporting the Indian position, he was imprisoned by the Indian regime when his views at a later date failed to coincide with the position of the Indian Government. His release from prison in 1964 has implications not only on the broad problem of finding a solution to the Kashmir problem, but also on the narrower problem of maintaining order along the truce line.

[3] *Two Nations and Kashmir* (London: Robert Hale, 1956), pp. 20–21.

areas under Indian control contain half the population of the state. There-fore, partition furnishes no easy solution, since neither India nor Pakistan has been willing to consent to a partition of the vale. It must also be remembered that Nehru himself was descended from an influential Hindu family in Kashmir and seemed to be emotionally incapable of consenting to a solution permitting the vale to be a part of Pakistan.

The Indian Government has consistently taken the position that the original decision of accession of Jammu and Kashmir to India by the Maharajah Sir Heri Singh was effective and justified the presence of Indian troops in Kashmir. For the same reason, Pakistani military forces would have no legal basis for their presence. At the same time, India has from time to time acknowledged that the ultimate disposition of Kashmir should be decided by a plebiscite.

The Indian and Pakistani armies facing each other on the line of battle had more in common with each other than the military of either had in common with the civilian elements in their own state. The two armies had originally been one, and their officers had, in the main, received their training in England.

These and other factors have largely determined the course of UN action. The problems of peace observation, while difficult, were far simpler than those of solving the political questions. With some exceptions, which will be considered later, there are in Kashmir neither fanatically antagonistic military forces nor hostile populations. Thus the conditions were favorable for maintaining a relatively quiet armistice line. However, the same con-ditions made it impossible to solve the basic political problem through military accommodation or through reconciling divergent populations. The political problem could be solved only in the capitals, which were miles from the front. Thus early in the UN consideration of the problem, the issues and machinery of peace observation were separated from the functions of mediation and good offices. This study deals with efforts to mediate only in the few instances where they affected the peace-observation activities.

UNITED NATIONS COMMISSION FOR INDIA AND PAKISTAN AND THE UN REPRESENTATIVE

On January 1, 1948, the Government of India charged in the Security Council that Pakistan was assisting the raiders who were attacking Jammu and Kashmir, which India considered a part of its territories. On January 20, the Security Council established a United Nations Commission for India and Pakistan (UNCIP), composed of representatives of three UN members, one selected by Pakistan, one by India, and the third chosen by the other two. India selected Czechoslovakia, and Pakistan selected

Argentina. The President of the Security Council designated the United States as the third member when the other two members failed to agree.

Terms of Reference

The resolution directed UNCIP to "proceed to the spot as quickly as possible," with a dual function of investigating the facts pursuant to Article 34 of the Charter and exercising a "mediatory influence likely to smooth away difficulties." [4]

The initial activities of UNCIP were directed toward working out a procedure for the restoration of peace and order followed by a plebiscite. These efforts resulted in a resolution passed on April 21, 1948, which enlarged the commission to include Belgium and Colombia, and called for the restoration of peace and order. [5] Pakistan should withdraw from the State of Jammu, and Kashmir "tribesmen and Pakistani nationals not normally resident therein who have entered the state for the purpose of fighting and to prevent any intrusion into the State of such elements and any furnishing of material aid to those fighting in the State." [6] India should reduce its forces in Kashmir and prepare for a plebiscite. Detailed procedures for appointment of a plebiscite administrator and for conduct of the plebiscite were included in the resolution. Although both India and Pakistan objected to this resolution, they agreed to cooperate with UNCIP.

The resolution provided for military observers in Jammu and Kashmir and invited India and Pakistan "to nominate a representative to be attached to the Commission for such assistance as it may require in the performance of its task." The resolution reaffirmed the earlier resolution of January 20, 1948, and reiterated the direction to the commission to proceed to the subcontinent to take measures to restore order and arrange for the plebiscite.

UNCIP was originally set up to meet a situation outlined in its initial interim report. [7] The sequence of events which led to its being dispatched to the subcontinent was: (1) religious disturbances, violence, and mass movements of population directly after the partition; (2) Moslem tribesmen, inflamed by reports of violence and "bent on avenging their co-religionists swarmed from the mountains," penetrating as far as the southern borders on the east and outskirts of Srinagar; (3) nationals of Pakistan entering Kashmir to fight; (4) after the accession of the state to India, the Indian forces advancing into Kashmir; (5) the tribesmen were pushed back but were not expelled from the borders. Therefore, UNCIP anticipated that its main task would be to influence the tribesmen to withdraw, which would be followed by the withdrawal of the Indian Army.

[4] UN Security Council, Resolution adopted at the 230th meeting, Jan. 20, 1948, S/654. Hereafter cited as S/654.

[5] UN Security Council, Resolution adopted at the 286th meeting, April 21, 1948, S/726. Hereafter cited as S/726.

[6] S/726.

[7] UN Security Council, S/1100, Nov. 9, 1948, pp. 56–58. Hereafter cited as S/1100.

When the commission arrived on the subcontinent, it learned for the first time that regular Pakistani troops had been introduced into Kashmir.[8] As a result, the main task of UNCIP changed to that of mediation between two governments. The commission adopted a resolution calling for a cease-fire and truce agreement, and indicated that a plebiscite would follow the truce.[9]

Shortly after the adoption of the resolution, UNCIP conferred in Geneva and Paris with the representatives of India and Pakistan, and, in the latter part of December, apparently obtained the agreement of both parties to a plebiscite. With the acceptance of these proposals, India and Pakistan saw no reason for continuation of hostilities. Accordingly, the cease-fire in Kashmir came into effect on January 1, 1949, with the first military observer named by UNCIP arriving on the subcontinent on January 2.

The terms of reference of the military observers have not changed substantially since January 1, 1949, despite the many efforts to transform the cease-fire into a truce and to arrange for a plebiscite. A cease-fire line was established on July 27, 1949. On March 14, 1950, the Security Council appointed a United Nations Representative[10] to assist in the preparation and to supervise the implementation of the program of demilitarization (included in the truce provisions of the August 13 UNCIP resolution); to make suggestions for solution of the disputed matters; "to exercise all of the powers and responsibilities devolving upon the United Nations Commission by reason of existing resolutions of the Security Council and by reason of the agreement of the parties embodied in the resolutions of the United Nations Commission of 13 August 1948 and 5 January 1949"; to arrange for the plebiscite administrator to assume his functions; and to report and make recommendations to the Security Council.

The resolution terminated UNCIP and transferred its powers to the UN Representative. At this time, a decision was made by the Secretary-General and the UN Representative, without any formal UN authorization, that the military adviser and observers should report directly to the Secretary-General and not to the UN Representative. At a later date, the UN Representative was assigned a separate military adviser and staff having no relation to the observers.

The Security Council, on March 30, 1951, adopted a resolution, the main purpose of which was to provide new procedures for settling the dispute.[11] It stated that "the Military Observer group shall continue to supervise the cease-fire in the State." The numerous resolutions since that

[8] S/1100, p. 60.
[9] For the cease-fire provisions see S/995, Aug. 13, 1948.
[10] UN Security Council, Resolution adopted at the 470th meeting, March 14, 1950, S/1461.
[11] UN Security Council, Resolution adopted at the 539th meeting, March 30, 1951, S/2017/Rev. 1.

time have dealt with the problems of obtaining a truce and arranging a plebiscite and have left the peace-observation procedures and machinery unchanged.

The UN Representative in 1958, Dr. Frank Graham, recommended that India and Pakistan reaffirm their request for the integrity of the cease-fire line and refrain from crossing the line, and that consideration be given to stationing a UN force on the Pakistani side of the border after withdrawal of Pakistani troops.[12] India objected to several features of the report and no action was taken. None of the UN actions since 1958 have affected the peace-observation activities.

Organization

The initial organization of UNCIP did not differentiate between peace-observation and mediation functions. The delegations consisted of five representatives, one for each state, four alternate representatives, two advisers, both from the United States, and two secretaries, both from the United States.

The UN secretariat personnel numbered sixteen: the personal representative of the Secretary-General, five deputy principal and assistant secretaries, a legal adviser, a press officer, an interpreter, an administrative and financial officer, a photographer, and five stenographers.[13]

On its arrival, UNCIP established two groups: one to go to Rawalpindi on the Pakistan side of the line, the other to Srinagar, occupied by the Indian forces. The commission also established a military affairs subcommission to draft a military questionnaire to be sent to the two governments. However, the main tasks of UNCIP were to discuss the problem with interested groups and to draft proposals for a cease-fire, truce, and plebiscite. The commission did not at this time organize for peace observation.

In November 1948, the Foreign Minister of Pakistan complained that India was strengthening its army in Kashmir with the objective of driving the groups favoring Pakistan from the areas which they occupied. At UNCIP's request, the Secretary-General obtained a Belgian officer, Lieutenant General Maurice Delvoie, as military adviser.[14]

General Delvoie with several assistants arrived on the subcontinent on January 2, 1949, which by coincidence was one day after the cease-fire had come into effect. UNCIP immediately requested the designation of "an adequate number" of military observers "to enable the Military Adviser to report to the commission on the observance of the cease-fire and the truce agreement."[15] In other words, the military adviser was to be used for a different purpose than originally contemplated.

[12] UN Security Council, S/3984, March 28, 1958.
[13] S/1100, p. 9.
[14] UN Security Council, S/1196, Jan. 10, 1949, pp. 12–13. Hereafter cited as S/1196.
[15] S/1196, p. 6.

On January 15, 1949, the Commanders-in-Chief of the Indian and Pakistani armies met at Indian Army headquarters to implement Part I of the UNCIP resolution of August 13, 1948, relating to the cease-fire. In contrast to the endless delays in political negotiations, the military commanders in one day agreed on the following:[16] (1) slight adjustments in troop dispositions to avoid minor incidents; (2) use of specified supply roads by both armies; (3) withdrawal of all "raiders" from Kashmir as soon as possible; (4) the Azad Kashmir forces to be relieved in the forward areas by Pakistan regular forces and concentrated in the rear areas; and (5) both the Indian and Pakistani armies would give all facilities to UNCIP required for establishing observer teams in the area of Jammu and Kashmir. Observer groups should consist of neutral observers appointed by UNCIP each with one Indian and one Pakistani officer. General Delvoie "communicated his satisfaction at the agreements which had been reached."[17]

The January 15 meeting also reached agreement on exchange of prisoners, return of abducted women, and efforts to stop the burning of villages. In short, the meeting settled all issues in connection with the cease-fire except the demarcation of the cease-fire line.

Under a commission decision of April 28, 1949, accepted by India and Pakistan, UNCIP took on the duty of observing the maintenance of order in the mountainous and sparsely settled regions in the north (occupied by Pakistan), and if it became necessary for the defense of the area, could request the Government of India "to post garrisons at specified points."[18] After repeated attempts "to negotiate agreements on military and political aspects of the Truce simultaneously," the commission held another all-military meeting from July 18 to 27 and successfully worked out the demarcation of the cease-fire line. The agreement provided that UNCIP would "station Observers where it deems necessary."[19]

The detailed explanation is needed to contrast the atmosphere accompanying the military functions with that of the political negotiations. The military leaders obviously wished to diminish violence and consequently reached agreements calculated to produce that result with scant regard for "face saving" gestures. UNCIP was welcomed by both sides and given unlimited authority to observe the enforcement of the cease-fire. This attitude inevitably led to the separation of the peace-observation functions of UNCIP from its mediation functions. The pattern of mediation has changed many times as new approaches are hopefully sought. The peace-observation machinery and methods established by the two meetings have remained virtually unchanged.

[16] UN Security Council, S/1430/Add. 1, Annex 47, Dec. 9, 1949, pp. 2–3. Hereafter cited as S/1430.

[17] S/1430, p. 4.

[18] S/1430, p. 71.

[19] S/1430, p. 38, Add. 1, Annex 26, p. 5.

To return to the development of the UN Military Observer Group (UNMOGIP), after the January 15, 1949, meeting, General Delvoie asked the UN Secretary-General to furnish military observers as requested by the Commanders-in-Chief of both India and Pakistan. By July 1949, General Delvoie had thirty-two observers from the United States, Canada, Belgium, Mexico, and Norway.[20] The report of the Secretary-General from July 1, 1950, to June 30, 1951, shows thirty-five military observers lent by Belgium, Canada, Chile, Denmark, Norway, Sweden, and the United States.[21] The number has varied since then from thirty to sixty-five. The Secretary-General commented in his annual report a year later:

> In Kashmir, the Secretary-General has considered it essential, in view of the rugged terrain and the difficulties of transportation, to increase the number of military observers from thirty-five to sixty-five. In doing so, he has broadened the geographical distribution of the United Nations military observer group.[22]

In 1954, when the United States extended military aid to Pakistan, India requested that the American observers be replaced as their terms of service expired, on the ground that they were no longer neutral. Nineteen Americans left during the next year.[23]

In 1949, General Delvoie returned to New York for consultations and was replaced by a Canadian officer, Brigadier Henry Angle, who was killed in a plane crash in 1950.[24] In September 1950, Major General R. H. Nimmo, from Australia, was appointed. He continues to be chief of the United Nations observers.

As a part of the January 15 agreement between the Indian and Pakistani military, both army headquarters issued orders to their troops to (1) hold the lines of forward-defended localities as they were at the time of the cease-fire order, (2) ensure that no further advance was made from these positions, (3) ensure that there was no patrolling forward of the forward-defended localities, and (4) carry out reliefs as ordered before and help the local refugees to settle in their homes.[25] The military observers were stationed with troops on both sides and were to accompany them in their investigations, gather as much information as possible, and report to the chief of military observers.

Under the organization and procedures established in 1949 by the chief of the military observers, the field observer teams consisting of two

[20] Birdwood, *op. cit.*, p. 153.

[21] UN General Assembly, *Official Records*, Sixth Session, Supplement No. 1, A/1844, p. 201.

[22] UN General Assembly, *Official Records*, Seventh Session, Supplement No. 1, A/2141, p. 176.

[23] Birdwood, *op. cit.*, p. 155.

[24] S. Lourie, "United Nations Military Observation Group in India and Pakistan," *International Organization*, IX: 1 (Fall 1955), p. 24.

[25] UN Security Council, S/AC.12/MA/1.

or three military observers and one radio operator are stationed with Pakistani and Indian military units on either side of the cease-fire line. Each team is rotated from one side to the other to avoid a spirit of partisanship on the part of the observers from remaining too long with one army.[26] The headquarters staff consists of the chief military observer, the chief of military staff, who represents the chief military observer during his absence, acts as liaison with the staff, and is director of the headquarters staff, an operations officer to recommend the location and strength of the field observer teams, an intelligence officer, who is responsible for keeping records, and a United Nations administrative officer, who is responsible for maintaining contacts with the Secretary-General and arranging for funds and expenditures. In addition, staff and liaison offices have been established both in India and in Pakistan to maintain relations with the governments.

The headquarters of UNMOGIP is located six months of the year (winter) in Rawalpindi, Pakistan, and six months of the year in Srinagar in the portion of Kashmir occupied by India. The staff and liaison offices move to Delhi and Srinagar when the headquarters is in Rawalpindi, and to Rawalpindi when the headquarters is in Srinagar.

Beginning in 1950, teams of civilian radio operators and technicians were posted with each military observer team. A United Nations communications network was set up centering in Karachi and Rawalpindi, with mobile transmitters and generators furnished to the observation posts. All personnel, both civilian and military, are assigned for service with the United Nations and report through the United Nations.

The observer teams receive their salaries from their respective national armies, but are paid a subsistence allowance and an allowance of $100 for personal field clothing and equipment while serving with UNMOGIP. The United Nations assumes responsibility for total disability or death of observers, and India and Pakistan provide hospitalization and other medical expenses in case of temporary disability.[27]

UN expenditures for UNMOGIP have remained approximately the same from year to year, as indicated by the following figures.:[28]

1958	$362,532
1959	$435,039
1960	$421,915
1961	$446,336
1962	$456,322
1963 appropriation	$433,200

[26] Lourie, *op. cit.*, p. 26.

[27] Lourie, *op. cit.*, p. 27.

[28] These figures do not include the salaries and allowances of "staff detailed from the regular establishment" and neither do they include expenses of the UN Representative for India and Pakistan. Figures taken from UN General Assembly, *Budget Estimates for the Financial Year 1961*, A/4370; *1962*, A/4770; *1963*, A/5205; *1964*, A/5505.

The 1964 estimated expenditure has also stayed within the range indicated by the above figures — $447,400. The components of this figure are as follows:[29]

Staff Costs:

Salaries and wages of staff recruited for mission	$ 45,500
Subsistence and travel of staff recruited and detailed	68,500
Subsistence and travel of military observers	187,900
Total	$301,900

Operational Costs:

Maintenance and rental of premises and equipment	$ 17,800
Operation and maintenance of vehicles	15,000
Communications, freight, supplies and services	48,800
Rental of aircraft	41,000
Purchase of furniture and fixtures	13,700
Purchase of vehicles	9,200
Total	$145,500

The salaries and allowances of the staff detailed from the regular establishment ($215,578)[30] must be added to the above figures, thus bringing total costs to approximately $600,000 and total *staff* costs to $517,478.

The total staff costs for 1964 covered the salaries and wages of sixty-four persons:[31] one chief military observer, thirty-six local staff and twenty-seven officers from the regular establishment (two administrative and finance officers and twenty-five field service personnel). Their travel and subsistence were also provided for as well as the travel and subsistence of thirty-six military observers and an air crew of four persons.[32]

Performance

The nature of the tasks performed by UNMOGIP is outlined in some detail in Lourie's excellent article and also in Lord Birdwood's book on the Kashmir question. As previously pointed out, the function of UNMOGIP is to supervise the implementation of the cease-fire agreement. In carrying out this function, the group has three activities: (1) investigation of complaints and efforts to settle the complaints, (2) determination of the order of battle of the two armies and other troop information, and (3) control of civilians.

[29] UN General Assembly, A/5505, p. 108.
[30] Professional staff from regular establishment, $29,578; Field Service, $186,000.
[31] The salaries of observers were paid by their national armies.
[32] Most of the expenses of the observers when they are on duty in the field are borne by the Indian or Pakistani armies.

UNMOGIP has adopted regular procedures for visits and inspection tours and investigation of incidents. When an incident occurs, it is usually checked by observer teams on both sides of the line. As soon as the investigation is complete, the team reports its findings, conclusions, and recommendations to headquarters. In the case of fighting, the military observer is expected to proceed immediately to the area and "endeavor to calm the troops on his respective side." Frequently, the jeeps with United Nations markings and flying the UN flag move into the line of fire to stop the clashes. Most of the work of UNMOGIP involves patrol clashes on the border.[33]

The second operation of determining general troop information is directed primarily to ensure against dangerous build-ups of troops on either side. It involves highly classified information, the disclosure of which would create grave problems for the opposing side. So far as is known, no other peace-observation group has ever been furnished with this information—a testimony to the confidence of both armies in the United Nations military observers. The sparseness of published reports from UNMOGIP stems largely from their responsibility for this function. All information of this nature is classified as "top secret."

The third concern of the military observers, the problem of civilian activities, is not strictly within their function but belongs to the civil police. The agreement of demilitarization provided for a 500-yard demilitarized zone on each side of the cease-fire line. The civilian police were to maintain authority in this area. Occasionally, however, the military commanders have used their troops for this purpose. The function of the observers has been to discourage this type of activity. When civilian encroachments cause violent incidents, frequently the military observers have investigated them and made recommendations with both sides agreeing to the procedure. This extension of the jurisdiction of the military observers beyond the terms of the initial India-Pakistan agreements reflects the confidence of both armies in the military observers. In one of the three major incidents occurring in February and March 1964, they were called on to settle the controversy even though the incident took place on the international frontier between India and Pakistan, which was not within the jurisdiction of UNMOGIP, and not along the cease-fire line.

While it is possible to describe the general operations of UNMOGIP, the records do not permit any close study of day-to-day operations. The first report of the United Nations Representative pointed out that the operations of UNMOGIP "were based on the assumption that the boundary framed by the cease-fire line would continue until the plebiscite was held notwithstanding demilitarization. Neither Prime Minister sought to depart from this assumption." The Representative recommended that India and Pakistan "reduce the military strength holding the cease-fire

[33] Lourie, *op. cit.*, p. 29.

line to the normal protection of a peacetime frontier."[34] The sole reference in this report to incidents is as follows: "Incidents in which the troops on one side fired on troops on the other side or upon a civilian or civilians occurred frequently at some point or another on the line but the incidents nearly all proved of small importance relatively and none threatened a general outbreak of hostilities."[35] The next year the Representative, Dr. Graham, reported:

> In the State of Jammu and Kashmir itself the United Nations organization for supervision, by means of the Military Observer Group, of the cease-fire line, was working effectively and, despite incidents, was continuing its successful assistance to the two Governments in their will to fulfill their commitments under the cease-fire arrangements.
>
> During the two and one half years that had elapsed since the coming into effect of the cease-fire, some decrease in forces on both sides of the cease-fire line had taken place and, to some extent, certain provisions of part II of the UNCIP resolution of 13 August 1948 had, for practical purposes, been implemented. [36]

This is the end of official public reporting by the UN Representatives to UNCIP.

Largely through visits of State Department officials to the area and through discussions with General Nimmo and representatives of the UN Secretariat, it is known that in 1954 the conditions along the border were relatively tranquil, with not more than some twenty incidents. By 1961, the number had grown from two dozen to two thousand, and there has been little change since that time.

The increase in incidents between 1954 and 1961 stemmed from the policy of Krishna Menon, then the Indian Defense Minister, that the cease-fire line should become a fixed international boundary. Apparently, he had concluded that neither a plebiscite, nor an international agreement for partition, nor any other alternative would assure Indian control of the vale. He therefore evacuated civilians from the 500-yard demilitarized zone on the Indian side of the cease-fire line and encouraged the Kashmir police to use force to prevent the Pakistanis from crossing the border. The Pakistanis did not follow a similar policy and continued civilian activities within the 500-yard demilitarized zone on their side of the line, since they have always contended that the cease-fire line is not a boundary. Most of the incidents arose when Pakistani civilians approached or crossed the line.

After the removal of Krishna Menon from the Indian Government and the advent of difficulties between India and Communist China, the incidents declined during 1962 and the first five months of 1963. Beginning in June

[34] UN Security Council, S/1791, Sept. 15, 1950, pp. 12, 30. Hereafter cited as S/1791.

[35] S/1791, p. 4.

[36] UN Security Council, S/2375, Oct. 15, 1951, p. 9.

1963, General Mohammed Ayub Khan concluded that despite India's fear of the Chinese Communists, the Indian Government was unlikely to take any steps to solve the Kashmir question in the absence of continuous pressure from Pakistan. Pakistan from that time on had been exerting this pressure in a number of ways. Before 1963, negotiations had commenced with the Chinese Communists to rectify the boundary between Kashmir and China. The agreement extended even to areas controlled by India. As a part of this campaign, the Pakistani Government seems to be trying to exert pressure on the United States to influence the Indians to agree to a settlement. Pakistani pressure also stems from the fact that the Pakistani influence with the Afro-Asian group is increasing while Indian influence declines.

It is difficult to estimate the effect of Nehru's death on the possibility of a political settlement of the Kashmir problem. For many years, Nehru adopted an intransigent policy which may have been influenced by the fact that his family was from Kashmir. In the last year of his life, however, Nehru seemed more conciliatory on this problem than other Indian leaders.

Until recently, General Ayub Khan had apparently believed that violence along the cease-fire line would be a method of exerting pressure on the Indians. Two events have transpired which may have changed this view: (1) the incident of the stolen hair of the Prophet, which showed that the Kashmir Moslems were far less timid than anyone anticipated and could be swayed towards violence, and (2) the indications that the Moslems supporting Abdullah have become more and more hostile to Indian rule. Nevertheless, competent political observers of the situation believe that the General is still unwilling to use excessive violence on the frontier as a means of exerting pressure toward a settlement.

Despite this view, during the early part of 1964, three incidents occurred, which were far more serious than any that took place in the past, and were reported to the Security Council.

In the first incident toward the end of January, a group of Pakistani irregulars ambushed twenty-six Indians. Twenty disappeared, and three were killed. UNMOGIP is still investigating and has interviewed a number of the Indians who were taken prisoner by the Pakistanis.

The second took place on March 5, and consisted of an exchange of mortar fire around a graveyard. This incident was not within the jurisdiction of UNMOGIP since it took place along the international border rather than along the cease-fire line. However, with the consent of both sides the principal military observer arranged for a cease-fire and for an investigation.

The third took place on March 24. Apparently, twenty-four Pakistanis wandered across the cease-fire line and were either killed or captured by the Indians. This matter is still under investigation.

The three incidents coincided with an increase in Indian-Pakistani tensions accompanied by religious riots in both countries and renewed migration of Moslems to Pakistan and Pakistani Hindus to India. At the same time, agitation increased in Kashmir against the Indian regime, which was an off-shoot of the detested hereditary non-Moslem overlords of Jammu and Kashmir and had become thoroughly discredited through incompetence and corruption. The Indian Government, recognizing the weakness of its situation, released from prison Sheik Mohammed Abdullah. It is authoritatively reported that the release of Abdullah eased tensions in Kashmir. After March 1964 the number of border incidents became less, and the cease-fire line became relatively quiet.

The lull in the number of border incidents did not last beyond the summer of 1964. In the last quarter of 1964 and in 1965 the tensions have become greater than during any previous period. An increased number of incidents has inevitably accompanied the growing tensions.

One factor in the increase of tensions has been a change in the governmental structure of Azad Kashmir, which the Indians complain in effect makes the area an integral part of Pakistan. This Indian charge parallels the previous Pakistani charges on the effect of changes in the government of the portion of Kashmir occupied by the Indians. General Nimmo has made proposals intended to arrest the deterioration of conditions, but neither side has accepted them.

Prime Minister Shastri has not carried forward the dramatic moves made by Nehru near the end of his life for a rapprochement between India and Pakistan. "Evidence has accumulated since his death to indicate that the Kashmir settlement envisaged by Nehru presupposed a larger Indo-Pakistan accommodation based on confederal relation between the two countries."[37]

In lieu of such an accommodation, increased tensions have resulted in relatively large-scale warfare in another sector. Even though the center of hostilities is not Kashmir, the effect has been a deterioration in Kashmir.

Some persons close to the scene believe that the continued absence of progress toward a political settlement is finally producing a delayed reaction along the border. At least until 1955, the Indian and Pakistani military authorities successfully restrained violence along the border so that it could be truthfully asserted that the tension was greater in the capitals than along the cease-fire line. Even today, the relationships between General Nimmo and the top levels of Pakistani and Indian military leaders remain cordial. This situation raises the fundamental question of the relation between the continuing postponement of the political settlement and the maintenance of law and order.

All of the incidents over the past two or three years took place in relatively well-populated areas and not along the cease-fire line in the sparsely settled mountain regions. This eliminates any implication that the uncon-

---

[37] Selig Harrison, "Troubled India and Her Neighbors," *Foreign Affairs*, XLV (January 1965), p. 321.

trollable tribes from the northwest province of Pakistan were responsible for the violence as they had been in 1948.

Evaluation

Perhaps the most remarkable feature of the fairly successful peace-observation mission of UNMOGIP over a period of more than fourteen years is that tension has been less along the cease-fire line than in the capitals. Despite the total failure of many different UN-sponsored efforts to obtain a political settlement, at least until 1955, border violence was at a minimum. While incidents have multiplied ten-fold since 1955, only in 1964 has the increase in tension between the two countries resulted in serious and organized disorders along the cease-fire line. Doubtless the timidity of the natives of Kashmir, whose spirit was crushed by centuries of submission to tyranny, contributed to this result. However, an even more important reason was the favorable attitude of the military leaders of both countries, which established favorable conditions for neutral military observation.

The agreement on the military arrangements for an effective cease-fire, reached by the military leaders *in one day*, and the demarcation of a 500-mile cease-fire line accomplished in less than one week stand in sharp contrast to the never-ending political discussions which have led nowhere. It should be noted that in the military settlement both countries took positions which the political leaders, for reasons of saving face, would never have tolerated. The Indian military leaders agreed that Pakistani regular army units should replace Azad Pakistani irregulars on the front line at a time when Nehru was insisting that all regular Pakistani troops should leave Kashmir before political negotiations could commence. The Pakistani military commander, by coincidence, General Mohammed Ayub Khan himself, agreed to remove to rear areas the Azad Pakistani irregulars whom Foreign Minister Sir Zafrulla Khan claimed were volunteers operating independently.

It seems clear that the military wished an effective cease-fire. Accordingly, they granted more favorable conditions for operations than have ever been granted before or since to UNMOGIP: (1) A demilitarized zone 500 yards in width was established on each side of the border. (2) UNMOGIP had complete access to both sides of the border and could cross the border freely. (3) A UN radio communication system was set up that could communicate in code with stations on both sides of the border and headquarters in both countries. (4) UNMOGIP received regular reports from both countries of the "order of battle" and other secret military information, thus giving UNMOGIP assurance that no undue buildup of forces was taking place on either side of the line. (5) The observers were stationed with the Indian and Pakistani units and were rotated at regular intervals from one army to the other. Without these favorable military arrangements, it is difficult to see how UNMOGIP with only thirty to sixty-five military observers could have been effective.

One element in the success of UNMOGIP has been the absence of publicity. Because UNMOGIP has access to secret information from both countries, its reports to the Secretary-General have always been classified "top secret." The success with which secrecy has been maintained has generated a confidence in UNMOGIP which carries with it respect for its conclusions and recommendations to maintain the cease-fire.

In a situation where political tensions in the capitals have been greater than border tensions, it was probably inevitable that the peace-observation and mediation functions would be separated, even though initially both were entrusted to UNCIP and later to the UN Representative. Though UNMOGIP theoretically reports to the UN Representative under the Security Council resolutions, in fact, for more than twelve years, all reporting has been to the Secretary-General. The UNCIP recommendations at times outraged Pakistan and India. If UNCIP's unpopularity had rubbed off on the military observers, it would certainly have impaired the confidence in their unbiased attitudes, which has made possible their success. However, an argument can be made that General Nimmo, because of the respect of both states for his work, might have mediated the political issues more effectively than the UN Representative. Likewise an argument can be made that the very success of General Nimmo in restraining violence reduced the pressures for a political settlement.

The events of 1964 seem to bear out the view that long postponement of a political settlement will eventually erode and destroy the foundation for a cease-fire. Similarly, the reduction in border incidents after the release of Abdullah from prison indicates that renewed hope of a political settlement reduces border tensions.

The Kashmir experience may indicate that one of the easiest forums for obtaining international agreements may be negotiations of military leaders. In this instance, both Indian and Pakistani senior officers had received identical training in English military schools. Their common background of education and experience undoubtedly aided their successful negotiations. Similarly, the intimate association of the neutral military observers with the Indian and Pakistani military forces was indispensable to their success. This relationship made it possible for a small number of observers with a minimum of UN financial support to observe a long boundary in a rugged mountainous area. Effectiveness has depended on the advantageous positions and mobility of a few observers rather than a large number. UNMOGIP might be a favorable organization for testing technological advances to increase the effectiveness of peace observation.

Peace observation in Kashmir has lasted longer than in any area except Palestine. While the cost has been relatively low in comparison to other

peace-observation groups, there has been a continuing UN budget requirement, which shows no signs of diminishing. This raises a series of questions,
some of which have already been mentioned: Does a peaceful boundary
lessen the pressures for a political settlement? If the United Nations were
to require India and Pakistan to assume the full costs, would this hasten a
political settlement? What would be the effect on India-Pakistan relations
if UN peace observation came to an end? Do peace-observation missions
tend to perpetuate themselves either deliberately or because it takes less
effort to continue them than to end them? Should the United Nations
work out a termination timetable?

6

THE 1958 MIDDLE EAST CRISIS

In 1958, crises developed in Lebanon and Jordan that were brought
before the Security Council. In both instances the charges were similar—
the United Arab Republic was accused of interference in the domestic
affairs of the states concerned. On May 21 and 22, 1958, the Government
of Lebanon brought to the attention of the Council of the Arab League and
the United Nations Security Council the strife in Lebanon and accused the
United Arab Republic of inspiring, directing, and subsidizing it. The
Lebanese Government appealed to the Security Council charging that the
United Arab Republic, by intervening in the internal affairs of Lebanon,
was endangering the peace. [1] On July 17, the Jordanian representative in
the Security Council stated that for several months his country had been
the object of open hostility on the part of the United Arab Republic. He
stated that aggression can mean indirect aggression—a method of subversion and the attempt to overthrow constitutional authority. Indirect
aggression, he asserted, can be just as dangerous as the open variety.
"This," he declared, "is the common factor linking the situations in Jordan
and Lebanon, the factor of indirect aggression. Aggression by fomenting
civil strife in the interest of a foreign power is one of the gravest offences
against peace and security." [2]

[1] UN Security Council, S/4007, May 23, 1958.

[2] UN Security Council, *Official Records*, Thirteenth Year, 831st meeting, July 17,
1958, par. 32. Hereafter cited as S/Agenda/831.

UNITED NATIONS OBSERVER GROUP IN LEBANON

The Government of Lebanon stated that the intervention involved "the infiltration of armed bands from Syria into Lebanon, the destruction of Lebanese life and property by such bands, the participation of United Arab Republic nationals in acts of terrorism and rebellion . . . the supply of arms . . . to [insurgents] and the waging of a violent radio and press campaign in the United Arab Republic calling for strikes, demonstrations and the overthrow of the established authorities in Lebanon." [3]

The Security Council deferred consideration of the matter pending the outcome of the deliberations of the League of Arab States in the hope that the Arabs themselves would be able to solve their problems. This hope, however, was not realized. The Arab League Council held four sessions, the first on June 1. It developed a resolution sponsored by the delegations of Libya, the Sudan, Saudi Arabia, Iraq, and Jordan, later joined by Yemen. The operative part of the resolution contained the following paragraph:

The Council decides:

(1) To do all in its power to put an end to anything which may disturb the atmosphere of calm among member States;
(2) To request the Government of Lebanon to withdraw the complaint it has placed before the Security Council;
(3) To appeal to the various Lebanese groups to end the disturbances and to take the necessary measures to settle domestic disputes by peaceful and constitutional means;
(4) To send a committee selected from among the members of the Council in order to ease the situation and to give effect to the decision of the Council. [4]

The resolution was, as such instruments usually are, a compromise. It was acceptable to the Lebanese delegation and was not opposed by the U.A.R. delegation. But much to the dismay of the parties who worked on the resolution, the Lebanese Government rejected it on June 5. The reasons for the rejection can only be a matter of speculation. The Lebanese Government did not appear to be seriously interested in solving the crisis at the Arab League level. Nor did it have any confidence that the League, dominated by the U.A.R., would be able to solve the problem. What the Lebanese Government appeared to want was the internationalization of the crisis. The men who were at the helm of the government were bitter at Nasser, their archenemy. Some believed that, by internationalizing the crisis, these men hoped for foreign intervention with the resulting possibility that Camille Chamoun, the Lebanese President, and his administration, would retain the presidency of the republic whose constitution barred an incumbent president from succeeding himself.

[3] S/4007.
[4] UN Security Council, *Official Records*, Thirteenth Year, 823rd meeting, June 6, 1958, p. 24. Hereafter cited as S/Agenda/823.

On the Arab League's failure to solve the problem, the Lebanese Government pressed its case in the Security Council. The Lebanese Foreign Minister, Charles Malik, asserted that the United Arab Republic was involved in massive illegal and unprovoked intervention in the affairs of Lebanon aimed at undermining its independence. He contended that international peace and security would be threatened if the situation created by this intervention continued. No small country, he asserted, would feel secure if intervention in Lebanon were permitted. The United Nations, he pointed out, was Lebanon's last resort. [5]

The delegate of the United Arab Republic denied the charges and accused Lebanon of internationalizing a situation that was purely domestic in nature, in hope of diverting local and world public opinion from the disturbed conditions within Lebanon. The essence of the trouble, he contended, was the desire of President Chamoun to take action contrary to the Lebanese Constitution by succeeding himself as President in the forthcoming elections. [6]

The Security Council meetings were stormy and conducted in a tense atmosphere. The United States, the United Kingdom, France, China, and Iraq supported the allegations of Lebanon. Canada, Colombia, Japan, Panama, and Sweden avoided prejudging the issue. The U.S.S.R. rejected the Lebanese allegations and asserted that the purpose of the complaint was to prepare the ground for Western intervention in the internal affairs of Lebanon.

The Swedish representative submitted a draft resolution providing for the urgent dispatch of an observer group to Lebanon, which was passed on June 11 by a vote of ten in favor with the Soviet Union abstaining. [7] The U.S.S.R. delegate explained that he had not vetoed the resolution because neither Lebanon nor the Arab Republic objected to it.

Terms of Reference

The observer group was "to proceed to Lebanon so as to ensure that there is no illegal infiltration of personnel or supply of arms or other materiel across the Lebanese borders." It was "to keep the Security Council currently informed through the Secretary-General." [8]

The Security Council's terms of reference were ambiguous. Did the Security Council intend by the words "to ensure that there is no illegal infiltration of personnel or supply of arms" to imply that the observer group was to use force if necessary to carry out its mission? The language is

[5] S/Agenda/823, p. 22.
[6] UN Security Council, *Official Records*, Thirteenth Year, 824th meeting, June 10, 1958.
[7] UN Security Council, *Official Records*, Thirteenth Year, 825th meeting, June 11, 1958, p. 17.
[8] UN Security Council, resolution adopted at 825th meeting, June 11, 1958, S/4023.

cloudy, but the interpretation of the resolution given by the Secretary-General confined the task of the group to observation and fact finding. The United Nations Observer Group in Lebanon (UNOGIL) was given no power to investigate past occurrences nor the means to stop such infiltration or supply of arms. No time limit was set for the performance of its duties, and rightly so. Nor were the parties obliged to accept the decision or recommendation of the group. Such authority and effectiveness as it had rested on the cooperation of the parties concerned and on the moral authority of the United Nations.[9]

Pending the arrival of a UN staff from New York and Geneva, the Secretary-General, who was entrusted with the responsibility of implementing the resolution, immediately organized the observer group by borrowing, on an emergency basis, ten military observers from the UN Truce Supervision Organization (UNTSO), who arrived in Lebanon on June 12 and 13, and administrative personnel from the United Nations Relief and Works Administration for Palestine Refugees (UNRWA).

On June 13, the Secretary-General appointed a group of three: Dr. Galo Plaza, former President of Ecuador, chairman; Major General Odd Bull of Norway, executive member in charge of military observers; and Rajeshwar Dayal of India, member of the group. The standing of these three individuals in the international community was high. In what capacity they acted is not clear. Presumably, they were the Secretary-General's representatives since he chose them and they were to report through him to the Security Council. Two of the members were from states that are allies of the United States, and the third came from an uncommitted state. The subordinate military personnel came from a number of small states. They and the administrative staff were presumably international civil servants. The mission reported to the Security Council through the Secretary-General.

Two days after the Security Council adopted the resolution, initial reconnaissance in Lebanon by military observers in United Nations jeeps was begun—a rather extraordinary feat due in considerable measure to the organizing ability of the Secretary-General and the good fortune of the presence of UN personnel in the area. By June 16, UNOGIL headquarters was opened in Beirut, and the first fourteen observers took up their positions in the areas held by the forces of the Government of Lebanon. By June 25, ninety-five observers, supplied by eleven members, were on duty.

The work of the mission developed in three stages. In the first stage, a force of military observers was assembled and instructed and material procured. In the second stage, the prevailing situation was analyzed, and, on the basis of needs, additional men and material were assembled. In the third stage, the group operated on its planned strength. The methods of

[9] Although UNOGIL was given no power to mediate, Dr. Galo Plaza, chairman of the mission, made informal efforts to mediate.

operation were as follows: (1) All accessible roads were patrolled regularly and frequently from dawn to dusk primarily in border districts and in the areas adjacent to the zones held by opposition forces. The observers traveled in white jeeps with UN markings, equipped with two-way radio sets. (2) Permanent observation posts were set up where groups of military observers were stationed. These posts were in continuous radio communication with headquarters in Beirut, with each other, and with the patrols. (3) An emergency reserve of experienced military observers was formed at headquarters and at the main observation posts. These observers were available for making inquiries on short notice or could be detailed to places where instances of smuggling of arms might be reported. (4) An evaluation team was set up at headquarters composed of specialized observer personnel with responsibility for analyzing, evaluating, and coordinating the information received from observers and other sources. (5) Observation by helicopters and planes was established. These planes and helicopters were outfitted with aerial photography devices and radio sets to enable them to communicate with headquarters and military observers in the field. (6) A procedure was established to use the information which the Lebanese Government might secure regarding suspected infiltration.[10]

By September 20, a regular military headquarters to conduct the operation of the group was organized. By November, UNOGIL had reached its maximum strength of 591 military personnel (469 military observers, 32 supporting troops, and 90 air section personnel). By this time, 49 manned outposts, 290 vehicles, 12 fixed wing aircraft, and 6 helicopters were in use. Administrative support was provided by 118 civilian and military personnel.

An agreement was reached between the United Nations and Lebanon regarding the presence of UNOGIL in Lebanon. The agreement covered, *inter alia*, freedom of movement within the area of UN operation, including all facilities for access and communications necessary for the task, and immunity of most of the UN personnel from being tried by local courts. Moreover, it provided that the authority granted the United Nations could not be exercised either in competition with or in cooperation with the host government on the basis of any joint operation. A UN operation, the Secretary-General felt, must be separate and distinct from activities by national authorities; otherwise, the United Nations would become involved in internal conflicts, which would be contrary to the Charter.

Lebanon established a five-member ministerial committee to maintain liaison with UNOGIL. In addition, the Secretary-General invited representatives of Brazil, Canada, Ceylon, Colombia, India, Norway, and Pakistan to serve as an advisory group for UNOGIL.

Early in the operation, on June 13, the United States Government responded affirmatively to an inquiry of the Secretary-General and made supplies and equipment available to UNOGIL on a reimbursable basis.

[10] See UN Security Council, S/4040, July 3, 1958. Hereafter cited as S/4040.

These included jeeps, planes, helicopters, and automotive, signal, and field equipment and supplies, at a cost of over $500,000.[11]

In its first report[12] UNOGIL pointed out that the length of the land frontier with Syria is 278 kilometers, only eighteen of which remained under the control of the government's forces. By July 15, however, it reported to the Security Council that, by agreement with the opposition leaders in the various sections of the country along the frontier, it had achieved "access to all parts of the frontier." Thus UNOGIL could observe *ad liberum;* but it had no access to the Syrian side of the border, because the U.A.R. declined to give it.

The mountainous terrain in the frontier regions is very difficult, a factor that affected UNOGIL's work substantially. The areas of primary concern to UNOGIL were those where the problems of accessibility were the greatest, both from the standpoint of topography and of obtaining security of movement.

In its first report UNOGIL stated that:

> Its patrols have reported substantial movements of armed men within the country and concentrations at various places. . . . The arms seen consisted mostly of a varied assortment of rifles of British, French and Italian makes. . . . It has not been possible to establish from where these arms were acquired. . . . Nor was it possible to establish if any of the armed men observed had infiltrated from outside; there is little doubt, however, that the vast majority was in any case composed of Lebanese.[13]

The Lebanese Government took strong objections to these conclusions of UNOGIL. It characterized the sentence "it has not been possible to establish from where these arms were acquired" as misleading. With respect to the conclusion that it was not possible to establish whether any of the armed men had infiltrated from the outside, the Lebanese Government questioned the adequacy of UNOGIL's observation and reporting. As for the conclusion that "there is little doubt, however, that the vast

---

[11] The cost of the UNOGIL operation was borne by the United Nations. The Secretary-General, under the authority given him by the General Assembly resolution of December 14, 1957, was able to commit the Organization up to $2 million for unforeseen and extraordinary expenses relating to the maintenance of peace and security. When it became clear that the expenses would be in excess of $2 million, the Secretary-General obtained the approval of the Advisory Committee on Administrative and Budgetary Questions to enter into commitments up to $4 million. The expenditures for UNOGIL during 1958 were finally placed at $3.6 million, and the General Assembly in 1958 voted a supplementary increase in the regular UN budget for that year to cover this amount. In addition, it provided $40,000 in the 1959 UN budget for residual expenses connected with UNOGIL. See *United States Participation in the United Nations, Report by the President to the Congress for the Year 1958* (Washington: Government Printing Office, 1959), p. 240.

[12] S/4040.

[13] S/4040, pp. 8–9.

majority was in any case composed of Lebanese," the Lebanese Government branded this as "misleading and unwarranted." From the publication of the initial report, relations between UNOGIL and the Lebanese Government became strained.

In its second interim report dated July 17, 1958, UNOGIL informed the Security Council that it had 113 observers and had established 15 outstations, substations, and permanently manned observation posts.[14] Air reconnaissance was a most valuable adjunct to ground observation, and up to July 15, 82 missions had been flown. UNOGIL stressed the importance of an adequate number of planes and trained personnel to provide continuous air patrols over all sections of the frontier. A proportion of these planes, it believed, should have night photography capability. It proposed to locate helicopters and reconnaissance planes at the airport at Rayak in the center of the Bekaa Valley so that a constant aerial watch of the entire eastern and southern frontier between Lebanon and Syria could be maintained on a twenty-four hour basis.

In the middle of July 1958, the situation in the area became dangerous. The Government of Iraq was overthrown and the King, the Crown Prince, the Prime Minister, and other leaders were murdered. Fearing that the events in Iraq would result in grave consequences in Lebanon and in Jordan, the Government of the United States in response to the Lebanese Government's request and the United Kingdom Government in response to the Government of Jordan's request landed troops in those respective countries.

President Eisenhower, on July 15, explained why he had sent the troops and declared that:

> In the face of the tragic and shocking events that are occurring nearby, more will be required than the team of the U.N. observers now in Lebanon. Therefore, the United States will support in the United Nations measures which seem to be adequate to meet the new situation and which will enable the United States forces promptly to be withdrawn.[15]

An urgent meeting of the Security Council followed on July 15 to consider the situation in the Middle East. The United States representative took issue with the findings of UNOGIL that there were no "threats from outside" against Lebanon. "The presence of United States troops in Lebanon," asserted the representative of the United States, "will be a constructive contribution to the objectives the Security Council had in mind when it passed the June 11 resolution dealing with this problem."[16]

[14] UN Security Council, S/4052, July 17, 1958.
[15] U.S. Department of State, *Bulletin*, Vol. 39 (1958), p. 181.
[16] UN Security Council, *Official Records*, Thirteenth Year, 82nd meeting, July 15, 1958, par. 36.

The Secretary-General explained to the Security Council that the landing of United States troops and the international implication of that action were irrelevant, so far as his mandate was concerned. Moreover, he made clear that under the mandate given to him he could not change "the observation operation into some kind of police operation" without exceeding his instructions and violating the Charter. He stated that:

> In a police operation, the participants would in this case need the right, if necessary, to take the initiative in the use of force. Such use of force would, however, have belonged to the sphere of Chapter VII of the Charter and could have been granted only by the Security Council itself, directly or by explicit delegation, under conditions spelled out in that chapter.[17]

The Secretary-General thus rejected the plea of Lebanon to transform the operation into a police action and the contention of the United States to be acting along with and in lieu of the United Nations.

A draft resolution of the Swedish representative, which was defeated, would "suspend the activities of the observers in Lebanon until further notice."[18]

He considered that the landing of American troops in Lebanon had altered the conditions under which UNOGIL was set up and had rendered the operation under the changed conditions impractical.[19] A draft resolution of the Japanese representative, which was designed to strengthen and expand UNOGIL to permit the withdrawal of United States troops and which was welcomed by the Secretary-General but vetoed by the Soviet Union, was also defeated.

In spite of the Soviet veto, the Secretary-General stated that he would continue to develop the observation group in conformity with the Security Council resolution of June 11, 1958, and with the Charter. Were the Security Council to disapprove of the steps he proposed to take, steps of which he would keep the members informed, he would accept its judgement.[20] The United States proposal to set up a UN police force, which was vetoed by the Soviet representative, did not find favor with the Secretary-General. He believed that since the United States proposal would limit the force to self-defense, it would be difficult for it to operate outside the government-held area, that is, in areas held by those opposed to the Lebanese Government, where it might well meet with armed resistance.[21]

[17] *Ibid.*, par. 64.

[18] UN Security Council, S/4054.

[19] UN Security Council, *Official Records*, Thirteenth Year, 830th meeting, July 16, 1958, par. 48.

[20] UN Security Council, *Official Records*, Thirteenth Year, 837th meeting, July 22, 1958, pars. 10–17.

[21] UN Security Council, *Official Records*, Thirteenth Year, 835th meeting, July 21, 1958, par. 34.

At the General Assembly emergency special session, President Eisenhower explained that: "The lawful and freely elected Government of Lebanon, feeling itself endangered by civil strife fomented from without, sent the United States a desperate call for instant help. We responded to that call."[22] He reminded the Assembly that: "United Nations action would have been taken and United States forces already withdrawn, had it not been that two draft resolutions, one proposed by the United States, the other proposed by Japan, failed to be adopted by the Council because of one negative vote—a veto."[23]

Here was a unique situation of simultaneous activity in a country by both the United Nations and the United States. The relations between the United States forces and UNOGIL were correct but distant. Such liaison as existed appears to have been ineffective. The record indicates that the Secretary-General and the United States Government assessed the situation in somewhat different ways. The United States conceived the civil strife as fomented from without and the Secretary-General, relying on the reports of UNOGIL, considered that the infiltration of arms into Lebanon from the outside was minimal and that the basic problem was the opposition to the government from within.

Robert Murphy, a former Under Secretary of State for Political Affairs, who was sent to Lebanon during the crisis summed up the situation as follows:

> We agreed that much of the conflict concerned personalities and rivalries of a domestic nature, with no relation to international issues. Communism was playing no direct or substantial part in the insurrection, although Communists no doubt hoped to profit from the disorders, as frequently happens when there is civil war. The outside influences came mostly from Egypt and Syria. From talks with Chamoun . . . and others, my estimate of the situation was that arrangements should be made for an immediate election of a new President. . . . I hoped this would bring about a relaxation of the prevailing tensions and permit the withdrawal of American forces. The United Nations group would remain in Lebanon as observers. This, then, was the United States objective which was reported to and approved by the State Department.[24]

It is noteworthy also to record what he said regarding the basis for the difference in the assessment:

> . . . This international party of investigators had reported they were unable to confirm the Lebanese charge that arms were being smuggled in, and they

[22] UN General Assembly, *Official Records*, Third Emergency Special Session, 733rd plenary meeting, Aug. 13, 1958, par. 7. Hereafter cited as 733rd Plenary Mtg.

[23] 733rd Plenary Mtg., par. 14.

[24] Robert Murphy, *Diplomat among Warriors* (Garden City, New York: Doubleday, 1964), p. 404.

were inclined to minimize the extent of Egyptian and Syrian clandestine activities. But when I made contact with Galo Plaza and his associates, I learned they had been able to work in the mountainous frontier area only during daylight hours, leaving the road network uninspected at night. And when our Marines tapped the telephone line between the capital of Syria and the Basta at Beirut, it was proved conclusively that the Basta rebels were receiving outside support. The American troop landings had been a surprise and a shock to the UN group, which regarded our military action with mixed emotions, as it seemed to interfere with their own efforts to settle the civil war.[25]

It is interesting to note what UNOGIL said with respect to the landing of United States forces:

> . . . During the period under report, in spite of the set-back caused by the landing of United States troops on 15 July which resulted in a sharp reaction in the opposition-held areas, the ground lost was steadily regained through the tact, patience and perseverance of the Military Observers. The extension of the observation Group's activities, therefore, continued and posts have been established at most of the sensitive points along the borders and in the areas immediately adjacent to them. . . .
>
> . . . The presence of the United Nations Observers moving around in their white jeeps from village to village is welcomed both by Government supporters and by opposition elements. The independence and impartiality of the Observers is universally recognized and appreciated, and they are regarded as the symbol of the United Nations presence in the area; they help to inspire feelings of calm and confidence in the areas patrolled by them. Sometimes local disputes and difficulties have been referred to them by different parties, which they have occasionally been instrumental in solving.[26]

It is also interesting to note what UNOGIL said regarding the effect of the presidential election on the general situation in the country:

> . . . While there may have been a limited importation of arms into the areas prior to the Presidential election on 31 July, any such movement has since markedly diminished. A virtual truce has prevailed since about that time in most of the disturbed areas. However, acts of brigandage and lawlessness, unconnected with the political movement, are being increasingly reported. Many of these lawless acts are motivated by economic considerations, as normal life throughout the country has been severely disrupted by the prolonged state of civil strife.[27]

It concluded its third report: "It is evident that the nature and scope of the work of the Observers will inevitably be conditioned by the progress made in dealing with the internal political aspects of the Lebanese problem

[25] *Ibid.*, p. 402.
[26] UN Security Council, S/4085, Aug. 14, 1958, p. 14. Hereafter cited as S/4085.
[27] S/4085, p. 15.

and with the return to normal conditions both in the countryside and in the towns."[28]

In its fourth report of September 29, UNOGIL observed that "with the establishment of its extended network of posts the Group is confident that any infiltration which may still be occurring is on a small scale indeed."[29]

On November 17, UNOGIL issued its last substantive report. It noted that all "organized opposition forces have now to all intents and purposes ceased to exist and the government is in process of extending its authority over the whole country." Moreover, during the period covered by this report, October 21 to November 14, UNOGIL stated that there were no cases of infiltration. In view of the improvement in the general security situation and in the relations between Lebanon and its eastern neighbor, the group concluded that its task under the June 11 resolution could be regarded as completed.[30] It accordingly recommended its withdrawal. The Secretary-General agreed and a withdrawal plan was prepared at his request under which all the group's outposts were closed by November 30, and all observers were withdrawn in three movements from November 28 to December 10.

It is pertinent to record the conclusion of UNOGIL's estimate of its own work:

> . . . Apart from the effects of [UNOGIL's] mission of observation and reporting, its presence has had a reassuring effect on the population and has influenced the historic events which have taken place. By helping to free the Lebanese situation from its external complications, it has contributed to the creation of conditions under which the Lebanese people themselves could arrive at a peaceful solution of their internal problems.
>
> . . . The success of an operation such as the present one depends on the application of moral force to circumstances where otherwise only the use of arms would be effective. The Military Observers, armed only with the moral authority of the United Nations and their own determination and courage, have been able to fulfill their task of peace and have won for themselves the respect of the people in all areas in which they have operated. In doing so they have, even in the recent improved circumstances in Lebanon, repeatedly undergone hardship and dangers.
>
> . . . Observers from twenty-one countries from different parts of the world have co-operated effectively and in a spirit of comradeship not only in circumstances of danger and under the stimulus of urgent events but also in the carrying out of routine duties and patrols. If, as it believes, the Group has been able to make a useful contribution to the restoration of peaceful conditions in Lebanon, it is because it has been able to base its reports on the objective information faithfully supplied to it by its Observers on the ground and in the air.[31]

[28] S/4085, p. 15.
[29] S/4100.
[30] UN Security Council, S/4114, Nov. 17, 1958, p. 7. Hereafter cited as S/4114.
[31] S/4114, p. 9.

Evaluation

In assessing the results of the mission entrusted to UNOGIL, it should be borne in mind that its establishment was a compromise to avert a paralysis of the Security Council. The Lebanese crisis was the product of domestic and regional rivalries with cold-war overtones in the background, and, as already observed, the terms of reference given UNOGIL were not clear.

Moreover, the mountainous terrain in which the group operated created problems in spotting infiltration. During the period when Lebanon was under French mandate, the French found it difficult to fully suppress the smuggling of arms by the Syrians who operated in the same terrain notwithstanding the presence of thousands of armed French soldiers. In comparing the performance of UNOGIL, with a handful of men, and that of the thousands of armed French soldiers, it is not surprising that the former was handicapped in carrying out its mission. Clearly the task entailed more men and equipment than was originally believed necessary to execute its mission.

The reports of UNOGIL indicate that night air patrols without ground support were not sufficient to check on the movement of vehicles. Freedom of movement and unimpeded access are a necessity for the efficient discharge of an observation mission.

The build-up of the mission did not reach its maximum effectiveness until after the election of General Chehab as President, July 31, 1958. Following the coup in Iraq, the landing of American troops in Lebanon, the landing of British troops in Jordan, and the threats of the Soviet Union, the build-up of UNOGIL proceeded very rapidly, as shown by the following figures.

	Aug. 10	Sept. 20	Nov. 14
Number of observers (including air personnel)	190	287	591
Number of permanently manned stations	22	33	49
Number of vehicles	—	173	290

	Number of Sorties in Month	Total Flying Hours in Month
June—6 days only	15	23
July	160	360
August	210	494
September	317	775
October	305	767

The build-up appears to have been *pari passu* with the increase in international tension in mid-July. This was a large peace-observation force, 591, for a border of approximately 165 miles. It was about ten times the size of the Kashmir cease-fire group, which observes a border of some 500 miles.

The reports of UNOGIL appeared to be objective. The members, by conducting themselves in an impartial manner, won the confidence of the partisans and alienated the government, since their reports were generally unfavorable to the government's claim of widespread outside interference. The press, which was loyal to the government, was critical of UNOGIL. This constituted a psychological impediment since the mission had to work with the official bureaucracy, which was generally under the control of the government.

In the Lebanese crisis, the United Nations demonstrated that it was capable of mounting a large and complex operation, involving observers from many countries in a short space of time.

The total UN expenditure on the observation group in Lebanon amounted to some $3,700,000: $3,580,742 in 1958 and $117,000 in 1959.[32] The 1959 expenditure was nothing more than a residual expense, as the Security Council had decided on November 25, 1958 to withdraw UNOGIL.

A breakdown of estimated expenditures for the period June 13, 1958, to December 31, 1958, appeared in the report of the Secretary-General to the Advisory Committee on Administrative and Budgetary Questions (A/C.5/763) as follows:

1. Staff costs
   A. Members $ 47,000
   B. Military personnel   1,540,000
   C. Civilian staff   613,000

   Total $2,200,000

2. Operational costs
   A. Rental and maintenance of premises   90,000
   B. Rental of aircraft and related expenses   155,000
   C. Equipment   1,109,000
   D. Operation and maintenance of equipment   77,000
   E. Supplies and services   84,000
   F. Communication services   30,000
   G. Freight, cartage and express   36,000
   H. Insurance   19,000

   Total $1,600,000

   Total Staff and operational costs $3,800,000

[32] UN General Assembly, *Official Records*, Fourteenth Session, Supplement No. 7, A/4170, p. 12.

Staff costs, therefore, represented approximately 58 percent of the total cost of the observer group. They included travel and subsistence for all three categories as well as salaries and wages for the civilian staff and honoraria for the three members.[33]

Operational costs represented about 42 percent of the cost and of the $1,600,000 estimated for operations, some 40 percent was recovered when UNOGIL was liquidated and the equipment disposed of.

The principal contribution to the settlement of the crisis may be said to be the moral influence of UNOGIL's presence, the symbol of concern of the international community, and its contribution to the creation of conditions that helped to untangle the Lebanese internal crisis from its external complications.

The simultaneous activity of the United Nations and the U.S. military presence created a unique situation. While the ultimate objectives of both were similar, their immediate missions were different. Each operated in its own and separate way. Relations between the two, it appears, were distant and correct, and such liaison as existed was ineffective.

The Secretary-General, as in the case of UNEF, set up an advisory group with which he could take counsel on the problems arising with respect to UNOGIL. The more the power of the Secretary-General has grown in these peace-observation and peace-keeping instrumentalities, the greater the need has been for the Secretary-General to use this device. It absorbs criticisms of his administration and acts as an arena in which he can give an account of the complex and difficult executive responsibilities lodged in him. In the management of his operation, he can resort to the advisory group without having to convene the General Assembly. Potentially, such an advisory group acts as a "cabinet" to give advice and to serve as a corrective.

UNITED NATIONS PRESENCE IN JORDAN

The Jordanian representative accused the U.A.R. of instigating the coup d'état in Jordan in April 1957, smuggling men and arms into Jordan, of inflammatory propaganda coming from the U.A.R. inciting the Jordanian people to rebellion, and of a recently discovered plot against his government. These threats menaced the independence and integrity of Jordan. To meet these threats, Jordan requested military assistance from the United Kingdom. The United Kingdom responded to the request and landed troops on July 17.[34]

---

[33] Both military and civilian personnel were allowed a daily subsistence of $12.50. The three members received a subsistence allowance of $20.00 per day and an honorarium of $50.00 per day.

[34] S/Agenda/831, pars. 24–25.

The Jordanian charges were denied by the U.A.R. representative who characterized the complaint of Jordan as a pretext to cover up the dispatch of British troops to reoccupy Jordan. A number of resolutions were introduced in the Security Council. But in view of the frustration brought on by the Soviet veto in the Council, an emergency special session of the General Assembly was convened on August 8. Several resolutions, one by the Soviet Union and one by Canada, Colombia, Denmark, Liberia, Norway, Panama, and Paraguay, were introduced. The Soviet proposal was unacceptable. The seven-power one did not meet with favor. The Arab states preferred their own resolution, one which would create a better image of themselves in the world at large.

Terms of Reference

Pursuant to a resolution developed by Iraq, Jordan, Lebanon, Libya, Morocco, Saudi Arabia, Sudan, Tunisia, the United Arab Republic, and Yemen, and adopted unanimously on August 21, 1958, the General Assembly, *inter alia*, requested the Secretary-General "in accordance with the Charter . . . [to make] such practical arrangements as would adequately help in upholding the purposes and principles of the Charter in relation to Lebanon and Jordan in present circumstances."[35]

The Secretary-General set up a United Nations Presence in Jordan. After negotiations with the governments concerned, he appointed a special representative in Jordan "to assist in the implementation of the resolution, specifically with a view to helping in upholding the purposes and principles of the Charter in relation to Jordan."

With respect to Lebanon, the Secretary-General informed the General Assembly that UNOGIL constituted for the time being an adequate and practical arrangement in the sense of the relevant sections of the August 21 resolution. In contrast to the Suez situation, where the United Nations interposed an emergency force between regular national military forces which were subject to a cease-fire agreed to by the opposing parties, the Secretary-General argued against establishing a UN police force in Lebanon or Jordan. In these countries, where the situation was described as a "domestic conflict," it would not have been possible to preserve a natural distinction between the presence and functions of any UN force and those of government troops.[36]

As for the withdrawal of United States forces from Lebanon and British forces from Jordan, the Secretary-General reported that he was discussing this matter with the governments concerned. The United States Government made known that its forces would be withdrawn by the end of October provided the internal security situation in Lebanon continued to improve. A similar assurance was given by the British Government with respect to its

[35] UN General Assembly, Res. 1237 (ES III), Aug. 21, 1958.
[36] UN General Assembly, A/3943, Oct. 9, 1958, par. 151.

troops in Jordan. In letters dated November 6, the United States Government and the British Government informed the Secretary-General that the withdrawal of United States forces from Lebanon had been completed by October 25 and of United Kingdom forces from Jordan by November 2.

Organization

The organization and the character of the United Nations Presence in Jordan, which was established as part of the implementation of the Arab states resolution passed by the emergency special session of the General Assembly on August 21, 1958, is given in detail for the bearing it may have on future peace observation and fact-finding.

The Secretary-General designated Pier Spinelli, one of the Under Secretaries of the United Nations, as his UN Presence in Jordan and conferred on him the rank of ambassador. The establishment of this presence entailed negotiations by the Secretary-General with the various Arab governments concerned. The headquarters of the UN Presence was lodged in Amman with supporting liaison offices to be set up in Damascus and Beirut.[37]

Unlike the UNOGIL mission in Lebanon, which made public reports to the Security Council through the Secretary-General, the UN Presence in Jordan was to report privately to the Secretary-General. The UN Presence was a diplomatic mission with a limited and special assignment, notwithstanding the broad terms of reference that would have permitted an operation of any kind short of that permitted under the "enforcement measures" of Chapter VII of the Charter. Its staff in Amman was to be from 60 to 100 men. The group was to (1) monitor at the Hashemite radio station in Jerusalem, (2) ride the borders, and (3) observe and report to the Secretary-General any evidence of foreign intervention.[38] It was separate from the UNTSO operation in Jerusalem, which has responsibility for questions arising under the various Arab-Israeli armistice agreements.

As of the spring of 1964, the United Nations Presence was still officially operating in Jordan with a reduced staff. The Jordanian Government desires to have this UN symbol in Jordan, and the UN Secretariat is disposed to leave it there for the time being.

[37] The U.A.R. rejected the UN Presence on its territory presumably on grounds that it would be tantamount to admitting U.A.R. interference. Nasser agreed to a UN office in Damascus on condition that it be purely administrative and that its activities be confined to facilitating communications. By the time agreement was reached with Nasser, the situation had eased to the point where the Secretary-General abandoned the idea of opening offices in Damascus and in Beirut.

[38] The existence of the radio monitoring team must have become known to Cairo and to "Radio Free Jordan" operating from Syria, for they soon ceased operating. Whether the Cairo and "Radio Free Jordan" broadcasts ceased because of the Secretary-General's intervention is not known. The monitoring device was also used effectively by UNSCOB.

Evaluation

This UN Presence, the first of its kind and a symbol of the United Nations interest in the area, can be said to have had a salutary effect, particularly a psychological one. The Secretary-General appears to have been satisfied with the experiment of using a United Nations diplomatic mission to deal with a localized political problem. It appears to have been successful enough to encourage the Secretariat to use the same instrument elsewhere. The Secretary-General characterized the Jordan UN Presence as an effort in "quiet diplomacy," in contrast to the public diplomacy through published reports of UN commissions established in various other trouble spots.

The UN Presence concept is of recent origin, and there has not yet developed a sufficient amount of experience from which definite conclusions might be drawn. A few preliminary observations might, however, be made regarding the use of this modality as contrasted with a UN representative or multiple type of commission, which serves as a subsidiary organ of the General Assembly or the Security Council.

Theoretically a UN Presence consisting of international civil servants who owe their loyalty to the United Nations and report to the Secretary-General instead of to the General Assembly or the Security Council can be and perhaps is more objective than the UN representative or multiple commission type reporting to the Security Council or the General Assembly. But here neither the character of the Secretary-General, who was an outstanding international servant, nor the kind of UN Presence he chose should be overlooked. Pier Spinelli, who headed the mission, is an accomplished and experienced diplomat. The single or multiple type of commission made up of representatives from various member states of various international political views gives rise to compromise, which quite often weakens the capacity of the commission to carry out its task. The members of a commission are instructed by the states they represent. Their loyalty is colored by political considerations and the commission itself frequently does not have the interests of the United Nations at heart.

Moreover, the character of reporting is radically different in the two types of modalities. The UN Presence reports to the Secretary-General are private and are not and need not be published. Accordingly, there is in these reports expression of views and ideas more freely given because they are protected from the public eye. The reports are made frequently and as often as the exigencies of the situation require. The reports of the UN representative or commission are public and periodic. In the General Assembly, the reports are usually rendered annually, in the Security Council, as required. While the UN representative and the commission both have their terms of reference, members of a commission representing states interpret and apply them in such a way as to reflect the policies of the countries they represent.

These shortcomings have been recognized by the members of the Secretariat and others who now have a strong preference for the UN Presence type of modality. They recognize, however, that this type cannot be used indiscriminately.

7

THE PROBLEM OF LAOS

In the early phases of United Nations involvement in the 1959 crisis in Laos, the Secretary-General actively applied his concept of "preventive diplomacy" to the Laotian situation. Consultations with Laotian representatives revealed the desirability of sending observers to the area, but it was apparent that North Vietnam would not accept observers on its side of the border. Mr. Hammarskjold was reluctant to bring the issue before the Security Council or the General Assembly where it would become embroiled in cold-war polemics. Another possibility under consideration involved the two co-chairmen of the 1954 Geneva Conference—Great Britain and the Soviet Union—working out a joint arrangement and seeking the consent of both Laos and North Vietnam. Also considered was a fact-finding mission to Laos alone without Security Council or General Assembly authorization and at the invitation of the Laotian Government.

While the Secretary-General was exploring these alternatives with the representatives of Laos and other interested United Nations members, the military situation in Laos worsened, and the Laotian Government asked the Secretary-General for the prompt dispatch of an emergency force to halt alleged North Vietnamese aggression and prevent it from spreading. This action forced the Secretary-General to bring the issue before the Security Council.

THE SECURITY COUNCIL SUBCOMMITTEE

The UN Security Council on September 7, with the U.S.S.R. opposing,[1] decided to send an observation mission "to examine the statements made before the Security Council concerning Laos, to receive further statements and documents and to conduct such inquiries as it may determine neces-

[1] The U.S.S.R. argued that unanimity was required and that, in any case, the ICC/Laos should be required to resume activity. The unanimity claim was rejected on grounds of precedent.

sary, and to report to the Council as soon as possible."[2] The mission consisted of Ambassador Shibuzawa (Japan), chairman; Brigadier General Ahrens (Argentina), Minister Plenipotentiary Barratieri (Italy), Ambassador Habib Bourguiba, Jr. to September 30, and Ambassador Ben Amman after September 30 (Tunisia). It met in New York with the President of the Security Council and Secretary-General Hammarskjold, largely in connection with the terms of reference. On September 12, having heard the Laotian Minister of Foreign Affairs, they left for Vientiane where they arrived on September 15. On October 10, part of the subcommittee returned to New York, and by October 21, the entire group met again. It submitted its report to the Security Council on November 3.[3]

The Italian representative, President of the Security Council, emphasized the distinction between "inquiry" and "investigation." "Inquiry" meant "fact-finding," and this meant that the subcommittee must receive information on facts from the government concerned, rather than to seek facts on its own initiative. He noted that the subcommittee should not make recommendations.[4]

The subcommittee decided that if any government other than the Royal Laotian Government offered evidence, it would receive it. However, since the Democratic Republic of Vietnam offered no communication subsequent to a letter to the Security Council of September 6, the subcommittee decided to restrict its inquiry to Laotian authorities. The subcommittee indicated the subjects to be covered in the inquiry: crossing of Laotian border by foreign troops since July 16, 1959; engagement of these troops against Royal Laotian units; dependence of attacking forces for supplies from abroad; participation of North Vietnam elements in attacks, particularly of August 30, 1959.

The report of the observation group describes the terrain, the organization of the Laotian Army, and the disposition of various forces in four separate groups of military actions. There follows a review of the military situation according to witnesses. Of particular interest is the line of questioning used to identify Viet Minh troops by uniforms, language, food (common rather than glutinous rice), and weapons.

In its summary the subcommittee declared:[5]

1. All four periods of military action were guerrilla in character.
2. Certain hostile actions must have had centralized coordination.
3. Practically all witnesses (forty out of forty-one) stated that the hostile elements received support from territory of the Democratic Republic of Vietnam consisting mainly of equipment, arms, ammunition, supplies, and the help of political cadres. The same emerges from the official Laotian documents submitted and from some of the material exhibits.

[2] UN Security Council, resolution adopted at 848th meeting, Sept. 7, 1959, S/4216.
[3] UN Security Council, S/4236, May 11, 1959. Hereafter cited as S/4236.
[4] S/4236, p. 7.
[5] S/4236, p. 31.

The last sentence of the report, which is the most important, answered the real question at issue: "The ensemble of information submitted to the Sub-Committee did not clearly establish whether there were crossings of the frontier by regular troops of the Democratic Republic of Viet-Nam." The subcommittee failed to confirm Laotian charges of overt North Vietnamese aggression and thus was unable to provide the basis for further action by the Security Council.

There seems to be no question, however, that the arrival of the subcommittee had a calming effect. One pro-Western observer wrote:

> On September 6 the fall of Sam Neua was considered inevitable, but on the 9th the enemy columns then sighted only about 6 miles away from the village did not advance. On the 10th, the Viet Minh offensive had practically halted. This sudden cessation of the rebel march at the very moment when it had swept aside everything in its way provoked general astonishment. The presence of the UN was clearly taking effect. . . . Fighting soon stopped completely, and it was in a country of almost peaceful appearance that the UN observers began their investigation. [6]

The fact that two alternate members of the subcommittee were left behind when the members departed for New York on October 13 constituted a further stabilizing influence.

The Secretary-General saw the potential benefits of a continuing United Nations Presence in Laos, and he accordingly resumed the behind-the-scenes discussions, which had been interrupted by the Security Council's involvement in the issue. Since the limited terms of reference and controversial origins of the subcommittee ruled out its further use in Laos, the Secretary-General decided to visit the country again (he had been there in March 1959 as part of a Southeast Asian tour) and to leave behind him a personal representative. He consulted with members of the Security Council and then informed them of his plans.

The reactions of the two major cold-war protagonists to his proposed *démarche* are largely conjectural. According to some observers, the Russians, though committed to denounce publicly any United Nations intervention, were privately not as strongly opposed to a UN Presence. This view was based on an interpretation of the Soviet Union's support of their Asian satellites' cause in Laos as somewhat less than whole-hearted. There is no evidence, however, that the Soviet delegates gave any intimations of approval for the Secretary-General's initiative. Joseph Lash reports that:

> Hammarskjold had talked with the Russians before sending his own letter to the Council. He wanted to find out whether their protest was one intended for the record, to assuage Chinese feelings rather than to intimate any withdrawal of confidence. He tried to get Dobrynin to give him some kind of lead,

[6] Sisouk Na Champassak, *Storm over Laos* (New York: Praeger, 1961), pp. 99–100.

but Dobrynin left him on his own. He decided to go anyway. It was a carefully calculated political risk. [7]

The expected Soviet denunciation appeared the day after the Secretary-General announced his visit. The Soviets released the text of Chief Delegate Sobolev's note replying to the Secretary-General's letter to the Security Council. As Soviet denunciations go it was fairly mild:

> The visit to Laos of the United Nations Secretary-General and the proposed stationing of a personal representative of the Secretary-General in Vientiane, as well as any other action on the part of the United Nations in this question, can only further complicate the situation obtained.

The United States was, of course, committed to support the move publicly, but the private views of government officials were less clear. While the stabilizing effect of a United Nations Presence was undoubtedly attractive to some, the prospect of the Secretary-General and his personal representative actively seeking the neutralization of Laos on the scene must not have pleased those influential officials who favored a pro-Western regime in Vientiane.

THREE-PHASE UNITED NATIONS PRESENCE

During the Secretary-General's visit to Laos, November 12–19, 1959, it was announced in New York that he had called Sakari Tuomioja, Executive Secretary of the United Nations Economic Commission for Europe and a former Prime Minister of Finland, to join him in Vientiane. Mr. Tuomioja was instructed to review the economic situation in the country, particularly the role of United Nations economic and technical assistance in promoting economic growth and stability, and to report his findings to the Secretary-General within four weeks. In addition, he would "follow up the discussions initiated by the Secretary-General and provide him with such further information as would be of importance for a judgment regarding the assistance which he might most appropriately render under the Charter." [8]

Mr. Tuomioja's report, received on December 17, 1959, reviewed the problems and shortcomings of the Laotian economy and set forth recommendations for coordinated action by the United Nations and the specialized agencies to assist Laos in agricultural development, education, health, transport and communications, and public administration. The

[7] Joseph Lash, *Dag Hammarskjold: Custodian of the Brushfire Peace* (Garden City, N.Y.: Doubleday, 1961), p. 143.

[8] United Nations, *Yearbook of the United Nations, 1959* (New York: Columbia University Press, 1961), p. 66.

report also recommended the appointment of a high-level official to co-ordinate in Laos the various development programs and activities of the United Nations and its specialized agencies.

After a preliminary study of Mr. Tuomioja's report by the Secretariat, the Secretary-General sent Roberto M. Huertematte, United Nations Commissioner for Technical Assistance, to Laos to discuss with authorities there the technical and organizational questions relating to the implementation of Mr. Tuomioja's recommendations. Mr. Huertematte assessed the specific needs of the Laotian people and determined which specialized agencies might be able to meet them most effectively.

Then in February 1960, it was announced that Dr. Edouard Zellweger of Switzerland had been appointed as a special consultant to the Secretary-General for the coordination of United Nations activities in Laos. Although Dr. Zellweger's assigned task was to implement the recommended program of technical and economic assistance, his background as an experienced diplomat and lawyer suggested that he would also serve as a political adviser to the Secretary-General. According to Joseph Lash, "when Hammarskjold described this modest technical assistance mission at the monthly Council luncheon, Sobolev twitted him that the mission under an economic hat would also serve political functions, but he did not object to the program." [9]

EVALUATION

It is difficult to evaluate the impact of the United Nations Presence on the political stability of Laos. The UN Presence coincided with a marked lessening of violence in the country's civil strife during the last months of 1959 and the first half of 1960. A coup d'état in August, however, ushered in a new period of fighting and crisis that led to the 14-nation Geneva Conference on Laos in 1961–62. The United Nations Presence was able to serve as a restraining influence in 1959 when the conflict was primarily domestic, but when foreign intervention on both sides was stepped up considerably in 1960, this restraint could no longer be effective.

Even in 1959, Laos was well on the way to becoming a cold-war battle-ground, and the major protagonists were already involved in the domestic struggle. This added an urgency to the Secretary-General's efforts to stabilize the situation, for a major East-West confrontation in Laos would represent a grave threat to international peace and security. But Mr. Hammarskjold's initiatives were more risky than the similar moves he had made in Jordan and the Cambodian-Thai dispute. His emphasis on technical and economic assistance was an effective way of diverting attention from the underlying political nature of his *démarches*. In addition, the

[9] Lash, *op. cit.*, p. 144.

impartiality of the Secretary-General's program of neutralization, internal reconciliation, and economic development contributed to the tolerance with which the major powers viewed his intervention.

The political objectives of the UN Presence were basically two-fold. The first was to obtain full information on a situation that might threaten international peace and security. This was accomplished both through the Secretary-General's personal visit in November 1959 and through the continuous reporting of his personal representatives on the scene. The second objective was to advise the Laotian rulers and thereby steer the country's political development along neutral lines. Events in Laos suggest that this effort was fairly successful in the short run only.

8

UNITED NATIONS PRESENCE IN THAILAND AND CAMBODIA

The origins of Cambodia's long-standing rivalry with its neighbors to the west, Thailand, and to the east, Vietnam, are found in the era of Khmer (Cambodian) dominance of the Southeast Asian peninsula from the ninth to the twelfth centuries. Thai (Siamese) pressure from about the twelfth century and Vietnamese (Annamese) pressure beginning in the seventeenth century whittled away at the Khmer Empire. In the nineteenth century, the French prevented the complete dissection of Cambodia by establishing a protectorate there.

In the first half of the twentieth century, the border provinces of Battambang and Siem Reap, which changed hands frequently, were the major source of tension between Thailand and Cambodia. These conflicts seem to have focused on the dispute over possession of the temple of Khao Phra Viharn, located in a contested border area. Under a settlement of 1904 and 1907, Thailand had ceded the provinces of Battambang, Sisophon, and Siem Reap to France. The territorial dispute was settled in Cambodia's favor in 1946 by the Treaty of Washington, but disagreements between Cambodia and Thailand have continued.

The cold war has added another dimension to this historic conflict. Thailand, which is a party to SEATO, and South Vietnam are both members of the Western alliance. Cambodia has cultivated a "neutralist" foreign policy that leans heavily in Communist China's direction. Cambodia fears that its two neighbors will seek Western support for their alleged drives to undermine Cambodian independence. Thailand and South Vietnam view their common neighbor as a Communist Trojan horse. Prince Norodom Sihanouk charges that Thailand and South Vietnam, supported by the United States, are assisting dissident Cambodian elements who hope to overthrow his "neutralist" regime and establish a more right-wing, pro-Western government.

THE 1958 CRISIS

Relations between Thailand and Cambodia during the second half of 1958 alternated between periods of tensions and accommodation, which has characterized the recent history of their relationship. On July 4, 1958, Prince Norodom Sihanouk was again named Premier by Parliament and promised to make "personal and friendly contacts with South Vietnam and Thailand to show that Cambodia doesn't want to make trouble for anyone."[1] On July 12, he made a brief visit to Bangkok and conferred with the Prime Minister and Foreign Minister of Thailand. From these talks emerged an agreement to negotiate the two countries' problems, notably border questions, press campaigns, and cooperation in economic, communication, and health matters.

Thai-Cambodian relations worsened, however, when Cambodia recognized the government of the People's Republic of China on July 18, and Prince Sihanouk announced his plan to visit Red China during August. In response to these moves, Thailand proclaimed on August 4 a state of emergency in six border provinces to check what a Thai minister described as the increasing banditry and infiltration of Communists activated by Cambodia's recognition of Communist China. Prince Sihanouk arrived in Peking on the same day that the Cambodian delegation arrived in Bangkok for the negotiations. Sihanouk's well-publicized state visit to Red China and the Thai-Cambodian talks thus unfolded simultaneously.

On August 24, Prince Sihanouk and Premier Chou En-lai issued a joint declaration in which the latter expressed his regrets that Cambodia had been the victim of violations and blockades by neighboring countries. On the same day as this thinly veiled reference to Thailand's border conflicts with Cambodia, the negotiations in Bangkok were broken off when the Cambodian Foreign Minister flew back to Phnom Penh to report to Prince Sihanouk. The next day Prince Sihanouk left Peking, inviting Chou En-lai to visit him "in the near future."

As expected, the Cambodian delegation returned to the negotiations with a tougher line, and the talks ended on September 4 without even a

[1] *New York Times*, July 5, 1958, p. 3.

joint communiqué. The Cambodian Foreign Minister made a statement blaming Thailand for the failure of the negotiations and announcing that Cambodia would submit the temple dispute to the International Court of Justice. In a communiqué issued the following day, the Thai Government outlined the areas of disagreement between the two delegations: the major conflict was over the terms of reference of a proposed mixed commission whose duty it would be to demarcate the Thai-Cambodian boundary and thereby settle the temple dispute and other related problems. On September 7, an anti-Cambodian demonstration in Bangkok, reportedly encouraged by Thailand's Minister of Interior, erupted in violence when some 10,000 demonstrators marched on the Cambodian Embassy. Police and firemen stopped the march in a two-hour battle in which more than 100 persons were injured.

A period of relative calm lasted until late November. One reason for this lull was Thailand's involvement in its own domestic political situation. On October 20, a bloodless coup brought to power a military clique headed by Field Marshal Sarit Thanarat. The new revolutionary party annulled the constitution and proclaimed martial law. The new regime, which appeared more militantly anti-Communist than its predecessor, promised a continuation of Thailand's international commitments and pro-Western foreign policy.

A month after the coup, a border incident marked the beginning of a new period of crisis in Thai-Cambodian relations. According to Thai frontier police, on November 20, a uniformed Cambodian force "kidnapped" thirty-two inhabitants of a Thai village in the border area, holding them in Cambodia on false charges. On November 24, Cambodia suspended "temporarily" diplomatic relations with Thailand. Cambodia stated to the Ministry of Foreign Affairs that the purpose of the move was to "smooth out the difficulties" between the two countries "in the interest of better relations in the future." The Ministry of Foreign Affairs, however, has revealed that "the Cambodian Ambassador stated orally that the reason for the . . . step . . . stemmed from attacks conducted by the Thai press which impaired the good relationship between the two countries." [2] Thai diplomats privately suspected that Red China was backing Cambodia's action.

Caught somewhat off balance by the surprise move, the ruling military clique countered the next day by sealing off Thailand's border with Cambodia and recalling its ambassador in Phnom Penh. On November 29, Cambodia indicated its willingness to retain a chargé d'affaires in Bangkok if Thailand would agree to keep one in Phnom Penh. The Thai Government declined the offer, stating its desire to restore diplomatic relations to the previous ambassadorial level. In addition, Thailand informed its

[2] Thailand, Ministry of Foreign Affairs, *Relations between Thailand and Cambodia* (Bangkok, 1959), pp. 9–10.

neighbor that it considered the release of the thirty-two Thai nationals
detained by Cambodian authorities as an essential condition of the restoration of normal relations.

THE 1958–1959 PRESENCE

In a letter to the UN Secretary-General on November 29, the permanent
representative of Cambodia charged that Thailand was concentrating
troops on a war footing and large amounts of military equipment on the
Cambodian frontier.[3] Cambodia held that this constituted a threat to the
peace, although it had not taken any retaliatory action. On December 8,
the representative of Thailand declared that the alleged concentration of
troops and military equipment was nonexistent and that it had only increased police reinforcements at the border posts to prevent unwarrantable
entry and armed raids.[4] Furthermore, Thailand indicated that it was prepared "to welcome any United Nations representative to observe the
situation in the border area between Thailand and Cambodia," and stated:
"If . . . Your Excellency should consider the present case as falling within
the purview of Article 99 of the Charter, my Government would be happy
to welcome your representative to Thailand and would afford him every
possible facility to inspect our border area."[5]

[3] UN Security Council, S/4121, Dec. 2, 1958.

[4] UN Security Council, S/4126, Dec. 8, 1958.

[5] There is a precedent for Thailand's invitation to a UN representative to observe the
Thai-Cambodian border situation. In 1954, Thailand feared that the war in Indochina
might spill over into its territory, and drew the attention of the Security Council to a
situation which, in its view, represented a threat to the security of Thailand, the continuance of which was likely to endanger international peace and security. Large-scale
fighting had repeatedly taken place in the immediate vicinity of Thai territory, and
there was a possibility of direct incursions of foreign (Viet Minh) troops. The Thai
Government stated that it was bringing this to the attention of the Security Council in
order that the Council might provide for observers under the Peace Observation Commission set up by the "Uniting for Peace" resolution. The representative of Thailand
eventually submitted a draft resolution according to which the Council would request
the Peace Observation Commission to establish a subcommission of from three to five
members with authority to (1) dispatch observers to Thailand, (2) visit Thailand if
necessary, (3) make such reports and recommendations as it considered necessary to the
Peace Observation Commission and to the Security Council. The majority of the
Council members, including the United States, supported the draft resolution because
they believed that the situation disclosed by the Thai representative warranted quick
response and United Nations observation. The Soviet Union which would benefit from
Communist inroads in Thailand opposed the measure on the ground that it represented a camouflaged attempt by the United States to deepen the conflict in Indochina
and to prepare for military intervention under cover of the United Nations flag on the
model of the Korean adventure. The Soviet delegation's negative vote, the only one
cast, defeated the measure. Thailand considered taking the request for observers to the
General Assembly but eventually decided not to do so.

Operating on the basis of Article 99, which states that the Secretary-General "may bring to the attention of the Security Council any matter which in his opinion may threaten the maintenance of international peace and security," Dag Hammarskjold began to explore the problem. Private discussions with representatives of Cambodia and Thailand indicated that both sides desired to restore diplomatic relations and that the assistance of a neutral third party might facilitate the reconciliation. The possibility of sending a special representative to the area was discussed more with a view to solving the basic problems of peace and confidence than to responding to Thailand's request for a frontier observer.[6] The members of the Security Council were consulted informally, and they raised no objection to a UN Presence in that area. On December 22, the Secretary-General announced that the two governments had invited him to send a representative to assist them in finding a solution to their difficulties. He designated Ambassador Johan Beck-Friis of Sweden as his Special Representative for the purpose.

Terms of Reference and Performance of the Mission

The Secretary-General described this mission as a "good offices operation."[7] This same interpretation was put forth by Ambassador Beck-Friis when he arrived in Bangkok on January 20, 1959. He declined to describe his mission as that of a "mediator," and said he considered himself "to be at the disposal of the two governments."[8] In a later statement, Ambassador Beck-Friis described his mission in these words: "I was not sent here to act as judge or arbitrator. My principal aim has been to help the two governments find a path toward better relations."[9]

[6] While these discussions were going on in New York the Cambodian Government made a request for border observers which paralleled closely the original Thai invitation, except that it was addressed to the International Control Commission, Cambodia (set up at the 1954 Geneva Conference), instead of the United Nations. In December 1958, the Cambodian Government repeated the charges of November 29 made to the Secretary-General about the concentration of troops and war materials by Thailand along the Cambodian border. The Royal Government requested the commission to send observers to the border provinces and verify the good faith of the Cambodians. The Polish delegation's proposal to send a team was outvoted by the other two delegations of the ICC, Canada and India. It was decided by a majority vote to inform the Royal Government that the commission could not take any action regarding the relationships between Thailand and Cambodia. See *Seventh Interim Report of the International Commission for Supervision and Control in Cambodia* (London: HMS, November 1959), Cmnd. 887, p. 4.

[7] Press Conference, Feb. 5, 1959, in *The Servant of Peace: A Selection of the Speeches and Statements of Dag Hammarskjold* (London: Bodley Head, 1962), p. 264. Hereafter cited as *The Servant of Peace.*

[8] "Thai-Cambodian Question," *United Nations Review*, V: 8 (February 1959), p. 5.

[9] "Thai-Cambodia Agreement," *United Nations Review*, V: 9 (March 1959), p. 2.

From January 20 to February 23, the Special Representative visited the two countries concerned, where he engaged in consultations with the officials of the two governments and made inspection tours of the frontier. Arrangements were made for the release of nationals detained by both sides, and both governments cooperated in restoring calm and confidence in their relations. As a result, diplomatic relations were resumed. The representatives of both governments expressed gratitude and appreciation for the assistance given by the Secretary-General and his Special Representative, which had led to the easing of the difficulty between them.

Evaluation

The Beck-Friis mission represented the first example of what has been called an "informal" Security Council—the Secretary-General's private consultation with members of the Council about the feasibility of sending a special representative to an area of political tension. Dag Hammarskjold evaluated this experiment at a press conference on February 5, 1959:

> Normally, a conflict of the type we had there would probably have gone to the Security Council, and we would have had a decision which, perhaps, in substance would have meant the same as the decision now taken. However, the parties agreed not to raise the issue in the Security Council but, anticipating a possible outcome, to direct parallel invitations, as it were, to the Secretary-General to send someone to assist them in getting over the difficulty. Without in any way making this a precedent, I responded to the invitations and a representative was sent there, with the acquiescence of members of the Security Council. You can see how much more effective and smooth-working such a technique is than the regular one, which involves all the meetings and debates and so on.[10]

This approach provided greater freedom of action and flexibility since there were no precise terms of reference calling for formal reports and verbatim records as would have been the case if the Security Council had formally considered the question. The success of this procedure depended on the tacit agreement of the United States and the Soviet Union not to raise any objections when consulted by the Secretary-General. This was partly because neither great power felt that its vital interests were at stake in the dispute, and that they were involved with such major issues as the Berlin crisis and summitry.

While there is no doubt that this mission represents one of the more successful efforts in the peaceful settlement of disputes, it is uncertain how wide a range of situations would be suitable for this approach. As the Secretary-General said in a press conference on February 26, 1959, it was "a fairly simple case with fairly few substantive issues involved and where we had full agreement on inviting a representative of the Secretary-

---

[10] *The Servant of Peace*, p. 264.

General to assist them."[11] The willing cooperation of both sides made Ambassador Beck-Friis' task of reconciliation considerably easier.

In addition, only the immediate sources of friction—the detention of nationals of the other country, the press attacks, and the rupture of diplomatic relations—were removed during Ambassador Beck-Friis' mission. This is not to denigrate these accomplishments, for presumably the improvement of relations could lead the way to a resumption of the negotiations begun in August 1958 on the more fundamental problems, such as the temple dispute. The détente proved in fact to be of short duration, for in 1961 Thai-Cambodian relations deteriorated to the point where Cambodia again broke off diplomatic relations in October of that year.

DETERIORATING SITUATION, 1961–1962

Despite the marked improvement in Thai-Cambodian relations early in 1959 as a result of the Beck-Friis mission, no progress was subsequently made toward the solution of the two countries' major disputes, particularly their rival claims to the ancient temple of Khao Phra Viharn. In October 1959, Cambodia instituted proceedings against Thailand before the International Court of Justice in the hope of getting international legal backing for its claim to the temple. Thailand had accepted the Court's compulsory jurisdiction, but sought to test its competence on this matter. In May 1961, the Court ruled that it possessed competence and began to consider the case.

The Thai Prime Minister ruled out the possibility of negotiations while the temple dispute was before the World Court.

Renewed press and radio attacks and an exchange of supposed threats in 1961 led Cambodia to break off diplomatic relations with Thailand for the second time in less than two years. The Cambodian Government put its army on alert to resist the allegedly imminent Thai aggression. The Thai Government thereupon closed its border with Cambodia.

For the remainder of 1961 and the first half of 1962, Thai-Cambodian relations remained hostile, but there were relatively few border incidents or other clashes between the two countries. In the summer of 1962, however, the tension again reached a critical point. On June 15, the International Court of Justice declared in a 9 to 3 decision that Cambodia held sovereignty over the disputed temple. In Bangkok, the Thais protested violently against the Court's judgment, but on June 21 Prime Minister Sarit Thanarat announced that Thailand would honor its obligations under the UN Charter. He told his people that "the communists hope to touch off clashes along the Burmese, Thai and Cambodian borders," and that in the

[11] Quoted by Richard I. Miller, *Dag Hammarskjold and Crisis Diplomacy* (New York: Oceana, 1961), pp. 229–30.

prevailing circumstances in Southeast Asia, peace with Cambodia was in the interest of the nation.[12] Prince Norodom Sihanouk, the Cambodian Prime Minister, had publicly stated that Cambodia would no longer tolerate Thai occupation of the temple, and a top emissary had been sent to Peking for consultations. The Thai leaders therefore realized that a fight with Cambodia would serve only the objectives of the Communists, and surrendered sovereignty over the temple on July 16.

It was clear, however, that the Thai withdrawal would not end the quasi-belligerent relationship between the two countries and would not restore diplomatic relations. Prime Minister Thanarat stated that Thailand reserved its "inherent right" in the temple affair, "especially the right to have recourse to any legal processes which may offer themselves in the future and will result in the recovery of our rights over the temple at an opportune moment."[13]

In mid-August, reciprocal charges of aggression again brought tensions to a critical point. Prince Sihanouk charged that Thai troops had occupied Cambodian territory since August 11. He proposed a fourteen-nation conference (with the same nations which had reached an accord on Laos in July) to guarantee Cambodian neutrality. The Soviet Union and Communist China supported the proposal, but the United States and other Western powers did not. Prince Sihanouk threatened on September 3 to ask Communist China for troops to "discourage aggression" if no one else guaranteed Cambodian neutrality. He held that the assurances of Prime Minister Macmillan and President Kennedy were insufficient.

THE 1962–1964 PRESENCE

The United States suggested privately in New York that the United Nations or the Secretary-General might be able to play a useful role in the crisis, but Secretary-General U Thant concluded that there was no basis for an initiative on his part at that time. Further discussions, however, led both governments to request the appointment by the Secretary-General of a personal representative to investigate the difficulties between their two countries. In a letter dated October 19, the Secretary-General told members of the Security Council that he believed such a step would be a constructive measure within the scope of the Charter and that he had appointed Nils G. Gussing of Sweden[14] as his personal representative after receiving

---

[12] Quoted by L. P. Singh in "The Thai-Cambodian Temple Dispute," *Asian Survey*, II: 8 (October 1962), p. 25.

[13] *Ibid.*, p. 26.

[14] Mr. Gussing had served in the office of the UN High Commissioner for Refugees since 1958. In 1961, he was appointed the High Commissioner's representative in Tunisia to deal with the problem of Algerian refugees, and in 1962, he was director of the Elizabethville refugee camp in the UN Congo operation.

the agreement of the two governments. On December 18, the Secretary-General informed the President of the Security Council that the permanent representatives of Cambodia and Thailand had agreed on the desirability of appointing a Special Representative of the Secretary-General in the area for one year, beginning January 1, 1963. [15] The two governments indicated their willingness to share on an equal basis all costs involved in the mission of the Special Representative (who would be assisted by a small staff). On December 10, 1963, the Secretary-General told the Security Council that the two governments had informed him of their desire that the Special Representative continue his mission during the calendar year 1964. They had further agreed that a small increase in the existing staff of the Special Representative should be provided to enable him to travel more frequently between the respective capitals. [16] The mission of the Special Representative ended on December 31, 1964, by mutual consent of the parties.

Terms of Reference

Mr. Gussing's original mandate, as formulated in the Secretary-General's letter of October 19, 1962, was "to inquire into the difficulties that have arisen" between the two countries. In announcing a more formal arrangement for a one-year period, the Secretary-General outlined the Special Representative's duties in more detail:

His terms of reference would, in general, require him to place himself at the disposal of the parties to assist them in solving all problems that have arisen or may arise between them. The most immediate among these would be the reactivation of the agreement concerning press and radio attacks, concluded between the parties in New York on 15 December 1960, and the lifting of restrictions on nationals of the two countries who are now forbidden to land on the airports of the other country while in transit. It is hoped that in due time consideration may be given to the question of the resumption of diplomatic relations. [17]

The Special Representative's mission was extended for 1964 under the same terms of reference.

Operation and Performance

The Special Representative arrived in the area on October 26, 1962, and had discussions with high officials of both countries. He also conducted a number of investigations in the border areas, on both sides of the international frontier. In December, the Secretary-General reported that these

[15] UN Security Council, S/5220, Dec. 18, 1962, Annex. Hereafter cited as S/5220.
[16] UN Security Council, S/5479, Dec. 10, 1963.
[17] S/5220.

"activities . . . have coincided with a lessening of tension between the two countries, to which the tone and the contents of the press and radio broadcasts bear witness."[18]

Early in 1963, the Special Representative accomplished one of the major tasks with which he had been charged—the revival of the 1960 agreement on the mutual cessation of press and radio attacks. The renewed accord included a provision for resort to the good offices of the Special Representative. The agreement proved to be ephemeral, however. In the two weeks following the renewal of the agreement, the Thai Government brought three alleged attacks by Prince Sihanouk, two of them in speeches broadcast over Peking radio, to the attention of Mr. Gussing. The Thai Government's attempts to implement the agreement angered Prince Sihanouk. His secretariat issued a communique on the subject:

> Prince Sihanouk has voluntarily . . . promised Mr. Nils Gussing . . . to avoid, in his speeches outside Cambodia, all criticism of Thailand. But the attitude of the Bangkok authorities renders worthless all the efforts towards reconciliation undertaken in recent months. In these circumstances, the Prince considers himself released from his promise and free to discuss at will the past and present difficulties between Cambodia and Thailand.[19]

Although the agreement on press attacks was short-lived, there was a significant decline during the first half of 1963 in the number of attacks by the Thai press on Cambodia. There was no corresponding decrease in the number of Cambodian attacks on Thailand.

Evaluation

Although there have been few advances toward a lasting improvement in Thai-Cambodian relations, the Gussing mission helped to prevent them from worsening, no mean accomplishment considering the deep antagonisms between the two countries. This made a constructive contribution in Southeast Asia, for there was a strong possibility that overt hostilities between these two countries might bring intervention by one or both of the major cold-war protagonists in the area—Communist China on the Cambodian side, the United States on the Thai side. The danger of escalation from local to more general conflict was thus particularly acute in this case.

The Gussing mission had a restraining influence on both sides and was a useful safety-valve or channel for handling complaints. In effect, the mission provided a substitute for diplomatic relations by acting as an intermediary between the two governments.

[18] S/5220.

[19] Quoted in *Facts about the Relations between Thailand and Cambodia, III* (Bangkok: Ministry of Foreign Affairs, March 1, 1963), pp. 10–11.

The UN Presence in Cambodia performed the additional function of serving as a symbol of international concern for the fate of this small country wedged between two hostile neighbors. It represented an authority above the rival blocs and provided Cambodia with an alternative to reliance on the Chinese Communists, whose pledges of assistance Prince Sihanouk frequently brandishes to intimidate his opponents.

The Gussing mission had the further benefit of providing the Secretary-General with continuous, on-the-spot observation of the situation in the area. Although the fact-finding aspect of the Special Representative's mandate implied some possibility of his judging the merits of the frequent charges and countercharges of aggression made by the two governments, he studiously avoided issuing any findings of right or wrong. One suspects that any such judgment would have quickly rendered him *persona non grata* in at least one of the two capitals.

An interesting lesson seems to have been learned from the experience of the earlier Beck-Friis mission. This mission was terminated slightly more than a month after its primary objective, the restoration of diplomatic relations, had been accomplished. When relations between the two neighbors again deteriorated and diplomatic relations were broken off after less than two years, it was apparently realized that more permanent representation of the Secretary-General was necessary. Thus the Gussing mission was extended first for the calendar year 1963 and then for 1964.

9

—◆—

UNITED NATIONS OPERATION IN THE CONGO, 1960–1964

The Republic of the Congo achieved independence on June 30, 1960, abruptly by comparison with other recently independent states, and, in retrospect, without adequate preparation. Following nationalist disorders commencing in January 1959, the Belgian parliament enacted a provisional constitution in May 1960 to serve until the Congolese parliament, which is also a constituent assembly, should draft new organic legislation.

At the Security Council meeting on July 7, 1960, which unanimously recommended the admission of the Congo to the United Nations, the United States representative, the Honorable Francis O. Wilcox, expressed the hope that the Congo would receive strong material support from the

United Nations. On July 11, an insurrection in the Congolese Army (Force Publique) caused Prime Minister Patrice Lumumba to request UN assistance to restore discipline.

THE FIRST PHASE

With the arrival of Belgian forces to protect Belgian lives and property, the Congolese Government specifically requested United Nations military assistance, "justified by the dispatch to the Congo of metropolitan Belgian troops" in violation of the treaty between Belgium and the Congo. "The essential purpose of the requested military aid is to protect the national territory of the Congo against the present external aggression which is a threat to international peace." [1]

In July and August 1960, the Security Council passed three resolutions which (1) called on Belgium to withdraw its troops, and authorized the Secretary-General to provide the Congolese Government with military assistance; and (2) called on all states to refrain from action that might impede the restoration of law and order and might undermine the territorial integrity and political independence of the Congo. The Council also invited the specialized agencies of the United Nations to render such assistance as the Secretary-General might require, [2] and called on the Belgian troops to withdraw from the Province of Katanga, and reaffirmed that "the United Nations force in the Congo will not be a party to or in any way intervene in or be used to influence the outcome of any internal conflict, constitutional or otherwise." [3]

Up to this point, UNOC was purely a peace-keeping operation intended to restore law and order. The August 9 resolution specifically disclaimed any authority to intervene in the internal conflict. This excluded even the simple fact-finding activities usually associated with peace-observation missions.

THE SECOND PHASE

The next phase of the Congo operations began in September 1960 with a conflict between Prime Minister Lumumba and President Joseph Kasavubu. The Soviet Union supported Lumumba and sought without success to remove the United Nations Command which, in its view, sup-

[1] The above background material is paraphrased from *United States Participation in the United Nations, Report of the President to the Congress for the Year 1960* (Washington: Government Printing Office, 1962), pp. 41–43.

[2] UN Security Council, Resolution adopted at the 879th meeting, July 22, 1960, S/4405.

[3] UN Security Council, Resolution adopted at the 886th meeting, Aug. 9, 1960, S/4426.

ported Kasavubu. The Soviet Union vetoed a series of resolutions calling on states to refrain from giving military aid except through the United Nations.

Until this development, the Secretary-General seemed to have in mind the termination of UNOC's military activities as soon as most of the Belgian troops were removed and the Congolese Army firmly established.[4] The United Nations activities would then be confined to technical assistance.

However, the Soviet support of Lumumba opened the possibility of an internal conflict like the Spanish Civil War in the late 1930's, with the antagonists receiving support from conflicting power groups. To avoid this situation, Ceylon and Tunisia proposed in the Security Council a resolution that would have permitted UNOC to act to restore order even though the governmental authority in the Congo was divided or in doubt. In effect, this would have given UNOC some authority to influence the ultimate structure of the Congo Government as well as to maintain law and order. The Soviet Union vetoed resolutions to accomplish this objective, and the United States brought the Congo problem before a special session of the General Assembly.

The special session was convened on September 17, 1960, and on September 20 passed a resolution by a vote of 70 to 0 with 11 abstentions (the Soviet bloc, France, and the Union of South Africa), which appealed to all Congolese to solve their internal conflicts by peaceful means "with the assistance . . . of Asian and African representatives appointed by the Advisory Committee on the Congo, in consultation with the Secretary-General, for the purpose of conciliation."[5]

The Conciliation Commission established under this resolution was of relatively little importance to the history of the Congo. It went to the Congo, made investigations, and reported to the regular session of the General Assembly along the same pattern as previous United Nations peace-observation commissions. It was theoretically independent of UNOC. To be sure, the conflict in this situation was among factions of one government (receiving some support from abroad) rather than between independent states. However, this was not very different from the situation in Indonesia in 1948 or in the Aaland Islands during the League of Nations period.

THE THIRD PHASE: THE CONCILIATION COMMISSION

The Conciliation Commission arrived in the Congo on January 3, 1961, and submitted its report to the General Assembly on March 21, 1961. The

[4] Arthur Lee Burns and Nina Heathcote, *Peace-keeping by UN Forces, from Suez to the Congo* (New York: Praeger, 1963), p. 46.

[5] UN General Assembly, *Official Records*, Fourth Emergency Special Session, Annexes, Res. 1474 (ES-IV), A/4510, Sept. 20, 1960. Hereafter cited as Res. 1474 (ES-IV).

situation in the Congo, theoretically, might have developed from that point along the lines of most other conflicts. The General Assembly might have accepted the recommendations of the Conciliation Commission and have recommended their implementation by the various factions with a reduced United Nations group to observe and report on the results. This would have been a typical peace-observation mission.

However, after the murder of Lumumba, emergency action became necessary to avoid civil war. The Security Council passed a resolution on February 21, 1961 (with France and the U.S.S.R. abstaining) which urged the United Nations to take "appropriate measures to prevent the occurrence of civil war in the Congo, including arrangements for cease-fires, the halting of all military operations, the prevention of clashes, and the use of force, if necessary, in the last resort." [6]

This procedure in effect nullified the paragraph of the resolution of August 9, 1960, cited above: "that the United Nations force in the Congo will not be a party to or in any way intervene in or be used to influence the outcome of any internal conflict, constitutional or otherwise."

From this point on, the Security Council furnished the main guidelines: reorganization of Congolese armed units and elimination of interference by such units in the political life of the Congo; withdrawal of all Belgian and other foreign military and political advisers not under the United Nations Command; [7] and opposition to the secessionist activities in Katanga. [8]

The Secretary-General was authorized "to take vigorous action, including the use of . . . force, if necessary, for the immediate apprehension, detention pending legal action and/or deportation of all foreign military and para-military personnel and political advisers not under the United Nations Command" and to prevent the return of "such elements." [9]

The steps taken by the Secretary-General were both political and military. The political steps included persuading the warring factions to reconvene the Congolese parliament and establish a fully legal central government; and efforts to obtain cease-fires and agreements concerning the status of Katanga, culminating in the Kitona agreement of December 23, 1961. The military steps included a full-fledged United Nations military operation in Katanga against the Katanga forces and Belgian mercenaries and cooperation with the central government in quelling a rebellion by the Communist-supported regime of Antoine Gizenga in Stanleyville.

Even before the United Nations military operations in Katanga, the Secretary-General had characterized the United Nations operations as follows: "Through combined military and diplomatic efforts, the United

[6] UN Security Council, *Resolution adopted at the 942nd meeting, Feb. 21, 1961,* S/4741. Hereafter cited as S/4741.

[7] S/4741.

[8] UN Security Council, *Resolution adopted at the 982nd meeting, Nov. 24, 1961,* S/5002. Hereafter cited as S/5002.

[9] S/5002.

Nations had, during that difficult period characterized by wide-spread political break-down, intense political rivalry and tribal conflicts, achieved a *pacification* which was far preferable to repression." [10]

Thus, the United Nations operations in the Congo were and are far removed from the practices of peace observation. After February 1961, the chief task was pacification, not conciliation or good offices. The policies had been set by the United Nations Security Council. When the various factions acted in a manner which threatened the Security Council objectives, UNOC did not "report" to the Security Council and "recommend" to the various factions, but took action in conjunction with the central government, or on its own. UNOC had at its disposal some 25,000 troops in contrast to the small cadres never exceeding 1,000 available for peace-observation missions.

The Secretary-General and UNOC arranged for cease-fires and for conferences among the factions which led, among other things, to the restoration of constitutional government in the Congo. Also the Secretary-General reported on occasion to the Security Council or General Assembly, which were guided by his views. All of this resembles "peace observation." It is significant that in this type of activity the Secretary-General relied primarily on his civilian advisers (Ralph Bunche, Robert Gardiner, Mahmoud Khiari, and others) rather than on military advisers.

Thus, except for the short period of the Conciliation Commission, the chief significance of the Congo operation in a study of peace observation is to point out the differences between the peace-observation approach and the peace-keeping approach. It is difficult to draw any sharp lines. A policy of peace-keeping (or in this case pacification), in contrast to peace observation, brings with it United Nations directives rather than recommendations to the parties and the threat or use of force instead of moral prestige to achieve the objectives. This in turn involves a military or semimilitary operation with many times the personnel requirements of the typical peace-observation mission.

Terms of Reference

The Conciliation Commission differs from UNOC in that the commission was established by a General Assembly resolution while UNOC was established by the Security Council. The Assembly resolution confirmed most of the policies and provisions set forth in the previous Security Council resolutions and appealed to all member governments for voluntary contributions for a United Nations fund for the Congo to be used under United Nations control and in consultation with the central government to render the fullest possible assistance to remedy the unsatisfactory economic and political conditions in the Congo.

[10] UN General Assembly, *Official Records*, Sixth Session, Supplement No. 1, A/4800, p. 27.

The third paragraph of the main resolution, which provided the terms of reference for the Conciliation Commission, appealed to all Congolese "to seek a speedy solution by peaceful means of all their internal conflicts for the unity and integrity of the Congo, with the assistance, as appropriate, of Asian and African representatives appointed by the Advisory Committee on the Congo, in consultation with the Secretary-General, for the purpose of conciliation."[11]

This in general follows the United Nations Charter provisions for peaceful settlement of disputes between states—the parties should settle the dispute by means of their own choosing with advice from a United Nations group. The chief difference in this case is that this formula is used in connection with a dispute between factions within a state rather than between states. While the resolution does not note that the various factions were receiving support from outside states, it does speak of "vigorous action" by the Secretary-General "to safeguard its territorial integrity and political independence in the interests of international peace and security."

Organization

The Conciliation Commission was intended to consist of representatives from each state serving on the Advisory Committee on the Congo and appointed by the Advisory Committee in consultation with the Secretary-General. These states were Ethiopia, the Federation of Malaya, Ghana, Guinea, India, Indonesia, Liberia, Mali, Morocco, Nigeria, Pakistan, Senegal, Sudan, Tunisia, and the United Arab Republic. However, Guinea, Indonesia, Mali, and the United Arab Republic, because of the hostility of President Kasavubu, withdrew from the Advisory Committee and therefore were not represented on the commission.

The chairman, vice-chairman, and rapporteur of the commission, representing respectively Nigeria, the Federation of Malaya, and Ethiopia,[12] arrived at Léopoldville on December 19, 1960, to make arrangements for the arrival of the full commission. The officers received an unfriendly reception, Kasavubu having issued an order prohibiting hotels in Léopoldville from providing accommodations for members of the commission. The President of the Congo insisted that the membership of the commission be changed before it arrived to eliminate representatives of states which the Congo Government regarded as unfriendly. The commission officers replied, however, that the composition of the commission was a matter exclusively for the United Nations and could not be altered. They also pointed out that "the members of the Commission, although designated by their respective governments, were coming to the Congo as representatives of the United Nations and that, in conformity with the

[11] Res. 1474 (ES-IV).
[12] Jaja A. Wachuku, Mohamed Sopiee, and Mallas Andòm.

Commission's terms of reference, they would not interfere in the internal affairs of the Congo."[13]

The full commission arrived in Léopoldville on January 3, 1961, and remained in the Congo until February 20, 1961. It then went to Geneva to draft its report which was approved on March 10, 1961.

The commission was assisted in its task by eleven members of the United Nations Secretariat headed by Mr. Dragoslav Protitch and Mr. F. T. Liu. Administrative support was no problem because of the presence in the Congo of UNOC. For this same reason, an analysis of the cost of the Conciliation Commission is of no significance since most of its costs were absorbed in the budget of UNOC.

Performance

The commission attempted to meet with groups and to form a clear idea of the positions held by the different factions. On the basis of the information which it obtained during its stay in the Congo, however incomplete, the commission suggested a summit conference of Congolese leaders in a neutral place, if necessary outside the Republic.[14] The object of such a meeting would have been to work out changes in the fundamental law with a view to submitting amendments to a reconvened parliament.

The commission in its report, in addition to reiterating its recommendation for a summit meeting of Congolese leaders, made other recommendations concerning military operations, reorganization of the Congolese National Army, foreign interference and other subjects, most of which were carried out in substance at a later date. However, the commission played no role in their implementation. As previously indicated, after the murder of Lumumba, the emergency action to avoid civil war eliminated the role of the commission. The General Assembly considered the report of the commission and adopted a number of resolutions, in one of which a new Commission of Conciliation of seven members to be designated by the President of the General Assembly was established to assist the Congolese leaders to achieve reconciliation and to end the political crisis. This commission, however, never played an active role in the events that followed. On the other hand, the Special Representative of the Secretary-General and UNOC played a great role.

Evaluation

The experience of the Conciliation Commission shows the inherent difficulty of carrying on a function of conciliation simultaneously with an

[13] See UN General Assembly, A/4711. March 20, 1961, p. 5. Hereafter cited as A/4711.

[14] A/4711, par. 136.

active military operation. The chairman of the Conciliation Commission in notes on its report pointed out that:

> It had been suggested by those responsible for the Operation in the Congo that the Commission has no right to comment on the activities of the UNOC or to make comments on the operations there. I, on the other hand, hold the view that the terms of reference of the Commission which empower the committee to study the situation throughout the Congo are inclusive enough to bring the United Nations Operation in the Congo within the scope of this study, and therefore the Commission is competent to comment on the operation of UNOC insofar as the nature of the operation affected the possibilities of conciliation of the opposing political factions in the Congo.[15]

The commission's report in fact commented favorably on the work of UNOC, but its treatment of UNOC as just another faction undermined the commission's effectiveness after the Security Council granted UNOC the use of force to attain its objectives.

The Conciliation Commission never obtained much cooperation from any of the important factions in the Congo. The Kasavubu government refused to permit it to interview Lumumba and, despite the protest of the commission, removed Lumumba from Léopoldville when the commission insisted on seeing him. Lumumba's death took place while the commission was in the Congo. Kasavubu did not permit the commission to interview any of the leaders on its list whom he held captive and indeed executed several of these leaders during the commission's stay in the Congo.

The Gizenga faction with Communist backing permitted the commission to interview the principal officers at its capital, Stanleyville, and even to interview two "detainees" who had not supported Gizenga's position. However, the commission characterized the Gizenga attitude as uncooperative and discourteous and pointed out that the morale of the two interviewed "detainees" was low and that the dominant thought in their minds was that of release.

Moise Tshombe in Katanga stated that he had no special problem to submit to the commission and would not receive the commission officially. He did, however, entertain the commission at dinner. Mr. Albert Kalonji, the other powerful factional leader, also declined to see the commission officially.

The attitudes of all the factions indicate that the Conciliation Commission was not regarded as the neutral and impartial agent of an international organ, the *sine qua non* for a successful peace-observation mission. The reason for this was not that the commission was deemed to favor one faction against another—all factions were uncooperative. While the commission, like UNOC, was a symbol of the United Nations, it was completely overshadowed by the UNOC activities. The UNOC participation

[15] A/4711, Annex XXII, p. 104.

in military operations by its nature prevented UNOC from appearing as an impartial arbiter. Its image, figuratively speaking, rubbed off on the Conciliation Commission.

The Conciliation Commission could nevertheless have functioned in a limited way as a political adviser to UNOC. However, in this capacity, it would be in competition with the Advisory Committee on the Congo where the nationality of the members was substantially identical. In this capacity, moreover, the commission would also be in competition with the UN Secretary-General and his political advisers. Clearly no significant role remained.

The chief conclusion to be drawn from the experience of the Conciliation Commission relates to the problem of combining a role of mediator supported only by moral sanctions with an operation that can impose military sanctions. The Congo situation shows that the peace-keeping operation will tend to overshadow the mediation and render the latter ineffective unless the mediation can be effectively separated.

The Cyprus situation today presents the identical problem. It is significant to note the main differences between the Cyprus mediation effort and the Congo conciliation.[16]

1. The United Nations in Cyprus obtained the consent of all factions both to the establishment of the position of mediator and to the appointment of the particular mediator chosen for the position.

2. The mediator in Cyprus came from Finland, which has no troops in Cyprus. The Conciliation Commission consisted of representatives of the same states which had sent troops to the Congo.

3. The UN military force in Cyprus is not large enough to assume a positive role in pacification of the country and therefore, to a much greater degree than in the Congo, presents an image of impartiality.

4. The UN military force in Cyprus has never received Security Council authority to play a positive role in pacification such as was granted to UNOC by the Security Council resolution of February 21, 1961.

Thus, the mediation effort in Cyprus started off under theoretically more favorable auspices both because of the more limited peace-keeping functions in Cyprus, functions that imply strict neutrality among factions, and because of the care taken in Cyprus to differentiate between peace-keeping and mediation and to establish a separate public image of the mediation.

[16] See "The Problem of Cyprus, 1964–1965," pp. 436 ff.

10

THE PROBLEM OF WEST IRIAN, 1962–1963

The western half of the island of New Guinea was governed as part of the Netherlands East Indies prior to the establishment of an independent Indonesia. However, the political status of West New Guinea was not settled by agreements leading to the independence of Indonesia. The Netherlands claimed that its sovereignty over the territory was unaffected by the Charter of Transfer of Sovereignty, while Indonesia maintained that West New Guinea became an integral part of its territory on the date of Indonesia's independence. The Netherlands continued to administer the territory. The dispute was brought before the General Assembly in 1954, 1955, 1956, and 1957 without any significant change in the position of either party.

In 1961, the Netherlands announced that it wished to end its administration of the territory provided the rights of the Papuan inhabitants, including their right of self-determination, could be guaranteed. Foreign Minister Luns stated that the Netherlands was prepared to relinquish sovereignty to the peoples and place the territory under an international authority established by or operated under the United Nations.

Indonesia urged that the Netherlands transfer its administration immediately to Indonesia, though if the Netherlands preferred to use the United Nations for the transfer, Indonesia would consider the proposal.[1]

The General Assembly in the 1961 session failed to work out an agreed solution. In December 1961, it became apparent that Indonesian infiltrators had landed in West Irian, and during December 1961 and January 1962, a number of serious clashes took place between Dutch and Indonesian troops, with a substantial number of Indonesians captured by the Dutch. After considerable effort, the United Nations Secretary-General arranged for Dutch and Indonesian delegations to negotiate in the presence of a neutral moderator, Ambassador Ellsworth Bunker of the United States. An agreement for the transfer of administration from the Netherlands was signed on August 15, 1962.

---

[1] *United States Participation in the United Nations, Report by the President to the Congress for the Year 1962* (Washington: Government Printing Office, 1963), p. 169. Hereafter cited as *1962 President's Report.*

UNITED NATIONS OPERATIONS

The agreement provided for the United Nations to assume a number of functions, which involved peace observation and fact-finding, during the period before the transfer of administrative authority to Indonesia, which turned out to be May 1, 1963. General Rikhye, senior military adviser to the Secretary-General, arrived in West Irian on August 17, 1962, before the General Assembly had considered the agreement and consented to assume the functions assigned to it. United Nations consent was given by a vote of 89 to 0 with 14 abstentions on September 21, shortly after the opening of the General Assembly. Thus, the United Nations groups performed their functions from August 17, 1962, until May 1, 1963.

Terms of Reference

The agreement between the Netherlands and Indonesia provided for two phases of United Nations operations. [2]

During the first period, after the cessation of hostilities on August 18, 1962, the Secretary-General agreed to undertake the following functions: (1) to observe the implementation of the cease-fire by both parties and their agreement not to reinforce their military forces nor resupply them with military materiel; (2) to take necessary steps for the prevention of any acts endangering the security of the forces of both parties; (3) to receive reports of any incidents and take the necessary measures to restore the situation in consultation with both parties; and (4) to make advance arrangements to permit the rapid installation of a United Nations Temporary Executive Authority (UNTEA) on General Assembly approval of the agreement between the Netherlands and Indonesia. [3]

During the second period, after the General Assembly approved the agreement, the functions conferred on the Secretary-General were as follows:

1. Administration of the territory would be transferred from the Netherlands to a United Nations Temporary Executive Authority under the jurisdiction of the Secretary-General. A UN administrator acceptable to Indonesia and the Netherlands would be appointed by the Secretary-General and would have "full authority under the direction of the Secretary-General to administer the territory for the period of the UNTEA administration." [4]

2. The Secretary-General would supply UNTEA with such security forces as the administrator deemed necessary to supplement the Papuan

[2] UN General Assembly, A/5170 (mimeo.), Aug. 20, 1962, Annex A, pp. 1–9. Hereafter cited as A/5170.

[3] A/5170, Annex B, p. 11. The memorandum goes into some detail in describing the methods of dealing with specific problems largely arising from the nature of the area.

[4] A/5170, Annex A, p. 2.

police and Indonesian armed forces, both of which would come under the control of the administrator.

3. Full administrative responsibility for the territory would be transferred from UNTEA to Indonesia no earlier than May 1, 1963. The agreement contained elaborate provisions for replacing Netherlands officials, bringing Papuans into technical and administrative positions, employing personnel provided by Indonesia, and taking the numerous other steps incident to the transfer of administration.

4. UNTEA had responsibilities in connection with informing the population of the transfer, preparing them for ultimate self-determination, and advancing the education of the inhabitants—responsibilities that continued even after the transfer of administrative responsibility to Indonesia. The agreement described in detail the participation of the Secretary-General in the act of self-determination. It provided that the Netherlands and Indonesia would bear the expense of its implementation in equal shares and would reimburse the Secretary-General for all expenses.

Organization

During the period from the cessation of hostilities until the establishment of UNTEA on October 1, 1962, the functions assigned to the Secretary-General were performed by the military adviser to the Secretary-General, Brigadier General Rikhye, and twenty-one military observers provided by six member states—Brazil, Ceylon, India, Ireland, Nigeria, and Sweden. These observers were stationed in four main centers. Their duties were to assist the Dutch and Indonesian troops in preparing for the take-over of authority of UNTEA in October.

On September 21, 1962, the United Nations observer team reported that it had completed its task. In accordance with the General Assembly recommendation, the Secretary-General's representative arrived in the territory and in cooperation with Dutch officials prepared a detailed plan for the transfer of authority to UNTEA.[5] The Netherlands Governor left the territory on September 28 and appealed to the population to support the United Nations administration. The transfer of administration took place on October 1 with the raising of the United Nations flag, which was flown side by side with the Netherlands flag. A temporary administrator, the personal representative of the Secretary-General, was appointed and served until the appointment of the United Nations Administrator, Dr. D. J. Abdoh, on October 24.

The United Nations administrator reorganized the civilian administration by replacing eighteen top Dutch officials with United Nations-appointed personnel who were neither from Indonesia nor from the Netherlands. The vacancies caused by the departures of large numbers of Dutch

[5] UN General Assembly, *Official Records*, Eighteenth Session, Supplement No. 1 (A/5501), p. 36. Hereafter cited as A/5501.

civil servants were filled wherever possible by promoting Papuan officials. The Indonesian Government was also requested to provide civil servants and responded with speed. However, large numbers of Indonesian personnel did not begin to arrive until February 1963. To maintain the government services a number of Dutch officials agreed to work for UNTEA on a temporary basis. During the period of UNTEA administration, the number of Papuan officials increased from approximately 7,000 to 7,600.[6]

In response to the Secretary-General's request, the Government of Pakistan provided a force of approximately 1,500 to serve as the main element of the United Nations Security Forces (UNSF). The government of Canada furnished two planes and the United States three DC-3s and crews to support the UNSF.[7] At the end of November, the United States had supplied ninety-nine officers and men, and the Canadians twelve. The American group gradually decreased to forty-nine at the end of March, one month before the Republic of Indonesia took over the administration. All of these forces were under the command of the United Nations administrator.

Also under the administrator's authority were the Papuan volunteer corps, the civil police, the Netherlands forces awaiting repatriation, and the Indonesian troops, totaling approximately 1,500.

In the Papuan volunteer corps, Dutch officers and noncommissioned officers were gradually replaced by Indonesian officers. By January 21, 1963, this process had been completed.

The maintenance of law and order was entrusted to the Papuan police, originally under Dutch officers. The Dutch officers were gradually replaced by Philippine officers who in turn were replaced by Indonesians. By the end of March 1963, the entire officer corps was Indonesian.

When UNTEA assumed administrative responsibility on October 1, there were still Indonesian troops in the territory who had been parachuted in during the Dutch-Indonesian conflict. Since many of these "volunteers" were starving, they were repatriated to Indonesia and replaced by fresh Indonesian troops. Under the agreement, the number of Indonesian troops could never exceed the contingent of 1,500 provided by Pakistan. The Netherlands forces were completely withdrawn by November 15, 1962. The United Nations contingent was completely withdrawn on May 1, 1963, when the Indonesian Government assumed authority.

Performance

The Secretary-General's report contains General Rikhye's summary of the immediate emergency actions that were required prior to the organization of UNTEA. These included "the concentration of the Indonesian forces, in four main areas, the provision to them of emergency

[6] A/5501, p. 37.
[7] See A/5501, p. 36, and *1962 President's Report*, p. 174.

supplies, and the repatriation of over 500 Indonesian detainees."[8] All this, as might have been anticipated, was accomplished without incident by the twenty-one military observers. The main problem with the Indonesian infiltrators was to inform them of the end of hostilities. This was accomplished by radio broadcasts and pamphlets dropped from the air. As soon as they were informed of the end of hostilities, they proceeded to the four main centers where they were assembled.

As pointed out, UNTEA had a wide variety of functions beyond peace observation. Most important, it was responsible for the administration of the territory for the period from October 1, 1962, until the Indonesians assumed responsibility "no earlier than May 1, 1963." Second, it was responsible for maintaining law and order by using a United Nations military contingent, the Papuan police, and Indonesian armed forces. Third, it had certain responsibilities in connection with informing the population concerning the transfer, preparing them for ultimate self-determination, and advancing the education of the inhabitants. These latter responsibilities continued after the transfer of administrative responsibility to Indonesia.

As pointed out, UNTEA replaced the Dutch officials with neutral officials who in turn were replaced by Indonesian officials. UNTEA increased the number of Papuan personnel occupying official positions but not in sufficient numbers to replace all the departing Dutch officials. Indonesians filled the gap. Within a very short time the Indonesian officials outnumbered the United Nations personnel. "This immediately jeopardized the development of an independent United Nations administration."[9] The same writer points out that the UN officials could not speak the native language and thus had little contact with the Papuans.

It is difficult to estimate the effectiveness of the UNTEA administration because standards of comparison in such a primitive country are lacking. During the period of fighting, the Dutch slowed down the supply of essential commodities in the realization that in all probability they would be leaving the country. UNTEA provided supplies not only for itself but also for the country. However, large quantities of supplies with United Nations markings were seen in the black market in Djakarta. Van der Veur contends that the level of employment declined, but concedes that UNTEA developed a small number of economic projects.

In connection with the second function of maintaining order, the UNTEA administrator stated that his administration had assured "a peaceful transition from the Dutch to the Indonesian authority."[10] This was unquestionably true. Only two incidents of violence were noted by

[8] A/5501, p. 35.

[9] Paul W. van der Veur, "The United Nations in West Irian: A Critique," *International Organization*, XVIII: 1 (Winter 1964), p. 59.

[10] UNTEA, Department of Information, News Bulletin No. 20, April 24, 1963, p. 4.

the Secretary-General in his report to the General Assembly. They involved the police and a small group of Indonesian troops, occurred on December 15, 1962, and resulted in one death and four wounded. Order was immediately restored by the United Nations Security Forces.[11] As pointed out, the Indonesian troops almost equaled in number the United Nations Security Forces, and Indonesian officials by the end of March 1963 were commanding the Papuan police. There is some evidence that the absence of violence may have arisen from fear of what would happen after the transfer to Indonesia.[12] During the entire period, the Indonesian Government was waging a campaign to transfer the government to Indonesia prior to May 1.

The third area of UNTEA's concern—the preparation of the Papuan people for self-government and for a plebiscite—is related only indirectly to peace observation. The Secretary-General in his report stated "that he was confident that the Republic of Indonesia would scrupulously observe the terms of the Agreement concluded on 15 August 1962 and would ensure the exercise by the population of the territory of their right to express their wishes as to their future."[13] The United Nations stood ready to give the Government of Indonesia all assistance in implementing this and the remaining parts of the agreement. On October 21, 1963, the Secretary-General reported that he had continued to consult on this subject with Indonesia and had established a United Nations fund for the economic and social development of West Irian.[14] Some students of the United Nations have suggested that the Government of Indonesia has shown more enthusiasm for receiving the funds than for arranging a plebiscite.

Evaluation

The objectives of the UN activities in connection with the transfer of West Irian from the Netherlands to Indonesia went far beyond peace observation and even peace-keeping. For example, UNTEA had for a time full administrative responsibility for the territory; the duty of supervising the replacement of Dutch officials; responsibilities in connection with preparing the native population for self-government and laying the ground for a future plebiscite; and duties in connection with providing economic assistance. It is possible, indeed probable, that the operations from the long-range standpoint will be deemed a complete failure. It is doubtful whether the Papuans will ever have a chance to determine their political future in a plebiscite. Much of the UN economic assistance for the Papuans ended up in black market bazaars in the Chinese section of Djakarta where such items as canned goods and "Kleenex" with UN labels could be purchased.

[11] A/5501, p. 37.
[12] Van der Veur, *op. cit.*, p. 68.
[13] A/5501, p. 40.
[14] See UN General Assembly, A/5578 (mimeo.), Oct. 21, 1963.

An appraisal of the entire UN operation in West Irian thus might reach a different conclusion from that reached through concentrating on the aspects of the operations relating to the maintenance of peace. If the appraisal is confined to these latter activities: (1) the military observer team was successful in implementing the agreement for cessation of hostilities; and (2) UNTEA achieved the transfer of authority from the Dutch to the Indonesians with a minimum of violence.

The task of the military observer team was less controversial but possibly more difficult than the task of UNTEA. It was less controversial because both the Dutch and Indonesians wished to end the fighting. Since the Netherlands was committed to leave West Irian, it wished to accomplish its departure peacefully. The Indonesian "volunteers" were widely dispersed in unhealthy jungle country, were being decimated by a cholera epidemic, and in many cases, were starving. Five hundred were detainees of the Dutch and undoubtedly more would have surrendered as soon as they could find their way through the jungle to Dutch posts. The authorities in West Irian undertook the main tasks of assembling the Indonesian forces and repatriating most of them. Twenty-one neutral military observers in four processing centers cooperated with the local authorities and assured the peaceful take-over by UNTEA on October 1.

The UNTEA military force consisted of approximately 1,500 UN troops, 350 Papuan troops (originally officered by the Dutch but later by Indonesians), and almost 1,500 Indonesian troops, all under the command of UNTEA. This situation, where the majority of the troops were officered by one of the parties to the dispute, was indeed unfortunate. It might have led to violence especially when Indonesia launched a propaganda campaign for an early take-over. It almost certainly influenced the decision to allow the Indonesians to assume administrative control on May 1, 1963, the earliest permissible date under the General Assembly resolution.

The UN troops except for some Canadian and U.S. pilots were all Pakistani. This was the first instance of a UN operation with personnel from only one country. The experiment worked out quite well. It is doubtful that a multinational force could have been assembled in so short a time.

The time element was most significant. The cease-fire was signed on August 15, 1962; the first observers arrived on August 17; and the preliminary task was completed by October 1. The General Assembly authorized the formation of UNTEA on September 21. UNTEA and its military force arrived on October 1 and completed its main tasks by May 1, 1963. The ability of the UN Secretariat to take on these functions on such a close schedule is a high tribute to the competence of UN peace-keeping organization, personnel, and procedure.

The financial arrangement under which the full costs were shared by the Dutch and Indonesians successfully avoided some of the problems that have confronted the United Nations in other cases.

While both the Dutch and Indonesians were interested in a peaceful transfer of authority, there were nevertheless many opportunities for disorders. It is clear that many Papuans wished greater freedom and were annoyed by the situation where Indonesians were merely replacing the Dutch. The hold-over Dutch officials doubtless encouraged such attitudes. Furthermore, the Indonesian officials, even before May 1, were in control of many areas and were suppressing freedom of speech. The Indonesian propaganda campaign for a take-over at an earlier date than that permitted by the General Assembly resolution could have caused disorders. Finally, economic deterioration such as took place in West Irian is a frequent cause of disorder. The presence of UN troops prevented clashes which might otherwise have occurred between the Indonesians and the Papuans. The absence of disorders could have the effect of diverting world attention from the long-range problem of the plebiscite and the future of West Irian.

11

UN OBSERVATION IN YEMEN, 1962–1964

On September 26, 1962, the royal government of Imam al-Badr was overthrown in favor of a group led by Abdullah Sallal, a former chief of the palace guard. To this coup, President Nasser of the United Arab Republic gave immediate support. The coup was heralded as republican in character, a revolution against the despotic rule of the Imam and expressive of a yearning for Arab unity and social reform.

The geographic location of this backward kingdom tells much about its strategic importance to the West, to the Soviet Union, and to President Nasser's ambition to extend his sway over the area. The kingdom is situated near the southwestern corner of the Arabian peninsula. In the north of Yemen and to the east, the desert reaches out to Saudi Arabia. To the south lie the British-controlled Federation of South Arabia and the British colony of Aden, which, together with Singapore, is one of the most important outposts of British power. At Aden is the world's greatest bunkering port and the seat of the British Middle East Command. With Yemen as the back door to the Arabian peninsula, adjoining Aden provides the vital strategic defense link to the Indian Ocean and Southeast Asia.

The Arabian peninsula with its oil riches is of enormous economic, political, and strategic value. Yemen is the only country of the Arabian peninsula that never was under British or United States protection or influence. Following World War II and up to the revolution in September, there was relative stability in the area. From September 1962 on, the country has been in a state of civil war, with Nasser, aided by the Soviet Union, supporting the Sallal government and Saudi Arabia the royal government of the Imam. The aim of Nasser in assisting Sallal, it appears, was to take over or dominate the area in accordance with the plan in his *Philosophy of the Revolution*.

Soon after civil war broke out, the United Arab Republic began sending troops to support the regime of Sallal, and Saudi Arabia gave arms and supplies to the royalists. The British Government, fearing Nasser's ambition to control the area on the doorstep of Aden, supported the royalists and withheld recognition of the Sallal regime. The United States, on the other hand, recognized the Sallal regime on December 19, 1962, while the Imam was still fighting to regain control of his country. One purpose underlying this recognition presumably was to maintain United States influence in an area where Soviet activities seemed threatening. In addition, the Department of State justified the recognition of Yemen because of the Sallal government's declaration that it would honor Yemen's international obligations, and President Nasser's assurance that he would withdraw the Egyptian troops in Yemen, then believed to be some 12,000. He predicated this assurance on the stopping of armed support from Saudi Arabia. The United Nations accepted the credentials of the new Yemen Government. Thus in this crisis, as in the Middle East crisis of 1958, the problem had three facets—national, regional, and international.

President Kennedy, it was reported on November 25, 1962, sent letters to the Middle East leaders outlining a proposal to end the Yemen crisis. [1] He suggested, as a first step, the withdrawal of U.A.R. forces from Yemen and the abandonment of Saudi Arabian support for the royalist government. Premier Faisal of Saudi Arabia rejected and Sallal welcomed the President's proposal, while the Imam protested because he was not consulted. Meanwhile, the U.A.R. continued to build up its forces in Yemen.

ACTION OF THE SECRETARY-GENERAL

Late in February 1963, the Secretary-General sent Under Secretary Ralph Bunche to Yemen on what was described as a fact-finding mission. This appears to have been the first step of the United Nations to take a hand in solving the crisis. Also quietly at work was Ellsworth Bunker, whom President Kennedy had asked to try to persuade President Nasser

[1] Harold Ingrams, *The Yemen* (London: John Murray, 1963), p. 141.

and the Saudi Arabian Government to stop giving aid to the warring factions in Yemen. After several weeks of separate negotiations with Nasser, Faisal, and Sallal (the Yemen royalists were not included), Bunker obtained their agreement to a phased withdrawal of Egyptian troops on condition that the Saudi Arabian Government halt its aid to the royalists. The United Nations, it was expected, would play a role in observing and verifying the disengagement.

The Secretary-General reported to the Security Council on April 29, 1963, that he had received from the U.A.R., Saudi Arabia, and the Arab Republic of Yemen formal confirmation of their acceptance of identical terms of disengagement in Yemen, terms that Bunker had negotiated. The substance of the agreement was: the Government of Saudi Arabia would terminate support and aid to the royalists of Yemen and would prohibit the use of Saudi Arabian territory by royalist leaders. The United Arab Republic would withdraw its troops from Yemen, the withdrawal to be phased and to take place as soon as possible. The United Arab Republic also agreed not to take punitive action against the royalists of Yemen for resistance prior to the beginning of their disengagement, and there would be an end to any actions on Saudi Arabian territory by U.A.R. forces. A demilitarized zone of twenty kilometers on each side of the Saudi Arabian-Yemen border was to be established from which military forces and equipment were to be excluded. Impartial observers would be stationed to check on the observance of the terms of disengagement. The United Arab Republic and Saudi Arabia would "co-operate with the representative of the United Nations Secretary-General or some other mutually acceptable intermediary in reaching agreement on the modalities and verification of disengagement."[2]

The Secretary-General asked Major General Carl Von Horn, Chief-of-Staff of the UN Truce Supervision Organization in Jerusalem, to proceed to the three countries to consult with the authorities on details relating to the nature and functioning of UN observation in implementing the disengagement terms and to report on the size of the set-up that might be required to discharge this responsibility.

The Secretary-General expressed to the Security Council his preliminary view that "the requirements of both men and equipment will be modest and will be needed for three or four months, at the most." He was thinking in terms of not more than fifty observers, with suitable aerial and ground transportation for patrol purposes. The Secretary-General thought he would ask Saudi Arabia and the U.A.R. to bear the cost.

In his report to the Security Council of May 27, 1963, the Secretary-General, basing his conclusions on the information provided by General Von Horn, gave his findings. (1) UN observers in the Saudi Arabia-Yemen area were vitally necessary and could be the decisive factor in avoiding

[2] UN Security Council, S/5298, April 29, 1963, p. 2.

serious trouble there. All parties concerned desired their presence. The need was urgent, and they should be sent without delay. (2) The terrain and climatic conditions in parts of the area would be difficult, and considerable danger might be encountered. Although problems of movement and logistics would be great, stationing of observers could be accomplished. (3) Personnel required for the mission would not exceed 200, including a small number of officer-observers; a ground patrol unit of about 100 men, carrying only arms for self-defense, crews for about eight small aircraft for reconnaissance and transport; and personnel for such supporting services as communications, logistics, medical aid, transportation, and administration. (4) The observation function was estimated to require no more than four months. (5) Some of the personnel required for this observation operation could be recruited from UNEF, UNTSO, and possibly UNMOGIP, subject to clearance with the governments concerned. General Von Horn would be designated Chief of the Yemen Mission. (6) The total cost of the Yemen Observation Mission was estimated at less than $1,000,000. The Secretary-General hoped that the two parties principally involved would bear the costs of the mission. He was sure the parties would agree to bear at least part of the costs, in money or in other forms of assistance.

The Secretary-General stated that because of the importance and urgency of the UN observation function to the peaceful resolution of the Yemen issue, he was establishing the operations as soon as the necessary arrangements could be made. This should mean, he stated, that a small advance party could be sent to the area within a few days. The Secretary-General had not yet received any authorization or instruction from the Security Council for establishing the instrumentality. Under what authority the Secretary-General was dispatching the mission was not clear.

In his report to the Security Council of June 7, 1963,[3] the Secretary-General stated that Saudi Arabia had orally agreed to accept a "proportionate share" of the costs of the operation and the United Arab Republic agreed in principle to provide assistance in an amount equivalent to $200,000 for a period of two months, which would be approximately half the cost of the operation over that period. He did not rule out an appeal to the U.A.R. Government for additional assistance at the end of two months, should it be necessary to extend the operation beyond that period. He also reiterated his intention to organize and dispatch the observation mission without delay and stated that General Von Horn would leave for the area in a day or two with a small advance party.

The Soviet Union's reaction to the zeal of the Secretary-General in setting up and dispatching the mission was indicated in its letter of June 8, 1963, asking for a meeting of "the Security Council . . . to consider the reports of the Secretary-General to the Council on developments relating

---

[3] S/5325.

to Yemen."[4] The letter reminded the Secretary-General that the Security Council is charged with the primary responsibility for the maintenance of international peace and security, and under the Charter, the Security Council makes the decisions on such matters, not the Secretary-General. Even though the interested parties had consented to a UN observation group in Yemen, the Soviet Union insisted that nothing be done until the Council met and acted.

ACTION IN THE SECURITY COUNCIL

The Security Council began its deliberations on June 10, 1963 (civil war in Yemen had broken out on September 26, 1962) with the Secretary-General referring briefly to the four reports he had circulated to the members of the Council regarding the situation in Yemen. His brevity underscored his irritation at the representative of the Soviet Union. General Von Horn had not been sent but was "ready to proceed to the area with elements of an advance party on twenty-four hours' notice," said the Secretary-General. The Security Council adjourned to consult, and when it resumed the following day, the Secretary-General uncertain of the Soviet position and fearing a veto said: "I feel strongly that it would not be in the interest of peace in the Near East, and certainly not in the interest of this Organization, if it should for any reason fail to provide the observation assistance requested by the parties, or to delay doing so much longer." He further warned the Council that "there is growing evidence that the agreement on the terms of disengagement may be jeopardized if the UN observation personnel is not on the spot."[5]

Before casting his abstention on the proposal by Ghana and Morocco to send an observation team, the Soviet Union representative made clear a few considerations that related not only to the parties directly concerned, but also to what he called "the entire problem of United Nations action in the maintenance of international peace and security." He pointed out that the sending of UN observers or the deployment of UN forces in various parts of the world in recent years had been a method used by the "imperialist" powers to establish their own control over specific regions under the flag of the United Nations. This, he asserted, was not the most effective way to safeguard against the continuation or renewal of agression. What must be done was to bridle the aggressor and not to deploy UN forces or observers on the borders between the foreign aggressor and its victim. This was another way of stating the Soviet philosophy of encouraging and assisting wars of national liberation. The Soviet representative, however, went on to say that a UN observer team might prevent further hostile

---

[4] S/5236.
[5] UN Security Council, S/PV.1038, June 11, 1963. Hereafter cited as S/PV.1038.

actions against Yemen and again reminded the Council that the Security Council is the only organ under the Charter competent to take decisions relating to UN action for the maintenance of international peace and security.

With respect to defraying the cost of the observer operation, he asserted that the Soviet Union adhered to the same position it had taken toward the maintenance of "the so-called emergency armed forces of the United Nations in the Middle East and the United Nations troops in the Congo." He characterized the Soviet Union's position as one of principle. "Action to liquidate the consequences of aggression should be paid for by the countries responsible for the aggression."[6] In view of the fact that the parties concerned had reached an agreement to pay the cost of the undertaking and that the duration of the observation would be limited to two months, he saw no reason to object to sending an observation group.

UN OBSERVATION MISSION IN YEMEN

The resolution proposed by Ghana and Morocco was carried by a vote of 10 to 0 with the Soviet Union abstaining. The substantive parts of the resolution requested the Secretary-General to establish the observation operation; urged the parties concerned to observe the terms of disengagement and to refrain from any action which would increase tension in the area; and requested the Secretary-General to report to the Security Council on the implementation of the decision.[7]

The United States representative had hoped that the Secretary-General might proceed promptly and without objection to dispatching the UN observation mission in compliance with the request of the parties. He described the delay as unfortunate. As for limiting the duration of the operation to two months, he pointed out that the disengagement agreement between the parties carried no time limitation. The reference to two months arose solely because the Governments of Saudi Arabia and the United Arab Republic agreed to finance the operation for two months, but without prejudice to the manner of financing thereafter if a longer operation should prove necessary.

The Soviet representative took issue with the U.S. representative's interpretation of the time limit. He felt that it was inconceivable for the Security Council to take a serious decision without at the same time taking into account a specific time limit. A close reading of the relevant documents supports the view expressed by the U.S. representative, who merely drew a distinction between the length of time the cost of the operation would cover and the unspecified length of time of the disengagement

---

[6] S/PV.1038, pp. 11–12.

[7] UN Security Council, Resolution adopted at the 1,039th meeting, June 11, 1963, S/5331.

operation itself. If the cost of the operation was to be borne by the parties for a two-month period only, what was to happen to the operation after that period? The Secretary-General would report the situation to the Security Council, thus giving the Council an opportunity to take whatever measures might be appropriate. This was the point the Soviet representative wanted to make clear. His intervention reflected again the unalterable Soviet position that the Security Council is the body charged with the responsibility for the maintenance of international peace and security.

ORGANIZATION AND PERFORMANCE

On the adoption of the resolution by the Security Council on June 11, 1963, the advance party of the Observation Mission in Yemen (UNYOM), under the command of Major General Carl Von Horn, arrived in Yemen on June 13. It set up its headquarters in Sana, the capital of the Republic of Yemen, with a liaison office in Jedda, Saudi Arabia. The United Nations Emergency Force (UNEF) liaison office in Cairo was to assist in maintaining contact with the appropriate authorities of the United Arab Republic. A small civilian staff of twenty-eight international members and twenty locally recruited employees was set up at Sana.

The operation of UNYOM began on July 4, 1963. The military side of the operation included a reconnaissance unit and an air unit. The reconnaissance unit, made up of 114 officers and men came from the Yugoslav contingent serving with UNEF. The air unit of some fifty officers and men was provided by the Royal Canadian Air Force.

The function of UNYOM was to *check* and *certify* the two parties' observance of the terms of the disengagement agreement. This entailed ground patrolling in the buffer zone and surrounding areas and air patrolling in the mountainous central part of the buffer zone, where land patrolling was deemed impossible. The military observers stationed in Sana and Hodzia were responsible for observing and certifying the withdrawal of troops.

This operation was not given any *peace-keeping* functions. Its role was to *observe, certify,* and *report.* Its terms of reference gave it a more restricted range of activity than UNTSO and UNMOGIP, UNEF, or UNOC. It had no mediation or conciliation functions. Since the disengagement agreement involved only Saudi Arabia and the United Arab Republic, UNYOM was not concerned with Yemen's internal affairs nor with that government's relations with other governments and bordering territories. UNYOM was not given authority to issue orders or directives.

In his report to the Security Council, the Secretary-General described the conditions under which UNYOM was operating: The physical conditions in Yemen were severe, the terrain was rugged, and local supplies and facilities were meager. UNYOM personnel and aircraft were subjected to gunfire and were frequently in danger. "In the circumstances, the members of the Mission are due great credit for their courage and devotion to duty, and their persistence, often beyond the call of duty." [8]

In August 1963, General Von Horn resigned. Colonel Branko Pavlovic, the Deputy Commander of UNYOM, was appointed Acting Commander. The reason for the resignation has not been made public, but press reports attributed to General Von Horn accused the Secretary-General of failing to give adequate support to UNYOM. Specifically, the reports carried charges that the mission was undermanned, discouraged, desperately short of rations, and lacked sufficient aircraft to supply their remote outposts in the deserts and mountains. The reports went on to say that despite these conditions, United Nations observers in Yemen were able to determine that neither Saudi Arabia nor the United Arab Republic was fully living up to the disengagement agreement. There were also reports of direct Soviet participation in the conflict in such activities as flying bombing raids in Soviet jets against the royalists. [9]

The Secretary-General called the press accounts of conditions relating to UNYOM "rather irresponsible and reckless." He informed the Security Council that he had sent General Rikhye, his military adviser, to the area to inspect the mission and assist it in solving its problems. General Rikhye and Colonel Pavlovic cabled the Secretary-General that "despite personal hardships, difficulties in supplying fresh rations and unavoidable lack of amenities, the morale of Mission personnel is indeed very high." They further assured him that the ration stock position "never reached a critical stage" and that the ration scales were maintained "in accordance with United Nations standards." [10]

The Secretary-General assured the Security Council that both General Rikhye and Colonel Pavlovic advised that the personnel was adequate to carry out its tasks "if these are limited to observation and report only." General Rikhye and Colonel Pavlovic implied that General Von Horn had gone beyond his terms of reference by having undertaken tasks such as investigation of incidents. It was on the important problem of terms of reference that the basic difficulties arose between General Von Horn and the Secretary-General; the former felt he had to stretch them to do an effective job, and the latter insisted that the activities of the mission be kept within the terms.

As for the withdrawal of U.A.R. troops and the reduction of assistance by Saudi Arabia, the Secretary-General reported to the Security Council that UNYOM reported it had no firm figures on the number of U.A.R. troops withdrawn and the number that have arrived as replacements.

---

[8] UN Security Council, S/5412, Sept. 4, 1963, p. 3. Hereafter cited as S/5412.

[9] *New York Times*, Sept. 1, 1963, and *Washington Post*, Aug. 31, 1963.

[10] Quoted by the Secretary-General in S/5412, p. 3.

U.A.R. sources in Yemen withheld exact information on grounds of security, but stated that some 13,000 troops had been withdrawn, and a figure of 1,500 new arrivals had been cited but not verified as accurate. UNYOM observers had noted departures of U.A.R. troops in substantial numbers, but had also seen replacements arriving, in apparently lesser numbers. There had been a reduction in the extent of assistance from Saudi Arabian territory to royalist ranks and supporters in Yemen, but such traffic had not come to an end. In fact, UNYOM air and ground patrols reported a recent possible increase in vehicular and animal traffic across the border.[11]

In some important respects, the Secretary-General reported, the terms of the disengagement agreement had not been fulfilled by either of the parties. Complaints about U.A.R. air actions had been investigated by military observers, and on occasion UNYOM personnel had witnessed such actions. UN patrols had also observed trucks and camels carrying weapons and ammunition as well as food and other stores crossing the Saudi Arabian border toward areas held by Yemeni royalists. The limited size and function of the mission permitted it to observe and certify indications of the implementation of the disengagement agreement, but it could not be said that encouraging progress had been made toward effective implementation of it.[12]

The Security Council authorized the Secretary-General to set up an observation mission on the understanding that Saudi Arabia and the U.A.R. would defray the expenses for a two-month period which would expire September 4. The Secretary-General approached both parties to defray the expenses of the operation for another two-month period starting September 4. Both governments gave oral assurances that they would do so.

As the end of the second two-month period was approaching, the Secretary-General reported to the Security Council on October 28, 1963, on the functioning of UNYOM and the implementation of the terms of disengagement, saying: "There has been no decisive change in that situation in the subsequent two months."[13]

In making a broad appraisal of the situation in Yemen and of the complexities there, the Secretary-General's report stated:

> The lack of allegiance of certain tribes and the . . . presence and activity of the Imam and Prince Hassan among them, evidently with sizable stocks of ammunition . . . continues to be a serious problem for the Government of Yemen and, therefore, for the UAR troops. This problem is aggravated by the apparent fact that the Yemeni army has not yet reached . . . training and competence which would enable it to cope with the situation without outside assistance, or perhaps even to defend Republican controlled areas, should one

[11] S/5412, p. 4.
[12] S/5412, p. 5.
[13] UN Security Council, S/5447, Oct. 28, 1963, p. 1. Hereafter cited as S/5447.

or more of these areas be attacked by hostile tribes. This dependence on outside military aid, which in practice means aid from the United Arab Republic,
inevitably impedes the improvement of relations, both between the United
Arab Republic and Saudi Arabia and between Saudi Arabia and the Yemen.
The problem is further complicated by both religious and political factors in
the Yemen itself.[14]

As for the two parties to the disengagement agreement, the Saudi
Arabian Government maintained that it was complying with the agreement, was no longer supplying war material to the royalists, and was
cooperating with UNYOM in verifying this contention. It further maintained that the U.A.R. had not withdrawn the main part of its military
forces from Yemen and continued military activities, including bombing
of royalist areas and over-flying of Saudi Arabian territory. This unilateral
implementation of the agreement, the Saudi Arabian Government warned,
could not continue indefinitely.

The U.A.R., on the other hand, maintained that, whatever might be the
present situation with regard to Saudi Arabian assistance to the royalists,
the arms and supplies sent previously or that would again be available to
them after the U.A.R. withdrawal would permit and encourage them to
continue operating in Yemen. Thus the resistance and active hostility of
the royalists constituted a serious obstacle to the withdrawal of U.A.R.
forces.

In this complex situation, and in the light of UNYOM's mission of observing, certifying, and reporting, the Secretary-General stated that he did
"not believe that the solution of the problem, or even the fundamental
steps which must be taken to resolve it, can ever be within the potential of
UNYOM alone—and most certainly not under its existing limited
mandate."[15]

In his consultations with the parties, the Secretary-General made clear
his own dissatisfaction with the mandate of UNYOM. Its role was so
limited that it was virtually impossible for it to play a really constructive
part in Yemen. The situation and the terrain made it impossible for
UNYOM to observe fully or to certify what was being done in the way of
disengagement. He had no doubt, however, that "a continuing United
Nations presence . . . of some kind but not necessarily having military
attributes, would be . . . helpful and might . . . be indispensable to an early
settlement of the Yemen problem, which clearly is primarily political and
will require a political solution."[16]

Having secured the agreement of the Saudi Arabian and United Arab
Republic Governments to participate in the financing of the UNYOM for
a further period of two months from November 5, 1963, the Secretary-

---

[14] S/5447.
[15] S/5447, p. 7.
[16] S/5447, p. 8.

General canceled the preparations that were under way for the withdrawal of the mission. His original estimate on May 27, 1963, was that the observation function in Yemen would not be required for more than four months. Since the continuation of the mission went beyond his original estimate, he was careful to consult the Council members to ascertain whether there would be any objection to the extension. There was none.

It was becoming increasingly clear that the restrictive mandate of UNYOM prevented it from playing a constructive role in Yemen. The mission had neither the authority nor the military power at its disposal to force the two outside parties to withdraw and let Yemen solve its civil war. It was also becoming clear that while the United Arab Republic forces controlled the main cities and roads, the mountainous and difficult terrain stood in the way of a U.A.R. victory.

President Sallal's republican regime proved weak and ineffectual. It appeared to have abdicated almost all real power to an embarrassed and unpopular Egyptian military force. Although it was believed Sallal had some support from the majority of Yemenis, he had not been able to create an effective administrative apparatus. Without the Egyptian troops, it was generally conceded his regime would not be able to survive against the fierce mountain tribes supporting the feudal monarchy.

All the contending parties involved realized the impossibility of ending the dispute by military means. Some form of reconciliation between the contending forces in Yemen appeared to be the best means of resolving the issue. There were indications, moreover, that the U.A.R. with its more than 30,000 troops in Yemen was becoming unpopular in Sana and that Nasser had undertaken a more costly and complicated venture than he had foreseen. Withdrawal for both sides was difficult unless a compromise between the contending parties could be found to save faces all around.

The Secretary-General, on November 4, 1963, accordingly announced the appointment of Pier P. Spinelli, Under Secretary and Director of the European Office of the United Nations, as his Special Representative in Yemen, in which capacity he would also head the Yemen Observation Mission. In appointing him, the Secretary-General had in mind supplementing the mission of military observation with its limited mandate by a United Nations political presence which, by exploratory conversations with the parties concerned, would get at the root of the trouble. This dual role would permit the Special Representative to try his hand at conciliation and at the same time shift the emphasis of the mission from military to political.

The appointment of Pier Spinelli was welcomed by the U.A.R., Saudi Arabia, and the Yemeni Republican Government. He had served on other United Nations missions of a special and difficult nature. These included his role as Special Representative in the former Trust Territory of Togoland, where he demonstrated the tact and firmness that go into the making of an astute diplomat.

At the Arab Summit Conference in Cairo in January 1964, the Yemeni civil war, among other problems, was discussed. It was agreed that Algeria and Iraq were to take a hand in mediating it. The aim underlying this effort, it was believed, was to accomplish initially two objectives: (1) restore relations between Saudi Arabia and the United Arab Republic; and (2) solve the Yemeni problem by endeavoring to find a way by which Saudi Arabia could be persuaded to recognize some form of republic in Yemen. Were these two objectives to be accomplished, it was hoped, the stage would be set for the withdrawal of U.A.R. forces and the halting of Saudi Arabian assistance to the royalists.

The Yemen Observation Mission was extended three times for two-month periods in March, May, and July 1964, each time after the Secretary-General's "informal consultations with the Council revealed no objection." [17] Each time the formal mandate of the mission continued to be "to observe the implementation of the disengagement agreement," and for each bi-monthly period the Secretary-General reported to the Council on the functioning of the mission, whose members had now been reduced from two hundred to twenty-five.

In his report of March 3, 1964, the Secretary-General disclosed that extensive and coordinated fighting had taken place in Yemen. [18] There were indications that arms and ammunition in appreciable amounts had been reaching the royalists from some source, presumably from across the border of the South Arabian Federation, which was not included in the disengagement agreement and therefore was not subject to observation. The U.A.R. forces were active in ground and air operations directed to safeguarding their communications which were under attack. The observers reported that the U.A.R. forces, contrary to the agreement, had increased by some 2,000 men and now were estimated to number about 32,000. The report indicated that the U.A.R. and republican forces were in control of the cities and lowlands while the royalists, armed and financed by the Saudi Arabian Government, operated freely from mountain strongholds.

The Secretary-General, however, saw encouraging factors in the results of the Conference of Arab States held in Cairo in January 1964 which, *inter alia*, urged direct conversations on the Yemen question between the parties and appointed the Presidents of Algeria and Iraq to assist as mediating delegates.

In his report of May 4, the Secretary-General informed the Council that instead of a reduction of U.A.R. forces as called for by the disengagement agreement, there had been some increase. No end to the fighting appeared to be in sight. However, a high-level meeting between representatives of the United Arab Republic and Saudi Arabia had taken place, and some progress had been made on the problem of Yemen, both governments de-

[17] See A/5681, May 4, 1964; S/5794, July 2, 1964; and S/5927, Sept. 2, 1964.
[18] UN Security Council, S/5572, March 3, 1964.

claring that they had no ambitions in Yemen apart from supporting the independence of the country and the freedom of its people. In view of this, the Secretary-General advised extending the mission another two months.

In his July report, the Secretary-General noted that although some reduction in the U.A.R. forces had taken place, "the implementation of the disengagement agreement is far from complete in so far as the U.A.R. troops in Yemen are concerned." He was convinced that progress toward stability in Yemen could be hoped for "only through talks between Crown Prince Faisal and President Nasser." But he saw no indication that such a meeting was imminent. He believed, however, that the observation mission, despite its limited function and authority, had helped to lessen the threat to international peace and security and toward keeping open possibilities for a final settlement. He wished to provide a further opportunity for negotiations and, therefore, reluctantly advised another two-month extension of the mission. But he advised the Council that if no substantial progress toward fulfillment of the agreement were made in this period, he "would find it difficult to envisage a further extension of the mission in its present form and with its present terms of reference and purpose."

On September 4, 1964, the observation mission was terminated. In his final report, the Secretary-General described the military position as somewhat improved. No military supplies were discovered crossing the northern frontier to the royalists, and some further reductions in U.A.R. troops had been made. However, a substantial amount of fighting was going on against royalist strongpoints in north Yemen supported by the U.A.R. Air Force. He noted with regret "that during its year of operation the mission had been able to observe only a disappointing measure of disengagement." Moreover, the hoped-for high-level discussions between the U.A.R. and Saudi Arabia had not taken place. He had addressed identical notes to the two governments to ascertain their wishes regarding termination of the mission, and both replied they had no objection. The Saudi Arabian reply stated that the United Arab Republic had not carried out its responsibilities, and added that it found itself unable to continue its payment of the mission's expenses.

The Secretary-General concluded his final report by again stating the difficulties resulting from the restrictive terms of reference of the mission—observe and report only—and the failure of the parties to fulfill their disengagement agreement. He felt, nevertheless, that the threat to peace and security had diminished during the mission's existence, "to a considerable extent because of its activities." It was clear to him "that during the fourteen months of its presence in Yemen, the U.N. mission exercised an important restraining influence on hostile activities in the area."

Some thirteen member states had provided personnel for the mission. Despite some incidents there were no casualties. The total expense for the fourteen-month period was approximately two million dollars.

EVALUATION

While the United States has no direct interest in Yemen, it does have an interest in the peace and security of the strategically placed and oil-rich area. President Kennedy's initiative in seeking a solution of the Yemen crisis was motivated chiefly by these important interests. With President Nasser's ambitions to control the Arabian peninsula, the civil war in Yemen, in the United States view, became a serious threat to United States interests in maintaining stability in the area under a regime which it supported. The disengagement agreement between the U.A.R. and Saudi Arabia negotiated by Ambassador Ellsworth Bunker reflected that concern.

The United Nations through the Security Council took on the role of observing and verifying the disengagement. Neither party carried out its commitments under the agreement. Although UNYOM was given access to the area and reported periodically on the status of the disengagement undertaking, neither its presence nor its reporting constituted a sufficiently strong sanction to secure compliance.

While there was no disengagement as contemplated in the agreement, another form of disengagement did take place—the breaking off of direct confrontation of the Saudi Arabian and U.A.R. military power after the United Nations entered the picture. Whether this was a coincidence, or whether the United Nations presence in the area made itself felt on both the United Arab Republic and Saudi Arabia is speculative. With the Saudi Arabian Government taking the lead in cutting down the shipment of arms across its borders to the Yemeni royalists—a lead which may well have been influenced by the presence of UNYOM—the United Arab Republic stopped bombing the supply trains and depots on the Saudi Arabian side. This, it should be pointed out, was one of the objectives of the disengagement agreement and reduced the possibility of an all-out military confrontation between Saudi Arabia and the United Arab Republic. Another purpose served by UNYOM was to provide the Saudi Arabian Government with an acceptable political reason for reducing assistance to the royalists.

The other principal objective, namely, the withdrawal of U.A.R. forces from Yemen, was not effected because of the political situation which developed in Yemen in this period: the inability of the Sallal government to establish its authority as an effective instrument and the growing resistance of the tribes to the presence of U.A.R. troops.

The Secretary-General, observing this course of development, decided that a new approach was needed. UNYOM's terms of reference had to be expanded to include the political function of mediation and conciliation. This the Secretary-General did by appointing Pier Spinelli as chief of UNYOM. In so doing, he shifted the emphasis of UNYOM's mission from observing and certifying to the role of mediator and conciliator with a view to political settlement. The change in emphasis and in purpose reflected the realities of the stalemated military situation in Yemen.

One might ask why the Secretary-General waited so long to bring about a change in UNYOM's terms of reference. Timing here was of the essence. Not until the United Arab Republic and Saudi Arabia had reached a military stalemate did it appear timely to try the political settlement approach.

UNYOM's task as a fact-finding instrumentality was well carried out. That the parties failed to honor the disengagement agreement cannot be placed at the door of UNYOM.

One of the problems in managing the terms of reference was the restrictive interpretation placed thereon by the Secretary-General. It was on this problem that the difference between the Secretary-General and the first Chief of UNYOM arose. The latter felt that he was unable to carry out his mission to observe, certify, and report without additional powers of investigation and interposition. In any peace observation, this difference is likely to arise since it stems from the need to bridge what is politically feasible and technically desirable. To have compelled compliance, UNYOM would have had to be given the necessary means. This would have meant a military force large enough to take on the forces of the parties to the disengagement agreement. And this the Secretary-General wisely did not even wish to contemplate. The further question which arose was whether the Security Council would sanction such a force.

While both parties continued to pay the costs of the operation for two months at a time, the life of UNYOM was conditional on the parties' willingness to pay. This created uncertainty on several occasions when the expiration of the two-month period approached and the cost agreement had not been renewed. This obliged the Secretary-General to announce that he would withdraw the mission. The principle of making the parties bear the cost was a necessity in view of the current financial plight of the United Nations, and indeed it may be a desirable principle in certain cases even where the Organization is in a sound financial condition. However, to put the life of a mission at the mercy of the contending parties is risky business when one is dealing with matters relating to international peace and security. The Yemen experience in this respect illustrates the need for reappraising the manner in which peace observation and fact-finding should be financed. The problem here is no less urgent than it is in the case of peace-keeping.

12

---•◆•---

THE PROBLEM OF CYPRUS, 1964–1965

For over 300 years, the island of Cyprus, which lies forty miles off the Turkish coast, was a province of Turkey. From 1878 until 1960, when it became independent and a member of the United Nations, it was under British occupation and administration by agreement with the Ottoman Empire. After Turkey entered World War I on the side of Germany, the British formally annexed the island, and by the Treaty of Lausanne of 1923, to which Greece and other allied powers were also parties, Turkey recognized the annexation of the island by Great Britain. To the British, Cyprus has strategic importance in the eastern Mediterranean, and since the British military withdrawal from the Suez Canal, its importance has been enhanced.

The population of the island, some 600,000 in number, is four-fifths Greek following the Cypriot Orthodox faith; the remainder is Turkish in origin and of the Moslem faith. The Moslem Turks and the Orthodox Christian Greeks did not intermarry but lived in comparative harmony. Cyprus has never been a part of modern Greece.

Following World War II, the desire for union of the island with Greece grew in intensity both among the Greek-speaking Cypriots and in Greece. But among the Turkish-speaking Cypriots, union with Greece was anathema. Turkish Cypriot leaders called for partition of Cyprus if Britain were to relinquish the island. The agreements worked out in London and Zurich in 1959 by the Greek, Turkish, and British Governments, which led to independence the following year, ruled out union with Greece and partition. To reassure the Turkish Cypriot minority, the agreements gave it rights under the constitution far in excess of its numbers. The Turkish Vice-President under the constitution was given a veto over matters relating to defense and foreign policy, and the concurrence of a majority of Turkish deputies in the legislature was necessary on fiscal legislation. In the civil service also, the ratio of Turkish Cypriots to Greek Cypriots was 30 to 70; and in the police and army 40 to 60.

From the moment of independence, the Greek Cypriot leaders were determined that the constitution should be revised, while the Turkish Cypriot leaders guarded it to the letter with passion and ferocity. A show-down was inevitable. The minority Turks feared the Greek majority would seek to impose its will by force, and the majority Greeks feared that a forced revision of the constitution would be met by Turkish Government intervention. Antagonism thus grew, and in this feverish atmosphere both sides began to arm.

On December 21, 1963, Greeks and Turks exchanged fire in Nicosia. Who fired the first shot was not clear, but two Turks were killed. Terror spread and loss of life on the island was considerable. The Greek Cypriots insisted that the Treaty of Guarantee, by which the British, Greek, and Turkish Governments were given the right to intervene, be declared null and void and the Government of Cyprus placed in the hands of its majority, while the Turkish Cypriots demanded partition.

After British Government appeals to both sides to stop the conflict had failed, the Governments of Great Britain, Greece, and Turkey, on December 24, 1963, offered their good offices to the Cyprus Government. When it became apparent that the situation was continuing to deteriorate, the three guarantor powers informed the Government of Cyprus—including both the Greek and Turkish elements—of their readiness to assist, if invited to do so, in restoring peace and order. A joint peace-keeping force under British command would be composed of the forces of the United Kingdom, already stationed in Cyprus under the Treaty of Guarantee between the United Kingdom, Greece, Turkey, and Cyprus, and the forces of Greece and Turkey under the Treaty of Alliance between Greece, Turkey, and Cyprus. The Government of Cyprus accepted the offer, and a joint peace-keeping force was established under a British commander.

On December 26, 1963, the Government of Cyprus asked for a meeting of the Security Council. In its letter of December 26, it complained against

. . . the Government of Turkey for the acts of (a) aggression, (b) intervention in the internal affairs of Cyprus by the threat and use of force against its territorial integrity and political independence, perpetrated . . . through the following acts:

(1) the violation of the air space of Cyprus by Turkish military aircraft . . . ;

(2) the violation of the territorial waters of Cyprus by the appearance and the presence of Turkish warships . . . ;

(3) threats of use of force by the Prime Minister of Turkey, made on 25 December 1963 before the Turkish Parliament . . . ;

(4) the movement of Turkish troops into Nicosia who joined the Turkish Cypriot insurgents in their fights against the police. . . .[1]

The representative of Cyprus did not initially ask for an urgent meeting of the Council because he was informed that a cease-fire had already been agreed upon. However, on December 27, his Foreign Minister informed him that: "The cease-fire is in danger, because Turkish ships have been sighted . . . speeding towards Cyprus. They were sighted by RAF airplanes."

[1] UN Security Council, S/5488, Dec. 26, 1963, p. 1.

The Foreign Minister, fearing an invasion, asked for an immediate meeting of the Security Council. The Council met and heard the representatives of Cyprus, Turkey, and Greece.

The representative of Cyprus stated that he did not come to discuss the whole subject of the complaint but "to call upon the Council to take steps so that the cease-fire does remain." He said that shortly after he had requested the urgent meeting "we were informed that the ships were not speeding towards Cyprus but were turned in another direction."[2] He then stated the root of the trouble, that is, the Constitution of Cyprus, with what he called "the divisive provisions of the Constitution" which divide the Greek Cypriots from the Turkish Cypriots and make them hostile to each other. Moreover, he asserted that the Constitution cannot even be amended by the consent of all the Cypriots, Greeks, and Turks without the consent of the other three powers. He clearly implied that the Constitution must be amended to give "true" independence to Cyprus, which he claimed did not then have it. This in effect would mean control of the Cyprus Government by the Greek Cypriots.

The Turkish representative denied the charges and accused the Greek Cypriots of a campaign of annihilation of the Turkish Cypriots by massacre. He referred to the history of the provisions of the Constitution which protect the Turkish minority and the role that the British, Turkish, and Greek Governments play in Cyprus as parties to the Treaty of Guarantee.

No proposals were introduced by any of the members of the Council, which adjourned December 28, 1963, and none appeared to be necessary.

On January 2, 1964, Duncan Sandys, the British Secretary of State for Commonwealth Relations, who flew to Cyprus, announced that Archbishop Makarios, President of Cyprus, and Mustafa Fazil Kutchuk, the Vice-President, had accepted the offer of good offices of the British, Greek, and Turkish Governments, which agreed to meet in London on January 15.

In the meantime, the Governments of Great Britain, Greece, Turkey, and Cyprus jointly requested the Secretary-General of the United Nations to appoint a representative to act as a United Nations observer in Cyprus. His role would be to observe the progress of the cease-fire and report to the Secretary-General. The Secretary-General appointed Lt. General P. S. Gyani. The cost of the observer was to be borne by the Government of Cyprus. At the same time, the Secretary-General agreed to send Mr. José Rolz-Bennett, his Deputy Chef de Cabinet, to London to be present at the good offices conference which opened on January 15, 1964.[3]

At the London conference, it became evident that the approaches of the two Cypriot communities to the solution were radically different, and the task of reaching agreement was going to be difficult and protracted. In Cyprus, tension was rising and intercommunal disorders had not abated.

[2] UN Security Council, S/PV.1085, Dec. 27, 1963, p. 8.
[3] UN Security Council, S/5514, Jan. 13, 1964; and S/5516, Jan. 17, 1964.

In these circumstances, the British Government felt it desirable that the burden of keeping the peace in Cyprus, which in practice fell exclusively on the British element of the joint force, should be shared by the participation of additional countries in the force. The British accordingly proposed augmenting the peace-keeping forces, first to the Greek and Turkish Governments who accepted them, and then to Archbishop Makarios and Dr. Kutchuk. The United States Government associated itself in the presentation of the proposals.

Sir Patrick Dean, the British representative to the United Nations, described the plan as follows:

> The . . . proposals provided for the establishment of an enlarged peace-keeping force drawn from countries friendly to Cyprus. This force would remain in Cyprus for the shortest possible period necessary to accomplish its peace-keeping mission, and national contingents would be committed for a period of not more than three months. It would be under a British Commander, who would receive political guidance from an inter-governmental committee of representatives from the participating countries sitting in London. The Greek and Turkish contingents in Cyprus would be part of the peace-keeping force, but neither contingent would be augmented. Meanwhile, the Governments of Greece and Turkey would undertake not to exercise their rights of unilateral intervention under article 4 of the Treaty of Guarantee . . . for three months on the understanding that the peace-keeping force would be in place during that period and the parties concerned would agree to accept mediation of their differences in a spirit of mutual accommodation, and to the appointment of a mediator for this purpose. [4]

The proposals of January 31 were not acceptable to Archbishop Makarios in the form presented to him. His position was that he accepted the stationing of an international force, whose composition must be agreeable to him; the force must be under the United Nations; Greek and Turkish units must not participate in the force; its terms of reference should include the protection of the territorial integrity of Cyprus and assistance in restoring normal conditions.

The British Government, acting in conjunction with the United States Government, consulted with the other guarantor powers on revision of the January 31 proposals, and on February 12 presented proposals to the Archbishop, described by Sir Patrick Dean as follows:

> An international peace-keeping force would be established, comprising contingents from those countries whose Governments agreed to participate. The force would include the existing Greek and Turkish contingents, which would come under the command of the Force Commander in the same way as contingents from other countries and would not be augmented. The force would remain in Cyprus for the shortest period necessary to accomplish its mission,

[4] UN Security Council, S/PV.1095, Feb. 18, 1964, p. 32. Hereafter cited as S/PV.1095.

and the countries providing contingents would commit themselves to leaving these forces in Cyprus for a period of not more than three months. The mission of the international force would be to prevent a recurrence of inter-communal fighting, to suppress disorders, to reduce inter-communal tension and to create conditions in which free movement and the ordinary life of the people could be resumed. The force would operate under a British Commander to be appointed by the British Government, who would receive guidance from the Governments concerned, acting through an inter-governmental committee in London.

The creation of this force would not affect any of the existing treaty rights and obligations of the British, Greek and Turkish Governments relating to the Republic of Cyprus, including the obligations in respect of the independence and territorial integrity of the Republic. . . .

In view of the common effort thus undertaken with respect to Cyprus, the three guarantor Powers would recognize that the question of unilateral action would not arise during the period of such concerted action and President Makarios and Vice-President Kutchuk would give assurances that they would do their utmost to restrain their respective communities.

Britain, Greece, Turkey and the two Cypriot communities would jointly appoint a mutually acceptable mediator whose function would be to assist the parties concerned in finding an agreed solution of the differences between them. The mediator would be appointed in his personal capacity and would act as an independent agent. He would keep the Secretary-General of the United Nations advised of the progress of his task.

The Cyprus Government would ask the Security Council to take note by consensus of the arrangements made for the creation of this peace-keeping force and for the appointment of the mediator. The Government of Cyprus would also request the Secretary-General of the United Nations to arrange for his representative to remain in Cyprus, so that he might maintain liaison with the Commander of the peace-keeping force. [5]

Once again Archbishop Makarios found the revised proposals unacceptable and made a number of counterproposals.

With the lack of progress in the London negotiations and the failure to reach agreement on the proposals for increasing the peace-keeping force to an adequate level, the situation on Cyprus continued to deteriorate with shootings taking place almost daily in February and with fear and terrorism mounting.

Moscow also took a hand in the Cyprus trouble. It could not resist giving its views on the events in that island. Accordingly, on February 7, 1964, the Minister for Foreign Affairs of the U.S.S.R. gave the Ambassadors of the United Kingdom, the United States, France, Turkey, and Greece a message from Chairman Nikita Khrushchev to Prime Minister Sir Alec Douglas-Home, President Lyndon Johnson, President De Gaulle, Turkish

[5] S/PV.1095, pp. 33–34.

Prime Minister Ismet Inonu, and Greek Prime Minister Ioannis Parasker-opoulos, concerning "the situation developing in the eastern Mediterranean area in connexion with Cyprus."[6] It warned the NATO powers to refrain from interfering in the internal affairs of Cyprus. This letter removed any doubt concerning where the Soviet Union stood. Indeed, it was known that President Makarios's intransigence to the proposals for a peace-keeping force from NATO countries was due in considerable measure to the support he was receiving from the Soviet Union.

The United States Government sent Under Secretary of State George W. Ball to Europe to throw its weight in favor of the British proposals, which were acceptable to all save Archbishop Makarios. In London, Athens, and Ankara, Ball conferred with various officials, and in Nicosia with Archbishop Makarios. But the latter would not swerve from his opposition to the revised British proposals.

In these grave circumstances, with the Government of Cyprus unable to accept the proposals, the British representative to the United Nations, on February 15, requested an early meeting of the Security Council to take steps to resolve the problem, having regard for the rights of both Cypriot communities, of the Government of Cyprus, and of the governments party to the Treaty of Guarantee. Following the British request, the representative of Cyprus also requested an immediate meeting of the Security Council.

APPEAL TO THE SECURITY COUNCIL

The Secretary-General's appeal of February 15 to (1) Archbishop Makarios and to the Foreign Ministers of Greece and Turkey to refrain from acts that might lead to a worsening of the situation and further bloodshed; and (2) all concerned, including the members of the two communities in Cyprus and their respective leaders, to show understanding and restraint did not alter the situation on the ground.

In the Security Council on February 18, 1964, Sir Patrick Dean described in detail the proposals considered in London which were unacceptable to Archbishop Makarios. He outlined a draft resolution that would have the support of his government: (1) endorsement by the Council of the Secretary-General's appeal; (2) a call on the parties concerned, including the guarantor powers, to secure the establishment of an effective peace-keeping force as soon as possible; (3) the appointment of an impartial mediator to assist the parties in achieving an agreed settlement; and (4) a call on all states and authorities concerned to respect the independence, territorial

---

[6] The message which was also circulated to all the members of the United Nations at the request of the Soviet representative to the United Nations is contained in: UN Security Council, S/5534, Feb. 18, 1964, p. 2.

integrity, and security of Cyprus, in accordance with the Treaty of Guarantee and as established and regulated by the basic articles of the Constitution.[7]

In the Security Council, Mr. Rossides, the representative of Cyprus, described the divisive provisions of the Constitution of Cyprus, and the impossibility of conducting the affairs of state under such an arrangement. Such a situation, he said, could not continue in peace and quiet. Archbishop Makarios, he informed the Council, had proposed in a letter to the Vice-President that they meet to discuss the problem of the Constitution with a view to finding a commonly agreed solution. Copies of the letter were sent to the three representatives of the United Kingdom, Greece, and Turkey. The letter contained proposals for changes which, in the view of the President, would make the Constitution workable, but the Vice-President had rejected the letter. The representative of Cyprus placed all the blame for the events of December 21 on the Turkish Government, which, he said, incited the Turkish community and its leaders in Cyprus to reject any tampering with the Constitution.

The exchange of charges and countercharges between the representatives of Cyprus and Turkey was not very enlightening, but it revealed the fear and hatred that prevails in Cyprus between the Greek and Turkish communities, which had been heightened by the bloody events after December 21. The statements by the Turkish and Cypriot representatives in the Security Council made clear that President Makarios was bent on revising the treaty structure and the Constitution of Cyprus and maintaining the territorial integrity of Cyprus, while the Turkish Government was adamant on maintaining the treaty structure and the Constitution or, as an alternative, partitioning Cyprus.

The Soviet representative, in supporting the position of President Makarios, charged that certain NATO powers had contravened the principles of the Charter by militarily intervening in the domestic affairs of a sovereign member of the United Nations, thus threatening the freedom, integrity, and independence of Cyprus. He pointed out that the primary source of the present complications in Cyprus lay in the agreements which were not based on a foundation of equality, and which were forced on that small country. He referred to a letter of January 1, 1964, which President Makarios addressed to "Heads of State and Government of the world" wherein he stated that these agreements are the source of the present abnormal situation in Cyprus. The Soviet representative said:

> As a result of these unequal agreements, there are at present on the territory of Cyprus military forces of three foreign Powers members of the NATO bloc and there are British foreign bases. . . . The dangerous actions of the NATO Powers in Cyprus are cynically and candidly aimed at destroying the

[7] S/PV.1095, p. 44.

independence of Cyprus, tying Cyprus to NATO and converting it into a NATO military bridgehead. [8]

The Soviet representative was in true cold-war form. On this occasion, he cloaked himself with the Charter of the United Nations, which he defended. His was a simple remedy. The Security Council, he said, "must take immediate steps so as to protect the Republic of Cyprus from aggression and to put an end to any foreign intervention in the domestic affairs of that small Member State." [9]

The Soviet position provided Moscow with an opportunity for maneuver in the Cyprus crisis. Moscow has long sought to establish a focus of power and influence in the eastern Mediterranean. Turmoil in Cyprus with Communist strength in the Greek labor unions on the island could lead to a left-wing bid for power with Moscow's aid. With Greece and Turkey, two members of the NATO alliance, intervening militarily on opposite sides of the Cyprus conflict, the situation could lead to a disintegration of the alliance and escalate into a general conflict.

Ambassador Adlai Stevenson, reviewing the events, told the Security Council that the plan for the establishment of a "larger and more broadly based peace-keeping force was required to augment the British forces if order were to be re-established and maintained throughout the island." He regretted that the President of Cyprus would not accept the proposal of an international peace-keeping force, acceptable to all the guarantor powers, and also to the United States. He stated that:

> Strenuous efforts will also be required to bring about agreement between the two parties on a political settlement which will permit them to live in peace with each other. Therefore, we would also strongly urge that the Government of Cyprus and the Guarantor Powers, in consultation with the Secretary-General, be asked to designate an impartial mediator to assist in achieving a settlement. . . . [10]

During the Council debate, five of the six nonpermanent members, the representatives of Bolivia, Brazil, the Ivory Coast, Morocco, and Norway, were working with the Secretary-General and others in drafting a resolution that would meet with the approval of the Council as well as the contending parties, including Greece and Turkey. Throughout these intense negotiations, the Secretary-General kept the members of the Council informed of the discussions. Sensitive of the prerogatives of the Council, he made clear that he was engaging "in these informal discussions because it was clearly the wish of all the parties that I should do so, and especially because, in

[8] UN Security Council, S/PV.1096, Feb. 19, 1964, p. 7. Hereafter cited as S/PV.1096.
[9] S/PV.1096, p. 23.
[10] S/PV.1096, pp. 32, 38.

view of the seriousness and urgency of the Cyprus situation, it is my desire to do everything possible to help resolve this dangerous crisis." [11]

Again, sensitive to the prerogatives of the Council, he explained that he responded favorably to the request of the Government of Cyprus, which was supported by the Governments of Greece, Turkey, and the United Kingdom. He appointed General Gyani as his "personal representative to observe the progress of the peace-keeping operation in the island. The presence of General Gyani in Cyprus has been most useful to keep me informed about the situation . . . and . . . I believe, has contributed to alleviating tensions in the island." [12]

The Secretary-General, who in the discharge of his functions treads on "a hundred or more spears," told the Council that the discussions which he had held on the problem had been undertaken "within the context of the Charter and bearing in mind . . . the authority of the Security Council." And as though addressing the representative of the Soviet Union directly, he assured the Security Council that "without the concurrence of the Security Council the question of the Secretary-General sending a peace-keeping force to Cyprus will not arise." [13] He had learned from his Yemen experience that matters of this nature lie within the prerogative of the Council. [14]

THE DRAFT RESOLUTION

On March 2, Bolivia, Brazil, the Ivory Coast, Morocco, and Norway introduced a draft resolution in the Security Council. [15] The Brazilian delegate, speaking for all the sponsors, said the draft was a fair and balanced document; it was the product of lengthy negotiations lasting a fortnight, and it reflected much give-and-take and compromise. It would not have been introduced had it not met with the general, though not with the entire, satisfaction of the parties concerned. Nor would it have been introduced if there were a risk of a veto by any of the five permanent members.

The first paragraph of the preamble notes that the situation with regard to Cyprus was likely to threaten international peace and security and might further deteriorate unless measures were promptly taken to maintain peace and to seek out a durable solution.

In the second paragraph, the treaties (signed at Nicosia on August 16, 1960) on which the political life of the Republic of Cyprus is based are mentioned in relation to the views on them of the interested parties and the

[11] UN Security Council, S/PV.1097, Feb. 25, 1964, p. 6. Hereafter cited as S/PV.1097.

[12] S/PV.1097, p. 6.

[13] S/PV.1097, p. 7.

[14] See case study on Yemen, pp. 421–35.

[15] UN Security Council, S/5571, March 2, 1964.

members of the Council. This paragraph, which entailed an important compromise, leaves the contending parties holding the views they expressed in the Council debate, but does not in any legal way affect the validity of the treaties.

The third paragraph refers to the relevant provisions of the Charter and, in particular, to Article 2, paragraph 4, in which the members of the United Nations are called on to refrain from the threat or use of force against the territorial integrity or the political independence of any state.

The operative part of the draft resolution reads as follows:

1. *Calls upon* all Member States in conformity with their obligations under the Charter of the United Nations, to refrain from any action or threat of action likely to worsen the situation in the sovereign Republic of Cyprus, or to endanger international peace;

2. *Asks* the Government of Cyprus, which has the responsibility for the maintenance and restoration of law and order, to take all additional measures necessary to stop violence and bloodshed in Cyprus;

3. *Calls upon* the communities in Cyprus and their leaders to act with the utmost restraint;

4. *Recommends* the creation, with the consent of the Government of Cyprus, of a United Nations peace-keeping force in Cyprus. The composition and size of the force shall be established by the Secretary-General, in consultation with the Governments of Cyprus, Greece, Turkey and the United Kingdom. The commander of the force shall be appointed by the Secretary-General and report to him. The Secretary-General, who shall keep the Governments providing the force fully informed, shall report periodically to the Security Council on its operation;

5. *Recommends* that the function of the force should be, in the interest of preserving international peace and security, to use its best efforts to prevent a recurrence of fighting and, as necessary, to contribute to the maintenance and restoration of law and order and a return to normal conditions;

6. *Recommends* that the stationing of the force shall be for a period of three months, all costs pertaining to it being met, in a manner to be agreed upon by them, by the Governments providing the contingents and by the Government of Cyprus. The Secretary-General may also accept voluntary contributions for that purpose;

7. *Recommends further* that the Secretary-General designate, in agreement with the Government of Cyprus and the Governments of Greece, Turkey and the United Kingdom, a mediator, who shall use his best endeavors with the representatives of the communities and also with the aforesaid four Governments, for the purpose of promoting a peaceful solution and an agreed settlement of the problem confronting Cyprus, in accordance with the Charter of the United Nations, having in mind the well-being of the people of Cyprus as a whole and the preservation of international peace and security. The mediator shall report periodically to the Secretary-General on his efforts;

8. *Requests* the Secretary-General to provide, from funds of the United Nations, as appropriate, for the remuneration and expenses of the mediator and his staff.

As the foregoing draft had already been informally approved by the members of the Security Council, there was little discussion. The Soviet representative, however, stated that although the draft did not meet all the requirements which should be embodied in a decision of the Security Council, it was aimed at preventing aggression against the Republic of Cyprus and at safeguarding the lawful rights and interest of Cyprus. He stated that operative paragraph 4 circumvented the Security Council. As to the provision wherein the commander of the force would be chosen by the Secretary-General, this to him was "not adequate." He therefore requested a separate vote on paragraph 4 and informed the Council he would abstain. Regarding the draft resolution as a whole, since the Government of Cyprus regarded it as useful despite its defects, since the United Nations forces would be sent for a limited period of three months, and since there would be no financial obligations on the members whose contingents do not participate in the forces, the Soviet representative would vote for it. He gave notice that if the forces would be required beyond the three-month period, a new decision of the Security Council would be necessary. The separate vote on paragraph 4 was 8 for, 0 against, and 3 abstentions (Czechoslovakia, France, and the Soviet Union). The resolution as a whole was adopted unanimously.

The French representative explained that since there was unanimous agreement by the parties concerned to the setting up of a force under the aegis of the Security Council, he did not oppose the proposal despite his reservations concerning the principle of intervention by the United Nations in a military form. His government's reservation was increased by the contention that the Security Council was divesting itself of responsibilities which are its own. The French delegation, he said, "considers that it is really going very far indeed in the direction of the delegation of powers to grant them in this way to a single individual [the Secretary-General]. It wishes, in any event, to point out that this decision can in no case be considered as a precedent." [16]

The essential points in the plan were worked out in the resolution by the Secretary-General and then transposed as a Security Council plan through the efforts of five nonpermanent members of the Council. This approach was designed to soften Soviet adamancy against peace-keeping operations run from the 38th floor [17] with Western and neutral advisers, rather than from the Security Council.

President Makarios, under this resolution, prevailed in blocking the creation of a force composed exclusively of contingents from NATO, as proposed by Great Britain and the United States before the Cyprus crisis was brought to the Security Council. The resolution made clear that the

---

[16] UN Security Council, S/PV.1102, March 4, 1964, p. 22.

[17] The official quarters of the Secretary-General are lodged on the 38th floor of the United Nations Secretariat building.

composition and size of the force was to be established in consultation with various named governments including that of Cyprus. With British troops in Cyprus, some 7,000 in strength, a number of these units came under the United Nations command. This is the first policing operation since Korea where troops of a major power have been included.

THE SECRETARY–GENERAL IN QUEST OF A FORCE

The resolution adopted on March 4, 1964, gave the Secretary-General vast executive powers in addition to the administrative powers he already possessed under the Charter. [18] He would establish the size and composition of the peace-keeping forces in consultation with the Governments of Cyprus, Greece, Turkey, and the United Kingdom. He would appoint the commander of the force who would report to him. In a sense, the resolution made him a commander-in-chief. It placed on him the obligation to keep the suppliers of the force fully informed and to report periodically to the Council on its operations. The UN force was to use its best efforts to prevent a recurrence of fighting and to contribute to the maintenance and restoration of law and order and a return to normal conditions. This language implies that the UN force may use force not only in self-defense but to take appropriate steps to maintain and restore law and order.

The task entrusted to the Secretary-General was very complex, entailing dealing with a series of military, diplomatic, financial, and logistic problems in assembling a volunteer police force. He appealed to all members for voluntary contributions to help meet the cost of the operation, and to Brazil, Canada, Finland, Ireland, and Sweden to provide contingents.

In the midst of the difficulties that beset the Secretary-General in implementing the resolution, the Cyprus representative, Ambassador Zenon Rossides, on March 13, 1964, called for an emergency meeting of the Security Council to consider what he described as "the clear threat of imminent invasion of the territory of the Republic of Cyprus by Turkish forces." The meeting was convened within three hours of the call.

Early that day, the Turkish Government, in a note to the Government of Cyprus, said it was determined to use its right of intervention as provided in the Treaty of Guarantee unless the Cypriot Government immediately put an end to bloodshed and the killing of Turkish Cypriots. Some observers believed Turkey issued the "ultimatum," although they denied it was that, to jolt the United Nations into getting its peace force to Cyprus as fast as possible. The note caused concern in Washington and London. Both capitals urged restraint on Ankara and Athens, which had responded to the Turkish threat by announcing that any Turkish move would cause Greece to react

---

[18] UN Security Council, Resolution adopted at the 1102nd meeting, March 4, 1964, S/5575.

decisively. A war between two allies of NATO could cause great damage to the Western Alliance, already shaken by internal dissension.

Great Britain was concerned about how long it would have to carry almost the entire burden of the peace-keeping. Some two weeks after the resolution was adopted, there was still no UN force. The delay prompted Duncan Sandys to tell the House of Commons that "we have repeatedly made it clear that we cannot discharge these thankless duties except in full cooperation and good will of the Cyprus authorities and of both communities." He complained that lately there had been very little of either cooperation or good will. "We have therefore warned the Secretary-General . . . that we cannot carry this burden alone, not only unaided but actively obstructed by those whom we are trying to help."

Thus the Secretary-General was besieged from all sides. He was aware of the growing impatience of the British concerning the vulnerability of British troops in Cyprus and at the United Nations delays in assuming the peace-keeping task. Yet he could not be blamed for the delays, for he was merely the instrument of the Organization which was no better or worse than its membership.

The Afro-Asian and Latin American countries appear to have regarded the Cyprus crisis as a NATO affair and primarily a European concern. Their attitude was that the rich industrial states of the West would have to supply the men and the money. They themselves had neither to spare, as has been evident from the reluctance of some of them to pay assessments for policing elsewhere. Many of them have been in default. There is a growing feeling among those who pay the bill that if they are to bear the greater share of the peace-keeping burden, they must be given a greater share in the decision-making power.

At the meeting of the Security Council on March 13, 1964, which dealt with the Turkish "ultimatum," much the same ground was covered as at the previous meetings that culminated in the resolution of March 4. The representatives of Cyprus and Turkey engaged in familiar recriminations. The members of the Council appeared to understand the motive underlying the Turkish note. Shortly after the Security Council met, the same members who sponsored the March 4 resolution submitted another:

The Security Council

Noting the progress reported by the Secretary-General that the United Nations peace-keeping force in Cyprus envisaged in the Council's resolution of 4 March 1964 . . . is about to be established, and that elements of that Force are already en route to Cyprus,

1. *Reaffirms* its call upon all Member States, in conformity with their obligations under the Charter of the United Nations, to refrain from any action or threat of action likely to worsen the situation in the sovereign Republic of Cyprus, or to endanger international peace,

2. *Requests* the Secretary-General to press on with his efforts to implement the Security Council resolution of 4 March 1964 and requests Member States to cooperate with the Secretary-General to that end.[19]

The resolution was adopted unanimously. Its objective was to encourage the Secretary-General to redouble his efforts to implement the resolution of March 4 and to stay the hand of Turkey. It also served as a hint to the members to expedite their troop contributions. Turkey did not invade, and by nightfall of the same day, the turmoil subsided in as mysterious a way as it had appeared earlier that day.

The Secretary-General was experiencing difficulty in organizing a UN force. Ireland agreed in principle to provide and pay for a battalion of 500 men on the condition that the force would be used only for maintaining peace and not for influencing or enforcing a settlement of the Cypriot crisis or for "imposing upon Cyprus a solution by partition while Irish troops are on the Island." Sweden agreed to supply a battalion if Ireland or Finland did so. Canada said its Parliament was expected to approve the sending of troops as soon as the terms of reference for the force were clarified.

The UN forces were moving into something in the nature of a civil war in Cyprus between the two communities. The contributors of troops were asking questions, undoubtedly prompted by the experience some of them had had in the Congo. If the terrorists of either side should fire on the UN forces, how should the latter respond? What about the hidden arms of the terrorists on both sides? Would the peace-keeping force be empowered to disarm the Greek and Turkish irregulars? These and many other problems confronted the Secretary-General as Commander-in-Chief of the international force.

To allay the concern of the troop contributors who were demanding clarification of the tasks of the UN force, under a resolution for which the two antagonists were advancing contradictory interpretations, the Secretary-General developed principles. He communicated them to the Commander of UNFICYP for his guidance and to the governments contributing forces. He made known that:

It was not his intention to negotiate instructions which he proposed to issue to the Commander with any Government either directly concerned in the situation or contributing contingents to the Force. . . . He would, however, . . . fully inform the representatives of the governments providing troops of the substance of the instructions and direction given to the Commander.[20]

At the end of March 1964, the status of the Cyprus peace-keeping operation was: (1) On March 27, Lt. General Gyani assumed command of UNFICYP at which time the force became operational and the three

[19] UN Security Council, S/5601, March 13, 1964.
[20] UN Office of Public Information, Note No. 2917, March 17, 1964.

months set out in the Security Council resolution began; (2) UNFICYP consisted of the Canadian contingent of some 950 men, about 6,000 British, and the Finnish and Swedish advance parties. A reconnaissance team arrived from Ireland, but Irish troops were withheld until Dail approval, which was expected in early April.

British troops were being withdrawn from the UN Command as they were replaced by Canadian or other troops. This process was expected to continue until the British contingent had been reduced to the British commitment of half of the force, not to exceed 3,500 troops.

The troop commitments to UNFICYP were as follows:[21] United Kingdom, 3,500; Canada, 950; Finland, 700; Ireland, 600; Sweden, 700; Austria, 54; total, 6,504. This total fell short of the Secretary-General's estimated minimum of 7,000 and General Gyani's estimated minimum of 10,000.

General I. J. Rikhye, the Secretary-General's military adviser, was engaged in a variety of details, which included purchasing and scheduling the deliveries of equipment and other supplies, and working out air-lift timetables. The United States offered to provide, at no cost to the United Nations, the initial airlift of UNFICYP contingents when no other airlift was available. The Canadians provided their own air and sea lift, and the British troops were already on the scene. As to supplies and equipment, it was understood that the British would be able to meet most, if not all, requirements of other contingents from Cyprus stockpiles. The British would, however, expect reimbursement for logistical support of UNFICYP.

THE SECRETARY-GENERAL IN QUEST OF A MEDIATOR

The Secretary-General had no difficulty in finding a Commander, Lt. General P. S. Gyani, Indian, who had served for several months as his observer in Cyprus and occupied other important UN military posts. But he had trouble finding a mediator who would be acceptable to the parties concerned. His first choice was José Rolz-Bennett, one of his close advisers. But he was unacceptable to the Turkish Government on the ground that he lacked stature and the requisite competence for the task. After securing the approval of the interested parties, the Finnish Ambassador to Sweden, Sakari S. Tuomioja, was chosen. After his death, in September, Galo Plaza, former President of Ecuador, was appointed.

The mediator's task is indeed a difficult one. Nothing short of a miracle will enable him to produce a solution in the near term, and no reasonable person can expect that he will.

[21] By June 1964, the size of the British force was reduced to 1,792; with increases on the part of the others, the total force in June was 6,411. (See UN Security Council, S/5764, p. 2.) The main body of the troops from Finland, Ireland, Sweden, and Austria were to arrive in April. Austria contributed a medical unit in lieu of troops.

THE SECRETARY–GENERAL IN QUEST OF MONEY

The Secretary-General estimated that the cost of the United Nations operation in Cyprus would be about $6 million for the three-month period. With the United Nations on the verge of bankruptcy, the Security Council authorized him to accept voluntary contributions for the operation. The United States Government pledged $2 million; Great Britain, $1 million; Greece and West Germany, $500,000 each; Italy, $250,000; Australia, $112,000; Belgium, the Netherlands, and Turkey, $100,000 each; Denmark and Switzerland, $75,000 each; Norway, $50,000; New Zealand, $42,000; and Luxembourg, $5,000. The total amount pledged as of April 1, 1964, was just under $5 million as against the estimated requirement of $6 million for the three-month mandate. Conspicuous by their absence from the list are the Latin American and Afro-Asian countries, with the exception of Japan. While these are the "have-not" countries, their failure to make even a token or symbolic contribution reflects their attitude toward the maintenance of international peace and security by the United Nations.[22]

In his report to the Council on September 10, 1964, the Secretary-General stated that in spite of the limitations in its terms of reference as laid down in the Council resolution of March 4, the force "functioned extremely well." Its presence, though not able "to prevent a recurrence of fighting [there had been two serious engagements since its arrival], was a major factor in bringing the fighting . . . to a quick end and in preventing those episodes from escalating." There was no doubt, he said, that if the force had not been deployed "there would have been far more fighting on the island." He noted "a considerable improvement in the security situation" since the force took up its positions. There was more freedom of movement and less harassment on the roads, harvesting was less molested, public services were restored in many places, and sieges were lifted on a number of Turkish communities.[23]

However, conditions in Cyprus were far from good, he said. Indeed they were very unsatisfactory when viewed in the hopes of the March 4 resolution. The "return to normal conditions" was far from realized due to a basic difference in the two communities as to what would constitute "normal conditions." The Turkish community held that the UN force was obliged to restore the constitutional situation by force if necessary, while the Cypriot Government with its Greek majority held this to be impossible. This fundamental difference has continued to remain unresolved.

The Secretary-General has refused to accept either of these positions, pointing out that the Security Council did not indicate such intentions. The force is not an arm of the Cypriot Government. He said that the force

---

[22] Liberia and Nigeria later contributed $3,000 and $2,800, respectively. S/5764/Add. 1, June 19, 1964.

[23] See UN Security Council, S/5950, p. 62.

"is in the most delicate position that any United Nations Mission has ever experienced, for it is not only in the midst of a bitter civil war, but it is dangerously interposed between the two sides of that war." Thus, the UN force "had to exert every effort to maintain objectivity, to serve fairness and justice, and to avoid taking sides while doing all possible to alleviate suffering." Its major effort in mid-1964 was to eliminate or lessen hardships experienced by many Turkish communities as a result of economic restrictions imposed by the Government.

The fighting was ended in August by the "cease-fire" called for by the Security Council. However, the economic siege imposed by the government against the Turkish elements indicated that economic pressure was used as a substitute for military action. This situation hardened the Turkish position and led to serious threats by Turkey to bring forcible relief to the Turkish Cypriots. Aerial attacks were launched by Turkey. The Cyprus Government substantially relaxed the economic restrictions in late August.

A further obstacle to the effectiveness of the UN force resulted from restrictions on their freedom of movement imposed by the Cyprus Government. The Secretary-General protested these restrictions, stating that the force could not "fulfill the mandates of the Council from a virtually static posture."[24]

Another crisis arose from the intended rotation by Turkey of a part of the Turkish contingent stationed in Cyprus. Though provided for in the agreement establishing an independent Cyprus, the Cyprus Government's opposition led to an impasse, which was only resolved some months later through the good offices of the United Nations. As part of the agreement, the Nicosia-Kyrenia road was reopened and placed under the exclusive control of the UN force instead of remaining under Turkish and Turkish-Cypriot personnel.

Despite all its handicaps, the Secretary-General, in view of the existing situation, recommended, and the Council agreed to, a further three-month extension of the UN force in Cyprus, under its present terms of reference, until December 26, 1964. He informed the Council that some clarification was needed of the mission's mandate, and that he intended to proceed on the assumptions that: (1) the Council intended the force to have "complete freedom of movement"; (2) to prevent fighting, the force is entitled to remove positions and fortified installations where these endanger peace and may take all necessary measures in self-defense if attacked in performance of this duty; and (3) the force commander may demand separation of opposing armed forces to reasonable distances in order to create buffer zones in which armed forces would be prohibited. There was no opposition to his proposal.

In December 1964, the Council again reviewed the Cyprus situation in the light of the Secretary-General's report.[25] From March to August, the

[24] *Ibid.*, p. 64.
[25] See UN Security Council, S/6102, Dec. 12, 1964.

major effort of the UN force was focused on stopping the shooting and arranging separation of the combatants. After the August session of the Council calling for a cease-fire, the active fighting had virtually ceased and "owing to UNFICYP's steady efforts and the restraint of the parties" the military situation in general remained quiet. These developments enabled the UN force "to concentrate its activities on promoting a return to normal conditions" as called for in the Council's March 4 resolution. An agreement was reached with the Governments of Cyprus and Turkey for the rotation of the Turkish national contingent, and for the reopening of the Kyrenia road under UNFICYP control. The easing of economic restrictions against the Turkish population, together with an easing of restrictions on freedom of movement, led to a general relaxation of tension in most parts of the island.

However, the Secretary-General reported that "the basic factors of the Cyprus situation remain essentially unchanged."[26] The deep distrust between the leaders and peoples of the two communities maintained a state of potential civil war causing the life and economy of the island to remain disrupted and abnormal. Certain areas controlled by the Turkish Cypriots remained inaccessible to the government administrative and other services, with the result that UNFICYP had to provide its good offices and act as the link and channel of communication between the two communities.

While this situation was better than active hostilities, the Secretary-General felt that the prolonged stalemate would produce steadily diminishing results. But he informed the Council that for the time being and in the immediate future "there seems to be no reasonable alternative to the continuation by UNFICYP of its functions in helping to keep the peace, supervising the cease-fire, and contributing to the maintenance of law and order and to a return to normal conditions."[27]

As all the parties directly concerned wished the force to be extended, he recommended and the Council agreed that it be continued for another three-month period until March 26, 1965. It was maintained at the same strength of approximately 6,000 and financed in the same manner and at the same rate as before.

Mediation efforts were unrelentingly continued by Ambassador Sakari Tuomioja, and after his death, by Galo Plaza. Repeated consultations were held in Nicosia, Ankara, Athens, and London with a view to finding "an agreed settlement of the problem." But these patient and persistent efforts had not succeeded in bringing about an agreement. In March 1965, the Council resolved to continue the efforts of both the mediator and the United Nations force.

[26] *Ibid.*, p. 77.
[27] *Ibid.*, p. 78.

When the Council on March 22 extended the stationing of the force for another three months, conditions in Cyprus could not be said to be fundamentally improved. Although the military situation had remained quiet, there was tension and continued danger of a renewal of the fighting. Both sides, the Secretary-General reported, had increased their military strength and were "better prepared to fight." He appealed to the parties to make the most sincere and determined effort, by direct negotiations and through the mediator, to find an agreed basis for long-term solutions of their inter-communal problems.[28] He offered the assistance of the force to bring about a progressive dismantling of all fortifications not needed for security against external attack.

At the same time, the mediator submitted a limited proposal to the parties asking them to meet "if only to look for a basis for discussion."[29] He considered both enosis and partition as impractical, and stressed a solution that would guarantee minority rights and avoid excessive dominance of one community over another.

The mediator's suggestions did not satisfy the Greeks, the Turks, or the Cypriots. The Turkish opposition was the most vocal. The recent development had been the impending supply of ground to air missiles by the U.A.R. to the Cypriots. This would seriously affect the balance of military strength in that area where heretofore the Turks had military superiority.

EVALUATION

The Cyprus case is the fourth instance in the history of the United Nations, excluding the Korean police action, where the Organization has engaged in a peace-keeping operation.[30]

Cyprus is the first instance where a permanent member of the Security Council has supplied forces in a peace-keeping operation. This instance does not mean a precedent. The circumstances of British troops on the ground and a British base in Cyprus, together with the fact that from 1878 to 1960 there was a historic British tie with the island, provided the *raison d'être* of British participation. While President Makarios objected to a NATO force, the Soviet Union could have insisted, but did not, that no permanent member participate unless the U.S.S.R. also participated, the British special position notwithstanding.

[28] See UN Security Council, S/6228, March 11, 1965.

[29] See UN Security Council, S/6253, March 26, 1965.

[30] UNEF, UNOC, and UNTEA were the other three. For a brief period of time in the latter part of 1949, the Palestine Truce Commission furnished the UN Mediator a small military force of 682 officers and men for peace-keeping purposes. This peace-keeping function terminated with the coming into force of the Armistice Agreements. Also for a limited period of time, June and July 1949, the Consular Commission in Indonesia performed limited peace-keeping functions.

Although no peace-keeping operation has ever been vetoed by one of the five permanent members of the Security Council, Cyprus is the first instance where the five permanent members voted unanimously to set up the force. This may in part be attributed to the fact that the compromise worked out was acceptable to the interested parties, particularly to President Makarios, who had the support of the Soviet Union. In previous instances, there have been abstentions. While this is an advance, it does not constitute a precedent. No permanent member would, through precedent, deny himself the right of veto.

The resolution setting up the peace-keeping force also provided for the appointment of a mediator. This instrumentality was not present in the other three peace-keeping instances. The character of the conflict in Cyprus made the appointment of a mediator desirable, whereas in the other three, the circumstances apparently made a mediator neither appropriate nor feasible at the time the peace-keeping force was created.

The Security Council constituted the Secretary-General as a "Commander-in-Chief" of the peace-keeping force. He was to select the commander of the force, and it was he who, being answerable to the Security Council, was to give the commander his orders. This the Secretary-General communicated to the governments supplying the troops. In addition, he made known to them that he did not intend to negotiate the instructions which he proposed to issue the commander with any government either directly concerned or contributing to the force. Thus the Secretary-General in clear language made known that the United Nations is not in Cyprus to provide simply a United Nations umbrella, but to take charge as directed by the Security Council.

An appreciation of the Secretary-General's constitutional position in this peace-keeping operation may be gleaned from an *aide mémoire* which he published on April 10, 1964. [31] Because of its importance it is quoted in full at the end of this case.

In his report to the Security Council on April 29, 1964, [32] the Secretary-General pointed out the savage acts occurring on the island and increasing tension which was developing between the two main groups of the population. Further steps were necessary by UNFICYP to abate this tension and facilitate the resumption of normal life in Cyprus. Accordingly, he announced the need for strengthening the mission by adding a top-level political officer who, on behalf of the Secretary-General, could conduct negotiations for the implementation of the program outlined in his April 29, 1964, report relating to a return to normal conditions in Cyprus. The need for appointing such an official was underscored by General Gyani, "who for too long now has been carrying . . . the dual load of commanding the Force and conducting negotiations on a variety of

[31] UN Security Council, S/5653, April 11, 1964.
[32] S/5671.

essentially non-military matters." On May 11, 1964, the Secretary-General appointed Galo Plaza of Ecuador to conduct discussions and negotiations with the parties concerned towards achieving the resumption of normal life in Cyprus, thus relieving the commander of the force of the responsibility of negotiating on nonmilitary matters.

As already noted, the Secretary-General encountered great difficulty in securing forces for the task. The presence of British troops on Cyprus diminished the sense of urgency in sending a UN force more expeditiously. While in the cases of Suez and the Congo, there was generally an interest and willingness by many members to take part, in the case of Cyprus some of the members asked to contribute forces were hesitant and indeed apprehensive about what they might be stepping into. A less important but inhibiting factor was having to pay their own way. Whereas in Suez and the Congo, the paramount problem was the restoration of the status quo ante, in Cyprus the United Nations intervention carried with it the implication of a new constitutional arrangement. Thus the United Nations for the first time was intervening in a crisis to bring about a new constitutional arrangement between two hostile parties. Here was a situation that, but for the international obligations undertaken by Greece, Turkey, and the United Kingdom, was a kind of civil war.

The question might very well be asked whether the United Nations may intervene or permit itself to be used after it has intervened in a civil war situation. The answer is that in certain situations, a civil war if not ended quickly is likely to develop into a threat to the peace. In the case of Cyprus, the internal strife was complicated by the obligations of the Greek, Turkish, and British Governments—the Greek Government supporting the Greek Cypriots, the Turkish Government supporting the Turkish Cypriots, with the British Government caught between the two, from which position it desired to extricate itself. Not far in the background was the Soviet Union supporting the Greek Cypriots. The situation in Cyprus had the makings of a serious conflagration, and the intervention of the United Nations was indeed a turning away from that road.

The method of financing the peace-keeping force leaves much to be desired. Cyprus is obviously too poor to pay the costs of such a force, and the United Nations is in difficult financial straits. The United States suggested that the members participating in the force pay their own expenses. This was acceptable to the Secretary-General and to the members of the Security Council. By and large, the members participating in the force are bearing the costs of their units with the exception of overseas allowances. The problem of expenses beyond this was solved when the United States agreed to donate $2 million and the United Kingdom $1 million toward the $6 million estimated cost for a period of three months.

Voluntary contributions have been the pattern for many years in financing the United Nations Technical Assistance program. But there is a vast difference between this and a peace-keeping operation which has far-reaching ramifications for the international community, not to mention the powerful influence that large donors can exert on the life or death of such an operation. Maintaining international peace and security should not be based on donations.

The delay in creating a peace-keeping force for Cyprus points up the necessity for advance planning. The earmarking of forces by member states and advance arrangements for financing such forces should be made by the General Assembly. The experience of the United Nations in financing the Congo operation, which at its peak came to over $100 million a year, indicates "that there may be no alternative to compulsory assessments by the General Assembly,"[33] particularly in the large and costly operations. In working out a special scale of assessments for this kind of operation, a distinction will have to be drawn between the richer and the poorer countries. Tied to this special scale is the problem of the decision-making process for peace-keeping operations in which agreement will also be necessary.

Some of the lessons which have thus far emerged from the Cyprus case also bear on peace-observation arrangements for the future. Two are of particular importance—the need for creating a cadre or a corps of peace observers, preferably a cadre, and advance arrangements for the financing of a UN peace-observation mission.

While in general a situation calling for a peace-observation mission is not as dangerous to the maintenance of international peace and security, improvising and gathering a group of observers to dispatch to an area is not an efficient nor an effective way to proceed. A standing UN cadre is clearly indicated by the UN experience. While the Secretary-General has been fortunate in the past in being able to draw on UNEF, UNOC, UNTSO, and other missions for cadres for Lebanon and Yemen, this may not always be possible.

As for financing a peace-observation mission, here too, the practice of the parties paying the costs is questionable, as was seen in the Yemen case. Peace observation is as much a responsibility of the international community as is peace-keeping. While peace observation is of a different species than peace-keeping, it belongs to the same genus financially and should be treated in the same way.

Aide-memoire concerning some questions relating to the function and operation of the United Nations Peace-Keeping Force in Cyprus

Function of the Force

1. The Security Council, by paragraph 5 of its resolution S/5575 of 4 March 1964, recommended that the function of the United Nations Peace-Keeping

[33] Richard N. Gardner, "Needed: A Stand-by U.N. Force," *New York Times* Magazine Section, April 26, 1964.

Force in Cyprus should be "in the interest of preserving international peace and security, to use its best efforts to prevent a recurrence of fighting and, as necessary, to contribute to the maintenance and restoration of law and order and a return to normal conditions."

2. In carrying out its function, the United Nations Force shall avoid any action designed to influence the political situation in Cyprus except through contributing to a restoration of quiet and through creating an improved climate in which political solutions may be sought.

Guiding principles

3. The Secretary-General has the responsibility for establishing the Force and for its direction. The Force, whose composition and size are to be established in consultation with the Governments of Cyprus, Greece, Turkey and the United Kingdom, is a United Nations Force, whose Commander has been appointed by the Secretary-General.

4. The Force is under the exclusive control and command of the United Nations at all times.

5. The Secretary-General is responsible to the Security Council for the conduct of this Force, and he alone reports to the Security Council about it.

6. The Commander of the Force, who is responsible to the Secretary-General, receives, as appropriate, directives from the Secretary-General on the exercise of his command and reports to the Secretary-General. The executive control of all units of the Force is at all times exercised by the Commander of the Force.

7. The contingents comprising the Force are integral parts of it and take their orders exclusively from the Commander of the Force.

8. The Force has its own headquarters whose personnel is international in character and representative of the contingents comprising the Force.

9. The Force shall undertake no functions which are not consistent with the definition of the function of the Force set forth in paragraph 5 of the Security Council resolution of 4 March 1964. Any doubt about a proposed action of the Force being consistent with the definition of the function set forth in the resolution must be submitted to the Secretary-General for decision.

10. The troops of the Force carry arms which, however, are to be employed only for self-defence, should this become necessary in the discharge of its function, in the interest of preserving international peace and security, of seeking to prevent a recurrence of fighting, and contributing to the maintenance and restoration of law and order and a return to normal conditions.

11. It would be desirable from the standpoint of effective operation of the United Nations Force that the Greek and Turkish troops now stationed in Cyprus should be placed under the over-all command of the Commander of the Force. Although the United Nations has no specific mandate to require this, the Secretary-General has urged this course on the Governments concerned.

12. The personnel of the Force must refrain from expressing publicly any opinion on the political problems of the country. They must also act with restraint and with complete impartiality towards the members of the Greek and Turkish Cypriot communities.

13. There is a clear distinction between the troops of the British contingent in the United Nations Force and the British military personnel in Cyprus, such as those manning the British bases not included in the United Nations Force.

14. The Status of the Force Agreement, concluded between the Government of Cyprus and the United Nations, covers matters such as freedom of movement, jurisdiction, responsibilities, discipline, etc., and has been circulated as a Security Council document (S/5634).

15. The operations of the Force and the activities of the United Nations Mediator are separate and distinct undertakings and shall be kept so. Nevertheless, in the nature of the case, the activities are complementary in the sense that the extent to which the Force shall be able to ensure quiet in Cyprus will help the task of the Mediator, while on the other hand any progress effected by the Mediator will facilitate the functioning of the Force.

Principles of self-defence

16. Troops of UNFICYP shall not take the initiative in the use of armed force. The use of armed force is permissible only in self-defence. The expression "self-defence" includes:
  (a) the defence of United Nations posts, premises and vehicles under armed attack;
  (b) the support of other personnel of UNFICYP under armed attack.

17. No action is to be taken by the troops of UNFICYP which is likely to bring them into direct conflict with either community in Cyprus, except in the following circumstances:
  (a) where members of the Force are compelled to act in self-defence;
  (b) where the safety of the Force or of members of it is in jeopardy;
  (c) where specific arrangements accepted by both communities have been, or in the opinion of the commander on the spot are about to be, violated, thus risking a recurrence of fighting or endangering law and order.

18. When acting in self-defence, the principle of minimum force shall always be applied, and armed force will be used only when all peaceful means of persuasion have failed. The decision as to when force may be used under these circumstances rests with the commander on the spot whose main concern will be to distinguish between an incident which does not require fire to be opened and those situations in which troops may be authorized to use force. Examples in which troops may be so authorized are:
  (a) attempts by force to compel them to withdraw from a position which they occupy under orders from their commanders, or to infiltrate and envelop such positions as are deemed necessary by their commanders for them to hold, thus jeopardizing their safety;

(b) attempts by force to disarm them;

(c) attempts by force to prevent them from carrying out their responsibilities as ordered by their commanders;

(d) violation by force of United Nations premises and attempts to arrest or abduct United Nations personnel, civil or military.

19. Should it be necessary to resort to the use of arms, advance warning will be given whenever possible. Automatic weapons are not to be used except in extreme emergency and fire will continue only as long as is necessary to achieve its immediate aim.

Protection against individual or organized attack

20. Whenever a threat of attack develops towards a particular area, commanders will endeavor to restore peace to the area. In addition, local commanders should approach the local leaders of both communities. Mobile patrols shall immediately be organized to manifest the presence of UNFICYP in the threatened or disturbed areas in whatever strength is available. All appropriate means will be used to promote calm and restraint.

If all attempts at peaceful settlement fail, unit commanders may recommend to their senior commander that UNFICYP troops be deployed in such threatened areas. On issue of specific instruction to that effect from UNFICYP headquarters, unit commanders will announce that the entry of UNFICYP Force into such areas will be effected, if necessary, in the interests of law and order.

If, despite these warnings, attempts are made to attack, envelop or infiltrate UNFICYP positions, thus jeopardizing the safety of troops in the area, they will defend themselves and their positions by resisting and driving off the attackers with minimum force.

Arrangements concerning cease-fire agreements

21. If UNFICYP units arrive at the scene of an actual conflict between members of the two communities, the commander on the spot will immediately call on the leaders of both communities to break off the conflict and arrange for a cease-fire while terms which are acceptable to both communities are discussed. In certain cases it may be possible to enforce a cease-fire by interposing UNFICYP military posts between those involved, but if this is not acceptable to those involved in the conflict, or if there is doubt about its effectiveness, it should not normally be done, as it may only lead to a direct clash between UNFICYP troops and those involved in the conflict.

Paragraph 2 of the resolution adopted by the Security Council on 4 March 1964

22. The Government of Cyprus, which has the responsibility for the maintenance and restoration of law and order, has been asked by the Security Council, in paragraph 2 of the resolution adopted on 4 March 1964, to take all additional measures necessary to stop violence and bloodshed in Cyprus. UNFICYP, therefore, shall maintain close contact with the appropriate officials in the Government of Cyprus in connexion with the performance of the function and responsibilities of the Force.

13

OTHER UNITED NATIONS CASES

In a number of cases, United Nations peace-observation and fact-finding missions were requested and in some instances authorized by the General Assembly, but never fully materialized, usually because one party refused to permit a UN mission to enter its territory. In some instances, however, observation has been carried on effectively without the cooperation of all parties to a dispute, especially when observation of a boundary was the chief task, and it has been permitted from one side of the frontier. Some of the missions authorized obtained useful information that enabled the United Nations to take a decision. Two cases, the Hungarian question and the situation in Angola are discussed in some detail below, and others are considered more briefly.

THE HUNGARIAN QUESTION

The Hungarian revolution of 1956 was touched off in Budapest on October 23 when peaceful demonstrations of students, workers, and soldiers erupted in violence. The turning point came when the hated and feared AVH (security police) opened fire on the defenseless crowd gathered in front of the Radio Building. The fighting spread as the insurgents acquired weapons and gathered strength. The first Soviet tanks appeared in Budapest on October 24. Until a cease-fire was ordered by Prime Minister Imre Nagy's government on October 28, the people of Budapest fought a hard and largely successful battle against the Soviet armor and the AVH.

On October 27, the United States, France, and the United Kingdom requested an urgent meeting of the Security Council on "The Situation in Hungary." This request was based on the situation "created by the action of foreign military forces in Hungary in violently repressing the rights of the Hungarian people which are secured by the Treaty of Peace to which the Governments of Hungary and the Allied and Associated Powers are parties."[1] Despite the claim of the representative of Hungary that the

[1] *United States Participation in the United Nations, Report by the President to the Congress for the Year 1956* (Washington: Government Printing Office, 1957), p. 83.

matter was exclusively within Hungary's domestic jurisdiction, the Security Council inscribed the item on its agenda on October 28 by a vote of nine to one (the Soviet Union), with Yugoslavia abstaining.

Imre Nagy, who had been named prime minister on October 23–24, met several of the insurgents' demands during the period from October 27 to October 30. These measures included the formation of a government of both Communist and non-Communist ministers, an agreement with the U.S.S.R. on the withdrawal of Soviet forces from Budapest, the abolition of the AVH and the "one-party" system, and the release of political prisoners, including Cardinal Mindzenty.

During the last days of October, Soviet armored and other vehicles began to evacuate Budapest. On November 1, however, additional Soviet military units entered Hungary, and Prime Minister Nagy announced Hungary's withdrawal from the Warsaw Pact and made a declaration of neutrality. He appealed to the Secretary-General for help of the United Nations and the four great powers in defending Hungary's neutrality and requested the forthcoming General Assembly session to consider this matter. The following day, he appealed to the Secretary-General to request the Security Council to instruct the Soviet and Hungarian Governments to start negotiations immediately on the withdrawal of Soviet troops. When the Security Council met on November 3 to discuss the question, both the Hungarian and Soviet representatives reported that negotiations for troop withdrawal were under way. Consequently the Council withheld voting on a draft resolution sponsored by the United States.

On November 4, however, Soviet troops began a new attack on Budapest and other Hungarian cities. At an emergency Security Council meeting, the Soviet delegation vetoed a proposed resolution calling on the U.S.S.R. to cease the introduction of additional forces into Hungary and to withdraw all its forces without delay. Ambassador Lodge tabled a resolution calling for an emergency special session of the General Assembly under the "Uniting for Peace" procedure, and the proposal was adopted by a vote of ten to one (U.S.S.R.).

Authorization of Secretary-General To Observe Situation

The General Assembly met the same afternoon in response to the Security Council resolution. It passed a resolution sponsored by the United States that called on the Soviet Union to stop its attack on the people of Hungary and withdraw its forces without delay. In addition, the resolution requested the Secretary-General to investigate and observe the situation through representatives named by him, to report to the General Assembly, and to suggest methods to "bring an end to the foreign intervention in Hungary." It called on the governments of Hungary and the Soviet Union to permit observers designated by the Secretary-General "to enter . . . Hungary, to travel freely therein, and to report their findings to the Secretary-General."[2]

Soviet troops had meanwhile gained control of the Danube bridges, the Parliament Building, and the central telephone exchange, thereby overthrowing the Nagy government and completing their occupation of the country. They installed a new government headed by Janos Kadar and three other former members of the Nagy government. The new Revolutionary Workers' and Peasants' government, however, was merely a shadow cabinet since the Russian commanders exercised real control. The Secretary-General received a cablegram on November 4 from Kadar and his Minister of Foreign Affairs, Imre Horvath, declaring that Imre Nagy's requests to the United Nations "to have the Hungarian question discussed in the United Nations have no legal force and cannot be considered as requests emanating from Hungary as a State."[3] From that point on, there was virtually no possibility of UN observers gaining access to Hungary.

On November 8 and 10, the Secretary-General requested the Hungarian Government to admit UN observers. The Acting Minister of Foreign Affairs refused, asserting *inter alia* that "the sending of representatives to be appointed by the Secretary-General of the United Nations is not warranted."[4]

Three-Man Observer Group

Despite his failure to gain the cooperation of the Soviet and Hungarian Governments, the Secretary-General announced on November 16 that he had appointed Judge Oscar Gundersen (Norway), Arthur Lall (India), and Dr. Alberto Lleras Camargo (Colombia) to investigate the situation in Hungary.[5] He reported on November 30 that this group was examining material available to the Secretariat, but the material did not provide a sufficient basis for a report.[6] The group, moreover, deemed it essential that its work be supplemented by direct observation. Since arrangements had not been concluded for observation in Hungary, it was not yet possible to present a comprehensive report.

[2] UN General Assembly, Res. 1004 (ES-II), Nov. 4, 1956. Adopted by 50 to 8 with 15 abstentions.

[3] UN General Assembly, A/3311, Nov. 4, 1956.

[4] UN General Assembly, A/3341, Nov. 12, 1956.

[5] Judge Gundersen had served as Norway's minister of justice from 1945 to 1953 and was a justice of the Supreme Court. Mr. Lall, a distinguished Indian diplomat, was his country's permanent representative to the United Nations from 1955 to 1959. Dr. Lleras had twice served as president of Colombia and was secretary-general of the Organization of American States from 1947 to 1954.

[6] UN General Assembly, A/3403, Nov. 30, 1956.

The General Assembly, which had passed a resolution on November 21 again urging Hungary to allow UN observers to enter its territory,[7] passed a stronger measure on December 4, which requested the Soviet and Hungarian authorities to communicate to the Secretary-General not later than December 7 their consent to receive UN observers.[8] In addition, the resolution recommended that the Secretary-General arrange for dispatch of his observers to Hungary and other countries as appropriate and requested all members to cooperate with them. The Secretary-General communicated the text of this resolution not only to the Hungarian and Soviet representatives but also to the permanent representatives of Austria, Czechoslovakia, Rumania, and Yugoslavia. Of these neighboring countries, only Austria complied with his request.

On January 5, 1957, the Secretary-General reported that the three-man group on the investigations stated that the Assembly's resolution of November 4 appeared to envisage the process of investigation, observation, and reporting as a unified one.[9] However, the available material did not put the group in a position to add anything significant to what was common knowledge about the situation in Hungary. It also noted that only one of the countries requested to offer facilities for observation had complied. Until further sources of reliable material were available through on-the-spot observation in Hungary and the cooperation of the governments directly concerned, there would be little purpose in attempting to assess recent events.

The General Assembly then established a special committee to take over the activities of the group of investigators established by the Secretary-General. Such a committee should serve as an organ of the General Assembly for a continued observation of developments in relation to Hungary in all those respects which might be of relevance to the Assembly.

Special Committee on the Problem of Hungary

The Special Committee on the Problem of Hungary, composed of the representatives of Australia, Ceylon, Denmark, Tunisia, and Uruguay, was established by the General Assembly on January 10, 1957.[10] The following representatives were appointed by their governments: K. C. O. Shann (Australia), R. S. S. Gunewardene (Ceylon), Alsing Andersen (Denmark), Mongi Slim (Tunisia), and Professor Enrique Rodriguez

[7] UN General Assembly, Res. 1128 (XI), Nov. 21, 1956, adopted by 57 to 8 with 14 abstentions.
[8] UN General Assembly, Res. 1130 (XI), Dec. 4, 1956, adopted by 54 to 10 with 14 abstentions.
[9] UN General Assembly, A/3485, Jan. 5, 1957.
[10] Res. 1132 (XI), adopted by 59 to 8 with 10 abstentions.

Fabregat (Uruguay).[11] The Secretary-General appointed W. M. Jordan as principal secretary of the committee and P. Bang-Jensen as deputy secretary. The committee held its first meeting at United Nations headquarters in New York on January 17, 1957, and elected Alsing Andersen as chairman and K. C. O. Shann as rapporteur.

The committee was instructed to provide the General Assembly and all UN members with "the fullest and best available information" on the situation in Hungary, and on developments relating to General Assembly recommendations on this subject. In fulfilling this objective, the committee was instructed "to investigate, to establish and maintain direct observation in Hungary and elsewhere, taking testimony, collecting evidence and receiving information," and to report its findings to the General Assembly.[12]

In its interim report of February 20, the committee stated that its primary concern was "to ascertain the extent and the impact of foreign intervention, by the threat or use of armed force or other means, on the internal affairs and political independence of Hungary and the rights of the Hungarian people." Since it was also requested to report on developments relating to the General Assembly recommendations, the committee said that it would "endeavor to throw as much light as possible" on the effects which the Assembly's recommendations had on developments in Hungary and the degree of current compliance with these recommendations.[13]

The main emphasis of the committee's investigation, however, would be on three areas: (1) the efforts of the Hungarian people in October-November 1956 to reassert their rights; (2) the precise circumstances of Soviet intervention; and (3) the consequences of this intervention on Hungary's constitutional, economic, social, and political evolution, its international commitments, and the fulfillment of its people's wishes.

> The Committee will attempt, in particular, to clarify the nature of the relations between the U.S.S.R. and its representatives in Hungary with the Nagy Government, the origin and significance of the communications addressed by the Government to the United Nations, as well as the role of the U.S.S.R. in connexion with the removal of that Government and the setting up of the present regime.[14]

[11] Mr. Shann had served as head of the UN Branch in Australia's Department of External Affairs from 1952 to 1955 and was then posted to the Philippines as Australian minister. Mr. Gunewardene was governor of the World Bank from 1954 to 1958 and his country's permanent representative to the United Nations from 1956 to 1958. Mr. Slim held ministerial positions in his country's government before being named ambassador to the United States and Canada in 1956; he later served as president of the General Assembly in 1961–1962. Mr. Alsing and Professor Fabregat had long served their countries' delegations to the United Nations.

[12] UN General Assembly, Res. 1132 (XI), Jan. 10, 1957.

[13] UN General Assembly, A/3546, Feb. 20, 1957, pp. 4–6. Hereafter cited as A/3546.

[14] *Ibid.*, p. 6.

In the resolution establishing the committee, the General Assembly called on the U.S.S.R. and Hungary to cooperate with the committee and, in particular, to permit it to travel freely in Hungary. However, the requests of the committee, through the Secretary-General, that the Hungarian Government assist the committee's work, especially with regard to the entry of the committee and its staff into Hungary, met with negative replies. The representative of Hungary informed the Secretary-General that in the opinion of his government the committee violated, in its function, the Charter of the United Nations, and that consequently it would not be permitted to enter Hungary.

The committee also requested the Secretary-General in March to inform the Government of Rumania that the committee desired to meet Imre Nagy in the interest of a full and effective performance of the functions entrusted to it by the Assembly. Rumania refused this request, stating it considered the establishment of the committee as contrary to the UN Charter, as well as to the interests of international cooperation.

Unable to observe the situation directly and obtain information from the two governments concerned, the committee was forced to rely on two sources of evidence in its investigation: the testimony of witnesses and documentary materials. In the preparation of its main report the committee heard 111 witnesses. The verbatim records of the testimony comprise some 2,000 pages of evidence.

The primary consideration in the selection of witnesses was their capacity to place before the committee evidence based on direct and personal knowledge of the events in Hungary. The need to draw witnesses from all segments of the Hungarian people and from all parts of the country was also considered. When requested, assurances were given that their identity would not be revealed.[15]

At the beginning of his testimony, each witness usually made an introductory statement regarding events of which he had special knowledge; he was then cross-examined by the members of the committee. Some witnesses submitted important documents and original drafts, and some prepared memoranda to support or elaborate their testimony. Among the prominent Hungarians who testified were Anna Kethly, Minister of State in the Nagy government; Major-General Bela Kiraly, military commander of the city of Budapest and commander-in-chief of the national guard during the Hungarian uprising; and Jozsef Kovago, Mayor of Budapest during 1945–47 and again from October 31 to November 4, 1956. Other high government officials, politicians, and military commanders testified as well as workers, technical cadres (engineers, technicians, and managers), Communist and non-Communist intellectuals, professional people,

---

[15] A serious controversy arose when the Secretary-General requested the list of names and the deputy secretary of the committee refused to give them on the ground that he had taken a personal commitment not to reveal them. The issue was whether anything filed in the Secretariat at that time could be kept from Soviet higher officials.

students, army officers, and soldiers. Some had been in the Parliament Building with Prime Minister Nagy until November 4 and were able to provide valuable information about events within the Hungarian Government during this critical period. The committee reported that the hearings greatly augmented the information at its disposal and contributed significantly to its understanding of the events in Hungary.[16]

The committee also received helpful material from seven UN members in response to its request through the Secretary-General that member states make relevant information in their possession available to it. Besides other documentary material, the Governments of Belgium, France, Italy, the Netherlands, the United Kingdom, and the United States submitted reports giving a detailed and extensive picture of events in Hungary based on information available to them. The Australian Government transmitted a memorandum based on interviews with thirty-eight Hungarian refugees in Australia. In addition, several nongovernmental organizations transmitted memoranda and documentary material, including a detailed study from the International Commission of Jurists.

Documentation of Hungarian origin included monitored reports of official Hungarian broadcasts as well as unofficial broadcasts during the revolution; official documents such as issues of the *Hungarian Gazette*, the *Hungarian White Book*, and official statements by the Hungarian Government; and Hungarian newspapers, including several revolutionary newspapers and leaflets published during the uprising.

Three reports resulted from the committee's investigations: (1) an interim report on February 20, 1957, which included a summary statement on the course of intervention in Hungary; (2) its full report on June 12, 1957, approved unanimously, which contained a detailed analytical account of the events in Hungary and presented the committee's main conclusions; and (3) a special report on July 14, 1958, on the circumstances of the execution of Imre Nagy, Pal Maleter, and two associates.[17]

UN Special Representatives

On September 14, the General Assembly approved a draft resolution sponsored by the United States and thirty-six other powers which endorsed the Special Committee's report and noted its conclusion that the events which took place in Hungary in October and November 1956 constituted a spontaneous national uprising.[18] In addition, the resolution condemned the U.S.S.R. and the Hungarian regime for the acts that were confirmed by the committee's conclusions. They were called upon, in view of the evidence contained in the report, to desist from repressive measures against

[16] UN General Assembly, A/3592, June 12, 1957, p. 1. Hereafter cited as A/3592.
[17] UN General Assembly, A/3546; A/3592; A/3849.
[18] Res. 1133 (XI), Sept. 14, 1957, adopted 60 to 10 with 10 abstentions. Hereafter cited as Res. 1133 (XI).

the Hungarian people, to respect the liberty and political independence of Hungary and the Hungarian people's enjoyment of fundamental human rights and freedoms, and to ensure the return of Hungarian citizens deported to the Soviet Union.

The resolution also requested the President of the Eleventh General Assembly, Prince Wan Waithayakon of Thailand,[19] "as the General Assembly's special representative on the Hungarian problem, to take such steps as he deems appropriate . . . to achieve the objectives of the United Nations . . . to consult as appropriate with the Committee . . . and to report and make recommendations . . . to the General Assembly."[20]

On December 9, 1957, Prince Wan reported to the General Assembly on his efforts to achieve these objectives: (1) humanitarian treatment in Hungary; (2) return of deportees from the Soviet Union; (3) withdrawal of Soviet troops from Hungary; and (4) free elections in Hungary.[21] Aware of the difficulties of his task, he proceeded step by step, and thus began by concentrating on humanitarian treatment in Hungary. He appealed to the foreign ministers of the Soviet Union and Hungary, who refused to discuss the matter. Prince Wan extracted an agreement from the Hungarian Foreign Minister to provide information on questions to be set forth in a memorandum, but subsequently, the Hungarian Government refused on the grounds that it could not negotiate on a matter that was an internal affair of Hungary. The Special Representative also offered to go to Budapest for the discussion, but the Hungarian Government refused to give him a visa as it would not admit observers from the United Nations.

Prince Wan was succeeded as UN Special Representative on the Hungarian question by Sir Leslie Munro of New Zealand on December 12, 1958.[22] By resolution 1312 (XIII), the General Assembly appointed him to report "to Member States or to the General Assembly on significant developments relating to the implementation of the Assembly resolutions."

Sir Leslie issued four reports from 1959 to 1962.[23] His statement of his activities during his first two years as UN Representative on Hungary provides the best summary of the four-year period:

> I have had two objectives in view: on the one hand, to pave the way if possible for the application of the Assembly's resolutions with regard to Hungary and, with this purpose in view, to keep in the forefront the proposal for

[19] Prince Wan was Thailand's ambassador to the United States from 1947 to 1952 and its permanent delegate to the United Nations from 1947 to 1959.

[20] Res. 1133 (XI).

[21] UN General Assembly, A/3774, Dec. 9, 1957.

[22] Sir Leslie served as his country's Ambassador to the United States and its permanent representative to the United Nations from 1952 to 1958. He was President of the Trusteeship Council in 1953–1954 and then President of the General Assembly in 1957–1958.

[23] UN General Assembly, A/4304, Nov. 25, 1959; A/4606, Dec. 1, 1960; A/4996, Dec. 1, 1961; A/5236, Sept. 25, 1962.

a visit by myself as United Nations Representative to Budapest: and on the other hand, to report to the General Assembly on developments in the situation in Hungary. From the outset it was apparent that little prospect of success faced me in regard to the first aspect of my task, since the Government of the Soviet Union and the Hungarian authorities have at all times declined to co-operate with the United Nations in this matter. The absence of agreement to any discussion in Budapest and the refusal by the Hungarian authorities of arrangements for obtaining information on the spot has not deterred me from the performance of my duties to the Assembly to the fullest extent within my power, and does not now. That my report has again to stress the basic character of the problem is exclusively the responsibility of the Government of the U.S.S.R. and the Hungarian authorities.[24]

In his final report, he noted "certain developments within Hungary which bring the situation within the country more in line perhaps with the Assembly resolutions on the observance of fundamental human rights and freedoms, though not in other respects." He observed, however, that "no change has taken place in the basic situation which has prevailed since 1956—the denial to the Hungarian people of the elementary right of self-determination as a result of the past use and through the continuing pressure of a foreign army."[25]

The easing of repressive measures, particularly the judicial processes that had facilitated the trial, sentencing, and execution of participants in the 1956 uprising, was partly attributed to the fact that there were few remaining participants to prosecute. Sir Leslie nevertheless found evidence in public statements of the Hungarian officials that they were seeking popular support by alleviating some of the worst practices of the immediate post-revolution period.

On December 20, 1963, the General Assembly passed a resolution sponsored by the United States that requested the Secretary-General to "take any initiative that he deems helpful in relation to the Hungarian question" and which considered that "in the circumstances the position of the United Nations Representative on Hungary need no longer be continued."[26]

Evaluation

In the background of the Hungarian revolution loomed a major confrontation of the world's most powerful nations, the United States and the Soviet Union. Yet the voting showed that many nations from all parts of the world were deeply disturbed by this ruthless intervention by the Soviet

[24] A/4606, pp. 17–18.

[25] A/5236, pp. 2–3.

[26] UN General Assembly, Res. 1857, Dec. 20, 1963, adopted by 50 to 13 with 43 abstentions.

Union. Because the Russians had committed themselves so heavily to maintaining their grip on Hungary, any intervention by the United Nations would have run a high risk of provoking a general war.

It was an especially difficult situation to deal with since the Soviet Union was able to stay in the background and work through the puppet regime of its small satellite. There were thus two elusive antagonists—a small country backed by a major power—neither of whom was responsive to the urgings of the General Assembly. In such circumstances, there seems to be little that the United Nations can do short of military sanctions.

If the United Nations had intervened militarily to drive out the Russians in a Korea-type action, the danger of escalation would have been much greater than in Korea. The situation was further complicated by the fact that the Hungarian revolution occurred during the Suez crisis. Because Suez was itself so critical, the Hungarian case was pushed somewhat into the background. Undoubtedly, this diversion of attention encouraged the Russians to play their cards boldly in Hungary. Suez marked the apogee of Western disunity in the 1950's, and the Soviet Union could thus discount any possibility of Western intervention in Hungary. One tentative conclusion from the coincidence of the Hungarian and Suez cases is that it may not be possible to deal with two major crises simultaneously, especially when they tend to aggravate each other and where the major powers are involved in an East-West situation.

The only period when a UN peace-observation group might have been granted permission to enter Hungary was during the Nagy regime between the first and second Soviet interventions. Prime Minister Nagy did not make his appeal to the United Nations until the second intervention was about to topple his government, but he might have been receptive to the support that an international peace-observation team could have given him from October 24 to 30 when the Soviets were being fought to a standstill, and he was able to make considerable progress in meeting the insurgents' demands. In the United Nations, this would have required (1) much earlier action in getting the issue from the veto-bound Security Council to the General Assembly under the Uniting for Peace Resolution, and (2) the rapid formation and dispatch of a peace-observation group. If there had been UN observers in Budapest, the Soviets might have hesitated in carrying out their planned second intervention, thereby giving the Nagy government the crucial time needed to consolidate its hold on Budapest and to negotiate the withdrawal of Soviet forces from the country. In particular, UN supervision of the cease-fire, which Nagy ordered on October 28, would have been an important step. Also, if the negotiations for Soviet withdrawal had been held under UN auspices, the seizure by the Russians of the Hungarian delegation, headed by General Maleter, might have been prevented. This is a somewhat tenuous chain of "might-have-been's," but it illustrates the vital importance of getting an observation group on the spot speedily while the situation is unsettled.

In conflicts where there are two or more roughly equal contending parties, such as border disputes, at least one of them is usually willing to admit observers. In this case, however, the area to be observed fell entirely within the confines of a single country. A secondary area of observation was that part of the Soviet Union adjacent to Hungary where troop movements and massing would have been observed. The authorities of both these countries refused to admit UN observers. Consequently, none of the UN instrumentalities—the three-man investigating group under the Secretary-General, the Special Committee, or the UN Representatives—was able to observe the Hungarian situation on the spot and obtain information from the governments directly concerned. The Special Committee was the most successful of the three in overcoming this major handicap. As the committee reported, "the range of information at its disposal has been far greater than could have been anticipated at the outset of its inquiry."[27] The committee was able to gather comprehensive and detailed documentation and testimony and synthesize this material into a factual report based exclusively on the careful examination of reliable evidence.

What effect did this report have on the situation? Like all reports in this case, it appeared after there was no further possibility of reversing the Soviet occupation of Hungary; this one came out nearly eight months after the revolution. It provided the basis for stronger condemnations of the Soviet Union and Hungarian authorities in General Assembly resolutions, particularly Resolution 1133 (XI). And it served to rebut Soviet and Hungarian charges that the revolution was fomented by reactionary circles in Hungary and was supported by Western "imperialists" at a time when the West was particularly sensitive as a result of the Anglo-French attack on Egypt over the Suez. Thus it may have had some value in correcting any distorted views of the situation. The only "sanction" ever applied to Hungary was in fact the General Assembly's refusal from 1956 to 1962 to take any action on the credentials submitted by the Kadar regime.

While the United Nations concern with the problem did not cause the Soviet Union to abandon its intervention in Hungary, it raised the political price for such intervention. The fact that a United Nations instrumentality, reflecting a wide political spectrum of UN membership, reported the facts of intervention and found that it constituted a clear violation of the Charter made it much more difficult for the Soviets to justify their action in Hungary. This international verdict against the Soviet Union, though unenforceable, had the effect of a moral sanction. While the Soviet Union seems impervious to such considerations, the possibility cannot be ruled out that the Hungarian episode might deter such conduct in the future.

[27] A/3592, p. 4.

THE SITUATION IN ANGOLA

The long-smoldering rebellion in the Portuguese colony of Angola erupted in violence during the early months of 1961. During the week of February 4–11, Angolan nationalists staged several attacks on prisons and police stations in Luanda, the capital, in an effort to free political leaders and Angolan patriots and to create international concern for their cause. These incidents led Liberia to bring the Angolan situation before the Security Council under Article 34 of the Charter.

The United Nations Subcommittee on Angola

A three-power draft resolution (Ceylon, Liberia, and the United Arab Republic) in mid-March aimed to establish a subcommittee to examine the statements made before the Security Council concerning Angola, to receive further statements and documents, to conduct such inquiries as it might deem necessary, and to report to the Security Council as soon as possible, but it failed of adoption.

Renewed fighting in Angola began in mid-March with large-scale rebel attacks on villages and settlements in northern Angola. In the wake of these events, forty United Nations members on March 20 placed "The Situation in Angola" on the General Assembly's agenda. Thirty-six Afro-Asian states sponsored a draft resolution that was identical with the three-power draft in the Security Council except for the references to the General Assembly instead of the Council. This resolution, with the additional provision that the Subcommittee on the Situation in Angola would consist of five members appointed by the President of the General Assembly, was adopted on April 20 by a roll-call vote of 73 to 2 with 9 abstentions.[28] On March 22, the President of the General Assembly nominated Bolivia, Dahomey, Federation of Malaya, Finland, and Sudan as members of the subcommittee.

The rebels' stepped up activity in April gave them control of a considerable area of northern Angola, but in May the reinforced Portuguese forces, reportedly numbering over 20,000, were able to begin full-scale "mopping-up" operations in certain areas. The increased tempo of the fighting led the Security Council to take up the matter again early in June. It passed Resolution S/4835 reaffirming the General Assembly's Resolution 1603 (XV), and requested the subcommittee to implement its mandate without delay, called on the Portuguese authorities to stop repressive measures and to extend every facility to the subcommittee to enable it to perform its task expeditiously, and to report to the Security Council and the General Assembly as soon as possible.

The subcommittee was composed of Carlos Salamanca (Bolivia),

[28] Res. 1603 (XV).

Ambassador to the Trusteeship Council in 1960, Chairman; Louis Ignacio-
Pinto (Dahomey), Ambassador to the United Nations and the United
States since 1960; Dato Nik Ahmed Kamil (Federation of Malaya),
Ambassador to the United States and Permanent Representative to the
United Nations from 1959 to 1962, rapporteur; Ralph Enckell (Finland),
Permanent Representative to the United Nations since 1959, Vice-Chair-
man; Omar Abdel Hamid Adeel (Sudan), Permanent Representative to
the United Nations since 1959.

The subcommittee's basic terms of reference were "to examine the
statements made before the Assembly concerning Angola, to receive
further statements and documents, to conduct such inquiries as it may deem
necessary and to report to the Assembly as soon as possible." The subcommittee considered that "its primary mandate was to inquire as fully
as possible into the situation in Angola,"[29] addressing itself to three main
aspects: the disturbances and conflicts in Angola since February 1961;
the background of the situation; and its repercussions within the context
of international peace and security.

On January 30, 1962, the General Assembly continued the subcommittee
defining its terms of reference as follows:[30] "To study ways and means to
secure implementation of the present resolution and to report thereon to
the Security Council and to the General Assembly."

Based on this and previous mandates, the subcommittee decided to
concern itself mainly with subsequent disturbances and conflicts in Angola;
repressive measures and armed action against the people of Angola;
measures and reforms in Angola; the situation's bearing on international
peace and security; and the question of peaceful solution. The subcommittee considered that it should examine such ways and means of securing
implementation of the resolution as good offices or other diplomatic
approaches, and formal and informal contacts with the Government of
Portugal, as well as other ways and means under the Charter and relevant
resolutions of United Nations organs to induce Portugal to give effect to
the resolution.

From the outset the subcommittee was convinced that its objectives
could be achieved only with the full cooperation of the Government of
Portugal, and that its mandate required a visit to Angola to obtain first-
hand information. Portugal, however, maintained that United Nations
consideration of the Angolan question constituted an intervention in its
domestic affairs and that the subcommittee was illegal. It therefore rejected the subcommittee's request to visit Angola. Portugal, however,
invited the chairman of the subcommittee, Mr. Salamanca, to visit Lisbon
"in a personal capacity" to give him the official Portuguese version of
events in Angola.

[29] UN General Assembly, A/4978, Nov. 22, 1961, p. 19. Hereafter cited as A/4978.
[30] Res. 1742 (XV), operative paragraph 6.

Thwarted in its attempt to obtain first-hand information, the subcommittee decided to continue its inquiry using the best sources of information available to it. It therefore requested and obtained permission from the Congo (Leopoldville) to visit that country in order to gather information from Angolan groups and refugees. Three members of the subcommittee, Mr. Enckell, the vice-chairman, Mr. Ignacio-Pinto, and Mr. Adeel, visited the Congo, heard representatives of seven Angolan groups and received statements or written material from them, and interviewed refugees in Leopoldville and in other places in the Congo where large numbers of Angolans were located.

In addition to the information gathered on this visit to the Congo, the subcommittee received information from the Government of Portugal, specialized agencies of the United Nations, nongovernmental organizations, and individuals with first-hand information on Angola. This material provided the basis of the subcommittee's first report, which examined the situation in Angola, its background and context, and international concern.[31]

With its mandate renewed in January 1962, the subcommittee launched another series of futile attempts to obtain the cooperation of the Portuguese Government, which questioned the integrity and objectivity of the subcommittee's first report. It continued to receive information from Angolan groups, refugees, and other sources in hearings at the United Nations headquarters, Leopoldville, and the areas of Matadi and Thysville along the Congo's frontier with Angola. While these sources of information helped the subcommittee continue its investigations of the situation in Angola, the Portuguese Government's uncooperative attitude prevented it from studying ways to implement Resolution 1742 (XVI), as paragraph 6(b) of that resolution requested. On November 14, 1962, the subcommittee issued its second and last report describing its work during 1962, the development of the Angolan situation, and its concluding observations.[32]

Evaluation

Portugal's refusal to cooperate with the subcommittee was inevitable from the outset: the subcommittee's work was backed by resolutions that had established Portugal as the villain before an inquiry was undertaken. Its mandate was to get Portugal to do something that country had steadfastly refused to do, namely, to agree to self-determination and implementation of the Declaration on Colonialism and to undertake reforms in that direction. The subcommittee was charged with this task because the majority of the members of the United Nations viewed the situation in Angola as a permanent source of international friction and a threat to

[31] A/4978.
[32] UN General Assembly, A/5286, Nov. 14, 1962. Hereafter cited as A/5286.

international peace and security. Portugal, on the other hand, had refused to acknowledge that Angola was a non-self-governing territory and therefore held that the situation was not a colonial issue within the purview of the United Nations. It maintained that the Angolan situation was a purely internal concern and that the subcommittee was interfering in Portugal's domestic affairs by investigating it.

In addition, the subcommittee and Portugal held diametrically opposed views on the best way to solve the problem. The Portuguese sought to eliminate the conflict by militarily crushing the rebellion while instituting some token reforms to improve their image abroad. As the subcommittee pointed out, this approach required a military response on the part of the Angolan nationalists, who otherwise faced a choice of annihilation or voluntary surrender. The Angolan nationalist groups, most of which would have preferred a peaceful settlement through political accommodation, were thus forced to wage a struggle in which they were at a clear disadvantage. They tried to offset their military inferiority to the Portuguese Government forces by resorting to guerrilla warfare, thereby prolonging the conflict.

The subcommittee, on the other hand, concluded that the Angolan problem could not be solved by military force and urged a political settlement. It pointed out the danger of the conflict expanding and threatening international peace and security. It thus urged Portugal to undertake real reforms in law and administration and to establish contacts with the Angolan political groups. When its direct efforts to persuade Portugal to change its policies proved fruitless, it could do little more than repeat its recommendations in its reports. Its second report did, however, foreshadow the possibility of stronger measures, perhaps in the form of sanctions, in stating the subcommittee's view that the Security Council and the General Assembly would have to consider "further measures in conformity with the Charter to secure the compliance of Portugal with United Nations decisions relating to Angola" if that compliance were not forthcoming. The report also stated that "the possibility of peaceful solution would be greatly enhanced if Member States made intensive efforts to convince the Government of Portugal of the need to face political realities and to adjust its policies thereto." [33]

Portugal's refusal to grant access to Angola hindered the subcommittee in the performance of its two main functions. In its investigating and fact-finding tasks, the subcommittee had to rely largely on the two parties to the conflict, the Portuguese Government and the Angolan nationalist rebels, who offered differing versions of events in Angola. Its task of gathering reliable evidence was made more difficult by the remoteness of the areas where most of the acts of violence occurred and the lack of adequate communications. It was thus frequently impossible to separate rumor from

[33] A/5286, p. 82.

fact. The subcommittee implicitly recognized the impossibility of verifying much of its information by its frequent attributive qualifications such as "reportedly," or "it was said that." Despite these obstacles, the broad outline of the events in Angola emerges from the subcommittee's reports, and its conclusions served to challenge the Portuguese assertions and charges, such as those concerning the alleged foreign and Communist origins of the rebellion. They also called attention, both in 1961 and 1962, to the deteriorating situation in the territory and thus effectively rebutted Portugal's claim to have completely put down the revolt.

In its second function, that of studying ways and means of implementing Resolution 1742 (XVI), the subcommittee was completely hamstrung by Portugal's refusal to grant it access to Angola. Without the consent of Portugal, the subcommittee could not enter Angola. Although Portugal was not swayed from its repressive policies by the UN instrumentality, its refusal to cooperate with the subcommittee was damaging to both its case and its international position and resulted in a further isolation of Portugal from the world community.

SITUATIONS IN SOUTH AFRICA AND CHINA

In three situations involving racial conflict in the Union of South Africa and in one situation in the Far East, the United Nations set up machinery for peace observation that was frustrated by denial of access to the area.

Union of South Africa

The first case relating to the problem of race relations in South Africa to be brought before the United Nations concerned the treatment of individuals of Indian and Pakistani origin in South Africa. It came before the General Assembly for the first time in 1946 and has been on the agenda of practically every session since that date. In 1952, the United Nations in addition was requested to take action in behalf of the entire colored population of South Africa because of the so-called apartheid laws. Since 1962, the General Assembly has considered these two cases simultaneously. The third situation relates to South West Africa, which was a League of Nations mandate administered by the Union of South Africa. This case does not strictly come within the definition of an action involving the maintenance of international peace. The effort has been to persuade the Union of South Africa to live up to its mandate obligations. However, in this case also, the efforts to obtain on-the-spot peace observations have rested at least partly on the ground that the apartheid policies of the Union of South Africa create a situation that endangers the maintenance of international peace.

There has been no on-the-spot peace observation in the first two cases.

South Africa has refused to cooperate with any of the committees or commissions set up by the United Nations on the ground that the matter is wholly internal, that under Article II (7) of the Charter, the United Nations has no competence. Nevertheless, the United Nations General Assembly set up a special commission in 1952, designated a personal representative of the Secretary-General in 1955, and set up a special committee in 1962 to deal with these problems. The latter committee consisted mainly of United Nations members who have been staunch supporters of UN proposals concerning human rights. It was instructed to keep South Africa's racial policies under review. Despite the South African denial of access of any of these groups to South Africa, they have obtained information concerning its racial policies from sources outside the country that has enabled the United Nations to make adverse findings and to censure that country.

In the case of South West Africa, the Union of South Africa has declined, ever since World War II and the disbanding of the League of Nations, to negotiate an agreement with the United Nations to place that territory under the UN trusteeship system. After several years of fruitless debate in the United Nations, the General Assembly, in 1949, requested the International Court of Justice to give an advisory opinion on this question. The Court held that South Africa continued to hold the territory as a mandate, with the United Nations competent to exercise the supervisory functions formerly assigned to the League.

The United Nations has set up a number of committees to implement the Court decision, which have tried without success to negotiate with South Africa. Relations between South Africa and other African and Asian states have become increasingly strained, and in 1961, the General Assembly established a special committee to visit the territory.

The South African government invited the chairman and vice-chairman of the committee to visit Pretoria and South West Africa. This visit was the first on-the-spot observation in the territory. Although the visitors were accompanied everywhere by South African officials, the presence of UN officials stimulated private discussions and enabled them to file a useful report on the territory. The UN observation in this case was essentially a fact-finding mission.

China

In 1949, China accused the Soviet Union of thwarting all efforts of the Chinese Government to re-establish its authority in Manchuria by aiding the Communist forces to take over areas evacuated by the Soviet armies in Manchuria, and of attempting to overthrow the Government of China by violent means. The Soviet Union sought to prevent UN consideration of the charges on the ground that the Chinese Nationalist Government no longer represented China. When this effort failed, the Soviet Union announced its refusal to cooperate in any manner with any action that might be taken.

The General Assembly referred the charges to the Interim Committee, an organization the Soviet Union had declined to recognize, to investigate the charges and suggest a solution. By the time the Interim Committee got around to serious consideration of the question, the hostilities in Korea had already commenced. The General Assembly in 1950 instructed the committee to continue the inquiry in order to obtain more information and facts. When the committee resumed its sessions early in 1952, emphasis had shifted to efforts to halt the hostilities in Korea. Since the Interim Committee had failed to investigate, China presented a large mass of material to the 1952 General Assembly and introduced a resolution which determined that the Soviet Union had violated its treaty obligations with China. The General Assembly passed the resolution by rather an indecisive vote. The significance of this situation is that the Interim Committee, despite its authorization, never conducted an investigation, thus reflecting the pragmatic approach that little would be gained from it. The results in this case lead to the conclusion that the main confrontations of the cold war are unsuitable for peace observation and fact-finding and that an organ such as the Interim Committee is not particularly suitable for peace observation.

OTHER REQUESTS FOR PEACE OBSERVATION

The Corfu Channel Case

The Corfu Channel case was one of the earliest cases in which the United Nations Security Council thought to use peace observation in an effort to settle a dispute. On October 22, 1946, two British destroyers were damaged by mines in the Corfu Channel, an international waterway between Corfu and Albania, and forty-four lives were lost. The British Government contended that the mines were part of a mine field recently laid by the Albanian government, and when negotiations with the Albanian Government failed to reach a settlement, it brought the matter to the attention of the Security Council.

The Security Council set up a subcommittee consisting of the Security Council representatives of Australia, Columbia, and Poland to sift the evidence and report on the facts of the case. When the subcommittee after ten meetings failed to reach a consensus, the Security Council recommended submission of the case to the International Court of Justice, and this took place.

This was the second instance of the UN establishing a fact-finding group (the Greek situation being the first) despite the fact that the issue was directly related to the cold war. The Soviet Union did not oppose the establishment of the subcommittee nor even the subsequent resolution sending the matter to the International Court. It did, however, veto a Security Council resolution that attempted to reach conclusions unfavorable to Albania on the basis of the subcommittee report. In short, in this case, when the technique of peace observation failed to solve the impasse, the United Nations Security Council shifted to another method of peaceful settlement.

Free Elections in Germany

In 1951, the General Assembly established a commission to make a simultaneous investigation in the Federal Republic of Germany, Berlin, and the Soviet zone of Germany to determine whether conditions were suitable for the holding of free and secret elections. Since the terms of the reference of the commission required simultaneous investigations in the Federal Republic, Berlin, and the Soviet zone, the failure of the East Germans to cooperate prevented the commission from carrying out any of its functions. The commission set up headquarters in Geneva in February 1952 and filed a report in August indicating its inability to proceed. The commission was still shown on General Assembly charts in 1959. The experience of the commission indicated that peace observation techniques are not particularly appropriate when applied to the major issues of the East-West confrontation without the consent of both parties and also that old committees never die.

Bacteriological Warfare in Korea

The United Nations General Assembly in 1953 set up a commission to investigate in North and South Korea, the mainland of China, and Japan, charges that U.S. forces were using bacteriological warfare in Korea. The commission was not to be organized until all of these states agreed to grant access to their territories. The United States, Japan, and the Republic of Korea agreed to grant access to the commission, but no reply was ever received from North Korea or the Chinese Communists. Therefore, the commission was never organized. However, the unsuccessful effort to organize an investigation was part of the background that enabled the General Assembly in 1953 to establish, from sources other than on-the-spot investigation, the facts which the non-cooperating parties were trying to conceal.

Czechoslovakia and Thailand

In two cases, the Soviet Union used its veto in the Security Council to prevent any investigation of matters alleged to endanger the maintenance of international peace. The first of these vetoes took place in February 1948 in order to thwart an investigation of the coup that brought the Communists into power in Czechoslovakia. The second took place in June 1954 when Thailand submitted a resolution requesting the peace-observation committee to establish a subcommittee and to dispatch observers to Thailand to investigate Communist Viet Minh activities in Laos, Cambodia, and Vietnam. After the veto, Thailand considered referring the matter to the General Assembly but never took any action in that direction.

Human Rights in Vietnam

One further case might have had some significance because it was the first instance of a UN mission investigating the violation of human rights within the accused state's territory, and at its invitation. A fact-finding mission was sent to South Vietnam, but before its mission was completed, the Diem government was overthrown, ending the mission's task.

In this final category of cases, peace observation never reached the stage of attempting to ascertain the facts from sources outside the area. In several of the cases, no organization was established. They are cited for the light they cast, first, on the problem of when states wish peace observation, and second, on whether the conditions of peace observation are propitious.

14

EVALUATION OF CASES UNDER THE UNITED NATIONS

In the first years of the United Nations the peace-observation missions were all authorized by the Security Council as the organ that, under the United Nations Charter, had primary responsibility for the maintenance of international peace. With the frustration of the Security Council through Soviet vetoes in the Greek case and Soviet opposition to the use of the United Nations in Korea, the General Assembly at the request of the Western powers established some peace-observation missions reporting to it, for example, Korea and the Balkans. The Security Council continued to have the responsibility for other missions: Palestine, Indonesia, and Kashmir.

From 1950 until 1956, while the existing peace-observation missions continued their work, new crises in the main were handled through international machinery outside the United Nations. This was the pattern followed in connection with the problems of Southeast Asia. With the outbreak of hostilities in Suez in 1956 and the prompt formation of the United Nations Emergency Force, it became apparent that the Secretary-General of the United Nations had developed machinery and procedures for dealing with emergencies that were superior to arrangements outside the United Nations. Since 1956, United Nations machinery has been frequently used. The General Assembly established the United Nations Emergency Force because of British and French vetoes of similar proposals in the Security Council. With this exception, however, peace-observation missions have invariably originated either in the Security Council or through direct action by the Secretary-General.

The Secretary-General has taken the position that because of his duties under Articles 98 and 99 of the Charter in bringing matters likely to affect international peace before the United Nations, he can initiate an investigation of trouble spots on his own authority. This procedure was followed in Southeast Asia and Yemen. In Yemen, however, the initiative of the Secretary-General was supplemented by Security Council action with the consent of the parties involved. The Secretary-General's initiative, however useful, is limited in scope to the provisions of Articles 98 and 99.

EXTENT OF USE OF PEACE OBSERVATION

The United Nations has used peace-observation machinery extensively in the period from 1946 to 1950, scarcely at all from 1950 to 1956, and more frequently than ever since 1956. In the Congo and Cyprus and in the Suez area, the United Nations efforts might be defined as "peace keeping" rather than "peace observation." However, in the Suez area after the initial activities, some of the functions of the United Nations Emergency Force have been analogous to those of typical peace-observation missions. In Yemen, Jordan, Lebanon, West Irian, and Southeast Asia, the United Nations activities in recent years clearly come under the rubric of peace observation.

COMPOSITION OF MISSIONS

Initially the peace-observation missions established by the United Nations were composed of states with instructed delegations. This pattern soon became unsatisfactory. The delegations experienced difficulty in obtaining their instructions from their governments. The personnel of the delegations were generally unsuitable for carrying on the wide variety of functions (many unanticipated) that the missions carried out. The personnel furnished by the United Nations Secretariat made the most important contribution to the success of the earliest missions. Therefore, the pattern of missions began to change as early as 1948. In general, the later missions have consisted of individuals rather than representatives of states. Occasionally, the United Nations designates the states from which the individuals will be chosen.

In the earliest cases—Palestine and Indonesia—most of the supporting personnel were initially drawn from the consulates of states in the area. The most important reason for this was that until the United Nations Secretariat perfected its organization, the consular establishments were the best source of readily available manpower. A political factor also entered into the use of consular personnel in Palestine and Indonesia: the only states with consular establishments in those areas were pro-Western. In Greece, a large portion of the supporting personnel attached to the delegations came from the Athens offices of the military attachés of the delegation members.

As the United Nations experience in peace-observation missions increased, Secretariat personnel began to replace delegation personnel in connection with the most important tasks. This change, in practice, reflected the fact that the Secretary-General was in a better position to choose personnel qualified for the specific tasks confronting the mission. It also reflected the fact that, as early as 1947, the supporting personnel of the missions found it advantageous to associate themselves as closely as possible with the United Nations through use of the United Nations flag and insignia. In the Greek and Kashmir cases, personnel originally furnished by the delegations began to report through the Secretary-General without any formal authority and to carry on their activities in the same manner as Secretariat personnel.

In the later peace-observation missions, all supporting personnel were furnished by the Secretary-General.

LOGISTIC SUPPORT

Initially, the United Nations Secretary-General had virtually no resources for giving logistic support to the missions. Therefore, the logistic support as well as most of the personnel were furnished by the delegations and, in particular, by the United States. Over the years, the Secretary-General has become the dominant factor in furnishing logistic support to the various missions. The United Nations worldwide radio network forms the basis for communications. The United Nations also furnishes radio equipment for communication between mission headquarters and the field, most of the transportation equipment required in the area, and even some long-range airplanes. In large operations, however, the United Nations has had to supplement its resources. For example, Canada, which has played a major role in many peace-observation and peace-keeping missions, has furnished much equipment and supplies. In the largest operations such as UNOC and UNEF, the Secretary-General has had to rely on the United States for some logistic assistance, even though from a political standpoint it was desirable to avoid great power involvement.

AGREEMENT OF PARTIES

Beginning in 1948, after several attempts to establish peace-observation missions without the consent of the states where the missions would operate, the Western powers began to insist on obtaining in advance the consent of the host countries. In the case of Palestine, this requirement was carried to the point where it seriously interfered with the effectiveness of UNTSO. In Korea and in the Balkans, peace observation took place on only one side of the border and with the consent of the state where the peace observation took place.

The consent of the parties is ordinarily obtained at the time of adopting the resolution establishing the mission and is, in effect, incorporated into the terms of reference of the mission. In recent years, whenever possible, consent of the parties has been reinforced through status agreements covering the details of the various operations.

Recently, in connection with the operations of UNTSO in Palestine, the Security Council has taken steps to clarify UNTSO's authority to act in specific situations without the consent of the parties. This should be regarded as an interpretation and clarification of the original consent of the parties to the peace-observation activities rather than as an authorization to act without consent of the parties.

The Soviet Union in recent years abstained or supported peace-observation missions in the Security Council only if the parties themselves desired the missions.

TERMS OF REFERENCE

The terms of reference of the early peace-observation missions under the United Nations were in some instances, for example, Greece and Korea, so detailed that they did not cover important functions the missions were required to perform. In other cases, for example, Indonesia and Palestine, the terms of reference were so ambiguous that either party was in a position to question the jurisdiction of the mission. In recent years, the United Nations has moved toward the former League of Nations practice of stating the terms of reference in broad comprehensive language that would cover all the functions the mission was likely to perform, but that avoids specifying details.

CHIEF TASKS

The earliest United Nations missions—in Palestine and Greece and to a lesser extent in Indonesia—believed that their central task would be to hear testimony of witnesses on the scene and report to the United Nations. Almost immediately, the missions realized that they could not adequately carry on their functions with such limitations on their activities. The chief activity of many of the missions has been to patrol a boundary and prevent violence on either side of the boundary. Largely in connection with such functions, the missions have assumed a wide variety of quasi-military and quasi-political functions going as far as interposing mission personnel between two armies (quasi-military) and arranging for the transfer of the entire government from one group to another (quasi-political). [1]

TERMINATION OF MISSION

In most instances, the United Nations has been able neither to set a definite time limit for a mission nor to adhere to the time limit where it has been set. A mission will ordinarily terminate with the solution of the controversy that resulted in the need for peace observation. Occasionally, even after the settlement of a controversy, the states involved desire to have the mission continued, as in the case of Jordan.

Where the parties cannot solve the controversy they usually wish the mission to continue indefinitely, fearing the effects of any change in the status quo. This indefinite continuance without hope of settlement of the controversy may lead to an erosion of its authority. Yet, its termination might result in a new crisis.

IMPROVISATION

Initially, when the United Nations established a mission, the Secretary-General had to improvise in each case. Over the years, the Secretary-General has developed procedures of general applicability, that is, a pattern for improvisation. Also, the existing missions furnish a reservoir of experienced personnel available to carry on new missions. The most important supply items are either already available or at least are known so that their procurement can proceed speedily. The original studies of the Collective Measures Committee, supplemented by UN Secretariat studies, have furnished guidelines for the chief steps required to insure an efficient operation. All this has resulted in somewhat less improvisation than in earlier years, when an emergency arose. In another section of this

[1] For a detailed description of the chief tasks in peace observation, see pp. 558 ff.

study steps are recommended that would further reduce the improvisation and lead to more efficient and expeditious programs for dealing with crises.[2]

The United Nations cases, taken as a whole, show steady progress away from complete improvisation to meet the needs of each crisis as it arises and toward established procedures and methods of operation. The United Nations experience furnishes a useful background for planning more extensive and effective peace observation under existing conditions and in a disarming world.

15

MULTINATIONAL ARRANGEMENTS FOR PEACE OBSERVATION

Three cases in which arrangements for observation and inspection were made outside the United Nations are of interest to this study and are discussed below. In Burma, a Joint Military Committee, composed of representatives of the United States, Thailand, Burma, and Nationalist China, was set up to assist in the evacuation of Chinese troops from Burma. In Indochina, three separate International Control Commissions, for Laos, Cambodia, and Vietnam, were set up at the Geneva Conference on Indochina of 1954. Under the Antarctic Treaty, inspection is by national rather than international or multinational observers and is within geographical limits set out in the treaty.

AGGRESSION AGAINST BURMA BY THE REPUBLIC OF CHINA

On March 25, 1953, Burma asked the General Assembly to place on its agenda an item entitled "Complaint by the Union of Burma regarding aggression against her by the Kuomintang Government of Formosa."[1] The Burmese Government alleged that early in 1950 some 1,700 Kuomintang troops had crossed the border from China into Burma. After being

[2] See pp. 547–53.
[1] UN General Assembly, A/2375, March 26, 1953. The title was revised to read "Complaint by the Union of Burma regarding aggression against it by the Government of the Republic of China."

dislodged from the area in Burma near the Chinese border, they had established a new headquarters at Monghsat near the Burma-Thailand frontier
and had prepared a regular airfield to receive supplies from outside of
Burma. Additional troops had been recruited until the force amounted
to about 12,000. The commanding general, Li Mi, had been moving freely
to and from Formosa, and there were other evidences of support from the
Chinese National Government.[2] The Burmese Government submitted a
resolution condemning the Nationalist Government for an act of aggression.
    The Chinese Government admitted the presence of the troops, which
had been forced out of China by the Communist victory. The troops in
Burma had formed the Yunnan Anti-Communist National Salvation
Army and had recruited additional forces. The Chinese representative
denied any connection between these forces and the Chinese Government.
    After considerable debate, the General Assembly on April 23, 1953,
adopted unanimously a resolution which, after deploring the presence of
foreign troops in Burma, recommended that the negotiations in progress
should be pursued, in order to put an end to the situation by means of the
immediate disarmament and withdrawal of the forces from the territory
of Burma or by their disarmament and internment. It urged all states to
assist Burma at its request to facilitate the evacuation of these forces.[3]

The Joint Military Committee

    The General Assembly neither set up nor recommended any peace-
observation machinery to implement its order. However, at the request of
the Burmese Government, the U.S. ambassador to Burma, aided by the
U.S. envoys to Thailand and China, set up a four-nation committee
(known as the Joint Military Committee) composed of representatives of
the United States, Thailand, Burma, and Nationalist China to discuss the
means and procedures for evacuating the troops.
    The committee met on May 20, 1953. The Burmese representative
withdrew from the committee on September 17, 1953,[4] following Chinese
refusal to make a definite commitment on how many troops could be
evacuated and how soon. The Burmese representative, in accordance with
the General Assembly resolution of April 23, 1953, reported to the General
Assembly on the progress of the troop evacuation in October 1953.[5] The

    [2] For more details on the involvement of the National Government of China, see
David Wise and Thomas B. Ross, *The Invisible Government* (New York: Random House,
1964), pp. 129–35.
    [3] UN General Assembly, Res. 707 (VII), adopted April 23, 1953, by 59 to 0 with 1
abstention (China).
    [4] *United States Participation in the United Nations: Report by the President to the Congress for
the Year 1953* (Washington: Government Printing Office, 1954), p. 64.
    [5] UN General Assembly, *Official Records*, Eighth Session, Annexes, Agenda item 25.
(A/C.1/L.70, Oct. 29, 1953.)

Joint Military Committee continued its efforts, even though the Burmese representative had withdrawn, and by the end of the Assembly session on December 8, some 1,500 troops had been evacuated. The Chinese representative to the United Nations expressed confidence that more than 2,000 and possibly as many as 5,000 troops would leave Burma. [6] Accordingly, the General Assembly, despite pressures for a more stringent resolution, generally reaffirmed the previous resolution expressing appreciation for "the efforts of the United States of America and Thailand in striving for the evacuation of these forces." [7]

On July 29, 1954, the Joint Military Committee reported that the regular program of evacuation of foreign forces from Burma had been completed. Nearly 7,000 had been evacuated, including dependents. [8] On September 18, the Chinese Foreign Office stated that the evacuation had been completed, the remaining guerrillas were beyond the influence of the Chinese Government, and the Chinese Government would grant them no assistance. After a short debate, the Assembly on October 29 unanimously approved a resolution terminating the General Assembly consideration of the problem. [9]

The operations of the Joint Military Committee are significant to the narrative of peace observation in two respects: (1) the organizational pattern is unique; (2) the Joint Military Committee carried on for a period of a year and accomplished successfully a variety of functions associated with peace observation.

As indicated, the committee was never authorized by the General Assembly but was organized by individual states to carry out an objective approved by the General Assembly. Nevertheless, it sent reports to the United Nations, which were circulated by the member states of the committee.

The United States and Thai personnel of the committee were drawn entirely from the military attachés at the embassies in Rangoon. The Chinese personnel had no official standing since Burma did not recognize the Nationalist Government. The Burmese personnel were government and military officials. The respective governments paid the expenses of the personnel assigned to the operation, and the United States, and, to a lesser degree, Thailand and China paid the costs of the evacuation. This was the third and latest occasion when the offices of the military attachés furnished personnel for peace observation in connection with problems before the United Nations. The previous instances were in Palestine for the armistice agreements and in Indonesia.

[6] *United Nations Yearbook 1953* (New York: Columbia University Press, 1954), p. 178.
[7] UN General Assembly, Res. 717 (VIII), Dec. 8, 1953.
[8] UN General Assembly, A/2740, Sept. 29, 1954.
[9] UN General Assembly, Res. 815 (IX), Oct. 29, 1954.

Peace-Observation Functions of the Committee

The Joint Military Committee performed a variety of functions commonly associated with peace observation: It arranged for a cease-fire in the Monghsat area and along a corridor from Monghsat to the Thai border to permit the evacuation. It worked out alternate plans for evacuation of the troops from Burma to Thailand either by road or by air. It persuaded the National Government of China, which had no relations with Burma, to take steps to facilitate the evacuation, such as disavowal of those who refused to leave Burmese soil. It arranged for the practical details of the evacuation: an air lift to Thailand supplied at U.S. expense; the dispatch of Burmese observers; the reception of evacuees at the border and their transit through Thailand at the expense of the Thai Government; the furnishing of food, shelter, and care to the evacuees in Thailand, and the provision of security troops at the expense of Thailand; the receipt of weapons surrendered by the evacuees at the border; the flight of the evacuees from Thailand to Formosa in General Chennault's planes at the expense of the Chinese Government.

Evaluation

The speedy evacuation of foreign troops from Burma was in the interests of three of the four states most vitally concerned: Burma, Thailand, and the United States which cooperated fully during the entire period of the evacuation. The fourth interested party, the National Government of China, at times was uncooperative.

It is most significant that the circumstances of the operation made it necessary for the interested parties to improvise their own machinery for peace observation. The improvised machinery had some advantages over regular United Nations machinery: the interested parties defrayed the entire cost of the operation; the logistic backing from the United States assured a speedy and efficient operation when the Chinese Government decided to cooperate fully.

The improvised arrangements had the disadvantage that the committee could not conceivably be deemed neutral or unbiased. When the Chinese representative began to drag his feet in connection with the plans, there was no easy way to use the prestige of the United Nations to influence his attitudes. The walkout of the Burmese representative was regrettable and probably would have been avoided if the committee had been an instrument of the United Nations. Likewise some of the recriminations in the General Assembly between the Burmese and Chinese arose as a result of misunderstanding, which a neutral mission might have avoided.

The task of the committee was relatively simple and uncontroversial. The General Assembly resolutions calling for the evacuation received unanimous support. The interested parties had both the desire and the capability of assuring the successful achievement of the mission.

PEACE OBSERVATION IN INDOCHINA, 1954–1965

By the end of the war in 1945, French Indochina was rapidly breaking up into three separate countries whose instability provided a fertile ground for direct and indirect Communist aggression from the north. The Japanese, after the fall of France in 1940, had attempted to incorporate the area into their "Greater East Asia Co-Prosperity Sphere," but had mainly succeeded in diminishing Western, particularly French, prestige without bringing any real stability into the area. Postwar French reoccupation was full of trouble and widely resisted. With the rise of Communism in China, the stage was set for southward Communist expansion, first into contiguous Laos, then into Vietnam, and with threats directed toward Cambodia and beyond to Thailand, Burma, Malaysia, and Indonesia as well.

In May 1954, the French surrender to the Communist North Vietnamese at Dien Bien Phu ended eight years of war and one hundred years of French colonial rule. The stakes for the Western world were considerable. Secretary of State John Foster Dulles urged united action by the free world. But President Eisenhower and Prime Minister Churchill rejected any military intervention. And even on the Communist side, Foreign Minister Molotov, probably thinking of Korea and United States nuclear power, was unwilling to risk further adventures that might bring the Sino-Soviet alliance of 1950 into operation.

Thus, on the initiative of Pierre Mendes-France, a conference of nine directly concerned powers was called in Geneva in June 1954. It led to an armistice based on the following accords:[10] (1) agreements on the cessation of hostilities in Vietnam, Laos, and Cambodia; (2) a final declaration, in which representatives of Cambodia, the Democratic Republic of Vietnam, France, Laos, the People's Republic of China, the State of Vietnam, the U.S.S.R., the United Kingdom, and the United States took part; and (3) several unilateral declarations by participants. The agreements were to be supervised by separate international control commissions: the International Commission for Supervision and Control, Laos (ICC/Laos); the Inter-

---

[10] U.S. Senate Committee on Foreign Relations, *Report on Indochina*, report of Senator Mike Mansfield on a study mission to Vietnam, Cambodia, Laos, 83 Cong., 2 sess. (Washington: Government Printing Office, 1954), p. 16. The United States participated in the negotiation of the Geneva Accords but was not a party to them, nor was South Vietnam. The true response of the United States to the military victory of Communism at Dien Bien Phu was the signature of the Southeast Asia Collective Defense Treaty and Protocol, signed at Manila on September 8, 1954. For text see U.S. Department of State, *United States Treaties and Other International Agreements*, TIAS 3170.

national Commission for Supervision and Control, Cambodia (ICC/
Cambodia); and the International Commission for Supervision and Control, Vietnam (ICC/Vietnam).

The Geneva Conference on Indochina

The Geneva Conference on Indochina operated under two co-chairmen
—the Foreign Secretaries of the United Kingdom and the Soviet Union—
who acted as a steering committee. One writer states that "a good deal
(though by no means the major part) of behind-the-scenes negotiations
occurred on their initiative or through their good offices."[11]

Their importance continued to grow throughout the 1954 conference.
The co-chairmen undertook to find a formula for financing the international control commissions.[12] Reports of the commissions were to be
received and distributed by them and, in effect, were to become the post-
office link between the commissions and the members of the conference.

The chart appended to the end of this section shows the structure and
functions of the peace-observation machinery in Indochina as it applies,
with slight differences, to the countries Laos, Vietnam, and Cambodia.

A key stipulation between Sir Anthony Eden and Chou En-lai, which
made the signing of the three agreements possible, was that Vietnam was
to be divided temporarily at the 17th parallel, while Cambodia and Laos
were to be recognized by both sides as neutral. An important part of the
package was that elections would be held in two years in North and South
Vietnam to determine the future of the country. Meanwhile, the international control commissions would supervise the agreements in all three
countries.

The origin of the "troika" principle, introduced in these commissions,
deserves some explanation. According to Sir Anthony Eden, Molotov and
Chou En-lai pressed for the inclusion of Poland and Czechoslovakia in
addition to India and one or two other Asian states. Sir Anthony could
not accept two Communist states and pressed for observation by the five
Colombo powers who were both Asian and neutral. This was rejected by
the Communists. "During the first two weeks of June, session after session
passed in mutual recrimination and endless argument over the question
whether or not a communist nation could be regarded as neutral."[13]

[11] George Modelski, "International Conference on the Settlement of the Laotian
Question, 1961–62" (Canberra: The Australian National University, 1962), p. 4 (mimeo.).

[12] One may well ask why it was necessary to create a special conference and special
international commissions to observe and supervise the terms of the armistice in Indochina when the United Nations was available with a Secretariat that had already
acquired some expertise. In this case the participation of Communist China was "well-
nigh indispensable" and Communist China was unwilling "to operate under the
auspices of an organization from which it was excluded." *Ibid.*, p. 5.

[13] Anthony Eden, *Full Circle: The Memoirs of Sir Anthony Eden* (London: Cassell, 1960),
pp. 116–17, 127–28.

It was not until two days before the end of the conference that the question was resolved.

> The first indication that the conference might at last be on the verge of success came on the afternoon of July 18th, when Chou En-lai proposed to me that the supervisory commission should consist of India, Canada and Poland. . . . From that moment the tangled ends of the negotiations began to sort themselves out.[14]

This, then, was the genesis of the "troika."

In all three Geneva Agreements the "troika" system was also to be carried out in the fixed and mobile inspection teams.[15] Voting in "troika" was on the basis of majority rule except that unanimity was required on recommendations for changes in the armistice agreements and questions that might lead to resumption of hostilities.[16]

The International Control Commissions

The tasks of the international control commissions were, in general, to supervise the execution of the terms of the armistice, and in particular: to control withdrawal of foreign forces; to control release of prisoners of war and civil internees; and to supervise the ban on introduction of foreign military personnel or war materiel.

In the case of Laos, the commission was also to supervise rotation of personnel and supplies for French Union security forces to be maintained in Laos. This task arose because, as an exception, the agreement provided for the retention of 1,500 French military personnel by Laos for training purposes and up to 3,500 additional for retention of French military bases.

The terms of reference were precise and adequate; the difficulties of execution that arose are traceable mainly to the political attitudes of the various factions involved.

The fixed teams were to be located at specific points, although these points could be varied by agreement between the government and the ICC. In general, the zones of action of the mobile teams were the regions bordering the land and/or sea frontiers of the respective countries. All three agreements provided:

> Within the limits of their zones of action, they shall have the right to move freely and shall receive from the local civil and military authorities all facilities they may require for the fulfillment of their tasks. . . . They shall have at their

---

[14] *Ibid.*, p. 141.

[15] See Cambodia Agreement (Article 12), Laos Agreement (Article 26) and Vietnam Agreement (Article 35).

[16] See Cambodia Agreement (Articles 20–21), Laos Agreement (Articles 34–35), Vietnam Agreement (Articles 41–42).

disposal such modern means of transport, observation and communication as they may require.

Outside the zones of action defined above, the mobile teams may, with the agreement of the Command of the party concerned, move about as required by the tasks assigned to them by the present Agreement.[17]

It was agreed at the Geneva Conference that the individual cease-fire was to become effective in Laos on August 6, 1954; in Cambodia on August 7, 1954; in North Vietnam on July 27, 1954; in Central Vietnam on August 1, 1954; in South Vietnam on August 31, 1954. The staggered dates reflected the recognition of the drafters of the Geneva Accords that conditions differed in the various areas and that varying amounts of time were needed to permit the cease-fire orders to reach the lowest combat echelons of the respective sides.

Some time was allowed for the three control commissions to organize. The time was insufficient, with the result that the early work was more of a token nature than real control. Only one commission was operative in time—the one having the longest lead time, South Vietnam. By October, however, all commissions were fully operative with fixed and mobile teams located in accordance with the cease-fire agreements.[18]

Size and Structure of Commissions. Each commission is composed of an Indian chairman, a representative of Poland, and a representative of Canada. Each country also has an alternate delegate. In addition, there is a group of administrative, communications, and secretariat personnel. The initial strength of the three international commissions was 160 Canadians, 300 Poles, and 500 Indians; today, these figures are somewhat smaller. The disproportionate share of the Indian delegation resulted from a commitment by the Indian Government to supply the major share of the administrative, communications, and secretariat personnel.

Each delegate has military and political advisers. The Indian chairman is ex officio Secretary-General and has three deputies, one each from India, Canada, and Poland.[19]

Each commission set up three committees for its operations. The first was a military committee whose principal function was the supervision of the fixed and mobile inspection teams. The second was a political committee which "examined, coordinated and determined priority of complaints

---

[17] Article 26 of the Laos Agreement. Similar provisions are found in Article 12 of the Cambodia Agreement and Article 35 of the Vietnam Agreement.

[18] Major Edmond A. Blais, "The International Commission for Supervision and Control in Indo-China," M.A. Thesis No. 1787, Georgetown University (June 1959), p. 31. (This is an unpublished monograph that was reviewed by several Canadian officers who participated in the work of the three Commissions.)

[19] International Control Commission for Supervision and Control in Laos, *First Interim Report, August 11, 1954–December 31, 1954*, Cmd. 9445, p. 2 (London: HMS, April 1955). Hereafter cited as Cmd. 9445.

and evaluated reports" for the public and the teams.[20] The third was an administrative committee which dealt with accommodations, transport, supplies, and general logistic problems.

Relationship between the ICC's and the Joint Commission. The Communist idea at the beginning of the 1954 Geneva Conference was that the agreements would be carried out by mixed commissions consisting of representatives of the belligerents. In the end, they agreed to have both joint and international commissions. The joint commission for Laos, for example, had specific terms of reference under the cease-fire agreement: (1) to fix the sites and boundaries of provisional assembly areas; (2) to ensure safety of troops on the move; (3) to determine routes of withdrawal for French Union and Vietnamese Peoples Volunteers (but not Pathet Lao—Article 4); and (4) to send groups of the joint commission to follow forces in movement.

Despite the basic hostility between the belligerents, it appears that some degree of cooperation developed in carrying out the agreements under the supervision of the ICC's.

Administrative Difficulties of the Control Commissions. The first difficulty of the ICC in Laos and also in Vietnam and Cambodia was the shortage of secretarial staff and particularly French-English and local language interpreters and translators. Thus, investigations sometimes had to be conducted with the assistance of interested parties.

Lack of adequate transportation was another problem. In Laos, for example, there was no railway, and only a few roads and bridges were in good condition. Surface travel was sometimes restricted to footpaths, pony tracks, or boats. In all three countries, there was a lack of airfields, and while the commissions had their own road transport, they relied in the beginning on the French for transport equipment. When the French withdrew, the commissions were forced to rely on such transport as the three governments made available. The Laotian Conference of 1961–1962 partially remedied this situation in Laos by providing the commission with transport and communications facilities. Radio communications of the three commissions and their subordinate bodies were more satisfactory, owing to the technical competence of the Indian Army Signal Corps.

Financing the Operation. The Geneva Agreements on the Cessation of Hostilities provided: "The costs involved in the operation of the Joint Commission and its joint groups and of the International Commission and its inspection teams shall be shared equally between the two parties." Nevertheless, the contributions were established in detail at the initial

---

[20] "Petition boxes" were erected in which the public could place their petitions. These would be collected and examined by the petition branch of the secretariat. The petition branch was supervised by the political committee, which also was concerned with democratic freedoms and freedom of movement.

meeting of the supervisory powers in New Delhi in 1954 and were adopted at the beginning of 1956 by the co-chairmen as follows:

1. Pay and allowances of delegation personnel—supervisory powers;
2. Common pool expenses (food, lodging, medical services and transport to and from home country of delegation personnel)—contributing powers (China, France, U.K. and U.S.S.R. in equal shares);
3. Local expenses (scheduled transport, board, etc.)—parties to Geneva Agreements (for example, Democratic Republic of Vietnam and France, in equal shares).

Audit was by the Government of India and, late in September 1956, it was agreed that certificates of audit by the various commissions would be acceptable rather than detailed audit.

For the first several years, the French authorities remaining in Indochina accepted financial responsibilities for the activities of the fixed and mobile international teams as provided in Article 26. Later, however, they claimed that they had paid more than their legitimate share of expenses, and in December 1956, the French National Assembly voted not to allow further sums for expenses of the commissions in Indochina and instead claimed refunds for overpayments. As a result, the Government of India agreed to advance funds for the commissions, but the French treasury demanded that these funds be used to satisfy past French claims.

Reporting Procedures. The three Geneva Agreements contained provisions for reports to be made both by the commissions and by their respective inspection teams. Article 31 of the Laos Agreement states:

> The inspection teams shall submit to the International Commission the results of their supervision, investigation and observations; furthermore, they shall draw up such special reports as they may consider necessary or as may be requested from them by the Commission. In the case of a disagreement within the teams, the findings of each member shall be transmitted to the Commission.

As time went on, the distinction between fixed and mobile teams largely disappeared. Both types of teams were required to submit to headquarters (1) daily situation reports, (2) special reports (on their own initiative or at the commission's request, including results of investigation), and (3) special situation reports. The latter, such as anticipated violations of the agreement or violations resulting in loss of life, were for immediate consideration of the commission. In addition, the fixed teams were to submit weekly activity reports including copies of documents received. All reports are in manuscript with a single copy retained by the team. All are classified secret.[21]

[21] See Cmd. 9445, pp. 62–65.

Although the Geneva Agreements did not require the control commissions to submit regular periodic reports, such reports have been made periodically by the Indian chairmen of the three commissions to the two co-chairmen of the Geneva Conference. These reports are simultaneously made available in the capitals of the members of the Geneva Conference.

Military Problems of the Control Commissions. In general, the military problems of the commissions did not present insuperable difficulties, despite their late start and the lack of cooperation of the parties. This was particularly true of the immediate problems concerning the cease-fires, disengagements, and withdrawals. The later problems, such as exchange of prisoners and supervision of the entry of troops and war materiel, were made difficult by lack of cooperation. In Laos, for example, the supervision of the entry of troops was made increasingly difficult by the presence of the Pathet Lao in the two northern provinces, a situation that has continued ever since.

The Role of the Co-Chairmen. The institution of the co-chairmen is not mentioned in the declarations or agreements on cessation of hostilities concluded at the Geneva Conference on Indochina on July 21, 1954.

Certain functions left to the co-chairmen "as a parting gift" of the conference are alluded to in the verbatim record of the Eighth Plenary Session of July 21, 1954.[22] These relate to the invitation to the Governments of India, Poland, and Canada to undertake the duties of supervision and the task of the co-chairmen to work out a formula on defraying the costs of the international commissions.

In 1954, no supervisory or guiding role was envisaged for the co-chairmen after termination of the conference, and it seems that whatever role they exercised thereafter simply evolved out of the needs. Even communications and reports from the commissions to the members of the conference were expected to be direct, rather than through the co-chairmen. The following provision appears in all three agreements on the cessation of hostilities:[23]

> If one of the parties refuses to put into effect a recommendation of the International Commission, the parties concerned or the Commission itself shall inform the members of the Geneva Conference.
>
> If the International Commission does not reach unanimity in the cases provided for in Article —, it shall submit a majority report and one or more minority reports to the members of the Conference.
>
> The International Commission shall inform the members of the Conference in all cases where its activity is being hindered.

[22] *Further Documents Relating to the Discussion of Indochina at the Geneva Conference, June 16–July 21, 1954,* Cmd. 9239, p. 6 (London: HMS, reprinted 1962).

[23] Article 22 of the Cambodian Agreement, Article 36 of the Laotian Agreement, Article 43 of the Vietnamese Agreement.

In the period from 1954 to 1962, the practice developed of appeals from the international commission to the co-chairmen for guidance, to act as a means of communication and for the circulation of reports. This development was regularized, so far as concerns Laos, in Article 8 of the Protocol to the Declaration on the Neutrality of Laos, concluded at Geneva, July 23, 1962, in the following terms:[24]

> The Co-Chairmen shall periodically receive reports from the Commission. In addition the Commission shall immediately report to the Co-Chairmen any violations or threats of violations of the Protocol, all significant steps which it takes in pursuance of this Protocol, and also any other important information which may assist the Co-Chairmen in carrying out their functions. The Commission may at any time seek help from the Co-Chairmen in the performance of its duties, and the Co-Chairmen may at any time make recommendations to the Commission exercising general guidance.
>
> The Co-Chairmen shall circulate the reports and any other important information from the Commission to the members of the Conference.
>
> The Co-Chairmen shall exercise supervision over the observance of this Protocol and the Declaration on the Neutrality of Laos.
>
> The Co-Chairmen will keep the members of the Conference constantly informed and when appropriate will consult with them.

Whether based on treaty provisions or not, the functions the co-chairmen were called on to discharge between 1954 and 1965 were to receive, publish, and circulate reports of the ICC, to arrange financial support for the control commissions, and to provide policy guidance and support.

The first responsibility assumed by the co-chairmen was in connection with the receipt and publication of commission reports. In a foreword to the First and Second Interim Reports of ICC/Vietnam,[25] the British Foreign Office noted that the Government of India, acting for the Indian chairman of ICC/Vietnam, transmitted to the co-chairmen on June 28, 1955, copies of the commission's First Interim Report. "Her Majesty's Government and the Soviet Government agreed that this report should be published in all capitals concerned once copies have been received by all members of the Geneva Conference."

Thus arose the first duty of the co-chairmen, which continues to the present for all the commissions. Generally speaking, the work is well done and is accomplished within a month after receipt. There seems to be increasing delay in the preparation of reports by the commissions, but this is not traceable to any fault on the part of the co-chairmen.

Financing is not a treaty obligation of the co-chairmen under either the

[24] *Declaration and Protocol on the Neutrality of Laos*, Cmnd. 2025, p. 27 (London: HMS, May 1963).

[25] International Commission for Supervision and Control in Vietnam, *First and Second Interim Reports*, Cmd. 9461, p. 3 (London: HMS, 1955).

Geneva Accords of 1954 or the Declaration of Laotian Neutrality of 1962. Nevertheless, the co-chairmen have taken some responsibility for financing.

For the first two years, the French liaison missions took up the slack until the French Government demurred and stopped providing working capital. The situation and response of the co-chairmen is described as follows in the Fourth Interim Report of ICC/Laos:[26]

> On 13th December 1955, the French Liaison Mission informed the Commission that the French Government was no longer in a position to maintain the French Liaison Mission in Vietnam unless finances were made available by the Commission . . . it was decided to pay the French Liaison Mission from 1st February 1958 at £12,000 per month in order to avoid dislocation of the services. . . . This arrangement was approved by the Co-Chairmen of the Geneva Powers also. . . .

The Eleventh Interim Report of ICC/Vietnam, September 18, 1961,[27] referred to the fact that the ICC called attention of the co-chairmen to the deteriorating financial position due to lack of adequate funds.

The Government of India had advanced working funds in the past and solicited payments as well. It, too, became weary of the task, for in June 1964, the report in Saigon was that the Government of India "in the future would not be inclined to pass the begging bowl again."

The habit of the international commission of looking to the co-chairmen for policy guidance and support grew by degrees. The first step was to invite the attention of the co-chairmen to particularly difficult situations.

In the commission's Third Interim Report of ICC/Vietnam there is a note by the Canadian delegation inviting attention of the co-chairmen to the unsatisfactory progress made in implementing Article 14(d) relating to freedom of movement of civilians from one zone to another and expressing the view that the task could not be done in the time period laid down.[28]

The Indian and Polish commissioners felt that the Third Report should be transmitted as the First and Second had been, that is, through the Government of India. But in view of the insistence of the Canadian delegation, it was sent to the British Foreign Office, with twelve copies in English for the conference members "as decided by the co-chairmen."

By the time the Fourth Interim Report of the ICC/Vietnam was published by the British Foreign Office in December 1955, the foreword carried an opinion concerning the role of the co-chairman.[29] The occasion was the

[26] International Commission for Supervision and Control in Laos, *Fourth Interim Report, May 17, 1957–May 31, 1958*, Cmnd. 541, p. 24 (London: HMS, October 1958). Hereafter cited as Cmnd. 541.

[27] International Commission for Supervision and Control in Vietnam, *Eleventh Interim Report, February 1, 1960 to February 28, 1961*, Cmnd. 1551, p. 27 (London: HMS, November 1961). Hereafter cited as Cmnd. 1551.

[28] Cmd. 9499 (London: HMS, June 1955), p. 4.

[29] Cmd. 9654, p. 2.

consideration of the Canadian note mentioned above concerning Article 14(d). The opinion reads:

> . . . There is no reference in the Agreements on the Cessation of Hostilities in Cambodia, Laos and Vietnam or in the Final Declaration of the Geneva Conference on July 21, 1954 . . . to the Co-Chairmen as such or to any special responsibilities devolving upon Her Majesty's Government and the Soviet Government by virtue of the fact that Sir Anthony Eden and M. Molotov had acted as Chairmen at alternate sessions of the Geneva Conference on Indo-China. In the view of Her Majesty's Government their obligations and responsibilities and those of the Soviet Government are neither more nor less than those of the other Powers adhering to the Final Declaration of the Geneva Conference. For reasons of practical convenience, however, it has become customary for Her Majesty's Government and the Soviet Government to act as a channel of communication between the International Supervisory Commissions and the Geneva Powers, to coordinate arrangements for the distribution and publication of the Commissions' reports and to initiate proposals for financing the work of the Commissions. On occasions, . . . Her Majesty's Government, the Soviet Government or other Powers have also employed this channel as a convenient means of bringing their views on matters concerning the implementation of the Geneva Agreements to the attention of members of the Geneva Conference as a whole. The existence of these informal arrangements does not, of course, in any way affect the position and obligations under the Geneva Agreements of Her Majesty's Government and the Soviet Government or derogate in any way from the responsibilities of members of the Geneva Conference as a whole in regard to the Geneva Agreements, under Article 13 of the Final Declaration of the Conference.

Having made the record clear, the British Government did what the Canadian delegation obviously hoped for. It stated its concern over the lack of cooperation the commission was receiving from the competent authorities in both zones in carrying out the article. This statement served as political support for the Canadian position.

In answer to the commission's appeal to the co-chairmen, which appeared in its Fourth Interim Report, the Governments of the United Kingdom and the U.S.S.R., in December 1955, dispatched messages to the other conference signatories and to the supervisory powers inviting suggestions for improving the implementation of the Geneva Agreements. Thus the process was started whereby the commission reports were considered by the co-chairmen in consultation with the conference signatories in an effort to improve the situation.

The co-chairmen discussed the matter in London and five months later, in May 1956, issued messages to the ICC/Vietnam, the Government of the French Republic, and the Governments of the Democratic Republic of Vietnam and the Republic of Vietnam. In these messages, they "strongly urged both the Governments in Vietnam to make every effort to implement the Geneva Agreements, to prevent any further violation of the military provisions of the Agreement and to ensure the implementation of the political provisions and principles of the Final Declaration of the Geneva Conference."[30] The parties were also asked to give the ICC their assistance and cooperation.

The efforts of the co-chairmen, however, proved to be of no avail, as evidenced by the continued appeals of the ICC.[31]

The co-chairmen under the 1954 Geneva Accords have no greater obligation to the ICC than have any of the other 1954 Geneva Conference signatories. The conference did not create an operational relationship between the co-chairmen and the ICC, and appeals of the ICC to the conference powers through the co-chairmen for help in discharging their obligations, as evidenced in its reports to the co-chairmen, arose out of the frustration the commission experienced. There was nothing for the co-chairmen to do but to send the reports to the Geneva signatories. Only the 1954 Geneva Conference powers could appropriately respond to the appeals of the commission.

The foregoing analysis indicates that the Geneva Conference of 1954 created an international peace-observation instrumentality without providing it with an international secretariat to give it the constant guidance and the backstopping such an operation requires and would have had if the Indochina problem had been brought under the United Nations. It is a wonder that the ICC functioned at all, but the greater wonder is that it did not collapse altogether.

Under Article 8 of the 1962 Declaration and Protocol on the Neutrality of Laos, the co-chairmen were mentioned specifically and were given the duty of circulating reports and any other important information from the commission to the members of the conference, as well as the duty of exercising supervision over the observance of the protocol and the Declaration on the Neutrality of Laos. The significant addition is the power given the co-chairmen to supervise the observance of the protocol and declaration. This, it might be said, was an explicit recognition of the operational gulf that previously existed between the commission and the conference signatories and an effort to correct it. However clear the language appears, one cannot overlook the fact that the co-chairmen can act only by unanimity, if they can act at all. Thus the problems over which the commission

[30] International Commission for Supervision and Control in Vietnam, *Sixth Interim Report, December 11, 1955 to July 31, 1956*, Cmnd. 31 (London: HMS, January 1957), p. 31.

[31] See International Commission for Supervision and Control in Vietnam, *Seventh Interim Report, August 1, 1956 to April 30, 1957*, Cmnd. 335 (London: HMS, December 1957), p. 20; *Ninth Interim Report, May 1, 1958 to January 31, 1959*, Cmnd. 726 (London: HMS, May 1959), p. 16; and *Tenth Interim Report, February 1, 1959 to January 31, 1960*, Cmnd. 1040 (London: HMS, June 1960), p. 25.

ORGANIZATION OF PEACE-OBSERVATION MACHINERY IN INDOCHINA

THE GENEVA CONFERENCE ON INDOCHINA, 1954

Members: Cambodia, Democratic Republic of Vietnam, France, Laos, People's Republic of China, State of Vietnam, U.S.S.R., U.K. and U.S. (U.S. present but not a signatory.)

Purpose: To take note of agreements ending hostilities in Cambodia, Laos and Vietnam and to organize international control and supervision of execution of these instruments.

THE CO-CHAIRMEN

Members: Foreign Secretaries of U.K. and U.S.S.R.

Duties: To guide the conference and provide continuing link among the members between conferences.

INTERNATIONAL COMMISSION FOR CONTROL AND SUPERVISION IN LAOS *

Members: India (chairman), Canada and Poland.

Duties: To control and supervise execution of the Agreement for Cessation of Hostilities in Laos.

Methods: Supervises work of the Joint Commission, which is initially responsible for executing provisions. Directs observation, investigatory and inspection work of its own fixed and mobile teams. Reports to the Co-Chairmen.

Subjects: Enforcement of cease-fire; withdrawal and transfer of troops, supplies, etc.; prohibition of introduction of fresh troops and supplies; exchange of prisoners and of civilian internees; removal of graves; prevention of retaliation on populations; general conciliation work with a view to establishment of unified, free, peaceful, and democratic government.

MILITARY COMMITTEE OF ICC, LAOS

Members: India, Canada, Poland.

Duties: Supervises work of the fixed and mobile teams of the ICC.

POLITICAL COMMITTEE OF ICC, LAOS

Members: India, Canada, Poland.

Duties: Examines, coordinates and sets priority for investigation of complaints.

ADMINISTRATIVE COMMITTEE OF ICC, LAOS

Members: India, Canada, Poland.

Duties: Provides housing, transport, communications, supplies and general logistical support.

JOINT COMMISSION FOR INTERNATIONAL CONTROL IN LAOS

Members: "The Parties," i.e. apparently Royal Laotian Government, France and Democratic Republic of Vietnam.

Duties: Execute the Agreement on Cessation of Hostilities.

---

* *This chart shows the organization of peace-observation machinery in Indochina, as typified by the Laos Commission.*

is divided and which are sent to the co-chairmen are treated in the context of unanimity. Should there be agreement among the co-chairmen, they still would not be able to act, since action can only be taken by the fourteen signatory powers. The defects of this structure and arrangements were appreciated by the negotiators, more especially by the Americans and British. This, however, was the maximum of accord possible at the 1961–1962 Conference at Geneva, particularly among the big powers. What they achieved was the alternative to no accord at all.

Peace Observation in Laos, 1954–1964

In August 1954, the cease-fire was declared throughout Laos. The Royal Laotian troops were to remain where they were, and plans were made to regroup in provisional assembly areas the other three forces involved in the fighting, that is, French, Pathet Lao, and Vietnamese Peoples Volunteers. By a fixed date, these forces were to be in the assembly areas. Two months later, the French and Vietnamese forces were to be withdrawn from Laos, and the fighting units of Pathet Lao not demobilized were to be transferred to other areas in Laos.

This operation was difficult because of the rugged terrain, the difficulty of identifying some of the forces without insignia, and the distrust and differences among the joint groups.[32] However, though largely unsupervised by the ICC/Laos or the joint commission, the withdrawal and transfer were in the main carried out. The withdrawal was relatively successful and the Laotian Government in February 1955 dissolved the joint commission. In addition, prisoners of war and civil internees were to be liberated under the Geneva Agreement. After much bickering, the exchanges were effected.

The Geneva Agreement on Laos also forbade the import of military supplies into Laos except specified quantities deemed necessary for defense. Provision was made between the ICC and the Laotian Government for checking the monthly statistics submitted by the French military mission regarding such imports. The Laotian Government, however, complained to the ICC that war materials and personnel were being imported into the northern provinces for use by the Pathet Lao. The commissioners disagreed about this complaint, but an investigation was undertaken.

The Canadian view was expressed as follows:

> While it has proved possible for the Commission to check the passage of war materials to and from parts of the nation under control of the Royal Laotian Government (and the Government has established a commendable pattern of co-operation with the Commission in this respect), there have never been procedures devised to investigate charges that the Pathet Lao in contravention of the Geneva Agreement received substantial military assistance from neighboring Communist North Vietnam.[33]

[32] Cmd. 9445, p. 13.
[33] Canada, Department of External Affairs, *External Affairs* (March 1957), p. 114.

The Geneva Agreement also called on the commission to get the lists of names and location of graves of war casualties, but it ultimately found it was unable to do so.

Certain complaints were received by the commission alleging forcible recruiting by the Pathet Lao, but these allegations could not be substantiated.

Cooperation of the Parties with the ICC. In its first Interim Report in January 1955, the ICC paid tribute to the cooperation of the high commands of the Franco-Laotian side, the Vietnamese Volunteers and the Pathet Lao. The cooperation of the Royal Laotian Government, however, was not as good after 1955. Some members of an observation team were threatened and manhandled by Laotian soldiers, some commission letters were ignored or answered in rude terms, and commission personnel were asked to evacuate quarters without alternate accommodations being made available. In early 1956, the Pathet Lao also began increasingly to create incidents calculated to hamper the commission's work.

In its first report, the ICC had stated that the most difficult problem was that of the two northern provinces.[34] The Geneva Accord called for the fighting units of the Pathet Lao to move into these two provinces "pending a political settlement." The latter term was not defined, nor was it clear whether only a part or the whole of these two provinces was meant. The Pathet Lao claimed control over the entirety, while the Franco-Laotian side claimed control over the western portions of the provinces. The Pathet Lao insisted that a "political settlement" had to precede their turning the provinces over to the Laotian Government. While the controversy continued, troops of both sides were in close proximity, and there was constant danger of clashes.

The commission, composed as it was, divided two ways on the action to be taken. A deadlock arose on a policy statement that aimed at preventing conflict without prejudice to the rights of either party under the Geneva Agreement.[35] The Canadian and Indian members voted in favor, but the Polish delegate held that this vote was invalid since the effect of the majority vote would constitute an amnedment to Article 14 requiring unanimity.

In August 1956, declarations were signed by neutralist Laotian Premier Prince Souvanna Phouma with his half brother Prince Souphanouvong, leader of the Pathet Lao, calling for new elections and the establishment of a National Union Government in which the Pathet Lao was to become a recognized political party. The fighting units of Pathet Lao were to be integrated into the Royal Laotian Army, and the two northern provinces

[34] Cmd. 9445, p. 41.

[35] International Commission for Supervision and Control in Laos, *Second Interim Report, January 1–June 30, 1955,* Cmd. 9630 (London: HMS, November 1955), p. 16. Hereafter cited as Cmd. 9630.

were to be returned to Royal Laotian control. This transfer took place in December 1957. The 1,500 members of the fighting units of Pathet Lao were integrated into the Royal Laotian Army at the Plain of Jars in a ceremony attended by the Military Committee of the ICC in February 1958. This transfer contained the seeds of future trouble.

Two days after this ceremony, Souvanna Phouma, in a letter to the chairman, requested "a winding up" of the control commission to take effect May 4, 1958, on the ground that the military and political integration constituted the last phase for the completion of cessation of hostilities in Laos.[36]

Adjournment of the ICC. Canada was anxious to terminate its commitments in Indochina and in May 1958 tabled a resolution calling for immediate dissolution of the commission. In his statement, the Canadian delegate expressed his views on the nature of the commissions' supervisory function: "I think we all agree that in accepting membership in the International Commission, all three Supervisory Powers did so as independent nations and as principals; they are not the agents of the Geneva Powers or of the Co-Chairmen."[37] Both the Polish and Indian delegations opposed this view, mainly on the ground that the three commissions were interdependent, and one could not be terminated without the others. Moreover, as to the Laos commission, one of the parties, the Democratic Republic of Vietnam, did not accept the proposal to terminate.[38]

On July 19, 1958, the ICC withdrew from Laos.[39] Thus ended the first period of international peace observation. It appeared that Laos was now unified and that a workable coalition government was installed with formerly hostile forces merged into a single army. This impression, however, proved to be wrong.

Within a year, the United Nations was requested to aid the troubled country by sending an observation mission, and in 1961, a second Geneva Conference on Laos was convened to send a reconstituted control commission to help the country out of the deepening crisis.[40]

International Conference on the Laotian Question, 1961–1962. The semblance of calm and peace resulting from the UN observation mission in the fall of 1959 did not last long. Prince Sananikone's government was overthrown in December 1959 by the anti-Communist "young ones,"

[36] Cmnd. 541, p. 112.
[37] Cmnd. 541, p. 113.
[38] Cmnd. 541, p. 114.
[39] The ICC withdrew but did not dissolve.
[40] Between the withdrawal of the ICC in 1958 and the reconstitution of the ICC in 1961, the United Nations in 1959 sent a subcommittee of the Security Council to Laos to investigate the situation and report to the Security Council. The UN Secretary-General also visited Laos to make a firsthand study of the country and arranged for a personal representative to be there to assist the country in its economic and social development. See pp. 390–95 above for an account of this period.

who put General Phoumi in his place. He won the May 1960 election, but in August, Souvanna Phouma was restored to power by a coup. General Phoumi withdrew to South Laos and set up a government under Prince Boun Oum, which received U.S. support. The U.S.S.R. charged the United States with "gross interference" in Laotian affairs and violation of the 1954 Geneva Agreement. A confrontation of the two super powers seemed possible.

In December 1960, General Phoumi captured the badly damaged capital, and Souvanna Phouma fled the country; Prince Boun Oum took charge. Captain Kong Le, undefeated, withdrew northward and on New Year's Day, 1961, took over the vital Plain of Jars.

> General Phoumi, backed by American instructors and equipment, an-
> nounced a "general offensive" against the Plain, with its three airfields, and
> which now had become the funnel for a vast Soviet airlift of equipment and
> North Vietnamese instructors. That Right-wing offensive, launched on Jan-
> uary 7, failed miserably. . . . A Pathet Lao-Kong-Le counter-offensive on
> April 24, 1961 completely routed the Right-wing forces who abandoned
> their American advisers (a Captain and 3 sergeants) in enemy hands. On
> May 2, 1961, fourteen nations, including Russia and the United States, met
> at Geneva to hammer out . . . what the United States had sought so strenuously
> to avoid: a neutral coalition government including Communist members in
> key posts. [41]

Despite U.S. opposition at the opening of the Geneva Conference in 1961 to the seating of the Pathet Lao delegation, the Soviets were adamant that the neutralist, pro-West, and Communist factions be seated even if one of them absented itself.[42] The delegation of the Royal Laotian Government considered itself the sole legitimate delegation and refused to participate.

Prince Sihanouk of Cambodia got the three Laotian princes to meet at Zurich with the result that a communiqué was issued on June 22, 1961, announcing the decision to form a government of national union comprising all three elements. Ambassador Averell Harriman went to Rangoon in September 1961 to make clear the conditions of U.S. support of the prospective government.

The pulling and hauling between the factions continued for a year, and the Geneva Conference was held up for six months on this account. After the stage had been set with the assistance of the ICC and the representatives of the co-chairmen, the three princes met in Laos at the Plain of Jars, June 7–11, 1962; the coalition government was formed and received the

[41] Bernard Fall, *Street without Joy: Insurgency in Indochina, 1946–63*, 3d rev. ed. (Harrisburg, Penna.: Bernard Fall, 1963), pp. 330–31.

[42] "Official Report of the United States Delegation to the International Conference on the Settlement of the Laotian Question, May 16, 1961–July 23, 1962" (mimeo.), p. 5. Hereafter cited as "Official Report."

sanction of the King, and the Geneva Conference was enabled to conclude
its labors.

Attitudes of the Powers.

United States. In 1961, the United States had three alternatives: (1) loss of
Laos to the Communists; (2) military action, involving U.S. troops and
other outside forces; and (3) settlement of the crisis through peaceful
international and internal negotiation to achieve a neutral status for the
kingdom that would permit it to survive as a nation.[43] After consultation
with congressional leaders, the administration chose the third alternative.

U.S.S.R. "In 1959 and 1960 the Soviet Union (as well as China, North
Vietnam, and Pathet Lao spokesmen) repeatedly called for the reconvening of the international commission." No doubt, they expected that this
would "improve the domestic situation of the Neo Lao Hak Xat [the Communist party], then hard pressed by government forces. But when the tide
of battle turned in their favor they made the return of the commission
conditional upon the holding of a Geneva Conference."[44]

India. Since mid-December 1960, when the neutralist government of
Souvanna Phouma collapsed, India (in concert with the United Kingdom
and France) had been urging the reconvening of the ICC/Laos.

Communist China. Tensions between the partners of the Peking-Moscow
axis began to be acute about the time of the calling of the second Laotian
Conference. Despite the divergencies, which were to intensify in 1962 over
Chinese military operations against India and Russia's withdrawal of
missiles from Cuba, both Communist powers tended to follow parallel
rather than competing policies in Southeast Asia.[45]

Convening of the Conference. Three messages were sent by the co-
chairmen: (1) an appeal to the parties in Laos for a cessation of hostilities;
(2) a request to the Government of India to reconvene the ICC/Laos; and
(3) invitations to fourteen nations to convene at Geneva on May 12, 1961.[46]

How was it determined which fourteen nations were to attend? On
January 1, 1961, Prince Norodom Sihanouk of Cambodia suggested the
pattern: six Western states (United Kingdom, United States, France,
Canada, Thailand, Republic of Vietnam), four Communist states (Chinese
People's Republic, U.S.S.R., Poland, Democratic Republic of Vietnam),
and four nonaligned states (India, Burma, Cambodia, and Laos).[47] The
rationale of this selection was that it included the parties to the 1954

[43] U.S. Department of State, Laos Desk, "Laos," Unclassified Briefing Paper (offset
print), p. 7.

[44] Modelski, *op. cit.*, p. 2.

[45] Russell H. Fifield, *Southeast Asia in United States Policy* (New York: Praeger, for the
Council on Foreign Relations, 1963), pp. 57–63.

[46] John J. Czyzak and Carl F. Salans, "The International Conference on the Settlement of the Laotian Question and the Geneva Agreements of 1962," *American Journal of
International Law*, LVII: 2 (April 1963), p. 302.

[47] Modelski, *op. cit.*, p. 6.

Geneva Accord, the United States, which was not a party, the three supervisory powers, and two states that border on Laos—Burma and Thailand.

> As delegations gathered at Geneva for the . . . opening of the Conference on May 12 the United States was chiefly concerned by (1) the continued absence of a satisfactory means of verifying the cease-fire in Laos, because of Soviet unwillingness to empower the ICC to take the . . . steps to achieve this, and (2) the fact that the problem of Lao representation at the Conference was . . . unresolved. [48]

The slow beginning of the Second Laotian Conference was accelerated by the issuance of a joint communiqué at Vienna, by President Kennedy and Chairman Khrushchev on June 4, 1961, in which they "reaffirmed their support of a neutral independent Laos under a government chosen by the Laotians themselves, and of international agreements for insuring that neutrality and independence prevailed, and in this connection they have recognized the importance of an effective cease fire." [49]

U.S. Secretary of State Dean Rusk stated the problem of the conference simply: (1) What is meant by a neutral and independent Laos? (2) What international agreements are necessary to insure it? (3) Can the first step of a cease-fire be made effective?

In his speech at the conference on May 17, Secretary Rusk dealt with the last point first. "An effective cease fire is a prerequisite to any constructive result from our proceedings." The Secretary then defined neutrality as: (1) nonalignment; (2) withdrawal of foreign troops; (3) cessation of supply of equipment; (4) no bases and no alliances; (5) a neutrality consistent with sovereignty, and hence with safeguards against subversion from abroad.

Of special interest are the Secretary's suggestions for improving the peace-observation machinery:

> 1. The control machinery must have full access to all parts of the country without the need for the consent of any civil or military officials, national or local.
> 2. It must have its own transportation and communication equipment sufficient to the task. These must be constantly available to and under the sole orders of the control body.
> 3. It must be able to act on any complaints from responsible sources, including personnel of the control body itself, responsible military and civil officials in Laos, the governments of neighboring countries and of the members of this conference.
> 4. The control body should act by majority rule with the right to file majority reports and minority reports. It should not be paralyzed by a veto.

[48] "Official Report," p. 5.
[49] U.S. Department of State, *Bulletin*, Vol. 44 (1961), p. 999.

5. There should be some effective method of informing governments and the world at large about a finding by the control body that the conditions of peace and neutrality, as defined, have been violated.[50]

Declaration of Neutrality of Laos.[51] This declaration consists of a statement of neutrality by the Government of Laos and a responsive declaration by the other conference members welcoming and taking note of that statement. The thirteen nations were bound to:

a) Refrain from impairing sovereignty, independence, neutrality, unity or territorial integrity of Laos.

b) Refrain from force or threat of force in relation to Laos.

c) Refrain from interference in internal affairs of Laos.

d) Impose no political conditions for aid.

e) Bring Laos into no alliance.

f) Respect the wishes of Laos not to recognize protection of any alliance, including SEATO.

g) Refrain from introducing foreign troops or military personnel into Laos.

h) Establish no foreign military bases in Laos.

i) Use no Laotian territory for interference in internal affairs of other countries.

j) Use no territory of any country, including their own, to interfere in internal affairs of Laos.

Point (i) is the so-called "corridor" provision. It was included on the proposal of the South Vietnamese since Laos has long been used by the North Vietnamese as a corridor for infiltration of armed men and equipment for the subversion of South Vietnam. This undertaking is incorporated in the Laotian statement as a reciprocal undertaking that Laos will not be used as a means of subverting South Vietnam.

The fourteen nations concluded a protocol, also signed on July 23, 1962, providing that:

a) All foreign troops and personnel must be withdrawn from Laos not later than thirty days after the ICC has notified the Government of Laos that its inspection terms are present at all points of withdrawal (or 75 days after June 23, 1964).

b) Withdrawal must take place only along routes and through points specified by the Government of Laos and the ICC.

c) Introduction of foreign regular and irregular troops is prohibited.

d) French military installations will be transferred to the Royal Government of Laos.

e) Prisoners of war and civilian internees will be released.

[50] *Ibid.*, p. 847.

[51] U.S. Department of State, *U.S. Treaties and Other International Agreements*, TIAS 5410 (Washington: Government Printing Office, 1962), pp. 3-4.

Functions of the Co-Chairmen. In the 1954 Geneva Accords, functions of the co-chairmen are not even mentioned. In the new agreement, they were to exercise "supervision over the observance of this Protocol and Declaration on the Neutrality of Laos."

Members of the U.S. delegation specializing in legal matters have held this to be the most important function assigned to the co-chairmen and interpreted it to mean "that the governments of the United Kingdom and the Soviet Union have assumed the responsibility of seeing to it that all of the parties to the declaration and protocol live up to those agreements, and of exercising diplomatic pressures, if necessary, to that end."[52]

Functions and Powers of the ICC. Articles 9 to 18 deal with the functions and powers of the ICC. Acting in concurrence with the Government of Laos, the commission supervises and controls the cease-fire in Laos. It supervises the withdrawal of foreign troops and personnel and investigates where it has reasonable grounds for considering that foreign troops or military personnel are being introduced into Laos. At the request of the Government of Laos, it investigates cases of violation of Article 6 prohibiting introduction of arms other than those required by the government for its defense.

The widest power of the ICC is contained in Article 15 of the protocol:

> In the exercise of its specific functions which are laid down in the relevant articles of this Protocol the Commission shall conduct investigations (directly or by sending inspection teams), when there are reasonable grounds for considering that a violation has occurred. These investigations shall be carried out at the request of the Royal Government of Laos or on the initiative of the Commission, which is acting with the concurrence of the Royal Government of Laos.
>
> In the latter case decisions on initiating and carrying out such investigations shall be taken in the Commission by majority vote.
>
> The Commission shall submit agreed reports on investigations in which differences which may emerge between members of the Commission on particular questions may be expressed.
>
> The Conclusions and recommendations of the Commission resulting from investigations shall be adopted unanimously.

The commission now has power on its own initiative and by majority vote to investigate suspected violations of the declaration and to send reports to enable the co-chairmen, who have the responsibility of exercising supervision and control of the declaration, to carry out this responsibility. "If, however, the Government of Laos requests an investigation, it must be made regardless of the views of the members of the Commission."[53] The Communist position is that the three elements of the coalition government must agree to the investigation.

[52] Czyzak and Salans, *op. cit.*, p. 310.
[53] *Ibid.*, p. 312.

Free access to all places is provided in the protocol as well as independent means of transport. The Supervisory Governments, as heretofore, pay the salaries and allowances of their nationals on the commission and its teams. Accommodations are provided by the Government of Laos, and all other capital or running expenses are paid for by a fund to which contributions are made in the following proportions: China, France, U.S.S.R., United Kingdom, United States, 7.6 percent; Burma, Cambodia, Democratic Republic of Vietnam, Laos, Republic of Vietnam and Thailand, 1.5 percent; Canada, India, Poland, 1.0 percent.

Neither the declaration nor the protocol have a stipulated term, but the protocol (Article 19) provides that the co-chairmen may at any time, in no case later than three years from the date of entry into force, present to the conference a report with recommendations on the question of termination of the commission.

The Work of the Reconstituted ICC. The first report of the Commission dealt exclusively with the immediate problem of withdrawal of foreign regular and irregular troops.[54] After the establishment by the Royal Laotian Government of the points and routes of withdrawal, teams and subteams were sent by the ICC to observe the withdrawals. The total figures for withdrawal were reported by the commission as follows: Democratic Republic of Vietnam, 40; Philippines, 403; United States, 666.

The U.S. Embassy in Vietnam reported to the commission that this represented all Philippine civilian technicians and all U.S. military personnel in Laos. The North Vietnam Embassy declared that all Vietnamese military personnel had been withdrawn. Laotian Foreign Minister Quinim Pholsena declared that unless he received proof to the contrary, he had to accept the assurances. The ICC stated that various radio and newspaper reports alleged that thousands of troops of various nationalities still remained in Laos, and the ICC would take appropriate steps if it had reasonable grounds for considering that a violation of the Geneva Protocol had occurred.

The message of May 17, 1963,[55] from ICC to co-chairmen is the first to reveal the basic differences between the Indian and Canadian commissioners on the one hand, and the Polish commissioner on the other.[56]

Hostilities broke out between neutralist and Pathet Lao forces on the Plain of Jars at the beginning of April. Heavy fighting ensued and abated only somewhat toward the end of the month. Constant vigilance paid by

---

[54] Australia, Department of External Affairs, *Current Notes on International Affairs* (November 1962), pp. 34–37.

[55] Great Britain, Foreign Office, "Exchange of Correspondence between Her Majesty's Government and the Soviet Government on the Situation in Laos," July 1, 1963 (mimeo.). This report is the most recent substantive communication from ICC/Laos on its work. Hereafter cited as "Exchange of Correspondence."

[56] For a later report on Polish non-participation in ICC/Laos see: ICC Message No. 33 of Dec. 17, 1964, to the co-chairmen.

the commission and its teams to the disturbed areas helped to bring some calm, but in general these efforts did not halt the fighting. "The Commission has been handicapped in its conciliatory role by the failure of the Pathet Lao to agree to the setting up of Commission's teams in other disturbed parts of the Plain of Jars area." [57]

By contrast, on April 12, 1963, the ICC received a letter from Prince Souvanna Phouma, as head of the Neutralist Party, stating:

> In order to allay possible doubts on the policy of strict neutrality that I have advocated for the Kingdom of Laos and in order to facilitate the task of the International Commission for Control, I have the honour to inform you that the ICC teams may proceed wherever they like in the areas under the control of the Neutralist forces. For that, it is enough that the ICC gives me a previous notice of 24 hours. [58]

General Phoumi Nosavan, as representative of the Prince Boun Oum Party, made a similar offer of free access and did not even require notice. [59]

It is thus clear that the Communist element alone refused free access to the ICC. The split between the Polish member, Dr. Marek Thee, and Chairman Avtar Singh and the Canadian member, Paul Bridle, occurred on April 28 over the question whether to send a provisional team to the headquarters of General Kong Le on the Plain of Jars and keep it there on a continuous basis, as had been requested by Prince Souvanna Phouma. The Polish member made several minor objections, but his major objection was that the request had not been approved by Prince Souphanouvong. [60]

Dr. Marek Thee withdrew from the commission's deliberations and sent a letter to the British and Soviet Ambassadors on May 22, 1963, which set forth his basic position. According to the Polish member, the basic problems disturbing the Laotian scene were:

1. Insecurity in Vientiane. This included the assassination of Foreign Minister Quinim Pholsena; assassination of Col. Siphasong, who was to become head of the mixed police force; fear of many other ministers for their lives. Dr. Thee endorsed the Neo Lao Hak Xat proposals that each force send a battalion to the capital to keep order and "liberate political prisoners."
2. Tense situation in the Plain of Jars. Violation of cease-fire by arrival of the Savannakhet group (pro-American) to join with General Kong Le in suppressing a dissident neutralist group.
3. Foreign interference in Laos. U.S. delivered arms to the Royal Laotian Government despite protests of Neo Lao Hak Xat. The United States maintains a para-military organization called "Air America." Activities of SEATO powers in Laos and concentration of U.S. fleet disturbing. [61]

[57] Exchange of Correspondence, Annex C, p. 16.
[58] Exchange of Correspondence, p. 5.
[59] Exchange of Correspondence.
[60] Exchange of Correspondence, App. XXI, p. 3.
[61] Exchange of Correspondence, Annex F, p. 2.

Dr. Thee interpreted the Geneva protocol to mean that the Royal Laotian Government could not act, except on the principle of unanimity among the three coalition parties and unanimity of the three ICC members. He charged that the Indian and Canadian delegations consciously violated these two basic principles of the Geneva protocol.

The flow of majority and minority communications to the co-chairmen continued, with Dr. Thee still boycotting the meetings. There ensued a sharp exchange of communications between the co-chairmen which embodied separate draft messages designed to be sent to the signatories of the Geneva Declaration and Protocol of 1962. Agreement on the text of the message was never reached by the United Kingdom and the U.S.S.R. However, the United Kingdom finally sent the exchange of correspondence to the signatories.

In general, the Soviet draft supported the Polish member's position and censured the U.S. Government; the British draft laid the blame on lack of progress in achieving a unified government, on restrictions placed on the ICC, and on the mistrust resulting from these two factors. As an annex to the exchange there is attached a letter from the Indian chairman, and concurred in by the Canadian member, to the effect that "Air America" is not in their opinion a para-military formation.

Evaluation. Four interim reports were made by the control commission during the first period, 1954–1958, which were of a high order. They did not gloss over unpleasant situations. Taken as a whole, they may be regarded as models for reporting by international peace-observation bodies charged with supervising cease-fire operations of large-scale hostilities.

In estimating the effectiveness of the ICC 1954–1958, it may be concluded that it produced quite good results on the nonrepetitive military tasks, that is, cease-fire, regrouping, and withdrawal, despite the fact that in this early stage it arrived late and was weak in personnel, resources, and experience. It was successful in varying degrees with respect to the continuing military tasks: prevention of introduction of fresh troops and guarantee of democratic freedoms.

A Canadian estimate of the value of the ICC in this stage is: (1) that promptings and exhortation of the ICC kept the parties in touch with each other; (2) that the mere existence of the ICC prevented *overt* support of the Pathet Lao by the Viet Minh; (3) that it prevented escalation of small incidents; and (4) that by preparing agenda and outline plans for joint meetings, the ICC expedited solutions of specific problems.[62] In short, this troika, in the early period, worked moderately well.

But basically it is clear that in the prevailing circumstances the modified troika observation commission could not work in Laos. The ICC never achieved an effective cease-fire. It did not have free access to Communist

[62] Blais, *op. cit.*, pp. 130–31.

territory, and the fact that forty Vietnamese withdrew as compared to 1,069 Philippine and American military personnel suggests strongly that the observation worked on one side only.

The changes in the voting procedure of the ICC introduced by Article 15 of the protocol were minimal in effect. Even the advantage of having its own helicopters and other means of transport was canceled by Pathet Lao determination not to admit the commission teams to its territories.

The main objection to the troika principle for peace observation is that it is easy for one of the parties to frustrate the agreement.

Was the 1962 ICC for Laos less effective than the 1954 ICC despite the slightly enlarged powers, independent transport, and modified voting procedure? The answer is: "Yes." The reason the 1954 ICC was somewhat effective in its early stages was because the Communist side welcomed a breathing space. In 1962, the Communist side felt that it had the pro-Western elements in Laos on the run, and the Viet Minh stepped up its aid to the Pathet Lao in the hope of taking over the control of the country.

There remains to be considered the role of the Indian chairman. Like the other members, the Indian member felt that he represented his government. His government's policy was nonalignment in the cold war. In the 1954–1958 stage of the ICC, it seems that the role of the nonaligned member, balancing Communist and non-Communist members, made the Indian member reluctant to embarrass the Communist side. In the 1962–1963 phase, he joined the Canadian member in the majority reports. By this time, Chinese aggression against India had influenced Indian thinking, and it seems likely that, in the future, India might be "neutral on the non-Communist side." [63]

Peace Observation in Cambodia, 1954–1964

The ICC/Cambodia had the same general structure and functions as those provided for Laos and Vietnam.

The Cambodian experience differed from those of Laos and Vietnam in the following respects. The country was not divided, but there were border troubles with Thailand and Vietnam. Also there were Communist Viet Minh soldiers in the country, and a dissident rebel group known as the Khmer Resistance Force (KRF) had to be quelled and demobilized. There were also French forces there, holding over from the French reoccupation after the Japanese defeat in 1945. Further, the geographical position of the

---

[63] An evaluation of the reconstituted ICC in Laos as well as a memorandum on it from the viewpoint of the American Government appears in U.S. House Committee on Foreign Affairs, *International Commission for Supervision and Control in Laos*, Hearings before the Subcommittee on Far East and the Pacific, 88 Cong., 1 sess. (Washington: Government Printing Office, 1964).

country favored neutrality. Prince Norodom Sihanouk, in an article in *Foreign Affairs*, wrote:

> Our neutrality has been imposed on us by necessity. A glance at a map of our part of the world will show that we are wedged in between two medium-sized nations of the Western bloc [South Vietnam and Thailand] and only thinly screened by Laos from the scrutiny of two countries of the Eastern bloc, North Vietnam and the vast People's Republic of China. What choice have we but to try to maintain an equal balance between the "blocs?" [64]

The French Government did little to prepare the country to assume the responsibilities of independence that the Japanese proclaimed for it in 1945. French occupation in 1945 made Cambodia "an autonomous kingdom of the French Union," but real independence was still withheld causing a rebel force (Khmer Issarak) to operate from the border province in favor of a free Cambodia. These irregulars interfered with Ho Chi Minh's political activities in Cambodia, and he attempted to win them over. King Norodom Sihanouk was opposed to the Khmer Issaraks, and when his cabinet failed to take firm measures against them, he took the post of Prime Minister himself. In this capacity, he greatly influenced the content of the 1954 Geneva Agreements.

The most important military tasks of the ICC related to completing the demobilization of the Khmer Resistance Forces and securing the withdrawal of the French and Viet Minh forces.

Functions and Powers of the ICC. Article 13 of the Geneva Agreement defined the ICC's task as follows:

> The International Commission shall be responsible for supervising the execution by the parties of the provisions of the present Agreement. For this purpose it shall fulfil the functions of control, observation, inspection and investigation connected with the implementation of the provisions of the Agreement on the cessation of hostilities and shall in particular:
> (a) control the withdrawal of foreign forces in accordance with the provisions of the Agreement on the cessation of hostilities and see that frontiers are respected;
> (b) control the release of prisoners of war and civilian internees;
> (c) supervise, at ports and airfields and along all the frontiers of Cambodia, the application of the Cambodian declaration concerning the introduction into Cambodia of military personnel and war materials on grounds of foreign assistance.

The KRF had been demobilized well within the required thirty-day period. They were fully demobilized by August 22, 1954, but the ICC was not operational until August 11, and the joint commission not until

[64] Prince Norodom Sihanouk, "Cambodia Neutral: The Dictate of Necessity," *Foreign Affairs*, XXXVI: 4 (July 1958), p. 583.

August 20. "As a result," reported the ICC, "no supervision could be brought to bear on this operation which was carried out unilaterally."[65]

This development had three consequences: (1) The Cambodian Government did not believe that all KRF were demobilized. (2) It did not believe KRF representatives that all arms had been destroyed on the spot. (3) KRF personnel did not get their identity certificates to facilitate their reintegration into normal life.

The withdrawal of the French forces was also largely carried out before the ICC became operational. The withdrawal of the Vietnamese forces was more difficult because of the need for appropriate river craft. But by mid-October, the ICC evacuated the first 500 Vietnamese soldiers with an ICC team accompanying them down the Mekong. A few days later, nearly 2,000 more were sent down, thus terminating the Vietnamese withdrawal.[66]

The Cambodian Government stated its conviction that some former Vietnamese soldiers were still in Cambodia, having merged with the large Vietnamese minority living there. The ICC investigated this and found that no military units, either Vietnamese or Khmer Resistance, remained in the country, but it could not pass judgment on the charge of infiltration by individuals or small groups.

Article 6 of the Cambodian Agreement took note of the declaration of the Royal Government that it would take all necessary measures to integrate all citizens without discrimination into the national community. The ICC viewed this obligation seriously and recommended the widest publicity of this policy. The distribution of identity cards went slowly at the beginning, for many KRF were reluctant to trust the government; others preferred the life of banditry.[67] In its second progress report, the ICC continued to find deep-rooted suspicion on the part of the KRF and petty harassment by over-zealous local Royal Government officials.[68] During this period, border raids from South Vietnam continued, and arms caches were discovered from time to time by the Royal Government. Investigation by the ICC showed that the caches consisted almost entirely of unserviceable arms.

Thus by the end of 1954, nearly all the substantive military problems were settled. These were: cease-fire, demobilization and withdrawal of former enemy units, exchange of prisoners, and removal of mines. Entry of war materials had, as yet, presented no problem. It was in the political

[65] International Commission for Supervision and Control in Cambodia, *First Progress Report for the period ending December 31, 1954*, Cmd. 9458, p. 5 (London: HMS, May 1955). Hereafter cited as Cmd. 9458.

[66] Cmd. 9458, p. 6.

[67] Cmd. 9458, p. 7.

[68] International Commission for Supervision and Control in Cambodia, *Second Progress Report for the period January 1 to March 31, 1955*, Cmd. 9534, p. 5 (London: HMS, July 1955).

realm that the real difficulties of the ICC existed, and these were just beginning.

A difference arose in 1955 between the King and the ICC over the King's proposal to reform the electoral system in a manner that would change "the character of the legislature and the powers of the executive."[69] These reforms seemed incompatible with Article 6 of the agreement under which Cambodia had undertaken to allow all citizens without discrimination to enjoy all the rights and freedoms the constitution provides. The ICC held that it was guided by certain principles:

1. that the elections were to be pursuant to the Cambodian Constitution and laws;

2. that the ICC had no authority to supervise the elections as a whole;

3. that it did have to discharge its responsibilities to the former members of the KRF under Article 6; therefore, (a) the ICC had to examine the laws to be sure they provided secrecy of ballot; (b) it had to study the application of the laws of the country in regard to democratic freedoms so as to understand the scope of Article 6; and (c) it had to satisfy itself there was no discrimination against the former KRF members.[70]

It was a delicate task for the ICC to steer between seeming to interfere in internal affairs and supervising Article 6 of the agreement. During the ensuing campaign and elections, the ICC and its teams had to assure, without seeming obtrusive, that everything was conducted fairly.

A further problem arose for the ICC in connection with the U.S. agreement of 1955 to supply military aid to Cambodia. Objection was raised by North Vietnam, a signatory to the Geneva Agreement, that this military aid constituted interference and made Cambodia, in effect, an ally of the United States in the "SEATO aggressive bloc." But in July 1955, the ICC unanimously concluded that:

> Although it may still be argued that some of the clauses of the new Military Aid Agreement in terms go beyond the limitations imposed by the Geneva Agreement, the Commission accepts the assurances given by the Cambodian Government and is confident that in practice the receiving of aid under the new Military Aid Agreement will be in conformity with the terms of the Geneva Accord.[71]

Neither in this decision nor in the subsequent check on war materials imported into the country did the Polish member make any difficulty. The

---

[69] *Ibid.*, p. 13.

[70] International Commission for Supervision and Control in Cambodia, *Fourth Interim Report for the period April 1 to September 30, 1955*, Cmd. 9671, p. 8 (London: HMS, January 1956). Hereafter cited as Cmd. 9671.

[71] International Commission for Supervision and Control in Cambodia, *Third Interim Report for the period April 1 to July 28, 1955*, Cmd. 9579, p. 6 (London: HMS, October 1955).

Royal Cambodian Government cooperated fully, and the fixed team at Phnom Penh easily made the checks on entry of war materials.

Competence of the ICC. The question whether the ICC was competent to investigate border disputes between Cambodia and its neighbors to east and west—South Vietnam and Thailand—caused an open split between the Canadian delegate and his Indian and Polish colleagues.

In 1956, the Cambodian Government charged South Vietnamese soldiers with violations of border areas, as well as attempted occupation of certain Cambodian islands.[72] At that time, the ICC felt that this matter should be resolved by direct talks between the two governments. But in 1957, the Cambodian Government complained of repeated violations by South Vietnam, and again the ICC did nothing. The commission, however, decided by majority vote, the Canadian delegate dissenting, that it was competent to deal with a case involving South Vietnamese military personnel operating two and one-half kilometers within Cambodia and in which attack one Vietnamese was killed and seven others taken prisoner. The Canadian position was that the ICC's task was with hostilities in Indochina as of 1954, and that the Geneva Conference did not intend that the ICC should supervise and control frontiers.[73] The co-chairmen were asked for their views on this question, but apparently they never replied.

Meanwhile, the difference in view sharpened, and in July 1959, when the ICC made its seventh report, the major portion dealt with border violations along the Cambodian-South Vietnamese frontier. In December 1958, the Cambodian Government requested the ICC to send a team to its border with Thailand regarding concentrations of Thai troops near the border. The Polish delegate's motion to send such a team was outvoted by the other two, and by majority vote, it was decided to inform the Cambodian Government that the ICC was not competent to take any action regarding relationships between Thailand and Cambodia.[74]

With the failure of the ICC to deal with this border question, Prince Sihanouk, in the early 1960's, requested the United States, the United Kingdom, and France particularly to guarantee Cambodian borders, failing which he would appeal for protection to Red China.

Evaluation. Unlike the commissions in Laos or Vietnam, the commission in Cambodia seemed to work quite smoothly notwithstanding its troika structure. The first tensions in the commission arose when the

---

[72] International Commission for Supervision and Control in Cambodia, *Fifth Interim Report for the period October 1, 1955, to December 31, 1956*, Cmnd. 253, p. 19 (London: HMS, September 1957).

[73] International Commission for Supervision and Control in Cambodia, *Sixth Interim Report for the period January 1 to December 31, 1957*, Cmnd. 526, pp. 4, 7 (London: HMS, October 1958).

[74] International Commission for Supervision and Control in Cambodia, *Seventh Interim Report for the period January 1 to December 31, 1958*, Cmnd. 887, p. 4 (London: HMS, November 1959). Two subsequent reports indicate that the situation in Cambodia and within the ICC has not changed.

Canadian member moved for an early termination of the commission's functions. Canada was eager to limit its commitments in Indochina.

The substantive military problems were relatively easy. Most were settled before the ICC appeared on the scene, and the remainder were promptly dispatched. Even the political problems of reintegration of former KRF and observation of the national election went off well.

The Canadian member aptly characterized the difference between the ICC/Cambodia and the ICC/Vietnam and ICC/Laos after the first year's operation. On the occasion of the impending departure of the Indian chairman, Ambassador G. Parthasarathi, he said:

> Driving a troika, while good sport, is not always easy, and I should like to pay tribute to the skill, patience and understanding with which you have accomplished this sometime tricky task. . . .
> The history of Cambodia and this International Commission during the past thirteen months has been the success story of the Geneva settlement. A war and civil war have been ended, a single regime established throughout the national territory, and now, as a result of the recent elections, a government chosen by the vote of all the people has taken over direction of the nation's affairs. We can all . . . be proud. . . .[75]

It is true that later the ICC/Cambodia became as divided and moribund as were the others, but the split did not occur in a cold-war context. It arose as a result of Canada's desire to reduce its commitments. Canada, not Poland, was here in the minority. Surprisingly, the Polish member did not vote against the other two on the question of whether U.S. military aid was a violation of the Geneva Agreement.

The explanation for the relative success in Cambodia, as compared to relative failure in Laos and Vietnam, lies in the absence of any conflict between Communists and non-Communists within Cambodia and of any dispute involving a Communist state. Cambodia was not partitioned as Vietnam was in law and Laos was in fact. There was no domestic Communist organization seeking to overthrow the Cambodian Government. In border conflicts, a Communist nation was not pitted against a non-Communist nation. In conflicts involving only non-Communist states, even a Communist member of a troika can afford to appear impartial.

Peace Observation in Vietnam, 1954–1965

There are about thirty million people in both Vietnams (Tonkin, Annam, and Cochin China), somewhat more than half in the north. The two parts are complementary—the north being mainly industrial and the south agricultural. This basic geo-economic factor taken together with the emergence of several major political figures in the north and south has largely determined the issues with which the ICC/Vietnam has been confronted since 1954.

[75] Cmd. 9671, p. 63.

The French colonial administration remained relatively intact through World War II, but with Japanese support, the Emperor Bao Dai proclaimed Vietnam's independence in March 1945. After the defeat of Japan, the native combat forces in the north under the leadership of Ho Chi Minh proclaimed the Democratic Republic of Vietnam. For a short time the "playboy" Emperor served Ho Chi Minh as "supreme adviser." He then moved off to exile for some years, first in Hong Kong and then in France. Though the Communists led the Viet Minh, at the beginning, Ho Chi Minh's public declarations were full of references to the spirit of 1776.[76]

When Dien Bien Phu fell in 1954, Bao Dai offered the premiership to Ngo Dinh Diem, who had served as his Minister of the Interior in 1953. Diem had refused to collaborate with either the Japanese or, since the war, Ho Chi Minh. Now, however, he felt that his two conditions were met by both Bao Dai and the French. These were: (1) complete independence for the country; and (2) all power to Diem, including civil and military. Relations with the Emperor deteriorating, Diem called for a popular election, and in October 1955, by a vote of 98 percent, Diem became president with the right to govern by decree. His dictatorial powers were confirmed from time to time, until he and his brother, Nhu, were assassinated in November 1963 in the political disturbances following his struggle with the Buddhist majority of South Vietnam.

Diem was more of an intellectual than Ho Chi Minh, but both were strong-willed nationalists. Diem was as firmly committed to the anti-Communist cause as Ho was to the Communist. This cold-war background was the most vital feature in the restoration of peace to Vietnam; it was against this background and with these personalities that the ICC had to deal.

Though the cold-war background was also common to the other two ICC missions, the Vietnam situation differed in the following ways:

1. The country was partitioned, and this resulted in an enormous exchange of populations.

2. The number of combatants was much larger in Vietnam than in Laos or Cambodia, and hence the regrouping plan and exchange of prisoners were much larger operations.

3. The Viet Minh was not, like the Pathet Lao and KRF, to be disbanded and integrated into a national army; the Viet Minh was already a national army and would continue to be such.[77]

[76] The American University, Special Operations Research Office, *U.S. Army Area Handbook for Vietnam* (1962), p. 221.

[77] The Agreement on the Cessation of Hostilities in Vietnam was signed by the Vice-Minister of Defense for North Vietnam and by a representative of the French Union Forces in Indochina. The validity of the agreement was questioned by South Vietnam on the grounds that its representative had not signed it, and South Vietnam, therefore, was not legally bound. This attitude was later repeated several times.

The 1954 Geneva Accord. The two principal features of the 1954 agreement were the division of the country at the 17th parallel and provision for an early election with a view to unifying the country. In addition, there were provisions for a cease-fire, establishment of the demarcation lines and demilitarized zone, regroupment of the Vietnamese and French Union forces, exchange of prisoners, and movement of refugees.

The agreement also established an international control commission and a joint commission of the same general structure and composition as in Laos and Cambodia. Fixed and mobile teams to act as "the eyes and ears of the commission" were established in each of the two parts of Vietnam.

Duties of the Commission. Article 36 of the Agreement on Vietnam defined the duties of the ICC as follows:

> The International Commission shall be responsible for supervising the proper execution by the parties of the provisions of the agreement. For this purpose it shall fulfil the tasks of control, observation, inspection and investigation connected with the application of the provisions of the agreement on the cessation of hostilities, and it shall in particular:
>
> (a) Control the movement of the armed forces of the two parties, effected within the framework of the regroupment plan.
>
> (b) Supervise the demarcation lines between the regrouping areas, and also the demilitarized zones.
>
> (c) Control the operations of releasing prisoners of war and civilian internees.
>
> (d) Supervise at ports and airfields as well as along the frontiers of Vietnam the execution of the provisions of the agreement on the cessation of hostilities, regulating the introduction into the country of armed forces, military personnel and of all kinds of arms, munitions and war material.[78]

The headquarters of the ICC were provisionally established in Hanoi, and the commission made periodic visits to Saigon. Later, it maintained a second headquarters in Saigon. In August 1955, the commission transferred its function to Saigon.

The First 300 Days. Although delayed in getting started, the commissioned achieved a number of positive results in the first period of its activity.

The agreement provided that the cease-fire should become effective between July 27 and August 4 in three separate zones. Although the commission was not able to supervise these operations, cease-fire orders were obeyed and, with minor incidents, carried out on schedule. The agreement also provided that a five-kilometer demilitarized zone was to be established

---

[78] U.S. Senate Committee on Foreign Relations, *Report on Indochina*, 83 Cong., 2 sess. (Washington: Government Printing Office, 1954), p. 23.

along the 17th parallel as a buffer between the belligerents. From the record, there appear to have been no violations.[79]

The regroupment plan called for all French Union forces to be south of the demarcation line and North Vietnamese forces north of that line. Provisional assembly areas were designated, and a time limit placed on execution of the plan, which was to be completed in 300 days, while the moves into the provisional areas were to take only fifteen days. These transfers were effected ahead of schedule and without incident. But transfer of civil administration workers was more complicated, since it involved the dismantling of establishments and the possible removal of equipment. Transfers, however, were effected in an orderly manner in advance of the date line.

Under the agreement, prisoners of war and civilian internees were to be liberated within thirty days after the cease-fire. Approximately 65,000 were released by the French and 12,000 by the North Vietnamese. The principal causes of dispute involved discrepancies in figures.

Between October 1954 and July 1955, more than 900,000 Vietnamese left the Communist-controlled north to go with the refugees to the south, while some 5,000 persons moved in the reverse direction. Southbound refugees were aided by French and U.S. shipping. Most of these refugees were Roman Catholics who moved sometimes by entire villages. About half (400,000) were resettled in the delta areas of South Vietnam. The North Vietnamese objected to foreign ships entering territorial waters, and as a result tens of thousands of refugees floated out to the three-mile limit in boats or on makeshift rafts. The ICC facilitated the move by cutting red tape and getting food and medical supplies to the desperate refugees. In general, the ICC found that those who wished to move were able to do so. There were no forced evacuations, but the attitudes of local authorities were sometimes obstructive and narrow. No movement was permitted after the final date of July 20, 1955.[80]

On the freedom of movement of the refugees, the Canadian delegate took exception to views of the Indian and Polish members and condemned the atmosphere of fear and suspicion in North Vietnam, charging that this served to inhibit and restrict the free exercise of the right of option and was in itself an impediment to an effective investigation.[81] He said there was no problem of freedom of movement in South Vietnam until the closing of the 300-day period.

[79] International Commission for Supervision and Control in Vietnam, *First and Second Interim Reports, August 11 to December 10, 1954, and December 11, 1954, to February 10, 1955,* Cmd. 9461, pp. 13–14 (London: HMS, May 1955).

[80] International Commission for Supervision and Control in Vietnam, *Fourth Interim Report, April 11 to August 10, 1955,* Cmd. 9654, p. 15 (London: HMS, December 1955). Hereafter cited as Cmd. 9654.

[81] Cmd. 9654, p. 19.

Although the problem of guaranteeing the freedom of movement of over a million evacuees was enormous, there is no doubt that the ICC played a beneficent role in this operation.

Activities of the ICC after the 300-Day Period. The continuing tasks of the ICC related to the ban on introduction of fresh troops, military personnel, arms and munitions, establishment of new military bases and possible resumption of hostilities.

As previously mentioned, certain difficulties in carrying out these duties occurred in South Vietnam owing to its "categorical attitude" that it had "not signed the Geneva Agreement," that it was "not legally bound by its provisions" and that it was "opposed both to the Agreement and the Final Declaration."[82]

The commission could wind up its activities only after the termination of the provisional arrangements for civil administration, both north and south of the line, through a general election which would bring about the unification of Vietnam as envisaged in the final declaration. The failure to settle the political problems thus meant that the ICC was faced with the prospect of continuing indefinitely. As indicated above, this indefinite continuance would be without any sanction for its work so far as the zone under control of South Vietnam was concerned.[83]

A demonstration against the Geneva Agreement and against the commission's personnel occurred on July 20, 1955, at Saigon. Papers, clothing, cars, and equipment of commission members were seized by the demonstrators and destroyed. The Diem government did little to prevent this action.

The French High Command withdrew from South Vietnam on August 28, 1956, and with it went the French Liaison Mission that had provided the transport for the ICC in both North and South Vietnam. The joint commission collapsed, and for years the ICC pleaded in vain for the restoration of a mechanism that had saved it from so much detailed work. The ICC appealed to the co-chairmen who in turn appealed to the two Vietnamese governments to restore the joint commission, but they took no action.[84]

So far as a political settlement was concerned, "the Co-Chairmen requested the two governments to transmit their views regarding the time required for the opening of consultations on the organization of elections and the time required for the holding of elections to unify Vietnam."[85]

Henceforth, the South Vietnamese authorities would remain rigidly opposed to an election with a view to unification, while the North Viet-

[82] Cmd. 9654, p. 16.

[83] Cmd. 9654, p. 17.

[84] Canada, Department of External Affairs, *Sixth Interim Report, ICC Vietnam*, Supplementary Paper No. 56/5, p. 14.

[85] *Ibid.*, p. 71.

namese were constantly to demand it. The Australian Government correctly predicted:

> Progress toward nationwide elections is unlikely in present political circumstances, and it seems certain that the International Commission's effective role in Vietnam will be restricted to continuing the work in which it has already been most successful, that is, in the maintenance of the cease-fire.[86]

Increasing Non-Cooperation with the ICC. Although the South Vietnam Government in April 1956 announced its intention to apply the main provisions of the cease-fire agreement and to cooperate with the ICC, there was little evidence of a change in attitude. In its Seventh Interim Report, covering the period up to April 1957, the commission charged the South Vietnam Government with violations of the provisions on democratic freedoms and the introduction of fresh military personnel and equipment. The South Vietnam Government did not reply to the commission's communications or permit the deployment of mobile teams.

The ICC also complained that in North Vietnam it could not observe the application of the agreement owing to lack of cooperation of the People's Army of Vietnam (PAVN).[87]

Political Background to Present Situation. The period from 1955 to 1959 was one of relative peace between the two Vietnams. In the north, the Communists were busy consolidating their power through reforms and expropriation of foreign industrial establishments. In the south, President Diem overcame the resistance of the religious sects and built a strong, authoritarian regime.

Still smarting under his failure to get the promised nation-wide election in 1956, Ho Chi Minh began to instigate guerrilla warfare on a large scale in the south.[88] The Viet Cong had long fought in the mountains, jungle, and rice paddies; now they were moving into the towns and even threw bombs in Saigon itself. In 1954, the Viet Cong numbered 10,000; by 1963, there were 25,000 regulars and 100,000 irregulars. (It has been estimated that anywhere from 10 to 1 up to 40 to 1 of regular troops are necessary to control guerrilla troops.)

By 1961, it appeared that the collapse of South Vietnam was dangerously near. In that year, Vice President Johnson and General Maxwell Taylor visited Vietnam, and subsequently Defense Secretary Robert McNamara made several trips. Direct aid to Indochina had cost the United States $1.2 billion up to 1954. From 1954 to 1962, in Vietnam alone, U.S. aid amounted

---

[86] Australia, Department of External Affairs, *Current Notes on International Affairs*, XXVIII: 4 (April 1957), p. 282.

[87] Canada, Department of External Affairs, *Seventh Interim Report, ICC Vietnam*, Supplementary Paper No. 57/9, p. 15.

[88] For the U.S. Government's view of Ho Chi Minh's responsibility, see U.S. Department of State, *A Threat to the Peace: North Vietnam's Effort to Conquer South Vietnam*, Publication 7308 (1961). For an opposing view, see Wilfred G. Birchett, *The Furtive War* (New York: International Publishers, 1963).

to $2 billion and in 1964 was running at $400 million. In 1961, the decision was made to increase U.S. military manpower in an advisory capacity to Vietnamese troops. From 1961 to 1963, the U.S.-Vietnamese strategy was: (1) to win over the non-Viet mountaineers; (2) to regroup rural Vietnamese into "strategic hamlets"; and (3) to increase U.S. military assistance.[89] Success seemed near, and many senior American military advisers felt that in a year or two the Viet Cong would be defeated.

President Diem made the serious error of underestimating the importance of the Buddhist unrest, which broke out in Central Vietnam in May 1963. The conscience of the world was shocked by pictures of Buddhist priests burning themselves to death. The world's sympathy was heightened by the callous remarks of Madame Nhu, sister-in-law of the President. The United Nations sent a fact-finding mission to inquire into the treatment of the Buddhists.

Early in November 1963, Diem and his brother, Nhu, were killed. Major General Van Minh headed the provisional government for a short time; he in turn was overthrown by Major General Nguyen Khanh, although Van Minh remained titular head. Viet Cong activities grew even bolder. There was already a Communist-controlled "Nation-wide Front for the Liberation of South Vietnam," pretending to be a government. Attacks now took place on U.S. barracks, movie theaters, and homes in Saigon. President Johnson, following repeated trips to South Vietnam by Secretary McNamara, dedicated the administration to increased efforts to maintain a pro-Western government in South Vietnam.

Present Status of the Vietnam ICC. The latest regular report of the ICC/Vietnam is the Eleventh Interim Report,[90] signed by the three commissioners on September 18, 1961. It carries a monotonous recital of violations by both sides and their failure to cooperate. The split between the Indians and Canadians against the Polish commissioner is foreshadowed. When the Polish commissioner contended that the number of citations of violations should constitute the measure of noncooperation, the majority commissioners objected that many cases "have not . . . reached the stage of formal citations because of evasions and lack of cooperation on the part of the Party concerned. For this reason, the two Delegations agree that, in the experience of the Commission, the number of formal citations itself is no fair measure of the degree of cooperation received from either Party."[91]

This regular report was followed by a special report to the co-chairmen, signed June 2, 1962.[92] Here the ICC was deadlocked.

[89] U.S. Senate Committee on Foreign Relations, *Vietnam and Southeast Asia*, 88 Cong., 1 sess. (Washington: Government Printing Office, 1963), pp. 5–6.

[90] International Commission for Supervision and Control in Vietnam, *Eleventh Interim Report, February 1, 1960, to February 28, 1951*, Cmnd. 1551 (London: HMS, November 1961). Hereafter cited as Cmnd. 1551.

[91] Cmnd. 1551, p. 25.

[92] International Commission for Supervision and Control in Vietnam, *Special Report to the Co-Chairmen of the Geneva Conference on Indo-China, June 2, 1962*, Cmnd. 1755 (London: HMS, June 1962). Hereafter cited as Cmnd. 1755.

The ICC majority declared that the special report was "made necessary by the serious deterioration of the situation in Vietnam in recent months." The South Vietnam Government charged the North Vietnam authorities with aggression and subversion, while the North Vietnam Government charged the South Vietnam Government with receiving aid from the United States. The ICC charged both sides with deliberate refusal of access to its teams, leading to near-breakdown of the commission.

The Legal Committee of the ICC examined the allegation of subversion and declared that subversion would be contrary to the fundamental provisions of the agreement, which enjoin mutual respect for the territory assigned to the two parties. The Legal Committee made the following report:

> Having examined the complaints and the supporting material sent by the South Vietnamese Mission, the Committee [concludes] that in specific instances there is evidence . . . that armed and unarmed personnel, arms, munitions and other supplies have been sent from the . . . North to the . . . South with the object of supporting, organising and carrying out hostile activities, including armed attacks, . . . against the Armed Forces and Administration of the Zone in the South. These acts are in violation of Articles 10, 19, 24 and 27 of the Agreement on Cessation of Hostilities in Vietnam.
>
> In examining the complaints and the supporting material . . . sent by the South Vietnamese Mission, the Committee has come to the further conclusion that there is evidence to show that the PAVN has allowed . . . the North to be used for inciting, encouraging and supporting hostile activities . . . in the South, aimed at the overthrow of the Administration in the South. The use of the Zone in the North for such activities is in violation of Articles 19, 24 and 27 of the Agreement on the Cessation of Hostilities in Vietnam. [93]

The Polish member submitted a separate statement to the co-chairmen, [94] asserting that the picture presented by the Indian and Canadian delegations did not correspond with the real state of affairs. He declared that they were wrong to admit charges of aggression and subversion by Communist North Vietnam against South Vietnam; he held the Government of South Vietnam guilty of violations in concluding a military alliance with the United States, in the introduction of a great number of U.S. military personnel, weapons, and war material and in direct participation of the United States in hostilities. [95]

In a special report, dated February 13, 1965, the Indian and Polish members of the commission signed a majority report while the Canadian member appended a minority statement intended, as he said, to set events "in their proper perspective." The Indian and Polish members called attention to the recent bombings in North Vietnam by South Vietnam and

[93] Cmnd. 1755, p. 7.
[94] Cmnd. 1755, p. 21.
[95] Cmnd. 1755, p. 21.

U.S. aircraft but said nothing about the aggressive policies of North Vietnam against the south. The Canadian member felt it necessary to repeat the findings of the Legal Committee, cited above, and to add that there was mounting evidence to show that the aggressive activities since then had been greatly expanded obliging the Government of South Vietnam "to request increased foreign aid for self-defence." It was the considered view of the Canadian delegation that the events referred to in the majority statement were "the direct result of the aggressive policy of the Government of North Vietnam . . . aimed at the overthrow of the South Vietnam administration . . . in direct violation of the Geneva Agreement."

Evaluation. ICC/Vietnam is, in the words of Professor Bernard Fall, "almost but not quite dead."[96] He credits the ICC with being, even today, an obstacle to large-scale infiltration from the North. Whether this gives too much credit to the moribund and divided ICC, certainly the commission has value and is worth retaining as a means of communicating with Ho Chi Minh. Ho denies that North Vietnam gives any support to the guerrillas in the South. He declares that this is a civil war led by the National Front for Liberation and carried out by the South Vietnamese themselves. Some day, it may be necessary to communicate with Ho; he may want to live up to the 1954 Geneva Agreement, and in that case, the ICC might be of value.

To summarize, the effectiveness of ICC/Vietnam has been in direct ratio to the cooperation of the parties. From mid-1954 to mid-1956, while the French were still there, and there was a sort of grudging cooperation on both sides, the immediate, nonrepetitive military tasks were done reasonably well. These covered the cease-fire, respect for demarcation line and demilitarized zone, freedom of movement of the civilian population, and even exchange of prisoners.

Where the ICC failed to function was in its long-run military tasks: prevention of aggression or subversion and the ban on the introduction of fresh troops, military personnel, and equipment. In both Laos and Vietnam, the commissions worked reasonably well for a brief period, initially, with respect to nonrepetitive military functions but failed almost entirely in their political tasks.

PEACE OBSERVATION AND FACT-FINDING AND THE ANTARCTIC TREATY ANALOGY

Antarctica is an area as large as Europe plus the United States, difficult of access and human existence. In this vast area, there appears to be no indigenous population. The few people who are there are engaged in scientific exploration. During the summer of 1959, there were some 600

[96] Bernard B. Fall, "Our Options in Vietnam," *The Reporter*, XXX: 6 (March 12, 1964), p. 20.

American personnel. During the Antarctic winter the number dropped to 200. In the International Geophysical Year (1957–1958), the total participating from the various states did not exceed 5,000.

The U.S. interest in Antarctica dates back to the latter part of the eighteenth century. Its explorers and scientists, along with those from other countries, have discovered and mapped large areas of the continent. The United States has never claimed sovereignty over any of the discoveries by its nationals, nor has it recognized the claims of seven other states that have advanced sovereignty claims over large tracts, some of which overlap. This view of the nonrecognition of claims was stated by Secretary of State Charles Evans Hughes on May 13, 1924: "The discovery of lands, unknown to civilization, even when coupled with a formal taking of possession, does not support a valid claim of sovereignty unless the discovery is followed by an actual settlement of the discovered country."[97]

The International Geophysical Year was an extraordinary venture in cooperation. Some seventy nations were involved, and 40,000 scientists and technicians were distributed at 4,000 stations blanketing the earth from pole to pole. While each nation involved in the IGY venture carried out its own program, international cooperation on a global scale was carried out in an unprecedented manner. How to further and preserve this unique and far-reaching spirit and method of international cooperation became the preoccupation of U.S. officials and scientists. The Antarctic region, it was decided, was the appropriate area to apply some of the lessons learned in IGY and perhaps create precedents that might be applied in other areas of international cooperation.

After soundings and exploratory talks with the various governments participating in the Antarctic program of the IGY, the United States Government on May 2, 1958, delivered identical notes inviting eleven governments[98] to a conference in Washington to discuss the possibility of concluding an agreement in the form of a treaty that would have the following peaceful purposes:

A. Freedom of scientific investigation throughout Antarctica by citizens, organizations, and governments of all countries; and a continuation of the international scientific cooperation which is being carried out so successfully during the current International Geophysical Year.
B. International agreement to ensure that Antarctica be used for peaceful purposes only.
C. Any other peaceful purposes not inconsistent with the Charter of the United Nations.[99]

[97] Green H. Hackworth, *Digest of International Law* (Washington: Government Printing Office, 1940), I, p. 399.
[98] The eleven countries with whom the United States had taken part in the Antarctic programs of the IGY were Argentina, Australia, Belgium, Chile, France, Japan, New Zealand, Norway, Union of South Africa, the Soviet Union, and the United Kingdom.
[99] For text of the U.S. note see U.S. Department of State, *Bulletin,* Vol. 38 (1958), p. 911.

The note of invitation specifically stated that such a treaty would not require any participating nation to renounce whatever basic historic rights it may have in Antarctica, or whatever claims of sovereignty it may have asserted. Indeed, it could be specifically provided in the treaty that such basic rights and such claims would remain unaffected while the treaty is in force, and that no new rights would be acquired and no new claims made by any country for the duration of the treaty. Stating it in another way, the legal status quo in Antarctica would be frozen for the duration of the treaty, permitting scientific and administrative matters to be carried out in a constructive, cooperative manner without being hampered by political considerations. The note of invitation went on to say that:

> Such an arrangement would provide a firm and favorable foundation for a continuation of the productive activities which have thus far distinguished the International Geophysical Year; would provide an agreed basis for the maintenance of peaceful and orderly conditions in Antarctica during years to come; and would avoid the possibility of that continent becoming the scene of international discord.[100]

The responses to this invitation were favorable; the invited governments met in Washington from October 15 to December 1, 1959, and produced what is known as the Antarctic Treaty.

The participants originally invited included the group of powers making territorial claims in the general area of the Antartic, plus a number of powers which, through their scientific expeditions and association with the Antarctic, should justifiably participate in any arrangements that may he agreed upon to make a treaty effective. This does not exclude others who may adhere to the treaty if they qualify. The treaty reserves the legal position of the signatories, the need to protect the rights of non-signatories, and the need for effectively preserving the Antarctic for peaceful uses, as well as anything that might unduly limit the activities of genuinely scientific expeditions.

Article VII

The treaty consists of fourteen articles. Article VII, which deals with the problem of observation and inspection of the area, is of primary interest to this study:

> 1. In order to promote the objectives and ensure the observance of the provisions of the present Treaty, each Contracting Party whose representatives are entitled to participate in the meetings referred to in Article IX of the Treaty shall have the right to designate observers to carry out any inspection provided for by the present Article. Observers shall be nationals of the Contracting Parties which designate them. The names of observers shall be communicated to every other Contracting Party

100 *Ibid.*, p. 912.

having the right to designate observers, and like notice shall be given of the termination of their appointment.

2. Each observer designated in accordance with the provisions of paragraph 1 of this Article shall have complete freedom of access at any time to any or all areas of Antarctica.

3. All areas of Antarctica, including all stations, installations and equipment within those areas, and all ships and aircraft at points of discharging or embarking cargoes or personnel in Antarctica, shall be open at all times to inspection by any observers designated in accordance with paragraph 1 of this Article.

4. Aerial observation may be carried out at any time over any or all areas of Antarctica by any of the Contracting Parties having the right to designate observers.

5. Each Contracting Party shall, at the time when the present Treaty enters into force for it, inform the other Contracting Parties, and thereafter shall give them notice in advance, of

(a) all expeditions to and within Antarctica, on the part of its ships or nationals, and all expeditions to Antarctica organized in or proceeding from its territory;

(b) all stations in Antarctica occupied by its nationals; and

(c) any military personnel or equipment intended to be introduced by it into Antarctica subject to the conditions prescribed in paragraph 2 of Article I of the present Treaty.[101]

The right of observation and inspection is far-reaching. It includes the right to inspect ships, aircraft, and stations, and the right of overflight. During the negotiations and drafting of this treaty the United States insisted on the right to go anywhere at any time with any number throughout Antarctica to see whether it is being used for anything but peaceful purposes. The right to observe and inspect is given a priori by Article VII and does not depend on the consent of the individual signatories. The right of observation and inspection is unilateral. For the first time in history, a large area of the world is devoted to peaceful purposes with adequate inspection. It is also the first treaty that prohibits nuclear explosions in a prescribed area. Some have characterized it as possibly constituting a precedent in the fields of disarmament, prohibition of nuclear explosions, and the law of space.

In his statement before the Senate Foreign Relations Committee, Professor Philip C. Jessup, now a judge of the International Court of Justice, asserted: "It would put into practice for the first time a plan of demilitarization with free inspection in which the United States and the Soviet Union would both participate." He further stated: "In taking this step, the United States and the 11 other signatory nations may well create a precedent which could be used to great advantage as a pattern for

[101] U.S. Department of State, *United States Treaties and Other International Agreements*, TIAS No. 4780.

international cooperation which the United States seeks in connection with the exploration of outer space."[102]

Under the Treaty (Article I) all military measures, bases, and fortifications are banned. The testing of weapons and the disposal of radioactive wastes in the continent are likewise prohibited. The observers are nationals under the jurisdiction only of their own states. No other state may exercise any authority or control over them. Should disputes arise, they will be settled by peaceful means. Resort to the International Court of Justice may be had with the consent of the parties to the dispute. The treaty provides for consultative meetings of the twelve signatories to convene at suitable intervals and plan ways to carry out the treaty effectively. The regime of the treaty is to last for at least thirty years.

Does the unilateral national system of observation and inspection under Article VII prejudice the idea of international inspection? This question was answered in a colloquy between Senator Humphrey and Herman Phleger, chairman of the United States delegation to the Antarctica Conference, as follows:

Senator Humphrey. But the article relating to inspection does not only provide for unilateral inspection but also, if it is agreed upon, for a cooperative endeavor if the parties so desire.

Mr. Phleger. That is correct.[103]

As for possible mineral resources in Antarctica, Laurence M. Gould, chairman of the U.S. Committee on Polar Research, National Academy of Sciences, who has spent some time in the Antarctic region, told the Senate Foreign Relations Committee:

My profession is geology and I would not give a nickel for all the mineral resources I know in Antarctica. The point is we don't know and to predicate a program or to presume that vast resources are there is nonsense. We haven't examined 1 per cent of the area geologically. We have only scratched the surface of our ignorance. So that for many, many years to come, maybe as many as 30 years, the most important export of Antarctica is going to be its scientific data. And that is terribly important indeed. There is no single field of geophysics which does not demand for its completion data which can come only from Antarctica, because the geophysical phenomena in which we are going to continue on a global pattern are global in scope and we shall not know completely the weather in Washington, D.C., until we know the role that this icecap in Antarctica—which is as big as the United States and Europe combined —plays in it.[104]

[102] *The Antarctic Treaty*, Hearings before the U.S. Senate Committee on Foreign Relations, 86 Cong., 2 sess. (1960), pp. 46–47.
[103] *Ibid.*, p. 70
[104] *Ibid.*, p. 75.

Implementing Article VII

Unlike most of the peace-observation and fact-finding instrumentalities set up by international organizations or by multinational agreements, whose purpose has been to deal with already existing situations, this treaty attempts to prevent situations from arising that would be a breach of the obligation undertaken.

The peace-observation groups set up by the Security Council of the United Nations in such instances as Palestine, Kashmir, and the recent case of the civil war in Yemen, or the tripartite commission regarding the neutralization of Laos, have been international or multinational in character. In the Antarctica Treaty, however, observation and inspection is to be by national components of the signatories to the treaty. A team made up exclusively of one signatory is indeed a novel departure from the hitherto established observation instrumentalities. Here the observation group is entitled to inspect at will. The inspection is unlimited in the area below the 60° parallel, and it includes the right of overflight at any time. The observers are not confined to a special area nor to a specific object. It is observation or inspection in the real sense of the term. With twelve signatories to the treaty, it is possible to have as many as twelve national inspection teams engaged in observing and inspecting each other simultaneously and *ad liberum*. The institution of inspection and observation is unique and all-pervasive, and each of the twelve signatories has accepted a supplementary agreement incorporating the recommendations of the First Consultative Meeting held by the signatories on July 24, 1961. This agreement provides for the exchange of information through diplomatic channels as early in each year as possible, and in any case before the end of November each year, in accordance with Article VII, paragraph 5, of the treaty. The information should include:

(1) The names, types, numbers, descriptions and armaments of ships, aircraft, and other vehicles introduced, or to be introduced into Antarctica, and information on military equipment, if any, and its location in Antarctica.

(2) Dates of expeditions leaving for, and arriving in, Antarctica, duration of stay, itinerary to and from Antarctica and routes followed within Antarctica.

(3) The names, location, and date of opening of the Party's bases and subsidiary stations established or planned to be established in Antarctica, listed according to whether they are for summer and/or winter operations.

(4) The names of the officers in charge of each of these bases, subsidiary stations, ships, and aircraft; the number and occupations and specialization of personnel (including any designated by other governments), who are or will be stationed at each of these bases and subsidiary stations and on board these ships and aircraft, including the number of personnel

who are members of the military services together with the rank of any officers and the names and professional affiliation of personnel engaged in scientific activities.

(5) The number and types of armaments possessed by personnel.
(6) The programme of work, including scientific investigation, being done and planned at each of these bases and subsidiary stations and on board those ships and aircraft; and also the area or areas of operation to be covered by such programme.
(7) Principal scientific equipment.
(8) Transportation facilities and communication equipment for use within Antarctica.
(9) Facilities for rendering assistance.
(10) Notice of any expeditions to Antarctica not organised by the Party but organised in or proceeding from, the Party's territory.[105]

The information exchanged is designed, *inter alia*, to tie in with any inspection or observation that might take place by the national teams.

The First American Team under Article VII

The Department of State announced on September 13, 1963, that the United States would conduct an inspection in Antarctica during the 1963–1964 austral summer season (November–March). There was no crisis in the area when the announcement was made, nor was there any suspicion that the treaty had been violated. "Indeed," the announcement stated, "the United States believes that any inspection conducted under the treaty, whether by the U.S. or any other signatory power, will in fact reinforce the basis of mutual confidence that prevails in Antarctica."[106] This was to be no surprise inspection, for the United States Government gave notice to the other signatory powers of its intention to inspect many months in advance, and its action was fully within the explicit provisions of Article VII. The announcement concluded by saying that the United States Government had informed the other signatory powers that it would welcome inspection of its own stations in the Antarctic.

What were the motives underlying the announcement? Perhaps the main motive was to establish a precedent. During the hearings on the treaty in the Senate Foreign Relations Committee, the Department of State representative stated that the United States "contemplated" designating "observers who would see to it that the provisions were respected."[107] This, it was believed, was a commitment to the Senate Foreign Relations Committee that the department felt obliged to carry out. It was also felt that the time to initiate inspection was when there was

[105] See U.S. Department of State, *United States Treaties and Other International Agreements*, TIAS No. 5094.
[106] U.S. Department of State, *Bulletin*, Vol. 49 (1963), p. 513.
[107] *The Antarctic Treaty*, Hearings, p. 67.

no suspicion of a violation rather than on the occasion of a crisis. The timing of the announcement also might bring home to the Senate that the test-ban treaty, then up before it for advice and consent, did not mark a softening of U.S. vigilance.

Composition and Findings of the Inspection Team

The men who composed the inspection team were selected with great care. Out of a large panel, nine were chosen, who were given thorough physical examinations and extensive briefing sessions by highly qualified experts. Three members of the nine-man team (seven observers and two alternates) were experts in nuclear test detection and had served in the Advanced Research Projects Agency in the Department of Defense, which is responsible for devising new means of detecting nuclear explosions. There were two specialists in Soviet affairs, two with general Foreign Service experience, and two specialists in polar wildlife. Members of the team were outfitted with special clothing and equipment to meet the rigors of the Antarctic, with the Navy Department supplying the transportation and logistic support in the area.

The United States observers reported that they had inspected the Antarctic stations of Argentina, Chile, France, New Zealand, the United Kingdom, and the Soviet Union. The "attitudes of host Government personnel to the inspections were frank, helpful, courteous and in keeping with the already existing cordiality of international relations and cooperation in the Antarctic area."[108] Access was freely accorded to all facilities, and there were no prohibitions on examining equipment. The observers found no evidence of measures of a military nature, and no indication that Antarctica was being used for nuclear explosions or for the disposal of radioactive waste material.

The report concluded that "observations made by United States observers during the inspection of ten Antarctic stations indicated that the activities of the stations visited were being conducted in consonance with the provisions and spirit of the Antarctic Treaty. No evidence was revealed by these inspections which would indicate that Antarctica is being used for other than peaceful purposes."[109]

For the United States, this "adversary inspection" was historic and unique in an area where international harmony and cooperation prevail. There is no cold war there. Territorial claims have been placed in abeyance, and an extraordinary tradition of scientific cooperation has been established.

[108] U.S. Department of State, *Report of United States Observers on Inspection of Antarctic Stations—1963–64 Austral Summer Season* (May 1964), p. 1.
[109] *Ibid.*, p. 4.

Significance of Antarctic Treaty to This Study

Assuming the existence of an international agreement on disarmament in which peace observation and fact-finding play a role, what aspects of the observation and inspection provisions of the Antarctic Treaty can be identified as being useful for a study of peace observation and fact-finding?

There are fundamental differences between a regime of demilitarization in the Antarctic and an international agreement obligating the signatories to cut armaments by stages until the world is totally disarmed. Demilitarization in the Antarctic entailed no removal or reduction of arms on the part of the signatories. In agreeing to demilitarization in an area where none of the signatories had any strategic or security interests to protect or defend, no strategic or security interest was sacrificed. The parties gave up nothing by agreeing to demilitarization and to inspection. They merely imposed on themselves a self-denying ordinance prospectively. Such rivalry as existed in the area, largely of a scientific character, still remains; the treaty has not affected that. And the rivalry over territorial claims has been put into deep freeze for thirty years and perhaps longer. However, the treaty (Article III) in providing exchange of information regarding plans for scientific programs, scientific personnel, and scientific observations and results, encourages a degree of governmental cooperation hitherto unknown. It is believed by some that encouraging the habit of cooperation in this important field of science is bound to rub off onto other fields.

In the United States treaty proposal for general and complete disarmament, the strategic and security interests involved go to the root of the modern state system. The risks entailed are enormous and predicate a degree of mutual confidence in the world that has hitherto been lacking. Whether this absence of confidence can be overcome in whole or in part by a rigorous system of inspection and verification remains to be seen. But since this study presupposes a treaty for general and complete disarmament in stages, it is confined to the problem of creating a peace-observation and fact-finding instrumentality in that setting.

The function of observation and inspection in the Antarctic Treaty is carried out by national as distinguished from international or multinational observers and inspectors and is accomplished within the geographical limits set out in the treaty. The system of observation and inspection here is what is described as "adversary," permitting each signatory to the treaty to go wherever it likes and to observe and inspect whatever it desires. This is different from "impartial" or "objective" peace observation and fact-finding, which implies observation and fact-gathering by an international or multinational agency. Presumably, in a disarming world, the system of peace observation and fact-finding would be carried out by an international body. It is therefore unlikely that the concept in Article VII could be incorporated in a treaty on general disarmament.

It is conceivable, however, that a form of adversary inspection in peace observation might be desirable. At any rate, such a possibility should not be ruled out. Indeed, "adversary" peace observation in the United Nations framework might be suitable in certain situations.[110] Prior consent in this treaty is the most extensive ever set forth, and along with the concept of adversary inspection might be a preview of the new techniques in peace observation in a disarming or disarmed world.

[110] On the Greek-Bulgarian border in 1947–1948 the local commanders of both sides occasionally permitted inspection of each other's border, an inspection which can be described as "adversary" in character.

PART TWO

STRENGTHENING PEACE OBSERVATION

PREFATORY NOTE

THE STRENGTHENING AND INSTITUTIONALIZATION OF PEACE-KEEPING, including peace observation, is now widely regarded as an indispensable device in moving toward the control of violence in the international community. Moreover, an expanding role of the United Nations in the peaceful settlement of disputes and control of international violence can provide a more auspicious environment for steps leading to the limitation and control of armaments.

The increasing use of peace-observation machinery, and peace-keeping machinery as well, need not, however, await a disarming world. Nor indeed has it. The preceding analysis of the cases under the League of Nations, the Organization of American States, and the United Nations indicates that considerable progress has been made in peace observation notwithstanding the absence of advances in the field of disarmament. Under the United Nations, the experience in the field of peace observation shows an extraordinary and unexpected growth. But this is only a beginning. The further development and use of peace observation as an instrument in preventing or stopping hostilities and in assisting in peaceful settlement is clearly indicated.

Having examined the past experience of peace observation and fact-finding missions, the study turns to an examination of the future character and role of peace-observation arrangements under the United Nations now, in the near future, and under conditions of a disarming or disarmed world. It considers the establishment of a United Nations Peace Observation Corps, or the alternative earmarking of peace-observation units by the various member states of the United Nations, which would make such units promptly available for use by the United Nations. It examines such practical problems as the selection, training, size, and composition of standing or *ad hoc* peace-observation groups; terms of reference; procedures and methods of activating a peace-observation operation under the United Nations; reports and reporting procedures; and the relation of a peace-observation corps to international military peace-keeping operations.

Finally, in an Annex to the study, the authors have presented a detailed plan for the organization and equipment of a United Nations Peace Observation Corps including estimated costs of establishing and maintaining a standing corps of different manning levels.

1

——•——

AREAS AND SUBJECT MATTER OF PEACE OBSERVATION

Since 1920, peace-observation procedures have been used in every continent and in every part of the world. But the areas in which they have been most frequently applied have shifted as new national states were formed after two world wars, giving rise to disputed frontiers, minority grievances, rival territorial claims and, more recently, indirect or direct ideological aggression.

After World War I, Europe was the scene of the most active trouble because of the many new nations resulting from the break-up of old European empires. Thus the League of Nations sent commissions of inquiry or observers to the Aaland Islands, the Vilna area, the Saar, Albania, Upper Silesia, Corfu, Memel, Bulgaria, and Greece. In each of these cases, the issue turned on disputed or undelimited boundaries, or on rival territorial and irredentist claims. However, the League was also involved in other areas. It sent commissions to the Near East (Mosul) and also to the Chaco and the Leticia areas in South America and to Manchuria. Ethiopia requested a League Commission when Italy attacked, but no agreement was reached to send one before the war ended in Italian victory.

After World War II, and the break-up of the colonial empires in Asia, Africa, and the Middle East, these areas became the scene of United Nations attention. The situations in Palestine, Indonesia, Korea, Egypt, Kashmir, Laos, Lebanon, and Yemen have called for various forms of peace-observation running from a one man UN Presence, as in Jordan and Cambodia and Thailand, to guarding a 500 mile cease-fire line as in Kashmir.

As many of the boundaries in Africa are artificial creations often running through and separating tribal communities, there are now, and will be in the immediate future, many occasions for hostilities in this area. Internal stability in a number of these new countries is also very fragile, and the threat of civil strife always lies near the surface. It may be expected, therefore, that the continent of Africa will require the close attention and assistance of peace observation, both regional and international.

Similarly, the situation in Southeast Asia is far from stabilized. It can be predicted that the need for peace observation in any of its forms will arise with some frequency, as it already has in Laos, Cambodia, and Vietnam. And the extent and nature of its application will, as in the recent past, depend on the degree of cooperation the great powers give in permitting others to prevent a conflict, which none of them wish to see escalate into a major war.

In Latin America, both border and internal situations that call for international attention have continued to exist. The continent has unstable areas. But these situations have generally been handled through regional rather than League or United Nations action, and this seems likely to continue in the future. However, nearly all of the Latin American nations that are now members of the United Nations were also members of the League of Nations, and the latter assumed peace-observation functions in this continent within the scope of its Covenant obligations and limitations.

The prospect in the immediate future is that the United Nations will be less likely to operate in Europe and the Americas than in Africa and Asia. In Europe, the United Nations can offer a forum for contact and discussion, as it did in 1948 during the Berlin blockade, but none of the great powers seem prepared to accept any form of direct UN intervention at present. For example, the UN Representative was not permitted to visit Hungary after 1956. In the Americas, it seems likely that the OAS rather than the UN will be the chosen instrument for peace-observation operations.

Where regional peace-observation machinery is as developed as it is in the Inter-American System, resort to the universal UN system is not usually taken as a first recourse. Indeed the Charter enjoins other procedures to be used first.

The newly formed Organization of African Unity (OAU) has been cited by Africans as permitting them to deal with African problems to the exclusion of "outsiders." However, when the army mutinies took place in Tanganyika, Kenya, and Zanzibar, the "insiders" called in the former metropolitan power to help quell them.

One difficulty with this argument, however, is that so-called outsiders frequently have a close and direct interest in such developments in other continents. Prolonged instability, civil strife, and dictatorships stimulated and aided from the outside can make the situation one of major concern for countries outside the region or area, for example, Greece, Korea, Iran, Vietnam. Thus the precarious new balance of power has created a situation in which the great powers, particularly the United States, must be vitally concerned whenever a marked shift in the balance occurs or is threatening to occur in any part of the world. This claim, however, cannot be made exclusively by the United States. Other great powers may assert an equal interest.

This assertion of world-wide interest and concern has the effect of carrying an issue beyond the scope of a regional organization. The Charter provides that solutions should be sought first by the states directly involved, then if necessary with the help of the regional organization, if one exists, and only finally by the United Nations. It also provides that any member of the United Nations may bring any dispute or any situation to the attention of the universal organization. The OAS has quite generally and successfully followed the former pattern. As for the newly formed OAU, it is too early to judge what the development may be. It has made an auspicious beginning in the Algerian-Moroccan frontier dispute, and is playing a role in the frontier dispute between Somalia and Ethiopia.

Experience has not shown an altogether clear and generally accepted procedure on how soon or at what point recourse should be had to the universal organization, or when the latter should assume the initiative. It can be assumed that states tend to use one or the other agency—regional or universal—where they believe that their interests will be best protected.

SITUATIONS GIVING RISE TO PEACE OBSERVATION

An examination of the cases since 1920, where situations or disputes arose requiring international attention, shows that these cases usually involved (1) conflicting border and territorial claims, (2) dangerous internal disorders, (3) ideological and ethnic conflicts, (4) minority grievances, and (5) arms build-ups. Most of these situations resulted from the break-up of old nations, and the rise of new nations, following the two world wars. Cutting across and aggravating them has been the ideological conflict that has stalemated and rendered far more difficult the smooth functioning of the United Nations as compared with the League of Nations. The League, until the rise of the dictatorships in the 1930's, was in effect a European club of like-minded peoples.

Japan, Italy, and Germany, the territorial revisionists, rendered the League unworkable and brought about its demise. It remains to be seen whether the Soviet Union will permit the United Nations to function, except perhaps in special situations where it is willing to have the lesser powers act to prevent a more direct confrontation. The role in this connection of the middle powers, for example, Canada, Sweden, Yugoslavia, Finland, and India, as well as that of the Secretary-General has increased as the awareness of the effects of a nuclear war has grown.

Since the time when primitive men fought over their favorite hunting grounds, rival border and territorial claims have continued to be a principal cause of disputes. As the basis of social organization has evolved from the tribe to the nation, the intensity of the claims has not diminished. Nor with the emergence of the many new African and Asian nations has the number of such conflicting claims lessened. When the claim for acres is coupled with claims for the minds of the inhabitants of those acres, the problem becomes even more complex.

In 1920, the League of Nations handled the dispute between Sweden and Finland over possession of the strategically located Aaland Islands whose inhabitants were of Swedish language and culture and who requested the right to exercise self-determination. Shortly thereafter, a similar conflict arose between Poland and Lithuania over possession of Vilna; between Poland and Germany over the partition of Upper Silesia; between Albania and Yugoslavia and Greece over the undelimited frontiers of Albania; between Turkey and Iraq over possession of Mosul; between Greece and Bulgaria over the border of Macedonia; between Paraguay and Bolivia over the Chaco; between Peru and Colombia over possession of Leticia; between Japan and China over Manchuria; and between Italy and Ethiopia over possession of the entire country of Ethiopia. In all these cases except the last, the League used a form of peace observation, usually called Commissions of Enquiry, with positive results in most cases.

After World War II, between 1945 and the present, territorial disputes were the occasion for United Nations action in Indonesia, Kashmir, Palestine and Korea to cite several of the more outstanding cases. [1] Boundary troubles are active in Africa today between Ethiopia and Somalia, and Somalia and Kenya. Although these and several other frontiers in Africa are active or disturbed, there are fewer such cases erupting at the moment than was thought probable several years ago when the independence movement began.

Internal instability and disorder had several times led to great power intervention in former years, for example, in Haiti, Morocco, the Dominican Republic, and Mexico, usually to protect the lives and property of the nationals of the intervening power. But as international organizations have assumed increasing responsibility for dealing with such situations, and as international agreements and understandings have limited the right to intervene to protect their interests, overt unilateral action is no longer an acceptable method to use in such cases.

Where the internal situation is such as to require assistance, and if such assistance is requested, the United Nations, as in the case of the Congo, is available to organize administrative, technical, and military assistance, making it unnecessary as well as undesirable for one or more of the powers to supply it. The lessons to be learned from the Congo are important in this connection. Here it will suffice to point out that the UN Congo operation has set many precedents for future consideration. The degree of innovation

[1] See pp. 293, 357, 242, and 323 ff. above.

that was necessary to overcome seemingly insuperable difficulties may not need to be repeated in other cases. It is also pertinent to observe that there is a limit to the number of such cases that could be simultaneously dealt with under present conditions.

In 1936, Italy used the backward internal conditions in Ethiopia as a pretext for aggression. The League of Nations, and Ethiopia itself, conceded that social and economic conditions—health, education, communications, administration—were not good, but that this could not justify Italy's claim to take over the country. The League proposed, and Ethiopia accepted, a broad five-year program of technical and economic assistance that was designed to overcome the backward and unstable conditions there, a program similar to the economic program the United Nations is carrying out in the Congo.[2] Italy, however, rejected the plan as inadequate.

Other countries in Africa, particularly some of the newly independent countries, as well as others in South Asia and in South America have internal situations of backwardness, poverty, and instability that are a potential danger, and call for remedial action. Technical assistance and mutual aid programs, both on a bilateral and multilateral basis, are operating in many places, and while often inadequate to the needs, their purpose, *inter alia*, is to contribute to lessening the danger of flare-ups where peace-observation procedures might be required, especially when the interests of other countries are affected.

Tensions arising from the ideological conflict inherent in the cold war will continue to be an active or potential threat as far as one can see into the future. Even if the tension becomes less acute, dangerous situations will inevitably arise where peace observation can be a factor in preventing the spread of conflict.

Peace observation as envisaged in this study is only applicable in situations where the super powers, or the smaller powers under their influence, give their consent, or at least do not actively oppose such arrangements.[3] Thus, the main objective in peace observation is not to *impose* but rather to *interpose*, not to enforce a solution but rather to bring about a cessation of hostilities and create an atmosphere in which a temporary or permanent solution may be found. Indeed, in most of the cases analyzed in this study, particularly in the UN period, peace observation was considered successful when it helped to bring about a cessation of hostilities rather than a settlement, for example, Palestine, Korea after the armistice, Lebanon, and Kashmir. A principal purpose of peace observation since 1945 has been to keep violence from spreading and to encourage peaceful settlement. And in

[2] See the Italian-Ethiopian conflict, pp. 71–72, for details of this plan.

[3] See UN General Assembly, *Official Records*, Thirteenth Session, Annexes, Agenda item 65, A/3943, Oct. 9, 1958, pp. 8–33, in which the late Dag Hammarskjold discusses the basic principles of peace-keeping.

pursuit of this purpose the Soviet Union, by acquiescence, has on occasion given a form of assistance.

Only in one case, Korea, was a UN force used to repel Communist aggression. In all other cases where the ideological conflict was a major or an important factor, as in Greece and Palestine, UN observers have been used to effect an armistice, supervise disengagement lines and demilitarized zones, and thus to afford an opportunity, perhaps through mediation, for negotiating a settlement. In Cuba, at the time of the missile crisis of 1962, UN observers could have been used to verify the removal of weapons but would probably not have had functions beyond that.

Ethnic, religious, and ideological factors have created situations where peace observation assisted in preventing or suppressing hostilities, in supervising armistice agreements, or in mediating a settlement. The Middle East conflicts—Palestine, Cyprus, Kashmir—are examples. In this category are intertribal conflicts in various parts of Africa that were active in the past and are not far beneath the surface now.

Another active or potential source of trouble is the existence of minorities within a state whose grievances are unredressed, and sometimes supported by irredentists in neighboring states. The Aaland Islands case between Sweden and Finland in 1920 was such, and the Cyprus case today arises from this source. Plebiscites, transfers of territory, exchanges of populations, or partitions, have sometimes been used to remedy such conflicts but not always with success. The League Commission of Enquiry sent in 1920 to investigate the facts and claims of the Swedish people on the Finnish Aaland Islands recommended against a plebiscite on the ground that it is impracticable to grant self-determination to every minority in every state lest it lead to general instability and the break-down of the state system. Instead, the commission recommended that language and cultural guarantees be given by the majority, which was approved by the League Council, and accepted reluctantly by the disputants. But when the conflict reaches a certain point, as in Cyprus, the capacity for reconciliation becomes more difficult. UN mediation has not had many successes in this type of conflict situation.

The record shows that dictatorships are more likely than democracies to create conflict situations. In the Latin American area, nine out of sixteen disputes considered by the Inter-American Peace Committee between 1948 and 1963 were cases arising out of dictatorships.

Democracies are open societies and cannot easily or precipitously take steps leading to war. Parliaments and people must first be consulted and convinced, unless an unprovoked attack has taken place. But dictatorships per se not only can create threats, they also tend to become the objects of personal rivalry and hatred. As human rights are denied, people take asylum in foreign embassies, flee to neighboring countries and carry on propaganda to overthrow the dictator who in turn retaliates by counterplots and assassination plans. All of this makes for instability, and civil and at times international conflict. This has been the familiar record in Latin America and elsewhere.

A sudden change in the arms position of country X as compared with country Y has frequently given rise to increased tension leading to complaints of hostile intent laid before the international body of which both may be members. Arms build-ups are a symptom and a cause of existing bad relations, of distrust, and of insecurity whose roots are political and require a political solution. But, in the absence of a basic understanding there is danger of an arms race or direct action, and the greater danger of a brush-fire war escalating into a full-scale war involving allies. Thus the presence of increasing armaments in the United Arab Republic in 1956 was a factor in the direct action of Israel and led to the Suez crisis. The United Nations Emergency Force (UNEF) was stationed between the rival parties, and succeeded in preventing a resumption of hostilities. Similarly, the dispute between Peru and Ecuador in 1955 was in part occasioned by an imbalance in the arms levels of the two countries, requiring the attention of the OAS.

Observation procedures have been and can be timely and effective both in reporting on the facts, often distorted, and in helping to defuse an explosive situation. Their effectiveness, of course, depends on the range of their observations and the backing given to their effort.

NONUSE OR INAPPROPRIATE USE OF PEACE OBSERVATION

In this study some seventy cases have been examined where some sort of peace-observation or fact-finding missions were sent to troubled areas. It will be useful to note cases where such observation procedures were not used and where they were used belatedly or perhaps inappropriately.

In 1936 when Italy invaded Ethiopia, and even before the invasion took place, Ethiopia strongly urged the League Council to send observers to report on various Italian allegations. Although sending an observation group might have been useful, none was ever sent. Italy was strongly opposed, and other members of the Council apparently believed that their influence to restrain Italy would be lost if such a group were sent. At a later stage, the League Council had before it a proposal to send technical and administrative advisers to Ethiopia to assist in modernizing the country and thus to overcome some of the complaints made by Italy. Ethiopia accepted, but Italy again objected and none was sent. Italy was then determined to occupy and annex the whole country, and in the face of this policy, observers could probably have done little to thwart the Italian ambition.

Another case where peace observation was not used occurred in 1959 when the Dominican Republic lodged a complaint against Cuba. No action was taken because of the widespread reluctance of the other members of the

OAS to come to the assistance of the unpopular Trujillo dictatorship. When India invaded the Portuguese enclave of Goa in 1960, Portugal brought the case to the United Nations Security Council. Prior to the invasion, Portugal proposed to India the sending of a peace-observation group. India did not respond to the proposal, since it was poised to strike at Goa and was not disposed to change its course.

The record also shows cases where peace observation was organized and sent to the spot too late to be effective. The Lytton Commission, sent to the Far East in 1931 to observe and report on Japanese aggression in Manchuria, arrived there seven months after hostilities had begun. By that time, the Japanese were in effective control of practically the entire province, and the commission could do little more than give a historical account of how the trouble started, what the issues were, and how Japan and China might regulate their relations by a series of new agreements. Many of the smaller states considered that this, in effect, amounted to a condonation of the Japanese aggression.

A government may be tempted to internationalize an internal conflict in an effort to achieve a specific end that may serve its purposes. While some internal conflicts, such as civil war, may hold dangers for the international community, the United Nations should be on guard that its proceedings are not abused. In the Lebanese case, for example, the government complained of infiltration and external threats from the United Arab Republic and sought help from the United Nations. The peace-observation group that was sent reported that the trouble was mainly from indigenous rebel groups opposed to President Chamoun's effort to continue in office beyond the time permitted by the Lebanese Constitution. Following the election of a new President, the rebellion ended.

An analogous situation of possible abuse of UN procedures arises when attempts are made to internationalize an essentially domestic matter contrary to Article 2(7) of the Charter. For example, the South Africans have contested the jurisdiction of the United Nations in considering the question of apartheid, a question brought before the Organization by the Afro-Asian members.

The Korean situation from 1947 to 1949, in some respects might be considered an ineffective use of the peace-observation function. It was proper for the United States to bring the Korean question to the attention of the General Assembly in 1947. The General Assembly proposals, however, depended for their effectiveness on the cooperation of both sides. When it became apparent that Korea was an area of great power confrontation and that Communist cooperation would not be forthcoming, it might have been preferable for the United Nations Temporary Commission on Korea (UNTCOK) to discontinue its operations rather than to carry on a different operation from that contemplated by the General Assembly. Two years later, the terms of reference of the United Nations Commission on Korea (UNCOK), the successor of UNTCOK, were broadened to include observation of any military build-up across the border in North Korea. UNCOK's main usefulness was in connection with this function, which could be carried out without Communist cooperation.

THE APPLICATION OF PEACE OBSERVATION

A special problem is sometimes presented in the application of peace observation when the case is already being dealt with on a bilateral basis or by a multilateral regional agency and one of the parties hopes to improve its position by bringing the case before another perhaps wider international body such as the United Nations. Such a situation existed in the early stages of the dispute between France and Algeria. Interested states sought to bring the case before the United Nations, while France considered the matter was essentially within its domestic jurisdiction and should be dealt with on a bilateral basis. Similarly, South Africa objected to having the complaint of India regarding the treatment of Indians in South Africa brought up in the United Nations on the ground that there was a treaty between India and South Africa that provided methods for regulating outstanding differences, and its possibilities had not yet been exhausted.

In the early stage of the Cyprus conflict, Great Britain, Greece, and Turkey, parties to the agreement setting up Cyprus as an independent state, sought to find a solution while the Government of Cyprus itself wished to bring the matter before the United Nations. Since Britain, Greece, and Turkey were members of NATO, it seemed to the NATO powers that the matter should be dealt with there. Eventually, however, Cyprus succeeded in bringing the matter before the United Nations, and an international force was sent in to assist in separating the combatants and in maintaining order, with a mediator appointed to seek a solution.

Some overlapping and interjurisdictional misunderstandings have also arisen between such regional bodies as the OAS on the one hand and the League of Nations and the United Nations on the other. Thus the Chaco dispute in 1933 was dealt with by the League of Nations, which sent a commission to the area. Later, however, when the OAS was created, the issue was considered under inter-American auspices, which eventually succeeded in bringing about a cessation of hostilities. In the Leticia dispute between Colombia and Peru in 1933, Colombia appealed to the League of Nations Council after attempts by Brazil and the United States to mediate the dispute had failed. A commission under the League was sent to administer the disputed area for a year during which the disputing parties were to negotiate a settlement. The plan was supported by the Latin American republics and the United States; no jurisdictional difficulties arose during the League's administration.

The cold war, as noted previously, has in a number of instances had the effect of preventing or partially frustrating peace-observation activities in situations where such observation would normally have been indicated. No peace observation has been possible in Eastern Europe where uprisings were ruthlessly suppressed by outside intervention. For example, in Czechoslovakia and particularly in Hungary, there have been situations where peace observation might have brought about a wholly different result. United Nations observation was able to control the northern frontier of Greece against invasion by guerrilla or other forces from Albania, Yugoslavia, and Bulgaria. It has not been possible, however, to use this device in the satellite states closer to the Soviet Union. Nor was it used in the 1962 Cuban affair. The attempt to get an investigation and report on the situation in Hungary by various General Assembly instrumentalities was prevented by Hungary backed by the Soviet Union. On the other hand, in the more distant area of Indochina, multinational commissions composed of Canada, Poland, and India were able to carry out observation functions agreed to outside the framework of the United Nations.

As the cold war has somewhat abated, the Soviet Union has abstained instead of vetoing some United Nations functions such as those exercised in Lebanon, Yemen, and Cyprus. There is reason to hope therefore that, in areas outside the Soviet sphere, increasing use might be made of peace-observation procedures, particularly when requested by the parties immediately concerned.

The late Secretary-General, Dag Hammarskjold, in the delicate and difficult situation between East and West as reflected in the Security Council, was at great pains to select and compose peace-observation bodies so that they would reflect the utmost detachment, impartiality, and neutrality. For this reason, he avoided including members from the great powers. Instead he relied heavily on persons chosen from the so-called middle powers—including Canada, Sweden, Brazil, and India.

2

AUTHORITY AND TERMS OF REFERENCE

In reviewing the cases of peace observation in the League of Nations, the Organization of American States, and the United Nations, it will be apparent that the specific grants of authority depend largely on the circumstances of the individual case. On the other hand, there are certain generalizations applicable to most situations, usually observed but occasionally disregarded, both under the League of Nations and under the United Nations, with adverse results.

548 STRENGTHENING PEACE OBSERVATION

INITIATIVE FOR PEACE OBSERVATION

Under the United Nations Charter, disputes that endanger the main-tenance of international peace may be brought to the attention of either the Security Council or the General Assembly by either or both parties to the dispute, by a third party, or by the Secretary-General. It is suggested that regardless of who initiates the peace observation, all parties to the controversy and the Secretary-General should be consulted prior to establishing the mission or framing its terms of reference.

Peace-observation missions may be established either by a regional organization, by the United Nations, or by special arrangements involving the parties directly concerned and perhaps other interested states. The latter procedure should be reserved for the exceptional circumstance where there is virtual unanimity on the necessity of the mission and where its success is within the control and resources of a few states. An example of a successful arrangement of this nature was the evacuation of Chinese National-ist troops from Burma in 1953 and 1954.

A regional organization should be used wherever the situation endanger-ing international peace is confined to states that are members of the regional organization and are willing to use it. The Arab League obviously could not deal successfully with problems involving Israel nor did it deal effectively with the Middle East crisis in 1948. The Organization of American States at this juncture cannot conduct peace-observation activities in Cuba.

Within the United Nations, the Secretary-General should not initiate a mission without authority from the Security Council or General Assembly except on occasions where both parties wish the Secretary-General to assume the initiative; and the mission will probably be successfully accom-plished in a short time and with minor costs; or the emergency is such that the Secretary-General must act prior to the convening of the appropriate United Nations organ. In other circumstances, the initiative of the Secre-tary-General is likely to be repudiated by one of the permanent members of the Security Council or by a bloc of smaller states, with adverse results, even if the Security Council or the General Assembly later assumes responsi-bility.

The Security Council as the organ with primary responsibility for the maintenance of international peace should be used for peace-observation missions wherever possible. The General Assembly could be used where the conflicts of interest between the great powers result in ineffective Security Council action because of the great power veto. However, direct confronta-tions of the great powers will usually be unsuitable for peace-observation missions. It follows that the situations where the General Assembly rather than the Security Council initiates the peace-observation mission will be few, that is, the situations involving conflicts among the great powers not amounting to great power confrontation.

AGREEMENT OF THE PARTIES

Neither the United Nations nor any regional organization is likely within the foreseeable future to be set up in such a manner that they can compel states to comply with their decisions. Therefore, the action of states to comply with decisions concerning peace observation and to cooperate with peace-observation missions will depend mainly on moral sanctions. Moral sanctions are most effective if the parties to a controversy agree to permit the peace-observation mission to operate within their respective territories. In this way, failure to cooperate will be a clear breach of the agreement. Such an agreement of the parties would supplement the recommendation of the United Nations or other international organization, which could either precede the agreement or confirm an agreement already obtained. Thus, the violator would be flouting both his own agreement and the recommendation of an international organization.

The agreement of the parties to permit peace observation within their territories and to cooperate with peace-observation missions may be of three types: (1) an *ad hoc* agreement applicable to a specific limited operation or activity; (2) a status agreement such as that existing between the United Nations and Egypt in connection with the operations of UNEF;[1] (3) a universal agreement might be included within a disarmament treaty, by which all states would permit peace observation within their respective territories on a determination by an appropriate organ of the United Nations that such peace observation should take place.

It is fundamental that neither party shall be in a position to limit the mission's activities by revoking a part of the agreement to permit the mission to carry on its activities and thus place obstacles in its path. This is considered in the following section.

The absence of agreement of both parties to peace observation does not necessarily destroy its effectiveness. The peace-observation operation in the Balkans produced excellent results even though the observers were confined to the Greek side of the border, and peace observation south of the 38th parallel in Korea established the aggression of the Communists operating in the north. In the future, some peace-observation missions might even be effective without agreement of either party to a controversy by using new techniques of detection.

TIMING OF INITIAL GRANT OF AUTHORITY

Most peace-observation missions derive their authority from the original resolution of an international organization establishing the mission. While it is always possible to increase or alter the authority of the mission after its

---

[1] The status agreements covering United Nations personnel would be generally applicable to peace-observation missions under the United Nations, but would not cover most of the day-to-day problems confronting the peace-observation mission.

establishment, and in a number of instances this has been done,[2] it is more satisfactory to grant adequate authority to the mission in its original terms of reference before the mission proceeds to the area. The parties are more likely to acquiesce in satisfactory terms of reference at the outset when world attention is focused on the controversy.

Therefore, defining the terms of reference of a mission is likely to be one of the first tasks of the international organization. The importance of this task underlines the necessity of careful study and negotiation with the interested parties. This is time-consuming.

On the other hand, successful peace observation often depends primarily on early and speedy action. If the peace-observation mission can get to the scene before conditions deteriorate too far, its chances of success are greatly enhanced. Examples of the importance of speedy action are: the League of Nations handling of the Greek-Bulgarian border dispute; the presence of United Nations observers at the 38th parallel when the North Korean forces attacked the Republic of Korea; the rapid dispatch of UNEF to Palestine at the time of the Suez crisis; and the speedy action to meet the Lebanese crisis in 1958. There are many examples both in the League of Nations and the United Nations where failure of timely and effective action adversely affected world peace—Manchuria, Ethiopia, Palestine.

In the Cyprus case, in the interest of timely action, the Security Council adopted a resolution containing considerably less than the optimum terms of reference. In each situation, the international organ must strike a balance. When the crisis demands immediate action the problem is: how far should the organization go, and how long should it take to perfect the arrangements for peace-observation?

ENUMERATION OF TASKS

The terms of reference should be broad enough to permit the peace-observation mission to carry on all activities reasonably necessary for efficient peace observation.

Ordinarily the League of Nations commissions of enquiry acted pursuant to broad resolutions giving them full authority to accomplish the objective of the mission. Under this authority, the League of Nations missions would proceed to the scene and use the most suitable means for obtaining their information.

Examples of too narrow terms of reference during the League of Nations period are in the controversy between Lithuania and Poland over Vilna, and in connection with the Lytton Commission on Manchuria, which could study and report but had no power to control military movements, initiate negotiations between the parties, or settle the dispute.

[2] For example, Mosul, Indonesia, Palestine, and Yemen.

The OAS missions likewise have had broad general terms of reference that have enabled them to send military observers to the field when necessary or to rely merely on interrogating witnesses if that appeared to be sufficient.

United Nations practice has varied greatly. There have been a number of instances where the terms of reference were so specific that the missions exhausted them without denting the problem, for example, the Security Council Balkan Commission. In other instances, the terms of reference have been so indefinite that the parties were in a position to contest the jurisdiction of the mission to carry out essential activities, as in Indonesia and Palestine.

In the United Nations period, one example of inadequate terms of reference was in connection with the Good Offices Committee in Indonesia, which the Dutch contended was not even permitted to make recommendations to the parties unless requested to do so by both parties. Another example relates to the armistice arrangements in Palestine, where neither the Chief-of-Staff of UNTSO nor UNTSO itself had adequate authority when the Mixed Armistice Commissions failed to agree.

As a result of these experiences, it is suggested that the terms of reference should so far as possible state the objective of the mission clearly, in broad terms. They should also specify the anticipated activities of the mission so far as they can be foreseen.[3] However, the list of activities should not be exclusive, and the mission should have a residual authority to carry on other types of activities reasonable for the achievement of its objectives. In general, this conforms closely to the League practice, which seems superior to the practice of both the OAS and the UN. However, it was unquestionably easier for the League than for the United Nations to obtain the consensus needed for such practices. The detailed methods of operation, in contrast to the statement of activities, should ordinarily be included in status agreements rather than in a resolution establishing the mission.

The nature of the mission may change radically during its operations. So far as this can be foreseen, provisions for phasing the mission operations should be included within the terms of reference. In any event, the possibility of changing the terms of reference should not be foreclosed. The experience in Korea and the Balkans indicates that the changes in the terms of reference should be made by the organ establishing the mission and should not be delegated by that organ to a subsidiary group.

RELATION OF MISSION TO INTERNATIONAL ORGANIZATION

It is clear that the terms of reference should provide for expeditious access by the mission to the international organization establishing it.

[3] See "Chief Tasks," pp. 558 ff.

There will be many occasions for such access—if either or both parties are hindering the activities of the mission or if there is a change in the political circumstances requiring the mission to transmit progress reports. In practice, the easiest access to UN organs by missions in the field has been through using the facilities of the Secretary-General. The mission chief will normally report to the Secretary-General, who will take action in the United Nations. This procedure has advantages in addition to expediting action by the United Nations. Many mission reports must remain classified. This, in effect, is impossible if they are submitted to the United Nations organs. However, the Secretary-General has successfully maintained the secret classification of military data submitted to him by both India and Pakistan in connection with the Kashmir dispute, a fact that has greatly enhanced the effectiveness of the peace observation.

While communication between the mission and the United Nations should ordinarily be through the Secretary-General, situations could arise where the Secretary-General might hold a contrary view, and the mission chief might wish to communicate with the United Nations organ to which he is responsible. It seems essential, therefore, that there be a right of direct access from the chief of mission to the United Nations organ. This would not apply where the mission is solely the creature of the Secretary-General.

As stated elsewhere in this study, missions consisting of an individual or individuals have been more effective than those consisting of representatives of states. However, the mission may wish to have the advice of representatives of states without going through the formalities of bringing each individual item to the attention of a United Nations organ. This can be achieved by the establishment of an advisory committee of representatives of states reporting to the Secretary-General. This procedure has been followed in connection with UNEF and UNOC. In summary, the channels of reporting should be specified in detail in the terms of reference.

TERMINATION OF MISSION

The United Nations experience has made it clear that wherever possible a time limitation should be set for the duration of the mission. In the absence of a time limitation, the missions may be unduly prolonged. The growth of vested interests in the status quo may arise not only within the mission but also within the governments of the parties to the controversy. This experience also reflects the basic difficulties of reaching peaceful settlements that would make the peace-observation missions unnecessary. In some cases, the establishment of a time limit for peace observation might be an incentive for a peaceful settlement of the case. It must be recognized, however, that in many cases the necessity for peace observation will continue after the expiration of the specified time limit. Then the United Nations is confronted with the necessity of further procedures to extend the life of the mission. The Yemen situation is an excellent example of this latter problem.

The terms of reference could in effect limit the duration of the mission in any of the following ways: (1) providing a specific time limit; (2) limiting the funds available for the mission; (3) providing for the termination of the mission on the request of either or both parties; (4) permitting the mission to determine whether its functions should continue beyond a specified time.

Despite the general desirability of indicating in the terms of reference the duration of the mission, no useful purpose is served in setting a termination date that cannot be met.

3

PEACE OBSERVATION AND COOPERATION OF THE PARTIES

The most effective peace observation takes place with the consent and cooperation of the country or countries directly concerned. Peace observers by definition go into a conflict situation to interpose rather than to impose. They assist in bringing about a cease-fire and in separating the combatants behind agreed lines. They help to establish and oversee neutral or demarcation zones between conflicting forces as in Kashmir. In short, they represent the will of the international community that hostilities should not be permitted to endanger the peace of the world. Peace observers with their United Nations flags, arm bands, and other symbols represent on an international plane the symbol of the mace used in many parliamentary bodies when disorder threatens to obstruct deliberation and orderly debate.

Action taken under Chapter VII of the Charter involves imposition or enforcement after a finding of a threat to the peace, breach of the peace, or act of aggression. Peace observation as an aspect of peace-keeping could be legally imposed. It appears possible also to carry out a limited form of compulsory peace observation under the investigative provisions of Article 34 to which members of the United Nations have in effect given prior consent in adhering to the Charter. However, the United Nations has not yet directed compulsory peace observation, even where, as in Palestine and in one phase of the Greek border situation, the Security Council had already made the preliminary decisions.

WITH THE CONSENT OF ALL PARTIES

In most cases since 1920, peace observers or commissions of inquiry have operated with the consent, if not always the full cooperation, of the countries concerned. This was particularly true under the League of Nations. Consent was most readily given when hostilities had not yet broken out. For example, in the Aaland Islands dispute between Finland and Sweden in 1920, both countries consented to the request of the League of Nations for an investigation on the spot of the dispute, even though Finland was convinced that the League had doubtful competence to operate within its domestic jurisdiction. In the Leticia case between Peru and Colombia in 1933, Peru objected to an international commission coming into the territory, and its consent was only obtained after a change of government. In a recent United Nations case, Lebanon, where the observation was wholly within the territory of one state, consent was with difficulty secured from those within the state who were opposed to the government.

The late Dag Hammarskjold in 1958, basing his view on the experience gained by the United Nations in Greece, Korea, Egypt, Lebanon, and Jordan—particularly on the experience of the United Nations Emergency Force—asserted that in practice the United Nations cannot undertake to station units on the territory of a member state without the consent of the government concerned. This consent, it should be pointed out, applies both to peace-keeping and to peace observation. The United Nations observations in the Middle East have conformed to these basic rules, and they hold valid for all similar operations in the future.

Before the establishment of UNEF, peace observation in Palestine had been seriously handicapped because consent to the peace-observation operations, derived from the various armistice agreements, was in many important respects inadequate to permit an effective operation. UNEF supplemented the already existing peace-observation machinery on the Israel-Egypt armistice demarcation line.

Israel, although it withdrew its forces from Egypt, has never agreed that the Emergency Force should operate on its territory even though the United Nations approved that it be placed "on" the armistice demarcation line. Israel's non-cooperation, however, has not been carried to the point of obstruction. The consent of Egypt was only secured when the United Nations, through the Secretary-General, agreed that contingents from certain countries would not be used. As a result, UNEF is composed of contingents from nations sympathetic to UN objectives, which at that time supported the Egyptian position.

A more important problem was whether Egypt would have the right to terminate UNEF. Egypt and the United Nations reached agreement that under the status agreement only the United Nations could terminate UNEF, but that the Organization would take into account the opinion of the host state. If Egypt as the host state decides unilaterally to terminate the status agreement, it is difficult to see how UNEF could remain in Egyptian territory. However, it is clear that Egypt cannot limit UNEF's powers so long as the force continues to exist. Despite these limitations, the existing consent of Egypt as expressed in the status agreement is far more comprehensive than the consents under which most UN peace-observation missions operate.

This problem of securing the cooperation and consent of the host state or states gave much concern to the late Secretary-General, who recommended that a valid basis for future arrangements of a similar kind might rest on an exchange of letters as in the case of Egypt where both sides undertook to "be guided by good faith in the interpretation of the purposes of the Force." It was agreed that if any differences should arise regarding this bilateral declaration "an exchange of views would be called for towards harmonizing the positions."[1] The consents are much stronger where, as in Kashmir and in UNEF, they are supported by status agreements.

A more difficult situation appears to exist in a case like the UN observation group in the Yemen, 1964, where the consent of the parties directly concerned was secured for a limited form of observation, but was also made dependent on the financial support of the two parties, which if terminated would affect the nature of the operation.

WITH THE CONSENT OF ONE PARTY

Although the consent and cooperation of the parties directly concerned is necessary for the full success of the observation, there are a few cases where observation activities were carried on when only one of the parties agreed. Thus in the dispute in 1921 between Albania and Yugoslavia regarding the demarcation of the frontier, a League Commission acted on the Albanian side without the cooperation of Yugoslavia. In the Manchurian case in 1931, China was willing to support a commission of enquiry from the beginning, but Japan consented only after some months had passed. The result was that the Lytton Commission got on the scene after much delay, and its work, although still valuable, was hampered by the initial opposition of Japan. The United Nations Special Committee on the Balkans had to operate only in Greece in observing the infiltration across the frontier from Albania, Yugoslavia, and Bulgaria. Similarly, in the various United Nations Commissions dealing with the Korean problem

[1] UN General Assembly, A/3943, Oct. 9, 1958, pp. 63–64.

before 1950, the activity was greatly hampered by the lack of cooperation of one of the parties. However, in both the Greek and Korean situations, the results amply justified peace observation conducted on only one side of the border. The Greek case, in contrast to the Korean case, underlined the wisdom of planning in advance for peace observation with the cooperation of only one party.

WITH INTERMITTENT COOPERATION

In certain instances, peace-observation activities enjoyed only the intermittent cooperation of the parties concerned, thus rendering the observers' work more difficult. Thus, for example, when the League attempted in 1921 to deal with hostilities between Poland and Lithuania over Vilna, there was cooperation at first with Lithuania, which was later withdrawn on the ground that a treaty had been made with Russia promising that no foreign troops would be brought into the Vilna area. On the Polish side, the cooperation was only half-hearted since the Polish Government did not feel able to disavow the action of the Polish general who led irregular forces into the area. As a result, the outcome was decided by superior Polish military force rather than by a reasoned international settlement. More recent examples of intermittent cooperation are shown in the United Nations truce operations in Palestine. Similarly, in Indonesia and Indochina, the observation activities have been hampered by changing attitudes of the parties directly concerned. In Indonesia, Dutch cooperation was far from whole-hearted as long as the Netherlands had the upper hand. The situation was reversed after the Republic of Indonesia became firmly established. In Laos and Vietnam, the international control commissions have been paralyzed by the non-cooperation of the Polish member. [2]

One may conclude from this experience, therefore, that where cooperation of the parties is not sustained and wholehearted, a positive result will be difficult to obtain. A detailed status agreement defining the terms of cooperation is the best method to prevent shifting attitudes from adversely affecting the operations.

WITHOUT COOPERATION

There have also been situations, particularly in the recent experience of the United Nations, where no cooperation was obtained from the party or parties directly concerned. For example, when the Soviet Union suppressed the uprising in Hungary in 1956, the General Assembly considered that more information on the facts in the situation was required and that

[2] See statement of Ambassador Stevenson, UN Security Council, *Official Records*, 119th Meeting, May 21, 1964, p. 9.

the Secretary-General should investigate the situation. Later it was decided that the former President of the Assembly, Sir Leslie Munroe, should go to Hungary to investigate the situation and make a report. After he made a number of unsuccessful attempts between 1957 and 1960 to obtain the permission of Hungary to make such an observation, the effort was dropped. Sir Leslie made reports to the United Nations based on information procured indirectly. However, the Assembly's wishes were frustrated because Hungary, backed by the Soviet bloc, did not cooperate.

Similarly in 1957, the Assembly established a commission to report on the racial conflict in the Union of South Africa and gave it authority to visit the area and base its report on first-hand observation. The South African Government, however, steadfastly refused to cooperate. The United Nations commission, nevertheless, rendered three voluminous annual reports to the General Assembly describing the racial situation in South Africa, based on official documents, newspaper reports, and inter-views with visitors. Thus valuable information was obtained indirectly. No appreciable result, however, was seen in the policy of the South African Government.

Similarly, with respect to the mandated territory of South West Africa on which the South African Government was required by the League mandate to render an annual report, there was no cooperation on the part of that government. South Africa's claim that its obligation to report to the United Nations did not exist after the demise of the League of Nations was rejected in an advisory opinion of the International Court of Justice, which held that the obligation to report continued to exist and that such reports should be made to the United Nations. The United Nations, nevertheless, was not prevented from following the situation closely, through a Committee on South West Africa, which the Secretariat supplied with voluminous data based on official documents of the Union itself and on newspaper reports and testimony from petitioners. These became the basis for United Nations resolutions.

In 1962, however, the Government of South Africa invited two members of a United Nations Committee to visit the territory of South West Africa. The visit was made and resulted in a report which, while adding no new knowledge, gave a first-hand account of the situation prevailing there.

A similar effort by the United Nations, in the situation in the Portuguese African territories of Angola and Mozambique, obtained only partial cooperation by Portugal, which in 1962 was willing to discuss the matter in Lisbon with the chairman of the UN Subcommittee on Angola but did not permit the subcommittee to visit the territory.

From the foregoing account, it is clear that peace observation to be fully effective must have the willing cooperation of the countries directly in-volved. It may not be wholly ineffective when cooperation is given by only one party or is intermittently given. Some results can be obtained even when cooperation by both parties is withheld.

The following conclusions may be drawn from this experience:

1. The consent of both parties is highly desirable.

2. In some situations, such as border disputes, peace observation can produce helpful results even if it is confined to one side of the border.

3. While peace observation could be legally imposed under Chapter VII, and within a limited scope under Article 34, it seems improbable that the United Nations will make extensive use of this authority.

4. The consent of the parties should wherever possible be obtained in advance of the entry of the observers and should be sufficiently broad so that the parties will be in violation of their agreements if they obstruct the operations.

5. The initial consent should wherever possible be buttressed by status agreements dealing with methods of operation in detail.

6. Consent, if possible, should not be terminable by either or both parties. However, if the parties have any right to terminate their consent, this should automatically terminate the entire mission; that is, the parties should not reap the benefits of peace observation and at the same time be permitted to obstruct the operation.

4

CHIEF TASKS OF PEACE OBSERVATION

The central task common to all peace-observation missions is fact-finding. Nowhere is this more clearly expressed than in the traditional one-sentence terms of reference of the Rio Pact Investigating Committee of the Organization of American States: "investigate on the spot the facts denounced and their antecedents and report." However, most peace-observation missions, especially under the United Nations, have far more complex tasks and terms of reference.

Fact-finding may consist of informing an international body of the facts concerning an international situation or dispute. Whether hostilities are only threatened or have commenced, each party is intent on giving its version of the facts. A sound solution will be greatly aided by an impartial finding of the facts. Fact-finding may also be required to verify that cease-fire agreements or resolutions of the UN Security Council or General Assembly are observed.

Another task of peace observation, and one which is frequently not mentioned in the terms of reference, is the task of conciliation or mediation. Mediation functions arise naturally. By tradition in the Inter-American System, though not specifically stated, mediation is considered to be the supreme task of peace observation, and investigating committees are loath to make a finding that one party is the aggressor precisely because such a finding may put an end to the possibility of mediation.

Also to be considered are the quasi-military and quasi-political tasks of peace observation. These will vary in accordance with the situation that brought the mission into existence. The mission may be one person, as in the case of Nils Gussing, Special Representative of the UN Secretary-General in Cambodia and Thailand; it may be a thirty-nine officer mission as in Kashmir; or it may be a 600-officer mission as in the case of Lebanon. The range of tasks will vary widely and is usually dependent on the degree of violence characterizing the dispute.

A peace-observation mission following threatened or small-scale hostilities is quite different from that following large-scale hostilities, for the latter leave in their wake a variety of difficult problems. Both types may require supervision of cease-fire and demarcation lines. Large-scale hostilities may require supervising the disengagement of opposing forces and their withdrawal or demobilization. Exchange of prisoners, de-mining and war graves are additional quasi-military tasks that peace observers are sometimes called on to supervise.

The quasi-political tasks, as exemplified by those entrusted by the Geneva Conference of 1954 to the international control commissions of Indochina, include: exchange of civilian populations; exchange of territory; guarantees of human rights; supervision of elections; and enforcement of neutrality provisions. Many of these tasks follow hostilities in the nature of civil war, and the armistice agreement adopts the principle that there shall be no reprisals for acts committed while under military command.

QUASI-MILITARY TASKS

A wide variety of terms have been used by various organs of the United Nations in describing the transition from a fighting to a non-fighting situation. "The three words most frequently used have been 'cease-fire,' 'truce,' and 'armistice.' " [1]

[1] Paul Mohn, "Problems of Truce Supervision," *International Conciliation*, No. 478 (1952), p. 53. In Palestine where the agreement to cease fire after a breach is regarded as a continuation of the original cease-fire, there are conditions of reciprocity expressed in the phrase: "I will cease fire if he does."

Cessation of Hostilities

Although the terms cease-fire, cessation of hostilities, and truce are often used interchangeably, the UN experience in the early cases of Palestine and Indonesia has given them a fairly precise content. Cease-fire implies the unconditional cessation of firing and in addition a freezing of the military situation by both sides. Cessation of hostilities is slightly different in that it implies both a cease-fire and the stoppage of other hostile acts such as naval blockade, air reconnaissance, and even hostile propaganda. A truce is the second step on the way to full peace; it is a cease-fire based on sets of conditions.

Where a fighting situation exists, it is essential to get the peace observers on the spot as quickly as possible. If the fighting is continuing when they reach the spot, they will assist in attaining a cease-fire according to the operating procedure for their respective organizations.

A time requirement in the case of a cease-fire is designed to allow the respective commanders adequate time to communicate their orders to the lowest echelons in the field. The appropriate period will vary, not only in accordance with the effectiveness of communications, but with the type of warfare that has been conducted. Where guerrilla-type warfare has been going on, the period will be considerably longer than in a situation of conventional warfare.

Synchronization of action is important. This was very difficult in Palestine where several armies had to act simultaneously. The situation was complicated by a time difference between Arabs and Israelis. A compromise was reached on Greenwich Mean Time. In the 1954 Geneva Agreements on the Cessation of Hostilities in Indochina, Peking Mean Time was used.

In Palestine, no distinction is drawn between the initial order to cease fire and subsequent orders to cease fire resulting from fire-fights between the opposing armies. In practice, UNTSO has allowed one half or one hour as the time in which the cease-fire is to become effective. These orders have been observed within the short time allowed because radio communication has been reliable and the opposing commanders have recognized that reliability. Thus it is clear that speedy, reliable, and adequate communications are essential to effective peace observation.

Establishment of Demarcation Lines

Demarcation lines are generally indicated in the agreements for cessation of hostilities, as, for example, in the cases of Palestine, Kashmir, and Indochina. Where a line has been indicated, it should be verified on the ground. Where it has not been indicated, the first task of the peace observers is to see that it is, for otherwise they would be unable to determine whether a violation has occurred. In the case of Korea, the establishment of markers for both the demarcation line and the boundaries of the demilitarized zone on each side of that line was confided to the Military Armistice Commission, which was a joint commission working with the peace observers.

An example of a good demarcation line is that in Kashmir. A single line was drawn on a map by mutual agreement of the parties and then verified on the ground by local commanders of each side with the assistance of the UN observers. The local commanders had slight authority to vary the line, and that authority was used to the mutual advantage and convenience of the peace observers. To say that the Kashmir demarcation line was good is not to say that it cannot be improved. The experience of UN personnel who participated in the verification of the line suggests the following steps: (1) require the survey parties to keep full and rigidly accurate field notes; (2) as soon as the field work is over, run a photo reconnaissance of the line (this will not only aid in fixing the line, but will reveal bunkers and similar military installations in the defensive zone along the line and facilitate policing the requirement that the level of military works may not be increased); (3) if feasible, obtain the authority for local commanders in agreement with the UN mission to make minor variations in the demarcation line *after* its establishment. Military commanders are not often impressed by arguments that villages should not be cut off from their water supplies or fields, but given time, and particularly when the cooperation of the parties is good, it may be possible to adjust the line in a way that will minimize such difficulties.

The experience of UNTSO in Palestine points to additional considerations. In Jerusalem, Arabs and Israelis often confronted each other across a single street. The demarcation line, drawn on a map of a scale of 1:250,000, led to the "Problem of the Greasy Pencil," because, when verified on the ground, it was found that the grease pencil mark was sixty meters wide.

The following are suggestions of one senior officer of UNTSO. (1) Follow an established international border if at all possible. The reasons are: everybody knows where it is; generally it already has its markers; property rights have already been sorted out on both sides of the line. An example of this kind of line is the Israeli-Lebanese border. This may be one of the major reasons for the effective operation of the Israel-Lebanon Mixed Armistice Commission. (2) Where it is not possible to follow an established international border, follow natural geographic features such as rivers, but carefully specify the thalweg controls. (3) Where it is not possible to follow natural geographic features, follow man-made features such as roads. Let the line run from point to point with the words of the agreement prevailing. Maps should be merely illustrative.

Local conditions will, of course, vary from case to case. For example, in Indonesia there was no continuous front line but pockets here and there, necessitating a status quo line worked out on the ground with the assistance of the UN observers. However, a good demarcation line, well-marked and agreed to by the parties, will go far toward reducing tension and the number of incidents.

Demilitarized and Defensive Zones

It is a common feature of agreements providing for the cessation of hostilities to establish a demilitarized zone or a defensive zone on both sides of the cease-fire or demarcation line. No rigid definitions of the terms have been crystallized from past experience. In general, a demilitarized zone means that no military personnel, equipment, or installations are permitted in the area; the term defensive zone means that the level of military personnel, equipment, and installations may not be increased during the life of the agreement.

Palestine was one of the first UN cases to use demilitarized zones. The most important in Palestine, the North, Center, and South Sectors of the demilitarized zone as described in the Israel-Syrian General Armistice Agreement, were along the Israel-Syrian armistice demarcation line. The only places where the Arabs had pushed across old international borders were in these areas. The Israelis refused to accept occupation by Arabs of any part of the old Palestine mandate since the Israelis considered that they were the heirs of the British. The Acting UN Mediator proposed the device of the demilitarized zone, and agreement between Israelis and Arabs was reached on this basis. The old international frontier delimited the eastern line of the zone, and limits of the Syrian advance marked the rest.

From the Palestine experience four types of demilitarized zones seem to emerge:

The first type has people living in it. Sovereignty of the land is disputed, and something in the nature of an administrative vacuum exists in such zones. The demilitarized zone along the Israeli-Syrian demarcation line is of this type.

The second type is strategic, and no people reside within its delimitations. With the exception of a small Arab village this is the case of Mt. Scopus. This spur from the Mount of Olives dominates the old city of Jerusalem. UNTSO has the task of seeing that the level of civilian police and arms is not increased. The process of erosion of UNTSO's authority in this area is particularly marked.

The third type neither has people nor is it strategic. The Latrun water works is an example. It was established because the parties could not agree on a common line. In effect, it defines "no man's land."

The fourth type is constituted by those areas that are set up for the sole use or convenience of the peace observers. These areas generally have no inhabitants. In Palestine, the area around Government House within the demilitarized zone between Israel and Jordan is reserved for the peace observers, although some people also live in this zone.

Whatever the category, a good demilitarized zone should be carefully marked and should specify the rights and duties of the peace observers. In addition, in those zones in which people live and will continue to live, a well-planned demilitarized zone should make detailed provision for the exercise of administrative jurisdiction.

Some of the present major difficulties in Kashmir arise out of the defensive zone that extends for 500 yards on each side of the cease-fire line. India established the Kashmir armed police for this zone. It is really a para-military body and operates with the military. In retaliation, the Pakistanis have armed the villagers living in the demilitarized zone. Most of the incidents occurring in the zone are betweeen Kashmir armed police and Pakistani villagers; the remainder are between the Indian and Pakistani armies.

In some defensive zones, the cease-fire agreement will specify the number of soldiers and military installations to be retained. In the first phase of the Honduran-Nicaraguan dispute of 1957, the number of soldiers permitted to remain was the subject of considerable dispute. The most usual justification, and a valid one, for maintaining military strength in a defensive zone is to alert the main army against surprise attack. From the standpoint of peace observation, it is preferable to have a demilitarized zone along the demarcation line rather than a defensive zone.

Violations and Their Treatment

A principal task of most peace-observation missions is to deal with violations. The terms of reference, whether incorporated in a cease-fire or truce agreement, or in a resolution of an organ of the United Nations, will necessarily determine how violations are to be discovered, treated, and reported.

The degree of access by peace observers to the territories of the respective parties will go far in determining the role that the peace-observation mission can play. For the most effective discharge of its mission, peace observers should have full and untrammeled access, that is, access to all persons, all installations, and all areas. This, however, has been the exception rather than the rule. Where a theoretical right of full access exists, it has frequently been sabotaged by indirection, as in the Communist-controlled portions of Laos and in North Vietnam. Lack of proper transport, physical insecurity, and illness of the liaison officer have been some of the excuses used in Indochina and Korea. Good faith and cooperation of the parties are essential elements in the success of a peace-observation mission.

The role of peace-observation missions in detecting violations varies greatly. A detachment commander of UNEF, who had previously served as a military observer under UNTSO, was recently asked the difference between peace observation and peace-keeping. His answer was: "When I was in UNTSO, I was a box-score keeper. I was called in after the event to observe what had happened and marked it down in my log. Here I am peace keeper because I apprehend people who try to infiltrate the border."

In practice, the UNTSO observers operating under the General Armistice Agreements have only limited independent power of movement or investigation. The observation usually begins when one party complains against an alleged violation by the other party. A violation committed in the presence of an observer is not entered in the log unless the opposing party has rendered a complaint on that particular incident.

On the other hand, an active view prevails on the peace-observation mission in Kashmir. This has been carried to the point where UN observers have driven right into the line of fire to call on the parties to cease fighting. One of the high officers of UNMOGIP remarked: "Interposition is not a function of peace observation. The UN wants no dead heroes. On the other hand, a fire-fight has a habit of spreading and when an observer sees one, he ought to call upon the nearest responsible officer—even if it is only a platoon commander—to stop the fight."

All UN peace-observation missions have standing regulations or standing operating procedures for officers. In model standing operating procedures, the preferable approach is that an observer who sees a violation being committed should call on the nearest responsible officer of the appropriate party to cease and desist at once. It is admitted that in certain reprisal cases, this guidance may not be practicable, as for example, where junior officers are inexperienced and undisciplined, or because of the locations and distances involved.

Usually, the only sanction against violations is to be cited as a violator by the peace-observation body. In the case of serious breaches, the incidents may be brought to the attention of the UN Security Council.

> It is sometimes urged that bringing serious breaches of the GAA before the Security Council served a useful purpose, in that "World Public Opinion" was informed of the facts of the case, and would consequently be a sort of moral sanction against the aggressor. I regret to say that this idea never seemed to work out. [2]

This may be a pessimistic estimate of the worth of world public opinion as a sanction behind UN peace observation. But for the foreseeable future, it is unlikely that there will be more than world public opinion as an ultimate sanction for UN peace observation. It is just as unlikely that a peace-observation mission will be sent to a territory or given full and untrammeled access without consent of the parties, or at least one of them.

However, in attempting to make efficient those tools that do exist, it might be more desirable to issue a citation in specific terms, accompanied by publicity, instead of a general statement that finds a particular country guilty of a violation. In some cases, such a citation and publicity might be uncomfortable for the general officer under whose jurisdiction the violation

[2] E. L. M. Burns, *Between Arab and Israeli* (New York: Obolensky, 1963), p. 280.

took place, and hence would be an inducement not to permit further violations. An example of a specific citation would be the following:

"The UN Mission finds as a fact that last night 200 soldiers of the X Army under the immediate command of Captain Y belonging to General A's sector of the demarcation line crossed that line to a depth of . . . yards and there committed the following acts in violation of the agreement between the Governments of X and Z."

It is desirable that the terms of reference of the mission indicate clearly the right of the chief of mission or his authorized agents to determine the existence of a violation and make recommendations to the parties to rectify the situation. Neither party should be in a position to question the jurisdiction of the chief of mission to make such recommendations or, if necessary, to bring the matter to the attention of a UN organ.

The Palestine and Indonesian cases have shown that it is advantageous to have as many cases as possible solved through agreement between the line commanders. The UN truce-supervision machinery should deal only with the complaints that the parties cannot solve through their own discussions.

In addition to violations by members of the armed forces, there may be violations of a demarcation line by civilians, both intentional and unintentional, and for many different motives. For example, in Palestine there are infiltrators, spies, thieves, fugitives from justice, smugglers, and adolescent delinquents as well as simple farmers in search of strayed cattle. Whether the mission has the power to apprehend violators, it nevertheless seems clear that no mission should attempt to punish a breach of its regulations concerning the demarcation line. The proper exercise of the peace-observation function is to hand over, or to preside at the handing over, of individuals from the authorities of one country to the other.

Where the armed forces of the parties are the violators, the case is more serious. But this would rarely occur in the presence of a peace observer. It is not unknown for a liaison officer to practice deception on an observation mission. The hostile operation may be calculated to terminate within the two hours or so that it will take for a peace observer to get on the scene. False information may be furnished; liaison officers may guide falsely; and other forms of deception may be used.

Disengagement of Opposing Forces

The problem of disengagement or withdrawal of the opposing forces is not so different where there have been only threats of violence or small-scale hostilities of armed forces. These are the cases where peace observation is more likely to be used. After large-scale hostilities or in case of breakdown of law and order, both peace-observation and peace-keeping missions are likely to be used. Peace-observation missions have at times been charged with the task of observing disengagement, and even with the task of inter-position between the opposing forces.

Peace observers were charged with the mission of observing and report-ing the disengagement of the U.A.R. and Saudi Arabian forces in the Yemen case, and the French Union and native forces in the Indochina cases. The disengagement aspects of the Yemen case were not fully carried out by the parties because, it appeared, the parties had mental reservations when entering into the engagement. In Indochina in 1954, disengagement was reported by the international control commissions in Vietnam, Laos, and Cambodia to have been successful. Indeed the peace observers arrived so late that the early part of the disengagement and withdrawal, including demobilization in the case of Cambodia, went unobserved. In Indochina, the joint commissions were sufficiently in agreement in their common objectives so that the entire task could probably have been done without the benefit of peace observation. Disengagement was successful because cooperation between the parties on this subject was good.

It is pertinent to inquire whether interposition between the opposing hostile forces is a proper task for peace-observation missions. Generally speaking, it probably is not because peace observers are usually few and unarmed. It is a proper task for peace-keeping missions because of their larger numbers and their arms.

The Yemen disengagement agreement provided for a demilitarized zone of twenty kilometers on each side of the Saudi Arabian-Yemeni border. In this zone, impartial observers were stationed to check on the observance of the terms of disengagement. While the UN observers were to be interposed between the hostile armies, the text of the terms of reference indicates that the purpose of the interposition was not to prevent a clash between the armies but to be in a strategic position to exercise the reporting function.

Although UNEF is stationed entirely in Egyptian-controlled territory, it is essentially an interposing force. UNEF standing regulations forbid any armed person from approaching the Gaza demarcation line any closer than 500 meters by day or night. By forbidding armed persons to approach the demarcation line and the international frontier, UNEF effectuates its interposition function.

The UN Military Observer Group in Kashmir in 1964 had thirty-nine observers stationed in six outposts on each side of the cease-fire line. There is a defensive zone consisting of 500 yards on each side of the cease-fire line. The opposing armies have been disengaged, and it is the avowed purpose of the UNMOGIP presence to keep them so. In a few cases of violations, the military observers have interposed themselves in the line of fire, but this is considered by the Commanding General to be excessive zeal.

Withdrawal or Demobilization of Forces

Many serious problems can arise in connection with the observation of withdrawal of forces after hostilities. Observations of this nature took place in Indonesia, Korea, Indochina, and West Irian. Although large numbers of troops were withdrawn by the Netherlands from Indonesia and by the United States from Korea, the problems of peace observers were minimal because the states supplying the troops and the local commanders were anxious to get them out, and the withdrawal operations encountered no obstacles. In West Irian, the number of Indonesian "volunteers" was relatively small, and the chief problem was to achieve assembly prior to withdrawal. The "volunteers" were starving, disease-ridden, and anxious to withdraw. The withdrawal of Chinese troops from Burma involves such unique political considerations that it does not furnish material for guidance. In Indochina, where the issues were complex, especially in Laos, there were far-reaching consequences of the withdrawal provisions.

Withdrawal is affected by three factors: first is the degree of cooperation of the parties; second is the condition of the road system and transport availabilities; and third is the kind of warfare that has preceded because if even an appreciable part of it was guerrilla warfare, it will be difficult to get the units and bands together and to feed them on the way out.

Withdrawal provisions of cease-fire or armistice agreements sometimes provide for provisional assembly and regroupment areas for the various forces. They may specify the routes for withdrawal, and provide for a joint commission of the opposing forces to bear the primary responsibility of fixing the sites and boundaries of the provisional assembly and regroupment areas. They may also provide for fixed and mobile teams of the peace-observation mission to supervise the work of the joint commissions. The purpose of the mission should be to prevent clashes during withdrawal and to certify the completion of the operation. This was the pattern in Indochina, Indonesia, and West Irian. In Korea, in 1947, the troops had already been assembled prior to the peace observation.

From the experience of peace observation in Laos, Indonesia, and West Irian, it may be concluded that:

1. The primary responsibility for withdrawal should rest on the parties. The joint commissions and their subgroups can be of great assistance to the international observation body, which necessarily must take time to get up to full operational strength, whereas the joint personnel are already on the ground and mobile.

2. The laying down of a timetable for regroupment and withdrawal should be for general guidance and should not be mandatory. The timetable tends to go awry not merely for the major phases of disengagement, provisional assembly, regroupment, and withdrawal but also with respect to the individual moves of particular units. Even with complete good will and cooperation, it is difficult to give precise advance information of moves, and there may be justification for deviation or changes.

3. The basic agreement should not make mandatory the places at which fixed teams should be established by the peace-observation mission. Local circumstances may make the provisions unnecessarily burdensome.

Thus any indication of the location of fixed peace-observation teams should be only a recommendation. This will also allow for adjustment to local situations if the observation continues over a long period.

4. The existence of guerrilla warfare means that there will be a problem of identification of units since guerrilla soldiers generally wear no uniforms or distinguishing insignia. Moreover, since they live off the country, food should be provided along withdrawal routes by the parties concerned. Identification is generally made by examination of arms carried, but this is not entirely conclusive.

5. A feature of the 1954 Geneva Agreement on the Cessation of Hostilities in Laos deserves special mention because it had significant political consequences. Article 12 provided that the Communist Pathet Lao forces were to have twelve provisional assembly areas in each of the twelve provinces of Laos. Pending a settlement, all fighting units of the Pathet Lao were to be moved from provisional assembly areas into the Provinces of Phong Saly and Sam Neua. Although the Communist side (Pathet Lao and the North Vietnamese) were to recognize the Royal Laotian Government's formal sovereignty over the two provinces in due course, the Pathet Lao meanwhile were allowed to station themselves throughout the provinces.

Political settlement was reached in November 1957, but the Pathet Lao continued to control the two provinces. This suggests that no regroupment area should be so large as to constitute an entire province. The supervision of regroupment and withdrawal was one of the most important of the peace-observation tasks in the early stages in Laos, Cambodia, and Vietnam, though less successful in Laos than in the other two countries. Nevertheless, the experience of peace observation in all three countries indicates that certification of withdrawal by impartial peace observers is beneficial since it makes it difficult for one of the parties to charge the other with noncompliance. In general, fact-finding by impartial observers tends to discourage false propaganda claims.

Demobilization differs from withdrawal in that, after concentration, the members of the military units are returned to civilian life in their country. The pertinent questions are: (1) What happens to their arms? (2) What document certifies their new status? (3) What guarantees are there that the demobilized soldiers will be effectively integrated into civilian life and be immune from punishment for acts committed while they were subject to military orders?

In this study, the only cases in which observation of demobilization was required were under the agreements on the cessation of hostilities in Cambodia and Indonesia.

The Cambodian Agreement provided for the on-the-spot demobilization of the Khmer Resistance Forces (KRF), and Article 6 took note of the declaration of the Cambodian delegation at Geneva in which the Cambodian Government stated it would: (1) take the necessary measures to integrate all citizens into the national community without discrimination; (2) affirm that all Cambodian citizens might freely participate as electors or candidates in general elections by secret ballot; (3) avoid reprisals and make certain that each national is entitled to the enjoyment of all constitutional guarantees concerning the protection of person and property and democratic freedoms.

Unfortunately, the time schedule was not realistic. The international control commission was not set up until August 11 nor the joint commission until August 20. The Khmer Resistance Forces were fully demobilized by August 22, 1954. For all practical purposes the demobilization was unobserved.

The delegation of the Khmer Resistance Forces claimed that arms were destroyed on the spot. Although this was doubted by the Cambodian Government, few serviceable concealed weapons were discovered by either commission.

No documents were issued to the KRF at the time of discharge. An identity card is indispensable in Cambodia to enjoy freedom of movement. Provincial authorities were directed by the Cambodian Government to issue these cards. Some former members of the KRF did not apply out of fear of reprisal or because they preferred to live the life of bandits. Eventually, however, all KRF who requested documents received them.

The first task of the ICC was the effective integration of the former Khmer Resistance Forces, and after some difficulties, this was accomplished.

In Indonesia, there was demobilization, and the round table agreements provided a guarantee against reprisals. However, about 11,000 Indonesians serving with the Dutch troops doubted that the provisions of the agreement against reprisals would be effective. They did not return to their homes but instead proceeded to the Netherlands. The remaining Indonesian troops who had served with the Dutch were either demobilized or joined the Indonesian Army. The UN Commission for Indonesia observed the process to assure that the choice was made freely and that there was no forced recruitment.

There are no particular guidelines for demobilization as distinguished from withdrawal except, perhaps, in the case of demobilization to emphasize the importance of the timely issuance of identity cards.

Bans on Introducing Fresh Troops or Arms and Establishing Military Bases

As one of the steps toward the peaceful settlement of disputes after large-scale hostilities, agreements for cessation of hostilities may establish a ban on the importation of fresh troops and military supplies and on establishment of military bases by foreign powers. This is a continuing military task. It is a logical extension of the process of cease-fire and withdrawal and transfer of troops. It is particularly appropriate where there has been great power intervention in the situation. A ban on alliances and the establishment of military bases as well as the prohibition against introducing fresh troops and arms is provided, with some differences, in each of the Indochina cases.

The Korean Armistice Agreement of 1953 makes provision in Article II for concrete arrangements to carry out the cease-fire and armistice and prohibits the introduction into Korea of reinforcing personnel except for rotation of units and personnel on a man-for-man basis; and of combat aircraft, armored vehicles, weapons, and ammunition, but provides that replacements might be made on a piece-for-piece basis of the same effectiveness and types. The Neutral Nations Supervisory Committee, Switzerland, Sweden, Czechoslovakia, and Poland was charged with supervision and inspection of rotation of units and personnel and of the specified arms and ammunition at five ports of entry in North Korea and five ports in South Korea.

The Swiss and Swedish delegations, however, soon discovered as they had predicted in advance of the armistice, that the Polish and Czech delegations were not impartial but acted as agents for the Communist side, that widespread evasion was taking place in North Korea, that mobile inspection teams could not operate unless a majority so decided, and the two-and-two organization of the NNSC resulted in a tie vote on most requests for inspection.

After a long history of noncooperation by the Communist side with the NNSC, the UN Command gave notice on May 31, 1956, suspending the activity of the NNSC teams in three South Korean ports because of Communist violations of the reinforcement, reporting, and supervision provisions of the armistice agreement. The NNSC survives merely as an empty shell.

The prohibition against alliances and new military bases is absolute in the case of the 1954 Geneva Agreements on the Cessation of Hostilities in Vietnam and Laos, although the French were permitted to leave behind a training mission of 1,500 personnel in Vietnam and 3,500 personnel in the case of Laos, and rotation of units was permitted on a man-for-man basis in the case of Vietnam. In the case of Cambodia, only alliances that are not in conformity with the principles of the UN Charter are prohibited; the prohibition against the establishment of foreign military bases is valid so long as Cambodia's territory is not threatened.

The prohibition against importation of arms and munitions in the case of Laos carries an exception—arms specified as necessary for the defense of that country. Such arms were to enter only at specific points. In the case of Vietnam, the importation of aircraft, ordnance, and armored vehicles was prohibited, while other arms could be replaced on a piece-by-piece basis.

The underlying purpose of the foregoing provisions was to limit the extent of the violence, should hostilities break out again, by imposing a ban on importation of arms.

There is a case where peace observers have attempted to achieve the same result by obtaining a ban on exportation or sale of arms. Toward the middle of the second phase of the Chaco War between Bolivia and Paraguay, the League of Nations Commission of Enquiry made a number of recommendations to the League Council in May 1934, one of which concerned the establishment of an arms embargo and strict control over the transit trade by neighboring countries. President Roosevelt complied at once. The United States Congress passed legislation empowering him to prohibit the sale of arms and ammunition, and the President promptly invoked the act by proclaiming a ban on shipments of arms to both Bolivia and Paraguay. Great Britain followed a parallel policy.

To what degree were the bans on fresh troops and arms observed? The prohibitions were completely ignored in the case of Vietnam and largely ignored in the case of Laos. The exceptions were so vast in the case of Cambodia that the prohibitions were practically nonexistent.

The export prohibition was effective in the Chaco case. Its success lies not in the method used but rather in the fact that the great powers wished to stop the traffic. On the other hand, in the case of Indochina, certain great powers considered it in their interest to ignore the prohibitions.

In the case of the Yemen disengagement agreement, the Government of Saudi Arabia was required to cease the supply of arms and ammunition to the Imam of Yemen. The Government of the U.A.R. was required to withdraw its troops. Both parties used subterfuges to nullify the agreement. While the government of Saudi Arabia ceased to supply arms, it provided the Imam with the money to purchase them. The government of the U.A.R. withdrew some troops, but at the same time sent in fresh troops, which in one instance exceeded the number withdrawn.

The foregoing experience indicates that:

1. If the parties to a cease-fire or armistice agreement are bent on not living up to it, there is very little that a peace-observation mission can do to compel performance, particularly if great power interests are involved.

2. The prime requisite of peace observers is impartiality. In matters involving a conflict of interest between Communist and non-Communist, Communists are not impartial. This was the experience of the NNSC in Korea and of the ICC in Laos and Vietnam.

3. When members of a peace-observation mission find that one side is a persistent violator, they should so report. When some members of the mission are accessories to the violations and obstruct the reporting of such violations, as happened in Korea, Laos, and Vietnam, the other members should make every effort to find proof of both the violations and the connivance of the mission members. When denied access, they should use whatever means are available to ascertain and obtain proof of the violations taking place. This will often mean interrogating refugees, deserters, and defectors. It may also mean radar, photo reconnaissance, or, in the future, outer-space observation.

4. In the case of the follow-up on minor hostilities, it may sometimes be helpful in implementing a ban on the introduction of fresh arms and supplies for the sponsors of the peace-observation effort to call on suppliers to prevent sale and export as well as to charge the peace observers with the responsibility of preventing importation.

Exchange of Prisoners of War and Civilian Internees

Special problems concerning the treatment and exchange of prisoners of war arose in French Indochina and in Indonesia. While the problem also arose under the Korean Armistice Agreement, the matter was handled separately by the military commanders and a neutral mission constituted solely for this purpose.

Where peace observers are given this function, they may be confronted with the problem of forcible repatriation. Peace observers are almost sure to find difficulties in reconciling statistics of prisoners claimed by one side as against prisoners released by the other side. This was characteristic of the exchange of prisoners after the war in Indochina. On exhaustive analysis, the International Control Commission for Vietnam reported in its first interim report that the glaring differences in the number and category of prisoners and civil internees were principally due to the difficulty in fixing the identity or category of the persons exchanged.

Discrepancies may also be due to faulty calculation, to the escape or prior release of prisoners, to desertions and defections, and to the important fact that in guerrilla warfare there are much greater losses of prisoners than in conventional warfare owing to death by exhaustion, malnutrition, and disease.

At the end of the first phase of the Chaco War, when U.S. military attachés acting as peace observers made a satisfactory exchange of Bolivian and Paraguayan prisoners of war, it was a surprise to the observers to find out how many Bolivian soldiers, believed to have been taken prisoner, had excused themselves from the belligerent life and had gone to live in Argentina.

Usually, truce or armistice agreements provide for the submission of lists of names and a time schedule for exchange of prisoners. Again it should be pointed out that it is rare for time schedules to be adhered to after large-scale hostilities, and that it is preferable for the terms of reference to give discretion to the peace observers in this matter.

The exchange of civilian internees presents no special problems. From past experience, these fall into two categories: (1) those who were interned because of political activities and hence were a security danger; and (2) ordinary civilian internees, most of whom were former civil administrators. Sometimes, as in Korea, there will be exchanges of displaced civilians across the demarcation line, under the auspices of the peace observers.

QUASI-POLITICAL TASKS

The range of political tasks of a peace-observation mission is wide and varied indeed. Even if the terms of reference do not specifically charge the peace-observation mission to deal with some political problem such as the supervision of an election, political problems requiring the attention of the mission will inevitably arise, and the successful and impartial observation mission will be fully aware of them. The principal objective is the restoration of peace, and this is a political matter.

Truce or armistice agreements frequently charge peace observers with the supervision of specific political tasks. This is particularly true after large-scale hostilities or where former members of opposing armies are expected to live peaceably in a single country. The logical sequence of events after a cease-fire is to draw a demarcation line, to disengage and withdraw the armies, and to exchange prisoners of war. Then the peaceful integration of former soldiers into normal civilian life should follow. Their fundamental freedoms should be guaranteed, and they should be free from reprisal. Exchange of civilian populations and transfer of territory are political tasks that may require supervision by peace-observation missions.

Political Reporting

Most peace-observation missions are required to make periodic or special reports to the international organization on the conditions—political, economic, and social—in the area, and on the progress of mission activities, in order to enable the organization to pass judgment on the issues presented to it. Occasionally, as in Indonesia and Korea, the organization itself called for specific reports on subjects of this nature. This function is akin to the reporting functions of diplomatic missions.

Radio Monitoring

In Korea and the Balkans, where on-the-spot observation was possible on only one side of the border, much information was obtained from monitoring broadcasts from the other side. The monitoring also disclosed the location of the source of the broadcasts. In Jordan, monitoring of Egyptian broadcasts disclosed violent denunciations that were in due course stopped when the UN Presence identified the source.

Exchange of Civilian Populations

The sheer size of the operation of exchanging civilian populations, and the degree of social and economic development of the people and the area, will affect the task of peace observation. One may compare the Honduran-Nicaraguan case in 1961 with the exchange of civilian populations between North and South Vietnam in 1954. In the Honduran-Nicaraguan case, there were only 4,000 people transferred, mostly from the disputed area to Nicaragua. In the Vietnam case, nearly a million people moved from the Communist North to the non-Communist South with only a few thousand moving in the opposite direction.

In both cases, the inhabitants were to have a free choice and freedom of movement. In both cases, complaints were made to the peace observers that pressure had been applied to the inhabitants. In the Central American case, the complaint was made that the government of Nicaragua was using pressure to force inhabitants to move to Nicaragua. In the Vietnam case, the charge was made that the Catholic Church was using pressure to persuade people to move to the South, and the countercharge was made that the government of North Vietnam was guilty of forced evacuation in some cases and guilty of hindering evacuation in others. But the Vietnam control commission observed that the parties made charges of forced evacuation and hindrance to evacuation more for the purpose of getting the commission to condemn one side or the other than out of any solicitude for the interests of the individuals whose right of freedom of movement was affected by these pressures of obstructions. By the due date, May 11, 1955, the transfer of populations was almost completed, and a brief extension of time took care of the remaining cases.

In the Honduran-Nicaraguan case, the task of moving 4,000 illiterate Indians presented difficulties. Trucks had to be sent in for the inhabitants and their cattle; arrangements had to be made for subsistence en route; and temporary housing had to be provided on arrival. On a vastly larger scale, the same procedure was followed in Vietnam except that a large part of the movement was by sea, and the government of North Vietnam would not admit French or U.S. ships to its territorial waters. Accordingly, the people had to move to the ships out on the high seas, often at considerable risk to their lives. There were concentrations of as many as 10,000 refugees at a single place unable to move, and procedures for granting permits were slow and clumsy.

The foregoing experiences suggest the following:

1. To prevent bogging down in infinite detail, the peace observers should require the representatives of the parties to do the absolute maximum for themselves. Appeals to the observers should be limited to differences between the national representatives involving questions of principle.

2. If the people do not already have identity cards, arrangements should be made well in advance to issue them. Without these cards, the individuals may switch sides from day to day, depending on their convenience. Smuggling and other illegal ventures may be involved.

Transfer of Territory

In the Honduran-Nicaraguan case, it was a relatively simple matter to hand over an underdeveloped territory with only a few villages that were so primitive that scarcely any records or installations were involved. The procedure was elementary: the Honduran-Nicaraguan Mixed Commission ordered the Nicaraguan authorities to move out one day; the next day the Honduran authorities were allowed to move in. Even the few municipal installations presented no problem. There was a gentleman's agreement that the Nicaraguan authorities could remove the electrical generators to Nicaragua. They took not only the generators, but the tin roofing and salvageable timber from the buildings as well.

Between the transfer of primitive villages and large urban concentrations, there is an intermediate type of territorial transfer as exemplified in the Leticia dispute between Colombia and Peru, 1933–1935. In this case, a League of Nations Administrative Commission consisting of an American colonel, a Brazilian commander, and a Spanish captain took over the government of the area for a year, repaired damaged property, restored sanitary conditions, and built several schools and hospitals. The operation was a success, and the local population was very happy with the commission's initiative.

The transfer of territory containing a large modern city, such as Hanoi, presents a different kind of problem. The Agreement on the Cessation of Hostilities in Vietnam made only the most general provision for the transfer of territory. Article 14 provided that "pending the general elections which will bring about the unification of Vietnam, the conduct of civil administration in each regrouping zone shall be in the hands of the party whose forces are to be regrouped there in virtue of the present Agreement." This article also envisaged that the transfers would take place in such a manner as to avoid any break in the transfer of responsibilities. The next article of the agreement required the parties to permit no sabotage or destruction of public property.

In such a large operation, two kinds of problems were encountered: (1) orderly transfer of civil and administrative services, including police; and (2) orderly transfer of essential public services such as electricity and water.

The ICC in Vietnam first realized that it had a serious problem when the postal workers of Hanoi sent a petition to the commission, complaining that the French postal authorities were dismantling the equipment, and stating that the workers feared that they would be thrown out of employment.

After consultation with the parties, the ICC arranged for the advance arrival of civil servants and police of the Democratic Republic of Vietnam. Hanoi was transferred sector by sector in five days using five ICC mobile teams. As to public offices and publicly owned utilities, the ICC required the submission of stock and equipment inventories, and it reviewed complaints on the inadequacy of inventories to be left behind.

Privately owned public utilities, such as water, electricity, and transport, presented more difficult problems. To prevent a break in service, the ICC proposed, and it was agreed, that all essential equipment, a supply of coal for two months, and spare parts for two years should be left behind.

These experiences suggest that: (1) In the truce or other agreement, the provision concerning the transfer of territory should be as specific as possible. (2) Peace observers should seek the cooperation of the parties as early as possible for an orderly transfer. (3) There ought not to be any break in the continuity of civil authority or essential public services. (4) If the agreement is silent on the matter of supplies and equipment, the peace-observation mission should require that a reasonable amount of supplies and equipment be left behind. (5) Malicious destruction of installations or supplies should not be countenanced.

Guarantee of Democratic Freedoms

An important provision frequently found in truce or armistice agreements is one guaranteeing to former combatants the enjoyment of democratic freedoms or forbidding reprisals or discrimination for acts committed during the hostilities. This is particularly important where, as in Indochina, the hostilities took on the character of civil war. In such cases, feelings will tend to remain bitter, and the incidence of reprisals will tend to be high.

The Agreements on the Cessation of Hostilities in Laos and Vietnam provided that each party would undertake to refrain from any reprisal or discrimination against persons or organizations on account of their activities during the negotiations and to guarantee their democratic liberties. The Cambodian Agreement differed slightly, but a Cambodian declaration incorporated in that agreement specifically provided that "all Cambodian citizens may freely participate as electors or candidates in general elections by secret ballot."

The Vietnam and Laos Commissions received thousands of complaints of violations of democratic freedoms. The Cambodian Commission received some complaints. These may be classified as follows: murders and torture; threats and acts of terrorism; arrests and detention of persons; and looting, illegal requisitions, illegal taxation, and destruction of property. To these may be added another, which is treated under a separate heading: forcible recruitment.

During the first year of operation, the Laos Commission received so many complaints that it had to draw up priority lists for investigation based on the nature, seriousness, number, and date of their occurrence. The highest priority, apparently, was accorded to those complaints that were so serious that they constituted a threat to the peace and order of the area.

The Laos Commission found that the parties made little effort to settle the complaints because of existing tension and bitterness. Sometimes complaints were forwarded to the commission without checking on facts. The ICC would issue a reprimand in such cases.

In West Irian, UNTEA was given wide responsibilities in connection with preparing the population for ultimate self-determination and in observing procedures for self-determination. UNTEA, as long as it was present in the area, could seek to carry out this function. On its withdrawal, the Secretary-General stated his confidence that Indonesia would scrupulously observe these terms of the agreement.

The following is suggested to enhance the effectiveness of peace-observation missions charged with protecting democratic freedoms. (1) Attempt to persuade the parties, if they have not already done so, to pass amnesty laws. This will give a basis in domestic law as well as in international law to the rights to be protected. (2) Mount a publicity campaign so that the general public and local officials—the latter being the most frequent offenders—will know the rights to be guaranteed by the peace-observation mission.

Supervision of Elections

Peace observers may be required to supervise an election or a plebiscite according to the specific terms of reference. Such a requirement may also be implied, as in the case of Cambodia, where one of the democratic freedoms guaranteed to former members of an army was the freedom to participate as electors or candidates in an election. Under the League, plebiscites were held in Upper Silesia in 1921 and in the Saar in 1935.

In the case of the Saar, the area had been administered for fifteen years by a League of Nations Governing Commission, and the plebiscite was to determine whether the territory was to return to Germany, become part of France, or remain under League control.

A Plebiscite Commission and a system of juridical tribunals of twenty experienced foreign judges was established to draw up the voting lists, supervise the balloting, and count the votes. The overriding objective was to assure the freedom, secrecy, and trustworthiness of the voting. The tribunals were to continue for one year after the installation of the new regime to hear possible complaints.

An international force consisting of 1,500 British, 1,300 Italian, 250 Dutch, and 250 Swedish members was established under the command of a British general. The task of this force was to maintain law and order during and after the plebiscite, should the local police prove inadequate.

The international force was stationed close to the polling places but not so close as to cause complaint of coercion. Troops were used to transport the ballot boxes to the central counting place.

Despite an atmosphere of threats and Nazi pressure, the plebiscite was conducted smoothly, and there were no incidents. The absence of disorder, according to the commanding general, was due to the moral influence of the troops' presence, which acted both as a deterrent to disorderly elements and as an encouragement to the local police.

Strictly speaking, there has been no supervision of elections in the Inter-American System, but recently a precedent has been established for provisional governments to invite a group of lawyers or diplomats, distinguished in inter-American affairs, to observe national elections. An example is the observation of the first free post-Trujillo elections in the Dominican Republic in December 1962. The provisional government invited a symposium of well-known personalities to visit the Dominican Republic for several days prior to the election.

On the day of the election, December 16, 1962, the members of the symposium dispersed to the various provinces and throughout the day visited polling places. They observed the organization of the polling places, verified the presence of representatives of the various parties, reviewed the methods for checking registration of voters, examined the blank ballots, verified the secrecy of marking ballots, and checked on the distance at which soldiers were stationed from the polling places. The only complaints received, other than a few unfounded allegations of illegal political activity around the polling places, were complaints by migratory workers who had been away from their residences at the time of registration and therefore were not registered to vote. The symposium found that the election, which resulted in a victory for candidate Juan Bosch, had been conducted in a free, fair, and orderly fashion.

A proposal for a similar observation of national elections in Honduras in October 1963 was frustrated by a military coup just before the term of President Villeda Morales expired. The timing of the coup was designed to prevent observation of the elections by an impartial body.

The United Nations Temporary Commission on Korea, as part of its task of expediting the program for Korean independence, was required "to observe and assure that elected representatives of the Korean people are in fact duly elected by the Korean people, and not mere appointees of military authorities in Korea." Its subcommittee defined the minimum requirements for a free atmosphere for elections as follows: "Freedom of expression, freedom of the press and information, freedom of assembly and association, freedom of movement, protection against arbitrary arrests and detention and protection against violence or threats of violence."

When the North Koreans declined to cooperate with UNTCOK on elections, the Interim Committee of the UN General Assembly decided that UNTCOK should proceed to observe elections in South Korea alone.

The subcommittee of UNTCOK reviewed studies prepared on the following subjects: the qualifications and disqualifications of the franchise; candidature; electoral districts and representation; electoral organization; registration of voters; electoral campaign and voting procedure; counting of ballots and declaration of election; and incompatabilities, litigation, and penal provisions.

After consultation with the United States authorities, all but one of the commission's recommendations were accepted and embodied in a revised electoral law. The commission recommended that elections be held on

May 9, 1948, but concurred in the ruling of the commanding general of the U.S. military government that it be postponed one day since a total eclipse of the sun was due on May 9.

The observation was divided into three periods: the registration period; the period following registration of candidates; and the election day and the days immediately preceding and following that day.

The commission had been alerted by complaints of arbitrary arrest or pressure by the national police and youth organizations and was particularly vigilant with respect to their activities both in the pre-election and election period. The youth organizations were warned that their behavior would be an important element in the commission's decision on the existence of a free atmosphere for the elections. The warning was effective. The police were given a warning by the military government not to interfere with the elections, and the conduct of the police gave no ground for complaint. Seventy-five percent of the potential voters went to the polls and the commission concluded that the election was a valid expression of the free will of the electorate.

The successor organization to UNTCOK, the UN Commission for the Unification and Rehabilitation of Korea (UNCURK), carried out a country-wide observation of the October 1963 elections in the Republic of Korea at the initiative of the incumbent administration.

UNCURK had nine observation teams. They observed no flagrant or relevant irregularities in the voting or vote-counting process and found all procedures proper. Almost 85 percent of the electorate participated in what was relatively a free and fair election.

The Nine-Power Geneva Conference of 1954 produced a final declaration in which the conference took note of the declarations of the governments of Laos and Cambodia, expressing their intention to permit all citizens to take part in general elections in 1955 in conformity with the constitutions, by secret ballot and in conditions of respect for fundamental freedoms.

On February 19, 1955, King Norodom Sihanouk informed the Cambodian Commission that he was making far-reaching reform proposals in the constitution and in the electoral system. The International Control Commission reserved its opinion of the proposals, and, while it was awaiting an official statement, the impetuous King abdicated in favor of his parents. There was much public speculation that the commission had opposed the reforms and that it was in consequence of this opposition that the King had abdicated. The commission publicly objected to this interpretation, and from Calcutta Prince Sihanouk issued a press release praising the commission and stating that it would assist at the September elections.

The commission decided that it had no authority to supervise the election as a whole, but that it had to observe whether the election took place pursuant to the Cambodian Constitution and laws, whether there was secrecy of ballot, and whether there was discrimination against former members of the Khmer Resistance Forces.

Indirectly, the observation amounted to much the same thing as supervision of the election. The commission had fourteen teams in the fourteen provinces covering the elections, the results of which were a clean, overwhelming victory for Prince Sihanouk's party.

The lessons in the light of the foregoing experience appear to be these: (1) An atmosphere devoid of fear in the pre-election period is essential to free and fair elections. (2) The presence of impartial observers in the registration, vote-casting, and vote-counting phases can do a great deal toward assuring a free and fair election. (3) Even where the electorate has not been educated to modern systems of democracy and government and where the police tend to be authoritarian, the presence of impartial and alert peace observers will tend to encourage conditions that will permit a free expression of the will of the people.

Observation of Neutrality Provisions

The Final Declaration of the 1954 Geneva Conference took note of the declarations of the governments of Cambodia and Laos, stating their intention not to join in any agreement with other states if the agreement obligated them to participate in a military alliance not in conformity with the principles of the UN Charter (or, in the case of Laos, with the principles of the Agreement on Cessation of Hostilities in Laos), and stating their obligation not to establish bases for the military forces of foreign powers so long as their security was not threatened.

Article 19 of the 1954 Agreement on the Cessation of Hostilities in Vietnam provides that the two parties shall ensure "that the zones assigned to them do not adhere to any military alliance."

In his opening statement on May 17, 1961, at the Laotian Conference in Geneva, Secretary of State Rusk expanded the definition of neutrality beyond the concept of nonalignment to mean no foreign military personnel, no foreign military supplies, no foreign military bases, a neutrality consistent with sovereignty, and hence safeguards against threats of subversion from within or without.

The Declaration of the Neutrality of Laos, signed July 23, 1962, had detailed provisions along the above lines.

The ICC has the responsibility for supervising the execution by the parties of these so-called "neutrality" provisions. Peace observers will probably be called on in the future to report on the observance of them. Past experience of the ICC indicates the probable ineffectiveness of peace observation in connection with the ban on alliances, at least in any area where the great powers have strong and conflicting interests in a cold-war environment.

5

ORGANIZATION AND SUPPORT OF PEACE–OBSERVATION MISSIONS

COMPOSITION OF MISSIONS

League of Nations peace observers were appointed by the Council in their individual capacities and not as representatives of governments. They were paid out of League of Nations funds especially allocated for that purpose. Most of the League missions in the decade 1920–1930 for example, Aaland Islands and the Greek-Bulgarian cases, were of relatively short duration. Where persons on active service for their governments were appointed, the additional expenses were defrayed in the form of a per diem.

In selecting observers, the practice was developed early for a committee of the League of Nations Council to nominate the persons to serve, and for the Council to confirm their nominations. The observers were responsible to the League of Nations Council and not to their respective governments.

General Frank McCoy's service with the Lytton Commission was a special case. U.S. Secretary of State Stimson was consulted about a choice and recommended General McCoy. General McCoy acted independently and was not known to have been in touch with the U.S. Department of State. Officers of the U.S. Government were not known to have seen and approved the commission's report before it was presented to the Council.

Subordinate personnel were supplied by the League of Nations Secretariat. There is no reason to doubt the quality or adequacy of the support furnished.

From the beginning to the present, OAS peace observers have been representatives of states and have not been chosen as individuals. This has been true both under the Rio Treaty and the Inter-American Peace Committee machinery. Members are compensated by the Pan American Union only for travel and per diem, not for their services.

Under the OAS Council rules of procedure, nominations of peace observers for Rio Treaty case investigations may be made by committee, but if this is not done, the President of the Council can make appointments. In practice, the latter procedure is generally used, and as with appointments to all other committees, the principle of geographic representation is observed. The Inter-American Peace Committee is a standing committee, but these general rules apply to it as well.

Those who are well acquainted with OAS peace observation say that although observers are instructed by their governments, generally speaking, this fact has not had adverse effects on the speed, impartiality, or efficiency of the operation. Reports are not submitted to the governments before going to the Secretary-General.

The subordinate personnel supplied by the Secretary-General of the OAS, particularly in recent years, has been of excellent quality. In 1962, a special staff unit was created under the Director of Legal Affairs to service the peace-observation operations of the OAS. This unit consists of five or six officers who can service both the IAPC and a Rio Treaty Investigating Committee.

The three international control commissions for Vietnam, Laos, and Cambodia, established by the Geneva Conference of 1954, are composed of one representative each of a Communist, non-Communist, and unaligned state. These states are: Poland, Canada, and India. The chairman of each ICC is the representative from India. Although the Geneva Conference on Laotian Neutrality (1961–1962) enlarged the conference membership, the ICC composition remained unchanged.

The peace observers are instructed representatives and appear to be held in tight rein by their governments. The disadvantages of the "troika" structure are set forth in detail in the analysis of the Indochina cases. [1] Experience has shown that the unanimity requirement of the structure has practically dead-locked the ICC/Vietnam and the ICC/Laos. Reports of the commissions have been subjected to review by both the home governments and the co-chairmen. This procedure has resulted in considerable delay in publication of the reports.

The subordinate personnel assisting these commissions have been supplied by the same three governments. India has supplied most of the signal-communications, administrative, and financial-audit personnel. Performance of signal communications has been quite good, but the performance of the other functions has been only fair.

It is suggested that there be two categories of personnel for a UN Peace Observation Corps: (1) those who qualify as staff officers; and (2) those who qualify for work in the field. The age limits for those in the first category might be from 35 to 50; those for field work from 25 to 40.

The requirement of good judgment has been stated in varying ways by several UN senior members of observation missions as follows: "he must have demonstrated stability;" "what you want is a calm sort who doesn't air his views but has a good personality and is able to get on with the parties' brigadiers and staff;" "he must have integrity, freedom from bias, be careful in his public utterances, conscious of political background but determined to help the mission carry out its terms of reference."

[1] See pp. 489 ff.

LIAISON WITH THE PARTIES AND THE ROLE OF
THE JOINT COMMISSION

The function of a liaison officer to a mission is to provide the day-to-day contact between the mission and the government. The liaison officer to a peace-observation group or team will provide that function at the lower level.

Where hostilities are on a small scale or only threatened, the records may not show that there are any liaison officers as such. However, certain officers do carry out such functions because of the need for making day-to-day contact, and for the purpose of making appointments for meetings. Generally, the liaison officer facilitates the procurement of housing, food, transport, communications, and interpreter services.

Where there have been large-scale hostilities, the liaison officer takes care of housekeeping and protocol matters while the substantive problems are handled by a joint commission of the disputant parties or by separate national delegations attached to the peace-observation body.

In the case of guerrilla warface or armies with a low level of discipline, the presence of a liaison officer may not provide the protection it should. Cases have occurred in which liaison officers displayed marked unwillingness to carry out on-the-spot investigations at night or where repetition of a fire-fight was likely.

Observation groups and teams in the field need to know the local military and civil personalities and local conditions as quickly as possible. In accomplishing this, the liaison officers can be very helpful. Liaison officers are instruments of the parties, and the attitudes of the parties may vary from a wholehearted desire to remove tension and restore peace to a desire to entrap the observers in some sordid or disgraceful situation in order to discredit the peace-observation mission or even to use the observers as spies.

Peace-observation bodies should use liaison officers, and joint commissions, in a way that will advance the objectives of the mission. They should be wary of any service, gift, or hospitality which entails, or even appears to entail an obligation to render some service in return.

In the previous section on "Chief Tasks of Peace Observation," reference is made to the degree to which peace-observation missions should try to use joint commissions. Skillful use by a mission chief of the joint commission can greatly lighten and facilitate his task.

An important problem concerns the appropriate rank for a chief on an observation mission operating in an area where symbols and titles are matters of prestige. His rank can affect the kind of working relationship he has with the officials of the host countries. It is suggested that all chiefs of UN peace-observation missions have a military rank at least that of brigadier, and a civil rank equivalent to that of an ambassador. The post of Under-Secretary of the United Nations has this status. This rank is frequently given to UN peace-observation mission chiefs.

IMPARTIALITY AND METHODS OF ASSURING IT

One of the most important attributes of a peace-observation mission is its impartiality. Several methods have been used to safeguard this attribute, principally with reference to the selection of the personnel for such missions. The first is to avoid the inclusion of any personnel in a UN peace-observation mission who are nationals of a government traditionally hostile to one of the parties. The second is to avoid the inclusion of personnel who are nationals of a government having a direct or substantial interest in the outcome of the dispute. The third safeguard is not an inflexible one and may change if the international political situation changes. In practice, the naming of nationals of the great powers among personnel engaged in substantive tasks has been avoided. This is a reflection of the current cold war and the desire of the UN Secretary-General to have the appearance as well as the reality of impartiality.

HEADQUARTERS AND FIELD OPERATIONS

With respect to the organization of headquarters and field operations, the experience of the League of Nations and the Organization of American States affords limited guidance. This together with the wide and varied experience of the United Nations indicates how the future character and role of UN peace observation will evolve.

Because of the "troika" composition of the ICC operations, the experience of the ICC in Indochina, both at headquarters and in the field, clearly indicates that resorting to this type of organization is undesirable. Nowhere could an investigation proceed unless there were members of the Indian, Canadian, and Polish delegations present. During the period of the 1954 agreement, for example, a typical mobile or fixed team in Laos consisted of an unwieldy organization of six officers, two representing each country. Such an organization should not be used unless there is no alternative.

The UNTSO operation provides a good illustration of a middle-sized establishment covering a fairly large geographic area. Its organization is described in the accompanying chart. The chain of command in the UNTSO operation is especially instructive since in a future middle-sized operation where the observers are deployed over a wide area, an intermediate link between headquarters and the team may be needed. The intermediate link, incidentally, provides more alternatives for communications.

The chart is also instructive in that it shows precisely how the civilian component is integrated into the command structures. The civilian component covers the political, legal, and public information advisers and the

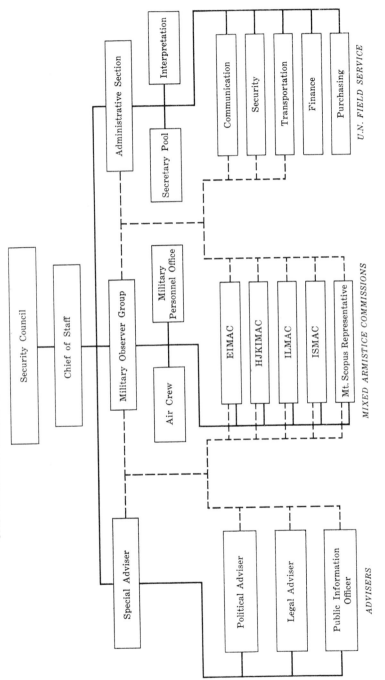

ORGANIZATION CHART OF U.N. TRUCE SUPERVISION ORGANIZATION

Security Council

Chief of Staff

Military Observer Group

Administrative Section

Secretary Pool

Interpretation

Military Personnel Office

Air Crew

EIMAC

HJKIMAC

ILMAC

ISMAC

Mt. Scopus Representative

MIXED ARMISTICE COMMISSIONS

Communication

Security

Transportation

Finance

Purchasing

U.N. FIELD SERVICE

Special Adviser

Political Adviser

Legal Adviser

Public Information Officer

ADVISERS

——— *Control channels* — — — *Co-ordination and liaison channels*

UN Field Service consisting of communications, security, transport, finance, and purchasing officers.

This chart is consistent with the illustrative Table of Organization and Equipment of a UN Peace Observation Corps.[2] Two clarifications are necessary. The provision for air crew should cover not only the operating crew for whatever aircraft are assigned, but the headquarters air transport officer as well. The provision for communications should not cover (although it does in UNTSO) communications between the mission headquarters and the UN worldwide network. The supply of equipment for the link between mission headquarters and New York is a responsibility of the United Nations headquarters itself as part of the worldwide network and hence provision for that equipment is not made in the illustrative table mentioned above.

There is a considerable diversity of opinion about what should be the basic element in the model UN peace-observation mission. Some experienced officers believe it should be the observer and his jeep. Others say that it should be a team of two observers since in some areas the risk of theft or damage to an unattended jeep is great. Moreover, if an observer has to do both observing and driving, it cuts down on his observing.

The usual practice seems to be to have a team of two observers and a jeep. This has been criticized on the ground that in those places where both sides of the line cannot be worked by the same team, the two-man team is wasteful of personnel. The rejoinder is that this is not necessarily so, for in those places where the same team cannot work on both sides of the line, the hostility must be very great. In such cases, it is helpful to have two UN observers of different nationalities who "find the facts."

The two-officer team concept has been criticized by others who say it should be a two-officer team plus an enlisted man. The enlisted man would not only guard the vehicle but would also be responsible for some of the maintenance, both actual and preventive. It ought not to be difficult to build into the enlistment qualifications the ability to operate CW (Morse Code) radio equipment and thus obtain even greater flexibility. The advocates of the two- or three-man teams would like to provide for walkie-talkie communication between the members of the team.

The concept of one-observer-one-jeep has been accepted for the purposes of planning a UN Peace Observation Corps because it provides the greatest flexibility for establishing teams. The objectives of the mission, the extent and character of the terrain in which the mission is deployed, and frequently the terms of reference, will dictate how many fixed and mobile teams are needed. After this is known, the commanding general will be in a position to deploy his observers.

[2] See pp. 634 ff.

OPERATIONAL AND LOGISTIC SUPPORT

Headquarters support did not appear to constitute a problem in the League of Nations. In the OAS, the frequency and complexity of peace observation has only recently been recognized as requiring support with the result that specific provisions in the organization of the Pan American Union have now been made for it.

The quality of support in the OAS has been good. This is due, in part, to the small-scale operations of the cases, and, in part, to the experienced and dedicated personnel with the missions. Some logistical support in the form of air transport has come from the U.S. Government.

The control commissions in Vietnam, Laos, and Cambodia have no superior headquarters to give them support and such backstopping as they receive comes from the respective governments of the individual delegations. The co-chairmen publish reports but provide no support and give no guidance to the commissions. However, since 1962 in the case of Laos, the co-chairmen are empowered to exercise general guidance and supervision.

The United Nations has provided headquarters support since the inception of its peace-observation work. To evaluate adequately its operational and logistical support would be beyond the scope of this study. It would be unfair to the UN Secretariat in general and its Field Service in particular to reach any conclusion without an exhaustive and careful review of the problem from all aspects. Without forgetting that authority must lie where responsibility lies, that is, with the Secretary-General, and that a great deal of improvisation has been unavoidable, the impression has been gained that some doubt exists about the adequacy of the logistical support rendered by the Secretariat to its field missions. Some senior military officers believe that the Secretariat supported their missions fully and efficiently. One officer, for example, declared that the quality of logistical support has been eminently satisfactory. He referred to a mission where the situation has been more or less stablized. A number of those contacted thought that the quality of UN logistical support has been good, given the difficulties of the situations presented. Several felt that UN support has been poor, inadequate, and late, and that the missions have been held on far too tight a rein by headquarters, which has continued to repeat the mistakes of previous cases. This view relates to the formative period of the missions.

Communications

From the hour a United Nations peace-observation (or peace-keeping) mission arrives in the place of operations, immediate, reliable, and secure radio communications with UN headquarters should be available on a twenty-four hour basis. Because a United Nations world-wide radio net exists, this is not particularly difficult to achieve.

The second requirement is reliable and secure radio communications with parties involved in the conflict. Such communications should likewise be set up immediately. This is generally not difficult to achieve and should extend to telephone and even teletype services. The importance of these communications cannot be overestimated, particularly where the situation is tense and hostilities may be resumed. It is not enough that the parties have confidence in the impartiality of a mission chief; they must also have confidence in the speed and reliability of his communications since military decisions depend on those communications.

The third requirement of a mission is internal communications with the groups and teams deployed in the field. In a fluid situation, the Secretary-General will need to have the facts ascertained and submitted by the observers as quickly as possible.

How to satisfy the requirements is a matter for experts. At present, the standard medium of communication between the observer and the mission headquarters is the jeep-mounted Motorola. This, however, is not always satisfactory due to the terrain, as in Kashmir, for example. The importance of radio communications between observer and headquarters is reflected in the illustrative Table of Organization and Equipment for a UN Peace Observation Corps by the amount allocated for radio equipment.

Transportation

It seems almost axiomatic that a peace-observation mission should have its own transportation, but until recently this has been more often the exception than the rule. Transportation has generally been supplied gratis by the parties or obtained commercially. This has both advantages and serious handicaps.

In Kashmir, jeeps and drivers are furnished to the UN mission by the Indian and Pakistani armies. Since there is relative good will among the parties and respect for the UN mission, this is an advantage: the mission does not have to worry about maintenance, fuel, or responsibility for accidents. In Yemen, the U.A.R. Army supplied UN vehicles with gasoline and lubricants.

In Indochina, except for local transport, the ICC relies on the parties. Since 1962, when the rules were changed for the ICC/Laos, it has had neither its own motor nor air transport. However, dependence on the parties for transport has given the Communists the excuse for denying access to the ICC by saying, "We don't have the means of transport."

Quite properly, UN missions have their own automobile transport. The jeep appears to be the favored vehicle for the field and the stripped-down version of the Citroen for town or short-range use. The principal question in regard to motor vehicle maintenance is how much the mission should attempt, that is, should it include motor overhaul? The availability of parts is so important that one UN motor vehicle maintenance supervisor recommends that the principal criterion in choice of vehicles should be whether spare parts are readily obtainable.

The illustrative Table of Organization and Equipment for a UN Peace Observation Corps rests on the concept of one-observer-one-jeep. A few three-quarter-ton four-wheel drives are also included for greater flexibility.

Because of the varying local conditions, it is difficult to state the requirements for air transportation. The initial air lift is one requirement; the operating requirement is quite different.

Almost all UN peace observers prefer the use of helicopters. The Italian helicopters in the Lebanon experience were very valuable in that rugged terrain. The ICC/Laos has four of its own, and the ICC/Cambodia uses a government Sikorsky helicopter when invited to observe. The Yemen operation has shown that they are extraordinarily difficult to maintain under desert conditions and so unreliable that they have to be sent in pairs. The UN administrative staff has reservations on the use of helicopters because they are costly to acquire and to maintain.

The initial air-lift requirements of a UN peace-observation mission are so small in relation to peace-keeping missions that they are much more easily supplied through private contract or by a UN member with a sizable air force. Some thought has been given to whether the proposed UN Peace Observation Corps should have a large transport airplane capable of transoceanic flight, but the idea was rejected because of the high cost. In recent years, the UN Field Service has provided air lifts by chartering planes or by calling on the U.S. Air Force. Sometimes charter planes are not available, and the U.S. Air Force may be engaged in an air lift of its own. It is understood that the U.S. Air Force is reluctant to earmark aircraft for UN peace observation or peace-keeping air lifts because operationally it is tantamount to "putting the units on the shelf" for the United Nations, and what ought to be a debit in the UN budget becomes a debit in the U.S. Air Force budget.

There are three ways to satisfy the requirements for UN air lifts: (1) to purchase and maintain aircraft and crews; (2) to charter planes for a single operation; (3) to contract with a large airline over a long period of time so that the airline will, when required, supply a certain number and kind of aircraft, crews, and maintenance. The preferred method, of course, would be to earmark aircraft from a national air force.

Lodging

Places to set up headquarters and lodging for personnel are often suggested and furnished by the parties. Sometimes the choices are plentiful and sometimes, as in Laos, so scanty as to constitute a bottleneck in the reception of observation officers. There is a general tendency to underestimate the life of a mission, so while a degree of improvisation may be understandable at the beginning, it is not satisfactory over a long period.

Other Services and Supplies

Several of the peace-observation and peace-keeping operations of the United Nations have been in the Middle East. UNTSO and UNEF have provided the experienced personnel and some initial supplies for the operations in Lebanon, Jordan, the Congo, Yemen, and Cyprus. Regardless of the establishment of a United Nations Peace Observation Corps, it appears likely that they will continue to provide them for some time to come.

The inventory of supplies in Gaza and Pisa is not so great that any plan may be based on this source. A considerable range of supplies is needed: tents, cots, bedding, mosquito nets, medical supplies, and office furniture. The delegation of a specified degree of procurement contracting authority to the commanding general might ease his difficulties.

DISCIPLINE, WELFARE, AND MORALE

The discipline problem of peace-observation missions is commendably small. Breaches of discipline are rare.

It is assumed that the United Nations will continue to conclude status agreements for peace-observation operations wherever appropriate. These provide for immunity of UN personnel from local jurisdiction. It is recommended that the terms of the contract between the United Nations and officer observers state that the Secretary-General may waive diplomatic immunity on the recommendation of the chief of the mission. In cases of very serious crime, the Secretary-General, no less than the U.S. Secretary of State, should be in a position to waive the immunity if that appears appropriate.

Welfare and morale are related matters, and success in welfare tends to lead to high morale. Mail call is as important for officers as it is for troops. When deployed over long distances, with poor internal transport, the problem will be difficult, as every commander knows. Mail and newspapers from home should have high priority. The prompt issue of pay and allowances is also an important factor in keeping morale high. In all UN operations visited, post exchange and leave facilities appeared to be limited but quite adequate. UN personnel were proud of their blue berets, scarves, and insignia, and although the matter was not touched upon, it was obvious they would feel distinguished to wear UN awards or medals as well.

The resources for medical services vary so greatly from place to place that the illustrative Table of Organization and Equipment for a UN Peace Observation Corps at the end of this study provides for the inclusion of a single hospital corpsman or male nurse. Experience has shown that U.S. Embassy Medical Centers abroad are generous in making hospital supplies and drugs available.

CONCLUSIONS

What is needed now, and will be increasingly needed in the future, is a clear-cut conception by all working elements of the relationship between UN Headquarters and the field operations. In the field, the relationship between the chief of the mission, if he is a military man, and the senior political adviser needs to be clarified. Conflict between headquarters and the field is a common occurrence in business and corporations engaged in international trade, in the relations between the Pentagon and the theatre commanders, and between the Department of State and embassies and consulates. Each may have a different viewpoint of the operation and hence arrive at a different judgment.

It is clear that the chief of a peace-observation mission, be he a military man or a civilian, must be the undisputed head of his mission. But missions frequently are neither wholly military nor wholly political in nature. They are mixed, and are manned by military and civilian personnel, and it is here that friction can arise. Where a mission is headed by a military man, requiring the support of a civilian political adviser who may also serve as the personal representative of the Secretary-General, conflict of authority is likely to arise. The civilian political adviser must respect the authority of the chief of mission, and a wise chief will take into account the guidance offered him by the political adviser.

The question of which logistical decisions should be made at headquarters and which in the field can be clarified by a guiding principle— authority to procure should be clearly spelled out and be delegated as close to the scene of action as practicable. However, competence must accompany such delegation, and if the competence is not there, it must be achieved by training or recruitment.

The experience of the United States Government in its operations abroad is illuminating. During 1961–1964, there have been broad changes. The power of procurement contracting by the Secretary of State has, within specified limits, been delegated to the Chiefs of Mission abroad.[3] This might well be the policy that the UN Secretariat should consider for peace-observation missions. Because of the great diversity of conditions, great distances, operations in primitive countries and the need for speed, a certain amount of flexibility appears essential.

[3] U.S. Department of State, Regulations, Delegation of Authority No. 23-G, May 28, 1964.

6

—•—

TERMINATION OF PEACE OBSERVATION

This subject has been referred to in the section of this study dealing with the terms of reference and authority of peace-observation missions. However, the problem transcends terms of reference. The nature of the controversy may be such that peace observation should continue beyond the specific term incorporated in advance in the resolution establishing the mission. In contrast, many missions have no specified time limits. In what circumstances and by what methods should such missions be terminated? The problems raise considerations beyond those dealt with in a study of terms of reference.

As was heretofore pointed out, once a mission is established, it tends to perpetuate its operations for a number of reasons: (1) Vested interests in the continuance of the mission develop not only among the mission personnel but among the government personnel of the states parties to the controversy. (2) The mere existence of the mission even after its active functions have ceased is occasionally deemed a protection against renewal of violence. Thus the mission performs the function of a security blanket, for example, UNCURK and POC in Greece. (3) It may be easier to continue the mission than to obtain a decision for its termination.

A TIME LIMIT IN THE TERMS OF REFERENCE

The practice in this matter has varied both in the League of Nations and in the United Nations. In one of the two League cases most closely approximating the type of peace-observation later carried on by the United Nations—the Leticia case—there was a time limit of one year. Unquestionably, this time limit facilitated the highly satisfactory results that were obtained. The mission was stationed in unhealthy and uncomfortable terrain near the headwaters of the Amazon River. The existence of a time limit must have had a good morale effect on its members. However, the accomplishment of its objectives within a year became possible largely through an accident—the assassination of the dictator of Peru—which made possible a substantive settlement within the specified time limit.

In another League case—the Mosul controversy—the peace-observation functions had no time limit but terminated with the settlement of the controversy.

In the United Nations, to mention only a few examples, no time limits have been established for the peace-observation missions operating in Palestine and Kashmir. They have continued for years with no indication that they can ever be abandoned until solutions of the political controversies that made the peace observation essential are reached. It is difficult to see how the incorporation of a time limit in the resolutions establishing the peace observation could have changed this situation. Undoubtedly, the original time limit would have had to be extended when it expired. This has proved necessary in connection with the mission presently operating in Yemen, which has always operated under time limitations, and the same experience has taken place in Cyprus. In contrast, the observation group in Lebanon, UNOGIL, which had no time limit was terminated quite promptly as a result of the disappearance of the political situation that required its establishment.

It appears that the termination of a peace-observation mission has little relation to the inclusion within terms of reference of a time limit for its operations. Where there is a reasonable chance of accomplishing the objectives of the mission in a limited time, it seems advisable to provide such a limitation in the terms of reference. This is partly to limit the financial support needed and partly for the morale effect both on the observers, whose enthusiasm is diminished through the prospect of a lengthy mission with small accomplishment, and on the public, which may not support a protracted operation. However, there seems to be little advantage in providing an arbitrary time limit that cannot be met, as in Cyprus. Such a time limit, however, may be necessary, as in Cyprus, because of the unwillingness of the parties or of a great power to assent to a mission of indefinite length.

TERMINATION OF STATUS AGREEMENT

UNEF operates on the Egyptian side of the border of Israel under a status agreement, which the Egyptians could terminate at any time. This arrangement arose because Israel never agreed to UNEF operating on its side of the border. In this case, the arrangement has advantages. The Egyptians, in order to obtain the benefits of UNEF, must continue to adhere to the status agreement that gives UNEF the broad powers and authority required for an effective operation. However, such a method of termination, from a long-range standpoint, seems unsatisfactory since Egypt might decide to terminate the peace-observation activities at the moment they are most essential. The United Nations would then have the choice of abandoning the peace-observation operation or establishing and imposing new emergency machinery.

SOLUTION OF CONTROVERSY

In the experience of the League of Nations, the Organization of American States, and the United Nations, obviously the best way of terminating a peace-observation mission has been through solving the controversy that led to the breach of the peace in the first place. As pointed out in other sections of this study, the relation of the peace-observation operations to the solution of the controversy varies. Occasionally, as in Indonesia, peace observation has focused on specific tasks directed toward facilitating a political settlement. In other situations, such as UNSCOB, peace observation tended to reduce the violence and disorder along the border thus facilitating the détente that took place following the Soviet-Yugoslav impasse. Certainly, the most satisfactory method of terminating a peace-observation mission is through the successful accomplishment of its objectives. Therefore, the peace-observation activities should be worked out wherever possible to facilitate a specific settlement. However, this formula gives no answer to the problem of termination where the controversy itself has not been solved.

CONTROL OVER FUNDS

A peace-observation mission can obviously be terminated through withdrawal of the funds for its activities. The threat of sudden death through denial of funds hangs over every mission regardless of the need for its continuance. Recently, financial support has been tenuous for four United Nations missions whose problems are far from any solution: the Congo—a peace-keeping rather than a peace-observation mission—which terminated on June 30, 1964 with major unsolved problems; the Yemen mission, the continuance of which depends on periodic agreement of the parties to defray expenses; the Cyprus mission (primarily peace-keeping), the continuance of which depends on voluntary contributions from United Nations members; and UNEF, which both parties desire to continue, but the Soviet bloc declines to pay its share of the expenses. The financial limitations of the operations may compel their reduction even where the funds are not completely cut off.

Terminating a peace-observation mission through denial of financial support from the standpoint of world peace may be irresponsible. It may result in the cutting off of a useful activity at a crucial time. The only remedy would seem to be through establishing firm, long-term financial support for the missions at the time of their establishment.

The present methods of financial support are: (1) through the United Nations budget, (2) through special contributions by UN members, (3) through reimbursement of the United Nations by the parties to the controversy. Although it is difficult to ensure long-term financing of a peace-observation operation through any of these methods, there are guidelines to minimize the danger that the mission will be cut off financially before its task is completed. Where the mission is to be financed through the United Nations budget, there should be some agreement among the great powers not only that the mission should be established but that at least for a reasonable length of time, it should be financed in this manner.

Where a great power such as the Soviet Union is willing to acquiesce in the establishment of the mission but is unenthusiastic, the mission should probably be financed through special contributions by the United Nations members. If this decision is made at the outset, the special contributions will probably continue at least during any period of crisis.

Where the parties to the controversy agree to defray the costs of the peace-observation mission, the probabilities are that financial support will continue as long as necessary. Particularly with this method of financing, the considerations leading toward the perpetuation of the operation of a mission come into play. Furthermore, it is suggested that if the mission is financed by the contributions of both parties, and both parties determine to withdraw their financial support, usually this would be a sufficient reason to terminate the mission. The serious problems of financial support of a mission financed in this manner could arise only where one of the parties desired to withdraw its financial support.

CONCLUSIONS AND RECOMMENDATIONS

1. A time limit for a peace-observation mission or at least a target date for the completion of its work should be included in the resolution establishing the mission whenever there is a reasonable probability that the time limit can be met.

2. Where the nature of the controversy or the circumstances surrounding it are such that it is difficult to foresee the length of the mission, either the mission should be established without a time limit or an easy procedure should be provided for extending the time limit.

3. A peace-observation mission will ordinarily terminate at the latest when the controversy leading to the disturbance of the peace has been solved. In some cases, progress toward solution of the controversy may result in the elimination of violence at an earlier date.

4. Wherever possible, the authority to terminate peace-observation should rest exclusively in the international organ establishing the mission. Neither party to the controversy nor both parties acting in agreement should have the authority to terminate the mission without the approval of the international organ establishing it.

5. In some instances, one or both parties to the controversy may in effect be in a position to terminate the mission through termination of the

status agreement under which the mission operates. If such a power exists, it is fundamental that the termination of the status agreement should terminate all operations. Neither party should be in a position to choose the portions of the status agreement to which they are willing to continue to adhere. They should be confronted with a choice of peace-observation as originally contemplated or no peace-observation at all. If both parties have signed status agreements and only one party terminates its status agreement, the international organ establishing the mission should be in a position to determine whether it should continue with access to only one side of the boundary.

6. Since every peace-observation mission can in effect be terminated through denial of funds for its continuance, every effort should be made to ensure at the time the mission is established that it will have the funds to continue for a period of time having some relation to the time anticipated to solve the controversy.

7. Peace-observation missions, once they are established, have a tendency to continue, sometimes after the need for the mission has lessened or has vanished. This tendency for a mission to perpetuate itself should be taken into consideration in working out the arrangements for financing it. If the states with vested interests in the continuance of the mission are the same as those primarily responsible for its financing, the likelihood is less that a mission will be terminated through denial of funds prior to the completion of its work.

7

RELATION OF PEACE OBSERVATION AND MEDIATION

The problem of the relation of peace observation to mediation or other efforts to effect a peaceful settlement of international controversies has arisen in connection with practically every controversy since World War II where peace-observation missions functioned. It arose in a different context in connection with League of Nations commissions of enquiry. In this section, except where otherwise specified, the term mediation is used to cover any method of peaceful settlement involving the use of an unbiased individual or group to obtain some sort of an agreed settlement of an international dispute. In this sense, the term mediation would include good offices, conciliation, and even arbitration. Mediation would include peaceful settlement of political problems incidental to the major political issues as well as peaceful settlement of the major issues.

At the outset, it should be observed that a study of the most important UN peace-observation missions, on the surface, leads to conflicting conclusions about the role of mediation in connection with such missions. In connection with the Palestine problem, the most knowledgeable students stress the necessity of separating the peace-observation machinery, for example, UNEF, UNTSO, and the MAC's, from the conciliation machinery, for example the PCC. They point out that Count Bernadotte, who at the outset combined both functions, was assassinated probably because of the antagonism in Israel for his mediation activities. The same individuals contend that no chief of UNTSO or UNEF could retain the measure of respect from both sides required to maintain a peaceful border if he had any responsibility for suggesting a settlement of the political differences between the Israelis and the Arabs.

On the other hand, there are two significant but contrasting examples where an original separation of the peace-observation and mediation functions hampered both functions, and where the functions were later successfully combined. In the controversies relating to the independence of Indonesia, two separate groups were set up originally, one responsible for peace observation, the other for mediation (in this specific instance to use its good offices). Within three months, it became apparent that the best way to eliminate violence was through a political settlement, and also that the lessening of violence would facilitate a political settlement. Therefore the peace-observation mission was subordinated to the conciliation mission—became its eyes and ears and carried on the activities that would best facilitate a peaceful settlement.

In the recent situation in Yemen, the UN mission started out with peace-observation functions, but the Secretary-General realized that some mediatory functions would facilitate the peace observation. Thus, the two functions as in the case of Indonesia were combined, with peace observation subordinated to mediation.

It should be pointed out that in Palestine and Kashmir, the two important UN cases where the peace-observation functions have remained separated from the mediation functions, the United Nations has achieved neither a political settlement nor a sufficient reduction of border tensions to make possible the termination of the peace-observation missions. However, in both these cases, a political settlement appears to be confronted with almost insuperable obstacles.

The question is whether some general conclusions can be drawn from the wide variety of patterns that have emerged in connection with the relation of peace observation to mediation.

PAST PROCEDURES INVOLVING PEACE OBSERVATION
AND MEDIATION

In the OAS, considerable emphasis has traditionally been placed on mediation in all cases of international conflict where there was a reasonable prospect of success. Accordingly, peace-observation missions frequently found themselves engaged in informal mediation efforts that strongly influenced their recommendations to the parent body—the Council. In some cases, the peace-observation mission was authorized to carry on mediation. In other cases, a technical distinction was drawn between the peace-observation mission as such and the mediatory body by abolishing the investigating committee and establishing a new group for the purpose of mediation that often included the same personnel. The strong desire to leave the door open for mediation, in some cases at least, tempered the presentation of evidence by the peace-observation group in their public report.

The League of Nations cases for the purposes of this analysis can be roughly divided into seven types:

1. The League of Nations commissions of enquiry in four instances were intended primarily to furnish a factual basis for the later League decisions to produce a pacific settlement—Corfu, Memel, Manchuria (excluding the Consular Commission at Shanghai), and the Aaland Islands. In these cases, the relation of peace observation and mediation did not arise as the commissions had no functions relating to mediation. Also in general these commissions were not concerned with the existence of violence or disorders in the respective areas.

2. In the Saar case, the commission maintained law and order and supervised a settlement previously determined by the League. Here again, the relationship of mediation and peace observation did not arise.

3. The Shanghai Consular Commission had only peace-observation functions. Some of its findings undoubtedly played a role in the unsuccessful attempts of the League to settle the Manchurian crisis.

4. In the Ethiopian crisis, there were attempts to mediate, but no peace observation. A suggested commission of enquiry never materialized.

5. The remaining League cases involved both peace observation and mediation. The usual League pattern was to separate the functions completely with mediation being carried out by organs outside the League (Vilna, the Albanian border, Leticia, and Silesia). In all of these instances except Leticia, the existence of separate mediation and peace-observation groups caused some problems. In the Vilna and Albanian cases, the relation between the League of Nations commissions and the Conference of Ambassadors outside the League, which ultimately worked out settlements, was far from satisfactory. In the Silesia case, the Interallied Force and Plebiscite commissions, responsible for functions that might be described

as peace observation, were far from neutral. The League worked out a settlement. In the Leticia case, the League commission did excellent work in keeping order and improving living conditions in the area. Simultaneously, a direct settlement between the parties became possible after the assassination of the Peruvian dictator.

6. The Greek-Bulgarian controversy involved both peace observation and mediation. In this highly successful case, the Council of the League insisted on the withdrawal of Greek troops from Bulgaria in sixty hours and used military attachés to observe the withdrawal. After the restoration of order, the Council used a commission of enquiry to work out a settlement that was accepted.

7. Mosul is the one League case in which a commission carried on both peace observation and mediation functions. Initially, the commission was merely seeking to establish the factual background for a settlement. However, the restoration of law and order became essential to a settlement, and the commission successfully dealt with both problems.

In the most important United Nations missions, the relation of peace observation to mediation may be summarized as follows:

On the Greek Border, peace observation took place on only one side of the boundary. The terms of reference of the peace-observation group included mediation functions. However, the attempts to mediate took place in another forum. The border was stabilized without any settlement of the underlying controversy because of changes in the world situation coupled with successful peace observation.

In Palestine during the first year of peace observation, the Mediator, Count Bernadotte, was responsible for both mediation and peace observation. Thereafter the functions were separated. Virtually no progress has been made in settling the Palestine dispute. From 1949 to 1952, there was some lessening of violence along the borders. From 1952 until 1956, violence increased. After the installation of UNEF along the Egyptian border in 1956, all of the Israeli borders became more stable.

In Indonesia, at the outset of the controversy, the United Nations Security Council set up separate groups for mediation and for peace observation. After three months the two groups were combined, with the peace-observation function ancillary to the main objective of obtaining a political settlement. The solution of the political problem eliminated the need for peace observation.

In Korea before the outbreak of hostilities in June 1950, the various UN commissions had both peace-observation and mediation functions. However, because of the failure of North Korea to cooperate, no mediation was possible and the peace observation was limited to areas south of the boundary. The peace-observation group achieved some success. The mediation functions of the group may have assisted its efforts to temper some actions of the South Korean Government.

The Neutral Nations Supervisory Commission after the Korean Armistice had no mediation functions. The Geneva Conference of 1954 attempted without success to solve the Korean problem. The main peace-observation efforts collapsed after the failure to achieve a political solution.

In Kashmir, the original commission had both peace-observation and mediation functions. After six months, however, a separate group reporting directly to the UN Secretary-General assumed responsibility for peace observation. Peace observation has been relatively successful in reducing border violence and continues without prospect of termination. The mediation to date has failed.

In Lebanon, the peace-observation mission had no authority to mediate but found that some unofficial mediation was necessary though unauthorized. The need for peace observation came to an end when internal conditions in Lebanon changed.

The United Nations Presence in Jordan, a mission that still continues, has only peace-observation functions of a passive character. There is no tangible controversy to mediate.

In West Irian, since the parties had already achieved a political settlement, the mission continued in the role of peace observation. It was successfully concluded within the time limits set in its terms of reference.

The functions of the international control commissions in Southeast Asia, acting outside the framework of the United Nations, were exclusively in the field of peace observation, to observe the implementation of an agreed settlement. Peace observation has been, in the main, effective in Cambodia; in Laos and Vietnam, however, many features of the settlements have not been carried out.

In Cyprus, the mediation function is separate from the peace-keeping function. It would be premature to predict the success or failure of either function.

CONCLUSIONS

It is suggested that neither the invariable combination of peace-observation and mediation functions in OAS missions nor their almost invariable separation under the League of Nations furnish a simple answer to the problem of the relation of mediation to peace observation in the existing world situation. The OAS practice stemmed from special conditions associated with the Latin American approach to foreign affairs and the nature of the cases. The League of Nations practice of separate commissions or groups dealing with the mediation and peace-observation or peace-keeping aspects of problems was largely a reflection of the constitutional structure of the League.

A cursory review of the principal United Nations peace-observation cases might lead to the conclusion that there are no guidelines to the relation of mediation to a peace-observation mission, and that each separate controversy must be judged on its specific facts. While the peculiar circumstances of individual cases must be borne in mind, there are certain broad principles that have considerable validity so long as they are not treated as inflexible rules. The League of Nations experience tends to confirm these principles, which may be summarized as follows:

Situation A: Where there is an apparently irreconcilable political controversy.

In general, where a political settlement appears impossible to attain in the near future, the peace-observation functions should be separated from the mediation functions. Peace observation can best make its maximum contribution to ultimate settlement of the political controversy through reducing tensions in the area. The peace-observation mission can establish the confidence of both sides needed to achieve this objective, if the mission does not have the extra burden of suggesting settlements that will probably be unacceptable to both sides. Two subsidiary situations should be differentiated. (1) Where a great deal of violence exists in the area, this is the clearest case for separation of the mediation and peace-observation functions since the reduction of violence is the best hope of accelerating an ultimate political settlement, for example, Palestine and Leticia. (2) Where the area is relatively tranquil and tensions are higher in the capitals than along the boundary, the advantage of keeping the area tranquil could be partially offset by the possibility that the absence of violent incidents would reduce the pressures for a political settlement, for example, Kashmir and the Aaland Islands. Nevertheless, it seems that in this type of situation, the peace-observation and mediation functions should be separated.

Situation B: Where the general principles of a political settlement have been agreed upon and the chief problem is to implement the political settlement.

This is the clearest case for combining mediation and peace-observation functions. The peace observers are often in the best position to suggest the best methods for implementing the political settlement and will not lose the confidence of either party through their suggestions since the final objective has already been determined, for example, the independence of Indonesia and West Irian.[1]

Situation C: Where elimination of violence in the area is more urgent than a political solution.

In this situation, it seems advisable to authorize the peace-observation mission to attempt to mediate at least localized political issues though not the entire political controversy. Such authority has proved useful in reducing violence in the area, for example, Mosul, UNSCOB, and Yemen.

---

[1] In most of the League of Nations cases, the danger of war or violence subsided after the political settlement of the case and therefore peace observation was not required after the political settlement.

However, where an ultimate political settlement seems impossible to achieve except through high-level political negotiations outside the area, it seems desirable to separate the peace-observation functions from the mediation functions or limit the mediation to highly localized issues.

Situation D: Where changes occur during the life of the mission.

Changes in the relation of peace observation to mediation may become necessary during the life of the mission, and, therefore, the terms of reference should be sufficiently flexible to facilitate such changes, for example, Vilna, Palestine, Kashmir, Yemen, and Cambodia.

8

PEACE OBSERVATION IN RELATION TO DISARMAMENT

Until the United States presented the "Outline of Basic Provisions of a Treaty on General and Complete Disarmament in a Peaceful World," in 1962, specific proposals for peace observation had never been included as a part of disarmament proposals. The purpose of this section is to sketch the historical background of the relation of peace observation to disarmament with a view to shedding light on the possible future character and role of peace-observation arrangements under the United Nations, now, in the near future, and under conditions of a disarming world.

HISTORICAL BACKGROUND

The relation of the equivalent of peace observation (the term itself is never used) and disarmament in the League of Nations period is sketched only briefly because of the different conditions prevailing under the League and because the United Nations approach toward disarmament represented a break with the past.[1] The League of Nations experience in

---

[1] "Two of the general activities of the League were, at least for the time being, left on the side—the organization of disarmament and the protection of minorities . . . the delegates who at Dumbarton Oaks and San Francisco laid the foundations of the United Nations, shrank from reopening old controversies." F. P. Walters, *A History of the League of Nations* (London: Oxford University Press, 1952), p. 813. For further elaboration, see Bernhard G. Bechhoefer, *Postwar Negotiations for Arms Control* (Washington: Brookings Institution, 1961), pp. 11–14.

disarmament, however, is useful in pointing out the general relation of disarmament to the maintenance of world peace. The United Nations Charter provisions on pacific settlement and nonmilitary sanctions, in contrast to the regulations of armaments provisions, stemmed largely from the League of Nations example.[2]

The heart of the League Covenant was in the provisions designed to prevent wars, Articles 8 to 17 inclusive. Section 1 of the first of these articles entitled "Reduction of Armaments" reads: "The Members of the League recognize that the maintenance of peace requires the reduction of national armaments to the lowest point consistent with national safety and the enforcement by common action of international obligations." Thus, reduction of armaments and international peace-keeping which would include peace observation were linked.

Article 8 specified the approach to arms reduction, which was an immediate task of the Council of the League. The chief characteristics of this approach may be summarized as follows. (1) The Council would suggest the amounts of the reductions or the levels of armaments. (2) The Council's suggestions, however, would not be binding on any state unless that state accepted the findings. (3) All states would agree not to exceed the fixed limits of armaments. However, the only provision for assuring fulfillment of agreements was: "The members of the League undertake to interchange full and frank information as to the scale of their armaments, their military, naval, and air programmes and the conditions of such of their industries as are adaptable to warlike purposes." Under conditions after World War I, these provisions were not as inadequate as under the conditions existing today. The provisions applied only to League members, which never included the United States and did not include the Soviet Union until 1934. Presumably, the military strength of the League members would always far exceed that of the nonmembers. There was no iron curtain dividing the members, and, therefore, failure to interchange full information might readily have been detected.

Article 8 was directly linked with the subsequent articles designed to prevent war. Article 9 provided for a permanent military, naval, and air commission to advise the Council on the execution of Articles 1 to 8 "and on military, naval and air questions generally." This provision greatly facilitated the effective commissions of enquiry.

Articles 10 to 17 inclusive contained the provisions for dealing with international disputes. The main effort was to channel the disputes into the various modes of peaceful settlement: arbitration, conciliation, or reference to the Permanent Court of International Justice. Sanctions were provided in case of resort to war in disregard of the Covenant. However, non-military sanctions required the unanimous approval of the Council of the

[2] Walters, *op. cit.*, p. 380.

League, and the Council could not go farther than to recommend military sanctions.

Commissions of enquiry, which in effect would be carrying out peace-observation functions, as pointed out in the studies of the specific cases, were contemplated under Articles 11 and 12.

The interesting feature of the disarmament negotiations, which were pursued vigorously during almost the entire period between World War I and World War II, is that their failure apparently stemmed from the inability of the great powers to provide concurrently for the solution of international political problems, which again in simplified terms may be described under the rubric "security."

Salvador de Madariaga, who in the twenties headed the section of the League Secretariat concerned with disarmament, concluded:

> If we now look back on the ground we have covered we find that the program of preliminary questions to be solved before disarmament can be a reality comprises:
> (a) A thoroughgoing organization of the World-Community having for its basis a universal League of Nations with power to take a hand in all the problems arising in the normal course of international life.
> (b) A thoroughgoing examination of all present discontents with a view to international solutions on world lines implying perhaps far-reaching changes in existing conditions of law and fact. [3]

This broad program of de Madariaga obviously goes much farther than the *Outline* in uniting the solution of other international problems with disarmament. It is significant that his disarmament views included the equivalent of international peace observation: "The League should possess an organization entrusted with the duty and the power of keeping its hand on the pulse of the world and of reporting the slightest tremor of armament fear." [4]

This program reflects his accumulated experience from years of negotiations. He points out specific failures and the reasons therefor: (1) The British proposal at the Washington Conference for land disarmament did not include naval disarmament. (2) Universal naval limitations depended on the concurrent political action to keep straits open and to protect non-riparian states; (3) A Draft Treaty of Guarantee (1924), coupling guarantees against aggression with reduction of armaments, was rejected by the British Government ostensibly because the guarantees were not sufficiently strong. The fault of the treaty was, however, its virtual neglect of arbitration as a useful instrument. (4) The Preparatory Commission established after the Locarno Treaties "though definitely created in order to tackle the prob-

[3] Salvador de Madariaga, *Disarmament* (New York: Coward-McCann, Inc., 1929), p. 339.
[4] *Ibid.,* p. 357.

lem of disarmament direct, could not get away from the problem of security." (5) The Preparatory Commission made considerable progress on some collateral matters affecting security—arbitration of international disputes, poison gas, and chemical warfare. However, a Disarmament Convention had not yet emerged by 1929. A main factor was that a third problem, international organization, had been added to the twin problems of security and disarmament.[5]

The United Kingdom and the United States, which by 1929 was participating in the technical discussions, ironically were insisting "that treaties rest on mutual confidence and their fulfillment should not be supervised nor in any way controlled."[6]

This brief outline is merely to point out that the League experience might well have been used in the United Nations discussions to avoid some pitfalls. It was not so used. However, the League experience makes it clear that any extensive progress toward disarmament requires simultaneous provision for protection against aggression (security) and for peaceful settlement of disputes (arbitration). This in turn requires the strengthening of international organization to maintain international peace. Peace observation is one instrument to accomplish this objective.

There was a complete break between the United Nations discussions of disarmament and all preceding disarmament negotiations.[7] Indeed only in 1952, after more than six years of UN negotiations, did any of the representatives in the commissions dealing with disarmament express interest in the League of Nations negotiations. The UN Secretary-General in February 1953 compiled a background paper on the League experience at the request of the Disarmament Commission.[8] The narrative portion of this paper occupied nine pages and satisfied the commission's requirements.

The Charter of the United Nations in effect set up a system of priorities for postwar problems relating to the regulation of armaments. The Allied Powers at the outset would disarm the Germans and the Japanese. The first task of the Security Council with its primary responsibility for the maintenance of world peace was to secure through agreements with states the forces necessary to maintain world peace (Article 43). A much less urgent task was to prepare plans to be submitted to the members of the United Nations for a system for the regulation of armaments. The least urgent task was for the General Assembly as a long-range planning organization to make recommendations but to take no action concerning "the principles governing disarmament and the regulation of armaments" (Article 11).

Obviously, it was never contemplated that active disarmament negotiations would commence at the very outset of the United Nations. The

[5] *Ibid.*, pp. 103, 105, 118 ff, 160, 198.
[6] *Ibid.*, p. 223.
[7] See Walters, *op. cit.*, p. 813.
[8] UN Secretariat, Department of Public Information, ST/DPI/SER.A./75, Feb. 20, 1953.

provisions permitting peace observation were in a different Chapter of the United Nations Charter (Chapter VI) and, unlike Article 8 of the League Covenant, were in no way related to disarmament.

The ideas of the United Nations founding fathers in giving a low priority to disarmament discussions were shattered by the explosion of nuclear bombs in Japan. Within a month, the President of the United States had stated:

> The atomic bomb is too dangerous to be loose in a lawless world. That is why Great Britain and the United States who have the secret of its production, do not intend to reveal the secret until means have been found to control the bomb so as to protect ourselves and the rest of the world from the danger of total destruction. [9]

The UN Security Council in its first month set up the United Nations Atomic Energy Commission to consider not only regulation of armaments but also atomic disarmament.

At the opening of the first regular General Assembly session in the fall of 1946, the Soviet Union called for a general reduction of armaments in addition to the prohibition of nuclear weapons.

The General Assembly resolution in response to this Soviet proposal recommended a second commission to deal with conventional armaments.[10] This resolution linked three phases involved in the problem of regulation of armaments: (1) elimination of nuclear weapons, (2) regulation of conventional weapons, (3) establishment of UN military forces, the task of the Military Staff Committee.

With this division of the problem, there was no basis for proposals involving peace observation in either the United Nations Atomic Energy Commission or in the Commission for Conventional Armaments, and none materialized. The Conventional Armaments Commission adopted over Soviet opposition a series of principles, which included the following: a system for the regulation and reduction of armaments "can only be put into effect in an atmosphere of international confidence and security." One condition essential to such confidence and security was "the establishment of an adequate system of agreements under Article 43 of the Charter."[11]

Thus the general association of disarmament and UN peace-keeping was recognized, but there were no details. Unfortunately, in a strange aberration, the United States representative in the Security Council on one occasion even denied the existence of a relationship.[12] This aberration was

[9] U.S. Department of State, *The International Control of Atomic Energy: Growth of a Policy*, Publication 2702 (1946), p. 108.

[10] UN General Assembly, Res. 41 (I), Dec. 14, 1946.

[11] UN Security Council, Commission for Conventional Armaments, S/C. 3/SR 1, March 26, 1947, p. 5.

[12] UN Security Council, *Official Records*, Second Year, 157th and 158th meetings, July 15, 1947, pp. 1297–98.

corrected by the Vandenberg Resolution approved by the Senate in 1948 linking "maximum efforts to obtain agreements to provide the UN with armed forces as provided by the Charter, and to obtain agreement among member nations upon universal regulation and reduction of armaments under adequate and dependable guaranty against violation."[13]

In the Essentials of Peace Resolution of the General Assembly in 1949, control of atomic energy and reduction of armaments were merely two of many essentials for a peaceful world.

In 1950, the General Assembly, profiting from the Korean experience, took substantial steps to improve the United Nations peace-keeping and peace-observation machinery. However, the General Assembly created a new suborgan, the Collective Measures Committee, to deal with these problems and did not refer them to the commissions having responsibility for regulation of armaments. The UN studies of collective measures took place in a section of the UN Secretariat that had no functions in the disarmament field.

In January 1952, the resolution establishing the Disarmament Commission[14] and abolishing the previous commissions recognized four separate subjects for discussion: (1) regulation, limitation, and balanced reduction of all armed forces and all armaments, (2) elimination of all weapons adaptable to mass destruction, (3) effective international control of atomic energy, (4) establishment of an adequate system of safeguards. All proposals until 1959 were directed toward one or more of these objectives. No proposal dealt with the relationship of peace-keeping or peace observation under the United Nations to arms reduction. This did not mean any lack of concern with the peace-keeping or peace-observation machinery. It simply meant that the Disarmament Commission was concentrating on other phases of the problem of maintaining peace: from 1952 until 1955 on a general program of arms control; and from 1955 through 1959 on separate partial measures of disarmament to reduce tension and lead to later extensive disarmament.

All the disarmament negotiations during this period were predicated on the proposition that some measure of agreement on arms control would in and of itself improve the international atmosphere and facilitate the settlement of other outstanding international controversies. Arms control negotiations contemplated simultaneous negotiations on other subjects. Therefore, the disarmament and arms control proposals need not include other issues even though their settlement might become essential at some stage of the disarmament program. There was no need for the West to propose in the disarmament negotiations improved United Nations peace-keeping or peace observation as long as the Soviet Union was willing to negotiate either a program of comprehensive disarmament or partial first stage measures of

[13] S. Res. 239, 80 Cong, 2 sess., June 11, 1948.
[14] UN General Assembly, Res. 502 (VI), Jan. 11, 1952.

disarmament. Peace observation proposals could be a partial first stage measure whether proposed in the disarmament negotiations or elsewhere.

In his 1959 address to the UN General Assembly, Premier Khrushchev, after advocating general and complete disarmament for something over an hour, spent the last five minutes suggesting a program of partial measures of disarmament:

> It goes without saying, that, if at present the Western Powers do not, for one reason or another express their readiness to embark upon general and complete disarmament, the Soviet Government is prepared to come to terms with other States on appropriate partial measures relating to disarmament and the strengthening of security.[15]

This statement opened the possibility that general and complete disarmament would be merely a long-range objective, which everyone, the West as well as the Soviet Union, must endorse. At most, it might be a general negotiating framework with specific negotiations on partial measures. In this context, peace-observation or peace-keeping proposals might still have remained separate from the disarmament negotiations, even though Khrushchev had specifically linked disarmament and the strengthening of security in describing partial measures. However, the Ten-Power Conference in 1960 made it clear that, for a time at least, the Soviet Union was determined to reap the full propaganda benefits from its advocacy of general and complete disarmament. The Western powers were therefore forced into the position of pointing out in their endorsement of general and complete disarmament the most important changes in world conditions that must accompany such disarmament, including the establishment of international machinery to ensure the maintenance of world order in a disarming world. International peace-observation as well as peace-keeping machinery would be required. When the decision was made to present the United States program in the form of an outline of basic treaty provisions, a format that has many advantages that need not be elaborated here, provisions relating to peace-keeping and peace observation were both logical and desirable. Thus, these subjects for the first time since the establishment of the United Nations became part of the disarmament negotiations.

PEACE–OBSERVATION MACHINERY AND THE INTERNATIONAL DISARMAMENT ORGANIZATION

The *Outline* might well have called for peace-observation machinery under the control of the International Disarmament Organization. It also might have called for a separate organization for peace observation that,

[15] UN General Assembly, *Official Records*, Fourteenth Session, Plenary, 799th meeting, Sept. 18, 1959, p. 37.

like the International Disarmament Organization, would function within the framework of the United Nations. However, the *Outline* called for a Peace Observation Corps within the United Nations. This study is confined to the future character and role of peace-observation arrangements under the United Nations. Therefore, the other possibilities need not be considered.

The decision that peace observation should be within the United Nations carried the further implication that suggestions for peace observation should be targeted to a period when the role of the United Nations would remain roughly as at present.

This dictates a pragmatic approach toward peace observation: What type of arrangements will work best in the foreseeable future rather than what is the ideal framework for peace?

PEACE OBSERVATION AND PARTIAL MEASURES

Historically, peace observation and peace-keeping became part of the disarmament negotiations during the discussions of general and complete disarmament where their relevance has already been pointed out. Proposals involving peace observation may be even more important as part of a program of partial and immediately realizable measures. The West has at all times recognized that little progress toward lessening the arms race is possible until the negotiations concentrate on immediately realizable steps. In 1964 and early 1965 the Soviet Union seemed willing once again to return to its 1955–1957 positions of meaningful negotiating on partial measures.

In such a context, peace-observation proposals can play an important role for two main reasons. First, the Secretary-General has already worked out some successful procedures to deal with peace-observation missions. These procedures have in some respects already advanced further than the U.S. proposals for peace observation in the first stage of disarmament. Therefore, the negotiations have something tangible with which to begin. Second, many students of arms control believe that the area of implicit East-West accord far exceeds in size the relatively small area of written agreements. Progress toward limiting the arms race therefore depends both on enlarging the area of implicit accord and reducing to treaty language the existing implicit accords. The latter process may achieve more immediate results than the former. International peace observation seems to be one area where a high degree of implicit accord already exists, evidenced by Soviet agreement or acquiescence to several missions, such as Lebanon and Yemen. Therefore, generalizations of the characteristics of agreed missions could be among the more promising avenues of negotiations.

As already indicated one of the earliest areas of East-West accord, achieved even during the Stalin era, was that settlement of political controversies need not precede progress toward disarmament as originally contended by the United States, and that disarmament need not precede political settlements as contended by the Soviet Union. Rather any agreement whether in the field of armaments or in other areas will lessen political tensions and facilitate further agreement. In this context, strengthening peace observation could be an important part of a package of immediately realizable measures to lessen international tension and control the arms race.

This does not imply that the United States should in the near future submit a specific written or even oral proposal for purposes of negotiation with the Soviet Union. The important objective is the continuing development of an area of implicit accord. A premature effort to reduce that accord to writing could be counter-productive. It could bring into the open areas of difference, such as the relation of peace observation to the Security Council or the General Assembly and a "troika" direction, which seem more likely to be resolved through development of continuing practices than through formulae. It could impair the steps contemplated in this study for improving the present machinery.

The factors that would govern a decision to formalize an area of accord including the timing of any such decision are beyond the purview of this study. It should merely be noted here that sufficient United States-Soviet Union accord seems to exist in the area of peace observation so that the United States should be prepared to submit proposals, particularly if a future détente in United States-Soviet relations should warrant this type of approach.

9

UNITED NATIONS EFFORTS TO STRENGTHEN PEACE-OBSERVATION MACHINERY

International crises come suddenly and unexpectedly. Even when they can be anticipated, they do not develop as expected, and no two crises ever present identical problems. Therefore, a certain amount of improvisation will always be necessary in meeting the crises. Nevertheless, over the years, certain basic principles of action in the crisis area entailing peace observation have arisen, the application of which has already somewhat reduced the improvisation that is required. It seems probable that on the basis of these principles, machinery and procedures can be developed that can further reduce both the areas and the amount of improvisation.

The handling of a crisis and the means available to facilitate its handling should at the outset be distinguished. While an international crisis may be *sui generis* and hard to predict, the international machinery for handling it should not and need not be the subject of improvisation. It is important that the machinery should be available and ready to function. This is no less true today than it would be in a disarming world. A critical situation involving peace observation generally requires prompt action. This lesson is amply borne out by the analysis of the cases over the past four decades.

As early as June 1948, the Secretary-General of the United Nations recognized the need for taking steps to systematize the machinery of peace observation within the Organization. At the Harvard University commencement exercises on June 10, 1948,[1] he described a plan for a United Nations Guard that could be recruited by him and placed at the disposal of the Security Council and the General Assembly. Later in his annual report, he wrote:

> Such a force would not be used as a substitute for the forces contemplated in Articles 42 and 43. It would not be a striking force, but purely a guard force. It could be used for guard duty with the United Nations missions, in the conduct of plebiscites under the supervision of the United Nations and in the administration of truce terms. It could be used as a constabulary under the Security Council or the Trusteeship Council in cities like Jerusalem and Trieste during the establishment of international regimes. It might also be called upon by the Security Council under Article 40 of the Charter which provides for provisional measures to prevent the aggravation of a situation threatening the peace.[2]

On September 28, 1948, the Secretary-General placed before the General Assembly the plan for the formation of a United Nations Guard of several thousand. His plan initially provided for an 800-man guard, 500 of whom would be held in reserve in their national homes. The guard would be "representative of the United Nations authority in support of United Nations missions in the field and provide a limited protection to United Nations personnel and property."[3] It would "patrol points or guard objectives neutralized under truce or cease-fire order of the United Nations." It would "exercise supervisory and observation functions at polling points during the conduct of referendums conducted under United Nations auspices."

[1] UN Press Release M/446, June 10, 1948.
[2] UN General Assembly, *Official Records*, Third Session, Supplement No. 1 (A/565), pp. xvii–xviii.
[3] UN General Assembly, A/656, Sept. 28, 1948. Hereafter cited as A/656.

The experience of the United Nations missions, the Secretary-General pointed out, had shown that "there must be available at their disposal adequate representative and protective authority to give effect to their decisions as well as technical service assistance to enable them to function with speed and efficiency." [4] This, he said was not to be an international army, nor was it to be used for enforcement purposes, nor for purposes of maintaining law and order in an area. It would be, he explained, an instrument that would strengthen the hand of United Nations missions established for the purpose of assuring pacific settlements without recourse to the use of force.

The response given the plan, as indicated by the debate, was mixed. The opposition, as might have been expected, was led by the Soviet bloc. This plan, the bloc contended, if adopted would be a violation of the Charter. The Communist bloc viewed it as an armed force designed to replace the forces contemplated in Articles 42 and 43. Others expressed doubts on budgetary and practical grounds. In view of this reception, the *Ad Hoc* Political Committee, realizing the need for a thorough study of the problem before taking concrete action, decided to establish a Special Committee to study the Secretary-General's proposal.

A FIELD SERVICE AND PANEL OF FIELD OBSERVERS

In the light of the debate in the *Ad Hoc* Political Committee, the Secretary-General submitted a substantial revision of his original plan. [5] In the revised plan, two new units would be set up, a Field Service and a Panel of Field Observers. The Field Service, made up of 300 uniformed men, would be a part of the Secretariat and would provide transport and communications for missions, guard UN premises at Headquarters and abroad, and maintain order at meetings, hearings, and investigations. It would have no truce or plebiscite funciton and would not carry arms, save side arms in certain instances when permitted by local authority.

The Panel of Field Observers would be a list of names of men in national service recommended by member states. The members of the panel would be called into service by a decision of the General Assembly or the Security Council, or an organ authorized by them, to carry out supervisory and observation duties with field missions. The size of the panel, the Secretary-General suggested would be 2,000, thus enabling him to do away with emergency recruitment of personnel for observation and supervision tasks.

The Special Committee approved the Secretary-General's revised plan with some modifications that were acceptable to him. The plan met with

[4] A/656, p. 2.
[5] UN General Assembly, *Official Records*, Fourth Session, Supplement No. 13 (A/959), p. 6.

widespread support in the Assembly's Fourth Session and was adopted by it. The American delegation described the revised plan as progress, and there was no question in their view that the Secretary-General had the legal right to reorganize Secretariat services in the manner proposed. Whatever one might think of the Secretary-General's original proposal, the revised plan as adopted was not an international force contemplated by Article 43. It was not capable of coercive action, but was designed as an instrument to further the maintenance of peace.

The Secretary-General established the United Nations Field Service, which has been used ever since to furnish the personnel responsible for the communications, transport, subsistence, construction, and equipment maintenance of individual missions.

The General Assembly resolution also established the United Nations Panel of Field Observers. It was to be based on the principle of equitable geographical distribution and kept up-to-date. The Secretary-General announced that he would formulate procedures under which certain qualified individuals drawn from all states would be listed as members of the panel. The Panel of Field Observers was drawn up but has been of minimal use.

Why has it not been extensively used for peace-observation functions? There are several factors that may account for its still-birth. When the Secretary-General is required to obtain personnel beyond the existing Secretariat personnel for missions, ordinarily the limitation on his freedom of choice is such as to prevent the use of persons listed on the Panel of Field Observers. The specialists he requires may not be found in the area from which he is obliged for political reasons to choose. Frequently, the individual is unavailable when his services are required. An up-to-date panel list is difficult to maintain. Moreover, it has usually been simpler to recruit personnel without first checking to determine the availability and suitability of the persons listed on the panel.

PANEL FOR INQUIRY AND CONCILIATION

To further the concept of peace observation and fact-finding, the General Assembly in 1949 provided for the establishment of a Panel for Inquiry and Conciliation. Each member of the United Nations was invited to appoint from one to five persons who might be called on by states or by the United Nations organs to act in a personal capacity as members of commissions of inquiry and conciliation. As in the case of the Panel of Field Observers, the lists have not been kept up-to-date. Once an individual is on the panel, it is difficult to remove him, even though he might not be able to serve. Moreover, as in the case of the Panel of Field Observers, it has usually been easier to obtain high-level personnel for inquiry and conciliation purposes without first determining whether the members of the panel are available.

PEACE OBSERVATION COMMISSION

In 1950, the General Assembly, following the Communist attack on the Republic of Korea, adopted a proposal submitted by the United States entitled "Uniting for Peace." This resolution sought to apply the lessons learned in the Korean case and to overcome some of the obstacles to effective United Nations action in the event of armed aggression. The resolution established a Peace Observation Commission that would observe and report on any area where international tension exists that is likely to endanger international peace and security.[6] Under this resolution, the Security Council, the General Assembly, or the Interim Committee if the Assembly is not in session, can avail itself of the services of the Peace Observation Commission only in a situation where the Security Council is not exercising its Charter functions with respect to the case in question. The Peace Observation Commission was authorized to appoint subcommissions and avail itself of the services of observers, including, if it wished, the United Nations Panel of Field Observers.

The Peace Observation Commission was composed of the following member states: the five permanent members of the Security Council, together with Colombia, Czechoslovakia, India, Iraq, Israel, New Zealand, Pakistan, Sweden, and Uruguay.

The Peace Observation Commission was used only once, in 1951, when the General Assembly abolished the United Nations Special Committee on the Balkans (UNSCOB) and requested the Peace Observation Commission to establish a Balkan Subcommission of three to five members with its seat at the United Nations Headquarters in New York. The subcommission was authorized to dispatch observers to the Balkans, to visit the area, and to consider any data that might be submitted to it by its members or observers. In January 1952, the Greek Government requested the dispatch of observers to the frontier areas of Greece, and the subcommission, composed of Colombia, France, Pakistan, Sweden, and the United States, responded by sending one observer each to Greece. It continued in existence for three years and made reports. When the situation along the frontier became quiet, the observers were withdrawn. The Peace Observation Commission was never used again, although its use was requested in May 1954 by Thailand in connection with incidents on the border of North Vietnam.

Why has the Peace Observation Commission not been used? The probable answer has two aspects: (1) The pattern for peace observation

[6] In 1926, the League of Nations began to study ways and means to make effective the functioning of the League in time of crisis. One of the arrangements it provided was "a list of persons who might be called on at short notice to hasten to the place where critical events were reported or expected, in order to be able to send information to the Council and to carry out its instructions on the spot." For further details see Walters, *op. cit.*, pp. 378–80.

reflected in the establishment and membership of the Peace Observation Commission turned out in practice to be unsatisfactory. (2) An alternative pattern was developing that became increasingly effective, as compared with the POC, which suffered from prolonged disuse.

Both aspects are reflected in the experience of four important and early United Nations peace-observation missions.

1. Both UNSCOB, which was established by the General Assembly, and its predecessor, the Balkan Commission established by the Security Council, were composed of states with instructed delegations. When the Balkan Commission determined, over Soviet opposition, to go to Geneva to write its report, it left a subsidiary group with headquarters in Salonika, Greece to observe the border. Since the bulk of the delegations had left Greece, the subsidiary group operated without instructions from the delegations and in effect was detailed to and reported through the Secretary-General of the United Nations. The results were so satisfactory that this organizational pattern was continued when the General Assembly established UNSCOB even though the delegations were located in Greece and could operate effectively with the Soviet bloc boycotting the commission.

2. The UN Temporary Commission on Korea (UNTCOK) and the UN Commission on Korea (UNCOK) consisted of representatives of states with instructed delegations. The record of these commissions has furnished a prime argument against the use of instructed commissions in peace observation. The delegations were in constant conflict with each other and with their national governments. Frequently action was delayed for months to obtain clearances from the home governments. Several times, when the delegates used their own best judgment in emergencies, they were reversed by the home governments. The most useful activity took place in the final three weeks preceding the initiation of hostilities by the Communists in North Korea on June 25, 1950. UNCOK had received authority in the fall of 1949 to establish a peace-observation group along the border, but had waited almost six months before requesting military observers. Immediately after the UNCOK request, the United Nations Secretary-General dispatched military observers to Korea who were in a position to report on the Korean situation when the Communists invaded. In short, the Korean situation furnished a dramatic contrast between the efficiency of the Secretary-General and the ineffectiveness of instructed delegations in peace observation.

3. The representatives on the Good Offices Committee and its successor the United Nations Commission for Indonesia were never certain whether they were acting as representatives of their governments or as individuals from states specified by the General Assembly. In fact, the U.S. representatives, who because of their personalities dominated the commissions, acted effectively on the latter hypothesis. The operation in Indonesia became increasingly identified with the Secretary-General of the United

Nations despite personnel and financial limitations. This development took place because it became apparent that the commission's effectiveness increased as their operations became more closely identified with the United Nations.

4. The United Nations Commission for India and Pakistan (UNCIP) established in 1948 to deal with the Kashmir problem consisted of representatives of states. The commission had responsibility for both peace observation and the pacific settlement of the Kashmir problem. As early as January 1949, peace-observation functions, however, were separated from the pacific settlement functions. The military adviser to the commission reported directly to the United Nations Secretary-General even though he was technically the adviser of the commission. When at a later date the United Nations representative required military advice in connection with the problems of pacific settlement, he was given a staff separate from the military group with responsibility for the peace-observation function. This change in the status of the personnel responsible for peace observation took place without any authorization from any organ of the United Nations. It was essential, however, to make an effective peace-observation operation and has never been challenged in the United Nations.

Thus as a result of the experience of these four missions, by 1950 it had become apparent that: (1) peace-observation commissions even with effective personnel are handicapped if they consist of delegates receiving instructions from their governments and reflecting the views of their governments rather than of the United Nations; and (2) the Secretary-General could produce an effective alternative to instructed delegations, an alternative that will subsequently be described.

The Peace Observation Commission was established in 1950 as part of the Uniting for Peace Resolution. Theoretically, it would have been possible for the sponsors of the resolution to have learned of the organizational inadequacies of the Peace Observation Commission through an analysis of the four peace-observation missions noted above. In fact, however, such an analysis was never made. Even if one had been made and indicated the inadequacies of instructed delegations, there is serious doubt that the Secretary-General could have brought the General Assembly to cure the difficulty. The membership was not ready for the change that was effected by the successor Secretary-General in the succeeding years. [7]

The trend in the United Nations has been away from the instructed-delegation modality. In more recent years, the Secretary-General has set up peace-observation missions, either on the request of the Security Council or the General Assembly, or on his own responsibility after consulting

[7] The studies of the U.S. delegation stressed the fields of activity of the Collective Measures Committee with the Peace Observation Commission added somewhat in the nature of an afterthought to meet the criticisms of states objecting to U.S. emphasis on military measures.

the members of the Security Council. Examples of the former are Lebanon and Yemen, and of the latter Cambodia-Thailand. Although in the former, the general terms of reference are set up by the Security Council, it is the Secretary-General who chooses the individuals who comprise the mission, spells out the specifics of the mission, and gives it policy guidance—guidance that is from him and not from governments. The Lebanese mission was made up of individuals chosen by him and reporting to the Security Council through him. In the Cambodia-Thailand case, the Secretary-General appointed a UN Presence who received his terms of reference and instructions from the Secretary-General to whom the reports were made. In this instance, one must not overlook the kind of servant the Secretary-General is. If he is an outstanding personality, capable and loyal to the principles of the Charter, trusted by the members of the Organization for his integrity and objectivity, they will entrust him with this great responsibility.[8]

A commission composed of representatives from states of various political views gives rise to compromise that quite often weakens the capacity of the commission to carry out its task. In a modality where the Secretary-General does the appointing, the appointees owe their loyalty to the Organization. Its reports, for that reason, can be and usually are more objective.

The character of the reporting by a mission whose members are selected by the Secretary-General is different from that of a mission consisting of representatives of states. If the mission reports to him, the reports are private and need not be published. Accordingly, there is in these reports expression of views and ideas more freely given because they are protected from the public eye. Moreover, the reporting to the Secretary-General is as frequent as the exigencies of the situation require. With the commission type of machinery, the reports are made to the Security Council or the General Assembly and are public. In the case of a General Assembly commission, the reports are usually rendered annually; in the case of a Security Council commission, the reports are rendered as required.

The foregoing briefly traces the legislative efforts made by the United Nations to place its peace-observation functions on a rational and systematic basis. The analysis indicates that the legislative steps taken by the General Assembly in that direction, with the exception of the Field Service, have not worked and that the Secretary-General, by various means, has sought to compensate for the faulty machinery the Assembly created.

The Charter is capable of growth, as shown under the direction of Dag Hammarskjold who gave the Organization a new and greater sense of

[8] In the League experience, commissions of enquiry were almost always composed of individuals appointed by the Council who functioned not on instructions from their respective governments but on the basis of terms of reference laid down by the Council. Their reports were made to the Council through the Secretary-General.

purpose and direction. It was this sense of purpose and direction among other things that led Mr. Khrushchev to propose a three-headed Secretariat that would have turned the clock back and would very likely have resulted in the ineffectiveness of the Organization. The defeat of the Soviet proposal indicates in some measure a will to strengthen the Organization.

10

—•▸•—

FUTURE CHARACTER AND ROLE OF A UNITED NATIONS PEACE–OBSERVATION INSTRUMENTALITY

As has already been pointed out, four alternative methods of dealing with the problem of peace observation and fact-finding are possible. The first is the method of improvisation—the creation of a separate and distinct peace-observation group for each individual crisis as it arises. This is the *ad hoc* method which, in the main, the United Nations presently employs. The second is the method by which the various member states identify a limited number of officers, say five to fifty, in their own military establishments to be specially trained for peace-observation work and placed at the service of the Organization as the occassion arises. The third is the earmarking and training of peace-observation officers in the military establishments of the various member states plus a small number of officers recruited and trained by the United Nations Secretariat, who would act as cadres in peace-observation missions. The fourth is a United Nations Peace Observation Corps whose personnel would be recruited, trained, and financed by the United Nations and under its full control at all times.

OBSERVERS ASSEMBLED *AD HOC*

Improvising a peace-observation mission is risky where time is of the essence. Delaying the control and containment of violence in the nuclear age carries with it the danger of escalation. In the absence of the already existing peace-observation missions, such as UNTSO and UNMOGIP and the peace-keeping mission of UNEF, from which trained personnel were chosen as cadres for the missions in Lebanon and Yemen, the Secretary-General would have been obliged to call on the various member states for personnel who did not have the know-how required by a United Nations peace-observation mission. Those who had had the experience in UNTSO, UNEF, and UNMOGIP were used in organizing rapidly the mission in Lebanon and deployed quickly throughout the area, not, however, without considerable stress, strain, and error. The Secretary-General went through a similar process when he was charged by the Security Council with the peace-observation responsibility in Yemen. It cannot be assumed that UNEF, UNTSO, and UNMOGIP will always be there to provide the experienced personnel on which to draw.

A United Nations peace-observation group in the field of operations resembles in some respects a small military unit. In addition to military personnel, however, the United Nations peace-observation teams must have political direction. In most peace-observation missions, as indeed in UN peace-keeping undertakings, where delicate political problems invariably arise and the goals to be attained are largely in the political field, there is need for skilled political direction on the spot. The UNOGIL mission was led by two civilians well versed in the art of diplomacy and a major-general who directed the operation in the field.

The members of a peace-observation mission confront situations unlike those of foot soldiers in a peace-keeping operation. The mission of peace observation may, for example, be to separate the contending parties, to oversee a cease-fire, to find the facts, to investigate and report on violations relating to infiltration, to settle disputes, and a host of other responsibilities with which it might be charged. The task is both quasi-military and quasi-diplomatic.

No two peace-observation missions are alike and in many respects each mission needs to be tailored to meet the particular circumstances. For example, the need may vary from one man with a supporting staff of three or four to serve as a UN Presence, as in Jordan and Laos, to some 600, which were used in Lebanon. In an underdeveloped country, almost everything is needed, including medical service, mechanics for aircraft and trucks, radio operators, and services such as the importation of food and water. In a more highly developed country, many of these needs can be met locally, and fewer UN administrative personnel are needed to supply the services.

Improvisation for so complex and, in many instances, so delicate an operation is hardly the way to meet the peace-observation task entrusted to the United Nations. The experience in peace observation in recent years points to the need for a high degree of versatility in preparing for possible United Nations service. Peace observers need to be trained and equipped in a manner that will permit immediate and effective response to United Nations requirements.

OBSERVERS EARMARKED BY NATIONS

The second alternative appears to be a considerable improvement over the first. Earmarking individuals, ready and available for United Nations service, has several advantages. The Organization, in the event of need or emergency, would know what to count on and could plan accordingly. The cost of maintaining these earmarked officers would be borne by the various member states, and not until these men were brought into the service of the United Nations would any expenditure be involved. The member states would continue to pay the regular salaries of the men when in the service of the United Nations, as they now do, and the United Nations would meet the extra costs.

Their training would be given at the UN Secretariat by senior Secretariat officers, extending over a period of several weeks and supplemented by field trips to gain first-hand experience. Since the United Nations would have to weigh carefully the political acceptability of peace observers, an important consideration is that the range of member states doing the earmarking must be broad enough to provide the Organization ample latitude in selection. In the past, the United Nations Secretariat has restricted itself to securing observers from the middle and small powers except in the special case of Cyprus. Should the present international climate continue, this is likely to be the practice in the future.

In addition to the earmarking and training of the military element of future missions, the United Nations should expand the Field Service to a degree that would permit it to support such missions. A similar expansion will have to be made in the UN Secretariat in New York to provide the political, legal, and press advisers who may be needed for future missions as well as to facilitate backstopping at Headquarters.

EARMARKED OBSERVERS AND A SMALL CADRE OF OFFICERS AT HEADQUARTERS

The third alternative appears to be an improvement over the second. Such a cadre, it might be pointed out, need not depend on earmarking, but it could be used in connection with the second alternative. It would entail an additional small cost for the Organization, but it would eliminate some improvisation and provide an element of expertise otherwise lacking in the second alternative. This Secretariat group would be supplemented by the expansion of the civilian element, that is, Field Service and UN Headquarters. They would be international civil servants paid by the Organization and loyal to the principles and purposes of the Charter.

This alternative, units small in number earmarked by the various member states and trained for special UN observation service, together with a small standing cadre of officers attached to the Secretary General, is an intermediate plan between the second and fourth alternatives outlined in this study. It has the merit of appearing to be more immediately realizable and raising fewer political, technical, and financial difficulties than the fourth alternative—the establishment of a sizable standing UN Peace Observation Corps. Moreover, the essential elements of this alternative are based on the recent experience of certain countries such as Canada, Norway, Sweden, and Denmark, which have supplied personnel for UN use both in peace observation and peace-keeping.

It is noteworthy that plans for earmarking and training peace-keeping forces, including peace-observation units, have been officially presented to the United Nations by the aforementioned countries, notably by Canadian Prime Minister Lester Pearson. It may be assumed that careful study has been given to all the advantages and disadvantages of this plan. The Canadian Government, because of the need for advanced planning, convened a conference in Ottawa in November 1964 of nineteen countries which had supplied peace-keeping forces for United Nations operations in the Middle East, the Congo, and Cyprus, to draft guidelines for future use.

The additional new element which the present study has shown to be necessary and indeed essential is the provision in the Secretary-General's office of a small group of specially selected and trained military observers, say twenty-five to fifty, who would be permanent international civil servants and subject exclusively to his direction. They would constitute a cadre based at Headquarters but available for service in various peace-observation missions in the field.

It can readily be seen how such a Headquarters cadre would soon acquire the techniques and skills, and above all, the attitude, so necessary for successfully handling the delicate situations that constantly and inevitably arise in peace-observing operations. The records show how effectively the late Secretary-General, and his all-too-few aides, functioned in the crises in Suez, Lebanon, Laos, and the Congo. However, the records, and the testimony of several of his aides, also show that there were a number of instances of a near breakdown often due to inadequate numbers of reliable and dependable officials either in the field or at Headquarters.

One of the most experienced aides of the late Secretary-General Hammarskjold has urged the strengthening of the UN Headquarters and field staff in order to avert certain of the difficulties encountered in the UN's peace-observation and peace-keeping experience.[1]

The training of such peace observers whether earmarked or standing, differs in many respects from the training required for peace-keeping forces. The latter are trained to keep the peace or terminate hostilities by the use of force if necessary. Observers have tasks that depend primarily on noncoercive procedures. When military units are used for peace-observa-

---

[1] See Andrew W. Cordier, "The Rule of Law in the World Community," *University of Pennsylvania Law Review*, III: 7 (May 1963), pp. 905 ff.

tion duties, some of their previous training has to be unlearned. Their new training would be more in the nature of policing—observing *inter alia* the withdrawal of hostile forces, supervising cease-fire arrangements, establishing demarcation lines and demilitarized zones, and fact-finding.

The largest observer corps assembled in UN experience comprised some 600 men in UNTSO drawn from some twelve countries. It is significant that this corps functioned as an intermingled group and not as separate national units. On the other hand, where the duties were largely peace-keeping and more of a military character, as in the Congo, the units were kept in their national formations.

Special problems and difficulties are bound to arise when a peace-observation (or peace-keeping) operation is carried out through separate national units. In the Congo, for example, certain governments continued to give instructions to their national units that were contrary to the UN commands or directives under which the operation was conducted. Such difficulties would not arise in a standing corps of the kind outlined in the fourth alternative where the personnel would be intermingled. Whether earmarked observers could be organized to obviate these difficulties would depend on the size of the group, their training and indoctrination, and especially their linguistic capability.

A STANDING UNITED NATIONS PEACE OBSERVATION CORPS

The fourth alternative calls for the establishment within the United Nations of a Peace Observation Corps, staffed with a standing cadre of observers who could be dispatched promptly to investigate any situation that might constitute a threat to or a breach of the peace. Elements of the Peace Observation Corps could also be stationed as appropriate in selected areas throughout the world. This Peace Observation Corps would then be one of the instrumentalities designed to strengthen the structure, authority, and operation of the United Nations so as to maintain international peace and security. Another would be the establishment of a United Nations Peace Force.

The fourth alternative would, however, seem to strengthen the capacity of the United Nations to maintain international peace and security. Many of the cases analyzed in this study testify to the need for such an instrumentality. However, there are certain political, technical, and financial difficulties that might delay the early establishment of a standing observation corps. Nevertheless, some of the details involved in organizing such a corps are given so that a plan would be available if and when circumstances permit its implementation. The following general description, together with a detailed Annex, outline the main features of this plan.

Within the present framework of the Charter of the United Nations, without the necessity of amending it, whether or not Stage I of a Treaty on General and Complete Disarmament is in effect, a United Nations Peace Observation Corps could be set up. The corps would be a subsidiary organ of the body creating it, its organization and function would be exclusively international in character, and its members would be international civil servants available for service at the request of the Security Council or the General Assembly.

While one may assume that a Treaty on General and Complete Disarmament would be signed in circumstances in which the cold war would have subsided with the veto still prevailing in the Security Council, it would be preferable to have the General Assembly create the corps rather than the Security Council. Should the occasion arise to amend the basic resolution, it would be easier to do it in a veto-free Assembly. However, it is problematic whether even the abatement or the termination of the cold war would permit the General Assembly to set up an instrumentality relating to international peace and security, an area the Soviet Union regards as within the Security Council's province.

The Organization and Function of the Corps

The size of the corps, staffed with a standing cadre of observers, could range from 250 to 1,000 or more. The number must be adequate for one or two or even three, four, or more simultaneous operations. At the present time, it is noteworthy that there are two peace-keeping operations in being, the United Nations Emergency Force and the United Nations Peace-Keeping Force in Cyprus; a number of peace-observation missions—including the United Nations Truce Supervision Organization; the United Nations Military Observer Group in India and Pakistan; the United Nations Yemen Observation Mission; and the United Nations Mission for the Unification and Rehabilitation of Korea; and the UN Presence in Jordan and Cambodia-Thailand. Its role would be set out in the basic resolution creating it, which would be so worded as to cover the range of activities and functions entailed in peaceful settlement, from fact-finding, investigating, reporting, and observing a cease-fire or a plebiscite, to conciliating and mediating. While the corps would be given a broad charter the specific terms of reference of a peace-observation mission would be determined by the principal organ responsible for the mission. The nature of the task to be performed by the mission would be determined by that organ.

The terms of reference given the mission should be elaborated clearly and with sufficient flexibility to enable the Secretary-General, on the basis of executive responsibility for the operation entrusted to him, to give the chief of the peace-observation mission the instructions and guidance necessary to further the objectives of the mission.

The question arises whether the Secretary-General might not be given discretionary authority to bring into being in all or certain types of cases a peace-observation instrumentality. In the instance of Laos and Cambodia-Thailand, the Secretary-General, on the request of the parties, appointed a UN Presence in the form of a personal representative, after consulting the members of the Security Council. In this case, the form of presence was one individual, assisted by a staff of three or four people. In the instance of Yemen, which was a large operation, at one time 250, the Secretary-General hoped to proceed as he did in the Cambodia-Thailand case but felt obliged to obtain a formal approval of the Security Council.

The precedents developed by the Secretary-General's initiatives since 1950 indicate that for certain limited purposes he can send a small mission such as a UN Presence without formal approval of the Security Council or the General Assembly. He can rest his authority for doing this on Articles 98 and 99 of the Charter. However, when it comes to a mission of the size of Yemen or Lebanon, it is doubtful whether under Articles 98 and 99, the requirement that he be personally informed, would cover such large and politically important missions entailing sizable expenditures.

It would not be easy to design criteria covering all instances where the Secretary-General might act on his own authority in bringing into being a peace-observation mission. No two cases here analyzed are alike. A politically important problem calling for the creation of a peace-observation group may be one that involves directly or indirectly the big powers, or the cost of the mission may be such as to require the approval of one or the other of the principal organs. In either case, the Security Council or the General Assembly might not wish to give to the Secretary-General powers that would appear to be an abrogation of their own responsibility. There might also be a question whether the General Assembly or the Security Council could properly delegate powers that under the Charter are for them to exercise. In any event, the Secretary-General should be in a position to act where the parties wish him to act and the expenditures are relatively small, consulting the appropriate organ where feasible.

The members of the corps must be capable of operating in any part of the globe, under conditions of consent by the host country or countries. Under the Charter of the United Nations, save in cases under Chapter VII, or within a much more limited scope under Article 34, Chapter VI, consent of the party or parties is required before a peace-observation mission may enter a country. To broaden that consent so as to include cases under Chapter VI requires either Charter amendment or a specific provision in a disarmament treaty. For member states to give up the right to withhold consent is a far-reaching act of sovereignty, and at present there appears to be no evidence that they would be willing to do so. Had this a priori consent existed among the members of the United Nations, the General Assembly, for example, could have sent its peace-observation and fact-finding mission into Hungary in 1956, to South West Africa, and to Cuba in 1962. Whether the Charter should be amended or consent incorporated into a treaty on general and complete disarmament should be given careful consideration when such a treaty is negotiated.

The corps would be headed by a commander appointed by the Secretary-General and serving under his executive and policy direction. The Secretary-General would be assisted by an advisory committee. In addition to heading the corps, the commander would, in consultation with the Secretary-General, recruit the military personnel of the corps from among the various member states and be responsible for its training and operations The possibility of recruitment of personnel from the five permanent members might be left open for the time being, but the possibility of including them in an environment of a disarming world should not be ruled out.

The corps would fly the United Nations flag and carry side arms as do the peace observers in some instances now. Members of the corps would wear a UN uniform, since they would be officials of the Organization, unlike the units that make up UNEF and UNFICYP, whose members wear the uniform of the state to which they belong save for the blue United Nations helmet liners and arm bands.

The Advisory Committee

The basic resolution should authorize the Secretary-General to set up an advisory committee made up of representatives from among member states with the Secretary-General as its chairman, with which he would consult on the planning and operation of the corps. There would be no voting at meetings. As was the case with the Advisory Committee on UNEF and UNOC, the Secretary-General would sum up his conclusions, with any participant free to record his objection to the summary.

It would not be desirable for the relationship to be given such form as to lead to divided responsibility. The ultimate decision must rest with the Secretary-General. The enormous burden he carries would, however, be considerably lightened by an advisory committee. In this way, the member states would participate in the planning and operation of the corps. The institution, which could be supplemented with advisory committees for appropriate missions as in the instances mentioned, would prove a helpful and highly useful method of consultation and would protect the Secretary-General from being accused of partiality. It would above all serve as a political lightning rod to absorb criticism of his stewardship and as a forum in which he could give an accounting of his activity without convening the General Assembly or calling a meeting of the Security Council. The advisory group would not only give advice but would serve as a corrective.

As for the composition of an advisory committee, a departure would need to be made from the precedents set in UNEF and UNOC where it was limited mainly to those contributing troops. In the instance of a United

Nations Peace Observation Corps which would be a subsidiary organ of the United Nations, the size would need to be small to be effective, yet large enough to reflect an equitable geographical distribution. Membership in the advisory committee might be limited in duration, thus permitting rotation among the various states.

With each observation mission, as under present procedures, the Secretary-General would negotiate a status agreement with the host country or countries regarding the stationing of the mission, the privileges and immunities required to fulfill its responsibilities, the inviolability of its premises, freedom of movement within its area of operations, the right of access, and the like.

Financing of the Corps

The financing of the corps should be borne by the United Nations itself as part of its regular budget. This was the method employed in the various peace-observation missions in the League of Nations and is now employed in the Organization of American States. Up to 1962, the United Nations paid its regular share of the cost of peace-observation missions from its regular budget. The first departure from this rule, occasioned by the financial plight of the Organization, was the United Nations Temporary Executive Authority in West New Guinea (UNTEA). There the entire cost of some $6,000,000 was borne equally by the Netherlands and Indonesia. The second departure came in the case of Yemen. Here Saudi Arabia and the United Arab Republic agreed to divide the costs of $400,000 for a two-month period equally between them. The life of the mission in Yemen has been extended several times for further two-month periods.

The cost of a standing United Nations Peace Observation Corps when not in service would depend on its size. [2] When it is engaged on a particular mission, the cost could be borne either by the United Nations, by the party or parties to whom it is rendering the service, or by voluntary contributions. While payment by the party or parties or by voluntary contributions would lift a financial burden from the Organization, the wisdom of such arrangements for a UN Peace Observation Corps particularly in a disarming world, is questionable. To make the existence of the mission while in service dependent on fees from the host countries or voluntary contributions is surely a questionable practice. The fee method would place in the hands of the host countries a powerful weapon that might jeopardize the existence of the mission and endanger the maintenance of peace. The Yemen observation mission where the parties share the cost and thus determine its life, and the Cyprus mission, which is financed by voluntary contributions and thus enjoys an uneasy existence, illustrate the

[2] The estimated cost of a UN Peace Observation Corps of 250, 500, or 1,000 men is set out in the Annex to this study.

need for finding a durable basis of financing an international undertaking that is a concern and a responsibility of the entire international community. The problem here is no less urgent than it is in the case of peace-keeping operations such as UNEF and UNOC.[3]

Training of the Corps

The task of observers, it has been noted, is both quasi-military and quasi-political. Whether for the immediate future UN observers are to be drawn from an earmarked pool established by the various states, or whether there is created a UN Peace Observation Corps, special training will be required. The analysis of the peace-observation cases since 1920 suggests that in many of them there are recurring common problems in which training would be highly desirable. Included in a curriculum of instruction would be: the role and philosophy of the United Nations in the maintenance of peace; the nature of a United Nations peace-observation mission— its organization and methods of work; the techniques of observing and reporting; the techniques of fact-finding; the art of negotiation and conciliation; the problems of logistics; the care and maintenance of equipment; and the problems of health and food under varying climatic conditions.

The component of the quasi-military and quasi-political type of mission usually includes a large civilian element. The lines of responsibility between the two must be clearly laid down. The political advisers must recognize that they are advisers to the chief of the mission and have no executive authority, and the administrative staff, that is, the Field Service personnel, is there to support the objectives of the mission. The UN field manuals should lay down clearly the lines of authority, and the basic principles and procedures that must be adhered to. Where the United Nations is dependent on nationally earmarked personnel, there are bound to be differences in the qualitative standards in training. To overcome these differences, a special training program would need to be developed.

A United Nations Training and Research Institute envisaged in General Assembly Resolution 1827 (XVII) is now on the way to being established. This institute can provide a focal point in the training and indoctrination

[3] John G. Stoessinger in his book *Financing the United Nations System* (Washington: Brookings Institution, 1964), in Chap. 11, which deals with new sources of revenue, examines the various proposals designed to strengthen the financial structure of the United Nations. They include such proposals as United Nations leasing and exploitation rights in the Antarctic on a royalty basis, revenue from ocean resources, and from outer space activities. "The overall lesson," he writes on page 292, "that emerges from this survey of long-range possibilities for United Nations revenue is this: the resources of the frozen polar zones, of the oceans, and of outer space will not become substitutes for the failure of states to meet their financial obligations to the United Nations here and now. Vision demands that these possibilities be explored in order to help the United Nations to evolve toward growing strength. But realism demands with equal force that a solution to the financial crisis of the Organization be found in our own lifetime."

of peace observers in the art of peace observation which is unique to the purposes and methods of the United Nations. The training in the institute would need to be geared directly to the requirements of the United Nations field operations. Training in the field would be carried out by attaching trainees to existing peace-observation missions where they would acquire experience in the various aspects of peace observation.

In describing some of the functions of the proposed institute, the Secretary-General stated that:

> There is a real need for an analysis of United Nations operations in troubled areas. This would involve analytical studies of the differences and similarities in the situations that have had to be met, in, for example, the Middle East, the Congo, Kashmir, West Irian, and Yemen, and the elements of strength and weakness in the operation, with a view to suggesting possible guidelines, should there be need for future United Nations operations of this nature.

He went on to add that: "There is also need for analysis of United Nations experience in the field of pacific settlement, covering comparative studies of various situations involving conciliation, mediation, investigation and procedures of settlement." [4] The product of research could provide the training materials for peace observers.

The responsibility for the training of field observers where earmarking of personnel is the alternative would essentially be that of earmarking states, but the United Nations Training and Research Institute could play an important role by placing manuals of instruction at the disposal of the earmarking states and by special lectures on the nature and requirements of UN field operations, including analysis, evaluation, and planning. This special type of training complementary to that which might be provided by the earmarking states would go a long way in building up a pool of personnel for service with the United Nations.

A sound training program might be organized as follows: a group of officers at Headquarters would be responsible for developing manuals and a general training program. They would go to the countries with earmarked units to train, lecture, and prepare them for field duty. However, the first exposure to peace observation should be at UN Headquarters. After this, the men would return to their earmarked units, and then the training interplay between Headquarters and the earmarked units would begin.

At the time of crisis, two-thirds or more of the Headquarters officers would go to the field to serve with the Headquarters personnel. They, therefore, would determine the tone and direction of the field operations.

Where a United Nations Peace Observation Corps is set up, the responsibility for training would of course be solely with the United Nations.

[4] United Nations Training and Research Institute: Note by the Secretary-General of the United Nations, February 1964.

United Nations Military Staff

The success of a peace-observation mission in the field, like that of a peace-keeping operation, depends in considerable measure on the effectiveness and efficiency of the United Nations Secretariat and the support the mission receives from it. One of the lessons derived from a study of the cases indicates that centralized direction in the field and at Headquarters is important and indeed necessary. The direction and logistic support that a peace-observation mission must have differs only in degree from the direction and support given to a peace-keeping mission. The two are akin to one another, and the present military adviser and his small staff serve the Secretary-General in both peace-observation and peace-keeping operations.

The experience derived from a study of the cases, particularly those under the United Nations, leads to the conclusion that, in addition to the political direction given peace-observation missions, and this is even truer in the case of peace-keeping, there must be a military unit in the United Nations to advise the Secretary-General in his capacity as "Commander-in-Chief" of peace-observation and peace-keeping missions. The role of this unit will be advisory to the Secretary-General, to ensure the proper execution of the responsibility given him by the Security Council or the General Assembly. It should also focus on the planning and direction of operations. The planning should relate to such problems as transportation, both in getting to and within the area of operations, communications with Headquarters, personnel administration, status of forces, and equipment.

The unit should be headed by a military officer who would be the Secretary-General's military adviser and his chief planner. During the Congo operation, the Secretary-General appointed in July 1960 a military staff consisting of three or four officers, headed by General Rikhye of India. Its function was not that of a military staff in the ordinary sense of the term. It had no command responsibility and was not part of the chain of command.

Initially, the military staff should be modest in size, and its development should take place in the light of experience. A large and full-blown apparatus at the outset should be avoided lest it encounter resistance. The officers of the staff should be engaged for short periods of time to ensure a balanced rotation from among the various member states and thus avoid developing a United Nations military oligarchy.

The Field Service, which is already in existence and is headed by an Under Secretary, has executive responsibility for procurement and supplying peace-observation missions. This service may be enlarged through recruitment of civilians from other United Nations establishments.

Equipment

A United Nations Peace Observation Corps would be assembled at an international base, trained for work in peace observation and equipped with standard equipment as peace observers. [5] To move a unit and its equipment to an operational area, commercial sea and air charter arrangements should be planned in advance. A peace-observation group must be prepared to be self-sufficient for a time, since it may have to operate in areas where the required equipment and supplies would not be readily available.

Public Information

At Headquarters, a unit which could provide information on such matters as terrain and climate in various parts of the world would be important. In the field, a peace-observation mission, as a peace-keeping mission, should be equipped with special communications personnel to give out as well as to collect information. The power of modern mass media is enormous. Rumors and propaganda have become significant factors in escalating a dispute. Accurate information about what is going on is important, as is scotching-rumors and lies. To secure the facts and to supply them to the Secretary-General, the Security Council, or the General Assembly is a basic requirement of peace-observation missions. This was recognized early by the commander of the League of Nations force that maintained law and order in the Saar plebiscite.

UN PEACE OBSERVATION CORPS AND UN PEACE FORCE AND DISARMAMENT VERIFICATION ARRANGEMENTS

Under a disarmament treaty, what would be the functional relationship between a UN Peace Observation Corps, a UN Peace Force, and the machinery set up to verify disarmament measures? In other words, what lines might be drawn between the activities of these three instrumentalities? While the three organizations would be related elements of international security arrangements, they would be separate in the functions they would be called on to discharge.

Peace-observation missions, in concept and practice, have at various times been referred to under such terms as "fact-finding," "commission of inquiry," "UN presence," or "visit to the spot." Such missions in recent years have been applied to a wide variety of international disputes. Where the hostilities are merely threatened, or slight, the peace-observation mission will probably be called on to find the facts and report back, as, for

---

[5] The Annex sets forth the kind of basic equipment a peace-observation mission is likely to need.

example, in the Yemen case. In Kashmir, the group watches over the implementation of the cease-fire agreement, and in Palestine UNTSO watches over the implementation of the armistice agreements and supervises the cease-fire. A peace-observation mission may be charged not only with observation functions but its terms of reference may include mediation, conciliation, or arbitration in order to achieve the peaceful settlement of international disputes. One of the virtues of peace observation is that it is a flexible instrument. As each international dispute differs from every other dispute or situation, so will the peace-observation body reflect that difference in its composition and terms of reference. Its size may vary from one person with a small staff, for example, the UN Presence in Jordan, to some 39 men in Kashmir, and 600 in UNTSO.

A United Nations Peace Force, in contrast, is a military force of considerable size, far larger than a peace-observation mission and presumably with a different kind of objective, "The Parties to the Treaty would progressively strengthen the United Nations Peace Force established in Stage II until it had sufficient armed forces and armaments so that *no state could challenge it.*"[6] This in other words would be a fighting force of the strength in men and arms designed to defeat any state that challenged it. It would be unlike UNEF, which is an international force of some 5,000 or more interposed between Egypt and Israel to prevent one of the adversaries from attacking the other. It would be unlike UNFICYP, which is a force of less than 7,000 men designed to maintain order in Cyprus. In other words, neither UNEF nor UNFICYP is a fighting force in the sense that the term is usually used. UNEF has no enemies; neither has UNFICYP. As one State Department official aptly described it:

> Members of U.N. peacekeeping forces are soldiers from the military establishments of the nations contributing units. They are commanded by professional military officers. They wear uniforms and carry guns. They sleep in tents or barracks and eat military rations.
> But once they put on the blue beret or, if need be, the blue helmet, they find they are supposed to be soldiers without enemies, fighters without rancor, members of an armed force without a military objective—their mission not to start shooting but to stop it, not to win a battle but to see to it there is no battle to be won or lost.[7]

Presumably, the United Nations Force contemplated in the *Outline* would be neither a UNEF, a UNOC, nor a UNFICYP, but a military establishment ready to take on any state that challenges it. In other words, it would be a fighting force with a mission to meet any challenger who thereby becomes its enemy.

[6] Stage II of the *Outline.* Italics added.

[7] Harlan Cleveland, Assistant Secretary of State, U.S. Department of State Press Release No. 128, March 20, 1964.

The *Outline* envisages the creation and maintenance of a peace-observation instrumentality associated with its arms control program. It also envisages the creation of machinery concerned with peace-keeping and inspection for disarmament. The three concepts in popular meaning are quite distinct, but two of the concepts—an Observation Corps and a Peace Force, are closely related both on the substantive and on the organizational sides. Each deals with a form of international conflict; the peace observers with small conflicts, potential or actual, the peace keepers with larger conflicts. The weaponry in one is usually but not always side arms, the military force and the weaponry in the other at its peak must be of a magnitude "so that no state could challenge it." The objectives of the two instrumentalities in a sense complement one another. A peace force should not be sent if a peace-observation mission can do the work. A peace-observation mission need not consist of military personnel, and in some instances it should not. Each observation mission needs to be tailored to the necessities of the case. A United Nations Peace Force, being a purely military arm with a different mandate, will need to be tailored in size in certain instances to attain its mission.

The peace-observation mission in the exercise of its main functions may find it necessary to take steps, such as the physical separation of antagonistic groups, which resemble peace-keeping. As long as this is only an incidental function, the activity comes within the concept of peace observation. Likewise a peace-observation mission, particularly where the matter to be observed is the level of armed forces or armaments, may use some of the techniques associated with inspection for disarmament, such as verification or authentication. Such activities, in connection with peace observation, however, are to determine the existence of facts likely to disturb the peace rather than to observe compliance with an arms control program.

Fact-finding may be associated with peace-keeping or inspection for disarmament as well as peace observation. Peace-keeping entails enforcement and envisages a military force of substantial size. Peace-keeping also entails peace observation, but peace observation where the numbers are relatively small and usually unarmed, and never involves more than minimal peace-keeping, usually of an episodic nature.

A United Nations Peace Observation Corps could draw on the men and equipment of a United Nations Peace Force and vice versa. In the large peace-observation missions such as UNTSO, UNOGIL, and UNYOM, the personnel was largely military, and the equipment it used in its work, communications, transportation and the like, came from military stores. With a Peace Observation Corps and a Peace Force under the United Nations, the military staff unit suggested as an advisory body to the Secretary-General could advise him on both instrumentalities.

Ultimately, in a largely disarmed world, the functions of a Peace Observation Corps and a Peace Force might be merged. This could take place when disarming had proceeded to a point where a relatively small force would be sufficient to cope with the forces of any state that might challenge it. This could not take place in a disarming world as defined for the purposes of this study, since the two activities, as pointed out, require such different approaches and organizational arrangements.

The role of peace observation is particularly significant for the part it can play in a disarming world. As pointed out elsewhere in this study, while observation and peace-keeping proposals were originally introduced in the context of negotiations for general and complete disarmament, they may likewise play an even more significant role as part of a program of partial and immediately realizable disarmament measures. The prospects for the inclusion of peace-observation measures in partial disarmament agreements are enhanced by two factors. First, the Secretary-General has already worked out a variety of approaches to peace observation acceptable to the Security Council and the General Assembly, which indicates the possibilities of developing this international instrumentality in the first stage of an agreed disarmament program. Second, there already appears to be a high degree of implicit East-West accord on international peace observation, providing a base that can be widened or formalized in treaties. With the recognition by both the United States and the Soviet Union of the interdependence of political settlement and disarmament progress, peace-observation agreements could contribute to lessening international tension and controlling the arms race.

ORGANIZATION AND EQUIPMENT OF A
UNITED NATIONS PEACE OBSERVATION CORPS

The *Outline* provides for "the establishment within the United Nations of a Peace Observation Corps, staffed with a standing cadre of observers who could be dispatched promptly to investigate any situation which might constitute a threat to or a breach of the peace." This study notes that the responsibilities of a peace-observation mission entail a wide variety of tasks. These may include fact-finding, observation of a cease-fire, transfer of populations, supervision of an election, settlement of border disputes, conciliation, mediation, and even for limited periods minor peace-keeping functions.

The size of the Peace Observation Corps is not specified in the *Outline*. In estimating the establishment and the annual maintenance costs of such an international organization, it was felt necessary to develop a set of general assumptions based on strength levels of 267, 516, and 1,002 men who would constitute a pool out of which would be drawn teams for observation missions in the field. It should be observed from the attachments that in studying the requirements, it was necessary to design a prototype basic peace-observation unit before an intelligent costing exercise could be carried out. It was found further that no existing military unit in the United States military establishment quite corresponded to the needs of a peace-observation unit. While the cost data are realistic for the design of peace-observation units, the design itself may need to be modified in the light of the tasks a mission will be required to perform. The basic units outlined here, however, provide room for the kind of flexibility which is needed to meet a wide range of situations.

The estimated costs of the three different sized corps (including major equipment and annual operating costs), organized and equipped as indicated in the attachments, are: $9,131,000 for the 267 man corps, $17,250,-000 for the 516 man corps and $34,500,000 for the 1,002 man corps. These estimates are believed to be accurate within 10 percent, plus or minus, for normal training operations at a location in the continental United States. They do not include estimates for deployed operations such as those that units of this kind might be expected to undergo as the most realistic test of their operational capability.

In addition, it should be pointed out that the complement of the basic observation unit does not include the UN civilian personnel who might form and always have formed a part of an observation team in the field. These as appropriate might include, *inter alia*, the political adviser, the legal adviser, the public information officer, interpreters, photographer, finance officer, administrative, security, and such indigenous personnel as may be required for unskilled tasks. The costs of the UN civilian personnel attached to observer missions in the field are not included in the estimates set out in the attachments, nor are physical security costs and the indirect staff costs, such as the increase in permanent staff at UN Headquarters itself to supervise, train, and administer the corps.

The following general assumptions underlie the Peace Observation Corps set out in the attachments:

1. Three different strength levels in the Peace Observation Corps, 267, 516, 1,002.

2. The Corps is to be quartered close to the New York metropolitan area, possibly in one of the closed U.S. military camps or one scheduled for closing.

3. The basic pay and allowance system is similar to that of the U.S. Army.

4. Medical services are available without cost.

5. Living quarters for married officers and enlisted personnel and their families are provided.

6. Retirement is based on the U.S. Military Retirement system.

7. Dependents' indemnity compensation is similar to that of the U.S. military.

8. The cost and maintenance of equipment necessary in connection with training are included.

9. Special training costs are likewise included.

The following is a glossary of the principal terms used.

AN/GRC-106	Portable communications radio
AN/GRC-108	Portable communications radio
AN/PRC-6	"walkie-talkie"
Avn	Aviation
Avn Det	Aviation Detachment
CONUS	Continental United States
E4	Corporal
E5	Sergeant
E6	Sergeant 1st class
E7	Master sergeant
EM	Enlisted men
Fld	Field
UH1B	Helicopter (Iroquois HV1B)
LOH	Light observation helicopter

MPA	Military Pay and Allowances
MT	Motor Transport
MT Maint Det, DA (modified)	Motor Transport Maintenance Detachment, Department of Army (modified)
O&MA	Operating and Maintenance Allowances
Peace Obsn Ctl Hqs	Peace Observation Control Headquarters
Peace Obsn Unit Hqs	Peace Observation Unit Headquarters
Sig Maint Det	Signal Maintenance Detachment
1/4 T Trk	1/4 Ton Truck
3/4 T Trk	3/4 Ton Truck

ESTIMATED COST

(Alternative Manning Levels)

1. It is estimated that the cost of a Peace Observation Corps organized and equipped as indicated on the following pages, will be as shown in the table below:

Force	No. of Officers in POC	Major Equipment Purchase Cost	Annual Operating Cost
A	267	$4,755,667	$4,376,124
B	516	8,904,151	8,347,938
C	1,002	17,808,302	16,695,876

2. Force composition for these estimates is derived from the following combinations of hypothetical Peace Observation Units and Peace Observation Force Headquarters. Enlisted strength, grade distribution, and major items of equipment are shown in the attachments:

Force	No. of Peace Observation Units	No. of Peace Observation Force, Hqs
A	3	1
B	6	1
C	12	2

3. All cost estimates except those for Dependents' Indemnity Compensation (DIC) and voluntary retirement have been factored from U.S. Army cost experience.

4. The estimates given above should be accurate within ±10% for normal training operations at a location in CONUS. They do not include estimates for deployed operations such as those that a unit of this kind might be expected to undergo as the most realistic test of its operational capability.

5. The estimates undoubtedly will seem to be high when compared with most other force estimates. Several factors influence this high apparent cost:

a. Retirement and survivor benefits are costed on a discounted present year basis. Conceptually, this means that the future cost of benefits is determined on an actuarial basis and discounted at 3% per annum to determine the sum one would have to put aside to finance these programs on a present or "pay as you go" basis.

b. The radio sets selected for cost estimates are single sideband models. Being newly developed, these sets are more expensive than the sets they will replace by a factor of three or four. They are, however, capable of reliable ground wave communication up to 100 miles and world-wide airwave communication. On the assumption that fast, reliable communications are essential to a Peace Observation Corps, a judgment was made that the capability provided is worth the extra cost. Many cheaper sets can be obtained, but only with a drastic decrease in operational reliability. It is assumed that radio personnel and equipment for contact with a higher headquarters will be provided by that headquarters.

c. Organizational maintenance personnel have been provided at a manning level exceeding that authorized for U.S. Army units. It is felt that the manning levels indicated are necessary if the corps is to be capable of deployment over great distances in areas of unimproved road networks.

d. Air transport type aircraft are not included, as such an aircraft could be contracted for on a specific mission basis as required.

CONCEPT OF ORGANIZATION

HYPOTHETICAL PEACE OBSERVATION UNIT

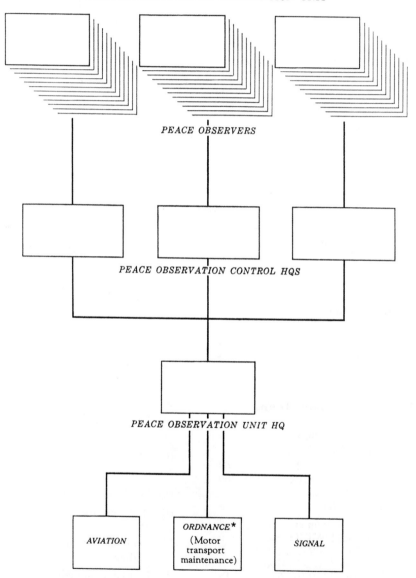

PEACE OBSERVERS

PEACE OBSERVATION CONTROL HQS

PEACE OBSERVATION UNIT HQ

AVIATION

ORDNANCE*
(Motor
transport
maintenance)

SIGNAL

* *In the current United Nations peace-observation missions, ordnance (motor maintenance) and signal operations are provided by United Nations civilian personnel.*

Peace Observation Unit

Personnel

(1) Officer

    (a) 60 Observers   60
    (b) 3 Ctl Hqs, 4 Off ea   12
    (c) 1 Obsn Unit Hqs, 6 Off   6
    (d) 1 Avn Det, 5 Off   5
                                    83

(2) Officer Grade Distribution

    (a) Maj/Capt   78
    (b) Lt Col   4
    (c) Col   1

(3) Enlisted

    (a) 3 Ctl Hqs, 4 EM ea   12
    (b) 1 Obsn Unit Hqs, 8 EM   8
    (c) Sig Maint Det, 6 EM   6
    (d) Avn Det, 12 EM   12
    (e) MT Maint Det, 13 EM   13
                                      51

(4) Enlisted Grade Distribution

    (a) E7   1
    (b) E6   5
    (c) E5   23
    (d) E4   22

Equipment, Major Items

(1) By unit sub groups

    (a) 60 Off obsr
        1 1 ea 1/4 T Trk ea   60
        2 1 ea AN/GRC-106 ea   60

    (b) 3 Ctl Hqs

        1 1 ea sedan ea   3
        2 3 ea 1/4 T Trk ea   9
        3 1 ea AN/GRC-106 ea   3
        4 1 ea AN/GRC-108 ea   3
        5 5 ea AN/PRC-6 ea   15

    (c) 1 Obsn Unit Hqs

        1 2 ea Sedan   2
        2 3 ea 1/4 T Trk   3
        3 1 ea AN/GRC-106   1
        4 2 ea AN/GRC-108   2

    (d) 1 Sig Maint Det

        1 3 ea 3/4 T Trk   3
        2 10% Equip float

    (e) 1 ea Avn Det

        1 4 ea LOH   4
            (cost 4 additional
            AN/GRC-106
        2 2 ea 3/4 T Trk   2
        3 2 ea 1/4 T Trk   2
        4 3 ea Avn Mech Tool Sets 3

    (f) 1 ea MT Maint Det, Da (Modified)

        1 9 ea 3/4 T Trk   9
        2 1 ea shop set, fld maint, basic   1
        3 1 ea shop set, fld maint, welding   1
        4 8 ea tool kit, auto maint   8

(2) By items

    (a) 3/4 T Trk   14
    (b) 1/4 T Trk   74
    (c) Sedans   5
    (d) AN/GRC-106   68
    (e) AN/GRC-108   5
    (f) AN/PRC-6   15
    (g) LOH   4
    (h) Avn Mech Tool Set   3
    (i) Shop set, fld auto maint, basic   1
    (j) Shop set, fld auto maint, welding   1
    (k) Tool kit, auto maint   8

Peace Observation Force Headquarters

Personnel

(1) Officer
- (a) Gen Off ... 1
- (b) Colonel ... 1
- (c) Lt Col ... 3
- (d) Maj/Capt ... 13

  18

(2) Enlisted
- (a) Hqs ... 20
- (b) Avn Det ... 6

  26

(3) Enlisted Grade Distribution
- (a) E6 ... 1
- (b) E5 ... 17
- (c) E4 ... 8

Equipment

(1) Sedans ... 5

(2) 3/4 T Trk ... 2

(3) 1/4 T Trk ... 3

(4) UH1B ... 2

(5) AN/GRC-106 ... 2

(6) AN/GRC-108 ... 2

INITIAL EQUIPMENT COST

(*Source—15 Mar 64 Equipment Cost Listing prepared by the DCSLOG Computer Center,
Radford, Virginia, except as noted*)

Item	Unit Price	Force Hqs Nr	Force Hqs Cost	Obsn Unit Nr	Obsn Unit Cost
Truck, ¾ Ton	$ 4,300	2	$ 8,600	14	$ 60,200
Truck, ¼ Ton	2,990	3	8,970	74	221,260
Sedan	a	5	8,900	5	7,500
AN/GRC-106 (Est 1968)	9,000	2	18,000	68	612,000
AN/GRC-108 (Est 1968)	40,000	2	80,000	5	200,000
AN/PRC-6 (Current AMC)	115	—	—	15	1,725
LOH (Sioux H-13)	44,350	—	—	4	177,400
UH1B (Iroquois HV1B)	235,000	2	470,000	—	—
Avn Mech Tool Set	6,250	—	—	3	18,750
Tool Kit, Auto Mech, Gen	93	—	—	8	744
Shop Set, fld auto maint, basic	8,700	—	—	1	8,700
Shop Set, fld auto maint, welding	8,700	—	—	1	8,700
Total			$578,270		$1,316,979
5% Misc b			28,913		65,849
Est Equip Cost			$ *607,183*		$ *1,382,828*

a Sedans are costed at $2,900 for one medium and $1,500 ea for the remaining light sedans.
b Included to cover tentage, typewriters, etc., as requested by military consultant.

ESTIMATED ANNUAL OPERATING COST[a]

(*Based on Fiscal Year 1965 Costs*)

	Force Hqs (18 Off; 26 EM)	Obsn Unit (83 Off; 51 EM)
Military Personnel Cost [b]		
Basic Pay	232,060	775,610
Basic Allowance for Subsistence	20,310	67,232
Basic Allowance for Quarters	58,550	190,984
Uniform Allowance	5,280	19,906
	316,200	1,053,732
Operation & Maintenance Cost		
Operating Forces [c]	55,610	169,100
School Specialist Training [d]	9,240	30,330
Central Supply Activities [e]	6,860	20,900
Major Overhaul & Maintenance [f]	4,530	13,800
Medical Activities [g]	7,920	24,150
Administrative Services & Recruiting	3,390	10,318
Finance Services	560	1,608
	88,110	270,206
Total Cost	$ 404,310	$ 1,323,938

[a] The estimated costs included above are based on average United States Army costs for U.S. Army personnel operating in CONUS.

[b] The cost for bi-annual leave assuming round-trip movement to Europe and return to CONUS is not included above. This home leave cost based on U.S. Army costs is estimated as follows:

Officer unaccompanied	$236
Officer with 3 dependents	944
Enlisted unaccompanied	236
Enlisted with 3 dependents	944

[c] Operating forces costs include all costs associated with Budget Program 2000 and cover such costs as replacement training of enlisted personnel replacements and unit operation and maintenance cost at home station to include unit, installation and aircraft operation and maintenance costs.

[d] School specialist training is Army Service School type training of replacements and is based on the per capita amount of training given U.S. Army personnel.

[e] Central supply activities cover operation of supply depots, supply management offices, centralized transportation services, operation of ports, terminals, and facilities and logistic control and direction.

[f] Major overhaul and maintenance covers major overhaul, modification, maintenance engineering services, and fabrication of parts and tools not available through the supply system or from commercial sources.

[g] Medical activity cost is based on per capita cost of providing all medical services including hospitalization, operation of dispensaries and dental service units, medical services in non-Army facilities, and medicare. One medical NCO included in force headquarters.

TOTAL COST ESTIMATES

(Alternative Manning Levels)

Force A—3 Obsn Units and 1 Force Hqs

Equipment Cost—Obsn Units	$4,148,484
Force Hqs	607,183
	4,755,667
Annual Operating Cost—Obsn Unit	3,971,814
Force Hqs	404,310
	4,376,124

Force B—6 Obsn Units and 1 Force Hqs

Equipment Cost—Obsn Units	8,296,968
Force Hqs	607,183
	8,904,151
Annual Operating Cost—Obsn Unit	7,943,628
Force Hqs	404,310
	8,347,938

Force C—12 Obsn Units and 2 Force Hqs

Equipment Cost—Obsn Unit	16,593,936
Force Hqs	1,214,366
	17,808,302
Annual Operating Cost—Obsn Unit	15,887,256
Force Hqs	808,620
	16,695,876

PER CAPITA COST FACTORS USED IN ESTIMATING COST

	Officer	*Enlisted*
MPA		
Basic Pay	8,860	2,791
Basic Allowance for Subsistence	548	383
Basic Allowance for Quarters	1,597	1,146
Uniform Allowance	200	65
	11,205	4,385
O&MA		
Operating Forces	1,203	1,273
School Specialist Training	781	137
Central Supply Activities	156	156
Major Overhaul and Maintenance	103	103
Medical Activities	208	179
Administrative Services and Recruiting	77	77
Finance Services	12	12
	2,540	1,937
Total Cost	13,745	6,322

DEPENDENTS' INDEMNITY COMPENSATION (DIC)
AND VOLUNTARY RETIREMENT COST ESTIMATES

1. *DIC*

a. The estimated average monthly cost, discounted at 3% per annum and based on actual death experience in the U.S. military establishment is $22.00 for enlisted men and $45.00 for officers.

b. Peace Observation Unit

    (1) 83 officers @ $45/mo × 12 = $44,820/year
    (2) 81 EM @ $22/mo × 12   =   21,384/year
                                           $66,204/year

c. Peace Observation Force Headquarters

    (1) 18 officers @ $45/mo × 12 = $ 9,720/year
    (2) 26 EM @ $22/mo × 12   =   6,864/year
                                         $ 16,584/year

2. *Voluntary Retirement*

a. The costs below are based on actual U.S. Army present mean years of service for pay proposed and estimated monthly cost, discounted at 3% per annum related to standard actuarial experience. This is the true cost of the present U.S. Military Retirement System. It is more expensive than retirement after 20 years service and upon reaching age 65. If the contractor prefers to use the latter basis, provided in his broad guidance, he can compute an alternative cost using mean ages at beginning of service: 18 years for EM and 21 years for officers.

b. Peace Observation Unit

    (1) 78 ea Maj/Capt, 12 yrs svc, @ $207/mo × 12 = $193,752/year
    (2) 4 ea Lt Col, 20 yrs svc, @ $311/mo × 12   =   14,928/year
    (3) 1 ea Col, 24 yrs svc, @ $345/mo × 12   =   4,140/year
    (4) 1 ea E7, 18 yrs svc, @ $148/mo × 12   =   1,776/year
    (5) 5 ea E6, 14 yrs svc, @ $124/mo × 12   =   7,440/year
    (6) 23 ea E5, 8 yrs svc, @ $73/mo × 12   =   20,148/year
    (7) 52 ea E4, 2 yrs svc, @ $11/mo × 12   =   6,864/year
                                                              $249,048/year

c. Peace Observation Force Headquarters

    (1) 1 ea Gen Off, 30 yrs svc, @ $609/mo × 12 = $ 7,308/year
    (2) 1 ea Col, 24 yrs svc, @ $345/mo × 12   =   4,140/year
    (3) 3 ea Lt Col, 20 yrs svc, @ $311/mo × 12   =   11,196/year
    (4) 13 ea Maj/Capt, 12 yrs svc, @ $207/mo × 12 =   32,292/year
    (5) 1 ea E6, 14 yrs svc, @ $124/mo × 12   =   1,488/year
    (6) 17 ea E5, 8 yrs svc, @ $73/mo × 12   =   14,892/year
    (7) 8 ea E4, 2 yrs svc, @ $11/mo × 12   =   1,056/year
                                                            $ 72,372/year

INDEX

A

Aaland Islands: in the Swedish-Finnish controversy before the League of Nations (1920), 11–15; report of Committee of Jurists, 12, 14; fact-finding on interests of parties, 13–14; Finland's sovereignty continued, 13; guarantees for the Swedish minority, 14–15, 543; League prestige raised by decision, 15

Abullah, King, 264

Abdullah, Shiek Mohammed, 370

Acheson, Dean, 119

Adlercreutz, M. de, 50

Africa: possible regional systems for newer states of, 215; emergence of new nations as basis of claims, 541

Aggression: sanctions against under the League, 7–8; collective measures against in the Inter-American System, 89–91; and Communist subversion, 206, 208, 209.

Agreement of parties: types of, 549

Albania: Yugoslavia-Greece dispute before the League (1921), 29–33; Conference of Ambassadors decision on frontiers, 30; invasions of, 30, 32; boundaries surveyed, 30–31; socio-economic reforms proposed, 31–32; survival of, due to League actions, 32–33; consent of one party in case, 555. *See also* Corfu Channel; Greece

Aldrovandi, Count Luigi, 58, 99

Algerian-Moroccan frontier dispute, 540

Allen, Ward P., 177

Alliance for Progress: in Latin American social development programs, 158; Declaration on Regional and International Economic Coordination, 178

Alvarez del Vayo, Julio, 99

Ambassadors: Allied Conference of, in League cases, 19, 20, 29–33, 35–39, 40–42, 78, 598

American Treaty of Pacific Settlement. *See* Pact of Bogotá

Angola: UN actions in uprising against Portugal (1961–62), 472–76; conduct of inquiries into disturbances and conflicts, 473–76; access to colony denied by Portugal, 473–76 *passim*, 557; information from Angolans in the Congo, 474; deteriorating situation, 476; Portugal's world position damaged, 476

Antarctica: Antarctic Treaty, 485, 526–31; peace observation and fact-finding in, 525–34; history, 525–26; consultative meetings of twelve signatories, 529, 530; findings of U.S. team in, 531–32; harmonious international relations in, 532, 533; "adversary" inspection concept in, 533–34

Arab League, 548

Arbenz Guzmán, Jacobo, 125, 126, 130, 131

Arbitration: defined, 597, 605

Arévalo, Juan José, 118, 125

Argentina, 88, 94, 98, 105, 108, 119; direct negotiation settlement of boundary dispute with Chile (1963), 207n; leading role of, in the OAS and the UN, 213

Arias, Ricardo, 141

Armas, Colonel Castillo, 126, 127, 131, 132, 134

Armistice Demarcation Lines (ADL), 260, 286, 560–61

Arms control. *See* Disarmament

Asia; possible regional systems for newer states of, 215; emergence of new nations in, as basis for claims, 541

Askenazy, Simon, 17

Asylum in foreign embassies: inter-American treaties and conventions on, 170, 197; tactics against asylees, 196, 198; in dictatorships, 543. *See also* Refugees

Australia, 328, 464

B

Bacterial warfare: UN requested to investigate alleged use of by U.S. forces in Korea (1953), 479; Communist noncooperation on, in the General Assembly, 479

Baldwin, Stanley, 74

Balfour, Arthur, 18

Y

Yemen: civil-war crisis in (1963–64), 421–35; U.A.R. and Saudi Arabia in, 422–35; disengagement operation for, 423–35 *passim*, 566, 571; Soviet reaction, 424–27; observation and mediation in, 426–35; UN Presence for conciliation, 431; Conference of Arab States on, 432; threat to peace diminished, 433, 434

Yoshida, Isaburo, 58
Yugoslavia, 7n, 10n, 36, 80. *See also* Albania; Greece

Z

Zanzibar, 539
Zeligowski, Lucien, 16–17, 18, 19, 34
Zellweger, Edouard, 394
Zook, David H., 97n, 100n
Zuleta Angel, Alberto, 168